STELLENBOSCH HANDBOOKS IN AFRICAN CONSTITUTIONAL LAW

The Stellenbosch Handbooks in African Constitutional Law series engages with contemporary issues of constitutionalism in Africa. The first experiments in democratic and constitutional governance in Africa that started after independence were soon overtaken by dictatorships, and arbitrary and repressive rule. The pulling down of the Berlin Wall followed by the collapse of the Soviet Union unleashed new forces of democratization and new hopes for the establishment and entrenchment of constitutional governance and constitutionalism in Africa. This series is designed to identify, analyse, and promote serious discussion of the critical issues that can shape, refine, and deepen the consolidation of constitutionalism in Africa.

Although comparative constitutional law has become a major field of legal scholarship, most of the extensive research that has been carried out has focused on long-established democracies. The only African country that has attracted sustained research interest from a comparative law perspective is South Africa. The few books that present perspectives on African comparative constitutional law focus narrowly and exclusively on developments in either anglophone, francophone, or arabophone Africa without cutting across these divides. Yet, since 1990, Africa has been at the centre of profound and far-reaching constitutional developments. Little comparative research has been carried out to understand the nature of these constitutional changes, to review their impact on the ethos of constitutionalism on the continent, and to explore prospects for the future.

The objectives of the Stellenbosch Handbooks in African Constitutional Law series are, first, to stimulate interest in comparative constitutional research and the different constitutional traditions operating in Africa by presenting a comprehensive analysis of the latest thinking, research, and practice. In this way, the series intends to fill the huge gap in the existing literature on comparative African constitutional law as well as point to directions for future research. Second, each volume will bring together high quality innovative and original material from diverse perspectives written by scholars and legal practitioners drawn from the different constitutional traditions operating on the continent. In this respect, each volume will strive to cover anglophone, arabophone, francophone, hispanophone, and lusophone Africa. In many respects, this will ensure that African voices are heard in the global constitutional debates. Third, because most African countries share many common features, such as the colonial legacy, geographical proximity, and social, economic, political, and cultural conditions, the volumes in the series adopt a comparative approach that highlights gaps and good practices in a manner that will provide a rich source of authoritative information for promoting an inter-African legal dialogue and the cross-fertilization of ideas between different constitutional traditions. Finally, the volumes in the series are intended to act as a repository for the accumulation of knowledge, experience, and expertise on the continent. Each handbook stands alone and is intended to provide an invaluable source of authoritative reference material for academics, researchers, students at all levels, as well as legal practitioners and policy-makers.

STELLENBOSCH HANDBOOKS IN AFRICAN CONSTITUTIONAL LAW

Constitutional Identity and Constitutionalism in Africa

Edited by

CHARLES M. FOMBAD
and
NICO STEYTLER

OXFORD
UNIVERSITY PRESS

OXFORD
UNIVERSITY PRESS

Great Clarendon Street, Oxford, OX2 6DP,
United Kingdom

Oxford University Press is a department of the University of Oxford.
It furthers the University's objective of excellence in research, scholarship,
and education by publishing worldwide. Oxford is a registered trade mark of
Oxford University Press in the UK and in certain other countries

First Edition published in 2024

Published in the United States of America by Oxford University Press
198 Madison Avenue, New York, NY 10016, United States of America

British Library Cataloguing in Publication Data

Data available

Library of Congress Control Number: 2023948637

ISBN 978–0–19–890630–8

DOI: 10.1093/oso/9780198906308.001.0001

Printed and bound by
CPI Group (UK) Ltd, Croydon, CR0 4YY

This volume of the Stellenbosch Handbooks in African Constitutional Law is dedicated to honouring the lifetime contributions to constitution-making and constitutionalism in Africa by the two greatest African comparative constitutionalists, Professor Ben Nwabueze and Professor Yash Ghai, who both delivered the keynote addresses at the seminar during which the papers published in this book were presented

Professor Ben Nwabueze

Professor Ben Nwabueze SAN was born eighty-nine years ago in Atanị, a village on the bank of the River Niger in Ogbaru Local Government Area of Anambra State, where he grew up and spent the early years of his childhood. He was educated at the CMS Central School in Atani and Onitsha, Our Lady's High School (formerly Africa College) Onitsha, and later at the London School of Economics and Political Science and the School of Oriental and African Studies, both at the University of London.

His career, after university education, spans fifty years in various roles, both at home and abroad, as Minister of Education, Constitutional Adviser to the Governments of Kenya and Ethiopia, Member Constitution Drafting Committee and the First Constituent Assembly for Nigeria, Member Constitution Review Committee for Zambia; Chairman, *The Patriots* and Chairman, Project Nigeria, Deputy Chairman, Presidential Advisory Council. Fondly referred to as Professor of Professors by his numerous admirers, he is Nigeria's first academic Senior Advocate of Nigeria (SAN) conferred on him solely on the basis of his published works.

Professor Ben Nwabueze is the second (and since the death of Dr T.O. Elias) the only Nigerian and African holder of a higher doctorate degree in Law (LLD) by published work (not *honoris causa)* from the University of London. He is the recipient of many awards for academic excellence, including Hon. PhD, Caritas University, Hon. LLD, University of Nigeria, Hon. DLitt, Anambra State University of Technology, Nigerian National Order of Merit (NNOM), and Fellowship of many academic institutions, as well as awards for meritorious services, such as Education Minister of the Year, Awards as Role Model conferred on him by the Hallmark of Labour Foundation in 2005 and 2011, and This Day Newspaper in 2011, Living Legend Award by the Faculty of Law, University of Lagos 2012, and Nigerian Most Outstanding Constitutional Legal Icon Award by the African Leadership Magazine 2012; in the same year (2012), the Nigerian Institute of Advanced Legal Studies established a professorial Chair in his honour, called Ben Nwabueze Chair of Constitutional Law; earlier in 2010, the Institute of Government Research and Leadership Technology also established in his honour an Annual Lecture Series, called Ben Nwabueze Lectures in Constitutional Law.

He is Commander of the Order of the Niger (CON) and the recipient of several honorary traditional chieftaincy titles. He was the Secretary-General/CEO of Ohanaeze Ndigbo for more than twenty years from 1976, when the organisation was established.

He is the author of thirty-four full length books with an average page extent of 400 pages, two of which, *Constitutionalism* and *Presidentialism*, have been translated into some European languages. He has also written over 200 articles in academic journals and delivered over 100 keynote addresses, public lectures, and lead papers at local and international conferences.

It may be said with truth that only few academics have achieved such intimidating and record-setting repertoire of intellectual harvest. This has made him a household word among colleagues, students, lecturers, members of the bench and bar, and indeed the general public. Hardly any other author is known to have been so frequently quoted in court judgments both in Nigeria and abroad.

In Memoriam

On 30 October, just before the manuscript of this book was sent to the printers, the Editors received a sad message from Eni Nwabueze, writing on behalf of the family which partly read as follows; 'With great sadness, we announce the passing on of our patriarch, Professor B.O. Nwabueze SAN, NNOM, CON, pioneer Secretary-General of Ohanaeze Ndigbo and Oduah Afo-na-Isagba of Atani, Anambra State, on Sunday 29 October 2023, age 94. He lived an exemplary life of consequence'. We share the grief of the family at the passing of this great man and extend our profound condolences to the family and friends of Professor Nwabueze.

Charles M. Fombad

Professor Yash Pal Ghai

Few constitutional law scholars have combined theory and practice of constitutional law with such success as Professor Yash Pal Ghai has done during a stellar career spanning nearly sixty years: as teacher, writer, constitution-maker, and activist all in the cause of constitutionalism in the Global South in general and Africa in particular.

In his various roles in constitution-making processes across the world, he has sought that the identity of such constitutions articulated the voice and values of the people they would govern, reflected democracy and a respect for human rights, ensured that governments are not a law unto themselves but that executives are contained, entrenched self-rule by communities where they so desired, and adhered to and advanced the basic of values of constitutionalism.

After graduating from the two most prestigious universities of the world, Oxford (BA, MA, and DCL) and Harvard (LLM), he embarked upon an academic career. He was an outstanding teacher at universities across the world, with teaching posts at the universities of Dar-es-Salaam (1963–70), Yale (1971–3), Warwick (1974–89), and Hong Kong (1989–2005). For him law teaching was more than a rendition and critique of black letter law, but had to place law in the context of politics, sociology, and economics.

He has been a prodigious scholar; his nearly 200 published works focused on constitutional law in Africa and elsewhere in the Global South. His first major work, co-authored with James McAuslan, was the seminal *Public Law and Political Change in Kenya* (Oxford University Press 1970) in which he mapped the constitutional development of his country of birth, but which also made him unwelcome in that country for decades to come.

Appearing from his searing pen are publications on human rights, limited government, devolution and decentralisation, the perennial issue of the management of ethnicity, the courts, and the legal profession—all within the framework of his abiding concern for constitutionalism.

What make Yash Ghai exceptional among constitutional lawyers has been his extensive practical involvement in the making of constitutions in many countries of the Global South. He was never a hired gun, but his engagement was always based on his firm commitment to constitutionalism—the control of public power through law.

In the 1970s, he assisted a number of Pacific island countries in negotiating independence constitutions from their colonial master, Great Britain, including the constitutions of Solomon Islands, Papua New Guinea, and New Hebrides/Vanuatu. Closer to home, he was an advisor at the Seychelles' Independence Constitutional Conference. He became involved in South Africa's process of democratisation. I recall my first meeting with Yash in Harare, Zimbabwe, when he was an advisor to the ANC in their meeting with a number of white constitutional lawyers. Later on he assisted the Constitutional Assembly during the drafting the 1996 Constitution.

In 2000, Yash could apply his expertise to his motherland. He was appointed the chairperson of the Kenya Constitution Review Commission (November 2000–June 2004), and proceeded to put theory into practice. He showed how a constitution-making process could be conducted from the bottom up. The basics of the Commission's draft constitution, containing the elements of constitutionalism and devolution, survived government revisions and underpins of the 2010 Kenyan Constitution.

His services were highly sought after by the United Nations in a number countries emerging from civil war, to assist in the drafting of constitutions that could cement peace. He was an advisor to Constitutional Commission for Afghanistan (2002–3) and the head of the UNDP Constitution Advisory Support Unit in Nepal (2006–8). He was also an advisor in constitution-making processes in the Maldives, Iraq, East Timor, and Philippines. In Africa, his advice was brought to bear on Somalia, Libya, South Sudan, Tunisia, Zimbabwe, Zambia, and Tanzania.

His role often extended beyond constitution-making. From 2005 to 2008, he was the Special Representative of Secretary General of UN on Human Rights in Cambodia, and in 2008, he was also the Emissary of the Commonwealth Secretary General to Fiji to discuss Fiji's return to democratic rule and UN's participation as a facilitator.

Throughout his life, Yash was an activist in the cause of democracy and constitutionalism across the globe in general and over the past decade in his native Kenya in particular. He and his wife and collaborator, Jill Cottrell, with the first executive director, Waikwa Wanyoike, founded the Katiba Institute in 2011 which, through training, advocacy and litigation sought to unlock the promise the 2010 Kenyan Constitution held. He was very much a public intellectual, writing regularly in newspapers and reaching out to the general public for whom the constitution was written in the first place.

It is most fitting that we dedicate this book, with constitutional identity and constitutionalism as its theme, also to Yash Ghai for his life-long contribution to constitutionalism in Africa. And it is particularly gratifying that he could also participate in this conference on, as he notes, 'the topic so close to my heart'.

Nico Steytler

Preface

Discussions about the identity of modern constitutions have attracted the attention mainly of Western scholars, particularly in Europe and the United States. This seventh book in our *Stellenbosch Handbooks in African Constitutional Law* series is the outcome of the eighth Stellenbosch Annual Seminar on Constitutionalism in Africa (SASCA). As in the past, it was organised by the Institute for International and Comparative Law in Africa (ICLA) of the Faculty of Law, University of Pretoria, the South African Research Chair in Multilevel Government, Law and Development (SARChI) at the Dullah Omar Institute, University of the Western Cape, and the Stellenbosch Institute for Advanced Study (STIAS). This was done in partnership with the Konrad Adenauer Stiftung (KAS) Rule of Law Programme for Anglophone Sub-Saharan Africa, Nairobi, Kenya. The seminar took place from 15 to 17 September 2021 and had as its theme, 'Constitutional identity and constitutionalism in Africa'.

The quest for a new constitutional ordering that is emerging, particularly after the wave of new or substantially revised constitutions were adopted after the 1990s, has raised important questions about the identity of African constitutions. The main question is whether these new or revised constitutions reflect an African identity. In addressing this question, this book examines, firstly, how the concept of constitutional identity can be useful in understanding constitutional change in Africa; secondly, how constitutional identities enhance or limit constitutionalism; and thirdly, how constitutional identities may be decolonised to reflect an African identity. Could both constitutionalism and the decolonisation of constitutions produce a new African constitutional identity?

The 2021 seminar, as in previous years, attracted eminent and emerging young constitutional scholars from across Africa and abroad. A key objective of these seminars continues to be our desire to encourage and mentor up and coming scholars concerned with constitutional law and its practice in Africa. This important goal is reflected in the inclusion of papers in this volume written by young scholars who participated in the seminar. We have also endeavoured, in line with the fundamental objective of this series, to secure papers that would cover a cross-section of the continent's regions and its diverse constitutional traditions.

The special keynote speakers for the 2021 seminar were Professors Ben Nwabueze and Yash Ghai. After their keynote addresses, a special tribute was paid to them in recognition of their exceptional lifetime contribution to constitution-making and constitutionalism in Africa.

We would like to acknowledge and thank a number of persons and institutions that made this book possible. Firstly, the seminar would not have taken place without the financial support provided by Swedish Riksbankens Jubileumsfond to STIAS to fund the SASCA programme. We would like to thank in particular the director of STIAS, Professor Edward Kirumira, and his predecessor, Professor Hendrik Geyer, and the coordinator of strategic initiatives, Professor Johann Groenewald, for their enthusiasm and guidance. We also like to acknowledge the assistance of the very able Mrs Nel-Mari Loock for all the practical arrangements. Secondly, we are grateful to Dr Lukman Abdulrauf of the Faculty of Law, University of Ilorin, Nigeria; Dr Michelle Maziwisa; and Dr Shehaam Johnstone, postdoctoral fellow at SARChI at the Dullah Omar Institute, who also provided excellent assistance in the management of the papers as well as casting a critical eye on their content. Thirdly, we would like to acknowledge support provided by the South African Research Chairs Initiative of the Department of Science and Technology and National Research Foundation, through the SARChI. Fourthly, we much appreciate the financial and advisory support provided by KAS. Fifthly, thank you to all the peer-reviewers who helped in ensuring the quality of the end-product. Sixthly, we would also wish to thank Andre Wiesner for his incisive editorial eye. Finally, special thanks go to OUP staff, especially Mr Alex Flach, Mr Brian Stone, Ms Paulina dos Santos, and Mr Reyman Dickrose Joseph.

Charles M. Fombad and Nico Steytler
Pretoria and Cape Town
April 2023

Contents

Table of Cases

BOSNIA AND HERZEGOVINA

CAMEROON

CANADA

CAPE VERDE

FRANCE

INDIA

IRELAND

KENYA

NIGERIA

SOUTH AFRICA

SPAIN

TANZANIA

UGANDA

UNITED STATES

ZAMBIA

Table of Legislation

List of Abbreviations

AAC	All Anglophone Conference
ACDEG	African Union's Charter on Democracy, Elections and Governance
AfCFTA	African Continental Free Trade Agreement
ANC	African National Congress
AU	African Union
AZAPO	Azanian People's Organisation
BAC	Baccalauréat
BCEAC	Economic and Monetary Union of Central African States
BCEAO	West African Economic and Monetary Union
BiH	Bosnia and Herzegovina
CA	Constitutional Assembly
CAM	Cameroon Anglophone Movement
CCCV	Constitutional Court of Cape Verde
CCI	Council of Constitutional Interpretation
CCJA	Common Court of Justice and Arbitration
CDC	Cameroon Development Corporation
CFA	Communauté Française d'Afrique
CNU	Cameroon National Union
Codesa	Convention on a Democratic South Africa
CoR	Council of Representatives
CPP	Convention People's Party
DRC	Democratic Republic of the Congo
ECOWAS	Economic Community of West African States
EFF	Economic Freedom Fighters
EPRDF	Ethiopian Peoples' Revolutionary Democratic Front
EPRP	Ethiopian People's Revolutionary Party
ESM	Ethiopian Student Movement
EU	European Union
FBH	Federation of Bosnia and Herzegovina
FDRE	Federal Democratic Republic of Ethiopia
GCE	General Certificate of Education
GDP	gross domestic product
GDR	German Democratic Republic
HCJ	High Council of the Judiciary
HJC	Higher Judicial Council
HoP	House of Federation
HoPR	House of Peoples' Representatives
ICLA	Institute for International and Comparative Law in Africa
IFP	Inkatha Freedom Party
ISEN	Institute for the Study of Ethiopian Nationalities
KAS	Konrad Adenauer Stiftung

LOPE	Law on the Political Organization of the State (Lei de Organização Política do Estado)
MEISON	All Ethiopian Socialist Movement
NATO	North Atlantic Treaty Organization
NDP	National Democratic Party
NEBE	National Electoral Board of Ethiopia
NP	National Party
OHADA	Organisation for the Harmonization of Business Law in Africa (in French, 'Organisation pour l'Harmonisation en Afrique du Droit des Affaires')
OLF	Oromo Liberation Front
PAC	Pan-Africanist Congress
PAIGC	African Party for the Independence of Guinea and Cape Verde (Partido Africano para a Independência da Guiné e Cabo Verde)
PDRE	Peoples' Democratic Republic of Ethiopia
PIC	Peace Implementation Council
PMAC	Provisional Military Administrative Council
PP	Prosperity Party
RECs	Regional Economic Communities
RET	Radical Economic Transformation
RS	Republika Srpska
SARChI	South African Research Chair in Multilevel Government, Law and Development
SASCA	Stellenbosch Annual Seminar on Constitutionalism in Africa
SCAF	Supreme Council for the Armed Forces
SCARM	Southern Cameroons Restoration Movement
SCJ	Supreme Court of Justice
SCNC	Southern Cameroons National Council
SDF	Social Democratic Front
SNNPR	Southern Nations, Nationalities and Peoples Region
SONARA	Societé Nationale de Raffinage
STIAS	Stellenbosch Institute for Advanced Study
SYO	Socialist Youth Organization
TGE	Transitional Government of Ethiopia
TPLF	Tigray People's Liberation Front
UAR	United Arab Republic
UDHR	United Nations Declaration on Human Rights
UK	United Kingdom
UN	United Nations
UPC	Union des Populations du Cameroun
US	United States
USSR	Union of Soviet Socialist Republics
WPE	Workers Party of Ethiopia

List of Contributors

Carlson Anyangwe
Emeritus Professor, Faculty of Law, Fort Hare University, South Africa

George B.N. Ayittey
Free African Foundation, Washington, DC, United States

Sherif A. Elgebeily
Centre for the Study of International Peace and Security, London, United Kingdom

Charles M. Fombad
Director, Institute for International and Comparative Law in Africa (ICLA) of the Faculty of Law, University of Pretoria, Tshwane, South Africa

Yash Ghai
Katiba Institute, Nairobi, Kenya

Asnake Kefale
Addis Ababa University, Addis Ababa, Ethiopia

Heinz Klug
Evjue-Bascom Professor of Law, University of Wisconsin, Madison, United States

Karl Kössler
Institute for Comparative Federalism, Eurac Research, Italy

Trésor M. Makunya
Postdoctoral student, Centre for Human Rights, Faculty of Law, University of Pretoria, Tshwane, South Africa

Ben Nwabueze
First Academic Senior Advocate of Nigeria (SAN), Nigeria

José Pina-Delgado
Chief Justice of the Constitutional Court of Cape Verde, Associate Professor of Public Law and Legal Theory at ISCJS, Santiago Island, Cape Verde

Nico Steytler
Professor Emeritus at the Dullah Omar Institute, University of the Western Cape, Cape Town, South Africa

INTRODUCTION

Constitutional Identity

Yash Ghai

I have to confess that 'constitutional identity' is not a familiar phrase. Also, it does seem to have some ambiguity. Does a constitution have an identity (other than a particular legal label for the legal document)? Does a country have a constitutional identity—such as being a monarchy or a federation? Do the people of a country have a constitutional identity—in the sense that their country's constitution is part of their identity?

I would argue that for many Kenyans these days, the Constitution is part of their identity as Kenyans. As a law student in the early 1960s, I was very conscious of the constitution-making process at Lancaster House. I would even go and watch the political luminaries arrive at work, to the extent that they started recognising me and would even acknowledge my presence. But neither the process nor the document had a particularly Kenyan identity, and probably few Kenyans in Kenya were aware of it all.

In the 1970s, if they were conscious of the Constitution at all, I doubt that was something they felt was part of their identity. If you have a one-party state, your constitution is not going to be central to your or your country's identity. Look at China. By the 1990s, the politically engaged viewed the constitution as something they wanted done away with—rather like a cancer they wanted cut out of their systems.

If you ask people what it means to be Kenyan these days, the chances are that they will recognise a tension between being Kenyan and being Somali or Luo or Giriama, or whatever. But, as Kenyans, many would identify the Constitution. Between 2013 and 2015, an art project invited Kenyans to express in words and drawings who they are (the project and resultant book were called *Who I Am, Who We Are*[1]). Among the contributions were these:

- 'I won't ever forget that in 1963 we got independence. Then, in 2009 [actually 2010, of course] we got the Constitution' (a 35-year-old single mother from Meru).
- 'I am similar to other Kenyans through the Constitution . . . I am proud of this country because we have a good Constitution that includes everything' (a 47-year-old Luo widow).
- 'Devolution for many people is about tribal groupings which form the majority in the country even though that is not what the Constitution envisioned' (a 32-year-old man from Isiolo).

[1] A Public Art Project on the Kenyan Identity: Nairobi (Mukuru Lunga, Kenya Cultural Centre, Kenyans of Somali Origin, Kenyans of Asian Origin, Kenyans of European Origin), Kisumu, Isiolo, Lamu, and Nyeri (2016) https://whoweareke.wordpress.com/ (last accessed on 9 October 2023).

Yash Ghai, *Constitutional Identity* In: *Constitutional Identity and Constitutionalism in Africa.* Edited by: Charles M. Fombad and Nico Steytler, Oxford University Press. © Yash Ghai 2024. DOI: 10.1093/oso/9780198906308.003.0001

These comments were typical of the rest of them.

Of course, the next question is: To what extent does the identity of the Constitution mirror that of Kenyans themselves and their efforts to navigate the dual nature of being a Kenyan? I think I would argue that if Kenyans do view the Constitution as an element of their national identity, it is to a considerable extent not because of its content but rather its history and the process of making it.

But to return to the identity of the Constitution, it seems to me that the very concept is a slippery one. Is the identity something that one designs into the constitution from the beginning? Or is it—or is it also—something that it acquires?

And where do we find its identity? In the preamble? Or in the substance? Or in the way it is perceived and used? There is another interesting question that I shall not go into here: What is the relationship between the concept of identity of the constitution and the basic structure?

I am asked to address myself to the following question: 'How can African constitutions be imbued with an African identity through African values?' Let it be said that it is common for constitutional processes in Africa to be constantly assailed by demands to be 'African'. Very often, what this means is not made specific. The tendency is not limited to Africa: Pacific Islanders want 'Pacific constitutions'.

Perhaps there are three responses, hypothetically, to the 'How' question posed to me. They are: through the language, through the substantive institutions and mechanisms, and in the process of making the constitution. I shall of necessity draw my examples mainly from Kenya. I did work on the Somali Constitution, but in a way that precluded my having much contact with Somali values other than through contact with the Constitutional Commission.

The preamble is a possible source of identity. It is common to include a little history, and a little hope, in it. A little bit of religion often creeps in. We tend to assume that people will actually read the preamble and that it will be important to them and approachable because it is in language not weighed down by technicality. I have no idea how true this is. Some empirical study would be interesting.

In the Kenyan context, however, I would argue that the most influential piece of language in the Constitution is in article 1: 'All sovereign power belongs to the people of Kenya.' Close behind this comes clause (2): 'The people may exercise their sovereign power either directly or through their democratically elected representatives.' The concept of national values is also much-quoted (including by the courts), and many people might be able to cite a few of the values—perhaps transparency, accountability, social justice, and participation.

To what extent are these specifically African values? They have definitely appealed to the people of Kenya, and they responded to what people felt had been lacking in the Kenya of the 1960s–1990s. Then there are substantive provisions. I would maintain that some of these responded to certain conceptions of African values or practices. A brief list:

- the protection of marginalised communities defined in a way that specifically mentions pastoralist and hunter-gatherer communities;
- the recognition of customary law;
- the encouragement of settling land disputes through communities;
- devolution, intended to give communities more control of their affairs;

- for Muslims, the recognition of Kadhi courts and exclusion of the equality requirement from cases before the Kadhi courts; and
- the various emphases on language and culture.

The Constitution as a whole is an effort to bring together national and community identities. There is recognition of diversity but within a broad national framework. No one is to be excluded because of who they are and where they come from. They have a right—and are right—to be proud of their community and its values and traditions. But the Constitution's vision is of a nation of people who are primarily Kenyans. Are these African values? I think they are values Kenyans hold dear.

Let me tell you a story about the process. There was a move to have much more about culture and communities. Inspired by the Ugandan Constitution, it was proposed to have a list of all Kenya's 'tribes' and their dress, drink, and food. The process began, and forty-two tribes were listed. Over the next few days (at the Constitutional Conference), people kept coming forward and saying, 'Our tribe is not there.' We were heading towards a hundred! It was decided that it was too divisive.

I should also point out that there are a good number of provisions that are clearly intended to do away with certain African traditions. For some people, certain of these provisions are important.

Turning to process. Incidentally, when we began our work, the received wisdom was that process was what really mattered. 'Look at South Africa', they said. People would go to South Africa on pilgrimage to learn about process. I should say that I learnt a great deal about constitutions and constitution-making when I had the privilege of visiting South Africa as it developed what I believed, and still believe, was an excellent constitution. We in Kenya invited South Africa to come to us—in form of Pius Langa, Yvonne Mkgoro, Geoff Budlender, and Christina Murray, among others.

I think that the Constitution's place in the identity of Kenyans is significantly due to process. There is still a remarkable consciousness of the Constitution among Kenyans—many foreigners comment on it. Kenyans knew the process was happening; participation was central to the process. In very substantial numbers they turned out to comment on what they wanted. They walked in their hundreds to meetings, stayed all day, and walked home again afterwards.

If such a process is genuine—and if the people are encouraged to express what they really want in a new constitutional order—the resultant document should reflect their values. I recognise that public input can be shaped—and distorted—all too easily by those in charge of the process, who think they know what the people want (or ought to want).

But if the people of Kenya felt that the Constitution in no way reflected what they wanted, they would not feel the same commitment to it. The same document—or an even better document—that they felt no involvement in would not have the same impact or be part of their identity.

I am not sure whether I have answered your question! But thank you for asking me to try. And all the best in your remaining deliberations.

Let me also say how delighted I am to share this session with Professor Ben Nwabueze—a true constitutional luminary, to use a favourite Kenyan word.

Africa's Chequered Journey to Constitutional Democracy[1]

Ben Nwabueze

Africa's journey to constitutional democracy has been a chequered one, marked by variegated events of a devastating nature. It began with a life of bondage under a colonial, racist, and supremacist form of rule that lasted for a significant part of the continent's political history until the attainment of freedom from servitude, a moment which is rightly regarded as a revolution or, at any rate, an event as revolutionary in its proportions as colonisation itself.

The devastation of life of bondage under colonial rule is what made the journey a chequered one from inception. The impact of colonial rule on the backward societies of Africa, writes Lucian Pye, gave rise to chaos and bequeathed successive African governments with the 'tragically heroic and comically futile' task of trying to create a semblance of order from the situation.[2] The task is indeed a tragically heroic and comically futile one. J.M. Lee too speaks of postcolonial African states as being 'hostages' to their colonial past and of the 'humiliating' task bequeathed to them by 'the circumstances in which they were created'. Politics in Africa, he says, is a fight between opposing groups 'about the nature of the state' itself, its relationship and boundary with society, the legitimacy of government, and 'accepted procedures for conducting public business'.[3] In this fight, which has all the characteristics of a feud, governance or management of public affairs to the best advantage of the people is sidelined and often trampled upon under the feet of the contestants. Democracy can scarcely be sustained until these issues, which touch upon the preconditions for it, are settled. Such, then, were the tragically futile circumstances in which the journey took place.

Every one of the fifty-four countries in Africa, except Liberia and Ethiopia, was engulfed in the holocaust of colonialism. All acceded to independence on the model of one type of constitutional democracy or another, mainly the Westminster export model of the British parliamentary system or the model of the 1958 Constitution of the French Republic.[4] Lamentably, whilst independence freed Africa from the oppressive and dehumanising yoke of colonial bondage, it also brought in its wake the yoke of the authoritarian regimes of African indigenous rulers. This impacted less on the personality, mentality, and psychology

[1] This address is based largely on Ben Nwabueze, *The Story of Africa's Chequered Journey to Constitutional Democracy* (Safari Books 2018).
This chapter is a keynote address presented by Professor Ben Nwabueze at the Eighth Stellenbosch Annual Seminar on Constitutionalism in Africa, 16–19 September 2021.

[2] Lucian Pye, 'Armies in the Process of Political Modernization' in John Asher Johnson (ed.), *The Role of the Military in Underdeveloped Countries* (Princeton Legacy Library 1962) 74.

[3] J.M. Lee, *African Armies and Civil Order* (Frederick Praeger 1969) 623.

[4] See Nwabueze (n. 1) chapters 7 and 11.

Ben Nwabueze, *Africa's Chequered Journey to Constitutional Democracy* In: *Constitutional Identity and Constitutionalism in Africa*. Edited by: Charles M. Fombad and Nico Steytler, Oxford University Press. © Ben Nwabueze 2024.
DOI: 10.1093/oso/9780198906308.003.0002

of Africans, as did colonial rule, than on their freedom of action, expression, and movement, as well as their freedom to associate with one another for political purposes.

The African one-party state arrived on the scene like a menacing leviathan eroding, yet without completely jettisoning, principles of democratic governance—the rule of law, every kind of separation or division of powers, individual liberties.[5] Its evils, as manifested in particular acts of oppression and repression, were horrific.[6] The authoritarianism of the one-party state was followed more or less immediately by absolutist or supremacist military regimes instituted in military coup d'états. These regimes were characterised above all else by the abolition of the notion of a constitution as a supreme law that overrides all laws and other acts of government inconsistent with its provisions. In other words, a military regime that overthrows a pre-existing government in a coup d'état is not just absolutist in terms of its unlimited powers in the management of public affairs; more ominously, it is a supremacist regime as well, a fact which has far-reaching and devastating implications for the principles, requirements, and ethos of constitutional democracy.[7]

The most far-reaching and devastating implication deserving special emphasis is that it overthrows not only the pre-existing government and its constitution; it is also a forcible seizure of the state and the sovereignty invested in it on behalf of the people, to whom it belongs. Since sovereignty belongs to the people as represented and institutionalised by the state, a successful military revolution, involving, as stated, a forcible seizure of the state and its sovereignty, is a coup against the people as well. It robs them of their political sovereignty, the most cardinal attribute of which is the power to frame a constitution for their own governance and to define, through such constitution, the extent of powers being delegated to government. It also robs the people of other political attributes of sovereignty by reason of the takeover of the entire powers of government, the overthrow of the representative institutions of government and of elected political leaders, the dissolution of political parties, and the ban on politics and other forms of popular political participation.

With the take-over by the military of power to lay down the *grundnorm* (the cardinal attribute of sovereignty), the usurpation of the powers of government, in particular the law-making power in its entirety; the overthrow of the representative institutions of government and of the elected political leaders; the dissolution of political parties, the banning of politics, popular elections, and all other forms of popular political participation; nothing—absolutely nothing—is left of the sovereignty of the people, save for the bare legal title of sovereignty vested in the state on behalf of the people. Now, the state too is forcibly seized.

A military revolution thus has the same effect as the colonial subjugation of a people by conquest: both are a forcible seizure of the entire sovereignty inhering in the country. A military government established after a coup thus combines in itself the delegated power of the local colonial government and the residual power of the imperial government in and over the colonised country. Just as the imperial government in its legislative capacity is subject to no law by which its power in and over the colonised country is limited, so too is a military government in its legislative capacity not subject to any supreme law. Just as the imperial government, by virtue of the sovereignty seized from the colonised people, can make any law it likes, including a law authorising and directing the arrest and detention of a named person

[5] Ibid. chapter 12.
[6] Ibid. chapter 13.
[7] Ibid. chapter 17.

or the confiscation of his property—a *privilegium*, as it has been described—so can a military government do the same by virtue of the sovereignty forcibly seized from its own citizens. The analogy with colonialism, as an imperial authority, goes further than this, of course.

It follows from the notion that a military take-over is a coup against the people in which their sovereignty is forcibly seized that the power exercised by a military regime in the government of the country is not bestowed on it by, nor otherwise derived from, the people; it is exercised not by their consent, express or implied, but against their wishes. The doctrine of implied mandate has no application here at all: a power derived from the implied mandate of the people would constitute a military government as a democratic government of some kind—a blatant contradiction in terms. The source of the military government's power is simply force; such power rests on the regime's ability to compel acceptance of its authority—its ability to hold down the people in subjection to its authority by means of armed force or the threat of it. Its power flows merely from the 'barrel of the gun', not from popular consent, express or implied. When there is voting at elections (albeit that the elections are rigged), election campaigns, political rallies, public assemblies, and processions on public issues and other forms of popular participation in a democracy banned under military rule, it is as if the country has reverted to its previous condition as a colonial state. This epitomises, in its gravest dimension, the tragic misfortune of military seizure of government and the state.

The oppressive and repressive impact of the absolutist regimes, both military and civilian, has been tragically manifested in reigns of terror unleashed on the people in which thousands have been killed and millions forced to flee to other countries as refuges. Its evil reaches its apogee in the privatisation of the state, as distinct from the personalisation of rule.[8] The evils of absolutist rule took on a new dimension with the advent of the socialist state, but, mercifully, the African socialist state was not characterised by some of the obnoxious elements of its prototype in the former Soviet Union, such as a centrally planned economy; the concept of socialist legality in place of the rule of law; democratic centralism; the empowerment of the masses or the working people; and other elements, all of which combined to make the socialist state a totalitarian one. The uncertain extent to which these elements characterised the African socialist state accounts for the appellation 'African socialism',[9] one perhaps used derisively, as when President Kamuzu Banda of Malawi said: 'Talk about African socialism. What is African socialism? It makes me sick.'[10]

We are confronted at this point by an interesting question as to the reasons for the predilection of African rulers for authoritarian rule and for their predisposition to sit tight in office once they get there—a sit-tight syndrome, as it is called.[11] The last leg of Africa's journey to constitutional democracy was marked by the end of authoritarian rule which, like the end of colonial rule, is rightly denominated as a revolution. But the event was not an exclusively African affair; rather, it was part of a movement that swept across the globe from 1989, taking Africa along with it. It was nevertheless momentous and dramatic. In January 1990, forty-two African countries had authoritarian one-party or military regimes; only nine—Botswana, the Gambia, Mauritius, Senegal, Zimbabwe, Liberia, Madagascar, South Africa, and Sudan—were ruled under some form of democratic system, however restricted or attenuated in one way or another.

[8] Ibid. chapter 19.
[9] Ibid. chapter 20.
[10] Ibid. 407.
[11] Ibid. chapters 14–16.

Some absolutist, no-party military regimes still lingered on, or even sprouted up after 1990 in Nigeria, the Gambia, Sierra Leone, Niger, Algeria, Burundi, and Côte d'Ivoire. But these too were shortly to be swept away by the mighty wind of change blowing across the continent. By 2001, with but a few exceptions, all of the countries of Africa hitherto under authoritarian or non-democratic rule had shed the system. The only four exceptions were Libya, Uganda, Swaziland (all three are no-party civilian regimes), and Somalia. And so came the unlamented end of authoritarian rule in Africa, a period that had spanned three decades of Africa's postcolonial history.

Before the events of 1989–94, who would have believed that the once all-conquering, all-powerful life president Ngwazi Kamuzu Banda of Malawi, the tyrannous Mengistu Haile Mariam of Ethiopia, and the invincible, all-knowing founding president Mobutu Sese Seko of Zaire could be consigned so ignominiously to the rubbish dump of fallen dictators in Africa, or that the seemingly impregnable apartheid system in South Africa would take an exit and give way to a democratic dispensation of freedom and justice for all, irrespective of colour, creed, and place of origin.[12] But such is the uncertain, impermanent nature of absolute, personalist rule everywhere. The end of authoritarian rule is not like the death of an individual, however famous, or the collapse of a business enterprise, however prestigious. It is the passing of an era or of an age.

That doing away with a dictatorship does not mean the same thing as installing a sustainable democracy is borne out by experience in Africa, as entrenched regimes either merely went through the democratic motions, or as newly democratic regimes succumbed to various forms of authoritarian reversion. The rocky political coastline against which it broke has made this returning wave appear decidedly jagged. 'The recent democratic openings in Africa', writes Samuel Huntington, 'moved only a short distance away from authoritarianism'.[13]

Not inaccurately, therefore, Michael Bratton and Nicolas van de Walle speak of transitions in Africa as having manifested four outcomes: where transition was 'precluded' owing to, for example, an internal security situation, such as civil war, or to other factors that prevented it from getting under way (as in Somalia); where transition, after its onset, was 'blocked', prevented, or interrupted, either by the incumbent authoritarian ruler's tendentious manoeuvres or by military intervention, from following its desired course (as in Sierra Leone); where a transition was 'flawed' by perverse manipulation of its process, thereby enabling the incumbent authoritarian ruler to win the multi-party elections and stay in power (as in Kenya and most of the other fourteen countries in which the transition elections were won by the incumbents); and, lastly, where the transition culminated in the installation of a new government following a free and fair election, that is, a truly 'democratic' transition (as in Zambia and the other ten countries where the incumbent authoritarian rulers were defeated).[14]

The course of events in the transition from authoritarian rule to democratic governance prompts the following intriguing questions:

[12] Ibid. chapter 8.

[13] In Samuel P. Huntington, *The Third Wave: Democratization in the Late Twentieth Century* (University of Oklahoma Press 1991) 39.

[14] Michael Bratton and Nicolas van de Walle, *Democratic Experiments in Africa: Regime Transitions in Comparative Perspective* (Cambridge University Press 1997), 284–6.

- Was the process of transition designed to bring about, as its outcome, a democratic form of governance? For example, the first transition in Nigeria (1976–9) involved six processes:
  - o the setting up of a Constitution Drafting Committee (CDC);
  - o public discussion of the constitutional proposals drawn up by the CDC;
  - o the convening of a Constituent Assembly;
  - o promulgation of a new constitution by the military government;
  - o multi-party democratic elections; and
  - o hand-over to and installation of a democratically elected civilian government.
- Was the outcome of the process a truly democratic form of government, which depends, in the final analysis, on how free, fair, and credible the elections were?
- How truly constitutionalist was the transition?
- Will the change to constitutional democracy endure—can it be consolidated and sustained?[15]

Every one of the milestones in Africa's journey to constitutional democracy is rightly regarded as in nature of a revolution—colonial rule and bondage; the regaining of sovereignty seized by European imperialism, otherwise known as independence; the advent of authoritarian rule as well as its exit; and the return of democratic governance. Of the five milestones, colonisation is the most far-reaching and devastating in its consequences for Africa, which is still held hostage to its colonial past and may continue to be so indefinitely. Another revolution, this time a social and ethical one, is needed to resolve the continent's lingering and vexed problem of governance in this colonially created modern state system. It is probably at the end of such a revolution that Africa's search for a true constitutional identity would have meaning.

Bibliography

Bratton M. and Van de Walle N., *Democratic Experiments in Africa: Regime Transitions in Comparative Perspective* (Cambridge University Press 1997)

Huntington S.P., *The Third Wave: Democratization in the Late Twentieth Century* (University of Oklahoma Press 1991)

Lee J.M., *African Armies and Civil Order* (Frederick Praeger 1969)

Nwabueze B., *The Story of Africa's Chequered Journey to Constitutional Democracy* (Safari Books 2018)

Pye L., 'Armies in the Process of Political Modernization' in Johnson J.A. (ed.), *The Role of the Military in Underdeveloped Countries* (Princeton Legacy Library 1962) 82

[15] These issues are examined in Nwabueze (n. 1) part IV.

Introduction

In Search of Constitutional Identity and Constitutionalism in Africa

Nico Steytler and Charles M. Fombad

1. Introduction

In its modern history, Africa has experienced different waves of constitutional ordering. The latest wave, which began in the 1990s, has set the stage over the past decade for what is now a hotly debated issue: whether recent new or fundamentally revised constitutions truly reflect an African constitutional identity. The aim of this book is to examine, firstly, how the concept of constitutional identity can be useful in understanding constitutional change in Africa; secondly, how constitutional identities enhance or limit constitutionalism; and thirdly, how constitutional identities may be decolonised to reflect an African identity. Could both constitutionalism and the decolonisation of constitutions produce a new African constitutional identity?

The issue of constitutional identity brings a number of important research questions to the fore—historically, contemporarily, and prospectively. Firstly, it raises the question of whether the concept of constitutional identity provides a useful optic with which to look at and appreciate African constitutions. Is it something more than the main characteristics of a constitution (unitary or federal, presidential or parliamentary)? Is it about the relevance and aspiration of the constitution? Is it nominal or effective, descriptive or transformative? Is it about the way the constitution relates to a country's culture(s) and history? What are the prevailing theories of constitutional identity and their core elements? What is the balance between the universal versus the particular, and what is the relevance of external and internal influences?

The second question concerns the role of path dependency in forming constitutional identities. To what degree have colonial heritages shaped the constitutional identities that surfaced in independence and post-independence constitutional ordering? What are the principal differences between the francophone (including lusophone) and anglophone approaches to constitutionalism and diversity? Have remnants of such 'colonial' identities persisted in post-1990 constitutional identities?

A third issue relates to the widening gap between most African constitutions—which in many cases incorporate fundamental principles of modern constitutionalism—and the actuality of practice. The question is whether this gap exists because these constitutions lack an authentic constitutional identity. Is this the reason why entrenching a culture of constitutionalism, respect for the rule of law, and good governance remains a challenge? This, then,

Nico Steytler and Charles M. Fombad, *Introduction* In: *Constitutional Identity and Constitutionalism in Africa*.
Edited by: Charles M. Fombad and Nico Steytler, Oxford University Press.
DOI: 10.1093/oso/9780198906308.003.0003

takes us to the question of whether African constitutions need to be 'decolonised' to give them an African identity. If so, how would they be decolonised in form and content? Are there alternative principles that can replace some of the present ones? Have any innovative theories, principles, or practices been designed to address specifically African challenges, such as ethnic conflict?

A fourth question is whether African traditional authorities and institutions are part of national constitutional identity-building or merely a sentimental cultural relic of the past with little relevance today? Closely related to this is the question of whether constitutionalism should form part of an African constitutional identity. Does the project of having constitutional identities reflect also constitutionalism remain important? Have conditions since the pre-1990s changed to such an extent that a different approach to government is viable? Are all the elements of constitutionalism equally relevant?

In addressing these questions, the volume is organised in three parts. The first provides an overview of concepts and key issues, in particular of the notions of path dependency and colonial and traditional constitutional identities. The second consists of case studies exploring these questions in regard to specific countries. The final part contains concluding remarks.

2. Overview: Key Concepts and Issues

One of Africa's pre-eminent constitutional scholars, Yash Ghai, sets the scene for this volume in his introductory remarks by asking pointedly what the term 'constitutional identity' means. There is ambiguity. Does it depend on the text? Does it depend on the form of state, for example, that of a monarchy or federation? Or do the people of a country themselves have a constitutional identity in that their constitution is part of their self-identity? Ghai says the concept is 'a slippery one'. Is a constitutional identity purposefully constructed, or is it something that emerges from the experience of a constitution?

In addressing the question of whether and how African constitutions can be imbued with an African identity through African values, he suggests that it can done through the language of the text, namely what the constitution says about state institutions and mechanisms of governance, and through the process of making the constitution. As the former chairperson of the Constitution of Kenya Review Commission which conducted a highly participatory process of constitutional drafting, Ghai argues that many Kenyans see their identity reflected in the 2010 Constitution and that this is due largely to its history and the process of making it.

Ben Nwabueze, another doyen of the constitutional law in Africa, categorises constitutional development in Africa into five historical stages. The first involved colonial 'constitutions', which imposed bondage, servitude, and absolute rule. The second stage, of short duration, was the era of independence constitutions at the end of the colonial period. In the third stage, postcolonial constitutions enshrined authoritarian rule through one- or no-party states at the expense of democratic accountability. In the process, Nwabueze argues, the people's sovereignty was stolen by autocratic leaders. An extreme case was military rule, which he likens to the previous colonial state. The fourth stage saw the post-Cold War wave of democratisation sweep away authoritarian regimes. The fifth concerns constitutional changes that move way away from constitutional democracies towards 'authoritarian democracies'.

Reviewing this history, Nwabueze is convinced that colonisation was 'far-reaching and devastating in its consequences for Africa, which is still held hostage to its colonial past, and may continue to be so held indefinitely'. He argues for another revolution, a social and ethical one, which is needed to deal with the problems produced by the colonially inherited governance systems. He concludes that it 'is probably at the end of this revolution that Africa's search for a true constitutional identity may have meaning'.

In Chapter 1, 'Constitutional Identity and Constitutionalism in Africa: Concepts and Key Issues', Charles M. Fombad provides an overview of the issues addressed in this volume. He notes that debates about the identity of modern constitutions are not new and for a while have attracted the attention of mainly Western scholars, particularly in Europe and the United States. Fombad unpacks the elements of the work of two leading scholars on constitutional identity—Gary Jacobsohn and Michel Rosenfeld. For Jacobsohn, the concept provides the tools to understand the formation of constitutional identity, which occurs through a dialogical process driven by disharmonies in a constitutional text or between the text and the social order. Rosenfeld, in turn, outlines different notions of constitutional identity and focuses on the interplay between the text of the constitution and national identity. Both scholars agree that the formation of constitutional identity is never a completed process but one always subject to change.

Fombad points out that the colonial legacy remains the most dominant external influence on African constitutions, be this legacy anglophone, francophone, or lusophone. In addition, the wave of democratisation of the 1990s introduced 'universal' liberal democratic elements, as evident, for example, in bills of rights derived from international human rights instruments. These constitutions are now confronted with the issue of having an 'African constitutional identity'. This raises the question of whether, at a practical level, the existing constitutional paradigms, concepts, and normative ideologies are suited to developing a stable, sustainable constitutional system of governance based on the fundamental principles of modern constitutionalism. In this context, Fombad introduces the concept of 'constitutional culture', which refers in part to the disposition of citizens to recognise and accept that they are governed by a constitution which creates institutions of government and sets limits on what the government may do. There is thus a strong link between constitutional culture and the concept of constitutional identity.

Fombad sums up the concept of constitutional identity in five key points. Firstly, it is the combination, coexistence, and evolution over time of various identities at both the national and international level. Secondly, the constitutional text is merely indicative: it is its application in practice which reveals the identity. Thirdly, however, the text may reveal much about the identity through the entrenchment of specific provisions against arbitrary and casual change. Fourthly, constitutional identity helps to preserve and protect national identity from the encroaching forces of supranational, regional, and global constitutionalism. Fifthly, it may provide the stimulus for debate aimed at developing constitutional principles, values, and institutions adapted to contemporary African realities.

Fombad poses the question of whether the success or failure of constitutionalism in Africa depends on whether constitutions reflect a national and/or African constitutional identity. He also wonders if the search for an African constitutional identity is an illusion and distraction from fundamental issues of constitutional governance. Central to the chapter is an examination of the link between constitutional identity and constitutionalism in Africa. In concluding, Fombad contends that, unlike in the past, the issue of constitutional self-identification is now a critical factor that experts must take into account in constitution-making processes. However, the quest for a distinctive African constitutional identity should not detract a constitution from its primary role of protecting citizens from the abuse of power.

Central to the process of decolonising African constitutions is infusing them with indigenous values, principles, and institutions. What might these values, principles, and institutions be and, as Fombad asks in Chapter 1, how do they tie up with the principle of limited government?

In Chapter 2, 'Constitutional Checks and Balances in Traditional Africa', George B.N. Ayittey addresses this question from a historical perspective. He argues that it has been a fallacy that pre-colonial governance was without viable institutions and consisted only in tyrannical and despotic rule. This factually incorrect perception has been used by colonisers and post-independence regimes alike to justify authoritarian regimes. Ayittey sets out to debunk this fallacy, one that has caused immeasurable harm to postcolonial development, by showing that Africa's indigenous political systems are not to be equated with despotic rule seeing as they contained traditional checks and balances.

Ayittey argues that in indigenous African political culture there was a fear of state tyranny and that the state was thus structured to provide a bulwark against this threat. In most societies, he shows, autocratic rule was generally the exception rather than the rule, because communities could always leave the authority of the despot: 'voting with their feet' was, in effect, a check on the despot's power. Other forms of checks included systems of government highly decentralised through detailed devolution of authority and assignment of responsibilities. Yet other safeguards were embedded in the taboos and injunctions a ruler had to obey.

The chapter discusses such checks and balances in the four main traditional polities: empires, kingdoms, stateless societies, and chiefdoms with centralised authority. Empires were formed by a group of kingdoms, usually through voluntary association. Tyrannical rule was thus not a possibility as membership was by choice. Moreover, devolution of authority was common. Kingdoms comprised chiefdoms of people of the same ethnic stock. The community accepted their king as a necessary evil, because he was necessary for the preservation of the social order, but to prevent abuse of his powers at the expense of the independence and freedom of his people, most of his powers were delegated to subordinate chiefs. Also, a king was surrounded by councils and courts. If all else failed, regicide was 'an ultimate check upon the excesses of a king'. As for stateless societies, these were communities which elected not to have chiefs or any centralised authority at all. In such societies, there were only two units of government: a council of elders and a village assembly. Governance was based on kinship and the norms of kinship behaviour in a particular system of law and order.

Ayittey uses the terms 'chiefdom' or 'chief' to refer generically to a leader of a tribal group at the village level whose primary duty was to determine a consensual position, not to impose his own style of governing, and was characterised by four Cs: consultation, conciliation, compromise, and consensus—the very opposite to despotism. Overall, Ayittey suggests that despotism was not an integral characteristic of indigenous African political systems, even though it was always a possibility. Africans, 'after encountering it, took measures to prevent its recurrence'. His contention is that the real tragedy is that the establishment today of tyrannical systems with no checks and balances is not reflective of indigenous values and institutions.

In Chapter 3, 'Constitutional Identity and Traditional Authority in the Post-colony', Heinz Klug addresses the role of present-day traditional authority in sub-Saharan Africa, an institution that sits uncomfortably in liberal democratic constitutions yet remains a source of identity for many. Klug locates traditional authority within Jacobsohn's concept of constitutional identity as something formed by a dialogical process involving contending ideas, and James Tully's argument for the recognition of a multiplicity of identities within modern constitutionalism. This chapter thus focuses on the recognition and role of traditional authorities in postcolonial constitutions in sub-Saharan Africa. Klug identifies three main constitutional patterns of response to traditional authorities in the post-independence era.

The first was to eradicate them on ideological or political grounds, or otherwise let them fade away as African societies modernised. This response is apparent in a large number of African constitutions that make no mention at all of traditional authorities. Despite their lack of recognition, though, these authorities continue to play a role in the lives of their communities, often providing services which the central government fails to do. Moreover, traditional authorities cannot be ignored by the political elite because they wield enormous electoral influence in their communities due to their control over resources and people.

The second pattern extends the colonial practice of indirect rule, in that traditional leaders are allowed officially to continue performing functions relating to customary law and communal land management. Some constitutions provide an institutional role for traditional authorities at the national, regional, local, or multiple level of government. An increasing number of states give constitutional recognition to traditional authorities but confine their powers largely to local governance, which gives them significant influence and authority. The third pattern involves granting traditional leaders constitutional recognition but denying them any role in formal governance: it is thus only a symbolic gesture that does not vest any formal power in them.

Klug maintains that the multiplicity of ways in which traditional authorities are recognised and incorporated in constitutions demonstrates how a dialogical process of constitutional identity unfolds. Recognition of traditional authority inserts a 'disharmony' in an otherwise liberal democratic framework; these disharmonious elements within such constitutions might impact on the formation of constitutional identities in sub-Saharan African countries. He observes that an African constitution that makes no mention of traditional authorities, or merely recognises them symbolically, could undermine the authority of those attempting to govern under the formal constitution.

It is often noted that the predominant influence on the style and content of African constitutions is their colonial past, which thus contributes to the formation of constitutional identities. In Chapter 4, 'The Struggle for Constitutional Identity in Francophone Africa', Charles M. Fombad and Trésor M. Makunya focus on the francophone colonial legacy that bestowed a civil law system on countries in West and Central Africa. The authors pose the question of whether, given the French 1958 Fifth Republic constitutional identity inherited at independence, constitutional reforms since 1990 have resulted in a reimagining of the constitutional identity of these countries. Have these countries crafted, redesigned, adjusted, and adopted principles, doctrines, and institutions that reflect the wishes and aspirations of the people as well as address their peculiar challenges? More specifically, have any characteristics emerged that would contain the seeds of a distinctive constitutional identity?

The premise of the chapter is that an effective constitutional system must be able to address the idiosyncratic problems a country is facing; this aside, a constitution must also reflect the people's culture, tradition, and history, as this would increase the acceptance and legitimacy of the normative and institutional frameworks it establishes and enhance their enforceability. Throughout francophone Africa, the French handed over power only to linguistically, culturally, and religiously assimilated locals versed in the colonial system of governance, thereby creating a rootless new social class that ensured the continuation of French policies. Despite heightened awareness of the complexity of the social, economic, and political challenges that different African countries face, Gaullism, with all its defects, continues to reign supreme notwithstanding the variety of constitutional options which are available for dealing with these challenges.

The three key features of the Gaullist model of constitutional governance are the dominance of the president; the subordination to the president and the executive of the other two branches of government; and weak protection of human rights. This system of centralisation resulted too in the excessive centralisation of political power seen in francophone African constitutions. In spite of the third wave of democratisation, France's continued interference and presence in the economic, cultural, and political life of its former colonies has served to perpetuate the Gaullist constitutional model and its associated institutions.

The possible explanation of why the Gaullist constitutional model survives and thrives is that it suits the temperament and strategic interests of francophone African leaders, the ruling elites, and the French. The chapter concludes that francophone African countries remain under the spell of the Gaullist constitutional model and have been unable to exercise creativity in designing distinctive principles, doctrines, and institutions that could be effective in addressing the specific challenges that they face.

As almost all African countries are a colonial construct, no notice was taken constitutionally of the diversity of their ethnic, linguistic, and religious composition. How, then, could a constitutional identity be developed that took into account the range of their ethnic and other markers of social identity? This problem is not confined to Africa. In Chapter 5, Karl Kössler asks the question, 'Who are "we, the people"?' and considers pluralist constitutional identity after democratic transitions in the cases of Ethiopia, South Africa, Bosnia and Herzegovina, and Spain—all countries with a high degree of diversity which have undergone a transition from authoritarian rule to constitutional democracy. They all have multilevel systems of government that could accommodate a pluralist identity at two levels, particularly where the constitutional space exists for the adoption of subnational constitutions.

The chapter commences by explaining the concept of pluralist constitutional identity and why the image of 'the people' is one of its core elements. Kössler follows Jacobsohn's approach to the formation of constitutional identity in seeing disharmonies, both internal and external to the constitutional text, as providing catalysts for change. Such disharmonies are, of course, apparent in plurinational countries. How, then, is the notion of 'the people' of a country formed within the text? Kössler use three types of constitutional information: explicit formulations as to who 'we, the people' are, gleaned mainly from preambles; symbols representing 'the people' beyond the constitutional text in everyday life; and constitutional backward-looking narratives and forward-looking aspirations that interpret 'the people's' past and outline a vision for its future. He finds this information in both national and subnational constitutions.

In the four case studies, some elements of constitutional continuity were present in the new national constitutions of South Africa and Spain, while in Ethiopia and Bosnia and Herzegovina the new constitutions were revolutionary. In the case of subnational constitutions and the shaping of plurinational identities, the case studies show a diverse picture. Both Ethiopia and South Africa make very little use of the subnational constitutional space, mainly because of the presence of a dominant national political party not encouraging of experimentation. In the cases of Bosnia and Herzegovina and Spain, subnational constitutions were seen as important vehicles for penning down plural identities.

In discussing the framing of 'the people' as the constitutional subject, Kössler shows that the classic American expression—'We, the people'—is not uniformly used. In Ethiopia, different groups—'nations, nationalities, and peoples'—are the very constitutional subject; in Bosnia and Herzegovina, any reference to a united polity—'the people'—is missing. The framing of the images of the people in subnational constitutions depends on the scope for and use of subnational activism. The use of symbols to represent the constitutional subjects in everyday life conveys a similarly diverse picture. While South Africa sought to construct a united 'people' through inclusive symbolism at the national level (e.g. its flag, anthem, and public holidays), divisive symbolism is encountered in Ethiopia and Bosnia and Herzegovina. In all four case studies, use is made of constitutional backward-looking narratives and forward-looking aspirations that seek to unify 'the people'. The narratives of the past bring inclusion to the formerly excluded but emphasise differences. More neutral are the forward-looking aspirations, which can be built around vague sentiments about unity and non-discrimination.

3. Case Studies

The concept of constitutional identity is examined in depth in several case studies of individual countries, ranging from South Africa in the south to Egypt in the north, and from Ethiopia in the east to the Cape Verde Islands in the far west, with Cameroon halfway between the latter two. These countries exhibit a wide range of contexts—from the dominant military identity of Egypt, historical race-based identity in South Africa, Ethiopian ethnic-bound identity, and the democratic, tolerant, and human-rights identity of the Cape Verde Islands, to a clash of two colonial legacies—francophone and anglophone—in Cameroon.

In Chapter 6, 'A Century of South African Constitutional Identities', Nico Steytler traces the formation of several constitutional identities since the formation of modern-day South Africa in 1910. The chapter raises the question of whether the concepts used in analysing the formation of constitutional identity, as advanced by Gary Jacobsohn and Michel Rosenfeld, shed fresh light on a century of constitution-making that culminated in the democratic constitutions of 1993 and 1996. Steytler asks if the concepts used by these theorists give a better understanding of why, during the past decade, there is yet another round of constitutional dialogue, and if the insights so gained provide a guide for the future.

The chapter argues that the literature on the formation of a constitutional identity affords useful tools for unlocking a fuller understanding of the shaping of South African constitutional identity. Firstly, it is a long dialogical process of forming and reforming the imagined 'nation' or constitutional identity—the 1909 Constitution is inextricably linked to the 1996 Constitution and will not stop at the latter. The 1913 division of land settlement between black and white has remained the key issue of contention.

Secondly, South Africa is also an example of how constitutional writing is a purposeful project of defining constitutional identity. Each of the five constitutions (of 1909, 1961, 1983, 1994, and 1996) had their intended audience (circumscribed by the definition of 'the nation') and provided protection of their vital interests, sometimes using in the preambles the constitutional techniques of justification, for example, narratives about the past.

Thirdly, each of the constitutions contained 'disharmonies', both internal to the text and externally with society, which served as catalyst for the next iteration of the constitutional identity. The exclusion of blacks from constitutional compact in 1909 resulted in the development of an alternative 'imagined nation', one based on equality and justice, as articulated in the Freedom Charter of 1955. For Afrikaners, the 1909 constitution's link to the British Crown was a disharmony which ended only when South Africa become a republic in 1961. The tricameral Constitution of 1983, which sought to divide South Africa between Africans and non-Africans, led to a further conflict which was eventually mediated in the 1993 and 1996 democratic constitutions. Yet the 1996 Constitution carries its own disharmonies, by basing land distribution on the 1913 legislation.

Fourthly, as a fixed constitutional identity is illusory, changes depend on those who control the authors' pen in writing the next constitution.

Ethiopia has also a long history of fluctuation in constitutional identity. In Chapter 7, 'Constitutional Identity and Disruption in Contemporary Ethiopia', Asnake Kefale sketches out that history, arguing that a continuous and unifying constitutional identity remains elusive.

The first modern (written) constitution was introduced in 1931 by Emperor Haile Selassie soon after his coronation. Although it was revised, or modernised, in 1955, it did not prevent the dethroning of the emperor in 1974. It was then suspended by the Marxist-Leninist military government (Derg) that assumed state power following a popular revolution. The 1987 Peoples' Democratic Republic of Ethiopia (PDRE) Constitution in turn was scrapped by the Ethiopian Peoples' Revolutionary Democratic Front (EPRDF) when it assumed state power following its military victory over the Derg in 1991. The EPRDF-led government introduced its own constitution, the Constitution of the Federal Democratic Republic of Ethiopia (FDRE), in 1995. Various acts of resistance against the government since 2018 question the suitability of the 1995 Constitution to keep the country together, with the civil war in Tigray region the most extensive but not the only conflict.

Kefale argues that the various constitutional regimes provided for little institutional restraint on the powers of the rulers. Moreover, because of the overbearing dominance of the state and lack of tolerance of dissenting voices, 'political changes in the country generally come about through violent ruptures rather than peaceful reforms'. He maintains that the problem of constitutional disruption reflects the absence of an overarching constitutional identity. This lack of continuity he attributes to interrelated factors, chiefly limitations in constitution-making, inability to reconcile foreign ideas with the country's socio-political identities, and constitutional disharmonies.

Firstly, constitutional making has been characterised by limited public participation. After a violent overthrow of the incumbent regime, the newly established regime 'invents its constitution without ensuring the participation of competing political actors'. The absence of inclusive, protracted negotiation often results in a lack of buy-in from the full spectrum of political actors.

Secondly, the adoption of foreign constitutional principles also did not advance popular acceptance of the new constitution and the development of a stable constitutional identity. The chapter illustrates how the four constitutions transplanted foreign constitutional ideas and 'gave limited attention to the need to harmonise foreign ideas with local histories and cultures'. The 1931 Constitution was influenced by 1889 Meiji Constitution of Japan, consequently consolidating and centralising imperial power. The Revised Constitution of 1955, in turn, was influenced by Western ideas. The Derg's 1987 Constitution followed the Soviet Union's constitutional framework of institutionalising Marxism-Leninism. While the 1995 Constitution introduced many Western constitutional concepts, Kefala states that the ethno-federal structure was heavily influenced by the Stalinist approach to the 'national question' and the Soviet model of federalism.

Thirdly, the four constitutions suffered from internal contradictions as well as divergences with the society. The 1931 Constitution both cemented imperial rule and introduced limited popular institutions, but failed to recognise the ethno-linguistic and religious diversity of the country. The 1955 Revised Constitution recognised human rights, yet there were no formal restraints on the emperor's powers. It too failed to accommodate societal diversity. The Derg Constitution of 1987, while recognising diversity, imposed a Marxist-Leninist ideology on a deeply religious society with a negligible working class. The 1995 FDRE Constitution established a centralised form of ethno-federalism but at the same time allowed for unilateral secession.

Kefale concludes that unless these challenges are addressed, the formation of a more enduring constitution and constitutional identity will continue to be elusive.

At the far west, off the African coast, the Cape Verde Islands present a different context: a country without a pre-colonial history. Justice José Pina-Delgado of the Constitutional Court of Cape Verde addresses this circumstance in Chapter 8, 'Rooting Constitutional Identity in African Countries without Pre-colonial Institutional Traditions but with National Values: The Cape Verdean Experience and the Role of the Constitutional Court'.

The archipelago was first settled some five hundred years ago by the Portuguese, who brought Africans from the mainland as slaves; the islands also attracted Jews who sought a safe haven. Despite its being a Portuguese colony, Cape Verde saw the development of a mulatto population as well as the emergence of a 'national' identity among its inhabitants. There was a modicum of democracy through elected municipalities. As Pina-Delgado notes, 'Cape Verdean society developed in a way that allowed its inhabitants to amalgamate European, African, and Jewish or at least Crypto-Jewish influences, thereby creating distinctive and hybrid cultural features that led, very early on, to a sense of national identity'. A part of this culture was the notion of individual freedom, particularly so after the abolition of slavery in 1869. The Cape Verdean identity was neither a regional Portuguese one nor an African one, but a creole 'nation', characterised by tolerance, hospitality, and democracy. This identity was at odds with top-down colonial governance.

The resistance to colonial rule was led by Amílcar Cabral, a 'Cape Verdean by blood and Bissao-Guinean by birth', who sought to establish a Marxist-Leninist political system that would unite Cape Verde and Guinea-Bissau by de-emphasising the importance of the cultural differences of their respective peoples. In 1975, independence was declared and in 1980, the first constitution was adopted, based on Marxism-Leninism and with a centralised state controlled by the PAIGC (*Partido Africano para a Independência da Guiné e Cabo Verde*). The values were national independence, unity with Guinea-Bissau, anticolonialism, anti-imperialism, and the African destiny of the country. One-party rule collapsed in the late 1980s with the end of the Cold War, multiparty elections were held in 1990, and the opposition, 'appealing to long-repressed desires for freedom, political tolerance, and self-government by the people', came to power.

In the constitution-making of 1990–2, Pina-Delgado argues, the new ruling party rejected the values of the previous regime and sought to ensure that the constitution reflected the true 'Cape Verdean ethos and its communitarian disposition—namely, human dignity, national independence, individual freedom, equality, popular sovereignty, solidarity, peace, and justice'. It was thus a case of 'national identity' influencing the constitutional identity. However, the constitutional drafters borrowed from the Portuguese Constitution of 1976 its structure and form, as well as many of its norms. This influence is attributed to the drafting lawyers, who were steeped in Portuguese constitutional law and found inspiration in liberal democracy. It was not complete plagiarism, as several innovations were introduced. Pina-Delgado concludes that 'the founding fathers used the Portuguese Constitution in order to adopt a constitutional skeleton, assimilate universal or foreign values on which to organise the Republic, and articulate traditional Cape Verdean values as well as communitarian aspirations'.

The Constitutional Court of Cape Verde (CCCV), which was brought to life only in 2015, has been at the forefront of articulating the national ethos when interpreting the Constitution. It has done so by reducing dependence on foreign sources and locating constitutional interpretation in domestic sources. The Court has 'endeavoured to root constitutional values in Cape Verdean history, reality, and national institutional values'.

In Chapter 9, 'Cameroon and the Crisis of Constitutional Identity: Is Anglophone Identity Compatible with a Cameroonian Constitutional Identity?', Carlson Anyangwe and Charles M. Fombad return to the theme of inherited colonial legal frameworks, which in Cameroon are a compound of the francophone and anglophone legacies. This chapter provides context to the crisis threatening to end the fragile union between Cameroon's anglophone and francophone communities. On account of the two communities' distinctive colonial heritage and experience, language, culture, and disparity in population size, the federal arrangement that formed the basis of their union in 1961 seemed the ideal framework for forging unity in diversity. It was supposed to form the foundation for a common constitutional identity to emerge, but within a few months of what proved to be a highly centralised federation, the francophone-dominated government began dismantling the federal system. In 1972, the federal constitution was, in violation of its amendment provisions, replaced with a unitary constitution.

The chapter examines the country's historical background and the circumstances in which the federal constitution came to be adopted and eventually abrogated. It shows that its abrogation in 1972 was seen by many anglophones as a divorce, particularly since it was followed by policies designed to eliminate the distinctive features of the anglophone community and impose the francophone system on them under the pretext of harmonisation and national unity. At the heart of the current political crisis, which started in 2016, and the ensuing civil war, is the question of whether an anglophone identity is compatible with an imposed francophone constitutional identity. This is especially pertinent given that the constitutional framework fails to reflect the country's history or the respective hopes and fears of the two communities.

The crisis raises serious questions about the ability of Africans in the twenty-first century to rise above their colonised mindsets and design institutions capable of addressing recurrent governance challenges. Constitutional identity cannot be imposed, particularly in a complex society with competing identities at stake such as in Cameroon. It is an illusion to expect the anglophone community to sacrifice its distinct identity and culture in order to self-identify with the identity of the francophone community, which is promoted as the Cameroonian constitutional identity.

In Chapter 10, 'Taking Power from the People: Shifting Constitutional Identity in Egypt', Sherif A. Elgebeily tracks changes in Egypt's constitutional identities over a ninety-nine-year period. He shows that these identities have been subject to both external and internal influences, and asks: What is the indigenous constitutional identity of Egypt?

The first constitution of 1923 established the monarchy of King Farouk after the Unilateral Declaration of Egyptian Independence, but Egypt remained under British influence through the latter's control of the Suez Canal. The revolution in 1952 led by Gamal Abdel Nasser overthrew the monarchy and imposed a socialist framework influenced by the ideology of the Soviet Union. The revolution effected three policy shifts. Firstly, a socialist orientation was enshrined in the 1956 Constitution. Secondly, Egypt's membership of an Arab nation was prominent. In giving effect to the latter ideal, the United Arab Republic (UAR), created in 1958, comprised Egypt and Syria, but lasted only three years. Thirdly, the strongly militaristic identity that emerged thereafter was popular because the military was regarded as the saviour of the nation.

After the death of Nassar, Anwar Sadat assumed power legally in 1970, and the 1971 Constitution maintained Egypt's socialist leanings. However, Sadat sought to move towards a market economy, though it was only under Mubarak in 2007 that the constitution was amended to entrench a further shift towards capitalism. The Arab Spring of 2011 also affected Egypt, with a popular revolt, supported by the military, seeing the overthrow of the Mubarak regime. A revolutionary provisional constitution of 2012 was a short-lived pro-Islamist document adopted by the Muslim Brotherhood following the election of Mohammed Morsi. This regime in turn was removed by the military, and President el-Sisi was elected to power in 2014. The constitutional changes of 2016 and 2019 drastically shifted the locus of power, Elgebeily argues, away from representation of the people and in a more autocratic direction. At a policy level, there was thus a transition from a socialist ideal under Nasser to a militaristic capitalist constitution under el-Sisi.

Elgebeily argues that in Egypt's constitutional history, three trends come to the fore. Firstly, from 1952 onwards, the military assumed a leading role in the country. With the exception of President Morsi (2012–13), Egypt's head of state during this period has always been a member of the armed forces. However, the military has played an equivocal role as both saviour and oppressor. Under the Sisi-regime, its role 'in and over the constitution [increased], including its protection from being bound by [the constitution's] articles'. Secondly, the relationship between state and religion has evolved such that Egypt has changed from a country with a relatively secular and religiously tolerant initial constitution to one where religion plays a far more significant role in society. Although a measure of religious diversity is recognised in relation to Judaism and Christianity, Islam is the state religion and Sharia the source of law.

Thirdly, a highly centralised authoritarian regime has been in place since 1952. Nasser imposed a one-party regime, while both Sadat and Mubarak ruled by means of emergency powers. This has meant increased personal powers for the president, a weakening of the separation of powers, and reduced oversight of the military. Elgebeily argues that, in view of these three major trends, Egypt's constitutional identity has shifted—in the way a chameleon changes its colours—to match the environment in which it exists.

The chapters in this volume take one on a journey through the realities of constitutional identity and constitutionalism in Africa. They provide a broad overview that not only covers countries influenced by the two dominant constitutional traditions on the continent, namely the common law and civil law, but also take into account indigenous African legal systems. In the concluding chapter, 'Fostering a Sense of Constitutional Identity amid the Travails of African Constitutionalism', Charles M. Fombad's overarching argument is that the idea of a constitutional identity is important not just for its sake but because it is one of the important ways of promoting an ethos of sustainable constitutionalism as well as ensuring that the constitution reflects the aspirations and needs of society as a whole. The question he seeks to answer is whether this is happening and what lessons can be drawn from this study.

Fombad identifies a number of elements that are trying to combine to give African constitutions a sense of identity. The main one is the coexistence and evolution since independence of various identities at both the national and international levels that have combined and contributed to the establishment of some sense of constitutional identity in the different polities. Inherent in developing a sense of constitutional identity is the need for every polity to confront actual and potential economic, social, cultural, political, and other forces as it develops.

From this perspective, it has been particularly difficult for African countries to develop a clear and consistent sense of constitutional identity. Several disharmonious factors pose a formidable challenge. The main ones discussed in the different chapters include the undermining of constitutionalism through autocratic constitutionalism; the challenges of constructing a sense of common national identity in ethnically heterogeneous polities fragmented by, inter alia, racial, cultural, and religious diversity; the enduring debilitating effects of the colonial legacy; the challenges of reconciling national with competing international and global factors; and the elusive search for an authentic African constitutional identity.

In spite of these challenges, the chapters provide evidence of positive signs. For example, unlike before the 1990s, more effort has been made to adopt inclusive, participatory constitution-making processes, even if this has only been so in some anglophone countries. More attempts have also been made to infuse and entrench the role and powers of traditional authorities and traditional courts and institutions, even if this still falls short of the rhetoric of Africanisation and decolonisation. The enhanced powers and role of courts, as some chapters show, gives courts an opportunity to factor local circumstances into their judgements.

However, the slow yet steady decline in the quality of democracy and constitutionalism in the past decade remains an impediment to progress in developing a stronger sense of constitutional identity with local flavour. What is clear is that, unlike in the past, the issue of constitutional self-identification is now a critical factor that all constitution designers must take into account in the constitution-making process. The critical issue today is not how authentically African or reflective of a particular African country a constitution is, or how successfully it has embedded indigenous African values, principles, and institutions. Rather, it is whether the constitution, however distinctive, is not only able to enhance the prospects for good governance, democracy, respect for the rule of law, and constitutionalism, but also do so in a way that promotes political stability and economic development.

PART 1

OVERVIEW OF CONCEPTS AND KEY ISSUES, COLONIAL AND TRADITIONAL CONSTITUTIONAL IDENTITIES, AND PATH DEPENDENCY

1

Constitutional Identity and Constitutionalism in Africa

Concepts and Key Issues

Charles M. Fombad

1. Introduction

Debates about the identity of modern constitutions are not new and for a while have attracted the attention of Western scholars, particularly in Europe and the United States (US). It is only in the past decade, however, that they have begun to be taken seriously in Africa. The reasons for this are self-evident—they relate to Africa's travails in embedding constitutionalism in its body politic. In its short constitutional history, Africa has undergone different waves of constitutional ordering that relate both to drafting constitutions and to implementing them in ways that foster democracy and good governance.

Africa's first experience of constitutional ordering came with the imposition of colonial rule, which replaced or suppressed indigenous forms of governance. The constitutional order was characterised in the main by untrammelled centralised rule in the service of colonial interests rather than those of the indigenous peoples. This period unravelled soon after the Second World War with the rise of African nationalism and the acceptance of the right of peoples to self-determination. Thereafter came three important waves of constitutional ordering.[1]

The first wave saw independence constitutions being adopted in most of Africa from the late 1950s until the departure of the Portuguese in 1974 from their five colonies. Zimbabwe, Namibia, and South Africa were the exceptions: they were ruled by minority white settlers, with majority rule obtained only towards the end of the twentieth century. The independence constitutions were largely imposed by departing colonial powers. Typically, they (the constitutions) did not reflect the earlier systems of colonial rule but rather the ideals by which newly independent countries ought to be governed: democracy, limited government with a bill of rights, separation of powers, and the rule of law.

The second wave of constitutional ordering came swiftly after independence. Independence constitutions were replaced by constitutional arrangements closely resembling the centralist colonial orders, with concentration of powers in the executive and scant regard for separation of powers, limited government, and human rights. Under the pretext of promoting national unity and rapid economic development, the one-party state emerged,

[1] For a discussion, see Charles M. Fombad, 'The Evolution of Modern African Constitutions: A Retrospective Perspective' in Charles M. Fombad (ed.), *Separation of Powers in African Constitutionalism* (Oxford University Press 2016) 13; Yash Ghai, 'A Journey around Constitutions: Reflections on Contemporary Constitutions' (2005) *122 SALJ* 804.

Charles M. Fombad, *Constitutional Identity and Constitutionalism in Africa* In: *Constitutional Identity and Constitutionalism in Africa*. Edited by: Charles M. Fombad and Nico Steytler, Oxford University Press. © Charles M. Fombad 2024.
DOI: 10.1093/oso/9780198906308.003.0004

with a 'strong man', military commander, or imperial president at the helm. Separation of powers withered away with weak legislatures and compliant judiciaries. The results were dire. Instead of nation-building, there was internal conflict, engendered by ruling elites who, supported by either of the sides in the Cold War, clung to power through repressive, autocratic, or outright tyrannical rule; instead of a developmental state coming into being, the weak, dysfunctional, and corrupt patrimonial state emerged.

The international support that propped up these repressive constitutional orders vanished after the implosion of the Soviet Union in 1989, which came as a result of the third wave, with the triumphalist West driving a 'universalist' surge in democratic liberalisation that swept through the continent in the 1990s. It was a period marked by fervid revision or replacement of the post-independence constitutions in an attempt to entrench the fundamental principles, institutions, and values of modern constitutionalism. In all but two countries (Botswana, with its 1966 Constitution, and Mauritius, with its 1968 one), new or substantially revised constitutions were adopted. This wave was captured continent-wide in the African Union's Charter on Democracy, Elections and Governance (ACDEG), which came into operation in 2012.

The new constitutional order promised by these 'made-in-Africa' constitutions has not been realised. Few of them are being implemented in full, the prospects for constitutionalism are doubtful, and a wide gap exists between what they espouse and the lived realities that Africans experience. This has raised many questions about their ability to address current economic, social, and political challenges. Is it the case that these constitutions are not fulfilling the desires and aspirations of the people because of excessive reliance on Western-imposed constitutional concepts; a lack of resonance of the constitutions with indigenous culture and traditional values and structures; and a lack of alignment with the African social context, which differs from the historical context of Europe and the US, the two principal sources of liberal constitutionalism? In short, is there a constitutional identity crisis in Africa?

Questions about the identity of African constitutions took centre stage after the 'Rhodes Must Fall' (#RhodesMustFall) student protests of 2015 in South Africa, especially the question of constitutional decolonisation.[2] As part of this, questions have been raised about the legitimacy of recent constitutional reforms on the continent and whether these new or revised constitutions truly reflect an African identity. The issue of an African constitutional identity in the post-1990 constitutional renewal and post-'Rhodes Must Fall' era raises the question of whether, at a practical level, the existing constitutional paradigms, concepts, and normative ideologies are suited to developing a stable and sustainable constitutional system of governance based on the fundamental principles of modern constitutionalism.

With it being noted that the debates on constitutional identity have arisen mainly in the Western setting, the objectives of this chapter are twofold: firstly, to provide an overview of the general understanding of the concept of constitutional identity, and secondly, to explore

[2] See A.K. Ahmed, 'The Rise of Fallism: #RhodesMustFall and the Movement to Decolonise the University' (PhD thesis, Columbia University 2019) https://academiccommons.columbia.edu/doi/10.7916/d8-n7n3-e372 (last accessed 20 November 2022); Roseanne Chantiluke, Brian Kuoba, and Athinangamso Nkopo, *Rhodes Must Fall: The Struggle to Decolonise the Racist Heart of Empire* (Zed Books 2018); Achille Mbembe, 'Decolonising Knowledge and the Question of the Archive' https://wiser.wits.ac.za/system/files/Achille%20Mbembe%20-%20Decolonizing%20Knowledge%20and%20the%20Question%20of%20the%20Archive.pdf (last accessed 20 November 2022).

the possible scope of its applicability in the African context and the extent to which it could have an impact on fostering a culture of constitutionalism and democracy on the continent. One critical question is whether the success or failure of constitutionalism in Africa depends on whether the constitutions in African states reflect a national and/or African constitutional identity. Another is whether the search for an African constitutional identity is an illusion and distraction from the fundamental issues of constitutional governance or a worthwhile pursuit. These and many more questions are posed rather than answered.

The next section of this chapter provides a general overview of the concept of constitutional identity and examines some of the critical issues that it raises. It tries to answer questions such as: What is constitutional identity? What are the prevailing theories of constitutional identity? What are its main characteristics and core elements? The third section examines constitutional identity in the African context. It is against this background that the fourth section examines the link between constitutional identity and constitutionalism in Africa. In concluding, it is contended that, unlike in the past, the issue of constitutional self-identification is now a critical factor that experts must take into account in the constitution-making process.

2. The Concept of Constitutional Identity

Identity, in general, and constitutional identity, in particular, are enigmatic concepts. Not only is there no broad agreement on what these terms mean, but identity, in any form, is subject to contestation and negotiation, with processes of identity-formation being as much about change as they are about continuity.[3] In addition, as will be apparent below, most of the definitions attempted so far emanate essentially from a restrictive Americo-Eurocentric perspective, one unreflective of the historical, socio-economic, and other factors that continue to influence the evolution of African constitutions. This is understandable, in that the concept has been discussed mainly in the context of the impact of European Union (EU) law on EU member states and, more broadly, in the US.

We will look briefly at some of the definitions of constitutional identity before proceeding to consider key elements of the concept. Thereafter, we will see what tentative conclusions we can draw with regard to the nature and scope of the concept.

2.1 Theorising Constitutional Identity

As pointed out above, although the idea of constitutional identity has attracted much debate and commentary in the past two decades, its exact meaning and scope are far from clear. One may get some insight into the meaning of this vague concept from the diverse, often intertwined, and sometimes conflicting ways that writers on the topic have engaged with it.

Gary Jacobsohn,[4] one of the leading scholars on this topic, notes that constitutional identity 'neither exists as a discrete object of invention nor as a heavily encrusted essence

[3] See Barbara Oomen, 'Strengthening Constitutional Identity Where There Is None: The Case of the Netherlands' (2016) 77(2) *Revue Interdisciplinaire d'études Juridiques* 242.

[4] See Gary Jacobsohn, 'Constitutional Identity' in Sujit Choudhry, Madhav Khosal, and P.B. Mehta (eds.), *The Oxford Handbook of the Indian Constitution* (Oxford University Press 2016) 110–26; Gary Jacobsohn, *Constitutions*

embedded in a society's culture, requiring only to be discovered'.[5] According to him, identity emerges dialogically as a mixture of political aspirations and commitments that are expressive of a nation's past and which evolve in ongoing political and interpretative activities occurring in courts, legislatures, and other public and private domains.[6] He goes on to say that the texts of many constitutions point, explicitly and generally, to their identity.

Along similar lines are the views of Monika Polzin, who says that constitutional identity may be understood as a nation or people's constitution-related self-conception, something which can be inferred from the text of the constitution, its interpretation, and its application.[7] As such, constitutional identity goes beyond the text of a constitution; determining what it is requires understanding how a constitution's rules, principles, and values resonate in the practice and culture of the body politic.

Another influential writer on the topic, Michel Rosenfeld, sets out three distinct understandings of constitutional identity that have, in his opinion, emerged from recent literature.[8] The first of these equates constitutional identity with the constitution itself and can be inferred from the main features of the constitution, which include matters such as who the constituent and constitutional subject are, what is included and what is not, and the form of government. Based on this, Rosenfeld distinguishes between American, British, French, German, Spanish, European, and transnational models.[9]

The second understanding equates constitutional identity with culture, but the third is much wider and involves the interplay between the text of the constitution and national identity. It concerns how the collective dreams and aspirations of a people are expressed in the constitution and the culture that surrounds it. Rosenfeld points out, however, that the relationship between constitutional and national identity is complex. Whilst national identity can serve as a rationale for progress in constitutional theory, it could just as well be invoked to counter such progress.[10] According to him, constitutional identity in this sense refers to ideas of sameness, continuity, and selfhood that act as key markers for the imagining of a collective self.[11]

In spite of the differences in how they define the concept, all these scholars agree at least that constitutional identity is an important modern concept that provides a useful optic for analysing and understanding the evolution and workings of constitutions. As a product of a dialectic engagement, it is essentially a process that involves the reconciliation between

and National Identity (Harvard University Press 2010); Gary Jacobsohn, 'The Formation of Constitutional Identities' in Tom Ginsburg and Rosalind Dixon (eds.), *Comparative Constitutional Law* (Edward Elgar 2011) 129–42.

[5] Gary Jacobsohn, 'Constitutional Identity' (2006) *68 Review of Politics* 363.

[6] Jacobsohn, 'The Formation of Constitutional Identities' (n. 4) 129.

[7] Monika Polzin, 'Constitutional Identity as a Constructed Reality and a Restless Soul' (2017) *18*(7) *German Law Journal* https://bit.ly/2yNd1bo (last accessed 20 November 2022).

[8] Michel Rosenfeld, 'Constitutional Identity' in Michel Rosenfeld and András Sajó (eds.), *The Oxford Handbook of Comparative Constitutional Law* (Oxford University Press 2012) 756–64; by contrast, see J.L. Marti, 'Two Different Ideas of Constitutional Identity: Identity of the Constitution v Identity of the People' in Alejandro Saiz Arnaiz and Carina Alcoberro (eds.), *National Constitutional Identity and European Integration* (Intersentia 2013) 17–36, who opines that the concept involves two ideas, 'the identity of the constitution and the identity of the people or the political community ruled by such constitution'.

[9] Marti (n. 8) 2 summarises Rosenfeld's three understandings as (1) the *fact* of having a constitution; (2) the *content* of the constitution; and (3) the *context* in which the constitution operates.

[10] See R.G. Treitel, 'Reactionary Constitutional Identity' in Michel Rosenfeld (ed.), *Constitutionalism, Identity, Difference, and Legitimacy: Theoretical Perspectives* (Duke University Press 1994) 234.

[11] See Rosenfeld (n. 8) 757.

different identities, conflicts, and tensions within a state or political community. We now examine some of the diverse factors that may combine within a legal system to give its constitution a particular identity.

2.2 Ascertaining Constitutional Identity

Although there is no unanimity on how this concept is defined, the different definitions do provide useful indications of some of its key elements. In a general sense, it can be said that two main factors engender a country's constitutional identity: national, internal, or particular factors that lead to a national identity, on one hand, and international, external, or universal factors that emerge from an international identity, on the other. The nature and scope of their influence on what emerges as the country's constitutional identity differ from one country to another.

2.2.1 National identity

There is often a temptation to equate 'constitutional identity' with 'national identity'. The tendency to conflate national with constitutional identity has arisen mainly in Europe, and for good reason too. As is explained below, because of the supranational legal order of the EU, it has become increasingly important to distinguish and keep intact member states' national constitutional identities from the general EU European constitutional identity.[12]

National identity is conceptually different from constitutional identity even if the former can contribute to the formation of the latter. As Michel Rosenfeld points out, '[C]onstitutional identity is constructed in part against national identity and in part consistent with it.' The reason, as he puts it, is that 'one can easily conceive of the French or German nation, without reference to a constitution'.[13] This is so in plurinational constitutional states such as Canada (with the Quebecois nation), Belgium (with the Flemish nation), and Spain (with the Catalan nation). The situation is even more complex in Africa given the multi-ethnic composition of nearly all its countries. Some markers of national identity include common ethnicity, history, culture, and language. However, not all persons who share all or some of these markers necessarily share the same national identity. For example, the Tswana people are found in both Botswana and South Africa.[14] This means that the constitutional identity is the identity of the people as constituted by the constitution and according to the parameters laid out in it.[15]

National identity often symbolises national sovereignty and is a reflection of self-identification by a political community with fundamental cornerstones of national constitutionalism as opposed to supranational constitutionalism. As Martin Belov notes, it focuses on answering questions such as 'what is our collective constitutional self?'; 'what

[12] See Elke Cloots, 'National Identity, Constitutional Identity, and Sovereignty in the EU' (2016) *45*(2) *Netherlands Journal of Legal Philosophy* www.elevenjournals.com/tijdschrift/rechtsfilosofieentheorie/2016/2/NJLP_2016_045_002_006.pdf (last accessed 20 November 2022).

[13] Rosenfeld (n. 8) 758.

[14] See 'Tswana-Speaking Countries' https://www.worlddata.info/languages/tswana.php (last accessed 30 July 2021). They make up almost 80 per cent of Botswana's population and 8 per cent of South Africa's.

[15] See Marti (n. 8).

are the durable characteristics of our constitutional tradition?'; 'what differentiates us from other constitutionally organised political communities'; and 'what is the core of our value and institutional consensus?'[16] Many of the elements that go towards responding to these questions might contribute to the national constitutional identity.

All constitutions contain standard features such as provisions separating powers between the three branches of government and those regarding an independent judiciary and bills of rights. Constitutions may also have borrowed features common to other constitutions, or there may be constitutions that operate in a particular legal tradition, such as the common law tradition. International or global forces (discussed below) can influence both the standard and the borrowed features. Within the domestic sphere, the constitution may contain certain features that may provide it with a national identity and depending on the nature and impact of this, contribute to the country's constitutional identity. This may be constructed and reflected in different ways.

For example, a constitution may consist of unique constitutional norms designed to address specific problems peculiar to the country, whether of a historical, social, economic, or geographical nature. This may be reflected in values, principles, or ideals so integral to the constitution that eliminating them would make it something entirely different. For example, the distinctive bi-jural and bilingual nature of Cameroon's constitutional set-up was dictated by its unique historical background.[17] These have become critical features of the Cameroonian constitutional identity.

The distinctive aspect of a country's national constitutional identity may originate from the adoption of the constitution and thus be contained in the text of the constitution itself, or it may emerge with time through executive or legislative initiatives and practice. However, the latter would often require judicial sanction to take effect. For example, in laying down the basic structure doctrine, the Indian Supreme Court has confronted the problem of constitutional identity much more explicitly and directly than the courts in most countries.[18] By contrast, the eternity clauses, which many scholars regard as part of the French and German constitutional identities, are based on specific provisions in the constitution[19] and are not the result of a broad activist interpretation of the constitution, as is the case with the Indian basic structure doctrine.

As will be seen, some of the decisions of the Indian Supreme Court provide an example of how the collective self-image of the country and a constitutional identity could be constructed from the interpretation of vague and indeterminate constitutional norms. Monika Polzin[20] opines that the decision of the French Constitutional Council banning the use of the burka in public could be understood as reflecting a constitutional self-image of the French as free and equal citizens.[21]

[16] Martin Belov, 'The Functions of Constitutional Identity Performed in the Context of Constitutionalization of the EU and Europeanization of the Legal Orders of EU Member States' www.degruyter.com/downloadpdf/j/pof.2017.9.issue-2/pof-2017-0010/pof-2017-0010.pdf (last accessed 20 November 2022).

[17] See the discussion by Carlson Anyangwe and Charles M. Fombad in Chapter 9 of this volume.

[18] See Jacobsohn (n. 5) 375; for a full discussion of the doctrine, see A. Lakshminath, *Basic Structure and Constitutional Amendments: Limitations and Justiciability* (Deep & Deep Publications 2002); Peeyushi Diwan, *Amending Powers and Constitutional Amendment* (2nd edn, Deep & Deep Publications 1997).

[19] See Polzin (n. 7) 1608–9, who is one of the few who disagrees, arguing that 'constitutional identity and the content of eternity clauses should not be equated'. Her arguments, however, are rather circular.

[20] Ibid. 1612.

[21] See Constitutional Council Decision No. 2010–613 DC, 7 October 2010, Rec. 276.

However, some of the most contested questions of constitutional identity have arisen from the tensions involved in reconciling the specificities of national identity with the encroaching elements of international or universal identity.

2.2.2 International and universal factors

One of the biggest challenges to national constitutional identity today arises from the tension caused by attempts to balance it with the influence of external factors promotive of a received universal, global, and transnational constitutional identity. Perhaps the most dominant of these influences in Africa is the legacy of the common law constitutional identity received in anglophone Africa and the civil law constitutional identity received in francophone, arabophone, and lusophone Africa. The colonial legacy has left features of a general nature in these former colonies rather than of a specific nature peculiar to any particular country.[22] These colonial constitutional traditions shaped the way in which constitutional identities surfaced in independence and post-independence constitutional ordering. This accounts for the distinctive features of the anglophone common law approaches and the civilian approaches adopted in the francophone, arabophone, and lusophone African countries.

Whilst constitutions in these different traditions share a number of distinctive characteristics by dint of belonging to the same tradition, it is not clear whether they have developed any individually distinctive features within their membership of that tradition. However, the broader question in recent years is whether—since independence, particularly after the radical reforms and revival of constitutionalism in the 1990s—African countries have adopted constitutional identities either within or outside the inherited constitutional traditions that take into account the peculiar realities and challenges of each country.[23]

Besides these enduring features of the colonial past, there have also been features of a universal nature based on the incorporation within the domestic system of international and regional instruments. For example, most bills of rights or provisions dealing with fundamental human rights in national constitutions today have been substantially influenced by international and regional human rights instruments.[24] In many instances, the adoption of these international standards has been an imperative requirement for being part of the international community.[25] Whilst this has given all national constitutions an 'internationalised identity', that latter should not be equated with a national identity except where an international norm, after incorporation, has been transformed in a unique manner to address a specific national problem. In this respect, it may be argued that the special manner in which certain specialised institutions, such as the Public Protector (ombudsman) and the Human Rights Commission, have been designed and constitutionally entrenched in the

22 See Fombad (n. 1).

23 For the situation in francophone Africa, see Charles M. Fombad and Tresor M. Makunya in Chapter 4 of this volume.

24 The main international instruments are the Universal Declaration of Human Rights of 1948, the International Covenant on Civil and Political Rights 1966, and the International Covenant on Economic, Social and Political Rights 1966; the main regional instrument is the African Charter on Human and Peoples' Rights 1981.

25 See further Wen-Chen Chang and Jiunn-Rong Yeh, 'Internationalization of Constitutional Law' in Rosenfeld and Sajó (n. 8) 1166–82; Cheryl Saunders, 'The Impact of Internationalisation on National Constitutions' in A.H.Y. Chen (ed.), *Constitutionalism in Asia in the Early Twenty-First Century* (Cambridge University Press 2014) 391–415; Charles M. Fombad, 'Internationalisation of Constitutional Law and Constitutionalism in Africa' (2012) 60(2) *American Journal of Comparative Law* 439.

South African Constitution makes them a distinctive feature of the constitutional identity of the country's constitutional system.[26]

Other elements of an internationalised—or more specifically, regionalised—identity have also emerged under most African modern constitutions as a result of the incorporation of regional norms and other standards laid down in African Union (AU) treaties, conventions, and instruments aimed at promoting constitutionalism, respect for the rule of law, human rights, and good governance on the continent.[27] A combination of internationalisation and increasing regionalisation of constitutional law in Africa reflects the fact that the activities of states are not only regionally and universally interwoven and highly interdependent but also play a role in shaping the constitutional identities of the different states. Given the limited extent to which these developments have a supranational effect, there is little likelihood that they would generate the kind of conflicts between national and EU identities that have arisen in Europe.[28]

This is based on the distinction sanctioned in article 4(2) of the EU treaty.[29] It is clear, however, that the concepts of constitutional identity and national identity are used in this context as a defence against the overreaching supranationalisation of member states' legal orders by the EU and its institutions. Because of its high level of supranationalism, the EU, in order to gain loyalty and legitimacy, tried to ensure that its citizens did not feel alienated from its institutions and practices. The distinction between national and EU identity was introduced deliberately to enhance the sense of inclusiveness, make EU citizens feel 'at home', and allay fears of an encroachment on or threat to member states' national identities. Consequently, there is a clear effort to balance EU and national interests. Numerous cases of conflicts between national and EU identity have gone before the European Constitutional Courts, particularly the constitutional courts in the Czech Republic, France, Germany, and Poland.[30] At the present stage of regional integration in Africa, these types of identity conflicts have not yet arisen, but may do so with the

[26] See sections 181–94 of the 1996 Constitution of South Africa. These institutions have been replicated in articles 248–54 of the 2010 Kenyan Constitution and sections 232–63 of the 2013 Constitution of Zimbabwe. What distinguishes these institutions from similar ones provided for in other national constitutions or legislation is not only the fact that they are provided with special powers and protected from political interference through their constitutional entrenchment but also the fact that they operate more or less like a fourth branch of government. For a discussion of these institutions, see Charles M. Fombad, 'The Diffusion of South African-Style Institutions? A Study of Comparative Constitutionalism' in Rosalind Dixon and Theunis Roux (eds.), *Constitutional Triumphs, Constitutional Disappointments: A Critical Assessment of the 1996 South African Constitution's Local and International Influence* (Cambridge University Press 2018) 359–87.

[27] See Charles M. Fombad, 'The African Union and Democratisation' in Jeffrey Haynes (ed.), *Routledge Handbook of Democratisation* (Routledge 2012) 322.

[28] For discussion of the conflict between national and European constitutional identity, see Rainer Arnold, 'Constitutional Identity in European Constitutionalism' www.constcourt.md/public/files/file/conferinta_20ani/programul_conferintei/Rainer_Arnold.pdf (last accessed 20 November 2022); Belov (n. 16); Wojciech Sadurski, 'European Constitutional Identity' *EUI Working Papers LAW No. 2006/33* https://cadmus.eui.eu/bitstream/handle/1814/6391/LAW-2006-33.pdf?sequence=3&isAllowed=y (last accessed 20 November 2022).

[29] It states, inter alia: '(2). The Union shall respect the equality of Member States before the Treaties as well *as their national identities, inherent in their fundamental structures, political and constitutional, inclusive of regional and local self-government.* It shall respect their essential State functions, including ensuring the territorial integrity of the State, maintaining law and order and safeguarding national security. In particular, national security remains the sole responsibility of each Member State' (emphasis added). This 'identity clause' was introduced by the 1992 Treaty of Maastricht, albeit in a more concise form. Article F(1) of the original EU Treaty provided that '[t]he Union shall respect the national identities of its Member States, whose systems of government are founded on the principles of democracy'. The reference to democracy was dropped in 1997 when the Amsterdam Treaty amended the identity clause.

[30] See Cloots (n. 12); Belov (n. 16).

intensification of cooperation through the African Continental Free Trade Agreement (AfCFTA).[31]

Finally, there is also the impact of transnational constitutional influences on constitutional identity. These impacts could come about not only through the transplantation of foreign constitutional values, concepts, and institutions, but also through judicial cross-fertilisation of ideas due to courts' reliance on foreign precedents.[32] However, these are not the only factors that could impact on constitutional identity—others include constitutional culture.

2.2.3 Constitutional culture

To draw on Lawrence Friedman's definition of legal culture, it may be said that constitutional culture encompasses the idea of public knowledge of and attitudes and behaviour patterns towards the constitutional system in place, along with citizens' knowledge of it and their perceptions of its legitimacy.[33] R.C. Post postulates that constitutional law and culture are locked in a dialectical relationship, such that constitutional law both arises from and regulates culture.[34] Some scholars see constitutional patriotism as a means of strengthening constitutional culture and legitimacy.[35]

In its broadest sense, constitutional culture includes such things as the disposition of all citizens to recognise and accept that they are governed by a constitution that creates institutions of government and sets limits on what the government may do. It also includes an accepted belief that the constitution is created by the citizenry; the knowledge that it is not timeless but rather that citizens may change it or revoke it under certain circumstances; and the understanding that, until it is changed, it remains the supreme law binding on all.[36] Constitutional culture also includes the understanding that a constitution unifies the population beyond those in one's immediate sphere of acquaintance, such that other people in other parts of the country are likewise governed by it regardless of whatever differences of opinion they may have.

There is hence certainly a close link between constitutional identity and constitutional culture. However, knowledge of the constitution is of critical importance, and it is the absence of such knowledge that is among the serious challenges affecting the project of deepening and sustaining constitutionalism in Africa today. Because the post-independence constitutions were more or less imposed by the departing colonial powers, the people, apart from a few elites who took part in the constitution-making processes, had little or no knowledge of these constitutions, nor did they appreciate their significance.[37] Active participation of citizens in the making or substantial revision of many modern African constitutions

[31] For developments within the AfCFTA, see https://au.int/cn/cfta (last accessed 20 November 2022).

[32] See Randy Kozel, 'Precedents and Constitutional Structure' https://scholarship.law.nd.edu/cgi/viewcontent.cgi?article=2334&context=law_faculty_scholarship (last accessed 20 November 2022); Pietro Faraguna, 'Taking Constitutional Identity Away from the Courts' https://core.ac.uk/download/pdf/54549653.pdf (last accessed 20 November 2022).

[33] See Lawrence Friedman, *The Legal System: A Social Science Perspective* (Russell Sage Foundation 1975) 193.

[34] R.C. Post, 'Fashioning the Legal Constitution: Culture, Courts and Law' (2003–4) *117 Harvard Law Review* 8.

[35] See D. Abraham, 'Constitutional Patriotism, Citizenship and Belonging' (2008) *6*(1) *I.CON* 131–52; J. Habermas, *Between Facts and Norms: Contributions to a Discourse Theory of Law and Democracy* (Polity Press 1996).

[36] See Jason Mazzone, 'The Creation of a Constitutional Culture' (2013) *40*(4) *Tulsa Law Review* 672.

[37] See Muna Ndulo, 'Constitution-Making in Africa: Assessing Both the Process and the Content' (2001) *21*(2) *Public Administration and Development* 101.

has provided an opportunity for citizens to become familiar with the nature, content, and purpose of constitutions. The extent of such popular participation in the recent wave of constitution-making processes has varied considerably, with far more involvement of citizens in anglophone African processes than in those of francophone, arabophone, and lusophone Africa.[38] Ultimately, no matter how comprehensive and perspicuous a constitution, if it does not find a home in the hearts and minds of the people and is venerated and actively used, then it will lose its essence. A constitutional culture can hardly be built on a foundation of ignorance, and in its absence this factor can scarcely contribute to the building of a particular constitutional identity.

2.3 Distilling the Essence of Constitutional Identity

From whatever perspective we look at the concept, it is clear that it remains a fluid, contested, and permanently negotiated concept which is forged dialectically. In spite of this, all the different views regarding the concept of constitutional identity may be summarised in a number of key points that explain its potential nature and scope.

Firstly, it is the combination, coexistence, and evolution over time of various identities at both the national (from local to regional) and international levels (from subregional, regional, to global) that contribute to the establishment of the constitutional identity of a particular country. The close interaction of these identities over time may result in a dominant identity emerging in the constitution as a whole, or some aspects of it, such as values, principles, or institutions, acquiring a distinctive characteristic associated with the country. An example we noted earlier is the eternity clauses that some authors suggest have become a distinctive feature of sections of the French, German, and Italian constitutions.[39] The Irish Constitution of 1937 explicitly places the family and Catholicism at the centre of its constitutional identity, a fact that has been reaffirmed by the Irish Supreme Court.[40] Ultimately, it is the deeply contextualised balancing of the particular with the universal that may provide the markers of a constitutional identity.

A second point is that the constitutional text on its own is merely indicative of the nature of the constitutional order.[41] What is also required is long and consistent experience which shows that the document and its principles resonate with the praxis of the body politic.

[38] See further Coel Kirkby and Christina Murray, 'Constitution-Making in Anglophone Africa: We the People?' in Muna Ndulo and Mamoudou Gazibo (eds.), *Growing Democracy in Africa: Elections, Accountable Governance, and Political Economy* (Cambridge Scholars Publishing 2016) 86; Charles M. Fombad, 'Constitution-Building in Africa: The Never-Ending Story of the Making, Unmaking and Remaking of Constitutions' (2014) *13*(4) *African and Asian Studies* 429.

[39] This refers to the unamendable 'republican' clause in article 89 of the 1958 French Constitution and article 139 of the 1946 Italian Constitution. As regards Germany, this refers to article 79(3), which prohibits any amendments to the federal character and democratic nature of the country. See further V.B. Armin and Schill Stefan, 'Overcoming Absolute Primacy: Respect for National Identity under the Lisbon Treaty' (2011) *48*(6) *Common Market Law Review* 1417.

[40] See Tommaso Pavone, 'Constitutional Identity: An Overview and Some Conceptual Concerns' https://scholar.princeton.edu/sites/default/files/tpavone/files/jacobsohn-_constitutional_identity_critical_review.pdf (last accessed 20 November 2022).

[41] Important though the written text is, it is not conclusive on its own, otherwise unwritten constitutions such as the British, Israeli, and New Zealand constitutions would not have a constitutional identity.

Similarly, the constitution's language may be only indicative of a strong commitment on the part of its drafters, but it will, in addition, require evidence of its subsequent interpretation corroborated by an accumulated practice of the constitutional community to raise this to the status of constitutional identity. In Africa, the characteristics of a constitutional order that contribute to a country's constitutional identity may consist of the Islamic faith, placing the Quran as the highest source of law, a one-party state system, or a centrist and presidentially centred constitution.

Thirdly, constitutional identity relates to something of such a constitutive essence at the heart of the constitution that it may be regarded as stable and deserving of preservation and special protection against arbitrary and casual change. This usually involves core aspects of the constitution whose continuity is identified with the continuity of the polity as a whole. That is why some constitutional values such as democracy and federalism are subject to the eternity clause in the German constitution. Nevertheless, because constitutional identity is part of a process of negotiating the values and principles that should serve as elements of the self-identification of the community, some change is allowed, provided that it is effected within the institutional framework laid down in the constitution and is consistent with the consensus of the political community. From this perspective, the concept of constitutional identity offers an opportunity for self-reflection by a political community on the parameters of its constitutional tradition and culture, the core of its transgenerational constitutional project, and how to balance continuity with change.

Fourthly, constitutional identity serves a legitimating and safeguarding function.[42] It helps to identify, preserve, and protect national identity from the unavoidable competition brought in through the encroaching forces of supranational, regional, and global constitutionalism.[43] In other words, constitutional identity has the potential to legitimate the linking and differentiation of the networked, polycentric, and semi-hierarchical orders that have become an inevitable part of modern constitutionalism operating in an increasingly globalised world.

Finally, and perhaps most importantly, a critical consideration of constitutional identity, particularly in Africa, is that it may provide the stimulus for debate aimed at developing constitutional principles, values, and institutions adapted to contemporary realities. This is particularly so because, as noted earlier, most of the contemporary conceptualisations of constitutional identity are essentially Americo-Eurocentric. Insofar as Europe is concerned, this tends to reflect the challenges European countries face with the competing demands of EU identity and the national identity of member states. The nature and scope of the challenges that African countries face are not necessarily the same, and therefore the African context is important in considering how the concept is relevant in addressing the continent's governance problems.

[42] As Belov (n. 16) puts it, albeit in the context of the EU: 'The safeguarding function of constitutional identity consists of interrelated processes: the protection of the inviolable core of national constitutionalism through its definition, the delimitation of lines which must not be crossed in the course of the encroachment of supranational constitutionalism into the national order, and the provision of substantial limitations for the transfer of constitutional competences and sovereignty to supranational regimes.'

[43] This is particularly so in the context of competition between national and transnational or supranational identity. See further Polzin (n. 7).

3. Constitutional Identity in the African Context

The widening gap between African constitutions and practice raises many questions. The answers may lie in a number of factors particular to Africa. They include the following:

- The continued influence of the colonial legal paradigm on constitutions—Is the problem that these constitutions lack an authentic constitutional identity? Is this the reason that entrenching a culture of constitutionalism, respect for the rule of law, and good governance remains a challenge?
- The insignificant role of traditional leaders and institutions
- The multinational/ethnic/religious composition of nearly all African states, created by colonial borders
- Pan-African ideals of constitutionalism

3.1 The Influence of Colonial Legal Paradigms

The independence constitutions imposed by the departing colonialists and a few African elites certainly did not pretend to reflect the will of the people. The niceties of constitutional authenticity and legitimacy did not matter to those who handed down these constitutions. However, some countries, such as Germany with its Basic Law of 1949 and Japan with its 1947 constitutions, have become the leading economies in the world in spite of operating under constitutions that were virtually imposed by Allied forces after the Second World War.[44] By contrast, the quick distortion of African independence constitutions, combined with repressive, corrupt, and inefficient leadership, led to economic collapse and political instability in Africa and provoked campaigns to substantially revise these constitutions. As noted above, although there often was popular participation in the recent constitution-making processes, especially in anglophone Africa, elites still played a decisive role. This was particularly so in most of francophone, arabophone, or lusophone Africa, where elites either determined the agenda, such as in Benin, or completely controlled and manipulated the process, such as in Angola, Cameroon, and Gabon.

Since the 'Rhodes Must Fall' campaign in 2015, the feeling that present constitutions are an inauthentic expression of African values has grown stronger. The dominant narrative is the need for a decolonisation of these constitutions to give them an African constitutional identity. This raises the question of whether African constitutions need to be 'decolonised' to give them an African identity. If so, how is this to be done, in terms of form and content? Are there alternative principles that can replace some of the present principles? Are there any innovative theories, principles, or practices that have been designed to address peculiar African challenges? Are there any distinctive governance principles that have emerged in African practice?

[44] See Bruce Ackerman, *Revolutionary Constitutions: Charismatic Leadership and the Rule of Law* (Belknap Press of Harvard University Press 2019) 18.

3.2 The Role (or Not) of Traditional Institutions

Perhaps the most important issue African constitution-makers repeatedly avoid is the role of traditional authorities, principles, and institutions.[45] Can they be part of the national constitutional identity-building framework, or are they just a sentimental cultural relic of the past with little relevance today? This calls for a rational assessment of the actual and potential relevance of traditional authorities and institutions in the light of their complicity in facilitating slave trade, colonial rule, and postcolonial dictatorships as well as in stifling the transition to democratic governance in many countries.[46] The question today is how exactly traditional authorities, principles, and institutions can be made to play a role in promoting constitutionalism and good governance and enriching constitutions with traditional identity and legitimacy. The problem is not simply one of the presence or absence of traditional authorities, principles, and institutions in designing constitutions that reflect an African identity. It is rather one of identifying what problems they solve and what value they add to the goal of promoting constitutionalism. In the final analysis, the critical question is whether we want traditional African authorities, traditional principles, and traditional institutions because they are indigenous and relevant, or only because they are indigenous.

3.3 The Multidimensionality of African States

Although it took centuries, constructing constitutional identities in the West in the past century has been relatively easy. Just over three decades ago, the last remaining multi-ethnic states in Europe and along its borders collapsed, making room for more nationally homogenous entities (at least until the past two decades that have seen huge waves of migration from Africa and the Middle East). In Africa, constructing constitutional identities in countries that are deeply fragmented by ethnic, racial, religious, and linguistic diversity is bound to be difficult. How is the nation's identity to be defined? The question has arisen sharply in Ethiopia, where ethnic nationalism has become dangerously prevalent after years of dominant-party rule. This has prompted questions about what keeps Ethiopia together, the answer to which, as some commentators argue, is common loyalty to a constitution that entrenches an ethnic-based federation.[47]

[45] See Charles M. Fombad, 'Constitutional Entrenchment of Decentralization in Africa: An Overview of Trends and Tendencies' (2018) *62*(2) *Journal of African Law* 175, which points out that a majority of African constitutions either contain no references to traditional leaders and institutions or make only obscure references to them.

[46] See Richard Crook, 'The Role of Traditional Institutions in Political Change and Development' *CDD/ODI Policy Brief No. 4* (November 2005) www.odi.org/sites/odi.org.uk/files/odi-assets/publications-opinion-files/1967.pdf (last accessed 20 November 2022); Paolo Galizzi and Ernest K. Abotsi, 'Traditional Institutions and Governance in Modern African Democracies: History, Challenges, and Opportunities in Ghana' in J. Fenrich, P. Galizzi, and T. Higgins (eds.), *The Future of African Customary Law* (Cambridge University Press 2011) 266; M.L.J. Koenane, 'The Role and Significance of Traditional Leadership in the Governance of Modern Democratic South Africa' (2018) *10*(1) *African Review* 58; Christina Murray, 'South Africa's Troubled Royalty: Traditional Leaders after Democracy' *Law and Policy Paper 23* www.publiclaw.uct.ac.za/usr/public_law/staff/Troubled%20Royalty%20LPP%20No%2023%20Murray.pdf (last accessed 20 November 2022).

[47] See the discussion by Asnake Kefale in Chapter 7 of this volume.

3.4 Pan-African Ideals

Looking beyond the nation-state and taking a cue from the EU, one wonders whether there is still some scope for the Pan-African ideal to be reflected in an individual national or collective African constitutional identity. Or is this a dream best deferred? Have any distinct, innovative theories, principles, and practices been adopted by the AU and/or regional economic communities to address Africa's challenges? Is the ACDEG of 2012 a sufficient and effective instrument to pave the way for a constitutional identity across the continent that fortifies constitutionalism?

Major strides towards regional integration have been made with the entry into force of the Agreement Establishing the AfCFTA on 30 May 2019.[48] How will the national constitutional identity of member states be reconciled with the imperatives of supranational constitutional identity? This question is particularly important with respect to the existing supranational judicial bodies on the continent.

Many of these questions have been raised rather than answered by those who advocate for an African constitutional identity or decolonisation of the present African constitutions.[49] For instance, one of the proponents of decolonisation of contemporary African constitutions argues, with respect to the South African constitution, that 'a thoroughgoing programme of decolonisation cannot take place within the framework of the current constitution'.[50] It raises the fundamental question of whether the search for a constitutional identity is reconcilable with the goals of promoting modern constitutionalism.

4. Reconciling Identity and Constitutionalism

A constitutional identity is not static or set in stone at the time of the constitution's inception. Conflicting understandings of the constitutional self regularly play off against one another due to the normal struggle within a community or state to determine the correct and best meaning of a vague or indeterminate constitutional norm. While continuity and stability are critical to any coherent understanding of a common constitutional identity, preserving constitutions for their own sake cannot be a value in or of itself. What concerns us is whether changes to a constitution, driven by the impulse for decolonisation and authenticity, could be reconciled with the basic principles of constitutionalism.

The quest is not one that seeks to follow these principles blindly in a neocolonialist manner but to address the underlying ills they seek to address. The lack of democracy was experienced in the tyranny of dictators and one-party states; the lack of separation of powers

[48] As of that date, twenty-four countries had deposited their instruments of ratification. The operational phase of the AfCFTA was launched during the 12th Extraordinary Session of the Assembly of the Union on the AfCFTA in Niamey, Niger, on 7 July 2019.

[49] See, for example, P.W. Heydenrych, 'Constitutionalism and Coloniality: A Case of Colonialism Continued or the Best of Both Worlds?' https://dspace.nwu.ac.za/bitstream/handle/10394/19410/No_75_%282016%29_6_%20Heydenrych.pdf?sequence=1&isAllowed=y (last accessed 30 April 2020); Tshepo Madlingozi, 'On the Proposed Amendment of the South African Constitution: Finishing the Unfinished Business of Decolonisation or Perpetuating Colonisation?' https://criticallegalthinking.com/2018/04/06/the-proposed-amendment-to-the-south-african-constitution/ (last accessed 20 November 2022); Meera Sabaratnam, 'Decolonising Intervention International Statebuilding in Mozambique' http:www.rowmaninternational.com/media/1218/9781783482764_web.pdf (last accessed 20 November 2022).

[50] See Madlingozi (n. 49).

facilitated the rise of tyrannical presidents with no bounds to their rule. The absence of a bill of rights subjected the people to massive violations of basic human rights. The absence of the rule of law meant that there was no predictable governance other than the random use of power without courts. Constitutions could be changed at random to facilitate dictatorial rule. There will always be issues, such as a new generation, changed circumstances, and fresh knowledge, that necessitate changes in the constitution. Generally, it was inevitable that, in the desire for home-made constitutions, African constitutions had to be changed.

However, one of the major causes of the undermining of the fundamental tenets of constitutionalism in Africa's post-independence constitutions was the ease with which these constitutions were distorted through frequent and arbitrary amendments. Constitutionalism dictates that the political organs of government should not be placed in the position where they can easily and arbitrarily change constitutions. In addition, it prescribes that if the constitution is to be changed, this should be through clearly laid down procedures which ensure that the will of the people is not defeated in the process. The existence of a constitution that is not overly vulnerable to governmental manipulation through arbitrary amendment provides a sense of certainty and predictability that enhances the prospects for constitutionalism and protects the identity of the constitution.

Whilst changing the constitution may be good for adapting it to reflect current realities, it might not only threaten the country's constitutional identity but also undermine the prospects for constitutionalism.[51] Put differently, constitutional changes designed to reflect a country's constitutional identity may or may not promote the course of constitutionalism and respect for the rule of law. This would depend on two important considerations, namely the manner of the changes (procedural issues) and the nature of the changes carried out (substantive issues). The changes should not be carried out in a manner which undermines constitutionalism and has the effect of destroying the identity of the constitution. As such, the abiding quest for constitutionalism can be reconciled with the need to adjust African constitutions to better equip them to deal with contemporary challenges.

4.1 Constitutional Identity and the Mode of Change

Whilst constitutionalism is about ensuring that the constitution reflects the hopes, aspirations, and existential circumstances of the people at any time through democracy, it also entails limits and constraints on how this is done. Modern African constitutions usually spell out the manner in which changes to the constitution are to be carried out as well as the role of the different actors involved in the process.[52] This usually consists of politicians

[51] Although the concept of constitutionalism has been defined in different ways by different writers, for the purposes of this discussion it refers to a constitution that does not only limit government in a manner that checks against any abuses of power but does so in a manner such that citizens can effectively enforce these limitations. In this broad sense, such a constitution must contain at least six core principles: principles that recognise and protect human rights; provide for separation of powers; provide for judicial independence; provide for control of constitutionality of laws; check against arbitrary constitutional amendments (the crux of the discussion in this section); and provide for institutions that promote democracy and constitutionalism. See further Charles M. Fombad, 'Post-1990 Constitutional Reforms in Africa: A Preliminary Assessment of the Prospects for Constitutional Governance and Constitutionalism' in A.G. Nhema and P.T. Zeleza (eds.), *The Resolution of African Conflicts* (OSSREA & James Currey 2008) 179.

[52] See Charles M. Fombad, 'Some Perspectives on Durability and Change under Modern African Constitutions' (2013) *11*(2) *International Journal of Constitutional Law* 382.

(with the process being initiated by the executive and going to parliament for approval), ordinary citizens (usually where a referendum or plebiscite is provided for), and judges (who deal with disputes about procedural or substantive compliance with constitutional provisions).

Owing to the distortion of post-independence constitutions, serious attempts were made during the constitutional revisions of the 1990s to introduce more rigorous amendment procedures, particularly in anglophone Africa. In principle, this would have ensured that what may be considered as the constitutional identity of the country is not easily changed by opportunistic politicians without the consent of the people. In civilian jurisdictions where safeguards against arbitrary constitutional changes were not especially robust, politicians have exploited fragmented multi-ethnic communities and used dominant ethnic groups and elites to push through constitutional changes clearly at odds with the prevailing consensus in society. From this perspective, it is doubtful that the removal of the presidential term limits provisions in most African constitutions genuinely reflects the will of the people.

Whilst compliance with formal constitutional amendment requirements is critical, in a number of cases (discussed below) the Indian Supreme Court has, to the extent that changes made in compliance with the constitutional requirements were so radical as to eviscerate the identity of the constitution, declared them illegitimate and unconstitutional. There is therefore also a need to consider the nature of the changes carried out before concluding that they are compliant with the principles of constitutionalism.

4.2 Constitutional Identity and the Nature of Change

In considering the nature of constitutional change that is consistent with the principles of constitutionalism, a number of important questions arise. Does a change of constitution or a provision in it change the identity of the constitution? Put differently, when could it be said that a constitutional change has resulted in a state acquiring a new or a different constitutional identity?

In spite of the extensive revision of most African constitutions from the 1990s, it is doubtful that these constitutions could be said to have acquired new identities. What then is the nature or extent of change that can result in a constitution acquiring a new identity? The challenge is that of reconciling competing demands for transformation and change, on one hand, with the need for certainty, durability, and preservation of the constitutional identity. Who decides when a change destroys not only a country's constitutional identity but also the values of constitutionalism embedded in that constitution?

In principle, it should be the people, as the repository of all constitutional power and the ultimate constituent authority, who determine what the constitutional identity of the country is. The reality, though, is that few citizens, even in advanced countries, understand what the constitution is about; it is even less likely that the few who do, appreciate the intricacies of constitutional identity. Reliance on elected representatives, as could be seen from the arbitrary changes of presidential term limits in many constitutions, has hardly been influenced by the actual or perceived political consensus of the community. Ultimately, in spite of questions of democratic legitimacy and the fear of a 'government of judges', the judiciary may have an important role to play in both determining the existence of a distinct constitutional identity in a particular case and protecting it. The lead in doing this has been taken by the Supreme Court of India.

In the key Indian case of *Kesavananda Bharati v State of Kerala*,[53] one of the justices of the Supreme Court declared that 'one cannot legally use the constitution to destroy itself', and added that 'the personality of the constitution must remain unchanged'.[54] In the opinion of the justices, 'the word "amendment" postulates that the old constitution survives without loss of identity despite the change and continues even though it has been subjected to alterations'.[55] In their view, to 'destroy its identity' is to abrogate 'the basic structure of the Constitution'.[56] One of the justices went further to point out that Parliament's right to amend the constitution 'does not enable Parliament to abrogate or take away fundamental rights or to completely change the fundamental features of the Constitution so as to destroy its identity. Within these limits Parliament can amend every article'.[57]

In *Minerva Mills Ltd v Union of India*,[58] the proposed amendment purported to oust the jurisdiction of the courts to question its legal validity. The Supreme Court, in declaring it unconstitutional, declared:

> If by constitutional amendment, Parliament were granted unlimited power of amendment, it would cease to be an authority under the Constitution, but would become supreme over it, because it would have power to alter the entire Constitution including its structure and even put an end to it by totally changing its identity.[59]

The Supreme Court has also declared the provisions on secularism to be part of the basic structure of the Indian Constitution. The leading case on this is *S.R. Bommai v Union of India*.[60] The Court upheld the authority of the central government to dismiss the elected governments in three states because of the alleged failures of their administrations to implement and respect the constitutional commitment to secularism. It declared that secularism was 'part of the basic structure of the constitution and also the soul of the constitution'.[61] In doing so, the Court said, 'We have accepted [secularism] not only because it is our historical legacy and a need of our national unity and integrity but also as a creed of universal brotherhood and humanism. It is our cardinal faith.'[62]

India's unique approach has been described by Rajeev Bhargava as 'contextualised secularism', at the core of which is the strategy of 'principled distance' where the 'state intervenes or refrains from interfering, depending on which of the two better promotes religious liberty and equality of citizenship'.[63] Gary Jacobsohn aptly summarises the Indian cases thus: 'The identity that was the object of so much judicial concern in these cases was generic,

[53] 1973 SC 1461.
[54] Ibid. 1624.
[55] Ibid. 1860.
[56] Ibid. 1756.
[57] Ibid. 1565.
[58] AIR 1980 SC 1789.
[59] Ibid. 1824. Also see *Indira Gandhi v Raj Narain* AIR (1975) SC 2299.
[60] 3 SC 1 (1994).
[61] Ibid. 143.
[62] Ibid. 148.
[63] In Rajeev Bhargava, 'What Is Secularism For?' in Rajeev Bhargava (ed.), *Secularism and Its Critics* (Oxford University Press 1998) 515.

implicating a cluster of attributes or characteristics that makes *a* constitution (rather than *this* constitution) a distinctive governing code.'[64]

Perhaps the most important lesson to draw from this is that in India's complex and fragmented multireligious society, the courts have creatively adopted multicultural policies designed to maintain its democracy and represent its culturally diverse interests in an enduring manner and safeguard it from politically motivated opportunistic and potentially destabilising changes.[65]

Irish courts have also grappled with the issues of change in constitutional identity. However, the context is different because the country's constitutional identity, unlike that of India, developed in a more homogeneous environment and was clearly embodied in the constitution. The imprint of Catholicism, that is, the religion of the overwhelming majority of the people, is reflected in several provisions of the constitution as well as in its preamble and in the prominent place given to religion, the family, and issues such as abortion. Whereas the project of Indian constitutional identity is societal transformation, that of the Irish is the preservation of the country's Catholic roots.[66]

In dealing with the cases that have come before them, the courts in Ireland have to a large extent taken account of the steeply declining influence of the Catholic Church in state affairs as well as the increasingly pluralist environment. As Gerard Whyte observes, '[T]he influence of institutionalized religion is on the wane' while 'communal views of society are increasingly challenged by a growing emphasis on the rights of individuals'.[67] In *Ryan v Attorney General*,[68] the Irish Supreme Court had no difficulty in interpreting article 41(1) of the Irish Constitution of 1937, which in recognising the family as 'the natural primary and fundamental unit group of society', referred to it as possessing 'inalienable and imprescriptible rights, antecedent and superior to all positive law'.

Whilst this is a formal acknowledgement of the Constitution's prescriptive reality, it has raised the problem of taking into account changing attitudes on issues such as abortion, divorce, contraception, and gender equality. In his analysis of the Irish cases, Gary Jacobsohn concludes that the courts, in dealing with these potentially controversial issues, have facilitated a change in constitutional thinking and produced an outcome that 'was substantively inconsistent with the views and expectations of those who first formally stamped the constitution with an identity' but nevertheless in its construction preserved that identity.[69] However, the recent referendum vote in favour of abortion in Ireland clearly suggests that even the Catholic roots of the Irish constitutional identity can be changed by the popular will of the people and that once this is clearly expressed, the courts cannot interfere.[70] It is therefore doubtful if the courts today would decide the *Ryan v Attorney General* case in the same way they did in 1965.

[64] Jacobsohn (n. 5) 380.

[65] Many of the cases arose from then prime minister Indira Gandhi's political aggrandisement schemes and efforts to hold on to power illegally.

[66] It is worth noting, however, that before 1994, South Africa's constitutional identity was essentially racist, non-democratic, and centrist with no checks and balances, and strongly supported by apartheid judges.

[67] In Gerard Whyte, 'Religion and Irish Constitution' (1997) *30 John Marshall Law Review* 725.

[68] *Ryan v Attorney General* (1965) IR 294 308.

[69] Jacobsohn (n. 5) 389.

[70] See J. Henley, 'Irish Abortion Referendum: Yes Wins with 66.4%—As It Happened' (26 May 2018) *The Guardian* https://www.theguardian.com/world/live/2018/may/26/irish-abortion-referendum-result-count-begins-live (last accessed 20 November 2022).

Changing and adjusting constitutions to respond to the inevitable economic, social, and political changes that take place is both unavoidable and necessary to sustain a viable politic. Nevertheless, changes—however small and insignificant or profound, however slow and incremental or sudden—that completely change the identity of a thing into something else do no more than destroy what they purport merely to change. Such radical changes often arise from revolutions. The profound changes that brought about the Namibian Constitution of 1990 and the South African constitutions of 1994 and 1996 can hardly be described as ordinary instances of constitutional change. The apartheid system and the constitutional framework on which it was built could never be reformed; it had to be destroyed. These revolutionary constitutions, as Bruce Ackerman points out, usually mark a total transformation of society.[71]

Even if African courts have not yet pronounced on issues of values underpinning constitutional identity, there is no doubt these matters will arise as constitutional reformers think of principles, values, and institutions better adapted to dealing with the continent's present and future challenges. Presumably there are identity constraints within which these reformers would have to operate. In the recent case of *David Ndii & Others v Attorney General & Others*,[72] a Kenyan High Court invoked the Indian basic structure doctrine to declare a number of proposed constitutional amendments as unconstitutional.

However, in most other African jurisdictions where the basic structure doctrine has been invoked, the courts have either declared in their judgements[73] or in their *obiter dicta*[74] that there is no basis for its application. The situation in India when the basic structure doctrine was developed was peculiar. There was an overwhelming public perception of the Indian legislature as ineffective, unstable, corrupt, and anxious to use its dominant majority to repeal the constitution on its own without involving the people. Modern African constitutions not only have elaborate provisions dealing with all aspects of constitutional amendment, however extensive this may be, but also provide for the intervention of the people through a referendum. In most cases, this framework is not entirely satisfactory, but these are weaknesses that cannot be cured by the vague and uncertain scope of application of the basic structure doctrine.[75]

[71] See Ackerman (n. 44).

[72] See Petition No. E282 of 2020 (Consolidated with Petitions Nos. 397 of 2020, E400 of 2020, E401 of 2020, E402 of 2020, E416 of 2020, E426 of 2020, and 2 of 2021) (on file with the author).

[73] In the Ugandan case of *Mabirizi & Others v the Attorney General*, Consolidated Constitutional Appeal No. 2 of 2018 (on file with the author), both the Constitutional Court and the Supreme Court were unanimous in their view that the circumstances for invoking and applying the doctrine do not exist under the Ugandan Constitution. Similarly, in the Tanzanian case of *Mtikila v Attorney General* Misc. Civil Cause No. 10 of 2005, available at https://www.elaw.org/content/tanzania-rev-christopher-mtikila-v-attorney-general-civil-case-no-5-1993-high-court-tanzania (last accessed 30 April 2020), the Court of Appeal, after describing the doctrine as nebulous and with there being no agreed yardstick for determining what it means, declared that it had no place in the Tanzanian constitutional framework. In the court's opinion, what the Constitution did was to provide safeguards and not basic structures; once the amendment procedure was followed, then the change would be valid.

[74] See the South African cases of *Premier, KwaZulu-Natal v President of the Republic of South Africa* 1996 1 SA 769 (CC); *Executive Council, Western Cape Legislature v President of the Republic of South Africa* 1995 4 SA 877 (CC); *UDM v President of the Republic of South Africa* 2003 1 SA 495 (CC); and the Zambian case of *Zambia Democratic Congress v Attorney General* SCZ Judgment No. 37 of 1999.

[75] See further Charles M. Fombad, 'Limits on the Power to Amend Constitutions: Recent Trends in Africa and Their Impact on Constitutionalism' (2007) 6 *University of Botswana LJ* 27; Fombad (n. 52).

5. Conclusion

Constitutional identity is a relatively new concept that may provide a lens through which to rethink and reimagine constitutional reforms and similar developments in Africa. The history of constitutions shows both continuities and disruption, both to the good and the bad. The colonial 'constitutions' were authoritarian, undemocratic, and unaccountable. The independence constitutions during the decolonialisation period sought to impose Western constitutionalism, but the post-independence constitutions, which came rapidly thereafter, had the same characteristics of the colonial period—authoritarian, undemocratic, and lacking in accountability. Post-Cold War democratisation produced constitutions not dissimilar to the liberal independence constitutions. There is no doubt that, unlike the pre-1990 constitutions, there is a sense of self-identification with the post-1990 constitutions due to their generally indigenous origins as a result of the greater involvement of citizens in the drafting of these constitutions. Do they now reflect the needs, aspirations, and values of the citizens based on the latter's history, experience, traditions, and culture?

The reality is that, apart from the South African and Namibian constitutions, modern African constitutions have more continuities than discontinuities. Many of the weaknesses of colonial and postcolonial governance systems, such as the centralisation of powers and sidelining of indigenous systems of governance, have been perpetuated in these constitutions. For example, values once criticised as Western are now accepted in the ACDEG as universal, notwithstanding the increasingly loud calls for the decolonisation or Africanisation of constitutions.

Be that as it may be, constitutional identity is not an abstraction. Whether or not a constitution has a distinctive constitutional identity may not matter much; what matters is whether the constitution can achieve the purpose for which constitutions that promote constitutionalism are designed. As Cass Sunstein puts it, a constitution should be designed to protect a country from its most likely problems in its usual political processes, particularly those aspects of its culture, tradition, and history that will predictably produce harm through its ordinary politics or its most threatening tendencies.[76] In short, as Lon Fuller observes, the constitution should be able to 'save us from the abyss'.[77]

The critical question, in the final analysis, is not whether a constitution is authentically African, whatever that means, nor whether it is embedded in indigenous African values, principles, and institutions that make it unique. If it is, well and good. However, the quest for a distinctive constitutional identity should not trump the overriding goal of designing a constitution which is fit for purpose: that is, one that will save us from the threats of descending into 'the abyss' through hunger, repressive and dictatorial governance, corruption, and the multiplicity of ills that are the lot of the ordinary citizen. The crux of the search for and assertion of an African constitutional identity is therefore not to debunk and jettison everything that is foreign, whether universal or particular, but to determine how to incorporate the best of what is African whilst ensuring that our people benefit from principles of constitutional governance that promote the fundamental principles of constitutionalism, good governance, and respect for the rule of law.

[76] Cass Sunstein, 'Against Positive Rights' in Andras Sajó (ed.), *Western Rights? Post-Communist Application* (Kluwer 1996) 226–7.

[77] Lon Fuller, *The Morality of Law* (Yale University Press 1964) 44.

Since constitutions are not cast in stone but must be adjusted to take account of changing circumstances and mores, constitutional identity must be seen as a process of maturation involving ongoing interaction between a society's multiple actors within the parameters and context of the existing constitutional text and the country's history. This entails striking a careful balance between constitutional stability and certainty, on the one hand, and modernisation and adaptability, on the other. It also requires a transgenerational consensus within the political community.

Ultimately, the political stability needed to promote development can be achieved only within the framework of a constitution that promotes the basic principles of constitutionalism, as well taking account of the country's ethnic, religious, cultural, and linguistic diversity. There will continue to be tension as countries strive to accommodate the often divergent aspirations of the different communities, but this is critical to establishing the self-identification that is necessary for a firm sense of constitutional identity to emerge.

Bibliography

Abraham D., 'Constitutional Patriotism, Citizenship and Belonging' (2008) *6*(1) *I.CON* 131

Ackerman B., *Revolutionary Constitutions: Charismatic Leadership and the Rule of Law* (Belknap Press of Harvard University Press 2019) 18

Ahmed A.K., 'The Rise of Fallism: #RhodesMustFall and the Movement to Decolonise the University' (PhD thesis, Columbia University 2019) https://academiccommons.columbia.edu/doi/10.7916/d8-n7n3-e372 (last accessed 30 March 2020)

Armin V.B. and Stefan S., 'Overcoming Absolute Primacy: Respect for National Identity under the Lisbon Treaty' (2011) *48*(6) *Common Market Law Review* 1417

Arnold R., 'Constitutional Identity in European Constitutionalism' www.constcourt.md/public/files/file/conferinta_20ani/programul_conferintei/Rainer_Arnold.pdf (last accessed 20 November 2022)

Belov M., 'The Functions of Constitutional Identity Performed in the Context of Constitutionalisation of the EU and Europeanization of the Legal Orders of EU Member States' (2017) www.degruyter.com/downloadpdf/j/pof.2017.9.issue-2/pof-2017-0010/pof-2017-0010.pdf (last accessed 20 November 2022)

Bhargava R., 'What Is Secularism For?' in Bhargava R. (ed.), *Secularism and Its Critics* (Oxford University Press 1998) 515

Chang W. and Yeh J., 'Internationalization of Constitutional Law' in Rosenfeld M. and Sajó A. (eds.), *The Oxford Handbook of Comparative Constitutional Law* (Oxford University Press 2012) 1166

Chantiluke R., Kuoba B., and Nkopo A., *Rhodes Must Fall: The Struggle to Decolonise the Racist Heart of Empire* (Zed Books 2018)

Cloots E., 'National Identity, Constitutional Identity, and Sovereignty in the EU' (2016) *45*(2) *Netherlands Journal of Legal Philosophy* 82

Crook R., 'The Role of Traditional Institutions in Political Change and Development' *CDD/ODI Policy Brief No. 4* (November 2005)

Diwan P., *Amending Powers and Constitutional Amendment* (2 edn, Deep & Deep Publications 1997)

Faraguna P., 'Taking Constitutional Identity Away from the Courts' https://core.ac.uk/download/pdf/54549653.pdf (last accessed 20 November 2022)

Fombad C.M., 'Limits on the Power to Amend Constitutions: Recent Trends in Africa and Their Impact on Constitutionalism' (2007) *6 University of Botswana LJ* 27

Fombad C.M., 'Post-1990 Constitutional Reforms in Africa: A Preliminary Assessment of the Prospects for Constitutional Governance and Constitutionalism' in Nhema A.G. and Zeleza P.T. (eds.), *The Resolution of African Conflicts* (OSSREA & James Currey 2008) 179

Fombad C.M., 'The African Union and Democratisation' in Haynes J. (ed.), *Routledge Handbook of Democratisation* (Routledge 2012) 322

Fombad C.M., 'Internationalisation of Constitutional Law and Constitutionalism in Africa' (2012) *60*(2) *American Journal of Comparative Law* 439

Fombad C.M., 'Some Perspectives on Durability and Change under Modern African Constitutions' (2013) *11*(2) *International Journal of Constitutional Law* 382

Fombad C.M., 'Constitution-Building in Africa: The Never-Ending Story of the Making, Unmaking and Remaking of Constitutions' (2014) *13*(4) *African and Asian Studies* 429

Fombad C.M., 'The Evolution of Modern African Constitutions: A Retrospective Perspective' in Fombad C.M. (ed.), *Separation of Powers in African Constitutionalism* (Oxford University Press 2016) 13

Fombad C.M., 'Constitutional Entrenchment of Decentralization in Africa: An Overview of Trends and Tendencies' (2018) *62*(2) *Journal of African Law* 175

Fombad C.M., 'The Diffusion of South African-Style Institutions? A Study of Comparative Constitutionalism' in Dixon R. and Roux T. (eds.), *Constitutional Triumphs, Constitutional Disappointments: A Critical Assessment of the 1996 South African Constitution's Local and International Influence* (Cambridge University Press 2018) 359

Fuller L., *The Morality of Law* (Yale University Press 1964)

Friedman L., *The Legal System: A Social Science Perspective* (Russell Sage Foundation 1975)

Galizzi P. and Abotsi E.K., 'Traditional Institutions and Governance in Modern African Democracies: History, Challenges, and Opportunities in Ghana' in Fenrich J., Galizzi P., and Higgins T. (eds.), *The Future of African Customary Law* (Cambridge University Press 2011) 266

Ghai Y., 'A Journey around Constitutions: Reflections on Contemporary Constitutions' (2005) *122 SALJ* 804

Habermas J., *Between Facts and Norms: Contributions to a Discourse Theory of Law and Democracy* (Polity Press 1996)

Henley, J., 'Irish Abortion Referendum: Yes Wins with 66.4%—As It Happened' *The Guardian* (26 May 2018) https://www.theguardian.com/world/live/2018/may/26/irish-abortion-referendum-result-count-begins-live (last accessed 20 November 2022)

Heydenrych P.W., 'Constitutionalism and Coloniality: A Case of Colonialism Continued or the Best of Both Worlds?' https://dspace.nwu.ac.za/bitstream/handle/10394/19410/No_75_%282016%29_6_%20Heydenrych.pdf?sequence=1&isAllowed=y (last accessed 20 November 2022)

Jacobsohn G., 'Constitutional Identity' (2006) *68 Review of Politics* 363

Jacobsohn G., *Constitutions and National Identity* (Harvard University Press 2010)

Jacobsohn G., 'The Formation of Constitutional Identities' in Ginsburg T. and Dixon R. (eds.), *Comparative Constitutional Law* (Edward Elgar 2011) 129

Jacobsohn G., 'Constitutional Identity' in Choudhry S., Khosal M., and Mehta P.B. (eds.), *The Oxford Handbook of the Indian Constitution* (Oxford University Press 2016) 110

Kirkby C. and Murray C., 'Constitution-Making in Anglophone Africa: We the People?' in Ndulo M. and Gazibo M. (eds.), *Growing Democracy in Africa: Elections, Accountable Governance, and Political Economy* (Cambridge Scholars Publishing 2016) 86

Koenane M.L.J., 'The Role and Significance of Traditional Leadership in the Governance of Modern Democratic South Africa' (2018) *10*(1) *African Review* 58

Kozel R., 'Precedents and Constitutional Structure' https://scholarship.law.nd.edu/cgi/viewcontent.cgi?article=2334&context=law_faculty_scholarship (last accessed 20 November 2022)

Lakshminath A., *Basic Structure and Constitutional Amendments: Limitations and Justiciability* (Deep & Deep Publications 2002)

Madlingozi T., 'On the Proposed Amendment of the South African Constitution: Finishing the Unfinished Business of Decolonisation or Perpetuating Colonisation?' https://criticallegalthinking.com/2018/04/06/the-proposed-amendment-to-the-south-african-constitution/ (last accessed 20 November 2022)

Marti J.L., 'Two Different Ideas of Constitutional Identity: Identity of the Constitution v Identity of the People' in Arnaiz A.S. and Alcoberro C. (eds.), *National Constitutional Identity and European Integration* (Intersentia 2013) 17

Mazzone J., 'The Creation of a Constitutional Culture' (2013) *40*(4) *Tulsa Law Review* 672
Mbembe A, 'Decolonising Knowledge and the Question of the Archive'https://bit.ly/2PDdp3T (last accessed 20 November 2022)
Murray C., 'South Africa's Troubled Royalty: Traditional Leaders after Democracy' *Law and Policy Paper 23* https://bit.ly/3Wn1wh1 (last accessed 20 November 2022)
Ndulo M., 'Constitution-Making in Africa: Assessing Both the Process and the Content' (2001) *21*(2) *Public Administration and Development* 101
Oomen B., 'Strengthening Constitutional Identity Where There Is None: The Case of the Netherlands' (2016) *77*(2) *Revue Interdisciplinaire d'études Juridiques* 242
Pavone T., 'Constitutional Identity: An Overview and Some Conceptual Concerns' https://scholar.princeton.edu/sites/default/files/tpavone/files/jacobsohn-_constitutional_identity_critical_review.pdf (last accessed 20 November 2022)
Polzin M., 'Constitutional Identity as a Constructed Reality and a Restless Soul' (2017) *18*(7) *German Law Journal* 1595
Post R.C., 'Fashioning the Legal Constitution: Culture, Courts and Law' (2003–4) *117 Harvard Law Review* 8
Rosenfeld M., 'Constitutional Identity', in Rosenfeld M. and Sajó A. (eds.), *The Oxford Handbook of Comparative Constitutional Law* (Oxford University Press 2012) 756
Sadurski W., 'European Constitutional Identity' *EUI Working Papers LAW No. 2006/33* https://bit.ly/3FvtnFU (last accessed 20 November 2022)
Sabaratnam M., 'Decolonising Intervention International Statebuilding in Mozambique' www.rowmaninternational.com/media/1218/9781783482764_web.pdf (last accessed 20 November 2022)
Saunders C., 'The Impact of Internationalisation on National Constitutions' in A.H.Y. Chen (ed.), *Constitutionalism in Asia in the Early Twenty-First Century* (Cambridge University Press 2014) 391
Sunstein C., 'Against Positive Rights' in Sajó A. (ed.), *Western Rights? Post-Communist* (Kluwer 1996) 226
Treitel R.G., 'Reactionary Constitutional Identity' in Rosenfeld M. (ed.), *Constitutionalism, Identity, Difference, and Legitimacy: Theoretical Perspectives* (Duke University Press 1994) 234
'Tswana-Speaking Countries' https://www.worlddata.info/languages/tswana.php (last accessed 30 July 2021)
Whyte G., 'Religion and Irish Constitution' (1997) *30 John Marshall Law Review* 725

2
Constitutional Checks and Balances in Traditional Africa

George B.N. Ayittey

1. Introduction

> *Despotism and kleptocracy do not inhere in the nature of African cultures or in the African character; but they are now rife in what was once called British colonial Africa, notably West Africa.*[1]

There is still much mythology enshrouding traditional Africa, in particular in regard to how Africans governed themselves and to their indigenous institutions and political systems. The widespread fallacy that has endured over the centuries is the notion that Africa has neither history nor viable institutions and that its people laboured under tyrannical systems. Thus, colonialism was good for Africans because it liberated them from their terrible and despotic traditional rulers. This misconception is not only factually incorrect but also served as a perversely convenient alibi for the tyrannical regimes that proliferated in postcolonial Africa. Western donors and international organisations were readily accepting of strong-man rule in Africa and consequently did not aggressively push for democratic reform in Africa prior to the collapse of the former Soviet Union in 1989. After all, they reasoned, dictatorship had always been the order of the day in Africa's traditional systems.

The purpose of this chapter is to debunk this mythology, one that has done incalculable damage to postcolonial development, by examining Africa's indigenous political systems. Four main traditional polities are examined. These consist of empires, kingdoms, and two smaller polities—firstly, the ethnic groups that chose not to have any centralised authority, often referred to as stateless societies, and secondly, chiefdoms, which comprise those Africans who chose to have centralised authority.

The focus of the discussion is on the distinctive African constitutional identity provided in these polities through their systems of traditional checks and balances. The latter clearly show that dictatorship was incompatible with the political systems that existed in pre-colonial Africa, where decisions were taken by consensus and ring-fenced with an elaborate system of checks and balances. The real tragedy today is not so much the European propagation of mythology about traditional Africa but its continuation by modern African leaders who established tyrannical systems in postcolonial Africa with no checks and balances. This aided and abetted the postcolonial destruction of Africa.

[1] See Peter Bauer, *Reality and Rhetoric: Studies in Economics of Development* (Harvard University Press 1984) 104.

George B.N. Ayittey, *Constitutional Checks and Balances in Traditional Africa* In: *Constitutional Identity and Constitutionalism in Africa*. Edited by: Charles M. Fombad and Nico Steytler, Oxford University Press. © George B.N. Ayittey 2024.
DOI: 10.1093/oso/9780198906308.003.0005

2. The Enduring Myth of Despotism

Political practices vary across cultures, and thus language—in particular, its nuances—could pose an obstacle to the understanding of how various political systems are supposed to work. Indigenous African political systems are such examples. The early European explorers did not witness competitive politics, where the people were offered a choice of different candidates, or actual voting, so they concluded that the political systems were probably not democratic. This rush to judgment did much harm to Africa's history, prospects, and development.

Despotism is not a new phenomenon. It is a theoretical possibility in any political system that centralises authority or concentrates power in the hands of a single ruler. It is a construct that has engaged minds since ancient times—not just those in the West but also those in Africa. The heroes of the American Revolution (1775–83) and the French Revolution (1789) used liberal ideas to justify the armed overthrow of the tyrannical order. The American rebellion was against the colonial power, Britain, while the French counterpart was against Louis XVI, an absolute monarch, whose predecessor, Louis XIV, famously declared, '*L'Etat, c'est moi*' ('I am the state'). On 17 January 1793, Louis XVI was condemned to death for conspiracy against public liberty and general safety. He was guillotined (i.e. subjected to regicide).

The American revolutionaries overthrew the tyrannical colonial state, and the French revolutionaries abolished the absolute monarchy and established a republic. The two revolutions, however, differ fundamentally in terms of the constitutional results they produced.[2] While both produced constitutions that sought to prevent state tyranny, the French saw the state as the ultimate guarantor and protector of individual rights, while the Americans saw the state as a threat to individual liberty and, therefore, wrote a constitution to limit the powers of the state.[3] The more power the state has, the less free its people are.

Of course, it would be naive and even preposterous to assume that Africans have never considered the threat of despotism in their systems and never had revolutions, and that present-day despotism is 'acceptable' to them. Of course, they too had their heroes and 'classical liberals'. However, their works and thinking are not available to all. These are transmitted not through literature but by oral tradition, which is a poor means of communication over the ages since it relies on memory. Over time, memory becomes foggy and certain facts and details are mangled or lost forever. Such communication generally starts like this: 'Many moons ago . . .' Nonetheless, Africans have also had 'revolutions' which resulted in kings not only being overthrown but also killed (regicide). Here is an example from the Gikuyu (Kenya) taken from the late president Jomo Kenyatta's book:

> King Gikuyu ruled [for] many moons and his method of governing was tyrannical. People were prevented from cultivating the land, as he commanded all able-bodied men to join his army and be ready to move with their families at any time and to wherever he chose. At last,

[2] It is important to emphasise this point. A constitution reflects the political experience, history, and aspirations of a people. As such, it necessarily has a cultural imprint. One cannot just copy someone else's constitution and make it their own. Such a comedy of errors occurred in Ghana in 1979 when the government proudly declared that its constitution was a blend of the American and French constitutions.

[3] Is it not ironic that the Europeans who overthrew monarchical absolutism went on to establish tyrannical colonial rule over others?

> the people grew tired of wandering and implored the King to let them establish permanent homes, but he refused to consider their plea. The people became very indignant and in desperation they revolted against him. After King Gikuyu was dethroned, the government of the country was at once changed from a despotism to a democracy, which was in keeping with the wishes of the majority of the people. This revolution is known as itwika, derived from the word twika, which means to break away 'from', and signifying [a] breaking away from autocracy to democracy.[4]

Most traditional African societies have no written constitutions, although one of the oldest, *Kurukan Fuga* (Manden Charter), came from Africa.[5] Britain does not have one either. However, many ethnic groups took measures to prevent state tyranny. An intensive study of indigenous African political culture reveals an obsessive fear of state tyranny. Most Africans considered the state as necessarily tyrannical and structured their political institutions so as to provide an effective bulwark against this threat. Some, like the Igbo, the Somali, and the Gikuyu, went to the radical extreme of abolishing the state altogether and dispensing with chiefs or centralised authority. These are known as stateless societies.

Even in the most backward societies, autocracy was generally the exception rather than the rule because the foot has always served as an effective check. Rulers who acted despotically found themselves abandoned. Groups that were persecuted always moved, that is, voted with their feet. The history of Africa is replete with migrations of people. The cultural imperative was independence. The same operating principles applied when a group of states united to form a kingdom, and kingdoms, to form an empire. But the assertion of central control often led to rebellions and the break-up of the kingdoms and empires. Peter Wickins was emphatic in his conclusion that

> [s]trong centralised government was the exception rather than the rule in sub-Saharan Africa. Poverty of communications made it difficult to prevent states from breaking up, and it is no accident that some of the most stable and enduring ones had navigable rivers, notably the kingdoms of the western Sudan, served by the middle Niger. Secondly, even relatively wealthy rulers, like the Mwene Mutapa, could not maintain a professional army of any size to enforce commands. Executive weakness and bad communications, together with total or general illiteracy, necessitated a devolution of powers of administration, either to appointed officials or to subordinate rulers, and in the absence of currency those exercising such powers had to be paid in kind.[6]

However, colonialism, independence, and population growth substantially reduced the number of unoccupied spaces to which oppressed people could escape. Furthermore, the acquisition of more and better means of coercion after independence radically altered the

[4] Jomo Kenyatta, the founder of Kenya, became its first president after independence in 1963. The irony is that he never established a democratic system of governance but instead set up a one-party state. See further Jomo Kenyatta, *Facing Mount Kenya* (Secker & Warburg 1938) 180.

[5] See UNESCO, 'Manden Charter, Proclaimed in Kurukan Fuga' (2009) https://ich.unesco.org/en/RL/manden-charter-proclaimed-in-kurukan-fuga-00290 (last accessed 15 August 2021).

[6] Peter L. Wickins, *An Economic History of Africa from the Earliest Times to Partition* (Oxford University Press 1981) 228.

logistics of population control. Modern and sophisticated arms and aircraft now afford African dictators much tighter control over a greater number of people and over a much wider geographical area than in pre-colonial times. Thus, the potential for despotism has become much greater in modern than in pre-colonial Africa.

The burning fear of tyranny was also much evident among those ethnic groups that chose to constitute themselves into states. The evidence for this is afforded, firstly, by their highly decentralised systems of government; secondly, by the detailed devolution of authority and assignment of responsibilities; and thirdly, by the institution of a complex system of checks and balances to curb autocracy. Many put in place relevant safeguards and measures—not written, of course, but embedded in the taboos and injunctions that come with office and which a ruler has to obey. For example, the king must not speak directly to his people but do so only through a linguist, or spokesperson, as was required of the *Asantehene* (Ashanti king), while the Yoruba *oona* must never venture out of his palace except under the cover of darkness. It is hard to imagine how a despotic king could function with such taboos. He could go out at night and bark all the orders he wanted through his linguist—but his people would be fast asleep! Perhaps no other area of study is as fascinating as the checks and balances Africans built into their traditional political systems to prevent or punish abuse of power or misuse of office.

Despotism exists only in a political system that lacks effective checks and balances. The threat of deposition and recall always kept potential despots in check. The French had no such safeguards before the 1789 Revolution—Louis XVI could not be deposed—neither did many European monarchical systems before the Era of Enlightenment, when this threat was not a common feature of the indigenous systems of the Ashanti, the Zulu, and a range of other ethnic groups.[7] But like the old medieval European monarchs, today's despots running amok in Africa face no threats of deposition or recall.

3. Pre-colonial Political Systems

In pre-colonial Africa, four main polities were established by the people: empires, kingdoms, stateless societies, and chiefdoms. We examine the prospect of dictatorship in each of them.

3.1 Empires

Many empires in ancient times were in fact confederacies that were formed through voluntary association. In this case, tyrannical rule was not a possibility as, by definition, a confederacy is an association. Furthermore, a number of factors checked any measure of harsh rule and rigid central control. The first was the language barrier. In the absence of written literature and formal education, it took a considerable amount of time to learn the language of the imperial overlords. This difficulty constrained rapid assimilation of the subjugated group. The second factor was that lines of authority in indigenous societies

[7] See further George B.N. Ayittey, *Indigenous African Institutions* (2nd edn, Transnational Publishers 2006) 265–310.

were based on kinship and ancestral connections. It was difficult to supplant these and substitute authority from imperial officers who lacked kinship relations and, thus, legitimacy.

The third check was geographical. In ancient and medieval times, Africa was sparsely populated and ethnic groupings were fluid. Those who found themselves under alien tyranny always moved into the great expanses of unoccupied land to uphold their independence and protect their cultures. Those who could not move because they were hemmed in by the sea and powerful ethnic groups on their sides either revolted or transferred their allegiance to an adjacent and stronger kingdom and sought its protection. Many groups formed such alliances, even with European traders who declared protectorates over them. The Fante of Ghana and the Kabaka of Buganda were such examples in their alliances with British colonialists.

The fourth factor was the lack of efficient population-control instruments. These were unavailable due to the underdeveloped state of technology, transportation, and communication networks. When subjugated people on the outer reaches of an empire broke away, it would often take weeks for the news to reach the capital by footpath. Talking drums reduced the informational lag somewhat but not by much.

In the eighteenth and nineteenth centuries, the main weapons were the bow and arrow, and the spear, which everybody could make. They were, in that sense, democratic weapons. As James Gibbs put it:

> No man [could] be a despot for long, especially where the technology [was] relatively primitive. It was only in the latter part of the last century, after the introduction of guns, that the *kabaka* [of Buganda] had even a small standing army.[8]

Devolution of authority was a common feature of ancient African empires. This was particularly evident in such states as the Zande and Oyo empires. Very few African empires had rigidly centralised administrations. The exceptions included the Kingdom of Dahomey, the Asante Empire, the Kingdom of Kongo, other interlacustrine states in eastern Africa (Buganda, Rwanda, Nkore, Burundi, Buha, Bushubi, Bunyoro, Bushi, Karagwe, and Wanga), and the Zulu kingdom. Even so, regimes in the interlacustrine region 'varied from strong absolutism to moderate aristocracy. Buganda, Rwanda and Nkore were quite absolutist, while Burundi, by the end of the 19th century, could be described as a moderate aristocracy'.[9] Furthermore, the degree of centralisation tended to be exaggerated, as was noted of the Zulu kingdom.[10]

Historical evidence also suggests that those empires characterised by strong, centralised administrations were inherently unstable and chronically threatened by internal revolts. Although a superior military kept rebellious vassal states in check, it was only a matter of time before the subjugated states successfully asserted their independence or bolted for freedom.

[8] James Gibbs, *Peoples of Africa* (Holt, Rinehart and Winston 1965) 91.

[9] See V.G. Simiyu, 'The Democratic Myth in the African Traditional Societies' in Walter O. Ougi and Afrifa K. Gitonga (eds.), *Democratic Theory and Practice in Africa* (East African Educational Publishers 1988) 55.

[10] See Paul Maylam, *A History of the African People of South Africa: From the Early Iron Age to the 1970s* (David Philip 1986) 28.

3.2 African Kingdoms

Below the empires, the African people organised themselves into kingdoms, which could comprise chiefdoms of people of the same ethnic stock. Several kingdoms are confederations of independent republics of chiefdoms—the Ashanti and Ga kingdoms, for example—and kingdoms may have vassal states.

Although different tribal societies may have different conceptions of their kings, Africans accepted their kings as a necessary evil. The king was necessary for the preservation of the social order, but he was also a danger: he could abuse his powers and be all-intrusive, restricting the independence and freedom of his people. To resolve this dilemma, many African ethnic groups created, to various degrees of success, a 'person' hidden from public view but whose awe-inspiring authority could be invoked to maintain order and harmony. This is akin to the tooth fairy or Santa Claus, figures which in Western culture awe Western children. The equivalent in traditional African political systems was the divine king. He was secluded and his everyday life planned to the minutest detail and loaded with socially useful burdens.

The outward signs of his sacredness were onerous personal taboos, which he had to observe in the interests of the polity. His sex life, symbolically fused with his fertility and vigour, might be severely restricted. His most elementary physical functions, such as crying, eating, drinking, or defecating, were ritually controlled, while his movements were hemmed in by taboos, such as those against touching the soil in fields or seeing a corpse. Sometimes, he might not even be allowed to reach the frailty of old age or, when at the point of death, expire naturally by himself. Taboos of this sort applied, it should be noted, not only to secluded and unmistakably 'sacred' kings but also to all African chiefs and kings.[11]

Most of these restrictions were designed to reduce the king to an executive nonentity, curtail the discretionary use of political power, and confine him to his palace where he would be safely out of people's private lives. They served primarily to take the gold out of royal glitter. The king was a remote, secluded, and ritual figure who could also serve as a convenient scapegoat if things went wrong. As long as he was prepared to obey these restrictions, some ethnic groups in fact did not care who the king was or from where he came. To the Goba of Namainga (Central Africa), their 'kings, *qua* rootless immigrants, were useful "slaves"'.[12] Along the Nile-Zaire divide, some small states requested that the Alur people furnish them with chiefs and kings. In Benin, 'the Edo elders were said to have requested the *Oni* of Ife to send them a king'.[13]

If he failed to perform, the king was deposed. Regicide was embedded in divine kingship, although it was outlawed in most traditional societies at the beginning of the twentieth century. In its classic form, divine kingship sanctioned killing the king if he became infirm or if things were going badly in the kingdom. The custom stems directly from the belief in the unity of the king and kingdom, such that the prosperity or failure of either may be regarded as that of both, and a king can thus be held responsible for conditions in the kingdom. Should he be ill or weak, the kingdom will be in danger; if conditions in the kingdom are

[11] See Igor Kopytoff (ed.), *The African Frontier* (Indiana University Press 1989) 66.
[12] Ibid.
[13] Ibid. 65.

bad, there must be something wrong with the king. Furthermore, it follows that a change in the person of the king will change conditions in the kingdom.[14]

An understanding of the role of the king necessitates a brief discourse on the traditional concept of the universe. Africans believed that their universe is composed of three elements: the sky, the world, and the earth. The sky is the domain of spirits of both the living and those yet to be born, as well as powerful forces such as lightning, thunder, rain, and drought. The earth is the domain of dead ancestors, other dead tribesmen, and the activities of the living: agriculture, fishing, hunting, and so on. The world is peopled by the living—the ethnic group and other tribesmen—and is therefore the domain of war, peace, trade, and relations with other tribes.

In most traditional African societies, each of the three elements is represented by a god and has to be in perfect harmony with the others. The king had a precise function to play: to appease or propitiate the three gods in order to achieve harmony among them and thereby ensure prosperity for his kingdom. If the sky god were 'angry', there would be thunder, heavy downpours, and flooding; if the earth god were 'angry', there would be poor harvests, famine, and barren women. In comparative terms, the kings of medieval Western Europe also had three fundamental duties: to ensure the spiritual welfare of their people through acts of piety and the protection given by the true faith; to defend their people against outside enemies; and, at home, to safeguard justice and peace. According to Basil Davidson, although the forms of kingship may have been different, their content in Africa and Europe was essentially the same.[15]

The king thus has two roles to play: a political one, as head of the kingdom, and a spiritual one, as the link to the universe. The political role, however, is subordinate. Most traditional constitutions require the king to delegate almost all of his political authority to other leaders and officials. For this reason, most kingdoms are characterised by decentralisation of power and delegation of authority. Custom and tradition set limits to the authority of the king, his cabinet, and advisors. Thus, the king's role in governance is small: he is the representative or symbol of the kingdom and may have some religious duties, but his participation in political decision-making is insignificant. He hardly makes policy or speaks. He has a spokesperson, called a linguist (as noted), through whom he communicates. He rarely decides policy. His advisers and chiefs would determine policies and present them for royal assent. His role in legislation and execution of policy is nearly zero and may be compared to that of the queen of England. His role is not political but to maintain cosmological, and therefore social, order. If the king were to die suddenly, there would be social upheaval, chaos, and calamities.

More emphasis is laid on the spiritual function of the king. This entails a separation of kingship and political leadership. In modern times, this tradition—the separation of the spiritual role from politics—has been maintained in most European kingdoms, for example Norway, the Netherlands, and Britain. The exceptions are two African kings: King Mohammed VI of Morocco and King Mswati III of Eswatini.

The traditional African king was stripped of executive power by means of cleverly designed taboos and injunctions. In some tribal systems, no one may see the king eat; he

[14] See James Vaughan, 'Population and Social Organisation' in Phyllis Martin and Patrick O'Meara (eds.), *Africa* (Indiana University Press 1986) 177.

[15] Basil Davidson, *African Kingdoms* (Time/Life Books 1970) 193.

should not walk in cultivated fields, lest the fertility of the soil be affected. He should not see a corpse or cry over the dead. He must not be allowed to die a natural death, for that would affect the power of his sacred 'medicines'. Among the Suku of Congo, James Gibbs notes,

> [w]hen the king drank, those present had to cover their faces while one of the attendants recited proverbs and sayings recapitulating historic events, praising the king for his good deeds and also hinting at those where he had shown himself to be unjust.[16]

Despite the puffed-up image of divinity, African kings were really scapegoat kings. They had little or no political function or role, only a spiritual one—to maintain social order, protect the people from such calamities as droughts and famine, and ensure the prosperity of the kingdom. If any of the three gods were 'angry' and there was famine, it meant the king had been derelict in the performance of his duties. He was also blamed for any other misfortune that befell his people. He was a useful scapegoat on whom to vent frustration and anger. Among the Kerebe of northwest Tanzania, Randall Packard says,

> [k]ings were expected to regulate rainfall and . . . the inability to conform to these expectations over an extended period of time was a major reason for deposing an *omukama*. Two kings are said to have been deposed in this manner at the beginning of the nineteenth century: Ruhinda, who was unable to prevent an excessive amount of rain from falling, and his successor, Ibanda, who fell victim to an extended period of drought.[17]

The Junkun of Nigeria, however, believed that

> kings were supposed to be killed if they broke any of the royal taboos on personal behavior, fell seriously ill, or ruled in time of famine or severe drought and whenever they could no longer be regarded as fit guardians of the 'right and natural'.[18]

The king was also put to death when the level of his vital force was perceived to have declined. For example, among the Serer, 'a *Bur* (king) who reached old age was subject to ritual murder because it was believed he could no longer guarantee that cattle and women would remain fertile'.[19] Similarly, among the Shilluk of the Nilotic Sudan, a sick or old king was to be killed. In the Kingdom of Cayor, the king could not rule when he was wounded. In other societies, an old king was not killed but revitalised. He would die symbolically, be born again, regain the vigour of his youth, and be fit once again to rule. This ritual was found among the Yoruba, Dagomba, Tchamba, Djukon, Igara, Songhai, Wuadai, Hausa of the Gobi, Katsena, and Daoura, the Shillucks, among the Mbum in Uganda-Rwanda, and in what was ancient Meroe.[20] Although regicide has been abolished, the belief in the practice reflected the existence of an ideological relationship between political authority and the problem of ecological control.[21]

16 James Gibbs, *Peoples of Africa* (Holt, Rinehart and Winston 1965) 460.
17 Randall Packard, *Chiefship and Cosmology* (Indiana University Press 1981) 6.
18 See Davidson (n. 15) 201.
19 Cited in Ayittey (n. 7) 212.
20 See Cheikh Anta Diop, *Pre-colonial Black Africa* (Lawrence Hill & Co. 1987) 61.
21 See Packard (n. 17) 6.

In other tribes, if the king failed to provide the vital link to the universe, he was dethroned. There were various procedures for divestiture. While the Serer ethnic group of Senegal adopted a distinctive drumbeat to signal the end of a king's reign, the Yoruba of Nigeria demanded the king's suicide 'with a symbolic gift of parrot's eggs'.[22] If he did not commit suicide within three months, a select group of young men seized and disposed of him.

3.2.1 Constitutional checks against tyranny

Though African kings played an insignificant political role in government, they were held accountable. Their traditional role was spiritual: to provide a vital link to the universe for the people by maintaining harmony or balance among the three cosmological forces of the sky, the world, and the earth. To enable the king to perform his function, he was, firstly, secluded in his palace—in order to keep his royal fingers out of people's business.

Secondly, he was not only secluded in his palace but entwined in a web of taboos and injunctions regarding the office of kingship. His daily life and conduct were planned down to the minutest detail. For example, he could not eat before strangers, speak directly to his people, or venture out of his palace except under the cover of darkness.

Thirdly, most of his powers were delegated to subordinate chiefs. Even then, most of the political organisations which had a king surrounded him with councils and courts. According to Paul Bohannan, almost all African political organisations have institutionalised means to keep the king from abusing his power.[23] Though Africans delighted in telling foreigners how 'powerful' their kings were so as to ward off foreign aggressive intentions, the kings were severely restrained in the exercise of those powers against their people. The Asante king appeared absolute, yet he had to procure the consent of the chiefs, and the chiefs the consent of the elders, in order to bring about group action.[24] Akan kings had no right to make peace or war, make laws, or be directly involved in important negotiations such as treaties without the consent of their elders and/or elected representatives.[25]

Even in the rigidly controlled Kingdom of Dahomey, Webster and Kramsky found as follows:

> Although the king's word was the law of the land . . . he was not above the law. Dahomeans like to recount how king Glele was fined for breaking the law. When gangs of men were working co-operatively on state roads, it was a law that a passer-by must offer a credible excuse as to why he could not break his journey to assist in the work. Permission was always given, the law being largely designed to reinforce courtesy. King Glele's procession passed one such group without asking to be excused. He was stopped and fined many cases of rum and pieces of cloth for breaking the law . . . The fact that the kings of Dahomey (now Benin) were prepared to obey the laws they themselves created was the difference between arbitrary despotism and despotism which realised that its power and position rested ultimately, no matter how indirectly, upon the will of the people.[26]

22 See Elizabeth Isichei, *History of West Africa since 1800* (Africana Publishing Company 1977) 71.
23 Paul Bohannan, *Africa and Africans* (Natural History Press 1964) 191.
24 See Kenneth Carlston, *Social Theory and African Tribal Organisation* (University of Chicago Press 1968) 127.
25 See Daniel Boamah-Wiafe, *Africa: The Land, People, and Cultural Institutions* (Wisdom Publications 1993) 169.
26 James Bertin Webster and Jiri Kramsky, *History of West Africa: The Revolution Years—1815 to Independence* (Praeger 1970) 106.

3.2.2 Regicide

James Vaughan has noted that, in many instances, the dependence upon the rule of law and a respect for law seems to have inhibited ambitious rulers; he adds that it should not be forgotten that regicide itself was an ultimate check upon the excesses of a king.[27] Regicide has been abolished, so kings are simply dethroned. Several *Asantehene* were deposed in the course of history. Among them were Kofi Kakari, who was deposed in 1874, and Mensa Bonsu, who was removed in 1883 for his avarice and refusal to raise an army and reconquer Gyaman.[28] *Itwika*, the Gikuyu equivalent of the French Revolution, may also be recalled.

Today, kings are still being dethroned. Consider the case of *Oba* Samuel Aderiyi Adara of the Ode-Ekiti community of Ekiti State in Nigeria, who was dethroned for non-performance. It was reported thus:

> The traditional ruler was accused of not contributing enough to the progress of the community and of frustrating the celebration of the yearly festival. He was invited to the community meeting where he was accused of failing in his duty of moving the town forward. But attempts by the monarch to extricate himself from the allegations failed. He was lambasted for not informing the state government of the pathetic socio-economic situation in his domain and asked to vacate the throne for a more progressive minded personality in the town. While the meeting was still going on, some youths in the town invaded the venue, removed the dress of the traditional ruler, including his royal beads and crown, and chased him out of the town. Shortly after, traditional trees in strategic shrines were cut down, symbolising the demise of the *Oba*. The spokesman for the community said it was the collective decision of both the old and young to dethrone the monarch, saying his reign was 'disastrous, woeful and sorrowful'.[29]

3.2.3 The Swazi kingdom

Evidently, African kings were not what they were seemed to be. The colonialists had difficulty dealing with some traditional rulers. Some ethnic groups did not have kings, so the colonialists created kings for them; others had kings but with very limited powers. In some such cases, the colonialists conferred enormous powers upon them which they did not have in their traditional systems. The Ga and Swazi kings[30] were classic examples of this.

In the indigenous system, the Ga *mantse* (king) was useful only in times of warfare. He had no political authority or executive function and was never an integral part of the native government. However, Europeans treated him as a king, showering him with respect and deference. Such European patronage emboldened a few obsequious Ga *mantse*s to act autocratically, which incensed the Ga people, who tried to dissuade the Europeans from dealing with such despots but to no avail. In response, the Ga destooled (removed leaders from the stool that was the symbol of their authority) many of these 'European' *mantse*s. One was Mantse Obli Taki, who was destooled in 1918 by his Labadi people 'for a number of offenses,

27 See Vaughan (n. 14) 178.
28 See Webster and Kramsky (n. 26) 128.
29 See *The Guardian* (24 July 2003) 4.
30 In 2019 the king changed the name of the country to Eswatini.

chief of which was the selling of Ga land in the name of the Ga people without consulting the owners of that land, and the pledging of the stool itself as security on a loan'.[31]

The Swazi king is another example of a meretricious caricature of the traditional counterpart. This kingdom was formed in the early nineteenth century when Sobhuza I, head of the Dlamini clan, crossed the Lubombo Mountains and conquered the resident clans. The kingdom is unique because it is a dual monarchy. The monarchy is built on a network of ties between the royal *Nkosi Dlamini* and commoners. The clans, more than seventy in number, fall into four major grades. At the apex is the *Nkosi Dlamini*, in which the lineage of the king, known as the *Malangeni* (children of the sun), is pre-eminent. The king, *Ngwenyama*, is the recognised lineal descendant of the first leader of the conquering *Nkosi Dlamini*. He performs executive, legislative, and judicial functions; holds land in trust for the Swazi nation and allocates its usage; performs sacred rituals; and is the symbol of national unity.

According to Ronald Libby, historically, the authority of the Swazi king was balanced by both *Ndlovukazi* (the queen mother) and two traditional institutions, the *Liqoqo* (inner or family council) and *Libandla* (general council or council of the nation). Libby put it thus:

> The *Liqoqo* was a small group of 10 to 20 senior princes, important representatives of the queen mother's *Nxumalo* clan, senior chiefs from outside the *Dlamini*, and *Nxumalo* clans, and a few commoners of outstanding importance in the country. The *Liqoqo* functioned in much the same way as a modern-day cabinet, meeting informally and with some of its members frequently consulted by the king. The *Libandla*, by contrast, was regarded as having binding authority on actions taken by the king on behalf of the Swazi nation. It comprised the *Liqoqo* members, all of the chiefs, their counsellors, and all adult men in the country. Although it normally met only once a year, in principle its approval was required for all important new laws and decisions.[32]

That is, without the *Libandla*, the Swazi king could not make any law. The relationship between the king and his councillors is expressed in two frequently quoted axioms: 'The king is king by the people' and '[t]he king is ruled by his councillors'.[33] Commoners participated in discussions with the king and their chiefs through regional forums called *Tinkhundla*. People could also voice their opinions through both the *Liqoqo* and the *Libandla*. No one was arrested for expressing a divergent opinion. In fact, the *Libandla*'s primary purpose was to reach consensus on important issues. Once a decision was reached, neither the *Liqoqo* nor the king could override it.

In the aftermath of the Anglo-Boer War, when the Swazi kingdom became a British protectorate in 1903, things began to change. In an effort to check Boer expansionism during the war, Britain ruled the kingdom indirectly through the king, Sobhuza II, and conferred enormous powers on him. In 1964, a constitution was imposed and the kingdom was required to hold democratic elections that same year, and again in 1967. After independence in 1968, Sobhuza II resorted to the same chicanery as other African nationalist leaders who, having made democracy their rallying cry during the struggle against colonialism, changed their tune upon winning independence. They claimed that democracy was alien to Africa

[31] See M.J. Field, *Social Organisation of the Ga People* (Government of the Gold Coast Printing Press 1940) 183.
[32] Ronald T. Libby, *The Politics of Economic Power in Southern Africa* (Princeton University Press 1987) 154.
[33] Ibid.

and proceeded to use their huge parliamentary majorities to outlaw the opposition, declare the countries one-party states, and install themselves as presidents-for-life. They justified this insidious concentration of power in their hands as necessary to protect their fledgling nations against the machinations of neocolonialism and imperialism.

In Swaziland, Sobhuza II jettisoned the British-crafted constitution that guaranteed individual rights and, in 1973, dissolved Parliament and rid himself of the annoyance of political parties. Mswati III succeeded his father in 1986 and, in 2005, promulgated a new constitution, a peculiar document that gave him absolute powers to appoint the prime minister and members of the governing cabinet and the judiciary. It was claimed that these changes were necessary to move away from the colonial model and revert to a reformed traditional system.

It should be recalled that in the traditional system, the Swazi king had no political role. Through the annual *ncwala* ceremony, he mediated between the world of the living and the world of supernatural beings. Furthermore, the little power that he had was checked by a slew of taboos and injunctions. Naturally, in 'modernising' the traditional system, the king got rid of all those taboos and encumbrances and thereby created a political system with no checks and balances—just as other African nationalist leaders had done. While they banned opposition parties, Mswati III banned *all* political parties.

King Mswati III abused this absolute power. In 2002, the Swazi government announced it was buying a USD 25 million luxury jet for the king, even though massive food shortages threatened an estimated 230,000 people with starvation. The cost of the plane was five times the impoverished nation's national deficit. People were outraged: 'Why an aircraft for the king? The money spent for the king's jet should have been used for buying food for the starving Swazis.'[34] Prime Minister Sibusiso Dlamini said the jet was urgently needed to help the king attract foreign investment and international aid.

King Mswati III is often portrayed as the prototypical 'traditional' ruler, with his bad deeds emblematic of an unsophisticated and backward political society. However, an examination of history reveals something altogether different. Rather than corruption and despotism being inherent to traditional rule, it is the undermining of traditional checks on executive authority by the colonial state that left the population exposed to the whims of their despotic king. Moreover, by writing traditional checks, such as destooling, out of the political narrative of Africa, the colonial legacy painted a false picture of African leadership. It is time to re-examine the traditional priority of executive accountability and once again hold Africa's leaders to task.

3.3 Stateless Societies

In 1787, Thomas Jefferson, one of America's Founding Fathers, wrote as follows in a letter to Edward Carrington: 'I am convinced that those societies [as the Indians] which live without government enjoy in their general mass an infinitely greater degree of happiness than those who live under European governments.'[35] He was presumably referring to stateless societies.

[34] 'Swaziland's High Flying King' *Mail&Guardian* (1 January 2022) https://mg.co.za/article/2002-01-01-swazilands-high-flying-king/ (accessed on 9 October 2023).

[35] See Founders online https://founders.archives.gov/documents/Jefferson/01-11-02-0047 (last accessed 15 August 2021).

'Government' is a necessary evil; it is the leader who can be dispensed with, as in stateless societies. According to Jean-François Bayart, 'the most distinctive contribution of Africa to human history has been precisely in the civilised art of living reasonably peacefully without a state'.[36]

A stateless society or 'non-state' would seem almost a contradiction in terms to Westerners, who may see the institution of the state as necessary to avoid tyranny yet recognise that a 'bad' state can impose tyranny. They see the absence of the state as a recipe for chaos. On the other hand, 'Africans who live in stateless societies tend to see the state as unavoidable tyranny; they seek and find order in other institutions'.[37] These societies pushed the concept of liberty to its most radical extreme and would fiercely resist tyranny. This was one reason why the Igbo fought a war (the Biafran War of 1967) to secede from Nigeria, and it also underlies the current chaos in Somalia.

Autocracy was always a theoretical possibility in government, a fact which concerned many ethnic societies. To guard against this, many elected not to have chiefs or any centralised authority at all. For example, 'the Tiv of Nigeria were a people who lived in fear of power and were compelled to place themselves under the possessors of power for protection against its abuse by others'.[38] Similar tendencies were also observed among the Ga of southern Ghana. The Ga *mantse* united his people and led them only in times of war; politically and in peacetime, he had no role in government. These tribal societies had a highly sophisticated understanding of the notion of liberty and pushed it to the extreme.

Most traditional African societies have four units of government: the chief, the inner or privy council, the council of elders, and the village assembly. In stateless societies, there are only two units of government: the council of elders and the village assembly. There is no leader, and the maintenance of justice as well as of cultural and territorial integrity is effected through extended family organisations and the invocation of kinship behaviour, not only in domestic but also in wider spheres. This was characteristic of hunting and pastoral peoples such as the !Kung, the Pygmies, and the Fulani.

But precautions were taken. A system of checks and balances was instituted in which two or more power centres were balanced against each other and applied at all levels of the community so that no single centre predominated. There was a wide dispersion of this system across Africa, one adopted by such ethnic societies as the Tiv and Igbo of Nigeria, the Nuer of Sudan, the Somali, and the Bedouin Arabs of North Africa. Both types generally used kinship idioms and the norms of kinship behaviour in their system of law and order. In general, there were no office-holders, only representatives of groups. Such societies reached compromises in conflict resolution rather than making judgments and applying sanctions.

A few of these societies had leaders. Among the pastoral Somali, he is the *suldaan* or sultan.[39] He is not a ruler. He symbolises the peace and prosperity of the clan and fulfils the functions of archivist and occasional ambassador. He is appointed for life, and when the clan engages in rituals, he is the master of ceremonies and the central figure. He is usually chosen from the family of his predecessor, but he is not necessarily the eldest son.[40] The headman among the !Kung (*Khwe*) is called *kxau*. In !Kung society, the headman is the

36 Jean-François Bayart, *L'Etat en Afrique* (Fayard 1989) 58.
37 See Bohannan (n. 23) 195.
38 See Carlston (n. 24) 211.
39 See Michael van Notten, *The Law of the Somalis* (Transnational Publishers 2006) 81.
40 Ibid.

eldest son of the previous headman. If the male line is cut off for a generation, headmanship passes through the eldest daughter to her eldest son. If a headman is too young, too old, or lacks personal qualities of leadership, the people turn informally to another man for leadership in their daily lives, asking him for help and advice.[41] But as John Marshall points out,

> in many acephalous societies, there was a clear separation between power (defined as the ability to influence events in a desired manner and direction) and authority (meaning the acknowledged or recognised right to exercise power). One did not necessarily flow from the other.[42]

The colonialists had the most difficulty in dealing with this arrangement in stateless societies. They sought leaders with 'power' in such societies. Finding none, they then 'created' these leaders. But the latter lacked authority since they were not part of the kinship group and were treated as the external appendages of an alien government. Within the ethnic group, they had little legitimacy or authority, and what little they had was considered tyrannical by the people under them. In fact, the Somalis mocked the titles which the British and Italian colonialists created for the officials of the first central government: 'The president of the Somali Republic, for instance, was called *madaxweyne*, which literally means "big head".'[43]

The Somalis pushed the concept of freedom to its most radical limit. They take orders from no one, but their country has been in chaos since 1991 and they have not had any effective government since they ousted the late dictator, General Siad Barre. To Westerners, the chaos in that country reflects the turbulence of traditional society and an inability to establish a democratic order. But nothing could be further from the truth on both counts. Traditional Somali society is peaceful. It is governed by customary laws, known as *xeer*, that come very close to natural law. Such societies are described as 'near-kritarchies'. Democracy is incompatible with kritarchy; hence, the Somalis have rabid contempt for 'government', which they dismiss as *waxan* (the thing). The chaos seen in Somalia is due not so much to the people's inability to establish a democratic order as it is to their rejection of any attempt to impose a *waxan* on them—they will fight any such 'thing'. Somali society may be described as a confederation of sovereign families, though Michael van Notten suggests a more appropriate description:

> A network of constantly shifting political alliances between independent *jilibs*, sub-clans, and clans. Given the fact that all of these entities are founded on respect for natural law, one might call their society a near-kritarchy . . . What all kritarchies or near-kritarchies have in common is that their judges apply a customary law. Because customary law approximates natural law, the term denotes a political system that is in accord with natural law.[44]

The Somalis are imbued with healthy self-esteem. Unimpressed by foreign political systems, they hold on to the institutions and rules of law they developed themselves. If a leader of

41 See Gibbs (n. 8) 268.
42 John Marshall, 'Hunting among the Kalahari Bushmen' in Elliot Percival Skinner (ed.), *Peoples and Cultures of Africa: An Anthropological Reader* (Natural History Press 1973) 110.
43 See Van Notten (n. 38) 82.
44 Ibid. 90.

any group of Somalis tried to lord it over his fellows, he would soon find himself alone: the others would simply pack up their belongings and start a new group elsewhere. The first European to note this may have been the British traveller Richard Burton, who in 1856 called the Somalis a 'fierce and turbulent race of Republicans'.[45] A century later, I.M. Lewis observed:

> The Somali have no indigenous centralised government. And this lack of formal government and of instituted authority is strongly reflected in their extreme independence and individualism. Few writers have failed to notice the formidable pride of the Somali nomad, his extraordinary sense of superiority as an individual and his firm conviction that he is the sole master of his actions.[46]

This discussion raises the question: Why has modern-day Somalia been in such chaos since the ouster of its dictator, General Siad Barre, in 1991? The simple answer is that the Somali people refuse to accept an alien system imposed on them by the political elites and the international community. Frank D. Heath expressed it well:

> Before being colonised, the Somalis based their society on respect for their customary law. The traditional political system of the Somalis is a near-kritarchy. In 1960, however, about the colonial powers pushed Somalis to adopt democracy. That system created such a chaotic situation that few were unhappy when, nine years later, a dictator stepped in to clean things up. Eventually, however, the Somalis became disillusioned with dictatorship as well. In 1991 they dismantled their European-style government altogether and went back to their traditional political system based on respect for the customary law.[47]

Most Somalis prefer their customary laws and institutions (*xeer*). In their experience, the *xeer* constitutes the heart of the Somali nation and is the cord that holds the house of the Somali people together. Without the *xeer*, the Somali nation would fall apart, lose its identity, forgo its solidarity, forfeit its civilisation, and surrender its culture. It is due to customary laws that the traditional political system of the Somalis takes the form of a kritarchy, not a democracy.

Of course, the politicians had other ideas: they prefer contrived statutory law that would allow them to lord it over the people. As Michael van Notten notes,

> During the 20th century, the Somalis were subjected to heavy-handed policies of the colonial powers. These powers left a form of government behind that was at odds with indigenous Somali political culture. It took the Somalis 30 years to get rid of it and return to their pre-colonial political structure. Many problems arose in the course of this, but gradually the Somalis are resolving them. Foreign observers fail to understand what they are

[45] Ibid. 30.

[46] I.M. Lewis, 'Lineage Continuity and Modern Commerce in Northern Somaliland' in Paul Bohannan and George Dalton (eds.), *Markets in Africa* (Northwestern University Press 1962) 1. Near-kritarchies such as Somali society have one fundamental weakness, however. They are defenceless against a powerful external aggressor. As a result, the Somalis found themselves cut up in five ways under colonial rule. Some found themselves in Ethiopia (Ogaden), Djibouti, Kenya, Italian Somaliland, and British Somaliland. The same can be said of the Hmong and the Kurds.

[47] Frank D. Heath, 'Tribal Society and Democracy' (2001) 5(22) *The Laissez Faire City Times*.

> doing; they think the Somalis have been trying to establish a democratic government and constantly failing to do so. In reality, the chief aim of many Somalis is to clean their indigenous legal and political system of its foreign elements.[48]

The Somalis are not the problem: the problem lies with the political elites, their allies in the international community, the warlords, the Islamic Courts Union, Al-Shabaab, and other groups who hold the *xeer*, the cord that keeps Somalis together, in contempt and are determined to sever it. It is not the Somali people but the intellectual backwardness of these groups that keeps Somalia in chaos. The Somali people will resist any foreign institution or law imposed on them.

3.4 Chiefdoms

The term 'chief' is used generically for a leader of a tribal group at the village level. As a central figure in the village, the chief plays many roles, least of which is that of autocrat. The survival of the people is the imperative and, by dint of reason as well as custom, consultation with his advisers and elders is mandatory. He must listen to as large a variety of viewpoints and proposals as possible, seldom dismissing any out of hand. His primary duty is to determine a consensual position rather than impose his own. He is required to explore every possible avenue, since his foremost prerogative is the preservation of his people. He acts as an umpire or guardian to ensure fair play and equal justice for all. He mediates in disputes and thus has to be impartial, weighing all sides to a dispute. Native courts exist to assist the chief in fair dispensation of justice. But as a judge, he is not infallible. His decisions at court can be overruled or even overturned. His style of governing is characterised by four Cs: consultation, conciliation, compromise, and consensus.

In his duties, the chief traditionally solicits and encourages dissenting or alternative viewpoints. Such solicitations are never considered demeaning. In fact, he is serving his traditional political role in making them. He frequently asks his people 'to bring their minds', which is the vernacular invitation 'to express an opinion'; those who 'bring their minds' do so willingly and freely, without fear of arrest.

The articulating principle of social organisation and government is kinship. Despotism does not fit into such a system. Firstly, if a despot brutalised and oppressed his own kinsmen, clan leaders would rise up against him. Secondly, many traditional societies had no standing armies. In the event of an external threat against the tribe, young men of certain ages would be assembled for combat. These men were provided by the leaders of the various clans or lineages and led into war by the chief or a war chief. After the cessation of conflict, this 'tribal or people's army' was disbanded. It was not under the permanent control of the chief. Were he to have despotic inclinations, the chief would have no coercive instruments (military or police force) to enforce his diktats.

Those states or chiefdoms that had standing armies were few in number. In Africa, out of more than two thousand ethnic groups, only in a few African kingdoms, such as the Asante, Dahomey, and Zulu, was the military given a prominent role in governance. But

[48] Van Notten (n. 38) 139.

other than these exceptions—about twenty—the military played little or no role in day-to-day government administration. It was understood that the role of the military was to defend the ethnic group or empire against external threats, not to rule. Military rule, therefore, is without question as alien and un-indigenous as colonial rule. Historical evidence does not show Africans being ruled by soldiers under the native system of government. In fact, some African tribes even took steps to limit the involvement of soldiers in government.

In the Yoruba kingdom, the *Kakanfo* was the field marshal, with his seventy war chiefs, the *Eso*, who were expected to be loyal to the *Alafin* (king). The army was responsible to the *Oyo Mesi* (Council of Notables), who appointed and promoted its officers. But could the *Kakanfo* not overthrow the *Oyo Mesi* and seize power? That was not possible, according to Boahen and Webster:

> Civil authority feared the potential power of the *Kakanfo* and in order to isolate him from politics he was usually of humble (slave) origin and was forbidden to enter the capital city. The political system was thus a complex and delicate balance with checks and counter-checks against concentration of power in one man's hands.[49]

Thirdly, the foremost prerogative of a chief—or a leader of an ethnic group—is the survival of the group. To achieve that objective, the social and political value systems stress unity and cooperation. These values or qualities are antithetical to despotism. A despot is intolerant of dissenting views and would weaken the tribe's social cohesion, thereby making the tribe vulnerable to conquest by a more powerful neighbour. A chief is expected to look 'powerful' and 'menacing' and act belligerently towards foreigners and other tribes or ethnic groups, but not towards his own people or kinsmen.[50] The corollary prerogative here is to protect his tribe.[51]

Writing about the Bantu, N.J.J. Olivier best summed up its native system of government:

> It is evident that the principle of free elections is unknown in Bantu society; that the tribal chief (who usually owes his position to the fact that he is the chief representative of the ruling clan) is neither autocrat or despot, but is continuously assisted, in the exercise of his various functions, by advisory councils and by the people themselves; that the tribal and territorial sub-divisions effectively curb the unitary power of the chief, and also form the

[49] A.A. Boahen and J.B. Webster, *History of West Africa* (Praeger 1970).

[50] This predisposition also led to the myth that chiefs were despots who acted belligerently towards their own people. The chief's people are members of his own ethnic stock, not of others. The Ga *mantse*'s people are the Ga people, not the Ashanti people. If the Ga *mantse* had the opportunity, he would depopulate the Ashanti kingdom, kill as many Ashantis, and enslave as many more. The fewer the Ashanti people, the less competition the Ga people faced for natural resources, and vice versa for the Ashanti. Thus, the Ga *mantse* sold Ashanti slaves and vice versa. But the Europeans saw it differently. To them, it was a black African chief selling off his own black people. The Ashanti were not the Ga *mantse*'s people—just as the German captors who carted off French slaves did not consider them Germans.

[51] Another nauseating myth was that, during the slave trade, chiefs sold their own people. This nonsensical myth was used to justify the trade. Firstly, the chiefs sold mostly war captives, who came from *other* tribes. But the Europeans made no such distinction. To them, it was a black African chief selling black African people. In medieval Europe, the French had German slaves and vice versa. But does one hear that Europeans were enslaving their own kind? Secondly, it does not make sense militarily for a chief to enslave his own people. He would be weakening his tribe for a stronger neighbouring tribe to conquer it.

basis of tribal government and in addition ensure active participation on all levels of the population in such government.[52]

3.4.1 Institutional checks against despotism

3.4.1.1 Private and public admonitions

Dictatorial tendencies in a ruler always caused disaffection among the people and brought shame to the royal lineage. A founding lineage member might be provoked to replace the 'dictator'. Those who chose or appointed the chief also had the power to recall or depose him if he did not perform the duties of his office satisfactorily.

Before a despotic ruler was removed from office, however, most indigenous systems gave him ample opportunity to reform. Often, the ruler was reminded of the oath he took upon assumption of power, which stated the standard of conduct expected of him. The oath he swore might require him to, inter alia:

- listen to advice,
- not abuse his power,
- not act dictatorially,
- not abuse his people, and
- not go after other people's wives.

The chief is advised to obey his own oath. The advice is cautionary, but the hidden threat of removal in case of breach or lapse of behaviour serves as an effective deterrent. In addition to the advice, a newly chosen chief is isolated for a number of days and given instructions on the proper code of conduct to follow.

3.4.1.2 Prohibitions against the office of chieftaincy

Most indigenous societies applied various restrictions and injunctions against the office of chieftaincy so that whoever occupied the 'stool' would act 'properly'. While some of these injunctions were intended to enhance the sanctity of the office, others were cleverly designed to check against despotic tendencies and misuse of power.

Of particular interest was the prohibition against property holding. The danger of a ruler using his position to amass wealth for himself was obviated by the custom that the king could not, except in a few circumstances, own any personal property while in office. Everything the ruler acquired while in office automatically became stool property or the property of the office, unless the elders knew he was acquiring it for himself and consented to it. That rule applied to the wives of the ruler as well. To make the rule effective, the administration of tribal funds and property was put in the hands of someone other than the chief. The ruler was debarred from any close contact with stool finances.

While this prohibition is fascinating and akin to requiring an American president to place his private holdings of stock in a 'blind trust', it may have contributed to the myth of communal ownership. When the Akan said, 'The chief does not own anything. Everything he owns belongs to the stool', it was easy for Europeans to misinterpret that as implying

[52] N.J.J. Olivier, 'The Governmental Institutions of the Bantu Peoples of Southern Africa' (1969) *Recueils de la Societies Jean Bodin XII* 112.

'communal ownership' rather than as an injunction against personal aggrandisement. Every gift to the chief would also belong to the stool.[53]

3.4.1.3 *The royal family*

Assume the year was 1723 and Ntonji, fed up with the despotic tendencies of his chief, gathered his family, packed their things, and left the village. They found a nice spot with arable rolling land by a river and settled down. Over time, assume that ten other clans joined them and the settlement grew. It would be called Ntonjiville and the Ntonji clan would be known as the royal family, for which would be reserved the right to provide a chief to govern the village. The leaders of the ten other clans would constitute themselves into a council of elders to assist the chief in governing.

The chief would be chosen by the royal family; he did not choose himself. The queen or clan mother would consult with elders and dignitaries of the royal family before the selection. This selection would be ratified by the council of elders. If the chief drifted towards despotism or shirked his responsibilities, he brought shame to the royal family. It is the duty of the queen mother to scold, reprimand, and rebuke an errant chief. If she failed in this duty, she herself could be deposed in some tribal systems. In fact, the king's fiercest critics are likely to come from the royal family because there are always rival claimants to the office when lines of succession become fuzzy or truncated. There are no written records; the keeper of royal oral tradition passed away years ago. So, when a chief dies and a new one has to be chosen, rival claimants emerge who will scrutinise every act of the new chief in the minutest detail. Obviously, the chief cannot lock up critics from his own royal family. If a chief brings shame to the royal family, the elders of the family may persuade the queen mother to recall and replace him. This often is the first line of defence against despotism.

3.4.1.4 *The inner privy council*

The second check against despotism is the privy or inner council of advisers. They are a small group of confidential advisers drawn mainly from the inner circle of the chief's relatives and personal friends, who may include influential members of the community. The duty of the advisers is not only to keep the chief in touch with happenings in the ethnic group but also to keep a check on his behaviour and, where he does wrong, speak to him privately or, if necessary, reprimand him. The role of the advisers is to see that the chief governs the ethnic group properly. If the chief ruled incompetently, the ethnic group would reproach the advisers for failing in their responsibility. In fact, Kofi Busia reported two cases where two Ashanti elders 'lost their stools and were fined in the one case sixteen pounds sterling (*ntanu*) and two sheep, in the other twenty-four pounds sterling (*ntansa*) and two sheep' for failing to advise their chief of his wrongdoing.[54] These advisers gauge public opinion and pass the information to the chief. If the chief persists in his despotic ways, the

[53] This is similar to modern-day practice in the United States. 'The National Archives and Records Administration stores gifts to the president—many of which end up in their official libraries—as well as the vice president and members of their families. Under a 2006 rule, recipients may not keep gifts from foreign officials that are worth more than $305, for fear of the potential influence on U.S. policy. They are accepted, however, on behalf of the American people.' See *The Washington Times* (8 December 2007) A2.

[54] Kofi Busia, *The Position of the Chief in the Modern Political System of Ashanti* (Oxford University Press 1951) 73.

advisers could abandon him. If this check also failed, there was a third, and most important, line of defence against despotism: the council of elders.

3.4.1.5 The council of elders

The council of elders is the representative body of the commoners. In crafting any law, the chief must consult with this council. It is composed of leaders of the various clans in the village. Without this council, the chief is powerless and cannot make laws. Generally, the elders tend to be interested only in the welfare of their lineages. Though the chief has his lineage in the village, it is his duty to reconcile the sectional and competing interests of the elders and serve as a unifying force. Council approval or unanimity is needed on all matters affecting the community. The chief cannot dismiss the councillors, since those offices are hereditary and restricted to non-royal lineages. In other words, the chief cannot use family ties to suborn the councillors. The officers come from different lineages.[55]

The Akan provided their people with an opportunity to admonish their rulers at certain festivals. For example, the Ashanti had the *odwira* festival at which the ruler gave a public account of himself. The people could express displeasure at his misrule by boos and hisses. In fact, they could do more: take legal action against the oppressive ruler.

A chief's subjects, acting through their representatives on the council, could present grievances concerning lapses in his conduct. The council would then constitute itself into a tribunal or court and hold an inquiry into these grievances. If found at fault in respect of any of the grievances, the chief would normally be cautioned and have to pay what the Akan call *mpata*, a pacification fee, which also served as a mark that an inquiry had been held into the case and appropriate steps taken. If it were found that the grievances were without factual basis, and therefore frivolously presented, those presenting them would be declared at fault, made to pacify the ruler, and also made to produce sheep and drink for the performance of religious ceremonies to pacify the spirits. Grievances generally related to a breach of one or the other of the contents of the admonition the elders offered him on his installation.

Olivier observed that the Bantu chief

> is surrounded and supported by various bodies and institutions which prevent him from becoming an abusive ruler and makes of Bantu government a peculiar type of democracy, although it is not based on the principle of free elections and on individual or communal voting.[56]

Furthermore, in exercising his powers, 'the chief cannot ignore the feelings of his people, nor the influence of those who are expected to advise him, otherwise he will be riding for a fall'.[57]

[55] The analogous situation in the United States is to imagine the existence of three political parties: the Republicans, the Democrats, and the Libertarians. The presidency in modern times is often drawn from the Republican Party, while the Democrats and Libertarians make up Congress. Although the president of the United States is one of the most powerful leaders in the world and could bring an end to the human race, without Congress he is powerless and cannot impose his will. The council of elders is to the chief what the US Congress is to the president of the United States.

[56] See Olivier (n. 51).

[57] Ibid.

Testimony before the South African Government Commission of Native Law and Custom was particularly telling. Asked to describe the Bantu system of government, Sir Theophilus Shepstone replied:

> It is a form of Government at the head of which is the chief, who is apparently arbitrarily supreme, and who possesses all power, but, practically, that power cannot be exercised by him safely, except with the consent of the people. That consent is given at assemblies of the chief men of the tribe. These men are not always entitled councillors, but they have the right of meeting at these assemblies, owing to personal influence, or the possession of riches, or to their being the heads of large families, or of hereditary descent in the tribe. These headmen again rely upon the opinions of their constituents, or people under them.[58]

3.4.1.6 The foot

If a tyrannical chief or a ruler manages to overrun the various lines of defence, the people could exercise the 'exit option', that is, vote with their feet and settle somewhere else. The history of Africa is full of such migrations of people, which still continue today, as is evidenced by the continent's millions of political and economic refugees.

3.4.1.7 Deposition

A bad chief may be recalled by the queen mother or removed by the council of elders at any time, not after any specified years in office. Even in modern times, chiefs are still held accountable and corrupt chiefs are deposed. Here are a few examples:

> An unspecified number of members of the Oyoko clan, King-makers of the Okumaning stools, have been rounded up by Kade Police for allegedly beating up their chief, Nana Karikari Appau II. The King-makers have preferred 13 destoolment charges against the chief. These include the alleged embezzlement of C50,000 ($18,182) land compensation belonging to the entire Oyoko family at Okumaning and the signing of a land agreement with an Italian firm, Greenwich Chemicals Company, involving some 16,000 acres without the consent of the entire family.[59]

Nana Sobin Kan II, the chief of Asansi Dompuase traditional area in the Ashanti region, was destooled on 7 February 2012. The charge was

> continuously showing gross disrespect and disregard to kingmakers and elders of the stool. He had continuously sown seeds of confusion and litigation in the traditional area through the rampant sale of stool lands to private developers without plot numbers and site plans. He was also accused of having received huge sums of money as compensation on behalf of the Adansi-Dompuase traditional areas from AngloGold Ashanti last year but failed to disclose the amount involved to kingmakers.[60]

[58] Cited in Ayittey (n. 19) 160.
[59] See *The Daily Graphic* (28 October 1981) 8.
[60] See *The Daily Guide* (10 February 2012) 17.

Oba Lawrence Omowole, the traditional ruler and the paramount ruler of Mahin kingdom, in Ilaje local government area of Ondo State in Nigeria, was removed from office for 'ceding Aboto community which is an important part of Mahin kingdom to another person either in the garb of a king or otherwise'. He denied the allegation.[61]

The 'primitive folks' of Africa had the sense to remove a king whose tenure was 'disastrous' but not so the 'educated' elites of modern Africa. The rule of so many postcolonial African leaders has been more than 'disastrous'.

4. The Modern Political Systems

There is a sharp contrast between the traditional and the modern political systems. Traditional rulers would not get away with the egregious crimes modern African leaders commit against their people, for example plundering the treasury. Firstly, the traditional systems were fairly stable, open, and inclusive. Stability, to a large extent, owed its origin primarily to the design and operation of the indigenous political system in which anybody—even slaves—could participate in the decision-making process. There was representation of slaves, the freeborn, and the nobility at the royal court in most African states. There was even foreign representation. The kings and chiefs of Angola and Asante, for example, allowed European merchants to send their representatives to their courts. No one was 'locked out' of the decision-making process, to use modern phraseology. As Boahen puts it, the Dutch dispatched an embassy to the *Asantehene*'s court as early as 1701.[62]

In Angola, King Alfonso allowed Portuguese merchants to send their spokesman, Dom Rodrigo, to his court. Europeans could even be selected as chiefs. For example, in 1873, the Zulu king Cetshwayo made an English hunter and trader, John Dunn, chief of an *isifunda*, or district: 'Dunn, not content to hover on the periphery of Zulu society, became fully integrated into the social system. He married forty-eight Zulu women, accumulated a large following of clients, and even rose to the rank of *isikhulu*.'[63] Also, there are several white chiefs in West Africa. One of them was the Englishman Jimmy Maxen, who in 1968 became the *odikro* (traditional chief) of Anyaisi at Aburi in Ghana. They were made chiefs not so much because they were white but because Africans really did not care who ruled them. They knew where power lies—with the people—and that the people could always take it back.

Africans should be proud of this heritage of theirs and not ashamed because it was 'backward and primitive'. In the nineteenth century, which Western countries allowed black Africans to take part in decision-making, let alone become president? Neither do most of our modern systems, the majority of which are often closed, measure up to this. In the one-party systems that proliferated across postcolonial Africa, a person did not participate in the decision-making process if he or she did not belong to the ruling party. Secondly, and more importantly, whereas traditional systems were embedded with checks and balances, modern systems either lacked these or made a mockery of them by placing institutions designed to check the head of state under his control—clearly a situation of conflict of interest.

[61] See *The Nigerian Tribune* (18 February 2017).
[62] Cited in Ayittey (n. 19) 265–310.
[63] See Charles Ballard, *The House of Shaka* (Emoyeni Books 1988) 55.

For example, Ghana's 1992 Constitution created a powerful executive. To decentralise power and check the executive, the following institutions were created and acknowledged:

- the council of state,
- district assemblies,
- the supreme court,
- the judiciary, and
- the electoral commission.

But the same Constitution authorises the president to appoint

- thirteen of the twenty-four members of the council of state,
- 33 per cent of all the members of the district assemblies,
- all the justices of the supreme court,
- most of the judges on the bench,
- the electoral commissioner, and
- the governor of the Bank of Ghana.

This effectively neutralises any restraint on the executive. A rogue president can break the law and get away with it because he appoints all the supreme court justices. At a minimum, the council of state, for example, may be constituted out of the council of elders in the traditional system—completely autonomous and independent of control by the executive. Furthermore, the panoply of taboos and injunctions that govern the behaviour of traditional rulers may also be adopted for modern African leaders, with the proviso that they are not crafted or written by the leaders themselves.

5. Conclusion

This chapter has sought to demonstrate that despotism was not a characteristic of indigenous African political systems. It was always a theoretical possibility, but Africans, after encountering it, took measures to prevent its recurrence. They built various safeguards into their political systems. Rulers were not elected by ballot but chosen by a clan mother, a queen mother of a royal family, or by a council of elders. They did not impose themselves on their people. Furthermore, they were enmeshed in webs of taboos and injunctions, the breach of any of which could result in their removal from office. That very possibility of deposition could in itself serve as a deterrent to autocracy.

Moreover, the rulers were surrounded by councils upon councils, without which they were powerless to initiate any action or law. Nor did the rulers have instruments of coercion—military and police forces—under their permanent control to enforce diktats. Even then, it did not make sense for a ruler to brutalise and oppress his own tribesmen, as this would weaken his own tribe to the benefit of a stronger neighbour; at any rate, if he did happen to do so, clan leaders would rise up against him. In the last resort, the people always had the final say: the exit option. They could vote with their feet and migrate to settle elsewhere.

Thus, a strong case can be made for Africa to return to its roots and build upon its own indigenous political systems. There is nothing wrong with them. As we have shown, dictatorship did not exist in them. As a matter of fact, one of the oldest constitutions in the world came from Africa. Known as the Manden Charter, it was proclaimed in *Kurukan Fuga*.[64]

Bibliography

Amoah G.Y., *Groundwork of Government for West Africa* (Gbenle Press 1988)
Ayittey G.B.N., *Indigenous African Institutions* (Brill 2006)
Ballard C., *The House of Shaka* (Emoyeni Books 1988)
Bauer P.L., *Reality and Rhetoric: Studies in Economics of Development* (Harvard University Press 1984)
Bayart J., *L'Etat en Afrique* (Fayard 1989)
Boahen A.A. and Webster J.B., *History of West Africa* (Praeger 1970)
Boamah-Wiafe D., *Africa: The Land, People, and Cultural Institutions* (Wisdom Publications 1993)
Bohannan P., *Africa and Africans* (Natural History Press 1964)
Busia K.A., *The Position of the Chief in the Modern Political System of Ashanti* (Oxford University Press 1951)
Carlston K.S., *Social Theory and African Tribal Organisation* (University of Chicago Press 1968)
Davidson B., *African Kingdoms* (Time/Life Books 1970)
Diop C.A., *Pre-colonial Black Africa* (Lawrence Hill & Company 1987)
Field M.J., *Social Organisation of the Ga People* (Government of the Gold Coast Printing Press 1940)
Founders online https://founders.archives.gov/documents/Jefferson/01-11-02-0047 (last accessed 15 August 2021)
Gibbs J.L. (ed.), *Peoples of Africa* (Rinehart and Winston 1965)
Heath F.D., 'Tribal Society and Democracy' (2001) *5*(22) *The Laissez Faire City Times*
Isichei E., *History of West Africa since 1800* (Africana Publishing Company 1977)
Jacobson L., 'Viral Meme says Constitution "Owes its Notion of Democracy to the Iroquois"' (2014) https://www.politifact.com/factchecks/2014/dec/02/facebook-posts/viral-meme-says-constitution-owes-its-notion-democ/ (last accessed 9 October 2023)
Kenyatta J., *Facing Mount Kenya* (Secker & Warburg 1938)
Kopytoff I. (ed.), *The African Frontier* (Indiana University Press 1989)
Lewis I.M., 'Lineage Continuity and Modern Commerce in Northern Somaliland' in Bohannan P. and Dalton G. (eds.), *Markets in Africa* (Northwestern University Press 1962) 365
Libby T., *The Politics of Economic Power in Southern Africa* (Princeton University Press 1987)
Marshall J., 'Hunting among the Kalahari Bushmen' in Skinner E.P. (ed.), *Peoples and Cultures of Africa: An Anthropological Reader* (Natural History Press 1973) 110
Maylam P., *A History of the African People of South Africa: From the Early Iron Age to the 1970s* (David Philip 1986)
Olaniyan R. (ed.), *Nigerian History and Culture* (Longman Group 1985)
Olivier N.J.J., 'The Governmental Institutions of the Bantu Peoples of Southern Africa' (1969) *Recueils de la Societies Jean Bodin XII* 112
Packard R.M., *Chiefship and Cosmology* (Indiana University Press 1981)
Simiyu V.G., 'The Democratic Myth in the African Traditional Societies' in Oyugi W.O. and Gitonga A.K. (eds.), *Democratic Theory and Practice in Africa* (East African Educational Publishers 1988) 49
UNESCO, 'Manden Charter, Proclaimed in Kurukan Fuga' (2009) https://ich.unesco.org/en/RL/manden-charter-proclaimed-in-kurukan-fuga-00290 (last accessed 15 August 2021)
Van Notten M., *The Law of the Somalis* (Transnational Publishers 2006)
Vaughan J.H., 'Population and Social Organisation' in Martin P. and O'Meara P. (eds.), *Africa* (Indiana University Press 1986) 177
Webster J.B. and Kramsky, J., *History of West Africa: The Revolution Years—1815 to Independence* (Praeger 1970)

[64] See UNESCO (n. 5).

3

Constitutional Identity and Traditional Authority in the Post-colony

Heinz Klug

1. Introduction

The notion of constitutional identity is often used as a basis for classifying constitutions according to their differing features, institutions, or approaches to rights and forms of constitutional review. As Charles M. Fombad notes in the introduction to this volume, the question of constitutional identity in Africa has been raised most dramatically in the context of debates about decolonising institutions in general and about 'the legitimacy of recent constitutional reforms on the continent and whether these new or revised constitutions truly reflect an African identity' in particular.[1] In exploring the place of traditional authorities in African constitutions, this chapter does not assume that these authorities are, as institutions, either unique to Africa or essential to the identity of African constitutions; rather, it seeks to understand their role in African constitutional orders and asks if their recognition or exclusion impacts on the legitimacy or practice of constitutionalism on the African continent.

While this chapter uses the term 'traditional authorities' to refer to a particular set of institutions that participate in different forms of governance or hold authority and enjoy the loyalty of communities across the continent, traditional authority is more properly understood as a source of social authority that extends far beyond any specific institutions. Kwasi Konadu has demonstrated that traditional authority may be located in relationships, biographies, and histories that extend beyond our conventional notions of such institutions.[2] It is thus important to acknowledge that the constitutional recognition and incorporation of 'traditional authorities'—the focus of this chapter—does not claim to include the myriad sources and forms of social and even political authority that exist sociologically either in African communities or, for that matter, in all communities worldwide, whether 'traditional' or 'modern'.

A recent Afrobarometer public attitude survey provides a snapshot of views on governance from across Africa that reveals the continued relevance of institutions of traditional authority on the continent.[3] Two questions in the survey asked respondents about their trust in leaders and to evaluate the performance of leaders, including traditional leaders, among various categories of leadership. On the issue of trust, 55.8 per cent of respondents

[1] See Chapter 1 by Charles M. Fombad, 'Constitutional Identity and Constitutionalism in Africa: Concepts and Key Issues', in this volume.

[2] Kwasi Konadu, *Our Own Way in This Part of the World: Biography of an African Community, Culture & Nation* (Duke University Press 2019).

[3] Afrobarometer, 'Round 7 (2016–2018)' https://afrobarometer.org/ (last accessed 24 August 2022).

Heinz Klug, *Constitutional Identity and Traditional Authority in the Post-colony* In: *Constitutional Identity and Constitutionalism in Africa*. Edited by: Charles M. Fombad and Nico Steytler, Oxford University Press. © Heinz Klug 2024.
DOI: 10.1093/oso/9780198906308.003.0006

indicated that they trusted traditional leaders either 'somewhat' or 'a lot', while only 15.9 per cent stated that they trusted them 'not at all'.[4] Responding to a question about the performance of leaders, 61.4 per cent 'approved' or 'strongly approved' of the performance of traditional leaders, while only 25.6 per cent 'disapproved' or 'strongly disapproved' of how they 'performed their jobs over the past twelve months'.[5] These results, while of a high level of generality, make it clear that whatever institutional role they might have, traditional authorities remain important to a significant percentage of the African population.

Gary Jacobsohn argues that constitutional identity 'emerges dialogically and represents a mix of political aspirations and commitments that are expressive of a nation's past, as well as the determination of those within the society who seek in some ways to transcend that past'.[6] This approach to constitutional identity regards constitutional provisions as reflecting different aspects of these often-contending commitments. In turn, beginning with a critique of modern constitutionalism, which he labels the 'empire of uniformity', the Canadian philosopher James Tully argues for a constitutionalism 'informed by the spirit of mutual recognition and accommodation of cultural diversity'.[7] Embracing Tully's argument for the recognition of a multiplicity of identities within modern constitutionalism and Jacobsohn's conception of the 'disharmonic constitution' in which there exists both 'conflicting, even radically inconsistent ideas',[8] this chapter will focus on the recognition and role of traditional authorities within postcolonial constitutions in sub-Saharan Africa. In exploring the status of traditional authorities in postcolonial constitutional orders, the various waves of postcolonial constitutions, and the different sources of identity and resistance that have struggled to reshape constitutional orders in moments of constitution-making, amendment, and contestation, this chapter attempts to identify what Jacobsohn describes as a broader constitutional identity—one consisting of 'identifiable continuities of meaning within which dissonance and contradiction play out'.[9]

Although colonialism conquered, co-opted, and corrupted traditional authorities, it was unable to destroy the institution of traditional authority in Africa. With the rise of African nationalism, independence, and the post-Cold War reconstitution of African states, traditional authorities have become part of constitutional orders across the continent. Setting out to explore the place and role of traditional authorities in African constitutional identities, this chapter briefly examines the history of traditional authorities in postcolonial constitutional orders. Firstly, there is a trajectory from when many nationalist leaders attempted to control or exclude traditional authorities to the more recent resurgence and constitutional recognition of these institutions. Secondly, the chapter notes that even when such institutions are recognised or are dominant, the form of their incorporation into the constitutional order has varied over time and from place to place depending on local histories and experiences. Finally, the chapter explores the different roles that traditional authorities

[4] Ibid. Responses to the question (in regard to traditional leaders): 'How much do you trust each of the following, or haven't you heard enough about them to say?'

[5] Ibid. Responses to the question (in regard to traditional leaders): 'Do you approve or disapprove of the way that the following people have performed their jobs over the past twelve months, or haven't you heard enough about them to say?'

[6] Gary Jacobsohn, *Constitutional Identity* (Harvard University Press 2010) 7.

[7] James Tully, *Strong Multiplicity: Constitutionalism in an Age of Diversity* (Cambridge University Press 1995) 209.

[8] Jacobsohn (n. 6) 3.

[9] Ibid. 4.

have been assigned or come to play in different constitutional orders across the continent. In conclusion, it reflects on the implications this history and process of recognition have for constitutional identity in Africa.

2. From Contestation to Recognition

African nationalist critiques of colonial rule rejected European domination but simultaneously embraced modernist notions of progress and development. As the nationalist leader and president of Tanzania Julius Nyerere argued,

> [O]ur political organization is only one aspect of the heavy task ahead . . . It must assist us to retain and expand personal freedom and human dignity and, at the same time, it must enable us to develop the economy of the country.[10]

From this perspective, many of the more radical, urban-based nationalists explicitly rejected traditional authorities and proclaimed their commitment to eradicating the institution of chieftaincy. Kwame Nkrumah's Convention People's Party (CPP) in Ghana exemplified this position, critiquing 'the arbitrary quality of a rural order dominated by those qualified to rule by birth rather than by achievement'.[11]

In spite of these challenges to traditional authority, the interaction between traditional authorities and governments, both during the colonial period and after independence, was always more complex.[12] Despite the CPP's early hostility, when Ghana's first post-independence constitution was adopted in 1960, it included a provision for regional houses of chiefs, albeit stating that these institutions 'shall have such functions relating to customary law and other matters, as may be provided by law'.[13] The key element of this recognition was that the traditional authorities were made subject to government recognition, thereby enabling the newly independent government to side with those claimants to traditional authority who aligned themselves with the new political order.

As Mahmood Mamdani argues in his analysis of the bifurcated colonial state and post-colonial African societies, the 'post-independence struggle tended towards deracialization, but not democratization. . . . [T]he hierarchy of the local state apparatus, from chiefs to native Authorities administering 'customary' law . . . was reproduced unproblematically, as part of tradition'.[14]

If there was a shared assumption across different constitutional regimes in the post-independence era, it was that traditional authorities, if not subject to active eradication, would simply fade away as societies 'modernised'. Despite this assumption, traditional authorities today remain a distinguishing feature of the African political and social landscape,

[10] Julius K. Nyerere, *Freedom and Socialism/Uhuru na Ujama: A Selection from Writings and Speeches 1965–1967* (Oxford University Press 1968) 40.

[11] Richard Rathbone, 'Kwame Nkrumah and the Chiefs: The Fate of "Natural Rulers" under Nationalist Governments' (2000) *10 Transactions of the Royal Historical Society* 45, 53.

[12] See Richard Rathbone, *Nkrumah & the Chiefs: The Politics of Chieftaincy in Ghana, 1951–1960* (Ohio University Press 2000).

[13] Constitution of the Republic of Ghana (1960), s 50.

[14] Mahmood Mamdani, 'The Politics of Civil Society and Ethnicity: Reflections on an African Dilemma' (1998) 12 *Political Power and Social Theory* 221–3, 229.

delivering 'essential services that African states do not always succeed in delivering', serving 'as intermediaries between the government and the local population', and, often, acting as 'a political force to reckon with, wielding enormous electoral and general influence in their own communities due to their control over resources and people'.[15]

Noting this resurgence in traditional authorities across sub-Saharan Africa, Helene Kyed and Lars Buur argue that three interrelated 'shifts' account for this phenomenon. Firstly, 'mainly bottom-up, self-assertive organizations, unions or associations of chiefs' have been emerging and 'been more or less successful in increasing their influence in local and national politics'.[16] Secondly, 'traditional leaders have often asserted their authority informally to execute state functions in local settings (such as dispensing justice, collecting rent and policing)'.[17] This has led in some contexts 'to competition with state authorities, while in others this has replaced or complemented state functions'.[18] Thirdly, in some countries, 'top-down, formal types of legislation, decrees and reforms . . . have (re)incorporated traditional leaders officially into state hierarchies in recognition of their ongoing influence as local players'.[19] To these one would add the more recent wave of constitution-making, which has seen traditional authorities gaining constitutional status and even guarantees of autonomy and resources that promise to ensure them an enduring position in the shaping of constitutional identity.

Indeed, a new wave of constitution-making and amendment swept across Africa from the 1980s to the early 2000s, marking a new effort to both incorporate and reshape the relationship between the constitution of formal democracy and individual rights and the recognition of traditional authorities. If the military regime that overthrew Nkrumah adopted a new constitution for Ghana in 1969 which guaranteed the 'institution of the chieftaincy with its traditional councils as established by customary law', the more recent processes of incorporation have sought to balance the recognition of traditional authorities with the embrace of constitutional supremacy, individual rights, and gender equality. In this form, the resurgence of traditional authorities is only partially constitutional, since most of the privileges and powers exercised by these institutions is now formally granted through legislation rather than by the constitution itself.

Whether they are embraced symbolically, as protectors of culture, trustees of community lands, or integral parts of governance in the new constitutional order, traditional authorities, Mahmood Mamdani argues, are a 'non-racial legacy of colonialism [which] needs to be brought out into the open so that it may be the focus of public discussion'.[20] Does the constitutional recognition of traditional authority represent an acceptance of Tully's multiplicity of identities, or are they simply elements of the constitutional disharmony that Jacobsohn sees as integral to the shaping of constitutional identities? Then again, is the phenomena of constitutional recognition simply a continuing reflection of Mamdani's bifurcated state?

[15] Janine Ubink, *Traditional Authorities in Africa: Resurgence in an Era of Democratisation* (Leiden University Press 2008) 5.

[16] Helene Maria Kyed and Lars Buur, 'Recognition and Democratization: "New Roles" for Traditional Leaders in Sub-Saharan Africa' (2006) Danish Institute for International Studies 2 https://www.jstor.org/stable/resrep13440 (last accessed 24 August 2022).

[17] Ibid.

[18] Ibid.

[19] Ibid.

[20] Mahmood Mamdani, *Citizen and Subject: Contemporary Africa and the Legacy of Late Colonialism* (Princeton University Press 1996) 4.

3. Recognition of Traditional Authorities in Postcolonial African Constitutions

The recognition of traditional authorities as part of the constitutional order has been a constant feature of postcolonial constitutions in Africa, but it has varied across time and within the different nation-states on the continent. In each new wave of constitution-making since decolonisation began, constitution-makers have responded in a range of ways to issues relating to indigenous cultures, traditions, and the institutions that govern them. While sovereign sub-Saharan African states now represent approximately forty-eight different postcolonial histories, there are several clear patterns in how traditional authorities are reflected in their constitutions.

These include, firstly, a division that reflects the colonial experience of direct and indirect rule, in which traditional leaders were either incorporated into the bureaucratic system of colonial government or provided with a degree of autonomy whereby traditional leaders and institutions coexisted with, but had to remain loyal to, the colonial state. Secondly, several newly independent states sought to suppress traditional authorities by excluding them from the new constitutional order on ideological or political grounds. Finally, there are those constitutions that from independence provided a specific institutional role for traditional authorities at national, regional, and/or local levels of government.

Whether traditional authorities are recognised or not, a large group of sub-Saharan African constitutions recognise customary or indigenous law as a valid source of law within their constitutional orders. While usually subject to the constitution, or explicitly subject to the rights of women, the recognition of indigenous law is not always correlated with the inclusion of indigenous institutions or traditional authorities. If in some cases traditional authorities are recognised as having jurisdiction to decide matters brought before them under indigenous law, this is constitutionally recognised only in a minority of African constitutions. Instead, if indigenous law or custom is considered a source of law, jurisdiction over its enforcement and development is often located in the ordinary courts. In the case of former British colonies, where the common law took root, both indigenous law and the common law are made subject to the constitution, even when constitutional supremacy is not enshrined. For example, in Uganda, the Constitution states that '[l]aws, cultures and traditions which are against the dignity, welfare or interest of women or other marginalized group . . . or which undermine their status, are prohibited by this Constitution'.[21]

Certain African states have, since the outset at independence, always included traditional authorities within the institutional framework of their constitutions. Apart from the formal monarchies—whether they be constitutional monarchies, such as Lesotho,[22] or an executive kingdom, such as Eswatini (formerly Swaziland), in which the constitution grants the king[23] and traditional institutions extraordinary powers[24]—the form of institutionalisation has varied. In most cases, those constitutions that provide institutional recognition of traditional authorities seek to include them in local government arrangements rather than at the national level. Even when included at the national level, for example, in the case of

[21] Constitution of Uganda (1995), art. 32(2).
[22] Constitution of Lesotho (1993), chapter V, ss 44–53.
[23] Constitution of Eswatini (2005), chapter II. Monarchy, ss 4–13.
[24] Constitution of Eswatini (2005), chapter XIV. Traditional Institutions, ss 227–235.

Botswana where the *Ntlo ya Dikgosi* ('House of Chiefs') is a national body,[25] their authority is limited—here, to giving advice and reviewing bills before Parliament that potentially affect traditional authorities, customary law, and 'tribal organization or tribal property'.[26] More recently, the adoption of multi-party constitutions in the post-Cold War era saw an increase in the number of states giving constitutional recognition to traditional authorities, even though the powers granted to them remain confined largely to local governance. This constitutional recognition might seem limited in comparison to the powers of national governments, but since local governance impacts people most directly, it gives significant influence and authority to these institutions.

The recognition of institutions representing traditional authorities takes different forms at both the national and regional levels of government. In addition to national houses of chiefs, such as the *Ntlo ya Dikgosi* in Botswana, the National House of Kings and Traditional Chiefs in Côte d'Ivoire,[27] or the College of Chiefs in Lesotho[28] and the Consultative Council of the Wise and Traditional Notables in the Republic of Congo,[29] there are also houses of chiefs at the regional level, such as regional houses of chiefs in Ghana[30] and South Africa,[31] or cases in which regional bodies include traditional authorities elected by their peers, as in Cameroon.[32]

Even more common is the recognition of traditional authorities at the local level of government. While those constitutions that provide national and regional roles for traditional authorities also provide a role for traditional authorities at the local level, several states provide constitutional recognition for traditional authority through local or community-specific institutions alone. Angola, for example, provides for the recognition of 'the institutions of traditional authorities',[33] which are defined as 'entities which personify and exercise power within the respective political and community organisations',[34] but incorporates them into formal governance only at the local level where, the Constitution declares, 'forms of local government organisation shall include local authorities, the institutions of the traditional authorities and other specific forms of citizen participation, under the terms of the law'.[35] Other constitutions that limit the institutional recognition of traditional authorities to local government include South Sudan, which despite its recognition of traditional authorities[36] provides that 'legislation of the states shall provide for the role of Traditional Authority as an institution at the local government level on matters affecting local communities'.[37]

Another large group of African constitutions makes no mention of traditional authorities at all, even at the local level. For example, the Constitution of Senegal, like that of many former French colonies, simply provides for democratically elected local government,

25 Constitution of Botswana (1966), part III, ss 77–85.
26 Ibid s 88(2)(d).
27 Constitution of Côte d'Ivoire (2016), title XIV, art. 175.
28 Constitution of Lesotho (1993), s 104.
29 Constitution of the Republic of Congo (2015), art. 230.
30 Constitution of Ghana (1992), s 274(1).
31 Constitution of South Africa (1996), s 212(2)(a).
32 Constitution of Cameroon (1972), art. 57(2).
33 Constitution of Angola (2010), art. 223(1).
34 Ibid. Art. 224.
35 Ibid art. 213(2).
36 Constitution of South Sudan (2011), s 167(1).
37 Ibid. s 168(1).

stating that 'territorial collectivities constitute the institutional framework of the participation of the citizens in the management of public affairs' and that '[t]hey administer themselves freely by assemblies elected by universal direct suffrage'.[38] Apart from the countries embracing the French constitutional tradition, there are others, such as Kenya and Tanzania, which, thanks to different historical processes, seem to have disentangled traditional and formal state authority such that their constitutions recognise customary law or legal traditions but incorporate this legal pluralism into the formal legal system and provide no recognition or role for traditional authorities as separate institutions.

In the case of Kenya, the incorporation of traditional authorities into the colonial bureaucracy carried over into the postcolonial state, with the result that traditional authorities today do not play a formal role outside of formal bureaucratic state structures. Tanzania, by contrast, explicitly abolished tribal chieftaincies at independence, with a recent study on accountability indicating that, while local government institutions compete with societal associations for legitimacy, traditional authorities have little influence, especially in comparison to religious organisations.[39] Interestingly, in the case of Tanzania, customary law was incorporated into the formal legal system even as separate customary law courts were disbanded. A study found that although traditional chieftaincy structures do not play a role, 'other authorities relying on customary or informal norms and sources of authority such as clan leaders, village elders, religious authorities or self-help groups mediate the relationships between the state and citizens'.[40]

Other constitutions may recognise traditional and cultural leaders but specifically deny them any role in formal governance. The Ugandan Constitution recognises that 'the institution of traditional leader or cultural leader may exist in any area of Uganda in accordance with the culture, customs and traditions of wishes and aspirations of the people to whom it applies',[41] but then states that 'a traditional leader or cultural leader shall not have or exercise any administrative, legislative or executive powers of government or local government'.[42] Indeed, the constitution goes even further, making it clear that while 'a traditional leader or cultural leader shall enjoy such privileges and benefits as may be conferred by the Government and local government or as that leader may be entitled to under culture, custom and tradition',[43] such person 'shall not, while remaining a traditional leader or cultural leader, join or participate in partisan politics';[44] moreover, no person may 'be compelled to pay allegiance or contribute to the cost of maintaining a traditional leader or cultural leader'.[45]

The absence of any constitutional recognition of traditional and cultural authorities does not mean that these institutions do not exist in society. Systems of legal pluralism, whether based on religious law or other informal rule-bound orders, exist in all societies. However,

[38] Constitution of Senegal (2001), art. 102.

[39] Andrew Lawson and Lise Rakner, *Understanding Patterns of Accountability in Tanzania, Final Synthesis Report* (Chr. Michelsen Institute 2005) http://www.gsdrc.org/docs/open/doc98.pdf (last accessed 24 August 2022).

[40] Swiss Agency for Development and Cooperation, 'Case Study 2: Insights on Customary and Informal Authorities in Iringa Region, Tanzania' SDC/IDS/Helvetas/Swisspeace Case Studies (2016) https://www.ids.ac.uk/download.php?file=files/dmfile/Tanzaniacasestudy.pdf (last accessed 24 August 2022).

[41] Constitution of Uganda (1995), chapter 16, s 246(1).

[42] Ibid. s 246(3)(f).

[43] Ibid. s 246(3)(c).

[44] Ibid. s 246(3)(e).

[45] Ibid. s 246(3)(d).

the failure to recognise such sources of social authority becomes salient for governance and constitutional legitimacy when these alternative sources of governing authority have as much or more legitimacy than the formal constitutional order. This difficulty was evident in cases where newly independent African states either attempted to formally abolish the institution of chieftaincy or simply excluded traditional authorities from the arena of governance yet were forced to backtrack and recognise traditional authorities after periods of conflict or concern that local government could not govern effectively without their participation. Angola and Mozambique adopted independence constitutions that provided no recognition of traditional authorities, yet in the post-Cold War wave of democratisation both countries reversed course and now explicitly recognise traditional authorities in their constitutions. This re-emergence of traditional authorities and indigenous law in the context of democratisation,[46] even if after armed conflict has destroyed efforts to build local alternatives—such as the attempt to build community-controlled courts and popular justice in Mozambique[47]—raises questions about exactly what powers are being granted to traditional authorities.

While many African constitutions recognise traditional authorities, the importance of this recognition to the question of constitutional identity depends in part on whether the recognition is purely symbolic or if the constitutions grant substantive power and protection to these institutions. Significantly, despite formal constitutional recognition, the formal powers granted to traditional authorities at national or regional levels of government are mainly advisory, even when the issues they are empowered to address directly affect the interests of traditional authorities and the cultural communities they represent. Even when they are granted more direct governance powers as part of formal local government structures, the powers are often dependent on national or regional government support, given the control over legislative and budgetary authority that these levels of government generally hold.

This formal distribution of power does not, however, reveal the significance of cultural and community-based power exercised by traditional leaders. Their power is demonstrated most clearly by the ability of traditional leaders to deliver votes to political parties during elections, especially in rural areas. As a result, it is evident that even dominant political parties, such as the African National Congress in South Africa and the Zimbabwe African National Union in Zimbabwe, have passed laws to empower traditional authorities so as to gain their cooperation in delivering electoral support in rural areas.

4. What Roles for Traditional Authorities in Postcolonial Constitutions?

Constitutional clauses recognising traditional authorities vary in both the form of the recognition and the roles assigned or implied by the nature of the recognition. At one end of the spectrum are those constitutions that guarantee the state's recognition of traditional authorities and specify the role they will play in the polity; at the other extreme are those

[46] Ubink (n. 15).

[47] Albie Sachs and Gita Honwana Welch, *Liberating the Law: Creating Popular Justice in Mozambique* (Zed Books 1990).

that merely acknowledge their existence or specify that they should play no role at all in the political process.

A striking example of the guarantee of traditional authority is the Constitution of Ghana, which states that '[t]he institution of chieftaincy, together with its traditional councils as established by customary law and usage is hereby guaranteed'.[48] It proceeds to deny the national legislature any authority to intervene in these institutions by stating that 'Parliament shall have no power to enact any law which' either '(a) confers on any person or authority the right to accord or withdraw recognition to or from a chief for any purpose whatsoever, or (b) in any way detracts or derogates from the honour and dignity of the institution of chieftaincy'.[49] The Constitution then establishes regional houses of chiefs that select a national house of chiefs with broad authority over matters pertaining to the chieftaincy and appellate jurisdiction, powers to be exercised by a judicial committee of the national house of chiefs 'in any cause or matter affecting chieftaincy which has been determined by the Regional House of Chiefs in a region', with an appeal to the Supreme Court if leave to appeal is given by either the National House of Chiefs or the Supreme Court.[50]

In addition to guaranteeing the institution, the Constitution of Ghana ensures the economic independence of these institutions by both protecting stool lands and providing for the allocation of a portion of the proceeds from these lands to sustain the stool as well as the traditional authority. Article 267 of the Constitution first states that '[a]ll stool lands in Ghana shall vest in the appropriate stool on behalf of, and in trust for the subjects of the stool in accordance with customary law and usage',[51] and then specifies that after '[t]en per cent of the revenue accruing from stool lands' is paid 'to the office of the Administrator of Stool Lands to cover administrative expenses',[52] the remaining revenue is to be divided proportionately,

> [with] twenty-five percent to the stool through the traditional authority for the maintenance of the stool in keeping with its status; twenty percent to the traditional authority; and fifty- five percent to the District Assembly, within the area of authority of which the stool lands are situated.[53]

The significance of stool land as a resource base for traditional authority is secured by another constitutional provision which ensures that it remains distinguished from any land market by providing that '[s]ubject to the provisions of this Constitution, no interest in, or right over, any stool land in Ghana shall be created which vests in any person or body of persons a freehold interest howsoever described'.[54]

While many other African constitutions valorise and recognise roles for traditional authorities, they rarely provide the detailed protection seen in the Ghanaian Constitution and instead usually subject the role of traditional authorities to legislative determination. Take for example the Constitution of Mozambique, which provides that 'the State shall recognise

[48] Constitution of Ghana, art. 270(1).
[49] Ibid. art. 270(2)(a) and (b).
[50] Ibid. art. 273(1).
[51] Ibid. art. 267(1).
[52] Ibid. art. 267(6).
[53] Ibid. art. 267(6)(a)(b) and (c).
[54] Ibid. art. 267(5).

and esteem traditional authority that is legitimate according to the people and to customary law'.[55] It then subjects this guarantee to legislative control by providing that the '[s]tate shall define the relationship between traditional authority and other institutions and the part that traditional authority should play in the economic, social and cultural affairs of the country, in accordance with the law'.[56]

Other constitutions provide even less guarantees or definition of the role that traditional authorities might play in governance. The South African Constitution, for example, recognises the 'institution, status and role of traditional leadership, according to customary law'[57] but states with less promise that '[n]ational legislation may provide for a role for traditional leadership as an institution at a local level on matters affecting local communities'.[58] The only explicit command is that the '[c]ourts must apply customary law when that law is applicable subject to the Constitution and any legislation that specifically deals with customary law'.[59] The Constitution of Chad simply acknowledges that 'traditional authorities are the guarantors of use and custom'[60] and that they 'concur in the control of populations and support the action of the Autonomous Collectivities'.[61]

Some of the constitutions that provide a role for traditional authorities also attempt to restrict the scope of their role in society, most often attempting to limit their political influence by specifically denying or restricting them from participating in partisan politics. On the one hand, this may be viewed as intending to hold these authorities above the political fray as symbols of social coherence; on the other, there is also clear indication that constitution-makers have attempted to separate the social and political authority of traditional authorities from electoral politics at both the national and subnational levels. While the Ghanaian Constitution provides some of the most explicit constitutional guarantees for traditional authorities, it defines a chief as a 'person, who, hailing from the appropriate family and lineage, has been validly nominated, elected or selected and enstooled, enskinned or installed as a chief or queen mother in accordance with the relevant customary law and usage'[62] and explicitly prohibits a chief from being 'active in party politics; and any chief wishing to do so and seeking election to Parliament shall abdicate his stool or skin'.[63] Most sub-Saharan African constitutions which recognise traditional authorities do not explicitly prohibit chiefs or traditional authorities from political engagement; however, the definition of their role in giving advice to the legislature or in being represented on various bodies from land boards to local government implicitly shapes the political realm in which these institutions are expected to be active.

How central, then, are traditional authorities to the constitutional orders of sub-Saharan African states? The answer to this question lies first in our conception of the relationship between the formal provisions of a constitution and the actual distribution of power in a society, and, more specifically, in how we understand the power that traditional authority may wield, whether it be constitutionally recognised or not. The recognition of traditional

[55] Constitution of Mozambique (2004), art. 118(1).
[56] Ibid. art. 118(2).
[57] Constitution of South Africa (1996), s 211(1).
[58] Ibid. s 212(1).
[59] Ibid. s 211(3).
[60] Constitution of Chad (2018), title XIV, art. 217 .
[61] Ibid. art. 219.
[62] Constitution of Ghana (1992), s 277.
[63] Ibid. s 276(1).

authorities in South Africa's 1996 Constitution and the continuing debates over their role, whether in the repeated attempts to pass constitutionally sustainable national legislation or in legal and political struggles over their assertion of authority,[64] be it in relation to land rights,[65] negotiations over mining rights, or constitutional cases over the interpretation of customary law, reveals the complexity and enduring character of this issue. A wealth of research since 1994 has explored the historical, political, social, and economic consequences of the resurgence of traditional authority within South Africa's new constitutional order. While the Constitutional Court has repeatedly adopted progressive interpretations of customary law,[66] others have argued that government policy has promoted the emergence of a 'neotraditionalism' which facilitates more conservative constructions of traditional authority.[67] The survival, even resurgence, of traditional authority within the constitutional order, whether formally recognised or not, is based on a combination of the ability of traditional authorities to leverage their political and economic resources[68] with the 'fact that many South Africans derive meaning from their African roots, values and customs, including some elements of culture that traditional authorities claim to embody'.[69] It is this combination of formal recognition, political mobilisation, and what Barbara Oomen describes as 'the constitutive effects of cultural rights legislation'[70] that informs the constitutional identities of many postcolonial states.

5. Traditional Authority and Constitutional Identity in the Post-colony

Of the forty-eight sub-Saharan national constitutions, approximately 52 per cent explicitly include traditional authorities in their institutional structures. If we include both institutional recognition as well as the inclusion of customary or indigenous law as a source of law, for either the regular courts or as the law applied in dispute management institutions under the auspices of traditional authorities, the number goes up to about 64 per cent. In addition, there is evidence that in some African countries traditional authorities are held in high esteem and have significant political and economic influence even if they have no formal recognition or role in the constitutional order, while in a few, such as Tanzania and Kenya, their status in society does seem to have been eclipsed by new political and social institutions.

Furthermore, the status of traditional authorities in those constitutional orders in which they have been formally incorporated varies dramatically both across and within these

[64] See Phathekile Holomisa, *A Double-Edged Sword: A Quest for a Place in the African Sun—Archival Records on the Formation and Missions of the Congress of Traditional Leaders of South Africa* (Red African Publishers 2011).

[65] Lungisile Ntsebeza, *Democracy Compromised: Chiefs and the Politics of Land in South Africa* (HSRC Press 2005).

[66] *Bhe v Magistrate*, Khayelitsha 2005 1 SA 580 (CC); *Shilubana v Nwamitwa* 2009 2 SA 66 (CC); *MM v MN* 2013 4 SA 415 (CC).

[67] Olaf Zenker, 'Land Restitution (Old and New) Neotraditionalism and the Contested Values of Land Justice in South Africa' in Jessica Johnson and George Hamandishe Karekwaivanane (eds.), *Pursuing Justice in Africa: Competing Imaginaries and Contested Practices* (Ohio University Press 2018) 243.

[68] Timothy Gibbs, *Mandela's Kinsmen: Nationalist Elites & Apartheid's First Bantustan* (Jacana Media 2014).

[69] Andrew Ainslie and Thembele Kepe, 'Understanding the Resurgence of Traditional Authorities in Post-Apartheid South Africa' (2016) *42*(1) *Journal of Southern African Studies* 19, 32.

[70] Barbara Oomen, *Chiefs in South Africa: Law, Power & Culture in the Post-Apartheid Era* (James Currey 2005), 241.

societies, depending on their access to public and private resources and political authority. Studies of the role of traditional authorities in post-apartheid South Africa indicate that the political and economic status of these authorities has depended to a large degree on their relative access to specific resources or political arrangements, such as the Royal Bafokeng nation which in 2007 was 'the largest single shareholder in the world's second largest platinum producing company'[71] or the late Zulu King, Goodwill Zwelitini kaBhekuzulu, who, in the context of South Africa's democratic transition, was made sole trustee of the Ingonyama Trust under whose control all the 'communal' and state lands of the former KwaZulu Bantustan were placed.[72]

Jacobsohn argues that constitutions include disharmonious elements that reflect tensions within the constitutional order and that constitutional conflict within the parameters of these elements produces ever-changing yet uniquely specific constitutional identities. The multiplicity of ways in which traditional authorities are recognised and incorporated in sub-Saharan African constitutions provides an expansive example of such elements and a broad canvas upon which to explore how disharmonious elements within these constitutions might impact on constitutional identities across the continent. While Jacobsohn's theory recognises that in some cases a constitutional identity may include a concerted attempt to preclude significant social forces, such as the long attempt to maintain a purely secular constitution in Turkey, the case of traditional authorities in Africa highlights another option that may be viewed as either a challenge to or supplement to the theory of constitutional identity.

Even if many African constitutions do include some recognition of traditional authorities, many others make no mention of traditional authorities at all. In these cases, we might consider whether the presence in society of social institutions that continue to play a significant role in the governance of people's lives may, if not recognised, also impact on constitutional identities. To the extent that these are simply symbolic institutions, they might not have much effect on constitutional identity, but where they command significant social loyalty and are looked to for both specific governance functions as well as legitimacy, they may provide a completely alternative source of identity. This alternative identity may merely be supplemental to the constitution, but at times it has clearly served as more than a symbolic alternative, even undermining the authority of those attempting to govern under the formal constitution.

Bibliography

Afrobarometer, 'Round 7 (2016–2018)' https://afrobarometer.org/ (last accessed 24 August 2022)

Ainslie A. and Kepe T., 'Understanding the Resurgence of Traditional Authorities in Post-Apartheid South Africa' (2016) *42*(1) *Journal of Southern African Studies* 19

Gibbs T., *Mandela's Kinsmen: Nationalist Elites & Apartheid's First Bantustan* (Jacana Media 2014)

Holomisa P., *A Double-Edged Sword: A Quest for a Place in the African Sun—Archival Records on the Formation and Missions of the Congress of Traditional Leaders of South Africa* (Red African Publishers 2011)

[71] Andrew Manson and Bernard K. Mbenga, *Land Chiefs Mining: South Africa's North West Province Since 1840* (University of the Witwatersrand Press 2014), 143.

[72] See 'Land Rights under the Ingonyama Trust', Rural Women's Action Research Programme, Center for Law and Society (University of Cape Town 2015).

Jacobsohn G., *Constitutional Identity* (Harvard University Press 2010)
Konadu K., *Our Own Way in This Part of the World: Biography of an African Community, Culture & Nation* (Duke University Press 2019)
Kyed H.M. and Buur L., 'Recognition and Democratization: "New Roles" for Traditional Leaders in Sub-Saharan Africa' Danish Institute for International Studies (2006) 2 https://www.jstor.org/stable/resrep13440 (last accessed 24 August 2022)
'Land Rights under the Ingonyama Trust', Rural Women's Action Research Programme, Center for Law and Society (University of Cape Town 2015)
Lawson A. and Rakner L., *Understanding Patterns of Accountability in Tanzania, Final Synthesis Report* (Chr. Michelsen Institute 2005) http://www.gsdrc.org/docs/open/doc98.pdf (last accessed 24 August 2022)
Mamdani M., *Citizen and Subject: Contemporary Africa and the Legacy of Late Colonialism* (Princeton University Press 1996)
Mamdani M., 'The Politics of Civil Society and Ethnicity: Reflections on an African Dilemma' (1998) *12 Political Power and Social Theory* 221
Manson A. and Mbenga B.K., *Land Chiefs Mining: South Africa's North West Province Since* 1840 (University of the Witwatersrand Press 2014)
Ntsebeza L., *Democracy Compromised: Chiefs and the Politics of Land in South Africa* (HSRC Press 2005)
Nyerere J.K., *Freedom and Socialism/Uhuru na Ujama: A Selection from Writings and Speeches 1965–1967* (Oxford University Press 1968)
Oomen B., *Chiefs in South Africa: Law, Power & Culture in the Post-Apartheid Era* (James Currey 2005)
Rathbone R., *Nkrumah & the Chiefs: The Politics of Chieftaincy in Ghana, 1951–1960* (Ohio University Press 2000)
Rathbone R., 'Kwame Nkrumah and the Chiefs: The Fate of "Natural Rulers" under Nationalist Governments' (2000) *10 Transactions of the Royal Historical Society* 45
Sachs A. and Welch G.H., *Liberating the Law: Creating Popular Justice in Mozambique* (Zed Books 1990)
Swiss Agency for Development and Cooperation, 'Case Study 2: Insights on Customary and Informal Authorities in Iringa Region, Tanzania' SDC/IDS/Helvetas/Swisspeace Case Studies (2016) https://www.ids.ac.uk/download.php?file=files/dmfile/Tanzaniacasestudy.pdf (last accessed 24 August 2022)
Tully J., *Strong Multiplicity: Constitutionalism in an Age of Diversity* (Cambridge University Press 1995)
Ubink J., *Traditional Authorities in Africa: Resurgence in an Era of Democratisation* (Leiden University Press 2008)
Zenker O., 'Land Restitution (Old and New) Neotraditionalism and the Contested Values of Land Justice in South Africa' in Johnson J. and Karekwaivanane G.H. (eds.), *Pursuing Justice in Africa: Competing Imaginaries and Contested Practices* (Ohio University Press 2018) 243

4

The Struggle for Constitutional Identity in Francophone Africa

Charles M. Fombad and Trésor M. Makunya

1. Introduction

The wave of constitution-making and remaking in Africa that began in the 1990s provided constitution-makers with an opportunity to imagine and construct new legal and institutional arrangements to address the enormous social, political, and economic problems the continent has faced since independence. In particular, constitution-makers had to deal with the legal and political legacy of constitutions that had been imposed on the eve of independence on an African leadership with little or no knowledge of constitutional governance. The new leaders simply perpetuated the repressive and authoritarian colonial system they knew best. This led inevitably to political and economic crisis, resulting in innumerable problems such as poverty, unemployment, and conflict that, by the end of the 1980s, brought pressure for reform.

The nature and extent of the constitutional reforms that took place varied from one country to another, with their purpose and orientation dictated by the national context and the peculiar problems of each country. The process also involved continuities and ruptures that differed between the various constitutional traditions in Africa.[1] Constitution-makers had to make hard decisions. For example, they needed to decide which aspects of the pre-colonial, colonial, and pre-1990 past had to be retained and how they would be combined with the emerging principles of modern constitutionalism. The focus of this chapter is, however, on developments specifically in former French colonies.[2] To set a comparative context for the discussion, the chapter will contrast this occasionally with developments in certain anglophone countries that belong to the common law constitutional tradition.

The central issue in the discussion is the extent to which constitutional reforms in francophone Africa in the past three decades have resulted, if at all, in a reimagining of the constitutional identity of these countries from the inherited French 1958 Fifth Republic constitutional identity. Have these countries crafted, designed, adjusted, and adopted

[1] For the different constitutional traditions in Africa, see Charles M. Fombad, 'The Evolution of Modern African Constitutions: A Retrospective Perspective' in Charles M. Fombad (ed.), *Separation of Powers in African Constitutionalism* (Oxford University Press 2016) 13–52.

[2] Although French is used in Africa by countries not colonised by France, expressions used in this study such as 'francophone Africa', 'former French colonies', and 'French-speaking African countries' refer to the thirteen former French African colonies of West and Central Africa. They are Senegal, Benin, Burkina Faso, Chad, Côte d'Ivoire, Niger, Mali, Togo, Guinea, Gabon, Cameroon, Republic of Congo, and Central African Republic. 'Francophone Africa' in this study does not include the Democratic Republic of Congo, Burundi, and Rwanda (former Belgian colonies where French is spoken and which also largely adopted Gaullism), Mauritius, Madagascar, Comoros, and the former French colonies of the Maghreb.

Charles M. Fombad and Trésor M. Makunya, *The Struggle for Constitutional Identity in Francophone Africa* In: *Constitutional Identity and Constitutionalism in Africa*. Edited by: Charles M. Fombad and Nico Steytler, Oxford University Press.
 DOI: 10.1093/oso/9780198906308.003.0007

principles, doctrines, and institutions that reflect the wishes and aspirations of the people as well as address their peculiar challenges?[3] Are any distinctive characteristics emerging, and to what extent do they contain the elements or seeds of a distinctive constitutional identity? To what extent do these elements of self-identity enhance the prospects for constitutionalism?

In responding to these questions, the chapter, in section 2, examines how the 1958 French Constitution, often referred to as the Gaullist constitutional model, was imposed. It briefly examines the background of this model and its main characteristics that were transplanted to Africa—characteristics that have dominated francophone African constitutionalism to such an extent that countries have been unable to develop their own constitutional identity. Against this background, section 3 discusses the perverse manner in which the Gaullist model operated in francophone Africa in the context of what is referred to as *Francafrique*. Section 4 examines the post-1990 constitutional reforms and the elusive search for constitutional self-identification in francophone Africa. In conclusion (section 5), it is contended that francophone African countries remain under the spell of the Gaullist constitutional model and thus have been unable to creatively design distinctive principles, doctrines, and institutions that could be effective in addressing the specific challenges they face.

2. The Imposition of the Gaullist Constitutional Model

This section provides a brief background of French colonial policy and describes the main features of France's constitutional model, one which continues to operate in Africa.

2.1 French Colonial Policy and the Gaullist Model

Gaullist constitutional culture and its continuing institutional and mental influence on francophone Africa today are partly explained by the nature and philosophy of French colonial policy in Africa. Unlike British colonial policy, which entailed the politics of indirect rule, France sought to assimilate the colonised population to French culture through a policy of assimilation.[4] Assimilation was grounded on an illusion of equality between French citizens (Europeans) and France's colonised African population. The crux of assimilation was that it sought not only to eliminate differences through a policy of cultural and sometimes political assimilation, but to eradicate all African traditional values, culture, and identities.[5] As Derwent Whittlesey puts it bluntly, 'France [was] in Africa to make Frenchmen out of the Africans.'[6]

One characteristic of French constitutional identity that has been an albatross around the neck of francophone African constitutionalism is the system of centralisation. The

[3] For a discussion of constitutional identity in the African context, see Chapter 1 by Charles M Fombad, 'Constitutional Identity and Constitutionalism in Africa: Concepts and Key Issues', in this volume.

[4] Emmanuelle Saada, 'Entre « Assimilation » et « Décivilisation »: L'imitation et le Projet Colonial Républicain' (2005) *44 Anthropologie & Sciences Humaines* 19–20.

[5] Mahmood Mamdani, *Define and Rule: Native as Political Identity* (Harvard University Press 2012) 1–2; Mahmood Mamdani, 'Historicising Power and Responses to Power: Indirect Rule and Its Reform' (1999) *66 Social Research* 862.

[6] Derwent Whittlesey, 'British and French Colonial Technique in West Africa' (1937) *15 Foreign Affairs* 367.

centralist state tradition, which dates to the French Revolution in 1798, was manifested in the way France ran its colonies. Inspired by the egalitarian ideas of the revolution, as well as beliefs about the superiority of French culture and the country's 'civilising mission', the French strove to lead native populations step by step to the higher plane of metropolitan culture.[7] Moreover, they saw the colonies as representing an extension of France, not only economically but also in every other aspect of life.[8] This informed the heavily centralised control they exercised over their colonies and, ultimately, the excessive centralisation of political power which is seen in francophone African constitutions.

To this centralising tendency, should be added the way that France governed its colonies. At the heart of its colonial policy was the notorious *indigénat* regime.[9] Through a regime of exception that operated side by side with a complex system of courts and colonial justice, this governance system, based on rule by decree, gave administrative authorities absolute discretion to inflict swift punishment for any challenge, real or perceived, to their personal authority. The *indigénat* regime provided legal cover for some of the worst administrative excesses of French colonial rule until its abolition in 1946.

Like all the other colonial powers, the French never administered their colonies in accordance with anything remotely related to the basic rules of constitutional governance, the rule of law, or respect for human rights. It was only on the eve of independence that they attempted to craft constitutions for the new colonies, and to do so, they had to model them on their own 1958 Constitution. Modelling post-independence constitutions on the French 1958 Constitution imposed constitutional texts on these African countries that scarcely reflected their culture, history, and traditions and which consequently lacked the ability to address problems peculiar to them. It also paved the way for the French constitutional identity, characterised by the centralisation of political power and scant regard for human rights and checks and balances, to find its way into the manner in which francophone African post-independence constitutions were designed.

Before we delve into these issues, having an overview of the French constitutional model will be helpful for understanding the challenges francophone African states have faced both in entrenching a culture of constitutionalism and respect for the rule of law and in finding a constitutional identity of their own.

2.2 Key Features of the Gaullist Constitutional Model

The Gaullist constitutional model was alien to the political and social situation of the newly independent African states, in part because it was designed under enormous pressure to prevent the collapse of the country and correct problems that bedevilled the 1946 French Constitution.[10] When it was transplanted and imposed on Africans in the 1960s, the French themselves little understood how it worked, given that they themselves had adopted it only in 1958.

7 Konrad Zweigert and Hein Koetz, *An Introduction to Comparative Law* (Clarendon Press 1998) 113.

8 Whittlesey (n. 6) 370.

9 See Gregory Mann, 'What Was the "Indigénat"? The "Empire of Law" in French West Africa' (2009) *50 Journal of African History* 331–53.

10 Samuel Finer, Vernon Bogdanor, and Bernard Rudden, *Comparing Constitutions* (Clarendon Press 1995) 8–9.

In France, President de Gaulle more or less dictated the content of the 1958 Constitution as a precondition for his assuming the office of president. The overriding objective was to eliminate the weaknesses of the 1946 French Fourth Republic Constitution. The power imbalance caused by the overbearing legislature established under this Constitution had led to economic difficulties, colonial problems, parliamentary logjams, political deadlocks, and futile coalitions that resulted in twenty-three changes of government within twelve years.[11] However, the 1958 Constitution merely swung the pendulum away from a dominant legislature towards an extremely powerful executive. Until far-reaching reforms in 2008 significantly modernised the French Constitution, its main features, described below, were the ones transplanted to Africa.[12]

Tailored to suit de Gaulle's ambitions, the 1958 Constitution signalled the dawn of a new form of constitutionalism at the centre of which was the president of the Republic. Three features of this system are worth noting: firstly, the predominance of the president; secondly, the subordination to the president and executive of the other two branches of government; and, thirdly, the weak protection of human rights.

The extraordinary powers conferred on the president were evident in his wide-ranging powers to appoint his cabinet, including the prime minister, as well as all senior officials in civil, military, and diplomatic posts. He also had powers not only to initiate laws but to make laws by decrees and ordinances.[13] Executive accountability to Parliament was limited to the prime minister, who, although appointed by the president and in principle tasked with implementing his programme, could be forced to resign if he lost a vote of no-confidence in that programme.[14] However, a possible check on the president could be applied if his party did not enjoy a majority in Parliament. In such circumstances, he would be forced to appoint a prime minister from the majority party in Parliament and 'cohabit' (share power) with such a prime minister, who would implement the programme of his own party rather than that of the president. This is an exceptional situation in the Gaullist model.[15] Hence, although Parliament has the powers to make law and hold the government accountable, the extensive law-making powers of the president, combined with limited powers for checking them, leaves him in a strong position.

Presidential dominance over the judiciary was sanctioned by article 64 of the Constitution, which made the president the 'guarantor of the independence of the judicial authority'. Judicial subordination was underscored not only by the fact that the judiciary was recognised only as an 'authority' rather than a 'power', but also by the fact that, if it were a coequal, as the branches of government should be, its independence should not be guaranteed by another power. Indeed, judicial appointments and promotions were effected by the High Council of the Judiciary (HCJ), which supposedly 'assisted' the president. Under the 1958 Constitution, the president presides over the HCJ, assisted by his minister of justice.

[11] Fombad (n. 1) 17.

[12] Martin A. Rogoff, 'Fifty Years of Constitutional Evolution in France: The 2008 Amendments and Beyond' *Jus Politicum. Revuew de droit Politique* http://juspoliticum.com/article/Fifty-years-of-constitutional-evolution-in-France-The-2008-amendments-and-beyond-373.html (last accessed 20 November 2022).

[13] See articles 37 and 38 of the French Constitution of 1958.

[14] See article 50 of the French Constitution of 1958.

[15] It occurred in France on three occasions: 1986–8 (cohabitation between President François Mitterrand and Jacques Chirac); 1993–5 (cohabitation between President François Mitterrand and Edouard Balladur); and 1997–2002 (cohabitation between President Jacques Chirac and Lionel Jospin).

The limited scope for presidential and executive accountability was underscored by the fact that the 1958 Constitution provided little avenue for judicial review of constitutional violations. Not only did individuals whose constitutional rights had been violated have no locus standi to directly petition the Constitutional Council, which had exclusive jurisdiction over these matters, but this body, a quasi-judicial, quasi-administrative entity, was composed of persons who were not necessarily jurists. Moreover, it exercised only abstract review.

A final point to note is that the 1958 Constitution dealt with human rights in a very peripheral manner. These are referred to only in the preamble, which states: 'The French people solemnly proclaim their attachment to the Rights of Man and the principles of national sovereignty as defined by the Declaration of 1789, confirmed and complemented by the preamble to the Constitution of 1946.' However, the recitations contained in these documents were interpreted by the French Constitutional Council as a bill of rights.[16]

As pointed out, and this bears repeating, these were the main features of the original 1958 Constitution prior to France's constitutional reforms of 2008 and the primary elements of the Gaullist model that was transplanted to Africa in the 1960s. In spite of more than half a century of independence, the way in which Gaullist constitutional identity has continued to influence developments in francophone African countries raises profound questions about the ability of these countries to design constitutions that cater to their specific needs.

3. Post-independence Francophone Constitutionalism

Although the enactment of the 1958 French Constitution coincided with rising demands for decolonisation in Africa,[17] France was reluctant to decolonise, fearing the loss of the economic, cultural, and military benefits it derived from its colonies. Pointedly, it abstained from voting in the United Nations General Assembly Declaration on Granting of Independence to Colonial Countries and Peoples, adopted two years later.[18] De Gaulle's insistence on retaining Algeria and waging a war most of France's citizens no longer supported[19] shows that, were it not for domestic and international pressure, France would not have embarked on decolonisation.

As the pressure to decolonise grew, France held referenda in 1958 in which it asked its colonial territories to choose between two alternatives: accept a constitution proposed by France and acquire internal self-government within the *Communauté Française* ('French Community'),[20] or gain immediate independence. France made it clear that it would sever

[16] André Cabanis and Michel-Louis Martin, *Le Constitutionnalisme de la Troisième Vague en Afrique Francophone* (Academia Bruylant 2010); Yves A Fauré, 'Les Constitutions et l'Exercise Du Pouvoir en Afrique Noire' http://www.politique-africaine.com/numeros/pdf/001034.pdf (last accessed 20 November 2022).

[17] Guia Migani, *La France et l'Afrique Sub-Saharienne, 1957–1963: Histoire d'une Décolonisation entre Idéaux Eurafricains et Politique de Puissance* (Peter Lang 2008) 25–6. The author indicates that the United States and Soviet Union were eager to have control over newly independent African states in order to strengthen their positions within the United Nations.

[18] Declaration on the Granting of Independence to Colonial Countries and Peoples http://digitallibrary.un.org/record/662085 (last accessed 8 July 2020).

[19] Charles-Robert Ageron, 'L'opinion Française Devant la Guerre d'Algérie' (1976) 63 *Outre-Mers. Revue d'Histoire* 256–85.

[20] The essence of the so-called French Community was to control African states behind the fig-leaf of equality. For example, although the *Communauté* member states agreed to cooperate as equal partners on foreign policy, defence, currency, economic and financial policy, as well as natural resources, justice, and higher education, France

all ties with any territory that opted for immediate independence. Guinea's Sékou Touré was the sole African leader to vote in favour of immediate independence, and he paid a heavy price for this.[21] It was hence clear that France was going to grant independence to its African colonies only on its own terms. In many respects, two of what can be regarded as French 'terms' for releasing African states from the yoke of colonialism have had an enduring legacy on the ability of African countries to shape the direction of their constitutional destiny—namely the so-called *Françafrique* and the independence constitutions that were imposed on the colonies.

3.1 In Thrall to the *Françafrique* Spell

The expression '*La Françafrique*' was first used by a French journalist in 1945, and subsequently by the first Ivorian president, Félix Houphouët-Boigny, in 1955, to define the wish of some members of the African elite to maintain special relations with France after their independence.[22] Since then, however, this expression has become a pejorative term referring to French neocolonial dominance in Africa and a relationship that reflects francophone Africa's alienated sense of self. Contemporary understanding of *Françafrique* is usually associated with François Xavier Verschave,[23] a French anti-neocolonial activist who investigated the practices de Gaulle and subsequent French regimes followed to sustain French presence and control in francophone Africa, practices that entailed supporting dictatorships and pillaging the resources of the various countries.[24]

Indeed, the dream of independence and the ability to develop norms and institutions that reflect each country's identity and aspirations was short-lived in view of the political, economic, and military agreements that de Gaulle brokered between France and its former colonies.[25] More so than any other former colonial power, France, through its *Françafrique*

ultimately defined the manner in which this was done among member states. See Stéphane Diémert, 'L'histoire Constitutionnelle de l'Outremer sous la Ve République' (2012) *35 Les Nouveaux Cahiers du Conseil Constitutionnel* 10 https://www.cairn.info/revue-nouveaux-cahiers-conseil-constitutionnel-2012-2-page-7.htm (last accessed 22 November 2022).

[21] Furious at the 95 per cent 'no' vote, de Gaulle decided to make a lesson of Guinea to other colonies considering full independence. France withdrew four thousand colonial servants from Guinea, including administrators, doctors, judges, technicians, and teachers. The departing civil servants burned blueprints, archives, and machinery manuals. In what a French commentator described as 'divorce without alimony', the French left the country almost in ruins. See Mairi S. MacDonald, 'The Challenge of Guinean Independence, 1958–1971' (thesis, University of Toronto 2010) https://tspace.library.utoronto.ca/handle/1807/19287 (last accessed 20 November 2022).

[22] Thomas Borrel, Amzat Boukari Yabara, Benoit Collombat, and Thomas Deltombe, *L'empire Qui Ne Veut Pas Mourir. Une Histoire de la Françafiruqe: Guerres, Pillages, Racisme, Coups d'Etat, Corruption, Assassinats* (Seuil 2021) 44–5; Tugba Korkmaz, '"La Françafrique": The Special Relationship between France and Its Former Colonies in Africa' *INSAMER English* (2 August 2019) https://en.insamer.com/la-francafrique-the-special-relationship-between-france-and-its-former-colonies-in-africa2307.html (last accessed 20 November 2022).

[23] The concept first appeared in his 1998 book. See François-Xavier Verschave, *La Françafrique: Le plus Long Scandale de la République* (Stock 1998).

[24] Ibid. 21–2; Fanny Pigeaud and Ndongo S Sylla, *L'arme invisible de la Françafrique: Une histoire du Franc CFA* (La Découverte 2018); Patrick Pesnot, *Les dessous de la Françafrique* (Nouveau Monde 2008). See broadly Lily Mburu, 'A Racial Capitalism Panorama. Africa's Last Colonial Currency: The CFA Franc Story by Fanny Pigeaud and Ndongo Samba Sylla (translated by Thomas Fazi), London: Pluto Press, 2021' (2022) *25 Journal of International Economic Law* 348–61.

[25] Antoine S. Gnagne, 'Les Raisons d'une Bipolarisation de l'Afrique: 1960–1988' in Emilia Robin-Hivert and Georges-Henri Soutou (eds.), *L'Afrique Indépendante Dans le Système International* (Sorbonne Pups 2012) 168, 177–8.

policy, ensured for itself a strong, continuing political, economic, and cultural presence among its erstwhile colonies. This policy is characterised by three key features.

The first way in which France maintains economic control is through the common currency, the CFA franc (African Financial Community franc).[26] The CFA operates in two blocs of mainly francophone countries in West and Central Africa. The first is the West African Economic and Monetary Union (BCEAO), made up of eight countries whose central bank is based in Dakar, Senegal;[27] the second is the Economic and Monetary Union of Central African States (BCEAC), made up of six member states with a central bank in Yaoundé, Cameroon.[28]

Two points must be noted about the CFA. Firstly, although there are two central banks in Africa which are supposed to oversee the zone's operations, the monetary policy of member countries is determined by the French Treasury. The currency is pegged at a fixed rate to the euro, with convertibility guaranteed by the French Treasury on conditions that include covering 20 per cent of sight liabilities by foreign exchange reserves and depositing 50 per cent of the foreign reserves of the countries in an operations account in the French Treasury. As a result, member countries cannot change monetary policies in response to particular macroeconomic needs. Consequently, the currency is exposed to extraneous volatility due to fluctuations in the euro. The countries have no ability to adjust to export shocks and are vulnerable to imported inflation.

The second point is that in June 2019, the Economic Community of West African States (ECOWAS), where francophone countries make up 53 per cent of the membership,[29] agreed to launch a new common currency, the Eco, by 2020. Many felt this sounded the death knell for the increasingly anomalous CFA franc in Africa. However, during a visit of the French president Emmanuel Macron to the Ivory Coast in December 2019, the Ivorian president Alassane Ouattara made the stunning announcement that the West African CFA franc would be retired sometime in 2020 and replaced with a new currency, also called the Eco.[30] France's Council of Ministers officially adopted a bill in May 2020 that ratified the reform of the monetary agreement that bound the French government to the eight member states of the West African CFA zone. The effect is that the Eco will replace the CFA franc and that these countries will no longer be required to deposit their foreign reserves in the French Treasury. Nevertheless, the Eco will remain pegged to the euro and be backed by the French Treasury. The Euro will guarantee the Eco's convertibility and stability, with the French Treasury remaining as guarantor for all eight member states.[31]

[26] See Charles M. Fombad, 'Comparative Overview of Measures and Devices to Shape the Economy in Some Modern African Constitutions' in Fombad C.M. and Steytler N. (eds.), *Constitutionalism and the Economy in Africa* (Oxford University Press 2022) 110–12.

[27] The member states are Benin, Burkina Faso, Côte d'Ivoire, Guinea-Bissau, Mali, Niger, Senegal, and Togo.

[28] The member states are Cameroon, Central African Republic, Chad, Congo Republic, Gabon, and Equatorial Guinea.

[29] The organisation has fifteen members: Benin, Burkina Faso, Cape Verde, Côte d'Ivoire, the Gambia, Ghana, Guinea, Guinea-Bissau, Liberia, Mali, Niger, Nigeria, Senegal, Sierra Leone, and Togo.

[30] In a statement, the Nigerian finance minister Zainab Ahmed said the December announcement was 'inconsistent with the decision of the Authority of the Heads of State and Government of ECOWAS for the adoption of the Eco as the name of an independent ECOWAS single currency'. See 'West African States Mired in Controversy over "Eco" Currency' *DW* (18 January 2020) https://www.dw.com/en/west-african-states-mired-in-controversy-over-eco-currency/a-52045052 (last accessed 20 November 2022).

[31] See Cindi Cook, 'Francophone Countries Get New Currency' *AA.com* (30 May 2020) https://www.aa.com.tr/en/africa/8-francophone-countries-get-new-currency/1858754 (last accessed 20 November 2022).

The Cooperation Agreement with the Member States of the West African Monetary Union that instituted the Eco is said to have been adopted in a condescending way, as there was no consultation, debate, and discussion between France, the francophone ECOWAS member countries, or the people themselves.[32] As a result of French machinations, an attempt to adopt a common African currency in West Africa was sabotaged and has never taken off the ground. Given that currency is an important symbol of sovereignty and self-identity, the problem is not only the continued reliance on a currency that has a foreign identity but, more significantly, the fact that France could intervene to prevent the francophone countries from collaborating in establishing an African currency. By contrast, Britain did not create a monetary union amongst its former colonies, most of which by now have established independent currencies with no strings attaching them to the pound sterling.

A second feature of the *Françafrique* link is the series of so-called military cooperation agreements that France signed with most of its former colonies, an arrangement which has ensured a continuous French military presence in most francophone states.[33] At present, France has military bases in Burkina Faso, Mali, Niger, Mauritania, Chad, Djibouti, Niger, Senegal, and Gabon.[34] There is extensive reliance on French intelligence officials to 'protect' African presidents. In fact, the military bases have been used to monitor the situation in the different countries and launch military operations to depose or reinstate presidents when it suits French interests to do so.[35] Recent initiatives that France undertook to review its military intervention in the Sahel region—such as the withdrawal of the Barkhane operation in Mali and its replacement with the Takuba Task Force—suggest that it is not yet ready to abandon its military influence in its former colonies and is still willing to support leaders who use the suppression of jihadist terrorism as an excuse to limit the political rights of their citizens.

The third, and perhaps most dubious, aspect of the *Françafrique* since independence has been the policy of ensuring that elites favourably disposed to France occupy prominent positions of power. This has often led to overt or covert intervention in the domestic politics of francophone African states to make, unmake, and remake presidents at France's convenience. Verschave suggests that in many francophone countries, such as Gabon, Djibouti, Togo, Cameroon, Republic of Congo, and Benin, France helped to rig elections to maintain authoritarian leaders in power against the will of the people in more than fifty elections between 1991 and 2003.[36]

France is also suspected of having been involved in political assassinations and removals of presidents to protect its economic interests. Some of the leaders who are alleged to have

[32] Assemblée Nationale, 'XVe Legislature: Session Ordinaire de 2020-2021. Séance du jeudi 10 décembre 2020' (10 December 2020) https://www.assemblee-nationale.fr/dyn/15/comptes-rendus/seance/session-ordinaire-de-2020-2021/premiere-seance-du-jeudi-10-decembre-2020 (last accessed 20 November 2022).

[33] Anna Sundberg, 'France: A Continuing Military Presence in Francophone Africa' https://webcache.googleusercontent.com/search?q=cache:EsQqYHQS_H8J:https://www.foi.se/rest-api/report/FOI%2520Memo%252066814+&cd=2&hl=en&ct=clnk&gl=za (last accessed 20 November 2022).

[34] 'Les Armées Etrangères en Afrique: Vers Une Compétition Stratégique' *RFI* (4 December 2019) http://www.rfi.fr/fr/afrique/20191204-forces-etrangeres-afrique-africom-barkhane-sahel-camp-lemonnier-terrorisme (last accessed 20 November 2022); Abdurrahim Siradag, 'Understanding French Foreign and Security Policy towards Africa: Pragmatism or Altruism' (2014) 3 *Afro Eurasian Studies* 118–19.

[35] Ronald Koven, 'French Troops, Negotiations Pushed Bokassa off Throne' *Washington Post* (22 September 1979) https://www.washingtonpost.com/archive/politics/1979/09/22/french-troops-negotiations-pushed-bokassa-off-throne/a43fa464-4c17-45b5-847c-edbd5a1efda0/ (last accessed 20 November 2022).

[36] François-Xavier Verschave, 'De la Françafrique à la mafiafrique' (2002) *21–22 Mouvements* 9, 21 https://www.cairn.info/revue-mouvements-2002-3-page-9.htm (last accessed 7 November 2022).

been assassinated or removed from power by France include Thomas Sankara (Burkina Faso), Sylvanus Olympio (Togo), and Hamani Diori (Niger).[37] For example, in Operation Barracuda, conducted in 1979 in Central African Republic, French troops deposed Jean-Bedel Bokassa whom they had previously installed in power. The former Chadian president Idris Debby made the startling revelation that France had forced him to amend the constitution in 2002 to run for an additional presidential term.[38] Unlike France, Britain has maintained a policy of non-interference in its former colonies and hardly ever interferes in their internal affairs.[39]

France's overbearing interference and constant presence in the economic, cultural, and political life of its former colonies has been particularly significant in perpetuating the Gaullist constitutional model and its associated institutions. These interventions have had a deleterious effect on the ability of francophone African states to develop governance systems that address their contemporary challenges, an issue to which we will now turn.

3.2 The Perverse Impact of the Gaullist Model

All constitutions have borrowed ideas from other constitutions.[40] However, each country adapts and tailors the borrowed ideas to address its circumstances. This has not happened in francophone Africa. In fact, the 1958 French Constitution was replicated lock, stock, and barrel, with there being few significant modifications in the constitutions that France crafted and imposed on its former colonies at independence. Given the harsh and exploitative nature of French colonial rule, and the fact that it had come to symbolise subordination, exploitation, repression, and violence against Africans, it was a surprise that the new leaders and ruling elites adopted the constitutions that were handed down to them.

There are a number of reasons why they did so. The first was the unequal power relations and the likelihood of economic and political dependence on France. As noted, given France's reluctance to grant independence to its African colonies and its barely disguised use of intimidation and blackmail, it coerced the new leaders into accepting the independence arrangements, however unfavourable these were. Secondly, since few Africans had been actively involved in colonial administration, their knowledge and experience of governance was limited. There was a realisation that, to achieve economic development, maintain public order, regulate commerce, and ensure proper functioning of the administrative and judicial services, they had to retain the system that they had known and with which they had some familiarity. If the foundations for continuous dependence and interference had been laid in the *Françafrique* policy, the independence constitution crowned it all.

The 1958 Gaullist constitution and its African prototype had been designed like a dictator's handbook and suited the temperament of the new ruling elites. As mentioned, it replicated all the main features of the French 1958 Constitution, particularly the extreme

[37] Ibid. 12; Pigeaud and Sylla (n. 24) 138–9.

[38] 'La France Est Intervenue Pour Changer La Constitution' (2017) https://www.youtube.com/watch?v=NczOkkR71IQ (last accessed 8 July 2020); Ésaïe Toïngar, *Idriss Deby and the Darfur Conflict* (McFarland 2014) 150–1.

[39] Laura Fenwick, 'British and French Styles of Influence in Colonial and Independent Africa: A Comparative Study of Kenya and Senegal' (American University 2009) 30 https://auislandora.wrlc.org/islandora/object/0809capstones%3A10/datastream/PDF/view (last accessed 20 November 2022).

[40] See Lee Epstein and Jack Knight, 'Constitutional Borrowing and Nonborrowing' (2003) https://scholarship.law.duke.edu/faculty_scholarship/3398/ (last accessed 20 November 2022).

concentration of powers in the president of the republic. The strong executive provided for under the 1958 Constitution certainly corrected the structural weaknesses that led to a dysfunctional system in France under the 1946 Constitution. However, in Africa, the excessive concentration of powers in the office of the president, combined with the absence of sufficient checks and balances and the retention of the unitarist and centralised system inherited from France, paved the way for the dictatorships that emerged soon after independence. The new ruling elites used the pretext of promoting national development and unity among the diverse communities that had been forced together artificially by the French to amass greater powers and silence critics of the government. Weak legislatures and judiciaries were unable to check the human rights abuses, corruption, and mismanagement that, by the end of the 1980s, had led to the near collapse of the economies of most francophone countries.

Although it is fair to say that by that point constitutionalism, good governance, and respect for the rule of law had collapsed in almost every country in Africa, the situation was far worse in francophone Africa.[41] The weak foundation for constitutionalism laid down by Gaullist constitutional framework, inherently flawed due to its ineffective system of vertical and horizontal governmental accountability, prepared the way for the economic mismanagement and ensuing economic and political crises that made revolution inevitable. The anger and frustration caused by years of repression, economic hardship, and political instability finally forced people out onto the streets to demand fundamental constitutional reform.

4. The Search for an Elusive Constitutional Identity

The political, institutional, and constitutional 'winds of change' of the 1990s were an opportunity to reimagine constitutions in francophone Africa and depart from models that entrenched powers in the hands of elites and consolidated authoritarianism.[42] The World Bank, International Monetary Fund, domestic social movements, and Western powers encouraged the adoption of new constitutions that provided for transparency in the management of public funds, the decentralisation of power, and the enhancement of free speech and participation[43] to give voice to citizens. Most francophone countries held so-called sovereign national conferences which, in spite of differences in outcome, provided a framework to establish appropriate checks and balances.[44] For the first time since independence, there was an attempt to involve the people actively in the revision of their constitutions.

What was equally significant was that it looked very much as if the French were going to allow francophone Africa to take control of its destiny. This came with a formal announcement by President Mitterrand at the June 1990 La Baule Franco-African Summit that democracy would henceforth be a condition for cordial relations with France. This was

[41] As Filip Reyntjens, 'The Winds of Change: Political and Constitutional Evolution in Francophone Africa, 1990–1991' (1991) *35 Journal of African Law* 44, 54, puts it, 'Francophone Africa has suffered more from bad management and gross human rights violations by incompetent, corrupt and authoritarian regimes, which have in most cases originated from military coups.'

[42] Stephen Riley, 'Africa's "New Wind of Change" ' (1992) *48 The World Today* 116; Reyntjens (n. 41) 44.

[43] Reyntjens (n. 41) 45.

[44] Jacques M. Nzouankeu, 'The Role of the National Conference in the Transition to Democracy in Africa: The Cases of Benin and Mali' (1993) *21 Journal of Opinion* 44.

reiterated with even more emphasis by President Jacques Chirac, who, in 1997, enunciated two new 'rules of conduct'.

Firstly, he said, France must 'refrain from any interference whatsoever, be it of political, military, or of any other nature', adding that 'France would not accept it at home; it must not resort to it in other countries'. Secondly, France must 'encourage our African partners to strengthen, in the manner and at the pace of their choosing, the rule of law and good governance', because this was essential for foreign investors to feel confident enough to do business in Africa.[45]

For what it is worth, successive presidents, including the current one, Emmanuel Macron, have repeated this, but with little conviction. Indeed, it has all turned out to be empty rhetoric. The reality is that France has devised subtler, more sophisticated means to tighten its stranglehold on francophone Africa. Not only have the so-called constitutional reforms in francophone Africa been half-hearted, but the Gaullist identity has proven impossible to reform.

4.1 Hesitant Substantive Reforms

Given that constitutions are a 'social contract'[46] between citizens and their governors on how they ought to be governed, citizens should play an important role in the constitution-making process. As noted, this did not happen with the independence constitutions, nor was it the case with the numerous amendments to these constitutions. Although the 1990s saw ordinary citizens presented with an opportunity to play a role in deciding their constitutional future, in francophone Africa, unlike the situation in anglophone Africa, the way in which the reforms were initiated and carried out ensured that, save for a few countries, ruling elites successfully stage-managed the process.[47]

The Benin 1990 Constitution is generally regarded as the most successful example of constitution-making in francophone Africa because it involved the participation of a wide range of citizens. However, participation in the process was still top-down, as participants were drawn from 'the political class and the educated elites of civil society'[48] and could not claim to represent the opinions of the larger population. The conference nonetheless led to constitutional and political reforms that established guiderails against authoritarianism and the holding of presidential elections where the incumbent lost to the interim prime minister.[49]

45 'Speech by Mr Jacques Chirac, President of the Republic, on the Role of Ambassadors in Promoting France's Cultural Influence and Economic Interests, on Europe and European defence and on African Policy, Paris 27 August 1997' https://www.vie-publique.fr/discours/172520-discours-de-m-jacques-chirac-president-de-la-republique-sur-le-role-d (last accessed 20 November 2022).

46 Louis Favoreu, Patrick Gaïa, Richard Ghevontian, Otto Pfersmann, André Roux, Guy Scoffoni, Jean-Louis Mestre (eds.), *Droit constitutionnel* (21st edn, Dalloz 2019) 8.

47 For the approaches, see generally, Tania Abbiate, Markus Böckenförde, and Veronica Federico (eds.), *Public Participation in African Constitutionalism* (Routledge 2017); Pearl T. Robinson, 'The National Conference Phenomenon in Francophone Africa' (1994) 36 *Comparative Studies in Society and History* 576–7; and compare with Christina Murray and Coel Kirkby, 'Constitution-Making in Anglophone Africa: We the People?' in Muna Ndulo and Mamoudou Gazibo (eds.), *Growing Democracy in Africa: Elections, Accountable Governance, and Political Economy* (Cambridge Scholars Publishing 2016) 86–113.

48 Robinson (n. 47) 576–7.

49 Aboya Manassé Endong, 'L'exorcisme de la révolution dans la Constitution béninoise du 11 décembre 1990' in Frédéric Joël Aivo (ed.), *La constitution béninoise du 11 décembre 1990: Un modèle pour l'Afrique? Mélanges en l'honneur de Maurice Ahanhanzo-Glélé* (Editions L'Harmattan 2014) 86–7.

Elsewhere, however, constitutional reforms were doomed in advance to failure since incumbents maintained control of the entire process.[50] For example, 81 per cent of participants in the 1990 constitutional reforms in Burkina Faso represented Blaise Compaoré's party, the Popular Front. Constitutional reforms also took place amid a state of emergency that limited participation by ordinary citizens. Unsurprisingly, 51 per cent of citizens abstained from the referendum held to approve the Constitution.[51] Jean du Bois de Gaudusson notes that citizens were called upon merely to approve the Constitution without a proper understanding of what it contained and what its implications were.[52] Similarly, the 'new' Cameroonian Constitution, presented as an amendment to the 1972 Constitution, perfectly illustrates the appropriation of people's aspirations by an entrenched regime, seeing as it was drafted by a technical committee on constitutional matters made up of eleven individuals appointed by the president.[53]

Although most of the constitutional reforms were approved in hastily organised referenda, these were often stage-managed to secure approval and were not as free and fair as those that led to the rejection of the draft new constitutions put before Kenyans and Zimbabweans in 2005 and 2000, respectively.[54] In fact, between 1990 and 2020, ten francophone countries held constitutional referenda in which all the proposed amendments were approved.[55] By contrast, the process that led to the adoption of the 1996 South African Constitution is estimated to have been the most consultative of all, considering the degree of political and public consultation that was achieved by way of the press, radio, television, and the Constitutional Assembly's website.[56] Similarly, an elaborate consultative process was involved in drafting the Kenyan and Zimbabwean constitutions, as compared to the practices in francophone Africa.[57]

[50] For example, this was Cameroon's experience.

[51] Céline Thiriot, 'Transitions Politiques et Changements Constitutionnels en Afrique' in Aurore Gaillet, Nicoletta Perlo, and Julia Schmitz (eds.), *Le phénomène constituant: Un dialogue interdisciplinaire* (Presses de l'Université Toulouse 1 Capitole 2018) 29–49.

[52] Jean du Bois de Gaudusson, 'Les tabous du constitutionnalisme en Afrique' (2012) *242 Afrique Contemporaine* 53, 56.

[53] Charles M. Fombad, 'Cameroon: Introductory Notes' https://nanopdf.com/download/1-cameroon-introductory-notes-prof-charles-manga-fombad_pdf (last accessed 20 November 2022).

[54] James T. Gathii, 'Popular Authorship and Constitution-Making: Comparing and Contrasting the DRC and Kenya Constitution Drafting in Post-Conflict States Symposium' (2007) *49 William and Mary Law Review* 1109; Masipula Sithole, 'Fighting Authoritarianism in Zimbabwe' (2001) *12 Journal of Democracy* 160–5.

[55] The Benin 1990 Constitution was approved by 93.2 per cent of voters. Burkina Faso approved its 1991 Constitution by 92.82 per cent, with a voter turnout of 48.8 per cent. The 1994 Constitution of Central African Republic was approved by 82.7 per cent, with a voter turnout of 45 per cent; the 2004 Constitution was approved by 91.3 per cent, with a voter turnout of 77.1 per cent; and that of 2015 was approved by 93 per cent. The 1996 Chadian Constitution was approved by 63.5 per cent, with a voter turnout of 61 per cent, whilst the 2005 one was approved by 66 per cent. The 1992 Republic of Congo Constitution was approved by 96 per cent, with a 70.9 per cent voter turnout; that of 2002 was approved by 87 per cent, with a voter turnout of 77.5 per cent; and that of 2015 was approved by 92.7 per cent. Reforms to the 1995 Constitution of Gabon were approved by 96.5 per cent, with a voter turnout of 64 per cent. The 1990 Constitution of Guinea was approved by 98.7 per cent, with a voter turnout of 97.4 per cent, whilst those of 2001 and 2020 were approved, respectively, by 98.36 per cent and 89.76 per cent. The 2000 Constitution of Côte d'Ivoire was approved by 86.5 per cent, whilst the 2016 one was approved by 93.42 per cent. The 1992 Constitution of Mali was approved by 99 per cent, with a turnout of 43.5 per cent. Niger's referenda in 1992, 1996, 2009, 1999, and 2010 were approved, respectively, by 89.79 per cent, 92.34 per cent, 89.6 per cent, 92.5 per cent, and 90 per cent. Senegal's 2001 Constitution was approved by 94 per cent, whilst reforms in 2016 were approved by 62.64 per cent.

[56] Charles M. Fombad, 'Constitutional Literacy in Africa: Challenges and Prospects' (2018) *44 Commonwealth Law Bulletin* 492.

[57] See generally Abbiate, Böckenförde, and Federico (n. 47).

Another point to note is that, again unlike the approach taken in most anglophone countries—where constitutional review commissions visited other countries outside the common law constitutional tradition, such as Germany, and also brought in experts from other African countries to assist in the constitution-making process—there was little effort in francophone Africa to learn from developments in other constitutional systems. As Filip Reyntjens observed, commenting on the approach taken in francophone Africa: 'Recent constitutional draughtsmen have again sought their inspiration in what they perceive as a reliable and unsuspected democratic model: that of France.'[58]

However, the most important issue is whether these new or revised constitutions provide better prospects for constitutionalism, good governance, and respect for the rule of law—and if the drafters took the opportunity to break out of the Gaullist mould and incorporate principles and institutions that reflect the desires and hopes of the people. In considering this, it is worth noting that much like the post-independence period, this new era of democratisation has been marked by an unrelenting process of making, remaking, and unmaking of constitutions.[59] It will suffice for our purposes here to highlight some of the key features that appeared in most of the 'made in Africa' francophone constitutions of the post-1990 era.

Among the first changes was dispensing with the single-party system, a major instrument for sustaining authoritarianism that had been entrenched, de jure or de facto, within a short while after independence. The revised constitutions or laws enacted to implement these changes formally recognised the existence of a plurality of parties.[60] Perhaps the main preoccupation of the constitution designers was with the problem of excessive concentration of powers in the executive, more specifically in the president of the republic vis-à-vis the other branches of government. Attempts were made to disperse such powers in several ways.

Firstly, to end the phenomenon in which power alternated only through the death of the president or his removal by coup, two-term presidential term limits were introduced in nearly all constitutions. Unfortunately, in most francophone countries, and in spite of the fact that in some of them, such as the Republic of Congo, this provision was declared unamendable, these term- limit provisions were repealed.[61] Although the removal of presidential term-limit provisions has occurred under most contemporary African constitutions, it has been more prevalent in francophone Africa than elsewhere on the continent.

Another measure to diffuse power was the introduction in francophone constitutions of the position of prime minister.[62] However, although these constitutions describe the prime minister as 'head of government', this attempt at dispersing power is more symbolic than substantive. For one thing, the prime minister is appointed and removed solely at the

[58] Reyntjens (n. 41) 51.

[59] In the light of this, it should be noted that all references here are to the latest amendments of the constitutions of these countries. For a discussion of this endless process of constitutional revision, especially in francophone Africa, see Charles M. Fombad, 'Constitution-Building in Africa: The Never-Ending Story of the Making, Unmaking and Remaking of Constitutions' (2014) *13 African and Asian Studies* 429–51.

[60] See, for example, articles 5–6 of the Benin Constitution of 1990; articles 11–13 of the Burkina Faso Constitution of 1991; article 3 of Cameroon's Constitution of 1996; and article 4 of Senegal's Constitution of 2001.

[61] See generally Jack R. Mangala, *The Politics of Challenging Presidential Term Limits in Africa* (Springer Nature 2020); Micha Wiebusch and Christina Murray, 'Presidential Term Limits and the African Union' (2019) *63 Journal of African Law* 131.

[62] See article 46 of the Burkina Faso Constitution of 1991; article 10 of the Cameroon Constitution of 1996; article 70 of the Côte d'Ivoire Constitution of 2016; and article 49 of the Senegalese Constitution of 2001.

discretion of the president, in addition to which he (or she) is appointed to implement the president's policies and political programme. In reinforcing the illusion of power dispersal, it so happens that only the prime minister is accountable to parliament; ironically, although he merely implements the president's political programme, it is he—and not the president—who may be forced to resign after a parliamentary vote of no confidence. This aside, under most francophone constitutions, the president's wide-ranging powers to appoint ministers, senior government officials, senior military officers, and members of the diplomatic corps remain undiminished.

The anomaly of retaining the imperial presidency in a new era of constitutionalism is all the more striking when it comes to relations with the legislature and the judiciary. As regards the legislature, extensive exclusive executive law-making powers in all areas of law-making not reserved to the legislature have been retained. So too are the executive powers to make laws by way of ordinances if and when the need arises in areas within the reserved legislative law-making domain.[63] In the final analysis, the president and his ministers have extensive powers to rule by presidential decrees and ordinances and ministerial orders, with the exercise of these powers exposed only to very limited parliamentary oversight.

However, it is with respect to presidential powers over the judiciary that the post-1990 reforms have been at their weakest and most illusory. The main innovation is supposed to have been the judiciary's transformation from a 'judicial authority' to a 'judicial power', yet in no way has this diminished the president's exorbitant powers over the judiciary. Firstly, the constitutions still state that the 'president is the guarantor of judicial independence'.[64] If all three branches were coequal, one of them would not be guaranteeing the independence of any of the others; instead, an effective system of checks and balances, which is absent in these constitutional models, would have served this purpose. Secondly, judicial appointments and promotions, as well as disciplinary actions against judicial officials, are decided upon by the president; in some cases, this is said to be upon receiving the 'opinion' of the Higher Judicial Council (HJC). Although a few of these constitutions no longer require the president and his minister of justice to act as chair and deputy chair, respectively, of the HJC, it makes little difference because the power to determine its composition and regulate its proceedings still leaves the president in a position to ensure that only persons likely to support his agenda sit in this body.[65]

Finally, with the exception of the Constitutional Court of Benin, it is the case that despite efforts to improve the centralised judicial review model of the constitutional council, the judiciary still has only limited jurisdiction to check against violations of the constitution.[66] In fact, the 1990 reforms have done little to diminish francophone Africa's culture of condoning oppression and grave human rights abuses, a situation often aggravated by judicial deference to government.[67] For example, whilst many citizens in anglophone countries

[63] See, for example, articles 100 and 102 of the Benin Constitution of 1990; articles 107–8 of the Burkina Faso Constitution of 1991; article 27–8 of the Cameroon Constitution of 1996; articles 103 and 106 of the Côte d'Ivoire Constitution of 2016; and articles 76–7 of the Senegalese Constitution of 2001.

[64] See article 134 of the Benin Constitution of 1990; article 131 of the Burkina Faso Constitution of 1991; article 37(3) of the Cameroon Constitution of 1996; and article 139 of the Côte d'Ivoire Constitution of 2016.

[65] See the different forms of this in articles 124–35 of the Burkina Faso Constitution of 1991; article 37 of the Cameroon Constitution of 1996; articles 145–7 of the Côte d'Ivoire Constitution of 2016; and article 90 of the Senegalese Constitution of 2001.

[66] See generally Charles M. Fombad, *Constitutional Adjudication in Africa* (Oxford University Press 2017).

[67] Trésor M. Makunya, 'The Application of the African Charter on Human and Peoples' Rights in Constitutional Litigation in Benin' in Frans Viljoen, Charles Fombad, Dire Tladi, Ann Skelton, and Magnus Killander (eds.),

such as South Africa,[68] Kenya,[69] Malawi,[70] and Uganda[71] have gone to court to challenge the legality and constitutionality of measures adopted by governments to deal with the spread of Covid-19, in francophone ones such as Cameroon, Central African Republic, Senegal, and Togo, they have endured abuses, restrictions, and human rights violations in silence. Francophone Africa's weak constitutional framework for promoting constitutionalism has had serious deleterious consequences for the quality of constitutional justice and the rule of law.

Traditional systems of governance and customary courts remain a daily African reality. The attempts by the French to undermine and eradicate them during the colonial period are reflected in the post-independence constitutions they designed. Thus, the independence constitutions of most francophone countries, such as Côte d'Ivoire,[72] Benin,[73] Togo,[74] and Senegal,[75] did not contain any provisions on traditional leadership and entities. It was anticipated that this important aspect of African constitutional identity would be revisited in the post-1990 constitutional reforms. However, only a few constitutions attempt to confer on them a formal status that promotes their participation in the political process.[76]

The constitutions of the Republic of Congo and Côte d'Ivoire provide interesting yet less-than-effective examples of how constitutional texts can ensure the participation of traditional authorities in modern governance. The former establishes an Advisory Council of the Wise and Traditional Leaders to provide 'opinions on the democratic, cultural and social governance of the state and for making suggestions to the Government'.[77] For its part, the Côte d'Ivoire Constitution provides for a National House of Kings and Traditional

A Life Interrupted: Essays in Honour of the Lives and Legacies of Christof Heyns (Pretoria University Law Press 2022) 406.

[68] Theo Broodryk, 'COVID-19, the Courts and Access to Justice Issue 9' *Juta Press Room* (22 May 2020) https://juta.co.za/press-room/2020/05/22/covid-19-courts-and-access-justice/#_ftn27 (last accessed 20 November 2022). Broodryk noted that, as of May 2020, there were twenty-one petitions against Covid-19 measures before South African courts.

[69] 'Petition 120 of 2020 (Covid 025)—Kenya Law' http://kenyalaw.org/caselaw/cases/view/192748/ (last accessed 20 November 2022).

[70] Hanibal Goitom, 'Malawi: High Court Temporarily Blocks COVID-19 Lockdown' (2020) http://www.loc.gov/law/foreign-news/article/malawi-high-court-temporarily-blocks-covid-19-lockdown/ (last accessed 20 November 2022).

[71] 'COVID-19: Petition for Legal Services during Lockdown' *Chapter Four* (23 April 2020) https://chapterfouruganda.org/articles/2020/04/24/covid-19-petition-legal-services-during-lockdown (last accessed 20 November 2022).

[72] Article 2 of the 3 November 1960 Constitution of Côte d'Ivoire.

[73] Article 2 of the 1960 Benin (Dahomey) Constitution.

[74] Article 1 of the 1963 Constitution of Togo. See also article 84, which, although proclaiming the unity and the indivisibility of the state, recognises the existence of territorial entities.

[75] Article 1 of the 1963 Senegalese Constitution.

[76] Under the 1996 Constitution of Cameroon, the role of traditional leaders is limited, in article 57(2), to their representation in the Regional Council. Although the Constitution imposes on the state the duty to 'recognize and protect traditional values', there is little clarity as to what this entails. The 2016 Central African Republic Constitution likewise 'recognizes and protects traditional values in accordance with the law and Customary Authorities' without further elaboration. Title XIV of the 2018 Constitution of Chad recognises traditional and customary leaders as the gatekeepers of customs. They are, in terms of articles 217–20, required to support the actions of local entities and of the administration in due respect of fundamental rights. Similarly, the preamble to the 1991 Constitution of Burkina Faso recognises customary authorities as the gatekeeper of customs but provides no elaboration. Article 167 of the 2010 Niger Constitution, as in the case of Chad, merely recognises customary leaders and indicates that they operate under conditions determined by the law. The constitutions of Senegal of 2001, Mali (1992), and Guinea (2010) make no reference to either customs or traditional leaders and institutions.

[77] Article 230 of the 2015 Constitution of the Republic of Congo.

Chiefs, which is required, inter alia, to promote peace, development, social cohesion, and non-judicial settlement of conflicts in villages and communities.[78] There is no clear indication of how this is to be done.

By contrast, the 1990 Ghanaian Constitution contains elaborate provisions that deal with issues of chieftaincy. It provides for national and regional houses of chiefs, and defines their roles and responsibilities as well as their judicial powers.[79] The Constitution also limits the powers of Parliament to legislate in the customary domain.[80] One of the duties of the houses is to

> undertake the progressive study, interpretation and codification of customary law with a view to evolving, in appropriate cases, a unified system of rules of customary law, and compiling the customary laws and lines of succession applicable to each stool or skin.[81]

This clearly demonstrates willingness to ensure appropriate cohabitation between modern and traditional leadership and to preserve traditional values. The important point to note, however, is that francophone constitution-makers have not made sufficient effort to incorporate the traditional institutions and traditional values formally in modern governance.

There was considerable pressure, especially from the World Bank and International Monetary Fund, for African countries to disperse powers through decentralisation as a way of promoting local democracy and accountability as well as of taking into account their ethnic, religious, and cultural diversity. In most francophone countries, with the exception of Cameroon, the constitutionalisation of decentralisation has been limited to one or two obliquely worded provisions.[82] Although the Cameroonian Constitution stands out for its detailed provisions on decentralisation,[83] the effect is the same as in all the other francophone countries. The timing of decentralisation, along with its nature, scope, and effect, is left to the discretion of central governments, which are mostly averse to sharing power with subnational units.[84]

This contrasts sharply with the approach adopted in most anglophone constitutions, where the matter is dealt with in elaborate provisions.[85] As a result of the limited scope for local self-governance, the wave of constitutional reforms has not given space or opportunity for much local governance, and the legacy of centralised rule prevails, with only limited opportunities for some degree of deconcentration of powers.

Ultimately, it is hard to see how modern francophone constitutions differ substantively from the independence constitutions, or how they have tried to develop an identity reflective of the major preoccupations of their countries. What could explain all of this?

[78] Article 175 of the 2016 Constitution of Côte d'Ivoire.

[79] Section 270 of the 1992 Constitution of Ghana.

[80] Section 270(2) of the 1992 Constitution of Ghana.

[81] Section 272(b) of the 1992 Constitution of Ghana.

[82] See, for example, articles 150–3 and 143–5 of the Burkina Faso Constitution of 1991; article 112 of the Constitution of Gabon of 1991; article 98 of the 1991 Constitution of Mauritania; and article 102 of the Constitution of Senegal of 2001.

[83] See articles 55–62 of the 1996 Constitution of Cameroon.

[84] For a detailed discussion of the different approaches to decentralisation in Africa, see Charles M. Fombad and Nico Steytler, *Decentralization and Constitutionalism in Africa* (Oxford University Press 2019).

[85] Ibid.

4.2 One Step Forward, Two Steps Backwards

Could francophone Africa escape the stifling shadow of the Gaullist constitutional identity? Whilst francophone scholars in literature,[86] history, philosophy,[87] and other disciplines have begun to imagine how epistemic colonial injustices could be eradicated by incorporating progressive concepts in order to help Africans self-identify themselves, francophone African legal scholars and jurists continue to restrict their thinking to the French civil law legal model and leave little room for any infusion of ideas from other legal models or even indigenous law. This stands in sharp contrast to the various anglophone legal scholars who have widened their focus to consider diverse influences not only in constitution-making but constitutional debates. Genuine constitutional transformation in francophone Africa thus faces a number of obstacles.

Firstly, many of the senior advisers who have the president's ear in francophone Africa today are French nationals. They are there to ensure not only that French legal, linguistic, and cultural hegemony is never threatened, but also that any senior officials who jeopardise these interests are sidelined. As a result, many legal scholars and jurists in francophone Africa who aspire to ministerial positions or senior positions in the judiciary indulge in strategic double-talk. Some commentators have expressed shock at the lack of imagination and creativity that certain of these scholars display.[88]

Two examples will suffice to illustrate France's continuing influence. Firstly, on the death of Togo's president Gnassingbé Eyadéma in 2005, the National Assembly quickly amended the Constitution to enable his son, Fauré Eyadéma, to replace him, while excluding the constitutionally sanctioned successor, the president of the National Assembly.[89] It is said that the French advisor to the late president was responsible for this attempt to manipulate the succession process.[90]

The second example concerns the Organisation for the Harmonization of Business Law in Africa (OHADA).[91] Created on 17 October 1993 in Port Louis, Mauritius, it is made up of seventeen, mostly francophone, countries in West and Central Africa.[92] The objective of OHADA, according to article 1 of the founding treaty, is the 'harmonisation of business laws in the contracting states by the elaboration and adoption of simple modern common rules

[86] Bidy C. Bodo and Adama Samaké (eds.), *La Théorie de la Décolonialité: Sémantique et Pratiques Textuelles* (L'Harmattan 2020).

[87] Marie Lechapelays, 'École Doctorale des Ateliers de la Pensée: « Décoloniser les Savoirs sur l'Afrique »' (*Le Point* (28 January 2019) https://www.lepoint.fr/culture/ecole-doctorale-des-ateliers-de-la-pensee-decoloniser-les-savoirs-sur-l-afrique-28-01-2019-2289443_3.php (last accessed 20 November 2022).

[88] Gertie Hesseling, 'La Réception Du Droit Constitutionnel En Afrique Trente Ans Après: Quoi de Neuf?' (1996) *International Association of Constitutional Law* 36–8 https://openaccess.leidenuniv.nl/bitstream/handle/1887/9357/ASC_1247243_137.pdf?sequence=1 (last accessed 30 July 2020).

[89] Thiriot (n. 51).

[90] Nicolas Vescovacci and Jean-Pierre Canet, *Vincent Tout-Puissant* (Lattes 2018) 187; Ali Al'Amin Mazrui, *Power, Politics, and the African Condition* (Africa World Press 2004) 76–7; Bal Ba Amadou, '«Charles DEBBASCH, pillier de la Françafrique» par Amadou Bal BA' (*Club de Mediapart*) https://blogs.mediapart.fr/amadouba19gmail com/blog/250619/charles-debbasch-pillier-de-la-francafrique-par-amadou-bal-ba (last accessed 2 July 2020).

[91] OHADA is the French acronym for 'Organisation pour l'Harmonisation en Afrique du Droit des Affaires'. On OHADA and constitutionalism, see Balingene Kahombo and Trésor M. Makunya, 'Constitutionalism, Regional Integration and the Harmonisation of Business Law in Francophone Africa' (2021) *1 Congolese Review of Social Sciences Research* 143–71.

[92] It includes the Comoros, which is from outside the region; Guinea-Bissau, which is lusophone; Equatorial Guinea, which is hispanophone; and Cameroon, which is, in principle, a bi-jural system. The francophone countries are Benin, Burkina Faso, Central African Republic, Congo, Ivory Coast, DR Congo, Gabon, Guinea, Mali, Niger, Senegal, Chad, and Togo.

adapted to their economies, by setting up appropriate judicial procedures, and by encouraging arbitration for the settlement of disputes'. Nine Uniform Acts have been adopted.[93] One of OHADA's major goals, as stated in its preamble and article 1 of the founding treaty, is to make common business laws which are simple, modern, and adaptable to present economic realities. There is no doubt that OHADA has made a valuable difference in regulating commercial matters amongst member states. However, serious questions surround its legitimacy. These relate not only to how it originated but also to how it operates and what its goals are.

Although a number of countries and international institutions were instrumental in OHADA's creation, the main actor was France, which provided most of the funds as well as ideas. Unsurprisingly, the most significant influence on the OHADA Acts is French civil law. Presumably to disguise the fact that it was a top-down, French-led reform, a distinguished African legal scholar and former vice president of the International Court of Justice, the late Judge Keba Mbaye, was given the responsibility of driving the process that led to the establishment of the organisation. The early drafts of the main treaty, as well as the early Uniform Acts, were prepared in France by French experts, while African 'partners' were required only to comment on the drafts.

This French influence in determining the content of modern commercial law in francophone Africa promotes not only French legal culture but also French economic and commercial interests. The mere fear of what the French would do if they do not have their way has held many francophone African leaders and their advisers *in terrorem*.

An enduring centralist mindset within which it is the president of the republic who dominates every aspect of economic, social, and political life leaves scant room for open discussion or local participation in governance. Indeed, Jean Baechler argues that the introduction to Africa of the unitary political system was '*l'erreur la plus tragique dans ses conséquences*' ('the most tragic error in its consequences') of France's involvement in the continent.[94] As Placide Moudoudou puts it, francophone constitutionalists have closed their minds to the adoption of alternative models, such as federalism, for taking into account the realities of African states.[95]

Compulsive centralisation has facilitated a top-down governance approach. Most of the few attempts at dispersing powers and giving the ordinary citizen an opportunity to participate in governance have been ignored, or the relevant constitutional provisions repealed. Perhaps the most notorious example of such a reversal of constitutional reforms is, as noted earlier, the repeal of presidential term limits. In other instances, progressive provisions in the revised constitutions have simply been ignored, with the ruling elites continuing to govern as if the reforms had never taken place.[96] The disconnect between constitutional provisions and lived realities in these countries is evidence of the fact that existing constitutional paradigms, concepts, and normative ideologies have not been drawn sufficiently

[93] See OHADA Uniform Acts, available at https://www.ohada.org/index.php/fr/actes-uniformes-de-l-ohada (last accessed 20 November 2022).

[94] J. Beachler, 'Des Institutions Démocratiques pour L'Afrique' (1992) *2 Revue Juridique et Politique* 163–81.

[95] Placide Moudoudou, 'L'Etat Africain: Entre Constitutionnalisme Libéral et Constitutionnalisme Identitaire' (2015) *2 Sciences Juridiques et Politiques* 129.

[96] For example, in Cameroon, articles 46–52 of the Constitution, which provide for a Constitutional Council, were implemented in 2018—that is, twenty-two years after the Constitution was adopted. The senate provided for in articles 20–4 was finally established only in 2013 (seventeen years later), while some degree of limited decentralisation provided in part X was partially implemented between 2004 and 2008. See further Charles M. Fombad, 'Designing Institutions and Mechanisms for the Implementation and Enforcement of the Constitution: Changing Perspectives in Africa' (2017) *25 African Journal of International and Comparative Law* 66–90.

from local conceptions of life and politics and instead aim generally to serve the interests of elites and those in power.

There is hardly any evidence to suggest that serious efforts have been made to introduce constitutional designs that can reduce the risks of authoritarian revival. One of the major innovations in the revised constitutions was, with the exception of Cameroon, the direct incorporation of provisions recognising and protecting human rights in modern francophone constitutions. Cameroon, however, followed the typical Gaullist style in which human rights are referred to only in the preamble.[97] Unfortunately, because (with the exception of Benin) individuals have no locus standi before constitutional courts or councils, they cannot directly challenge any legislation that violates these human rights provisions.[98]

Underlining the failure of a distinct constitutional identity to arise despite more than a half a century of flirtation with Gaullist constitutionalism is the sad case of Benin. After adopting the most progressive constitution in francophone Africa in 1990, its president Patrice Talon, who came to power in 2016, speedily returned the country to its deadening authoritarian past. The only francophone country that tried to break with its constitutional heritage has, in short, failed.

5. Conclusion

The use of imposed independence constitutions in the 1960s and shortly thereafter is understandable. Across Africa, the French handed over power only to linguistically, culturally, and religiously assimilated locals versed with the colonial system of governance, thereby creating a social class with home-grown roots to ensure the continuation of their policies. It is, however, difficult to understand how—in an era of heightened awareness not only of the nature of the social, economic, and political challenges that the different countries face, but also of the variety of constitutional options which are available to deal with these challenges—Gaullism, with all its defects, can continue to reign supreme. The only possible explanation of why the Gaullist constitutional model has survived and thrived is that it suits the temperament and strategic interests of francophone African leaders, the ruling elites, and the French.

The Gaullist constitutional model is good for France and works well for it: it is culturally and organically French, and serves this country well because its actual or perceived excesses and limitations are tempered by the broader European Union constitutionalism within which it operates. But it is certainly not good for francophone Africa, and certainly has not served it well. The new constitutions have failed to address the problems of excessive centralisation of power in the person of the president and the authoritarianism that arises from this—problems that have plagued all of these countries since independence.

The constitutional reforms of the 1990s provided opportunities for francophone African constitutional designers to think of innovative ways in which this inherited model could be

[97] Although the Cameroon Constitution of 1996 states in article 65 that 'the preamble shall be part and parcel of this constitution', the hortatory language in which this is formulated does not lend itself to legal enforcement. Election disputes aside, individuals do not have the locus standi to raise issues of constitutionality before the Constitutional Council, the body with exclusive jurisdiction over constitutional matters.

[98] The Benin Constitution of 1990 states in article 117 that the Constitutional Court shall rule, inter alia, on 'the constitutionality of laws and regulatory acts deemed to infringe on fundamental human rights and on public liberties, and in general on the violation of the rights of the individual'.

adapted to deal with their countries' particular challenges. It was the same challenge that anglophone constitution-makers faced. After three decades of constitutional reform, one can point to innovative ideas such as the adoption of principles of transformative constitutionalism and the constitutional entrenchment of special institutions to promote democracy and constitutionalism in the Kenyan, South African, and Zimbabwean constitutions,[99] yet there is hardly anything new that the wave of constitutionalism in the 1990s brought to francophone Africa, apart from a few trifling cosmetic changes.

There is little to suggest that any of these developments have enhanced the prospects for constitutionalism, good governance, and respect for the rule of law, or that they better reflect the African context and its major challenges. Worse still, francophone scholars and jurists have found it politically inconvenient to think outside the Gaullist box. Unless francophone Africa can wean itself off the stifling influence of Gaullism, progressive constitutionalism and a sense of constitutional identity and constitutional ownership will remain a forlorn hope.

Bibliography

Abbiate T., Böckenförde M., and Federico V. (eds.), *Public Participation in African Constitutionalism* (Routledge 2017)

Ageron C.-R., 'L'Opinion française devant la guerre d'Algérie' (1976) *63 Outre-Mers. Revue d'histoire* 256

Amadou B.B., '«Charles DEBBASCH, pillier de la Françafrique» par Amadou Bal BA' (*Club de Mediapart*) https://blogs.mediapart.fr/amadouba19gmailcom/blog/250619/charles-debbasch-pillier-de-la-francafrique-par-amadou-bal-ba (last accessed 2 July 2020)

Assemblée Nationale, 'XVe Legislature: Session Ordinaire de 2020–2021. Séance du jeudi 10 décembre 2020' (10 December 2020) https://www.assemblee-nationale.fr/dyn/15/comptes-rendus/seance/session-ordinaire-de-2020-2021/premiere-seance-du-jeudi-10-decembre-2020 (last accessed 20 November 2022)

Bodo B.C. and Samaké A. (eds.), *La théorie de la décolonialité: Sémantique et pratiques textuelles* (L'Harmattan 2020)

Borrel T., Boukari Yabara, A., Collombat, B., and Deltombe, T., *L'empire Qui Ne Veut Pas Mourir. Une Histoire de la Françafiruqe: Guerres, Pillages, Racisme, Coups d'Etat, Corruption, Assassinats* (Seuil 2021) 44

Broodryk T., 'COVID-19, The Courts and Access to Justice Issue 9' *Juta Press Room* (22 May 2020) https://juta.co.za/press-room/2020/05/22/covid-19-courts-and-access-justice/#_ftn27 (last accessed 20 November 2022)

Cabanis A. and Martin M.-L., *Le constitutionnalisme de la troisième vague en Afrique francophone* (Academia Bruylant 2010)

Cook C., 'Francophone Countries Get New Currency' *AA.com* (30 May 2020) https://www.aa.com.tr/en/africa/8-francophone-countries-get-new-currency/1858754 (last accessed 20 November 2022)

[99] On transformative constitutionalism, see Karl E. Klare, 'Legal Culture and Transformative Constitutionalism' (1998) *14 South African Journal on Human Rights* 146–88; Theunis Roux, 'Transformative Constitutionalism and the Best Interpretation of the South African Constitution: Distinction without a Difference' (2009) *20 Stellenbosch Law Review* 258; Theunis Roux, *The Politics of Principle: The First South African Constitutional Court, 1995–2005* (Cambridge University Press 2013); Theunis Roux, 'Principle and Pragmatism on the Constitutional Court of South Africa' (2009) *7 International Journal of Constitutional Law* 106, 106–38. For constitutional institutions to promote democracy and good governance, see Charles M. Fombad, 'The Diffusion of South African–Style Institutions? A Study in Comparative Constitutionalism' in Rosalind Dixon and Theunis Roux (eds.), *Constitutional Triumphs, Constitutional Disappointments: A Critical Assessment of the 1996 South African Constitution's Local and International Influence* (Cambridge University Press 2018) 359–87.

'COVID-19: Petition for Legal Services during Lockdown' *Chapter Four* (23 April 2020) https://chapterfouruganda.org/articles/2020/04/24/covid-19-petition-legal-services-during-lockdown (last accessed 20 November 2022)

Declaration on the Granting of Independence to Colonial Countries and Peoples http://digitallibrary.un.org/record/662085 (last accessed 8 July 2020)

Beachler, J., 'Des Institutions Démocratiques pour L'Afrique' (1992) *2 Revue Juridique et Politique* 163

Diémert S., 'L'histoire constitutionnelle de l'outremer sous la Ve République' (2012) 35 *Les Nouveaux Cahiers du Conseil constitutionnel* 7 https://www.cairn.info/revue-nouveaux-cahiers-conseil-constitutionnel-2012-2-page-7.htm (last accessed 22 November 2022)

Endong A.M., 'L'exorcisme de la révolution dans la Constitution béninoise du 11 décembre 1990' in Aivo F.J. (ed.), *La constitution béninoise du 11 décembre 1990: Un modèle pour l'Afrique? Mélanges en l'honneur de Maurice Ahanhanzo-Glélé* (Editions L'Harmattan 2014) 86

Epstein L. and Knight J., 'Constitutional Borrowing and Nonborrowing' (2003) https://scholarship.law.duke.edu/faculty_scholarship/3398/ (last accessed 20 November 2022)

Fauré Y.A., 'Les Constitutions et l'exercise Du Pouvoir En Afrique Noire' http://www.politique-africaine.com/numeros/pdf/001034.pdf (last accessed 20 November 2022)

Favoreu L., Gaïa P., Ghevontian R., Pfersmann O., Roux A., Scoffoni G., Mestre J-L. (eds.), *Droit constitutionnel* (21st edn, Dalloz 2019)

Fenwick L., 'British and French Styles of Influence in Colonial and Independent Africa: A Comparative Study of Kenya and Senegal' (American University 2009) https://auislandora.wrlc.org/islandora/object/0809capstones%3A10/datastream/PDF/view (last accessed 20 November 2022)

Finer S., Bogdanor V., and Rudden B., *Comparing Constitutions* (Clarendon Press 1995)

Fombad C.M., 'Constitution-Building in Africa: The Never-Ending Story of the Making, Unmaking and Remaking of Constitutions' (2014) *13 African and Asian Studies* 429

Fombad C.M., 'The Evolution of Modern African Constitutions: A Retrospective Perspective' in Fombad C.M. (ed.), *Separation of Powers in African Constitutionalism* (Oxford University Press 2016) 13

Fombad C.M., *Constitutional Adjudication in Africa* (Oxford University Press 2017)

Fombad C.M., 'Designing Institutions and Mechanisms for the Implementation and Enforcement of the Constitution: Changing Perspectives in Africa' (2017) *25 African Journal of International and Comparative Law* 66

Fombad C.M., 'Constitutional Literacy in Africa: Challenges and Prospects' (2018) *44 Commonwealth Law Bulletin* 492

Fombad C.M., 'The Diffusion of South African–Style Institutions? A Study in Comparative Constitutionalism' in Dixon R. and Roux T. (eds.), *Constitutional Triumphs, Constitutional Disappointments: A Critical Assessment of the 1996 South African Constitution's Local and International Influence* (Cambridge University Press 2018) 359

Fombad C.M., 'Comparative Overview of Measures and Devices to Shape the Economy in Some Modern African Constitutions' in Fombad C.M. and Steytler N. (eds.), *Constitutionalism and the Economy in Africa* (Oxford University Press 2022) 110

Fombad C.M., 'Cameroon: Introductory Notes' *Constitutions of the World* https://nanopdf.com/download/1-cameroon-introductory-notes-prof-charles-manga-fombad_pdf (last accessed 20 November 2022)

Fombad C.M., 'Constitutional Identity and Constitutionalism in Africa: Concepts and Key Issues' in Charles M. Fombad and Nico Steytler (eds.), *Constitutional Identity and Constitutionalism in Africa* (Oxford University Press, forthcoming)

Fombad C.M. and Steytler N., *Decentralization and Constitutionalism in Africa* (Oxford University Press 2019)

'La France Est Intervenue Pour Changer La Constitution' (2017) https://www.youtube.com/watch?v=NczOkkR71IQ (last accessed 8 July 2020)

Gathii J.T., 'Popular Authorship and Constitution Making: Comparing and Contrasting the DRC and Kenya Constitution Drafting in Post-Conflict States Symposium' (2007) *49 William and Mary Law Review* 1109

Gaudusson J. du Bois de, 'Les tabous du constitutionnalisme en Afrique' (2012) *242 Afrique contemporaine* 53

Gnagne A.S., 'Les Raisons d'une Bipolarisation de l'Afrique: 1960–1988' in Robin-Hivert E. and Soutou G.-H. (eds.), *L'Afrique indépendante dans le système international* (Sorbonne Pups 2012) 168

Goitom H., 'Malawi: High Court Temporarily Blocks COVID-19 Lockdown' | Global Legal Monitor' (2020) http://www.loc.gov/law/foreign-news/article/malawi-high-court-temporarily-blocks-covid-19-lockdown/ (last accessed 20 November 2022)

Hesseling G., 'La Réception Du Droit Constitutionnel En Afrique Trente Ans Après: Quoi de Neuf?' (1996) *International Association of Constitutional Law* 33 https://scholarlypublications.universiteitleiden.nl/access/item%3A2888530/view (last accessed 16 October 2023)

Kahombo B. and Makunya T.M., 'Constitutionalism, Regional Integration and the Harmonisation of Business Law in Francophone Africa' (2021) *1 Congolese Review of Social Sciences Research* 143

Klare K.E., 'Legal Culture and Transformative Constitutionalism' (1998) *14 South African Journal on Human Rights* 146

Korkmaz T., '"La Françafrique": The Special Relationship between France and Its Former Colonies in Africa' *INSAMER English* (2 August 2019) https://en.insamer.com/la-francafrique-the-special-relationship-between-france-and-its-former-colonies-in-africa_2307.html (last accessed 20 November 2022)

Koven R., 'French Troops, Negotiations Pushed Bokassa Off Throne' *Washington Post* (22 September 1979) https://www.washingtonpost.com/archive/politics/1979/09/22/french-troops-negotiations-pushed-bokassa-off-throne/a43fa464-4c17-45b5-847c-edbd5a1efda0/ (last accessed 20 November 2022)

Lechapelays M., 'École doctorale des Ateliers de la pensée: « Décoloniser les savoirs sur l'Afrique »' *Le Point* (28 January 2019) https://www.lepoint.fr/culture/ecole-doctorale-des-ateliers-de-la-pensee-decoloniser-les-savoirs-sur-l-afrique-28-01-2019-2289443_3.php (last accessed 20 November 2022)

'Les Armées Etrangères en Afrique: Vers Une Compétition Stratégique' *RFI* (4 December 2019) http://www.rfi.fr/fr/afrique/20191204-forces-etrangeres-afrique-africom-barkhane-sahel-camp-lemonnier-terrorisme (last accessed 20 November 2022)

MacDonald M.S., 'The Challenge of Guinean Independence, 1958–1971' (thesis, University of Toronto 2010) https://tspace.library.utoronto.ca/handle/1807/19287 (last accessed 20 November 2022)

Makunya T.M., 'The Application of the African Charter on Human and Peoples' Rights in Constitutional Litigation in Benin' in Frans Viljoen, Charles Fombad, Dire Tladi, Ann Skelton, and Magnus Killander (eds.), *A Life Interrupted: Essays in Honour of the Lives and Legacies of Christof Heyns* (Pretoria University Law Press 2022) 406

Mamdani M., 'Historicising Power and Responses to Power: Indirect Rule and Its Reform' (1999) *66 Social Research* 859

Mamdani M., *Define and Rule: Native as Political Identity* (Harvard University Press 2012)

Mangala J.R., *The Politics of Challenging Presidential Term Limits in Africa* (Springer Nature 2020)

Mann G., 'What Was the "Indigénat"? The "Empire of Law" in French West Africa' (2009) *50 The Journal of African History* 331

Mazrui A.A., *Power, Politics, and the African Condition* (Africa World Press 2004)

Mburu L, 'A Racial Capitalism Panorama. Africa's Last Colonial Currency: The CFA Franc Story by Fanny Pigeaud and Ndongo Samba Sylla (translated by Thomas Fazi), London: Pluto Press, 2021' (2022) *25 Journal of International Economic Law* 348

Migani G., *La France et l'Afrique sub-saharienne, 1957–1963: Histoire d'une décolonisation entre idéaux eurafricains et politique de puissance* (Peter Lang 2008)

Moudoudou P., 'L'Etat africain: Entre constitutionnalisme libéral et constitutionnalisme identitaire' (2015) *2 Sciences Juridiques et Politiques* 113

Murray C. and Kirkby C., 'Constitution-Making in Anglophone Africa: We the People?' in Ndulo M. and Gazibo M. (eds.), *Growing Democracy in Africa: Elections, Accountable Governance, and Political Economy* (Cambridge Scholars Publishing 2016) 86

Nzouankeu J.M., 'The Role of the National Conference in the Transition to Democracy in Africa: The Cases of Benin and Mali' (1993) *21 Issue: A Journal of Opinion* 44

Pesnot P., *Les dessous de la Françafrique* (Nouveau Monde 2008)

'Petition 120 of 2020 (Covid 025)—Kenya Law' http://kenyalaw.org/caselaw/cases/view/192748/ (last accessed 20 November 2022)

Pigeaud F. and Sylla N.S., *L'arme invisible de la Françafrique: Une histoire du Franc CFA* (La Découverte 2018)

Reyntjens F., 'The Winds of Change: Political and Constitutional Evolution in Francophone Africa, 1990–1991' (1991) *35 Journal of African Law* 44

Riley S., 'Africa's "New Wind of Change"' (1992) *48 The World Today* 116

Robinson P.T., 'The National Conference Phenomenon in Francophone Africa' (1994) *36 Comparative Studies in Society and History* 575

Rogoff M.A, 'Fifty Years of Constitutional Evolution in France: The 2008 Amendments and Beyond' *Jus Politicum. Revuew de droit Politique* http://juspoliticum.com/article/Fifty-years-of-constitutional-evolution-in-France-The-2008-amendments-and-beyond-373.html (last accessed 20 November 2022)

Roux T., 'Principle and Pragmatism on the Constitutional Court of South Africa' (2009) *7 International Journal of Constitutional Law* 106

Roux T., 'Transformative Constitutionalism and the Best Interpretation of the South African Constitution: Distinction without a Difference' (2009) *20 Stellenbosch Law Review* 258

Roux T., *The Politics of Principle: The First South African Constitutional Court, 1995–2005* (Cambridge University Press 2013)

Saada E., 'Entre « assimilation » et « décivilisation »: l'imitation et le projet colonial républicain' (2005) *44 Anthropologie & sciences humaines* 19

Siradag A., 'Understanding French Foreign and Security Policy towards Africa: Pragmatism or Altruism' (2014) *3 Afro Eurasian Studies* 118

Sithole M., 'Fighting Authoritarianism in Zimbabwe' (2001) *12 Journal of Democracy* 160

'Speech by Mr Jacques Chirac, President of the Republic, on the Role of Ambassadors in Promoting France's Cultural Influence and Economic Interests, on Europe and European Defence and on African Policy, Paris 27 August 1997' https://www.vie-publique.fr/discours/172520-discours-de-m-jacques-chirac-president-de-la-republique-sur-le-role-d (last accessed 20 November 2022)

Sundberg A., 'France: A Continuing Military Presence in Francophone Africa' https://webcache.googleusercontent.com/search?q=cache:EsQqYHQS_H8J:https://www.foi.se/rest-api/report/FOI%2520Memo%25206814+&cd=2&hl=en&ct=clnk&gl=za (last accessed 20 November 2022)

Thiriot C., 'Transitions Politiques et Changements Constitutionnels En Afrique' in Gaillet A., Perlo N., and Schmitz J. (eds.), *Le phénomène constituant: Un dialogue interdisciplinaire* (Presses de l'Université Toulouse 1 Capitole 2018) 29

Toïngar É., *Idriss Deby and the Darfur Conflict* (McFarland 2014)

Verschave F.-X., *La Françafrique: Le plus long scandale de la République* (Stock 1998)

Verschave F.-X., 'De la Françafrique à la mafiafrique' (2002) *21–22 Mouvements* 9 https://www.cairn.info/revue-mouvements-2002-3-page-9.htm (last accessed 7 November 2022)

Vescovacci N. and Canet J.-P., *Vincent Tout-Puissant* (Lattes 2018)

'West African States Mired in Controversy over "Eco" Currency' *DW* (18 January 2020) https://www.dw.com/en/west-african-states-mired-in-controversy-over-eco-currency/a-52045052 (last accessed 20 November 2022)

Whittlesey D., 'British and French Colonial Technique in West Africa' (1937) *15 Foreign Affairs* 367

Wiebusch M. and Murray C., 'Presidential Term Limits and the African Union' (2019) *63 Journal of African Law* 131

Zweigert K. and Koetz H., *An Introduction to Comparative Law* (Clarendon Press 1998)

5

Who Are 'We, the People'? Pluralist Constitutional Identity after Democratic Transitions in African and European Countries

Karl Kössler

1. Introduction

'How we are able to constitute ourselves is profoundly tied to how we are already constituted by our own distinctive history', which makes the constitution 'less something we *have* than something we *are*.'[1] This statement aptly emphasises the impact of past experience on any constitutional arrangement at a given point in time. Such an arrangement is indeed never fixed but always fluid. This perspective shall form the background of this chapter.

My aim is to explore how and to what extent the constitutional systems of four ethnically diverse countries created a pluralist identity in their initial design and how this constitutional identity, as understood by Jacobsohn,[2] has changed, or rather *has been* changed, over time by political and judicial actors. The focus is therefore not on the reflection of pluralism in constitutional norms regarding state structure and power-sharing between government institutions,[3] but on those norms framing the image of 'the people' as the constitutional subject.

The chapter looks at two European (Bosnia and Herzegovina (BiH), and Spain) and two African (Ethiopia and South Africa) countries with certain common features which guided their selection as case studies. Firstly, the history of all four countries involves a period of non-recognition of ethnic diversity, which I understand as an umbrella term referring to various kinds of diversity based, for example, on shared linguistic, cultural, and religious identity.[4] All four countries have been characterised by such non-recognition in the context of violent conflict and/or non-democratic rule, but have embarked over the past decades on a transition to constitutional democracy. In such cases, the promulgation of democratic (national) constitutions is then often regarded as abruptly ending the period of transition. Yet it needs to be recognised that 'transitional constitution making is frequently impermanent'.[5] Even if the new (national) constitution is certainly a milestone, it remains

[1] Hanna Pitkin, 'The Idea of a Constitution' (1987) *37 Journal of Legal Education* 167.

[2] See Gary Jacobsohn, *Constitutional Identity* (Harvard University Press 2010).

[3] This is the focus of many publications. See, for example, Sujit Choudhry (ed.), *Constitutional Design for Divided Societies: Integration or Accommodation?* (Oxford University Press 2008).

[4] See, for example, Yash Ghai, 'Introduction: Nature and Origins of Autonomy' in Yash Ghai and Sophia Woodman (eds.), *Practising Self-Government: A Comparative Study of Autonomous Regions* (Cambridge University Press 2013) 2.

[5] Ruti G. Teitel, *Transitional Justice* (Oxford University Press 2000) 196.

Karl Kössler, *Who Are 'We, the People'? Pluralist Constitutional Identity after Democratic Transitions in African and European Countries*
In: *Constitutional Identity and Constitutionalism in Africa.* Edited by: Charles M. Fombad and Nico Steytler, Oxford University Press.
 DOI: 10.1093/oso/9780198906308.003.0008

something fluid, an order subject to change through amendment, judicial interpretation, and the like. Moreover, it is sometimes complemented by significant subnational constitutions to form together the constitutional system of the country. Secondly, all four case-study countries have multilevel systems, ones in which pluralist identity may potentially be reflected at two levels. My comparative analysis therefore takes into account both of these levels. In this context, it is important to note that the national constitution in a multilevel system is typically an incomplete document that 'leaves "space" in its constitutional architecture to be filled by the constitutions of its subnational units, even while it sets parameters within which those units are permitted to act'.[6] This space is always limited to some degree by the national constitution through the detailed prescription of contents, homogeneity clauses ensuring conformity, and the requirement of ex ante approval of the subnational constitution or its restrictive judicial interpretation ex post.[7] Within these limits, it then depends on whether subnational entities actually use this space. If they engage in a nation-building project,[8] they will frame the image of the people differently and often in contradiction to the country-wide project. Yet subnational entities of course may also choose *not* to use their constitutional space (for this specific purpose or generally). As we shall see, both the limits of this space and its actual use vary considerably between the case-study countries as well as between subnational entities.[9] This in itself is telling and points to the value of examining constitutional systems composed of two levels.

In view of its research question, the chapter has five sections. This introduction is followed by further explanation of what I take pluralist constitutional identity to mean and why I consider the framing of the image 'the people' as one of its core elements (section 2). Subsequently, the chapter discusses which parts of a constitutional system actually frame this image (section 3), after which it undertakes a comparative analysis of Ethiopia, South Africa, BiH, and Spain (section 4). Section 5 concludes the chapter.

2. Pluralist Constitutional Identity and the Image of 'the People'

'Constitutional identity' is an increasingly popular notion among constitutional theorists and comparative constitutional lawyers,[10] yet its conceptualisation varies considerably from case to case. Michel Rosenfeld, for example, asserts that constitutional identity emerges through a discursive process that involves the devices of negation, metaphor, and metonymy.[11] My chapter, by contrast, relies on Gary Jacobsohn's very different conceptualisation. He posits that constitutional identity is something shaped by both *internal* disharmonies, that is, incongruities within a constitution, and *external* disharmonies, that is, the

[6] G. Alan Tarr, 'Explaining Subnational Constitutional Space' (2011) *115 Penn State Law Review* 1133.

[7] See Francesco Palermo and Karl Kössler, *Comparative Federalism: Constitutional Arrangements and Case Law* (Hart Publishing 2017) 321.

[8] See Karl Kössler, 'Conclusions: Beyond the Illusion of Ethno-culturally Homogenous Territory' in Tove Malloy and Francesco Palermo (eds.), *Minority Accommodation through Territorial and Non-territorial Autonomy* (Oxford University Press 2015) 261–3.

[9] In the case of South Africa, for instance, only one province (the Western Cape) indeed has a constitution.

[10] See Mark Tushnet, 'How Do Constitutions Constitute Constitutional Identity?' (2010) *8 International Journal of Constitutional Law* 671.

[11] See Michel Rosenfeld, *The Identity of the Constitutional Subject: Selfhood, Citizenship, Culture, and Community* (Routledge 2010) 45–65.

gap between the constitution and historical changes in the political, social, and economic reality within which it operates.[12]

This understanding of constitutional identity offers two main advantages. Firstly, it perceives constitutional identity, in line with this chapter's opening quote, as something which is never fixed but fluid and provides a lens through which to look at this mutability. According to Jacobsohn, disharmonies function as a stimulus to change inasmuch as they could prompt political and judicial actors to contest the inherited identity inscribed in the constitution, which is by nature imperfect and open to such contestation. Secondly, the concept takes due account, through the focus on external disharmonies, of the rootedness of constitutions in their respective social, political, and economic contexts. It thus stands, from a methodological perspective, in the tradition of contextualism.[13]

Since the chapter concentrates on *pluralist* constitutional identity, another conceptual clarification is required. It seems fair to say that 'we are living in an era of pluralism, both in fact and in legal terms'.[14] Precisely because of its ubiquity, pluralism has become an extremely multifaceted notion. For some, it denotes political competition among multiple interest groups,[15] and for others, diversity of values or sets of values.[16] In studies of law, the rise—since the mid-1980s—of legal pluralism has drawn attention to 'the fact that there are multiple uncoordinated, coexisting or overlapping bodies of law'.[17] Pluralism in this legal sense almost naturally calls to mind, among European scholars, the interrelated constitutional orders of the European Union (EU) and its member states.[18] In Africa, it is perhaps the coexistence of formal written law and customary law that first comes to mind. In contrast to these understandings, 'pluralist identity' refers in this chapter to reflections of ethnic diversity in the constitutional norms framing the image of 'the people' as the constitutional subject.

In this regard, the focus of comparative research so far has been mainly on such reflections in provisions about state organisation, especially those concerning federalism and power-sharing. State organisation has been considered *the* part of constitutions that is decisive for whether the pure fact of diversity risks becoming a political powder keg, and strategies for avoiding this have been widely discussed in the so-called Lijphart-Horowitz debate or broader controversy between integrationists and accommodationists.[19] My focus is, instead, on a rather neglected dimension of pluralist constitutional identity, namely how the image of 'the people' as constitutional subject is framed. The comparative analysis in this chapter thus includes three types of provisions: firstly, formulas that explicitly define 'the people' as constitutional subject; secondly, symbols representing this constitutional subject in everyday life and therefore projecting an image beyond the period of

[12] See Jacobsohn (n. 2) 335.

[13] For a concise introduction to contextualism, see Vickie C. Jackson, 'Comparative Constitutional Law: Methodologies' in Michel Rosenfeld and András Sajó (eds.), *The Oxford Handbook of Comparative Constitutional Law* (Oxford University Press 2012) 7f.

[14] Palermo and Kössler (n. 7) 111.

[15] See Robert A. Dahl, *Who Governs? Democracy and Power in an American City* (Yale University Press 1961).

[16] See Richard Bellamy, *Liberalism and Pluralism: Towards a Politics of Compromise* (Routledge 1999).

[17] Brian Z. Tamanaha, 'Understanding Legal Pluralism: Past to Present, Local to Global' (2008) *30 Sydney Law Review* 375.

[18] See Neil Walker, 'The Idea of Constitutional Pluralism' (2002) *65 Modern Law Review* 317.

[19] For an overview, see John McGarry, Brendan O'Leary, and Richard Simeon, 'Integration or Accommodation? The Enduring Debate in Conflict Regulation' in Sujit Choudhry (ed.), *Constitutional Design for Divided Societies: Integration or Accommodation?* (Oxford University Press 2008) 41–88.

constitution-making; thirdly, constitutional narratives and aspirations that, respectively, interpret 'the people's' past and outline a vision for their future.[20]

3. Constitutional Provisions Framing the Image of 'the People': Where to Look for Them?

3.1 National and Subnational Constitutions

Since this chapter looks at constitutional systems as integrated wholes, a perspective limited to *national* constitutional provisions would be clearly insufficient and miss a part of the bigger picture. This is because subnational constitutions are, in many countries, increasingly bound up with expressivist features related to identity,[21] even though this fact has long been largely unnoticed in legal research. Over the past decade, that has started to change. Some have compared the legally formalised 'distinctive identity claims'[22] of subnational entities and how the judiciary responds to them. With reference to European case studies, others have claimed that 'subnational identity constitutionalism'[23] has become an increasingly widespread phenomenon. My chapter intends to go one step further by adopting an integrated perspective on what we might call 'multilevel identity constitutionalism'.

3.2 Preambles and Beyond

It seems to make intuitive sense that our comparative analysis should focus on preambles, which acquire importance for imagining the constitutional subject through their legal and social functions. Legally speaking, a global comparison recently revealed a trend towards preambles having greater binding force than before, whether it be as independent sources of rights, in connection with the constitutional provisions that follow them, or as guidelines for constitutional interpretation.[24] This increasing importance of preambles is itself due in no small part to interpretation by courts. For instance, in perhaps its most seminal judgement ever, the Supreme Court of India ruled in 1973 that the preamble of the Constitution enjoys legal force.[25] More recently, the Canadian Supreme Court held in the 1998 *Secession Reference* that the principles enshrined in the preamble 'dictate major elements of the architecture of the Constitution itself and are as such its lifeblood': they are 'invested with a powerful normative force, and are binding upon both courts and governments'.[26]

In addition to their legal dimension, preambles have a key social function in that they should convince the people who are subject to the constitution of its underlying rationale.

[20] These three types determine the structure of the comparative analysis. See sections 4.2.1, 4.2.2, and 4.2.3.

[21] See Cheryl Saunders, 'The Constitutional Credentials of State Constitutions' (2011) *42 Rutgers Law Review* 853, 860.

[22] Antoni Abat I. Ninet and James A. Gardner, 'Distinctive Identity Claims in Federal Systems: Judicial Policing of Subnational Variance' (2016) *14 International Journal of Constitutional Law* 378.

[23] Giacomo Delledonne and Giuseppe Martinico, 'Legal Conflict and Subnational Constitutionalism' (2012) *42 Rutgers Law Journal* 881, 882.

[24] See Liav Orgad, 'The Preamble in Constitutional Interpretation' (2011) *8 International Journal of Constitutional Law* 714, 731.

[25] *Kesavananda Bharati v State of Kerala* (1973) 4 S.C.C. 225.

[26] *Reference re Secession of Quebec* [1998] 2.S.C.R. 217 [51], [54].

In Plato's words, much as a physician should explain an illness and its cure to a patient 'in order to gain his co-operation, so the legislator must explain and justify his laws. Hence every law must be headed by a preamble justifying its provisions'.[27] Another aspect of a preamble's social function is its potential as a political resource. While a preamble which is inclusive and enjoys broad acceptance may have important integrative effects,[28] a divisive and partisan text can have serious disintegrative effects.

Even if these legal and social functions make preambles particularly important for how the image of the people is framed, they are not the only part of the constitution fulfilling this role. In fact, they are complemented in this respect by introductory articles and sometimes even provisions dispersed in latter parts of the basic law. The comparative study in this chapter thus goes beyond a narrow focus on preambles and scrutinises these other provisions as well.

3.3 The Original Constitutional Design and Constitutional Change

Inspired by Jacobsohn's conceptualisation of constitutional identity, this chapter explores provisions framing the image of the people in both the original constitutional design and with regard to subsequent change through political and/or judicial means. I shall take the 'original' constitutional design to mean the first new democratic constitution that is not an interim order. The points of departure are therefore the year 1978 for Spain, 1995 for BiH as well as Ethiopia, and 1996 for South Africa. Obviously, these original constitutional texts are the historically contingent results of bargains struck between centralising and decentralising forces of the time rather than theory-informed blueprints.[29] Ethnically diverse countries often demonstrate a penchant for vague compromise language in the name of 'constructive' ambiguity and/or for constitutional silences through which overly delicate matters are deferred for future resolution.[30]

Whereas radical expressivism subscribes to a 'static view of constitutional identity, fixing its content in the codified affirmations of a specific time and place',[31] it seems more accurate to perceive this identity as something fluid. Yet, as Jacobsohn convincingly argues, this fluidity is bounded because the textual commitments of the original design 'set the topography upon which the mapping of constitutional identity occurs'.[32] Such commitments erect certain barriers against change, which is, after all, the rationale of entrenchment.

Importantly, however, these barriers are not insurmountable. As the original constitutional design is only part of the picture and the image of the people is then further shaped through constitutional change, this chapter's comparative study takes due account of the various channels for such change. In Jacobsohn's view, 'internal disharmonies' within the constitution,

[27] Plato, *The Laws* (Trevor J. Saunders ed., Penguin Classics 2005) 137.

[28] See Dieter Grimm, 'Integration by Constitution' (2005) 3 *International Journal of Constitutional Law* 193, 193–203.

[29] See Vicki C. Jackson, 'Comparative Constitutional Federalism and Transnational Judicial Discourse' (2004) 2 *International Journal of Constitutional Law* 105; Donald L. Horowitz, 'Constitutional Design: Proposals versus Processes' in Andrew Reynolds (ed.), *The Architecture of Democracy: Constitutional Design, Conflict Management, and Democracy* (Oxford University Press 2002) 17.

[30] See Rosalind Dixon and Tom Ginsburg, 'Deciding Not to Decide: Deferral in Constitutional Design' (2011) 9 *International Journal of Constitutional Law* 636.

[31] Jacobsohn (n. 2) 13.

[32] Ibid.

often at first deliberately obscured by ambiguous language, and 'external disharmonies' due to changing realities may bring political and/or judicial actors to contest the inherited identity. Mostly, such change occurs, politically, through constitutional amendment and sometimes 'sub-constitutional' reforms[33] and, judicially, through constitutional interpretation. In the latter regard, it is important to recognise that judicial interpretation 'produces constitutional identity and is at the same time shaped, filled, and molded by the latter'.[34]

While the comparative analysis of how the image of the people is framed will thus look at both the original constitutional design and subsequent constitutional change, the following section starts with a brief account of the constitutional transitions in the four case studies. This is key because, self-evidently, initial designs and any subsequent changes do not appear out of nowhere. It is crucial to realise that even

> [f]ounding choices are themselves a blending of continuity and change . . . Imagining a polity in which the live hand of the present was the animating and sole directive source for its constitutive choices is to imagine a polity without a constitutional identity.[35]

While the original design influences subsequent change according to the logic of 'bounded fluidity',[36] the very same logic also implies that this design is itself influenced by the pre-transition order. Be that as it may, with the multilevel systems of our case-study countries it is key to recognise that transition has taken place in two distinct but interrelated constitutional arenas, that is, the national and subnational arenas.

4. Comparing Two African and Two European Countries

4.1 The Constitutional Heritage and Its Contestation (or Not): The Old Order and the Transition to Constitutional Democracy

4.1.1 Transition in the national constitutional arena

Under the rule of Emperor Haile Selassie I (1930–74) and the Derg military regime (1974–91), Ethiopia's attempts to build a nation based on a single language, Amharic, sparked resistance by several ethnic communities.[37] When ethnic-based armed movements seized power in 1991, a Transitional Period Charter was adopted and, four years thereafter, a definitive constitution. Ethnic diversity had been suppressed in preceding constitutional eras, but it now took centre stage in both political and legal terms. For instance, article 8 of the Constitution vests 'the Nations, Nationalities and Peoples of Ethiopia'[38] with 'all sovereign

[33] Such reforms occur in particular when constitutional amendment proves impossible but political actors are willing to consider alternative routes. A case in point is the 2006 Canadian parliamentary motion recognising 'that the Québécois form a nation within a united Canada'.

[34] Michel Rosenfeld, 'Constitutional Identity' in Michel Rosenfeld and András Sajó (eds.), *The Oxford Handbook of Comparative Constitutional Law* (Oxford University Press 2012) 771.

[35] Jacobsohn (n. 2) 324.

[36] Ibid. 349.

[37] See Yonatan Fessha, 'Constitutional Déjà Vu: Reading Subnational Constitutions in Ethiopia' in Patricia Popelier, Giacomo Delledonne, and Nicholas Aroney (eds.), *Routledge Handbook of Subnational Constitutionalism* (Routledge 2021) 2.

[38] On these categories, see section 4.2.1 below.

power', while article 39(1) entrenches their 'unrestricted right to self-determination up to secession'.[39]

Similarly, the South African Constitution resulted from a two-step constitutional process tainted by violence. The country's emergence from apartheid was not as bloody as Ethiopia's protracted civil war (1974–91), but the transitional period witnessed violent escalation of conflict both between white and black as well as, within the latter group, between supporters of the African National Congress (ANC) and Inkatha Freedom Party (IFP).[40] South Africa's two-step transition consisted in the adoption of the 1993 Interim Constitution and the 1996 'final' Constitution. The latter was drafted by the bicameral parliament that emerged from the first democratic elections in 1994.

This process was based on an ambitious public participation programme[41] as well as on thirty-four constitutional principles enshrined in schedule 4 of the 1993 Interim Constitution. Compliance with them had to be certified by the Constitutional Court.[42] These principles were negotiated by the outgoing apartheid government before losing its power entirely to the parliament elected in 1994. They were 'the focus of a deliberate effort to incorporate contradictory visions – in other words, disharmony – within the project of constitutional design',[43] or, according to a more critical account, the tools by which 'the old order would ensure its survival'.[44] Yet, arguably, constitutional change prevails over continuity, and the South African basic law is generally regarded by academic observers as a highly transformative constitution.[45] Likewise, the Constitutional Court described the Constitution as representing 'a radical rupture with a past based on intolerance and exclusion, and the movement forward to the acceptance of the need to develop a society based on equality and respect by all for all'.[46]

In comparison with the two African case-study countries, BiH's transition to constitutional democracy was characterised by a different kind of rupture, one that did not involve a transition period of several years but which was effected in only a few weeks in late 1995. Three years earlier this former constituent republic within socialist Yugoslavia's federal system[47] had descended into a civil war that resulted in the displacement of almost half of the pre-war population. Until then, BiH had been hailed as a model of peaceful interethnic coexistence, as the three main groups—Muslims (later called Bosniacs), Serbs,

[39] For a comparative perspective on the design of this secession clause, see Karl Kössler, 'Territorial Referendums from a Constitutionalist Perspective: Functions, Justifications and Legal Design' in Alberto López Basaguren and Leire Escajedo San-Epifanio (eds.), *Claims for Secession and Federalism: A Comparative Study with a Special Focus on Spain* (Springer 2019) 278.

[40] Christina Murray and Richard Simeon, 'Recognition without Empowerment: Minorities in a Democratic South Africa' (2007) *5 International Journal of Constitutional Law* 699, 712–13.

[41] See Hassen Ebrahim, *The Soul of a Nation: Constitution-Making in South Africa* (Oxford University Press 1998) 246.

[42] *Certification of the Constitution of the Republic of South Africa* 1996 (4) SA 744 (CC); *Certification of the Amended Text of the Constitution of the Republic of South Africa* 1997 (2) SA 97.

[43] Jacobsohn (n. 2) 122.

[44] Makau wa Mutua, 'Hope and Despair for a New South Africa: The Limits of Rights Discourse' (1997) *10 Harvard Human Rights Journal* 63, 81.

[45] See Heinz Klug, 'Constitutional Identity and Change' (2011) *47 Tulsa Law Review* 46, 47.

[46] *Minister of Home Affairs v Fourie*, CCT 60/04 (2005) [10].

[47] See Mitja Žagar, 'The Collapse of the Yugoslav Federation and the Viability of Asymmetrical Federalism' in Sergio Ortino, Mitja Žagar, and Vojtech Mastny (eds.), *The Changing Faces of Federalism: Institutional Reconfiguration in Europe from East to West* (Manchester University Press 2005) 107–33.

and Croats[48]—as well as fifteen national minorities had for ages been living intermingled with each other. After a NATO intervention ended the fighting, the constitutional future of BiH was determined at the United States (US) military base in Dayton, Ohio. The General Framework Agreement for Peace ('Dayton Agreement'), signed in December 1995, aimed at creating security through stability and therefore forced the former warring parties together in a single state.

Three facts vividly demonstrate the current constitution's blatant lack, unlike South Africa's, of local ownership. Firstly, the Constitution is Annex 4 of the Dayton Agreement, an international agreement negotiated in only a few weeks. Secondly, its article 12(1) states explicitly that 'this Constitution shall enter into force upon signature of the General Framework Agreement as a constitutional act *amending and superseding* the Constitution of the Republic of Bosnia and Herzegovina' (emphasis added). This wording clarifies that the Dayton Constitution was not in line with constitutional amendment rules in force at that time and had come about in a revolutionary manner. Thirdly, whereas its closing provisions consider the whole Dayton Agreement to be authentic in the Bosnian, Croatian, Serbian, and English languages, the Constitutional Court regards only the English version as authentic and standard for correcting misleading translations in the other versions.[49] This also has to do with the fact that three out of nine court members are 'international judges' who are often not versed in local languages.[50]

Spain's transition to constitutional democracy was not as abrupt and driven by external actors as that of BiH, and it was certainly more peaceful than that in all the other case-study countries. This process began with the death in 1975 of General Francisco Franco, whose dictatorship of almost four decades had resulted from the victory of the right-wing nationalist faction in the Spanish Civil War (1936–9). According to most accounts, the transition lasted until the adoption of the Constitution of 1978, an event preceded by the first parliamentary elections in 1977. Spain's path towards democracy was less confrontational than in the other case studies, and aimed instead at a gradual transformation of Francoist institutions and laws. Importantly, however, the new order clearly distanced itself from Franco's suppression of ethnic diversity, which had resulted from an emphasis on Spain as a 'unity of destiny' (*unidad de destino*) that is organic, ordained by God, and predicated on the Castilian language and culture.[51] The new accommodation of diversity revolved around the 1978 Constitution's legal framework for the establishment of autonomous communities (1979–83). A key point is the individual adaptability of self-government through statutes of autonomy, or subnational quasi-constitutions, which are concluded bilaterally between each autonomous community and the national government. These statutes perfectly illustrate why the narrow view that the national basic law is the only point of departure for the formation of a new constitutional identity is, in multilevel systems, often

[48] In the 1991 census, 43.4 per cent of the population identified as Muslims by nationality, 31.2 per cent as Serbs, 17.4 per cent as Croats, 5.5 per cent as Yugoslavs, and the remaining population as belonging to national minorities.

[49] See Joseph Marko, 'Five Years of Constitutional Jurisprudence in Bosnia and Herzegovina: A First Balance' (European Diversity and Autonomy Papers, July 2004) 9–12.

[50] These judges are selected by the president of the European Court of Human Rights after consultation with the Presidency of BiH (article 6(1a)).

[51] See Daniele Conversi, 'Autonomous Communities and the Ethnic Settlement in Spain' in Yash Ghai (ed.), *Autonomy and Ethnicity: Negotiating Competing Claims in Multi-ethnic States* (Cambridge University Press 2000) 138.

insufficient: in some of these systems, the subnational constitutional sphere may be equally important.

4.1.2 Transition in the subnational constitutional arena

In Ethiopia, the 1995 Constitution, in articles 50(5) and 52(2b), grants the legislatures of the ten states the power to enact state constitutions.[52] According to the country's peculiar system of non-judicial review,[53] it is ultimately up to the House of Federation, the second chamber of the national parliament, to verify compliance with the national constitution.[54] Soon after the transition, all states adopted constitutions (1995–8) and all revised them around the same time (2001–4).[55] Importantly, however, these revisions were engineered in a top-down manner from the prime minister's office, 'on his order, and without involving the regional authorities; indeed, it took place without their knowledge'.[56]

It is this predominance of a single party functioning in a highly centralised manner that has been widely blamed for the ostensible uniformity of the state constitutions. It therefore hardly comes as a surprise that state constitutions 'do not feature in constitutional and policy debates. Neither do they generate interest among the public.'[57] However, some observers claim that the common view of these basic laws as mere copies of the national constitution is not justified anymore in the light of revisions in the early 2000s that arguably gave rise to some subnational constitutional activism.[58]

By contrast, South Africa is famous for an almost complete lack of such activism. To this day, only one of the country's nine provinces, the Western Cape, has a constitution. Under the South African Constitution, the speaker of the provincial legislature must submit the text of a subnational basic law to be certified by the Constitutional Court,[59] which requires compliance with national constitutional specifications concerning both procedure[60] and content.[61] Although the concept of certification stemmed from the two-step process of national constitution-making,[62] it also proved convenient as a means for national politicians to keep a lid on the (potential) constitutional ambitions of the provinces.[63]

That certification is indeed not something to be taken for granted became clear in the case of the KwaZulu-Natal Constitution. Drafted by the IFP-dominated provincial government,

[52] Zemelak Ayele, 'Subnational Constitutions in the Ethiopian Federal System in Light of the Demos, the Federalists and Deliberative Democracy Models of Subnational Constitutionalism' (2019) *31 Journal of Ethiopian Law* 153ff.

[53] See Yonatan T. Fessha and Zemelak Ayele, 'Giving "Shape and Texture" to a Federal System? Ethiopia's Courts and Its Unusual Umpire' in Yonatan T. Fessha and Karl Kössler (eds.), *Federalism and the Courts in Africa: Design and Impact in Comparative Perspective* (Routledge 2020) 60–1.

[54] Articles 83 and 84 of the Ethiopian Constitution.

[55] For an overview of the state constitutions, see Christophe van der Beken, *Completing the Constitutional Architecture: A Comparative Analysis of Sub-national Constitutions in Ethiopia* (Addis Ababa University Press 2017).

[56] Zemelak Ayele, 'The Politics of Subnational Constitutions and Local Government in Ethiopia' (2014) *6 Perspectives of Federalism* 89, 105.

[57] Fessha (n. 37) 1.

[58] See Christophe Van der Beken, 'Sub-national Constitutional Autonomy in Ethiopia: On the Road to Distinctive Regional Constitutions' (IXth World Congress of Constitutional Law, Workshop 2: Sub-national constitutions in federal and quasi-federal constitutional states, Oslo, 16–20 June 2014) 1.

[59] Section 144(1).

[60] Section 142.

[61] Section 143.

[62] See section 4.1.1 above.

[63] See Christina Murray, 'Provincial Constitutions in South Africa: The (Non)Example of the Western Cape' (2001) *49 Jahrbuch des Öffentlichen Rechts* 481, 504.

it failed to be certified. The Constitutional Court famously pointed to 'fundamental respects in which the provincial constitution is fatally flawed'.[64] In particular, it criticised the constitution's usurpation of national powers,[65] and held that the KwaZulu-Natal legislature seemed to have adopted the text 'under a misapprehension that it enjoyed a relationship of co-supremacy with the national legislature and even the Constitutional Assembly'.[66] After this damning verdict, the IFP refrained from submitting a revised constitution, mainly because Zulu nationalism was subsiding[67] and the ANC had ousted the party in 2004 from provincial power.

Probably influenced in part by the court's harsh reaction to KwaZulu-Natal's constitutional project, the Western Cape took a very cautious approach. Thirty-nine out of eighty-four sections copied the national constitution with only minor rephrasing, while another nineteen sections implemented sections of the national constitution or referred to them.[68] The Court at first withheld certification,[69] but granted it once provisions about the main contentious issue, namely the provincial electoral system, were removed.[70]

Whereas in 1999 one could arguably still claim that there was a 'developing jurisprudence of South African provincial constitutions',[71] provincial constitutionalism since then has turned out to be an 'empty promise'.[72] This has been attributed to various reasons: firstly, the mostly artificial creation rather than organic historical evolution of the provinces; secondly, their ability to manage on the basis of the default constitution contained in sections 104–41 of the 1996 Constitution, which even the Constitutional Court called a 'complete blueprint for the regulation of government within provinces';[73] and, thirdly, the ANC's deeply rooted suspicion of subnational constitutionalism, illustrated by its boycott of the ceremony celebrating South Africa's only provincial constitution.[74]

In comparison, the subnational constitutional arena is clearly far more important in the two European case studies. What distinguishes BiH from the other cases is that the constitutions of its only two entities—the predominantly Serb-populated Republika Srpska (RS) and the largely Croat-Bosniac Federation of Bosnia and Herzegovina (FBH)—preceded the national constitution. Both of these entities were established during the war as '"states" with proper constitutions'.[75] In 1992, little more than a month after BiH's declaration of independence, the country was itself faced with the proclamation of an independent unitary RS on its territory. The FBH was created in 1994 to end hostilities between Bosniacs and Croats and subdivided into ten cantons. In terms of the 1995 Dayton Constitution,

64 *Certification of the Kwazulu-Natal Constitution* 1996 (4) SA 1098 [13].
65 Ibid. [14ff].
66 Ibid. [15].
67 See Rod Alence, 'South Africa after Apartheid: The First Decade' (2004) *15 Journal of Democracy* 78, 82f.
68 See Murray (n. 63) 488.
69 *Certification of the Constitution of the Western Cape* 1997 (4) SA 795 (CC).
70 *Certification of the Constitution of the Western Cape* 1998 (1) SA 655 (CC).
71 Robert F. Williams, 'Comparative Subnational Constitutional Law: South Africa's Provincial Constitutional Experiments' (1999) *40 South Texas Law Review* 625, 647.
72 Nico Steytler, 'Provincial Constitutions in South Africa: An Empty Promise' in Patricia Popelier, Giacomo Delledonne, and Nicholas Aroney (eds.), *Routledge Handbook of Subnational Constitutionalism* (Routledge 2021) 1.
73 *Certification of the Constitution of the Western Cape* 1997 (CCT6/97) [1997] ZACC 8 ('*Certification WC* judgment') [15].
74 See Murray (n. 63) 481f.
75 Jens Woelk, 'Bosnia-Herzegovina: Trying to Build a Federal State on Paradoxes' in Michael Burgess and G. Alan Tarr (eds.), *Constitutional Dynamics in Federal Systems: Sub-national Perspectives* (McGill-Queen's University Press 2012) 110.

the two (henceforth subnational) entities were obliged to amend their basic laws within three months from the entry into force of the new national constitution.[76] However, they failed—in keeping with their general interest in preserving the status quo—to make these adaptations. It was eventually up to the Constitutional Court to demonstrate the limits of subnational constitutional space and enforce amendments.[77]

This contrasts with the statutes of Spain's autonomous communities, which are bilaterally negotiated organic laws approved by both the respective regional parliament and the national parliament.[78] Although these laws are not formally called constitutions, observers qualify them as such,[79] or at least as 'quasi-constitutional norms';[80] moreover, the Constitutional Court recognises them as superior to all regional and national law except for the Constitution.[81] Importantly, the latter are explicitly allowed, beyond compulsory core content such as institutional organisation and powers,[82] to address certain optional matters, such as regional flags[83] and other symbols, which are clearly relevant for the creation of constitutional identity. Like Ethiopia, Spain underwent a second wave of subnational constitution-making in which the statutes were reformed between 2006 and 2011, thereby enhancing their materially constitutional nature. Besides bills of rights, they contain plenty of provisions that frame the image of the people as constitutional subject. However, the most ambitious statute, Catalonia's, came face to face with the limits of regional-identity affirmation when the Constitutional Court declared fourteen provisions unconstitutional and, in regard to twenty-seven others, issued a binding interpretation that required them to be consistent with the national constitution.[84]

4.2 Framing the Image of the People as Constitutional Subject

4.2.1 'We the people(s)': Formulas explicitly defining the constitutional subject

Many constitutions contain explicit definitions of the subject that gives itself this basic law. With such formulas, the famous first words of the US preamble referring to '[w]e the people of the United States' have undoubtedly been influential. However, this homogenising phrase, one picturing a somewhat monolithic community, is not the only one in use. In fact, it is curious that the initial wording of the US preamble, as introduced at the 1787 Philadelphia Convention, referred separately to the people of the thirteen single states[85] and that there is no evidence as to why it was later changed.[86] Among preambles still in force, that of Australia, for example, follows the original US approach by stating that '[t]he people

[76] Article 12(2).

[77] On the seminal Partial Decision U5/98 III of 1 July 2000 (Constituent Peoples case), see section 4.2.1 below.

[78] Article 147(3) of the Constitution.

[79] See César Colino, 'Constitutional Change without Constitutional Reform: Spanish Federalism and the Revision of Catalonia's Statute of Autonomy' (2009) *39 Publius* 262.

[80] See Francisco Rubio Llorente, 'El bloque de la constitucionalidad' (1989) *27 Revista Española de Derecho Constitucional* 9, 25f.

[81] STC 66/1985 FJ 1 and STC 4/1981 FJ 3.

[82] Article 147(2).

[83] Article 4(2).

[84] STC 31/2010.

[85] 'We the people of the States of . . . do ordain, declare, and establish the following Constitution for the Government of Ourselves and our Posterity.'

[86] Orgad (n. 24) 718.

of New South Wales, Victoria, South Australia, Queensland, and Tasmania . . . have agreed to unite in one indissoluble Federal Commonwealth'. Switzerland's preamble demonstrates yet another option by defining the 'we' as 'the Swiss People and the Cantons', while Russia's wording aims to be pluralist in its reference to '[w]e, the multinational people of the Russian federation'.

Among our four case studies, it is Ethiopia that deviates most clearly from the homogenising phrase introduced and popularised by the US Constitution. Indeed, the preamble of its constitution begins with the words '[w]e, the nations, nationalities and peoples of Ethiopia', and goes on to say that the 'political community' they form is based on the 'full and free exercise [of the] right to self-determination'. The latter includes, besides language and cultural rights, political representation and territorial autonomy, as well as a right to secession.[87] While article 39(5) defines 'nations, nationalities and peoples' through both objective elements and subjective ones such as 'collective identity' and 'a common psychological make-up', there remains much ambiguity about how the constitutional subject is imagined.

Given the controversies during the transitional period on how to deal with Ethiopia's more than eighty ethnic groups, it seems probable that this vague terminology was indeed employed 'in the hope of avoiding highly sensitive questions about what the nature, and therefore status, of groups of people in the Ethiopian state is'.[88] Some observers today claim that the three notions of 'nation', 'nationality', and 'people' should be interpreted as denoting a hierarchy of groups in exactly that order with regard to population size and political clout.[89] But the Constitution does not distinguish between the three categories of groups and provides, in the aforementioned article 39(5), a single, common definition of them.[90] Unlike the solemn declarations that many other countries make about the unity and common destiny of the people, Ethiopia's preamble is striking for its pragmatic tone, one suggesting a dispassionate commitment to living together as opposed to entering a 'love marriage'. It merely states that the nations, nationalities, and peoples 'have, through continuous interaction on various levels and forms of life, built up common interest and have also contributed to the emergence of a common outlook'.

Similar to the case at the national level, the state constitutions start with preambles defining the constitutional subject. These generally characterise the basic law—in line with the logic of Ethiopia's ethnic federalism—as an emanation of the will of the group that the creation of the state was supposed to empower.[91] The preamble of Oromia, for instance, refers to 'we the Oromo people' and not to the people *of* the state of Oromia.

In stark contrast to Ethiopia, South Africa's preamble follows in the terminological footsteps of the US preamble. The use of the formula '[w]e, the people of South Africa' in the 1993 Interim Constitution has been called, due to its adoption by the unrepresentative tricameral parliament, a 'legal fiction'.[92] At any rate, the same homogenising phrase appears

[87] Article 39(1)–(3) of the Constitution.

[88] John M. Cohen, 'Ethnic Federalism in Ethiopia' (1995) *2 Northeast African Studies* 157.

[89] See Alem Habtu, 'Multiethnic Federalism in Ethiopia: A Study of the Secession Clause in the Constitution' (2005) *35 Publius* 313, 324.

[90] Yonatan T. Fessha, *Ethnic Diversity and Federalism: Constitution Making in South Africa and Ethiopia* (Ashgate 2010), 192ff.

[91] See Van der Beken (n. 58) 5.

[92] Heinz Klug, *The Constitution of South Africa: A Contextual Analysis* (Hart Publishing 2010) 77.

in the 1996 Constitution and makes it clear that South Africa, like the United States as described in *Texas v White*,[93] is conceived as a covenant among individuals. Although the further emphasis in the preamble on 'building a united . . . South Africa' and in section 1 on 'one, sovereign, democratic state' reinforces this conception, it is counterbalanced by recognition of diversity. Indeed, according to the preamble, the people '[b]elieve that South Africa belongs to all who live in it, united in our diversity'. This is a representation, in constitutional form, of the oft repeated idea that the country is a 'rainbow nation'.[94] Attempting to navigate between (at least) twelve different conceptions of South Africa,[95] the 1996 Constitution does recognise diversity but not in any territorialised form, which is in line with the ANC's commitment to non-racialism. Put differently, 'differences can be reflected in cultural and social life yet are not to be entrenched and institutionalised in the political process'.[96]

In fact, the provinces' lack of ethnic identity is also reflected in their approach to defining the constitutional subject. Ethnicity has not been their explicit basis because the provinces are rooted in the nine 'development regions' of the 1980s. Moreover, the territorial demarcation commission, formed in 1993, aimed primarily at the reduction of territorial disparities in social and economic development,[97] even if most provinces each ended up with one ethnic group in a majority position. The only explicitly ethnic-based provincial project, the idea of an Afrikaner *volkstaat*, was rejected by the ANC in 1996, and KwaZulu-Natal remained—in contrast to Ethiopian states—the only province whose name has ethnic connotations. However, even that province's uncertified constitution refrained in its preamble from focusing on its Zulu majority. 'We, the people of KwaZulu-Natal' was complemented by a declared mindfulness of the province's 'unique and diverse heritage'. In the case of Western Cape's preamble, no ethnic-identity language is used, but the people of the province declare that they act '[i]n humble submission to the Almighty God'. While this religious reference angered the ANC because it repeated the opening line of the apartheid constitution and contradicted the party's avowed secularism, the Constitutional Court did not see the statement as being contrary to diversity.[98]

In the case of BiH, a controversial preliminary question regarding the definition of the constitutional subject in the preamble was whether the latter actually has normative force. Invoking the examples of the French Constitution's preamble, which integrates the 1789 Declaration of the Rights of Man and the Citizen, and of the Canadian *Secession Reference* case,[99] the Constitutional Court clarified that provisions of the preamble are 'not merely descriptive, but are also invested with a powerful normative force, thereby serving as a sound standard of judicial review'.[100] As for the constitutional subject, this preamble states that

[93] *Texas v White* 74 US (7 Wall) 700 (1869).

[94] The term was coined by Archbishop Desmond Tutu and gained currency thanks to an early speech by President Nelson Mandela: 'Each of us is as intimately attached to the soil of this beautiful country as are the famous jacaranda trees of Pretoria and the mimosa trees of the bushveld—a rainbow nation at peace with itself and the world.'

[95] See Donald L. Horowitz, *A Democratic South Africa? Constitutional Engineering in a Divided Society* (University of California Press 1991) 3–9.

[96] Christina Murray and Richard Simeon, 'Recognition without Empowerment: Minorities in a Democratic South Africa' (2007) 5 *International Journal of Constitutional Law* 699, 714.

[97] See Anthony Egan and Rupert Taylor, 'South Africa: The Failure of Ethno-territorial Politics' in John Coakley (ed.), *The Territorial Management of Ethnic Conflict* (2nd edn, Frank Cass 2003), 105f.

[98] See Steytler (n. 72) 13.

[99] *Reference re Secession of Quebec* [1998] 2.S.C.R. 217 [51]. See above section 3.2.

[100] Constitutional Court of Bosnia and Herzegovina, U 5/98-III [26].

the new basic law was determined by 'Bosniacs, Croats, and Serbs, as constituent peoples (along with Others), and citizens of Bosnia and Herzegovina'.

A clash between this provision and the definitions of the respective constitutional subjects in the entity constitutions was inevitable. The RS Constitution of 1992, in article 1, had emphasised 'the natural, inalienable and untransferable right of the Serb people to self-determination' and defined the RS as 'the State of the Serb people and of all its citizens'. Similarly, the 1994 FBH Constitution, in article 1, determined who rules by referring only to Bosniacs and Croats as the entity's 'constituent peoples'. The Constitutional Court was thus faced with the fundamental question of whether the references in the national preamble to three constituent peoples and to the goal of 'peaceful relations within a pluralist society' allow such affirmations of ethnic domination in subnational constitutions.[101] In the seminal *Constituent Peoples* case,[102] the judges invalidated parts of the entities' constitutions. They ruled that the preamble, read in conjunction with articles 1(2) and 2(4) of the Constitution, guarantees the 'collective equality' of the three constituent peoples not only at the national but also at the subnational level.[103] The court stated emphatically that the creation of two entities through article 1(3) 'cannot serve as a constitutional legitimation for ethnic domination, national homogenization or a right to uphold the effects of ethnic cleansing'.[104]

The conception of the subnational constitutional subject as one group (in the RS) or two groups (in the FBH) also had to give way to equal status of the constituent peoples in both entities for another reason. Such a conception formed the basis of an empirically proven, systematic, and purposeful discriminatory practice on ethnic grounds,[105] which violated both the individual's right to non-discrimination (in article 2(4)) and refugees and displaced persons' right to return (in article 2(5)). To respect the latter right, both entities are obliged not only to refrain from harassment but also to 'establish necessary political, economic and social conditions conducive to the voluntary return and harmonious reintegration'.[106] As the two entities failed to change their constitutions in order to comply with the ruling, amendments were ultimately effected in 2002 by the High Representative for BiH.[107] This official, accountable only to the Peace Implementation Council (PIC), carried out the intervention on the basis of the 'Bonn Powers' granted to him by the PIC in 1997.[108]

While interventionism has been pervasive in the BiH case, transition in Spain was much more of an internal process but still quite a delicate one. The preamble to the 1978 Constitution first proclaims, fearing the disintegration of a state held together by Franco's repression, that the 'Spanish Nation' is acting 'in the exercise of its sovereignty'. However, this is balanced by article 2, which refers not only to 'the indissoluble unity of the Spanish Nation, the common and indivisible homeland of all Spaniards' but also to the 'right to self-government of the nationalities and regions'. This provision has been

[101] See Joseph Marko, '"United in Diversity"? Problems of State and Nation-Building in Post-Conflict Situations: The Case of Bosnia-Herzegovina' (2006) *30 Vermont Law Review* 503, 532.

[102] For an in-depth analysis of the ruling, see Woelk (n. 75) 120–2.

[103] U 5/98-III [56]–[61].

[104] U 5/98-III [61].

[105] For empirical evidence, see regarding the RS, U 5/98-III [86]–[89], and regarding the FBH, U 5/98-III [131]–[136].

[106] Regarding the RS, see U 5/98-III [95] and for the FBH, see U 5/98-III [139].

[107] See Florian Bieber, *Post-war Bosnia* (Palgrave 2006), 132.

[108] The PIC is an international forum of fifty-five states involved in the peace process.

aptly described as an 'authentic point of encounter between different conceptions of the Spanish nation'.[109]

But almost three decades later, 'encounter' would give way to open conflict. Whereas article 1 of its first statute in 1979 still defined Catalonia—in line with the terminology of the Spanish Constitution—as a 'nationality', the new text proposed by the Catalan parliament in 2005 went beyond that to talk of a 'nation'. After bilateral negotiations with the national government, this was watered down to more ambiguous wording. The preamble then stated that

> [i]n reflection of the feelings and the wishes of the citizens of Catalonia, the Parliament of Catalonia has defined Catalonia as a nation by an ample majority. The Spanish Constitution, in its second Article, recognises the national reality of Catalonia as a nationality.

Moreover, the agreed text stated, in article 1, that Catalonia as a 'nationality' (not as a 'nation') 'exercises its self-government by constituting itself as an Autonomous Community'. When the statute was challenged, the Constitutional Court refrained from striking down all these provisions but relied instead on rendering interpretations in conformity with the Constitution. It made clear that a community may define itself as a national reality in an ideological, historical, or cultural sense, but that under the current Constitution the only nation in legal-constitutional terms is the Spanish one.[110] To be sure, the Catalan Statute was exceptional in its attempts of self-definition as a nation. Yet, unlike in their old statutes, other autonomous communities also included provisions to characterise themselves at least as historical nationalities (e.g. Andalusia and Valencia) or 'historical and cultural community (Castile and León).[111]

4.2.2 Our symbols: representations of the constitutional subject in everyday life

Operating in a more indirect way than explicit formulas, the symbols enshrined in constitutions (for instance, flags, coats of arms, and anthems) also serve to characterise the people giving itself a constitution. Importantly, the social impact of such symbols depends very much on the extent to which, beyond their entrenchment in the basic law, they are present in everyday life as constant representations and reminders of collective identity, something which has been called 'banal nationalism'.[112] To be sure, symbols sometimes have disintegrative effects, as 'banal nationalism' may form the basis for violent nationalism, yet they also have significant integrative potential if national as well as subnational constitutions both adopt an approach of inclusive symbolism.

In the Ethiopian case, a tension between diffident unity- and identity-affirmations by groups dominating their own states characterises the symbols supposed to represent the constitutional subject at the national and subnational levels. Article 3(1) of the Constitution has retained, with certain modifications, Ethiopia's old flag.[113] But the yellow pentagram in

[109] Jordi Solé i Tura, one of the seven framers of the Spanish Constitution, quoted in Conversi (n. 51) 126.

[110] STC 31/2010, FJ 12. For a comprehensive analysis of the judgment, see the special volume, 'Especial Sentència 31/2010 del Tribunal Constitucional, sobre l'Estatut d'autonomia de Catalunya de 2006' of the *Revista catalana de dret public* (2010) http://revistes.eapc.gencat.cat/index.php/rcdp/issue/view/23 (last accessed 1 March 2022).

[111] See Delledonne and Martinico (n. 23) 881; Rosario Serra and Pablo Oñate, 'The Reform of the Spanish Subnational Constitutions: Rules and Regulations and Political Context', Paper presented at the VII World Congress on Constitutional Law, Athens, 2007, 12–17.

[112] Michael Billig, *Banal Nationalism* (Sage Publications 2005).

[113] See Fessha (n. 90) 195.

its centre, which is also the national emblem, is a new element and 'shall reflect the hope of the Nations, Nationalities, Peoples as well as religious communities of Ethiopia to live together in equality and unity'.[114] In addition, many states made use of the authorisation in article 3(3) of the Constitution to determine their own symbols and did so via ordinary legislation. In some cases, however, the state constitution itself provides binding indications. To cite Oromia's Constitution again, its article 3 stipulates that the 'Oda' sign, referring to the tree where the Oromos meet under the traditional Gada governance system, has to be in the middle of the state flag.[115] This appears alongside the above-mentioned definition of the constitutional subject, and is yet another element identifying the state of Oromia with the Oromo group.

In the South African case, an attempt to combine continuity and change is particularly evident in its regulations on the national anthem, which shall be determined, according to section 4 of the Constitution, by the president by proclamation. It is indeed impressive that an African hymn, sung at anti-apartheid protests, is blended with the old national anthem and that the anthem's text features five languages. Similar inclusive symbolism is also evident, for example, in the flag (Schedule 1 of the Constitution), which mixes colours of the South African republic (1852–1902) with those of the ANC flag. Moreover, the 'V' that joins together in the flag's centre is supposed to epitomise the coming-together of the country's diverse population. The coat of arms is especially noteworthy because it features this same motto of 'unity in diversity' in the ancient Khoisan language and symbolises it in the style of Khoisan rock art.[116]

Having sought to ensure inclusive symbolism at the national level and fearing separate identities in some cases, the ANC was generally sceptical about provincial symbols. Both the failed KwaZulu-Natal and the Western Cape constitutions enabled their establishment through a provincial law passed by a two-thirds majority.[117] But even in the latter case, a flag has never been designed, and a coat of arms, existing in the other eight provinces as well, features unpolitical symbols representing the areas around Cape Town.[118] Subnational constitutional activism thus did not play any role at all.

In a country as divided as BiH, symbols have been far more contentious, and it proved impossible to reach consensus in the Dayton Constitution. Article 1(6) therefore deferred the matter by stating that the country 'shall have such symbols as are decided by its Parliamentary Assembly and approved by its Presidency'. But seeing as divisions have persisted since 1995, it remained impossible for these two institutions—that is, the ethnically segmented bicameral parliament and the presidency comprising one Bosniac, one Serb, and one Croat[119]—to find a solution. Eventually, it again fell to the High Representative for BiH to impose a decision regarding the country's flag and coat of arms. Both of these feature references, through the use of blue, to Europe, but also emphasise the predominance of the constituent peoples, represented by the corners of a yellow triangle. As for the anthem of BiH, in an absurd development, the High Representative determined the melody but

[114] Article 3(2).
[115] See Van der Beken (n. 58) 7.
[116] See Fessha (n. 90) 100.
[117] See George Devenish, 'The Making and Significance of the Draft KwaZulu-Natal Constitution' (1999) 47 *Jahrbuch des Öffentlichen Rechts* 503, 515.
[118] See Steytler (n. 72) 13.
[119] Article 5.

not the text, on which the various groups still do not agree. Indeed, controversy continues to surround even what are arguably less important symbols, such as registration plates, bank notes, and passports.[120] In overall terms, then, state symbols have not had integrative power, and Bosnian Serbs and Croats, for instance, still identify themselves more so with Serbia and Croatia, respectively, than with BiH.

The situation is no better at the level of entities whose symbols have even been called 'the enemy of the return process'.[121] The Constitutional Court held that the flag and coat of arms of the RS and FBH are unconstitutional because their symbols represent only Serbs, in the first case, and Bosniacs and Croats, in the latter. The judges saw this as a violation of the above-mentioned constitutional principle of equality of the constituent peoples.[122] In the RS case, they also invalidated legislation about the anthem, a song that dates to 1872, glorifies the Serb people, and calls on God to unify the Serb brothers. Moreover, the Court ruled that article 3 of the RS Law on the Use of Flag, Coat of Arms and Anthem, which stipulated that symbols are to be used 'in accordance with the moral norms of the Serb people', was discriminatory and thus unconstitutional.

Compared to BiH, there has been much less controversy about symbols in Spain. Article 4(1) of the Constitution entrenches the Spanish flag. However, article 4(2) immediately points out that the regional statutes may recognise flags which 'shall be used together with the flag of Spain on their public buildings and in their official ceremonies'. All autonomous communities made use of this opportunity, and today have their own flags and coats of arms. By contrast, there is significant variation concerning the relevance of their anthems. Whereas some are little-known regional songs, others are politically loaded. For example, article 8(4) of the Statue of Catalonia entrenched an anthem (*Els Segadors*) which had already been officially recognised by a regional law since 1993 and is a symbol of anti-Spanish resistance. It refers to the Reapers' War (1640–59), in particular to the initial uprising of peasants against the royal army and their call to fellow Catalans to take arms.

Unlike in the case of BiH, though, the Constitutional Court was fairly relaxed and did not object to the anthem or other symbols in terms of their substance. What raised eyebrows was the formal qualification in article 8(1) of the Statute that '[t]he flag, the holiday and the anthem are the *national* symbols of Catalonia' (emphasis added), even though the same provision had made it clear that the latter is 'defined as a nationality by Article 1'. The judges felt obliged to reiterate that 'national' refers to 'nationality' and not to 'nation', and that the nationality of Catalonia is integrated in 'the indissoluble unity of the Spanish Nation', as mentioned in article 2 of the Constitution.[123]

4.2.3 Our past and future: narratives and aspirations

Invocations of the past are widely used to further characterise the people forming the constitutional subject, and they come in very different shapes. Some constitutions include lengthy history lectures on nearly everything that preceded the founding moment, while others limit themselves to passing mentions. The latter do not themselves provide a sufficient narrative. However, like the short reference in the preamble of the eventually unratified 2004

[120] See Christian Steiner and Nedim Ademović, 'Article I.6' in Christian Steiner and Nedim Ademović (eds.), *Constitution of Bosnia and Herzegovina: Commentary* (Konrad Adenauer Stiftung 2010) 117f.

[121] Ibid. 'Article II.4' 508.

[122] U 4/04 of 31 March 2006 [125ff].

[123] STC 31/2010, FJ 12.

EU Constitutional Treaty to the continent's 'bitter experiences', they may be considered a basis from which to create such a narrative.[124]

It is important to note that this 'constitutional storytelling' may shape common belonging by reminding people of quite different elements of history. These may be glorious struggles for independence or other stories of pride, as in the preamble of the Constitution of China, which declares that it 'is one of the countries with the longest histories in the world'. Yet, as Ernest Renan famously emphasised in 1882, it seems at least equally important as a foundation for common belonging to share stories of common suffering and grievances because there is hardly anything more unifying than surviving adverse conditions. Together, both positive and negative memories create a link between the past and the present.[125]

However, they do so only regarding the past and present from the historically contingent perspective of the framers of the constitution, and their narrative can become outdated. In this regard, an oft-cited blatant example is the Irish Constitution of 1937, which is adopted, according to its preamble, '[i]n the Name of the Most Holy Trinity, from Whom is all authority and to Whom, as our final end, all actions both of men and States must be referred'. Quite evidently, such a statement no longer fits the social reality of a country whose Roman Catholic character has been diminished by non-religious new generations and the advent of new religions due to immigration.[126] It has therefore become exclusionary.

Backward-looking statements serving as narratives about the constitutional subject are often complemented by forward-looking ones that outline its aspirations. In constitutional terms, supreme goals can be enshrined in different kinds of provisions. Notably, they are reflected in preambles and directive principles for policies. It is certainly true that such provisions often refer to ideas of such abstraction that their value may be open to question: 'The concern is that everyone in the world could agree with some such statements, which means that no one in the world will actually care about doing so.'[127] But instead of generally dismissing the entrenchment of goals, especially as directive principles, a more differentiated view should be adopted. While they evidently have an important guiding function in regard to legal, political, and/or moral obligations in some countries (e.g. India), this is less so in others (e.g. Ireland).[128]

Interestingly, the preamble of the Ethiopian Constitution is relatively silent on the past. There is a commitment to 'continuing to live with our rich and proud cultural legacies in territories we have long inhabited' and to 'rectifying historically unjust relationships'. But otherwise it stresses the recent past by highlighting 'struggles and sacrifices' in bringing about 'peace and the prospect of a democratic order'. By comparison, the preambles of several state constitutions are more outspoken. They remind the reader of hardship under the Haile Selassie and Derg regimes by citing human rights violations, ineffective policies, and the marginalisation of the state's main ethnic group (as in, e.g., the Oromia and Somalia constitutions).[129] The states have also used the opportunity to create their own narratives

124 See Armin von Bogdandy, 'The European Constitution and European Identity: Text and Subtext of the Treaty Establishing a Constitution for Europe' (2005) 3 *International Journal of Constitutional Law* 295, 310.

125 See Ernest Renan, 'What Is a Nation?' in Homi Bhabha (ed.), *Nation and Narration* (first published 1882, Routledge 1990) 19.

126 See Tushnet (n. 10).

127 Mark Tushnet, *Advanced Introduction to Comparative Constitutional Law* (Edward Elgar 2014) 27.

128 See Bertus De Villiers, 'Social and Economic Rights' in David Van Wyk, John Dugard, Bertus de Villiers, and Dennis Davis (eds.), *Rights and Constitutionalism: The New South African Legal Order* (Oxford University Press 1995) 618.

129 See Van der Beken (n. 58) 5f.

through public holidays in addition to country-wide ones and the naming of places or institutions,[130] even though these narratives are not always shared by other ethnic groups living in these states. The Harari state, for instance, celebrates the Chelenko Martyrs' day commemorating the (eventually broken) resistance in 1887 against the expansion of the Ethiopian empire under Menelik II. In a similar vein, other states, in particular Oromia, have reintroduced the old names by which certain towns were known before Menelik's expansion.

These narratives are complemented both at the national and subnational levels by forward-looking statements. Chapter 10 of the Ethiopian Constitution contains 'national policy principles and objectives' that concern a wide range of issues, including the political objective 'to strengthen ties of equality, unity and fraternity' among the nations, nationalities, and peoples.[131] Although these principles and objectives are explicitly binding for both government levels,[132] the state constitutions may contain complementary provisions. Some of the state goals are related to specific characteristics of their populations, for example, the promotion of the living standards of pastoralists (in Afar and Somalia) and the achievement of unity in (ethnic) diversity (in Gambella and Benishangul-Gumuz).[133] But for the most part, state constitutions merely repeat Chapter 10 of the national constitution nearly verbatim, with the result that reading their objectives amounts to 'constitutional déjà vu'.[134]

In South Africa, creative (re)interpretation characterises not only the above-mentioned national symbols but also historical narratives. This is best illustrated by the approach to public holidays.[135] Whereas 16 December, now the Day of Reconciliation, was a holiday under apartheid celebrating the victory of the *voortrekkers* over the Zulus in 1838, it is also the day when the ANC began its armed struggle in 1961. KwaZulu-Natal's Shaka Day, commemorating the famous Zulu king, is now Heritage Day, on which South Africa's diversity is celebrated. Apart from these narratives outside the Constitution, the preamble itself makes several references to history, both in its negative and positive aspects. It declares that the people '[r]ecognise the injustices of our past; honour those who suffered for justice and freedom in our land; [and] respect those who have worked to build and develop our country'.

The Western Cape Constitution similarly emphasises the ambition 'to heal the injustices of the past', but remains devoid of more concrete references. The only provision potentially implying a historical or cultural narrative is section 70, which obliges provincial legislation to provide for a 'cultural council or councils for a community or communities in the Western Cape sharing a common cultural and language heritage'.[136] The ANC claimed that the provision was designed to protect Afrikaner identity and to disadvantage councils with an interethnic mission. However, the Constitutional Court did not share the party's view that the creation of cultural councils in the provinces, in addition to a similar national commission, would not fall within their competences.[137]

[130] See Fessha (n. 90) 195.
[131] Article 88(2).
[132] Article 85.
[133] See Van der Beken (n. 58) 11–16.
[134] Fessha (n. 37) 1.
[135] See Fessha (n. 90) 196.
[136] See Murray (n. 63) 496.
[137] See Steytler (n. 72) 6.

In comparison, references to a narrative centred around a specific group are easier to identify in the failed KwaZulu-Natal Constitution. While the preamble declares the desire 'to progress away from a history of conflict' and to be mindful of the province's 'diverse heritage', the Constitution then, in chapter 1, section 1, goes on to establish a constitutional monarchy under the Zulu king. As a constitutional adviser frankly pointed out, this 'means that all the residents of KwaZulu-Natal and not merely Zulus would owe allegiance to the monarch'.[138]

With regard to forward-looking statements, KwaZulu-Natal's unsuccessful constitution merely featured passing references to certain public goods that the province shall promote,[139] whereas the Western Cape Constitution's chapter 10 on 'Directive Principles of Provincial Policy' has more substance.[140] However, these principles, which are 'not legally enforceable' but meant to 'guide the Western Cape government in making and applying laws',[141] do not really develop a vision for the province which is distinct from the rest of South Africa. The provincial constitution instead combines reformulations of rights in the national constitution as principles with a few additional policy goals. As for the latter, they seem either general or to reflect, as with 'the promotion of a market-oriented economy', the ideological preferences of the then ruling New National Party (in this case, as opposed to the preferences of the more interventionist ANC).[142] In any event, they do not carve out a specific vision for the province as a whole that would go beyond these ideological preferences.

As one might expect with a country like BiH, one which is not at peace with itself, the battle about the past has been fiercely contested. Interestingly, the national constitution itself is devoid of backward-looking statements, while even the entity constitutions refrain from lengthy narratives. However, the real battles take place in the entities at the level of ordinary legislation or through direct democracy. An example of the latter was the 2016 referendum in the RS in which 99.8 per cent voted for upholding a National Day of the Republika Srpska, something which the Constitutional Court had held to be unconstitutional just months before.[143] In the court's view, the holiday is discriminatory against non-Serbs because it is an Orthodox feast day and the date in 1992 when the Bosnian Serb Assembly declared a republic as a breakaway entity from BiH (which was itself seceding from Yugoslavia).

Another political and legal dispute revolved around ordinary legislation which renamed certain municipalities in the RS by adding the prefix 'Serbian' (and eliminating the prefix 'Bosnian' in some cases).[144] The Constitutional Court refused to believe that the renaming was only to distinguish municipalities from others with similar names, regarding it instead as ethnic labelling with the clear intention to declare these places purely Serbian and thus, in some cases, even to uphold the effects of war-time ethnic cleansing. In line with its rationale in the seminal *Constituent Peoples* case, the judges ruled that this was unconstitutional due to violations of the principles of non-discrimination and of the equality of the three constituent peoples.[145]

138 Devenish (n. 117) 503f.
139 Chapter 1, section 15.
140 See Dirk Brand, 'The Western Cape Provincial Constitution' (2000) *31 Rutgers Law Journal* 961, 970.
141 Section 82.
142 See Steytler (n. 72) 22.
143 Constitutional Court of Bosnia and Herzegovina, U3/13 of 26 November 2015.
144 See Steiner and Ademović (n. 120) 505–8.
145 U 44/01 of 24 January 2002 [49ff].

In terms of forward-looking statements, the national and subnational constitutions do not have much substance beyond very general references in the preambles to peace and human rights as enshrined in international treaties. On the one hand, this might be seen as the result of these basic laws' pragmatic focus on the business of governance; on the other, it is probably a sign of a lack of vision for the future.

This certainly contrasts with Spain's constitutional framework, where forward-looking statements abound. However, what is striking is the divergence which is evident in the backward-looking elements. Whereas the national constitution is generally silent in this regard, the revised statutes (2006–11) indulge in historical and cultural narratives. Unsurprisingly, Catalonia's statute has a particularly lengthy preamble highlighting 'a constant will to self-government over the course of the centuries, embodied in such institutions as the Generalitat [the Catalan government] created in 1359' and a 'civil and associative tradition' that has supposedly promoted a long list of characteristic values. But other preambles also make reference to ancient realms or institutions, such as the assembly of nationalists' adoption of the Federal Constitution for Andalusia in 1883.

A second type of narrative focuses on cultural traditions, such as in Andalusia's peculiar claim of a 'monopoly' on flamenco dance.[146] However, a third type has clearly proven to be controversial. While only two original statutes, those of the Basque Country and Aragon, invoked historical rights, this became common practice in the reformed statutes. Valencia claimed a right to apply its own historical civil law, with Catalonia's Statute going even further. According to the preamble, this autonomous community's 'self-government is founded on the Constitution, and *also* on the historical rights of the Catalan people' (emphasis added), something which is reiterated in article 5. Although the Constitutional Court refrained from invalidating these parts of the Statute, it did issue a binding interpretation requiring that the Statute be brought in line with the Constitution. 'Historical rights' must be construed as referring to Catalan traditions of private law or uncontroversial forms of public law, but certainly not as providing an independent foundation of self-government besides that in the national constitution.[147]

Concerning forward-looking provisions, the reformed statutes have similarly become more comprehensive. Today they complement the national constitution's chapter 3 on 'Principles Governing Economic and Social Policy' in many areas. Until the revisions, political objectives had been included in only some of the original statutes, although, curiously enough, not in Catalonia's. The latter's reformed Statute now, however, contains an entirely new Title I on 'Rights, Obligations and Governing Principles'.[148] While 'governing principles' are obviously meant to guide public policies, the 'rights' in the statutes of the autonomous communities were in part 'downgraded' by the Constitutional Court to a similar status. Only some, such as participatory rights, are deemed directly enforceable individual rights; others, especially the widespread social rights, are merely guiding principles for regional policy-makers.[149] Even if many of these principles were already enshrined in

[146] Article 68 of its statute declares that 'the Autonomous Community holds exclusive competence as for knowledge, preservation, research, formation, promotion and spreading of flamenco as a peculiar feature of the Andalusian cultural heritage'.

[147] STC 31/2010, FJ 10.

[148] See Josep-Maria Castellà Andreu, 'Spanish Autonomic State Reform: Catalonia's 2006 New Statute of Autonomy' (2008) *102 The Journal of Law and Political Science* 89, 101.

[149] STC 247/2007; STC 31/2010.

ordinary legislation, their elevation to the higher-ranking statutes can be interpreted as movements towards regional quasi-citizenship.[150] Thus, they are—together with the vision that they embody—clearly significant for how the image of the people as constitutional subject is framed.

5. Conclusion

It has been argued that in democracies a notion must prevail of the people as a political community 'whose identity will constantly be open to question, whose identity will remain forever latent'.[151] Such a perception of the people as something which is *not* monolithic and immutable must undergird pluralist democracy's core idea of multiple claims to representation—this is even more applicable in countries which are marked by a history of non-recognition of ethnic diversity and that have only rather recently embarked on a transition to democracy. While pluralism is also reflected (and mostly researched) in provisions regulating the state structure, this chapter has focused on how it is reflected in the manner in which constitutions (both national and subnational) frame the image of the people. Four main conclusions have emerged.

Firstly, the two above-mentioned categories of pluralist constitutional identity[152] are not only distinct but also interrelated. Arguably, it makes sense to draw an analytical distinction between these categories: on the one hand, the state structure, especially the (vertical) 'dislocation' of power through federalism and its (horizontal) 'disaggregation' through consociational power-sharing,[153] and, on the other hand, the image of the people. Yet these categories are not only complementary but interrelated, as the framing of the latter image is far from being only of symbolic significance. On the contrary, it often has major repercussions for pluralism in the state structure. A clear case in point is BiH, where narrow definitions of the people in subnational constitutions, ones that focused only on Serbs (in the RS) or Bosniacs and Croats (in the FBH), formed the basis for the discrimination of other groups in these entities' political institutions. Another example is Ethiopia, the preamble of which emphasises the supreme position of the country's 'nations, nationalities and peoples'. Beyond mere symbolism, this preambulatory statement, in combination with article 39(1)–(3) of the Constitution, has created the possibility of reorganising the state structure, one which was used for the first time with the establishment of the state of Sidama in June 2020.

Secondly, interrelations between the framing of the images of the people in national and subnational constitutions depend mainly on both subnational activism to this effect and the national reaction to this activism.[154] It is hardly surprising that subnational entities engaging in their own nation-building projects that rival the country-wide project

[150] See Michael Keating and Alex Wilson, 'Renegotiating the State of Autonomies: Statute Reform and Multi-level Politics in Spain' (2009) *32 West European Politics* 536, 550.

[151] Claude Lefort, *Democracy and Political Theory* (Polity Press 1988) 304.

[152] See section 2 above.

[153] Sujit Choudhry, 'After the Rights Revolution: Bills of Rights in the Post-conflict State' (2010) *6 Annual Review of Law and Social Science* 301, 303. On the importance of horizontal 'disaggregation' of power not only at the national but also at the subnational level, see Karl Kössler, 'Beyond Majoritarian Autonomy? Legislative and Executive Power-Sharing in European Regions' in Matteo Nicolini, Francesco Palermo, and Enrico Milano (eds.), *Law, Territory and Conflict Resolution* (Brill-Martinus Nijhoff 2016) 39.

[154] See sections 4.1.2 and 4.2 above.

(e.g. Catalonia, Oromia, and both entities of BiH) demonstrate a high level of activism and project different images of the people. As South Africa's provinces were simply created in Kempton Park (with the 1993 Interim Constitution) and do not have historically grown identities, 'multilevel identity constitutionalism' has developed there only to a very limited extent. Yet, as the Spanish case illustrates, even subnational entities without such identities sometimes start to develop a certain level of activism. With the second wave of statutes (2006–11), other autonomous communities emulated Catalonia by introducing characterisations of their people as historical communities—an example of 'ethnoterritorial concurrence'[155] that has also been observed in other areas.

Subnational activism in framing the image of the people can obviously meet with very different national responses. In Ethiopia and South Africa, such activism, to the extent that it exists at all, has been held in check politically by the respective dominant parties as well as, in the latter case, legally through the instrument of ex ante certification. As the Prosperity Party (PP) ruling Ethiopia since 2019 might prove less able than the preceding political coalition to dominate the country, there perhaps will be—at least in the long run—opportunities for identity creation through state constitutions.[156] However, this could also become a breeding ground for greater discrimination against internal minorities in the states and 'exogenous communities', with one constitution already differentiating, for example, between 'owners' of the state and others. By contrast, in BiH and Spain it is less the political constellation than constitutional jurisprudence that has set limits to identity creation through subnational constitutions. The courts have done so, respectively, by introducing the principle of the 'collective equality' of the three constituent peoples and by highlighting the distinction between the Spanish nation and Catalonia as a nationality.

Thirdly, change is driven, if it occurs at all, at least as much by judicial actors as by political actors. This chapter proceeds on the assumption that (pluralist) constitutional identity is something fluid and mutable that does not itself change but *is* actively changed over time, especially so by the actors above. It is important to note that even the identity distilled in the original constitutional design is, of course, not created in an abstract manner at a zero-point unaffected by the past.[157] Instead, while this design has been the point of departure for our comparative analysis, it is historically contingent and itself encapsulates, as this chapter demonstrates,[158] the disharmonies of the period preceding the founding era. Framers of the constitution are, in their deliberative process, detached neither from conflicts with other power-holders nor from individual motivations based on interests, rational grounds, or even emotional factors.[159]

While coexistence, in various proportions, of 'preservative and transformative elements'[160] characterises any original constitutional design, a mixture of these two opposing forces also shapes subsequent constitutional change. In the Ethiopian and South African cases, the initial design was, overall and also regarding the framing of the image of the

155 Ayele (n. 52) 97f.
156 See Ayele (n. 52) 170f.
157 See Jacobsohn (n. 2) 324.
158 See section 4.1 above.
159 See Jon Elster, 'Forces and Mechanisms in the Constitution-Making Process' (1995) 45 *Duke Law Journal* 364ff; András Sajó, 'Emotions in Constitutional Design' (2010) 8 *International Journal of Constitutional Law* 354ff.
160 Jacobsohn (n. 2) 214.

people, highly transformative, even if in the latter case the 1993 Interim Constitution and subsequent inclusiveness regarding symbols and narratives also ensured some continuity. Since the 1990s, however, constitutional imagery has not changed to the same extent as in BiH and Spain.[161] In the Spanish case the drivers of this process have been both political actors, ones introducing new provisions in the reformed statutes, and judicial actors, ones establishing limits to these efforts. In the case of BiH, the Constitutional Court has clearly been in the driver's seat due to a complete absence of political compromise. The preeminent role of judges in both countries appears to be linked with constitutional silences and/or ambiguities concerning matters too delicate to be solved politically (e.g. national symbols in BiH, and, in Spain, the implications of the definitions as 'nation' or 'nationality'), which then often entail clarification through judicial interpretation. However, these deferrals and ambiguities sometimes also tend to become controversial if political actors decide to lift the fog around them. In 2009, one could still claim that the Statute of Catalonia had managed the issue of different conceptions of Spain 'by a creative ambiguity and some tortuous language, which neither recognises plurinationality nor denies it'.[162] More than a decade later, it is evident that this has not worked too well.

Fourthly, a lack of pluralism in the framing of the image of the people both reflects and fuels intergroup tensions, as it may undergird tendencies of disintegration or hinder integration in the first place. As the chapter has demonstrated, a lack of pluralism is often apparent from the formulas used to define the people and from narratives about a country's past (less so from its aspirations for the future). However, it is arguably most visible in symbols meant to represent the people.[163] Whereas South Africa seems exceptional through its inclusive symbolism and narratives at the national level (for instance, the flag, anthem, and public holidays) and lack of provincial efforts to this effect, divisive symbolism is a well-known phenomenon in some of the other case-study countries. The provision in Oromia's state constitution that ensures the depiction of a traditional sign of the Oromo people on the flag is a good example because this excludes other groups in the state. Similar to the claim that Ethiopia needs, especially given the increasing conflicts of the past years, a model of federalism that 'takes ethnic concerns into account without making ethnic identity the only identity that matters',[164] the same balancing act of emphasising ethnic identity without overemphasising also seems key for symbols in the constitutions at both levels of government.

While the divisive symbolism of subnational entities may be seen in some cases as part of an effort to intensify tendencies of state disintegration, it is, with the two entities of BiH, linked to a complete lack of integration in the first place. To make matters worse, exclusionary symbols in both the RS and FBH are complemented by an outright absence of consensus on common national symbols. The fact that these symbols, eventually imposed by the High Representative for BiH as an external actor, have failed to acquire integrative power is a bitter reminder that the efforts of a constitution and its judicial interpretation to promote a pluralist image of the people face certain limits. Indeed,

[161] See sections 3.3 and 4.2 above.
[162] Keating and Wilson (n. 150) 554.
[163] See section 4.2.2 above.
[164] Yonatan Fessha, 'Ethiopia's Ethnic Federalism: Part of the Problem or Part of the Solution' *Verfassungsblog* (2019) https://verfassungsblog.de/ethiopias-ethnic-federalism-part-of-the-problem-or-part-of-the-solution/ (last accessed 19 August 2022).

> [a] constitution's language may indicate a commitment on the part of its authors and subsequent interpreters to establish a constitutional identity, but until confirmed in the accumulated practice of a constitutional community, the goal, however noble, will remain unfulfilled.[165]

Bibliography

Alence R., 'South Africa after Apartheid: The First Decade' (2004) *15 Journal of Democracy* 78

Andreu J.M.C., 'Spanish Autonomic State Reform: Catalonia's 2006 New Statute of Autonomy' (2008) *102 The Journal of Law and Political Science* 89

Ayele Z., 'The Politics of Subnational Constitutions and Local Government in Ethiopia' (2014) *6 Perspectives of Federalism* 89

Ayele Z., 'Subnational Constitutions in the Ethiopian Federal System in Light of the Demos, the Federalists and Deliberative Democracy Models of Subnational Constitutionalism' (2019) *Journal of Ethiopian Law* 153ff

Bellamy R., *Liberalism and Pluralism: Towards a Politics of Compromise* (Routledge 1999)

Bieber F., *Post-war Bosnia* (Palgrave 2006)

Billig M., *Banal Nationalism* (Sage Publications 2005)

Bogdandy V., 'The European Constitution and European Identity: Text and Subtext of the Treaty Establishing a Constitution for Europe' (2005) *3 International Journal of Constitutional Law* 295

Brand D., 'The Western Cape Provincial Constitution' (2000) *31 Rutgers Law Journal* 961

Choudhry S. (ed.), *Constitutional Design for Divided Societies: Integration or Accommodation?* (Oxford University Press 2008)

Choudhry S., 'After the Rights Revolution: Bills of Rights in the Post-conflict State' (2010) *6 Annual Review of Law and Social Science* 301

Cohen J.M., 'Ethnic Federalism in Ethiopia' (1995) *2 Northeast African Studies* 157

Colino C., 'Constitutional Change without Constitutional Reform: Spanish Federalism and the Revision of Catalonia's Statute of Autonomy' (2009) *39 Publius* 262

Conversi D., 'Autonomous Communities and the Ethnic Settlement in Spain' in Ghai Y. (ed.), *Autonomy and Ethnicity: Negotiating Competing Claims in Multi-ethnic States* (Cambridge University Press 2000) 138

Dahl R.A., *Who Governs? Democracy and Power in an American City* (Yale University Press 1961)

Delledonne G. and Martinico G., 'Legal Conflict and Subnational Constitutionalism' (2012) *42 Rutgers Law Journal* 881

Devenish G., 'The Making and Significance of the Draft KwaZulu-Natal Constitution' (1999) *47 Jahrbuch des Öffentlichen Rechts* 503

Dixon R. and Ginsburg T., 'Deciding Not to Decide: Deferral in Constitutional Design' (2011) *9 International Journal of Constitutional Law* 636

Ebrahim H., *The Soul of a Nation: Constitution-Making in South Africa* (Oxford University Press 1998)

Egan A. and Taylor R., 'South Africa: The Failure of Ethno-territorial Politics' in Coakley J. (ed.), *The Territorial Management of Ethnic Conflict* (2nd edn, Frank Cass 2003) 105

Elster J., 'Forces and Mechanisms in the Constitution-Making Process' (1995) *45 Duke Law Journal* 364

Fessha Y.T., *Ethnic Diversity and Federalism: Constitution Making in South Africa and Ethiopia* (Ashgate 2010)

Fessha Y.T., 'Ethiopia's Ethnic Federalism: Part of the Problem or Part of the Solution' *Verfassungsblog* (2019) https://verfassungsblog.de/ethiopias-ethnic-federalism-part-of-the-problem-or-part-of-the-solution/ (last accessed 19 August 2022)

[165] Gary Jacobsohn, 'The Formation of Constitutional Identities' in Tom Ginsburg and Rosalind Dixon (eds.), *Comparative Constitutional Law* (Edward Elgar 2011) 131.

Fessha Y.T., 'Constitutional Déjà Vu: Reading Subnational Constitutions in Ethiopia' in Popelier P., Delledonne G., and Aroney N. (eds.), *Routledge Handbook of Subnational Constitutionalism* (Routledge 2021) 2

Fessha Y.T. and Ayele Z., 'Giving "Shape and Texture" to a Federal System? Ethiopia's Courts and its Unusual Umpire' in Fessha Y.T. and Kössler K. (eds.), *Federalism and the Courts in Africa: Design and Impact in Comparative Perspective* (Routledge 2020) 60

Ghai Y., 'Introduction: Nature and Origins of Autonomy' in Ghai Y. and Woodman S. (eds.), *Practising Self-Government: A Comparative Study of Autonomous Regions* (Cambridge University Press 2013) 2

Grimm D., 'Integration by Constitution' (2005) *3 International Journal of Constitutional Law* 193

Habtu A., 'Multiethnic Federalism in Ethiopia: A Study of the Secession Clause in the Constitution' (2005) *35 Publius* 313

Horowitz D.L., *A Democratic South Africa? Constitutional Engineering in a Divided Society* (University of California Press 1991)

Horowitz D.L., 'Constitutional Design: Proposals versus Processes' in Reynolds A. (ed.), *The Architecture of Democracy: Constitutional Design, Conflict Management, and Democracy* (Oxford University Press 2002) 17

Jackson V.C., 'Comparative Constitutional Federalism and Transnational Judicial Discourse' (2004) *2 International Journal of Constitutional Law* 105

Jackson V.C., 'Comparative Constitutional Law: Methodologies' in Rosenfeld M. and Sajó A. (eds.), *The Oxford Handbook of Comparative Constitutional Law* (Oxford University Press 2012) 7f

Jacobsohn G., *Constitutional Identity* (Harvard University Press 2010)

Jacobsohn G., 'The Formation of Constitutional Identities' in Ginsburg T. and Dixon R. (eds.), *Comparative Constitutional Law* (Edward Elgar 2011) 131

Keating M. and Wilson A., 'Renegotiating the State of Autonomies: Statute Reform and Multi-level Politics in Spain' (2009) 32 *West European Politics* 536

Klug H., *The Constitution of South Africa: A Contextual Analysis* (Hart Publishing 2010)

Klug H., 'Constitutional Identity and Change' (2011) *47 Tulsa Law Review* 46

Kössler K., 'Conclusions: Beyond the Illusion of Ethno-culturally Homogenous Territory' in Malloy T. and Palermo P. (eds.), *Minority Accommodation through Territorial and Non-territorial Autonomy* (Oxford University Press 2015) 245

Kössler K., 'Beyond Majoritarian Autonomy? Legislative and Executive Power-Sharing in European Regions' in Nicolini M., Palermo F, and Milano E. (eds.), *Law, Territory and Conflict Resolution* (Brill-Martinus Nijhoff 2016) 39

Kössler K., 'Territorial Referendums from a Constitutionalist Perspective: Functions, Justifications and Legal Design' in Basaguren A.L. and San-Epifanio L.E. (eds.), *Claims for Secession and Federalism: A Comparative Study with a Special Focus on Spain* (Springer 2019) 278

Lefort C., *Democracy and Political Theory* (Polity Press 1988)

Llorente F.R., 'El bloque de la constitucionalidad' (1989) *27 Revista Española de Derecho Constitucional* 9

Malloy T. and Palermo F. (eds.), *Minority Accommodation through Territorial and Non-territorial Autonomy* (Oxford University Press 2015)

Marko J., 'Five Years of Constitutional Jurisprudence in Bosnia and Herzegovina: A First Balance' (European Diversity and Autonomy Papers, July 2004) 9–12

Marko J., '"United in Diversity"? Problems of State and Nation-Building in Post-Conflict Situations: The Case of Bosnia-Herzegovina' (2006) *30 Vermont Law Review* 503

McGarry J., O'Leary B., and Simeon R., 'Integration or Accommodation? The Enduring Debate in Conflict Regulation' in Choudhry S. (ed.), *Constitutional Design for Divided Societies: Integration or Accommodation?* (Oxford University Press 2008) 41

Murray C., 'Provincial Constitutions in South Africa: The (Non)Example of the Western Cape' (2001) *49 Jahrbuch des Öffentlichen Rechts* 481

Murray C. and Simeon R., 'Recognition without Empowerment: Minorities in a Democratic South Africa' (2007) *5 International Journal of Constitutional Law* 699

Mutua M., 'Hope and Despair for a New South Africa: The Limits of Rights Discourse' (1997) *10 Harvard Human Rights Journal* 63

Ninet A.A.I. and Gardner J.A., 'Distinctive Identity Claims in Federal Systems: Judicial Policing of Subnational Variance' (2016) *14 International Journal of Constitutional Law* 37

Orgad L., 'The Preamble in Constitutional Interpretation' (2011) *8 International Journal of Constitutional Law* 714

Palermo F. and Kössler K., *Comparative Federalism: Constitutional Arrangements and Case Law* (Hart Publishing 2017)

Pitkin H., 'The Idea of a Constitution' (1987) *37 Journal of Legal Education* 167

Plato, *The Laws* (Trevor J. Saunders ed., Penguin Classics 2005)

Renan E., 'What Is a Nation?' in Bhabha H. (ed.), *Nation and Narration* (first published 1882, Routledge 1990) 19

Rosenfeld, M., *The Identity of the Constitutional Subject: Selfhood, Citizenship, Culture, and Community* (Routledge 2010)

Rosenfeld, M., 'Constitutional Identity' in Rosenfeld M. and Sajó A. (eds.), *The Oxford Handbook of Comparative Constitutional Law* (Oxford University Press 2012) 771

Sajó A., 'Emotions in Constitutional Design' (2010) *8 International Journal of Constitutional Law* 354

Saunders C., 'The Constitutional Credentials of State Constitutions' (2011) *42 Rutgers Law Review* 853

Serra R. and Oñate P., 'The Reform of the Spanish Subnational Constitutions: Rules and Regulations and Political Context' (Paper presented at the VII World Congress on Constitutional Law, Athens, 2007) 12

Steiner C. and Ademović N., 'Article I.6' in Steiner C. and Ademović N. (eds.), *Constitution of Bosnia and Herzegovina: Commentary* (Konrad Adenauer Stiftung 2010) 117

Steiner C. and Ademović N., 'Article II.4' in Steiner C. and Ademović N. (eds.), *Constitution of Bosnia and Herzegovina: Commentary* (Konrad Adenauer Stiftung 2010) 485

Steytler N., 'Provincial Constitutions in South Africa: An Empty Promise' in Popelier P., Delledonne G., and Aroney N. (eds.), *Routledge Handbook of Subnational Constitutionalism* (Routledge 2021) 1

Tamanaha B.Z., 'Understanding Legal Pluralism: Past to Present, Local to Global' (2008) *30 Sydney Law Review* 375

Tarr G.A., 'Explaining Subnational Constitutional Space' (2011) *115 Penn State Law Review* 1133

Teitel R.G., *Transitional Justice* (Oxford University Press 2000)

Tushnet M., 'How Do Constitutions Constitute Constitutional Identity?' (2010) *8 International Journal of Constitutional Law* 671

Tushnet M., *Advanced Introduction to Comparative Constitutional Law* (Edward Elgar 2014)

Van der Beken C., 'Sub-national Constitutional Autonomy in Ethiopia: On the Road to Distinctive Regional Constitutions' (IXth World Congress of Constitutional Law, Workshop 2: Sub-national constitutions in federal and quasi-federal constitutional states, Oslo, 16–20 June 2014) 1

Van der Beken C., *Completing the Constitutional Architecture: A Comparative Analysis of Sub-National Constitutions in Ethiopia* (Addis Ababa University Press 2017)

Villiers B.D., 'Social and Economic Rights' in Wyk D.V., Dugard J., de Villiers B., and Davis D. et al. (eds.), *Rights and Constitutionalism: The New South African Legal Order* (Oxford University Press 1995) 618

Walker N., 'The Idea of Constitutional Pluralism' (2002) *65 Modern Law Review* 317

Williams R.F., 'Comparative Subnational Constitutional Law: South Africa's Provincial Constitutional Experiments' (1999) *40 South Texas Law Review* 625

Woelk J., 'Bosnia-Herzegovina: Trying to Build a Federal State on Paradoxes' in Burgess M. and Tarr G.A. (eds.), *Constitutional Dynamics in Federal Systems: Sub-national Perspectives* (McGill-Queen's University Press 2012) 110

Žagar M., 'The Collapse of the Yugoslav Federation and the Viability of Asymmetrical Federalism' in Ortino S., Žagar M., and Mastny V. (eds.), *The Changing Faces of Federalism: Institutional Reconfiguration in Europe from East to West* (Manchester University Press 2005) 107

PART 2
CASE STUDIES

6

A Century of South African Constitutional Identities

*Nico Steytler**

1. Introduction

South Africa stunned itself and the world by negotiating a constitutional democracy in 1993–4 after the decades of conflict that came in the wake of the formation of the Union of South Africa in 1910. In the years that followed, the oppressive white-minority regime strengthened its grip on power through the Republican Constitution of 1961 and then the Tricameral Constitution of 1983, which sought to pit non-Africans against Africans. Preceded by the 1993 interim Constitution, the 1996 Constitution, reflecting a democratic dispensation, was heralded as the 'birth certificate of a new nation' after centuries of white oppression and the black majority's struggle against it. The post-apartheid constitutions gave expression to the 'rainbow nation' and promised to transform South Africa from a highly unequal society to a more egalitarian one, a transformation that was to occur within the strictures of constitutionalism.

After nearly thirty years, however, the rainbow has lost its dazzle, levels of inequality and poverty are as high as they ever were, and the very basis of the democratic constitutions is being questioned. Decolonialisation scholars claim that the 1996 Constitution is illegitimate because it is based on a historical wrong: the theft of land by white settlers, which has gone unaddressed since the formation of modern-day South Africa. The Constitution is thus portrayed as a 'neo-apartheid' institution that protects and perpetuates the ill-gotten gains of apartheid.

The history of modern South Africa can be viewed from different perspectives—political, historical, and economic—with each bringing its own insights. One way of looking at the country's constitutional history is through the prism of the concept of constitutional identity. Gary Jacobsohn, a leading scholar on constitutional identity, uses the concept as a tool for analysing constitutional development and change. For him, a constitutional identity is shaped through a dialogical process driven by disharmonies in the constitution itself and between itself and society. Michel Rosenfeld, on the other hand, while agreeing with Jacobsohn, uses the concept of constitutional identity in a prescriptive manner, asking how a constitutional identity can be manufactured purposefully through various constitutional methods and strategies.

Jacobsohn refers to South Africa's 1996 Constitution as 'a textbook example of dialogical constitution making' thanks to its 'interaction of local participation, context and history

* The author wishes to thank the two anonymous reviewers whose constructive comments were so helpful in giving direction to this chapter.

Nico Steytler, *A Century of South African Constitutional Identities* In: *Constitutional Identity and Constitutionalism in Africa.* Edited by: Charles M. Fombad and Nico Steytler, Oxford University Press.
DOI: 10.1093/oso/9780198906308.003.0009

with international influences and conditionalities'.[1] The question that arises is whether the terms and concepts used in analysing the formation of constitutional identity could shed fresh light on a century of constitution-making processes in South Africa that culminated in the constitutions of 1993 and 1996. Do the concepts advanced by theorists in this area give us a better understanding of why we are, at this stage, in yet another round of constitutional dialogue? Moreover, do the insights so gained serve as a guide for the future?

The argument in this chapter is that the literature on the formation of a constitutional identity provides useful tools for unlocking a fuller understanding of the shaping of South African constitutional identity. Firstly, the country engaged in a long dialogical process of forming and reforming the imagined 'nation' or constitutional identity—the 1909 constitution is inextricably linked to the 1996 Constitution, and, indeed, the process will not end with the latter. Secondly, constitutional writing is a purposeful project of defining the constitutional identity by asking: '*To whom* shall the constitution be addressed?' '*What* should the constitution provide?' and '*[H]ow* may the constitution be justified?' (emphases in the original).[2] Each of South Africa's five constitutions has had its intended audience (one circumscribed by the definition of 'the nation'), afforded protection to that audience's vital interests, and used techniques of justification. Thirdly, each of the constitutions has contained disharmonies, both internal to the text and externally with society, with these disharmonies serving as a catalyst for the next iteration of constitutional identity. Fourthly, as a fixed constitutional identity is illusory, changes depend on those who control the authors' pen in writing the new constitution.

The chapter begins with a brief exposition of the approaches taken by two major theorists of the concept of constitutional identity—Jacobsohn and Rosenfeld—with the aim of constructing a framework within which to analyse a century's formation of constitutional identity. Section 3 examines that century of constitutional history, commencing with the Union of South Africa Act of 1909 and followed by the Republican Constitution of 1961 and the tricameral Constitution of 1983—collectively referred to as the apartheid constitutions—and the popular responses they elicited. Against this background, the two democratic constitutions of 1993 and 1996 are dissected. Section 4 deals with the ongoing debate as to whether the 1996 Constitution has indeed overcome the legacy of the apartheid constitutions. The chapter concludes with remarks on the value of the concept of constitutional identity.

2. The Formation of Constitutional Identity

The aim here is not to review theories and approaches to constitutional identity; that has been done in the introductory chapter and touched on elsewhere in other chapters. The aim is to distil those elements in the discourse on the formation of constitutional identity that resonate with the South African experience of constitution-making. The focus will be on the two prominent theorists Jacobsohn and Rosenfeld, whose work overlaps but emphasises different aspects of the formation of constitutional identity.

[1] Gary J. Jacobsohn, 'The Formation of Constitutional Identities' in Tom Ginsburg and Rosalind Dixon (eds.), *Comparative Constitutional Law* (Elgar 2011) 137, quoting Heinz Klug, *Constituting Democracy* (Cambridge University Press 2002) 3.

[2] Michel Rosenfeld, 'Constitutional Identity' in Michel Rosenfeld and András Sajó (eds.), *The Oxford Handbook of Comparative Constitutional Law* (Oxford University Press 2012) 756.

At the most basic level, constitutional identity starts with the characteristics by which a constitution can be identified or distinguished from others. For Jacobsohn, the material from which to infer these characteristics is, in the first place, the constitutional text, allowing that the text has value only to the extent that it has meaning in practice. As he states, '[t]he language may indicate a commitment on the part of its authors to establish a constitutional identity, but until confirmed in the accumulated practice of a constitutional community, the goal, however noble, will remain unfulfilled.'[3] For Jacobsohn, the constitution so described is only one element of a constitutional order; the other is the social order in which it is situated.

A constitutional identity is, however, never static: fluid by nature, it changes over time due to circumstances. Jacobsohn thus focuses on what drives such evolutionary change of identity and leads to the formation of a new identity, one which, inevitably, in turn is subject to change. Ironically, then, the seeds of change lie in each new constitution itself. The evolutionary dynamic is driven by 'disharmonies' within the constitutional text[4] as well as between the text and its social context—internal and external disharmonies. He writes:

> All constitutions are crafted over time in the sense that their meaning and identity evolve gradually in ways determined by a dynamic fueled by their internal tensions and contradictions and their confrontations with a social order over which they have limited influence.[5]

The evolution of the constitutional identity is then driven by seeking greater harmony within the text and between the text and society, a process involving dialogue between those seeking to conserve the existing constitution and those emphasising the disharmonies. For Jacobsohn, 'constitutional identity will be fashioned—and refashioned—through struggle over constitutional identity'.[6] In stable polities, disharmonies are often addressed through judicial interpretation or constitutional amendments.

Rosenfeld agrees with Jacobsohn's analysis, though only up to a point. He, too, is of the view that a constitution acquires an identity through 'experience', meaning the practice of implementation; likewise, he agrees that 'the *context* in which a constitution operates seems bound to play a significant role in the shaping of its identity' (emphasis in the original).[7] But he understands constitutional identity as a broader concept transcending the constitution and as equivalent to 'national identity' or the 'collective self'.[8] Rosenfeld draws a distinction between a national identity that exists irrespective of the particularities of a constitution, such as the ethno-linguistic French or German nation, and a modern concept of constitutional identity in a diverse or pluralistic society as the 'imagined nation' formed by

[3] Gary J. Jacobsohn, 'Constitutional Identity' (2006) 68 *The Review of Politics* 361–97, 365.

[4] There is also a narrow view that it is solely the text that matters; in this case, specially protected provisions, such as the eternity clauses in Germany's Basic Law, are seen as the crux of a constitution's identity. Monika Polzin, 'Constitutional Identity, Unconstitutional Amendments and the Idea of Constituent Power: The Development of the Doctrine of Constitutional Identity in German Constitutional Law' (2016) *14*(2) *International Journal of Constitutional Law* 411–38.

[5] Gary J. Jacobsohn, 'Theorising the Constitutional Revolution' (2014 Spring) *Journal of Law and Courts* 1–30, 30.

[6] Gary J. Jacobsohn, *Constitutional Identity* (Harvard University Press 2010) 135.

[7] Rosenfeld (n. 2) 756.

[8] Ibid. 757.

dialogical interaction.[9] The 'nation' is thus not divorced from the constitution but is inextricably defined by it. Such a constitutional identity, he writes,

> can be constructed on the basis of sameness or of selfhood, or more precisely, based on dynamic interaction between projections of sameness and images of selfhood. Moreover, the interaction in question may at times evoke complementarity and at other times contradiction.[10]

Rosenfeld's focus on the construction of the selfhood goes further than Jacobsohn's more descriptive approach to the evolution of constitutional identity; he sees a constitutional identity 'as belonging to an imagined community that must carve out a distinct self-image',[11] with the object 'to foster a functional constitutional order'.[12] Monika Polzin describes Rosenfeld's project as follows:

> This special, collective self-identity is—as Rosenfeld has aptly emphasized—ideally determined by a process which can abstractly be characterized as a reconciliation process between the different identities, conflicts, and tensions within a state or community. This ideal constitutional identity is developed through a process that emphasizes simultaneously certain common identities in a society and suppresses or reduces the importance of divergent identities.[13]

That imagined community—'the nation'—is, in Rosenfeld's words, '*a lack* that must be overcome through a discursive process that relies on three principal tools: negation, metaphor, and metonymy' (emphasis in the original).[14] He sees the formation of a constitutional identity not as a process that unfolds by its own dynamics, but one actively pursued by the authors of a constitution. 'A lack' of a (desired) community requires the smashing of the old conceptions, or imaginings, of the nation, which then requires fashioning a new imagined community with a distinct positive self-image by way of metaphor and metonymy, for instance, by evoking narratives about the past or symbolising the nation and constitution.[15] Rosenfeld concludes that '[b]ecause a self-image cannot be built up in a vacuum, negation, metaphor, and metonymy must combine to reprocess pre-constitutional materials and extra-constitutional ones into a serviceable, flexible, and adaptable constitutional

[9] Monika Polzin, for example, uses the term 'imagined' political community as the 'nation' or 'the people', namely those who are citizens of a country. Monika Polzin, 'Constitutional Identity as a Constructed Reality and a Restless Soul' (2017) *18*(7) *German Law Journal* 1599.

[10] Rosenfeld (n. 2) 757.

[11] Ibid. 758.

[12] Ibid.

[13] Polzin (n. 9) 1600.

[14] Rosenfeld (n. 2) 758.

[15] A similar idea is found in the literature on state-building and national-building. Armin von Bogdandy et al. write that '[a] successful nation-building process produces a cultural projection of the nation containing a certain set of assumptions, values and beliefs which can function as the legitimizing foundation of a state structure'. Armin von Bogdandy, Stefan Häußler, Felix Hanschmann, and Raphael Utz, 'State-Building, Nation-Building, and Constitutional Politics in Post-Conflict Situations: Conceptual Clarifications and an Appraisal of Different Approaches' (2005) 9(1) *Max Planck Yearbook of United Nations Law* 579–613, 585. They also mention three tools available for constitutional nation-building: 'the form and procedure of constitution-making itself, the institutional arrangements made in the constitution, and the values and symbols employed or referred to both during the political process and in the final text' (597).

identity'.[16] The result, he notes, can be a constitutional identity, 'defined, to some degree, by who "we" are not, as opposed to who we are'.[17]

He thus sees the function of the concept of constitutional identity as determined by

> the need for dialectical mediation of existing, evolving, and projected conflicts and tensions between identity and difference—or, more precisely, identities and differences—that shape the dealings between self and other within the relevant polity committed to constitutional rule and favorably disposed toward the aims of constitutionalism.[18]

Once constitutionalism is elected, he continues, 'constitutional identity must be molded' by answering three questions: '*To whom* shall the constitution be addressed? *What* should the constitution provide? And *how* may the constitution be justified?' (emphasis in the original).[19] The 'to whom' includes the constitution's authors, those who are addressed, and those expected to become bound by it. The 'who' may be difficult to define in the context of significant cleavages in a country: how to weave various strands into 'one single constitutional self'? The content of the constitution (the 'what') would be aimed at 'unify[ing] the various competing selves and others within a polity into a single polity-wide constitutional self'.[20] This includes the structural design of the rule of law and the protection of fundamental rights. With regard to the justification (the 'how'), he writes:

> [C]oncerning 'how' constitutions may be justified to a diverse and pluralistic constituency, constitutional identity figures at various levels of abstraction ranging from the highly theoretical to the fairly concrete ones relying on actual history or living traditions. The relevant justifications that must become integrated in an appropriate constitutional narrative are of three principal kinds: those based on a common history or traditions; those based on a hypothetical or actual consent; and those emanating from normative precepts deemed to be universally valid or indisputably valid for those meant to be subjected to the constitutional regime sought to be justified. Often these justifications or some of them may be combined.[21]

The constitution-making process comes in various forms, including through revolution, war, or a negotiated pact in which 'no clear-cut winners or losers emerge'.[22] In the case of negotiations between the *ancien régime* and the leaders demanding a new constitutional order, the constitution comes about without a break in legality.[23]

In both authors' views, the formation of a constitutional identity is work in progress. Polzin expresses this idea poetically: 'Constitutional identity can therefore only be compared to an intangible restless soul of a nation, and not an imagined stable heart.'[24] She also

16 Rosenfeld (n. 2) 759.
17 Ibid. 775.
18 Ibid. 761.
19 Ibid.
20 Ibid.
21 Ibid.
22 Ibid. 569.
23 Ibid.
24 Polzin (n. 9) 1615.

warns that 'the concept of constitutional identity itself is inherently fragile. There is always a risk that a constructed constitutional identity does not represent the overall picture, but only a subjective view'.[25]

Both Jacobsohn and Rosenfeld's use of the concept of constitutional identity may provide tools for examining South Africa's experience of a century of constitutions. The review of this constitutional history proceeds along two sets of questions. The first set, using Jacobsohn's focus, looks at the formation of constitutional identities through the catalyst of disharmonies in the constitutional text and between the text and the social order: What were (and are) the major disharmonies in the constitutional text, and how did they play a role in the continuous process of forming constitutional identities? The second set, using Rosenfeld's analysis, concerns the crafting of constitutional identity, which entails the questions: '*To whom* shall the constitution be addressed?' '*What* should the constitution provide?' And '*how* may the constitution be justified?'

For clarity, in this chapter the concept of constitutional identity is used in the sense of a constructed artifice, based primarily on the constitution, which, apart from regulating the exercise of power, seeks to define 'the nation' or 'the people' to which it is addressed.[26] It is not equated with the 'national identity', which may exist separately from any legal constructs.

3. South Africa's Century of Constitutions

The five constitutions that spanned the period since the foundation of South Africa in 1910 could be seen as part of a single trajectory in the formation and reformation of constitutional identities, as the disharmony in the 1909 Union constitution, that on land,[27] still reverberates in the decolonisation critiques of the 1996 Constitution. The property clause, on the one hand, protects the right to property, while, on the other, land restitution is envisaged for any person or community 'dispossessed of property after 19 June 1913 as a result of past racially discriminatory laws or practices'.[28] The 1913 date is based on the Native Land Act of that year, limiting African landholdings to 7 per cent of the land,[29] a law enacted by a whites-only parliament in terms of the 1909 Union constitution. More profound was the disharmony from the start of the negotiations on the formation of the Union (1908–9) on the contested 'imagined nation' of South Africa, the 'constitutional subject'. Although the 1996 Constitution promised a new rainbow nation of substantive equals, one overturning centuries-old economic oppression based on apartheid, race-based grinding poverty and excessive inequality are still the reality that give the promise a hollow ring.

Starting with the 1909 Union constitution, the well-known history of the next four is traversed using the tools of analysis provided by the concept of constitutional identity.

25 Ibid.
26 Following the approach by Polzin (n. 9) 1603.
27 Heinz Klug, 'Constitutional Identity and Change' (2011) 47(1) *Tulsa Law Review* 41–9, 47.
28 1996 Constitution, s 25(7).
29 A further 6 per cent was added by the Native Urban Areas Act of 1923.

3.1 The 1909 Union of South Africa Act: Imagining the New White Nation

South Africa, understood as a single political entity, commenced when the 1909 Union of South Africa Act established the Union in 1910 and was composed of four southern African dominions (Cape, Natal, Orange Free State, and Transvaal). Although the Act emanated from the imperial parliament at Westminster, the draft Act was penned by the National Convention (1908–9), comprising white political elites of the four dominions, and was approved by the legislatures of the Cape, Transvaal, and Free State and by a plebiscite in Natal.[30]

The imperial project of uniting the British dominions into a single political entity required the imagining of a new nation comprising the white 'races' of southern Africa, namely the Afrikaners of the conquered two Boer republics and the British members of the Empire. The aim was to reconcile the differences—cultural and political—between Boer and Brit, who had a common goal in the continuance of white domination over the black majority. But at the outset, there was a disharmony for Afrikaners: a choice between reconciliation with the British and the assertion of Afrikaner nationalism.[31]

The constitution reflected three narratives that would bind this 'nation' together. First and foremost, the new constitutional order would be the white man's domain. Election to Parliament was limited to the ruling white elite: only resident males (after five years of residency) who were 'British subjects of European descent' could be elected to it.[32] While that principle found favour among all parties, its foundation—the election of such members—presented a deep cleavage between the semi-liberal Cape and the arch racists of the north on voting rights irrespective of race, which led to a compromise: constitutionally protecting the continuation of coloured and African voters on the common voters' roll in the Cape.[33]

The second narrative was the protection of the language and culture of the conquered Boer republics. Afrikaner delegates, fearing English domination, demanded the constitutional protection of equality between the English and Dutch and bilingualism in the civil service.[34] This difference did not, as happened in Canada (1867), lead to opting for a federal state, the argument being that the aim of the Union was to bring the two white culture-linguistic groups closer together rather than keep them apart in self-governing federal arrangements.

The third narrative was that the imagined new nation would flourish on the back of a growing economy. Central to that objective was putting the necessary economic infrastructure across the four provinces by standardising and expanding railways and harbours. This was the theme of the only programmatic provision of the constitution:

> The railways, ports, and harbours of the Union shall be administered on business principles, due regard being had to agricultural and industrial development within the Union

[30] See H.R. Hahlo and Ellison Kahn, *The Union of South Africa: The Development of Its Laws and Constitution* (Stevens & Son, Juta & Co 1960) 118–27. See also Leonard Monteath Thompson, *The Unification of South Africa: 1902–1910* (Clarendon Press 1960).

[31] David Welsh, *The Rise and Fall of Apartheid* (Jonathan Ball 2009) 4.

[32] Sections 26(d) and 44(c).

[33] Sections 35 and 152.

[34] Hahlo and Kahn (n. 30) 125.

> and promotion, by means of cheap transport, of the settlement of an agricultural and industrial population in the inland portions of all provinces of the Union.[35]

The constitution thus contained two 'disharmonies': a 'white nation' that excluded the black majority, and, moreover, a 'white nation' which, under the British Crown, was premised on prosperity but composed of two culturally antagonistic groups, Afrikaners and Brits. Both of these disharmonies were the catalyst of evolutionary constitutional change. For Afrikaners, they would culminate in the 1961 Constitution, and for blacks, in the 1993 and 1996 constitutions.

From the outset of the Union talks in 1908, blacks saw that the constitution was to be an instrument of white domination and opposed it with petitions, deputations, and delegations.[36] The first petition was made in October 1908 by the Transvaal Native Congress, which demanded equality between whites and blacks and representation by Africans in a future national legislature. In March 1909, the South African Native Convention called for references to race or colour to be omitted from the new constitution. According to John Tengo Jabavu, one the leaders of the delegation to plead this cause in London, the draft constitution entailed that Africans 'had to accept "the crumbs of justice" falling from the new constitution'.[37] For a leading black lawyer of the time, Alfred Mangena, that law, which produced no justice, was no law at all.[38] The constitution, while ostensibly uniting the white minority, gave rise to an alternative 'imagined' South Africa and the founding in 1912 of an organisation championing that vision—the African National Congress (ANC).[39]

Following the Native Land Act of 1913 and consequential legislation in 1923 limiting black land ownership and freedom of movement (the Native (Urban Areas) Act of 1923), the ANC targeted the constitution as the source of evil and Parliament as the place for its correction. In 1923 the ANC adopted 'the African Bill of Rights', which proclaimed the freedom of movement, abode, and land ownership as well as the right of representation in Parliament and provincial legislatures.[40] It also envisaged the unrestricted ownership of land by Africans 'in the land of their birth'.[41] Lacking any power, the call was ignored both by Parliament and by the British government, which too had been petitioned.

With shifts in power on the international stage, a more receptive response was anticipated twenty years later during the Second World War when Franklin Roosevelt and Winston Churchill signed the Atlantic Charter (1941), which contained the following principle:

> [T]hey [Roosevelt and Churchill] respect the right of all peoples to choose the form of government under which they will live; and they wish to see sovereign rights and self-government restored to those who have been forcibly deprived of them.[42]

[35] Section 127.
[36] Tembeka Ngcukaitobi, *The Land Is Ours: South Africa's First Black Lawyers and the Birth of Constitutionalism* (Penguin Random House 2018) 233.
[37] Quoted in ibid. 241.
[38] Ibid.
[39] Thula Simpson, *History of South Africa: From 1902 to the Present* (Penguin Random House 2021) 29.
[40] Ngcukaitobi (n. 36) 247.
[41] Tembeka Ngcukaitobi, *Land Matters: South Africa's Failed Land Reforms and the Road Ahead* (Penguin Random House 2021) 84.
[42] Atlantic Charter, 14 August 1941 https://www.nato.int/cps/en/natohq/official_texts_16912.htm (accessed on 15 March 2023).

Directly inspired by the Atlantic Charter, the ANC adopted the African Claims in December 1943, containing two documents.[43] The first, the *Atlantic Charter from the African's Point of View*, drawing on the quoted principle, stated that 'full citizenship rights and direct participation in all the councils of the state should be recognised' in South Africa. The second document contained a Bill of Rights setting out civil and political rights on the basis of equality, including the right to own and occupy land. It also called for fair redistribution of land 'as a prerequisite for a just settlement of the land problem'.[44] In addition, positive obligations were imposed on the state to provide services in the fields of education, health care, and social security.[45] Emphasis was placed on corrective measures for Africans in these fields due to past discrimination.

The ANC's attempts to reach out to the Smuts government and the British government on the basis of the African Claims were dismissed out of hand. Smuts thought of it as 'propagandist',[46] and Churchill, for one, never thought that the Atlantic Charter applied to the British Empire.[47]

Afrikaner willingness to be part of the new 'imagined white nation' under the British Crown was equally fragile. While the new government of 1910 was led by former Boer generals—Louis Botha and Jan Smuts—in an embrace of the new nation and the British sovereign, a minority of Afrikaners rebelled against the new dispensation in 1914 at the outbreak of the First World War.[48] The armed rebellion, itself led by former Boer generals Christiaan de Wet and Koos de la Rey, was crushed by the government, but not the dream of resurrecting the Boer republics. In subsequent years the notion of an Afrikaner-dominated republic gained momentum, culminating in the election to power in 1948 of the National Party (NP), representing Afrikaner nationalists, and South Africa's becoming a republic in terms of the 1961 Constitution.

3.2 The 1961 Constitution: Celebrating Afrikaner Triumphalism

When Afrikaner nationalists came to power, two explicitly dissonant elements of the 1909 constitution became the catalyst for constitutional change: coloured voters in the Cape on the common voters' roll, and South Africa's attachment to the British Crown. The NP, with a slim majority of seats in Parliament but a minority of votes (31 per cent), sought to remove the coloured vote in the Cape as a factor in white politics and secure a clear majority of Afrikaners.[49] Using a variety of stratagems, it had succeeded by 1956 in removing the entrenched provisions.[50] The audience of the constitution was now unambiguously 'the white nation', a nation in turn with only partial loyalty to the British Crown.

[43] African Claims https://www.marxists.org/subject/africa/anc/1943/claims.htm (accessed on 15 March 2023).

[44] Ngcukaitobi (n. 41) 89.

[45] For example, under the heading of 'Full Citizens' Rights', clause 10 proclaimed '[t]he right of every child to free and compulsory education'.

[46] David Everatt, 'The Freedom Charter in Historical Perspective', in Nico Steytler (ed.), *The Freedom Charter and Beyond: Founding Principles for a Democratic South African Legal Order* (Wyvern 1991) 24.

[47] Jo Meachham, *Franklin and Winston: An Intimate Portrait of a Friendship* (Penguin Random House 2003); Ngcukaitobi (n. 36) 266.

[48] See Leonard Thompson, *A History of South Africa* (4th edn by Lynn Berat, Jonathan Ball 2014) 159; Simpson (n. 39) 42–5.

[49] Welsh (n. 31) 6.

[50] See John Dugard, *Human Rights and the South African Legal Order* (Princeton University Press 1978) 28–33.

Afrikaner nationalism eventually found expression in the adoption of the 1961 Constitution. Although effecting few substantial changes to the 1909 founding constitution, it was a momentous symbol of Afrikaner hegemony.[51] Declaring the country a republic, it severed the last strings to the British Crown, fulfilling an aspiration that had existed ever since the defeat of the Boer republics in the Anglo-Boer War. Unlike the 1909 constitution, which was a compact between Boer and Brit, the 1961 Constitution asserted Afrikaner control. Though a referendum showed a deeply divided 'white nation'—with 52.3 per cent for and 47.7 against the republic[52]—the NP could push the constitution through Parliament with a simple majority. The 'constitutional audience' was narrowed down to Afrikaner nationalists. Letting go of the British moorings and setting the country adrift in an increasingly hostile international community, the constitution employed a religious trope in its preamble, reiterating the myth of the Afrikaners as 'a chosen people' and evoking the notion that the primacy of the whites was the result of divine intervention:

> In humble submission to Almighty God, Who controls the destinies of nations and the history of peoples; . . .
>
> Who gathered our forebears together from many lands and gave them this their own;
> Who has guided them from generation to generation;
> Who has wondrously delivered them from the dangers that beset them.

The religious commitment went even beyond the non-binding preamble; the second substantive provision, following after the proclamation of republican status in section 1, declares in section 2: 'The people of the Republic of South Africa acknowledge the sovereignty and guidance of Almighty God.' Although it is no more than an exhortation, perhaps even an interpretative tool, the statement narratively binds the new imagined 'white/Afrikaner nation' to divine providence.

The NP's ascension to power led to deeper entrenchment and legalisation of apartheid in numerous aspects of social and economic life: separate settlements, job reservation, the requirement of passes for Africans to be in 'white' areas, and the slow formation of black self-governing areas. This total exclusion of blacks from the imagined 'white/Afrikaner nation' was the central disharmony between the constitution and the social order. Indeed, the increasing stringency of apartheid led to ever greater non-violent resistance in the 1950s. Of particular importance was the formulation of a diametrically opposed imagined South African nation, one comprising blacks and whites. In 1955, African (ANC), white, coloured, and Indian political organisations came together at Kliptown, a township south of Johannesburg, under the umbrella of the Congress of the People, and adopted the Freedom Charter. The non-racial composition of the Congress was resisted by Africanists within the ANC, however, and was one of the reasons for the splitting off of the Pan-Africanist Congress (PAC) in 1959.[53]

[51] Hercules Booysen and Dawid Hercules van Wyk, *Die '83 Grondwet* (Juta 1984) 5.
[52] Ibid. 5 n. 22.
[53] Ian Philips, 'The Political Role of the Freedom Charter' in Nico Steytler (ed.), *The Freedom Charter and Beyond: Founding Principles for a Democratic South African Legal Order* (Wyvern 1991) 63.

The Charter's imagined nation and society reflected the following characteristics. Firstly, non-racialism was its core principle: 'South Africa belongs to all who live in it, black and white.'[54] A new imagined nation—'we, the people of South Africa, black and white, together—equals, countrymen and brothers'—adopted the Charter. Everyone's civil and political rights should thus be protected 'regardless of race, colour or sex'. Secondly, substantive equality was the goal, reiterating the African Claims' emphasis on socio-economic rights.[55] Thirdly, equality also required a redistribution of wealth. The Charter proclaimed that '[t]he national wealth of our country, the heritage of all South Africans, shall be restored to the people'. More explicit was the demand: 'The mineral wealth beneath the soil, the banks and monopoly industry shall be transferred to the ownership of the people as a whole.' The demands regarding land were ambiguous, as they did not specifically call for the return of the land: 'Restrictions of land ownership on a racial basis shall be ended, and all land redivided amongst those who work it, to banish famine and land hunger.'

These economic clauses, which are described as no more than the social democratic principles then current in post-war Europe,[56] became the centrepiece of the 1956 prosecution for treason of the Congress of the People's leadership, a prosecution which failed: after a mammoth trial that lasted till 1961, the court found that this claim was not a call for a violent revolution.

While the 1961 Constitution's identity was for the Afrikaners that of their hegemony, it was perceived by the ANC and the PAC as a declaration of war. After the peaceful protests of the 1950s came to naught, the armed struggle commenced in 1961. On 16 December, the day the Afrikaners celebrated their 'God-given' victory in 1838 over the Zulus at the Battle of Blood River as a religious holiday,[57] the ANC's armed wing, Umkhonto we Sizwe, launched its first attack.[58] By the end of 1960s, the apartheid government had more or less crushed armed resistance and commenced implementing the grand apartheid of divide and rule—an elaborate vision of different South African nations each exercising their political rights in separate areas. Africans, already excluded from the 'constitutional audience' of 1910, would also lose their South African citizenship and be consigned to exercising political rights in ethnic-based homelands that were to develop ultimately into 'independent' countries.

Given that the imagined South African nation was of a white hue, the position within it of coloureds and Asians was problematic. At first, the approach was that coloureds were to be treated the same as Africans, namely as separate but still a 'nation in the making'; as for Asians, they would be repatriated. These solutions were pure illusions, and this internal disharmony in the 1961 Constitution eventually gave birth to an imagined 'non-African nation'.

[54] Preamble, Freedom Charter 1955.

[55] Dennis Davis regarded these provisions as 'one of the most important indigenous aspects of the Charter'. Dennis Davis, 'The Freedom Charter: A Challenge and Bequest' in Nico Steytler (ed.), *The Freedom Charter and Beyond: Founding Principles for a Democratic South African Legal Order* (Wyvern 1991) 10.

[56] Pieter le Roux, 'The Social Democratic Nature of the Charterist Economic Vision' in Nico Steytler (ed.), *The Freedom Charter and Beyond: Founding Principles for a Democratic South African Legal Order* (Wyvern 1991) 120–35.

[57] Hermann Giliomee, *The Afrikaners: Bibliography of a People* (University of Virginia Press 2009) 165.

[58] SA History online, uMkhonto weSizwe (MK) https://www.sahistory.org.za/article/umkhonto-wesizwe-mk (last accessed 3 October 2022).

3.3 The 1983 Tricameral Constitution: The Compound Non-African 'Nation'

While the government forged ahead vigorously with the grand apartheid scheme of bantustans, cracks in the apartheid edifice appeared in the 1970s. Widespread strikes by black workers in the early 1970s effectively ended the notion of black workers being only temporary sojourners in 'white cities'.[59] The 1976–7 Soweto uprising dented Afrikaner hegemony when black school children rejected Afrikaans as a medium of instruction in their schools.[60] In an attempt to shore up white dominance, the NP sought a non-African political alliance against the African majority. The 1983 Constitution thus sought to draw coloureds and Indians into the formerly white parliament from which the NP had fought so fervently to exclude them thirty years before. Drawing on the principles of consociationalism, it sought to bring the leadership of the three race groups under one roof in a type of 'racial federation',[61] albeit firmly under white control.[62]

The 1983 Constitution was meant to address a new 'imagined nation' of non-Africans. This attempt was remarkable for its ineptitude in not using any of the tools for constructing such a 'nation'. Deluded as to its omnipotence, the NP government did not involve the coloured and Indian communities in the constitution-making process at all.[63] It was strictly a parliamentary affair which in the end involved only the NP, seeing as the two main opposition parties vehemently opposed the Bill introducing the tricameral dispensation.[64] The official opposition, the Progressive Federal Party, representing liberals, pointed out its fundamental flaw—the exclusion of Africans—while the Conservative Party, representing segregationist Afrikaners, bemoaned the loss of complete white sovereignty. After adoption by a simple majority, the Act was submitted to a non-binding referendum by whites, who remained the primary audience of that constitution and received two-thirds majority support. No such referendum was extended to the coloured and Indian communities: their first opportunity to give voice would be the first elections for three separate houses of parliament, where their rejection of the new 'nation' was clear, given that the turnout of coloured and Indian registered voters (few in number to begin with) was only 21 per cent.[65]

The content of the 1983 Constitution focused on the organisation of the tricameral parliament and administrations. In Parliament, each of the three race groups had a chamber: the House of Assembly for whites; the House of Representatives for coloureds; and the House of Delegates for Indians. Legislative authority was divided between 'own affairs'[66] and 'general affairs', with the former falling in the domain of the 'ethnic' houses and the latter having to be dealt with collectively but separately. In case of a conflict between any of the houses, the final decision was made by the Presidential Council, which had a built-in majority for whites according to the following formula: four whites, two coloureds, and one Indian.

[59] Johann Maree, 'The Durban Moment: Turning Temporary Worker Action into a Permanent Democratic Trade Union Movement . . . and Then . . .?' (2019) *100*(1) *Transformation: Critical Perspectives on Southern Africa* 53–77.

[60] Welsh (n. 31) 142–71.

[61] Booysen and Van Wyk (n. 51) 45.

[62] See the National Party's defence of the Constitution in ibid. 28–31.

[63] Ibid. 36; K.P. Magyar and B. Ranchod, 'South Africa's New Constitution: The Indian Experience' (1985) *15*(1) *Africa Insight* 31–4.

[64] Booysen and Van Wyk (n. 51) 27–31.

[65] Magyar and Ranchod (n. 63) 33.

[66] Which included education, health care, welfare, culture, and local government (Schedule 1).

Building a constitutional narrative in support of the new dispensation was both contradictory and skimpy. The preamble repeated most of the 1961 'white nation' rhetoric, but 'national goals' were added, among them an injunction '[t]o uphold Christian values and civilized norms, with recognition and protection of freedom of faith and worship'—the latter phrases being an oblique reference to the sizeable numbers of Muslims and Hindus in the coloured and Indian communities. Nevertheless, the essence of the constitutional identity was still premised on separateness. The imagined 'white race' was no longer a single envisaged nation but a compound of 'population groups'. The national goal, '[t]o respect, to further and to protect the self-determination of population groups and peoples', captured both the new compound 'people' made up of three population groups, as well as the segregation of the African 'peoples'. Although the 1983 Constitution was a small step away from the hard-line racism of the 1961 Constitution, Welsh has argued that, through its inclusion of two other race groups, it sought to strengthen white dominance vis-à-vis the African majority.[67]

The exclusion of Africans from the future inclusive character of the South African state made the 1983 Constitution yet another declaration of war—the vital external disharmony. In protest against the constitution, the United Democratic Front emerged, an organisation that crossed race divisions and mobilised communities and trade unions under the banner of the Freedom Charter.[68] The revolt in black townships across the country was met by repeated declarations of states of emergency from 1985 onwards.[69] As the fragility of the white regime became more apparent, debates about a future constitutional identity flourished.

In 1988 the ANC published its Constitutional Principles when the first contact between the ANC and the minority government was surreptitiously under way.[70] Drawing on the Freedom Charter, the Principles were addressed 'to the people of South Africa' as a consultative document seeking 'to mobilise the widest sections of the population to achieve agreement on how to put an end to the tyranny and oppression under which our people live'.[71] The duty of the new state would be 'to promote the growth of a single national identity and loyalty binding all South Africans', while recognising linguistic and cultural diversity.[72] The foundations of the state were non-racialism and equality, further to which the injustices of apartheid would be corrected: 'The immediate aim is to create a just and democratic society that will sweep away the centuries-old legacy of colonial conquest and white domination, and abolish all laws imposing racial oppression and discrimination.'

Critical in this regard were 'constitutional provisions for corrective action which guarantees a rapid and irreversible redistribution of wealth and opening up of facilities for all'. More specifically, according to the section entitled 'Bill of Rights and Affirmative Action', corrective action was required to 'eradicate, speedily, the economic and social inequalities produced by racial discrimination'.[73] In general, there would be a bill of rights with the

[67] David Welsh, 'Constitutional Changes in South Africa' (1984) *83 African Affairs* 147; Welsh (n. 31) 221.

[68] Philips (n. 53) 73; Jeremy Seekings, *The UDF: A History of the United Democratic Front in South Africa, 1983–1991* (New Africa Books 2000).

[69] Welsh (n. 31) 269.

[70] On the pre-negotiations phase, see Mac Maharaj and Z. Pallo Jordan, *Breakthrough: The Struggles and Secret Talks That Brought Apartheid South Africa to the Negotiating Table* (Penguin Random House 2021); Sylvia Neame, *Drama of the Peace Process in South Africa: I Look Back 30 Years* (Best Red HSRC 2021).

[71] Preamble. See further Maharaj and Jordan (n. 70) 132.

[72] Paragraph g.

[73] Paragraph j.

usual civil and political rights as well as socio-economic rights. On the fundamental nature of a future constitution, nothing was said. Constitutional supremacy was yet to enter the ANC's lexicon: the courts were given no role in guaranteeing the Bill of Rights—the constitution would merely 'provide appropriate mechanisms for . . . [the Bill's] protection and enforcement'.[74]

The implosion of the Soviet Union, the fall of the Berlin War, and the end of the Cold War in 1989 caught the ANC off guard, as its main supporter in the armed struggle dramatically withered away and the white government saw an opportunity to take the initiative in bridging the constitutional gap between non-Africans and Africans. The unbanning in 1990 of the ANC, PAC, and other liberation movements, the release of Nelson Mandela and other political prisoners, and the commencement of negotiating a new constitution unleashed a new dynamic—a search for a new imagined nation, a new shared constitutional identity, which would end the deep constitutional division of the past eighty years.

3.4 The 1993 Constitution: The Rainbow Nation

Both sides came to terms with the fact that reliance on force would not achieve victory over the other. The white government knew that grand apartheid had failed and that, in the context of a hostile international community and a shrivelling economy, the violent suppression of the black revolt was not achievable. The ANC, despite its rhetoric, was not close to marching onto Pretoria as a victorious liberation army. Both sides saw that the continuation of the conflict would lead to the destruction of South Africa. How could the distinct 'imagined nations' of the past merge in a new constitutional identity for the future?

The main parties embarked on an inclusive process of constitution-making through negotiations. As Zephania Mothopeng, the leader of the PAC, remarked laconically in 1990, negotiations 'actually began in 1910 after the foundation of the Union of South Africa'.[75] As the first formal step, the Convention on a Democratic South Africa (Codesa) convened in December 1991. It was composed of nineteen parties from across the political spectrum, including bantustan leaders; absent were the right-wing Afrikaner party, the Conservative Party, and the left-wing Africanist parties, the PAC, and the Azanian People's Organisation (AZAPO). After much dithering, the PAC joined the negotiations in 1993.[76] While still holding formal negotiations, the NP government put before the white electorate the question of whether they supported a continuation of the reforms and negotiations and received 68 per cent support.

After the second meeting of Codesa deadlocked, the Multiparty Negotiating Forum resumed negotiations, signalling a shift in operation: attempts of obtaining consensus were abandoned, and 'sufficient consensus'—principally between the ANC and the NP government—would suffice. This left the Inkatha Freedom Party (IFP) out in the cold, which prompted its withdrawal from the process. The constitution-making process was,

[74] Paragraph h.

[75] Thami Ka Plaatjie, 'Internal Political and Administrative Re-organisation of the PAC and Negotiations in the 1990s' in South African Democracy Education Trust (ed.), *The Road to Democracy in South Africa* (Unisa Press 2013) 1074–107, 1101.

[76] Ibid.

however, kept open to entice two armed groups who could spoil the holding of the first democratic elections, namely Afrikaner and Zulu nationalists.[77]

In the end, this led to the claim in the Preamble that '[w]e, the people of South Africa' were broadly the authors of the constitution,[78] although they had no democratic mandate. But the challenge was huge: a projected constitutional identity had to accommodate, in the words of Jacobsohn, 'an aspirational aspect that is at odds with the prevailing condition of the society within which it functions'.[79]

The constitutional identity was based on three fundamental features. Firstly, a democratically drafted constitution was essential for legitimacy's sake; as such, an elected Constitutional Assembly (the elected Parliament) would be the final authors of the constitution, subject to a set of negotiated Constitutional Principles.

Secondly, an extensive bill of rights safeguarded fundamental rights. Critical for the whites was the protection of property rights. Dikgang Moseneke, a former vice president of the PAC and one of the drafters of the constitutional text, remarked that the property clause 'was perhaps the biggest give the liberation movement had to tolerate to go over the democratic winning line'.[80] While the latter was guaranteed, expropriation was permissible according to a scheme that had to provide for compensation that was 'fair and equitable', having considered a range of factors, including 'market value' and 'the history [of the land's] acquisition'.[81] Land restitution was specifically provided for regarding land that was 'dispossessed' by discriminatory laws at a date no earlier than 1913 when the Native Land Act was passed.[82] In the words of Moseneke, the property clause 'in effect, sanitised historical dispossession and entrenched property benefits and privileges of an unequal past'.[83]

Thirdly, the Constitution replaced parliamentary sovereignty with constitutional supremacy. The Constitution was 'the supreme law of the Republic and any law or act inconsistent with its provisions' would 'be of no force and effect',[84] which the courts were duty-bound to declare when it did occur. Also, the amendment procedures required a supermajority, with only the core pact—the Constitutional Principles—being unamendable.[85]

The new democratic dispensation would be affirmed by a narrative that allowed the white minority to hold on to its wealth and culture while promising new opportunities for the disadvantaged black majority. Firstly, a new 'imagined nation' was to be a negation of the past: it offered common and equal citizenship for all, a right denied for the past eighty-four years. The preamble articulated the goal as follows:

> [T]here is a need to create a new order in which all South Africans will be entitled to a common South African citizenship in a sovereign and democratic constitutional state in

[77] Nico Steytler and Johann Mettler, 'Federal Arrangements as a Peacemaking Device during South Africa's Transition to Democracy' (2001) *31*(4) *Publius: The Journal of Federalism* 93–106.

[78] The race-based and illegitimate Tricameral Parliament adopted the text agreed upon by the negotiated partners, affirming Rosenfeld's observation (n. 4 769) that where a constitution is a result of negotiations, legal continuity is usually present.

[79] Jacobsohn 2006 (n. 1) 380.

[80] Dikgang Moseneke, *My Own Liberator* (Picador Africa 2016) 302.

[81] Interim Constitution, section 28.

[82] Interim Constitution, section 121.

[83] Moseneke (n. 80) 302.

[84] Interim Constitution, section 4(1).

[85] Interim Constitution, section 74(1).

> which there is equality between men and woman and people of all races shall be able to enjoy and exercise their fundamental rights and freedoms.

In the post-amble, a narrative unifying the past and a better future was movingly told:

> This Constitution provides a historic bridge between the past of a deeply divided society characterised by strife, conflict, untold suffering and injustice, and a future founded on the recognition of human rights, democracy and peaceful co-existence and development opportunities for all South Africans, irrespective of colour, race, class, belief or sex. The pursuit of national unity, the well-being of all South African citizens and peace require reconciliation between the people of South Africa and the reconstruction of society.
>
> The adoption of this Constitution lays the secure foundation for the people of South Africa to transcend the divisions and strife of the past, which generated gross violations of human rights, the transgression of humanitarian principles in violent conflicts and a legacy of hatred, fear, guilt and revenge.
>
> These can now be addressed on the basis that there is a need for understanding but not for vengeance, a need for reparation but not for retaliation, a need for ubuntu but not for victimisation.

While the Constitution wove the history of white oppression and the need for corrective action into the narrative, the post-amble also provided for reconciliation and amnesty for committed crimes 'associated with political objectives and committed in the course of the conflicts of the past', clearly referring to apartheid repression even though this also applied to crimes committed by the liberation movements.[86]

Secondly, unity and diversity were the catchwords, with diversity no longer resting on race but on language and culture. The rights and freedoms protected key interests of the outgoing ruling class. Although Afrikaans became one of eleven official languages,[87] it nevertheless could be asserted. So, too, were cultural rights and the right to mother-tongue education where practicable.[88] Thirdly, the new 'nation' consisted of citizens each entitled to their rights and freedoms and bound together by a common commitment to constitutionalism.

This new identity was depicted by the high priests of the Constitution, the Constitutional Court justices, as one unifying a nation after centuries of division. In the Court's first decision, invalidating the death penalty, Justice Mahomed described the function of the Constitution in universal terms: 'All Constitutions seek to articulate, with differing degrees of intensity and detail, the shared aspirations of a nation; the values which bind its people, and which discipline its government and its national institutions.'[89] As South Africa's previous constitutions were testimony of the opposite, what Mahomed described was an ideal type of constitution capable of performing such an exalted function—by implication, the 1993 Constitution was an example par excellence of such an institution. And so it was that the 'rainbow nation'[90] rose from the ashes of centuries of conflict.

[86] Truth and Reconciliation Commission, *Truth and Reconciliation Commission of South Africa Report* Vol 2 (Truth and Reconciliation Commission 1998) 325–99.

[87] Interim Constitution, section 3.

[88] Interim Constitution, sections 31 and 32.

[89] *S v Makwanyane and Another* (1995) ZACC 3 para. 251.

[90] See Simpson (n. 39) 357 et seq.

3.5 The 1996 Constitution: The Soul of the Nation

The 1996 Constitution was to give the new constitutional dispensation the inclusive democratic legitimacy which the 1993 Constitution lacked. The drafting body, the Constitutional Assembly (CA), comprised the newly elected parliament of 400 members of the National Assembly and 90 senators. The proportional representation electoral system ensured that the National Assembly was highly representative of the full array of opinion across the political spectrum: the ANC received 63 per cent of the vote (252 seats); the NP, 20.5 per cent (82 seats); the IFP, 10.75 per cent (43 seats); the conservative Afrikaners' Freedom Front, 2.25 per cent (9 seats); the liberal white Democratic Party, 1.75 per cent (7 seats); the PAC, 1.25 per cent (5 seats); and the African Christian Democratic Party, 0.45 per cent (2 seats).[91] The 90 senators were much less proportional, as each provincial legislature elected 10 senators even if its population ranged from a million to 12 million. Reaching agreement within the two-year cut-off period, 86 per cent of the CA members voted for the Constitution, with only the IFP and the PAC voting against.

The democratic credentials of the Constitution were not seriously questioned given that the CA was encumbered by the Constitutional Principles. The first eleven Constitutional Principles required no more than a modern liberal constitution: a democratic state with a separation of powers between the three branches of government; a bill of rights of 'universally accepted fundamental rights, freedoms and civil liberties';[92] and constitutional supremacy, enforced by an 'independent and impartial judiciary'.[93] More contentious was the preservation of the federal elements in the constitution, a structure of the state the ANC vehemently opposed: it took eleven principles to pin down the essentials of a very weak form of federalism.

As with the interim Constitution, the 1996 update was also in the business of creating an 'imagined nation' from the wreckage of the past. The 1996 Constitution's preamble could now rightly claim that '[w]e, the people of South Africa . . . through our freely elected representatives' are the authors of the document. 'The people' are also inclusively self-defined as those who '[b]elieve that South Africa belongs to all who live in it, united in our diversity'. While the nature of the diversity is not disclosed but well understood—race, language, ethnicity, and religion—the question is: What 'unites' the people? How is the narrative constitutionally woven? The recognition of 'the injustices of our past' and the honouring of those 'who suffered for justice and freedom in our land' tell of different stories that divide the former oppressors and the oppressed. The aim, then, is to 'heal the divisions of the past and establish a society based on democratic values, social justice and fundamental human rights'.[94]

The Constitution's task is thus 'to lay the foundations' so as to '[i]mprove the quality of life of all citizens and free the potential of each person'. The 'imagined' South African nation of the future would be built on four premises: a commitment to democracy, social justice, fundamental human rights, and constitutional supremacy. The content of the Constitution cemented that.

[91] Jacques de Ville, 'The Electoral System in Terms of the South African Interim Constitution' in Jacques de Ville and Nico Steytler (eds.), *Voting in 1999* (Butterworths 1996) 23 table 5.

[92] Schedule 4, Constitutional Principle II.

[93] Schedule 4, Constitutional Principle II; Schedule 4, Constitutional Principle VII.

[94] Preamble.

The 'imagined nation' was also indirectly defined in the foundation values captured in section 1:

> The Republic of South Africa is one, sovereign, democratic states founded on the following values:
> (a) Human dignity, the achievement of equality and the advancement of human rights and freedoms.
> (b) Non-racialism and non-sexism.
> (c) Supremacy of the constitution and the rule of law.
> (d) Universal adult suffrage, a national common voters roll, regular elections and a multi-party system of democratic government, to ensure accountability, responsiveness and openness.

Paragraph (a) contains two narratives. The first brings to the fore implicitly the apartheid history of the denial of dignity, prompting the value of 'the achievement of equality'. Achieving equality can be promoted by the various provisions recognising the need for corrective action and the social welfarism of socio-economic rights. The second narrative comes in the universalisation of human rights and freedom in the Bill of Rights, which included, critically for whites, the inclusion of property rights. Section 25, the property clause, protects property rights as well as promises the restitution of land dispossessed since 1913 and land reform.

The inequality to be rectified was primarily linked to race and gender. The new nation would be 'non-racial and non-sexist', an example of Rosenfeld's observation that a constitutional identity is often 'defined, to some degree, by who "we" are not, as opposed to who we are'.[95] The value is not what South Africans are, but what they should not be. But only up to a point: they will all be democrats. Here again the narrative refers obliquely to the past struggle against separate voters' rolls. The grand narrative is thus a nation of substantive equals, bonded by a supreme constitution and the rule of law that provide the framework in which the deep disharmonies would be reduced. In this sense, the constitutional identity is constructed as 'an aspirational constitutional identity',[96] as an imagined nation yet to be built.

The 1996 Constitution was lauded locally and abroad as the crowning glory of a long process of peaceful transfer of power that united former antagonists in a new compact. The process of constitution-making was hailed as inclusive, open, and participatory. It was the beginning of a new nation. The title of Hassen Ebrahim's book on the constitution-making process, *The Soul of a Nation: Constitution-Making in South Africa*,[97] captures the symbolically loaded meaning first articulated by Justice Mahomed with reference to the interim Constitution. The latter's aim was to serve not only as a programmatic blueprint 'for thoroughgoing, state-led social and economic change'[98] but as the template for a new nation.

95 Rosenfeld (n. 2) 775.
96 Polzin (n. 9) 1612.
97 Hassen Ebrahim, *The Soul of a Nation: Constitution-Making in South Africa* (Oxford University Press 1999).
98 Theunis Roux, 'The Global South and Liberal Constitutionalism: Incommensurable Opposites', IACL-IADC Blog, 15 July 2021, https://blog-iacl-aidc.org/2021-posts/6-15-21the-global-south-and-liberal-constitutionalism-incommensurable-opposites (last accessed 15 August 2021).

4. Disharmonies in the Rainbow Nation

Twenty-five years later, South Africa's imagined nation of substantive equals exercising their individual rights within the framework of the rule of law seems to be receding further and further into never-neverland: the disharmony between the constitutional promise and experience is deep and intense. Grinding poverty abounds, inequality is the highest in the world, and there is no sign of it having decreased since the end of apartheid.[99] The economy is still highly skewed in favour of whites. Even the Constitutional Court has recognised this failure, which it attributes neither to the Constitution nor legislation but to governmental incapacity.[100] Such a bureaucratic failure, Justice Edwin Cameron warned, '[has] jeopardised not only the rights of land claimants, but the constitutional security and future of all'.[101] He added that 'South Africans have been waiting for more than 25 years for equitable land reform. More accurately, they have been waiting for centuries before'.[102]

Instead of effect being given to the section 1 value of democratic government by ensuring 'accountability, responsiveness and openness', South Africa has witnessed the emergence of a patrimonial state, one reaching a peak of state capture during Jacob Zuma's presidency.[103] Apart from high levels of crime, the frailty of the rule of law came sharply into focus with Zuma's arrest in July 2021 on being found guilty of contempt of court. It was followed by the collapse of law and order in KwaZulu-Natal and parts of Gauteng, where widespread looting, destruction of property, and loss of life occurred, with the state machinery seemingly paralysed and incapable of taking action.[104]

Even the symbol of the rainbow nation has come under attack over the past decade, with the 1996 Constitution being assailed for lying at the root of the country's slow implosion.[105] As Theunis Roux perceptively remarks:

> The 1996 Constitution, in its moral idealism and utopian social welfarism, was always going to be susceptible to attack if it was seen to be failing to deliver on its promises. The fact that South Africa's poor economic performance is not really a function of the 1996 Constitution, but rather of a combination of the enduring legacy of apartheid, international economic factors, poor policy choices, and the ANC's descent into corruption, does not make any difference.[106]

[99] Aroop Chatterjee, Léo Czajka, and Amory Gethin, 'Wealth Inequality in South Africa, 1993–2017' World Inequality Lab (2021) https://wid.world/document/wealth-inequality-in-south-africa-wid-world-working-paper-2021-16/ (last accessed 8 August 2021) 1: 'The top 10% of South African wealth holders own more than 85% of household wealth, while the top 1% wealth share reaches 55%. The top 0.01% (about 3,500 adults) own a higher share of wealth than the bottom 90% as a whole (about 32 million individuals). The average wealth of the bottom 50% is negative: the market value of their assets is lower than their liabilities.'

[100] *Mwelase and Others v Director-General for the Department of Rural Development and Land Reform and Another* (2019) ZACC 30 para. 41 .

[101] Ibid.

[102] Ibid.

[103] Judicial Commission on Allegations of State Capture, Corruption and Fraud in the Public Sector and Organs of State (Zondo Commission) 6 volumes (2022) https://www.statecapture.org.za/ (last accessed 30 September 2022).

[104] Abahlali baseMjondolo, 'KwaZulu-Natal and Gauteng Are Burning, We Need to Build a Just Peace' (13 July 2021) https://abahlali.org/node/17320/ (last accessed 20 July 2021).

[105] See D.M. Davis, 'Is the South African Constitution an Obstacle to a Democratic Post-colonial State? (2018) 34(3) *South African Journal on Human Rights* 359–74.

[106] Roux (n. 98) 22.

At both academic and political levels, disharmonies within the constitutional text and between the text and society have been headlined, contesting the carefully constructed elements of the constitutional identity—the imagined rainbow nation—of the 1996 Constitution. The very audience of the Constitution is questioned: were the 'freely elected representatives'[107] of the majority black Africans 'sell-outs' or liberators when it came to the land question? Was the entire Western liberal democratic edifice, including constitutional supremacy, in dissonance with African values? The attacks do not have a unified ideological or political base, with the two main strands being Africanist and populist, albeit that for many, these are mutually supportive.

The main attack against the 1996 Constitution is the legitimacy of its basis—or, to put it in the vocabulary of constitutional identity, the attack targets the disharmony between the constitution and society, meaning the majority black population. Joel Modiri contends that the Constitution's fundamental fault is its failure to address what its primary purpose should be—African historical justice.[108] He argues that

> South Africa's constitutional democracy has over the years been rendered empty by the absence of concrete historical justice and the non-realisation of an emancipatory experience of freedom and dignity in the lives of the black majority in South Africa.[109]

According to Modiri, the Constitution is more than a legal text but the embodiment of a larger political and cultural rationality that embeds Western liberal democracy to the exclusion of African values. The very notion that the Constitution is there 'to hold together the always-already fragile civic bonds of the nation' is questioned.[110] For Modiri, it is not a question of 'blaming' or 'rejecting' the Constitution, but of asking 'to what extent *this particular constitution* and liberal constitutionalism in general is able to provide for a framework, vision and language that is "purpose-made" to address the accumulated social contradictions of colonial conquest, racial capitalism, apartheid and neoliberalism' (emphasis in the original).[111]

Land and property remain the central disharmony. Land, in particular, is viewed as much more than a policy area: as Khwezi Mabasa and Bulelwa Mabasa argue, '[l]and ownership and power relations inform core building blocks of nation-building, such as political identity, social cohesion, citizenship and belonging'.[112] For Tembeka Ngcukaitobi, the land question remains the 'unfinished business of the liberation struggle: until and unless there is a confrontation with the negotiated settlement of the transitional in period, it is impossible to speak of freedom, equality and dignity, values we cherish'.[113] Tshepo Madlingozi, following a decolonisation approach to the Constitution, argues that in its entirety it is still built on the 'right of conquest' by the settler community.[114] For this very

[107] Preamble, Constitution 1996.

[108] Joel M. Modiri, 'Conquest and Constitutionalism: First Thoughts on an Alternative Jurisprudence' (2018) *34 South African Journal of Human Rights* 300–25.

[109] Ibid. 4.

[110] Ibid. 8.

[111] Ibid. 18.

[112] Khwezi Mabasa and Bulelwa Mabasa, 'Nation Formation, Citizenship and Rethinking Land Reform' in Khwezi Mabasa and Bulelwa Mabasa (eds.), *Land in South Africa: Contested Meanings and Nation Formation* (Mapungubwe Institute for Strategic Reflection 2021) 351.

[113] Ngcukaitobi (n. 41) 6.

[114] Tshepo Madlingozi, 'On Settler Colonialism and Post-Conquest Constitutionness: The Decolonising Constitutional Vision of African Nationalists of Azania/South Africa' https://www.academia.edu/33747352/

reason, the PAC rejected the Freedom Charter of 1955 and the 1996 Constitution.[115] As the foundation of the constitutional dispensation has not been addressed, he labels the constitutional order as 'neo-apartheid constitutionalism'.[116] For a constitution to be a rupture with the settler-colonial past, it must establish 'the restoration of complete, unencumbered and integral sovereignty to the conquered as at conquest'.[117] Magobe Ramose thus depicts the Constitution as 'a second conquest', as it validated the earlier 'right of conquest'.[118]

Madlingozi thus argues that, despite the democratic claims of its birth, the Constitution was no more than 'an elite compromise',[119] as the ANC at that juncture in time 'sold out' to international and local capital. The acceptance of the 1913 Native Land Act as the starting point for land restitution bears testimony of that.[120] Although Heinz Klug reminds us that the constitution-writing did not follow a victory in war or rebellion (there was no ANC or PAC military victory in sight after the collapse of their main supporter, the Soviet Union),[121] the salience of this fact recedes in the face of a new narrative spun by a growing popular mood for reimagining 'the nation' and its constitutional identity.

For others, the Bill of Rights is a 'Bill for Whites' because it entrenched the conquered land: for Ramose, a constitution will be postcolonial only if it ends colonialists' and successors' 'right of conquest'.[122] The Constitution is too restrictive in that it places obstacles in the way of the redistribution of land. Critical is the property clause in section 25 in the Bill of Rights. The ensuing debate has been whether section 25 is broad enough to accommodate expropriation of land without compensation, or if its amendment (or repeal) is essential to achieving one of the goals of the Constitution—the redistribution of resources. While many commentators have argued that section does not require compensation at market value[123] and that the poor track record of land restitution and reform is due primarily to government ineptitude, other political forces see an amendment as vital for reshaping property relations. The most vociferous are the Economic Freedom Fighters (EFF), a political party that hived off from the ANC, and elements within the ANC comprising its so-called Radical Economic Transformation (RET) faction, one much influenced by the rhetoric of the EFF.[124]

On_Settler_Colonialism_and_Post-Conquest_Constitutionness_The_Decolonising_Constitutional_Vision_of_African_Nationalists_of_Azania_South_Africa (last accessed 1 August 2021); Tshepo Madlingozi, 'South Africa's First Black Lawyers, AmaRespectables and the Birth of Evolutionary Constitution—a review of Tembeka Ngcukaitobi's *The Land Is Ours: South Africa's First Black Lawyers and the Birth of Constitutionalism*' (2018) *31 South African Journal on Human Rights* 517–29.

[115] Madlingozi 'Decolonising Constitution Vision' (n. 114).
[116] Tsepo Madlingozi, 'Social Justice in a Time of Neo-apartheid Constitutionalism: Critiquing the Anti-Black Economy of Recognition, Incorporation and Distribution' (2017) *Stellenbosh Law Review* 123.
[117] Madlingozi 'Decolonising Constitution Vision' (n. 114) 13, quoting Mogobe Ramose.
[118] Quoted in Madlingozi 'Neo-apartheid Constitutionalism' (n. 116), 139. See also Magobe Bernard Ramose, 'Towards a Post-conquest South Africa: Beyond the Constitution of 1996' (2018) *34*(3) *South African Journal on Human Rights* 326–41.
[119] Madlingozi 'Neo-apartheid Constitutionalism' (n. 116) 128.
[120] Ngcukaitobi (n. 41) 114.
[121] Heinz Klug, 'Decolonisation, Compensation and Constitutionalism: Land, Wealth and the Sustainability of Constitutionalism in Post-apartheid South Africa' (2018) *34*(3) *South African Journal on Human Rights* 469–91.
[122] Quoted in Madlingozi 'Neo-apartheid Constitutionalism' (n. 116) 140.
[123] Ngcukaitobi (n. 41).
[124] Theunis R. Roux, 'Constitutional Populism in South Africa' https://papers.ssrn.com/sol3/papers.cfm?abstract_id=3583270 18 (last accessed 6 July 2021).

A constitutional amendment bill has been before Parliament since 2019, but a lack of agreement between the ANC and the EFF had, by the time of writing (September 2022), not yet produced the requisite two-thirds majority. In a major concession seeking to narrow the dissonance, the ANC in August 2021 tabled a further amendment to the draft amendment Bill making the cut-off date for land claims the year 1800 and thus prior to conquest of the bulk of South Africa.[125]

Dissonance has also been heard in regard to the experience of constitutionalism and, more fundamentally, to the notion of constitutionalism itself. The immediate and pointed critique comes from the government which, after losing cases, castigates judges for not observing the separation of powers. Given the range of the Constitution, it was inevitable that the judiciary, the guardian of the Constitution, would cross swords with the executive and legislature.[126] The constitutionalised policy of socio-economic rights has clashed with government-directed policy on the same matter. After losing two socio-economic rights cases, the secretary-general of the ANC reportedly said the courts were 'acting as if they were the political opposition and in so doing seeking to arrest the functioning of Government'.[127] Suffering one legal defeat after the other, senior government ministers have attacked the courts for resisting 'transformation' and being in opposition to the government.[128]

A fundamental disharmony is that between constitutionalism and democracy. Although there have been populist attacks against the notion of constitutional supremacy,[129] critiques of it have been made by Africanist scholars not only on the basis of courts' intrinsic anti-majoritarian nature but also for its consequences. Ramose, for one, argues that the move from parliamentary sovereignty to constitutional supremacy 'consolidated historical injustices, and is, thus, tantamount to a second "conquest", a conquest by consent'.[130]

The post-apartheid constitutional identity, carefully cultivated since its inception, is contested; the 1996 Constitution is riven with disharmonies, and a dialogical process is under way in reshaping a new one. How will this dialogical process work out? While the Constitution may provide the catalysts of change, it is power play between two visions of the nation that will be determinative.

On the one hand, the ruling faction of the ruling party still sees South Africa's constitutional identity as the bedrock of the 'imagined nation': the Constitution must simply be given effect in 'experience'. Ngcukaitobi, for example, while recognising that the Constitution 'is also a symbol of our collective soul and vision', argues that 'it is time to take the Constitution off the shelf. Dust it off. And put it to work on the land'.[131] The Constitution is seen as a useful instrument that remains capable of delivering transformation within the confines of

[125] Jan Gerber, 'Section 25: Traditional Land Exempt from Expropriation without Compensation in New Draft Amendment', News24 (27 August 2021) https://www.news24.com/news24/southafrica/news/section-25-traditional-land-exempt-from-expropriation-without-compensation-in-new-draft-amendment-20210827 (last accessed on 31 August 2021).

[126] See H. Kawadza, 'Attacks on the Judiciary: Undercurrents of a Political versus Legal Constitutionalism Dilemma?' *21* (2018) *PER/PELJ*.

[127] Ibid. 7.

[128] Isabeau Steytler, '"Striking Back" and "Clamping Down" in South Africa: Responding to Adverse Judicial Decisions under Systems of Parliamentary Sovereignty and Constitutional Supremacy' (2020) *12 Hague Journal on the Rule of Law* 12 363–86.

[129] See Nico Steytler, 'The Dynamic Relationship between Devolution and Constitutionalism in South Africa' in Charles Fombad and Nico Steytler (eds.), *Decentralisation and Constitutionalism in Africa* (Oxford University Press 2019) 151–82, 178.

[130] Referred to by Madlingozi 'Neo-apartheid Constitutionalism' (n. 116) 141.

[131] Ngcukaitobi (n. 41) 7.

the rule of law. Dennis Davis, too, argues that the Constitution does not preclude 'a rigorous examination' of the colonial past and an understanding of the role of law in reproducing social order, something which would enable a reimagining of 'a legal system that can contribute to make the country whole'.[132] The most eloquent defence of the rule of law comes from a shack-dwellers' movement, Abahlali baseMjondolo:

> We remain committed to the Constitution because the law gives us some protection from the political gangsters in the ANC. Without the law, repression would be much worse. We would just be ruled by violence. Therefore, the Constitution must be defended at all costs.[133]

On the other hand, the ANC's populist faction of rentiers, along with the EFF and Africanists, are seeking fundamental constitutional change, with some of them envisioning a reversion to the 1909 constitution model, only now with different role-players. It is an assertion of black dominance, one refocusing power in Parliament as the locus of policy-making by restoring the latter's sovereignty and, consequently, black sovereignty over land and property. Time will tell whether they gain ascendancy amidst the debris of a failing state and popular discontent, dismantle limitations on state action, and reshape South Africa's constitutional identity yet again.

5. Conclusion

The question posed at the outset of the chapter was whether the analytical tools associated with the concept of constitutional identity provide a useful lens through which South African constitutional development over the past century can be examined. Do these tools unlock a fuller understanding of the shaping of the South African 'nation' by means of constitutional engineering? The short answer is yes; the longer answer lies in four observations.

Firstly, the notion of a dialogical process of constitutional identity formation reminds us again of the historical context of the drafting of the South African constitutions. As Jacobsohn noted, the 1996 Constitution is an excellent example of such a process.[134] Political actors and scholars trace clear linkages between the 1909 South Africa Act and the 1993 and 1996 constitutions (and the apartheid constitutions of 1961 and 1983 in between). The drafters of the 1996 Constitution draw the link,[135] and its detractors do the same, only more emphatically. The dialogue has been over the land, democracy, and equality. The fashioning and refashioning of a constitutional identity are an ongoing process that can slow down but never be terminated. The observation that 'American constitutional history is best understood as an ongoing struggle over our collective constitutional identity'[136] is equally true of South Africa. It was (and is) a struggle about who the South African nation is or is imagined to be.

[132] Davis (n. 105) 70.
[133] Abahlali baseMjondolo (n. 104).
[134] Jacobsohn (n. 1) 3.
[135] See Leon Wessels, *Vereeniging: Die Onvoltooide Vrede* (Umuzi 2010).
[136] Jacobsohn (n. 1) 366, quoting Bruce Ackerman.

Secondly, the dialogical process of constitutional identity formation is driven by the disharmonies immanent in the constitutional text and between the text and wider society. The explicit exclusion of blacks from the democratic institutions of the 1909 Union constitution engendered resistance and rebellion. Closely connected to this was the disharmony about land, which after a century now occupies centre stage. An alternative imagined nation—comprising all the inhabitants of South Africa—was present from the beginning. The African Bill of Rights of 1923, the *Atlantic Charter from the African's Point of View* of 1943, the Freedom Charter of 1955, and the ANC's Constitutional Principles of 1988 offered a different imagining of the 'the people'. More parochial was the disharmony in the 1909 constitution's subjection of Afrikaners to the majesty of the British monarch, which resulted eventually in Afrikaner hegemony and South Africa's republican status. The 1983 Constitution, which sought to foster an anti-African alliance among whites, coloureds, and Indians, was the final catalyst for smashing the old order and bringing forth the rainbow nation. The 1993 and 1996 constitutions, in seeking to eliminate those disharmonies, contained their own disharmonies, ones that may well drive the next iteration of South Africa's constitutional identity.

Thirdly, while we can view this process from a historical perspective, the formation of a constitutional identity at any given time, particularly at 'constitutional moments' of great significance, is, in Rosenfeld's lexicon, an active process of constructing such an identity. Constitutional authors purposefully set out to define the constitutional identity by asking, '*To whom* shall the constitution be addressed', '*What* should the constitution provide' and, '*[H]ow* may the constitution be justified?' (emphasis in the original).[137] The addressee of the 1909 constitution was explicitly the new 'imagined nation' of white South Africans who would bridge the deep, war-based conflict between Boer and Brit. Blacks were not part of that image (with minor exceptions); it was a case of seeking a common identity between the two 'white races', while simultaneously suppressing the importance of divergent black identities.[138] A part of the white 'nation' were the Afrikaners, who unshackled themselves from the British monarchy in 1961. Later, visceral racism was sacrificed at the altar of strengthening white domination with the tricameral Constitution of 1983 and its weak attempt to define a new compound 'non-African nation'. The negotiations between black and white, culminating in the 1993 and 1996 constitutions, saw the construction of the new 'rainbow nation' as an 'aspirational constitutional identity',[139] but twenty-five years later, proponents of decolonisation contend that their aspirations are not addressed in the Constitution. Establishing a fully inclusive imagined selfhood is, indeed, likely to elude the efforts of any constitutional author: the seeds of disharmony are difficult to dislodge.

As to the content of a constitution, its particular character is also gleaned from those provisions that receive special protection. The 1909 Union constitution, a compromise document, included protection of the Dutch language as well as coloured voters in the Cape Province. The entrenchment of the official status of Afrikaans and English in the subsequent 1961 and 1983 apartheid constitutions was of symbolic value only, as the removal of constitutional review during the 1950s entrenched Afrikaner/white power through parliamentary sovereignty. It was only with the construction of the rainbow nation, defined by

[137] Rosenfeld (n. 2) 756.
[138] See Polzin (n. 9) 1600.
[139] Ibid. 1613.

and epitomised in the 1993 and 1996 constitutions, that constitutional supremacy became important again.

The justifications in the constitutional text for new 'imagined nations' alert us to the need for close reading. The 1909 Union constitution was weak on justificatory rhetoric; it was business-like in setting out the organisation of state power, with only the commitment to economic development of the new nation finding expression, here in provisions relating to railways and harbours. The 1961 apartheid constitution brought into the text a divine guiding hand that would protect the fledgling nation as it sought its fortunes outside the British Commonwealth. The 1983 Constitution offered little justification as to why a breach with the racist past had been made in seeking to bring the coloured and Indian communities into the white nation's camp. Much stronger were the narratives surrounding the alternative vision of 'the people' of South Africa from 1908 onwards. Building on these narratives, the 1993 and 1996 constitutions explicitly tell the historical story of struggle and suffering (justification) and propound the features of the new aspirational nation which reconciles past disharmonies while seeking a new harmony.

Finally, as both Jacobsohn and Rosenfeld point out, the constitution cannot by itself carry out the task of constructing a constitutional identity. It is a mere text and is not self-executing: it must be animated by experience. This self-evident truth focuses our attention acutely on the fate of the 1996 Constitution. If the promise that the constitutional enterprise will '[i]mprove the quality of life of all citizens and free the potential of each person'[140] falls flat, so does the Constitution. As a symbol of the 'soul of the nation', it will also become the symbolic scapegoat and victim of the unrealised aspirational nation.

Where does this analysis leave South Africans? Change is inevitable; the only question is when and how radical. Since disharmonies will drive the process, they must be understood and dealt with. If the state and the ruling party are unwilling or unable to bring about the imagined 'rainbow nation' of 'a people' of substantive equals bonded by a commitment to democracy, social justice, and equality, the disharmony will only become louder and more raucous. The question that will have to be addressed is whether, in the process of refashioning a new constitutional identity, the current constitutional commitment to restraining the abuse of state power will expediently fall away and allow for the tyranny of the state, as occurred under parliamentary sovereignty in the apartheid era—or have the basic tenets of constitutionalism become part of South Africa's constitutional identity?

Bibliography

Abahlali baseMjondolo, 'KwaZulu-Natal and Gauteng Are Burning, We Need to Build a Just Peace' (13 July 2021) https://abahlali.org/node/17320/ (last accessed 20 July 2021)

African National Congress, 'African Claims' https://www.marxists.org/subject/africa/anc/1943/claims.htm

Booysen H. and Van Wyk D.H., *Die '83 Grondwet* (Juta 1984)

Chatterjee A., Czajka L., and Gethin A., 'Wealth Inequality in South Africa, 1993–2017', World Inequality Lab (2021) https://wid.world/document/wealth-inequality-in-south-africa-wid-world-working-paper-2021-16/ (last accessed on 8 August 2021)

[140] Preamble, Constitution of 1996.

Davis D., 'The Freedom Charter: A Challenge and Bequest' in Steytler N. (ed.), *The Freedom Charter and Beyond: Founding Principles for a Democratic South African Legal Order* (Wyvern 1991) 1

Davis D.M., 'Is the South African Constitution an Obstacle to a Democratic Post-colonial State?' (2018) *34*(3) *South African Journal on Human Rights* 359

De Ville J., 'The Electoral System in Terms of the South African Interim Constitution' in De Ville J. and Steytler N. (eds.), *Voting in 1999* (Butterworths 1996) 23

Dugard J., *Human Rights and the South African Legal Order* (Princeton University Press 1978)

Ebrahim H., *The Soul of a Nation: Constitution-Making in South Africa* (Oxford University Press 1999)

Everatt D., 'The Freedom Charter in Historical Perspective' in Steytler N. (ed.), *The Freedom Charter and Beyond: Founding Principles for a Democratic South African Legal Order* (Wyvern 1991) 21

Gerber J., 'Section 25: Traditional Land Exempt from Expropriation without Compensation in New Draft Amendment', *News24* (27 August 2021) https://www.news24.com/news24/southafrica/news/section-25-traditional-land-exempt-from-expropriation-without-compensation-in-new-draft-amendment-20210827 (last accessed on 31 August 2021)

Giliomee H., *The Afrikaners: Bibliography of a People* (University of Virginia Press 2009)

Hahlo H.R. and Kahn E., *The Union of South Africa: The Development of Its Laws and Constitution* (Stevens & Son, Juta & Co 1960) 118

Jacobsohn G.J., 'Constitutional Identity' (2006) *68 The Review of Politics* 361

Jacobsohn G.J., 'The Formation of Constitutional Identities' in Ginsburg T. and Dixon R. (eds.), *Comparative Constitutional Law* (Elgar 2011) 137

Jacobsohn G.J., 'Theorising the Constitutional Revolution' (2014 Spring) *Journal of Law and Courts* 1

Judicial Commission on Allegations of State Capture, Corruption and Fraud in the Public Sector and Organs of State (Zondo Commission) 6 volumes (2022) https://www.statecapture.org.za/ (last accessed 30 September 2022)

Ka Plaatjie T., 'Internal Political and Administrative Re-organisation of the PAC and Negotiations in the 1990s' in South African Democracy Education Trust (ed.), *The Road to Democracy in South Africa* (Unisa Press 2013) 1074

Kawadza H., 'Attacks on the Judiciary: Undercurrents of a Political versus Legal Constitutionalism Dilemma?' (2018) *21 PER/PELJ*

Klug H., *Constituting Democracy* (Cambridge University Press 2002)

Klug H., 'Constitutional Identity and Change' (2011) *47*(1) *Tulsa Law Review* 41

Klug H., 'Decolonisation, Compensation and Constitutionalism: Land, Wealth and the Sustainability of Constitutionalism in Post-apartheid South Africa' (2018) *34*(3) *South African Journal on Human Rights* 469

Le Roux P., 'The Social Democratic Nature of the Charterist Economic Vision' in Steytler N. (ed.), *The Freedom Charter and Beyond: Founding Principles for a Democratic South African Legal Order* (Wyvern 1991) 120

Mabasa K. and Mabasa B., 'Nation Formation, Citizenship and Rethinking Land Reform' in Mabasa K. and Mabasa B. (eds.), *Land in South Africa: Contested Meanings and Nation Formation* (Mapungubwe Institute for Strategic Reflection 2021) 351

Madlingozi T., 'Social Justice in a Time of Neo-apartheid Constitutionalism: Critiquing the Anti-Black Economy of Recognition, Incorporation and Distribution' (2017) *Stellenbosh Law Review* 123

Madlingozi T., 'South Africa's First Black Lawyers, AmaRespectables and the Birth of Evolutionary Constitution—a review of Tembeka Ngcukaitobi's *The Land Is Ours: South Africa's First Black Lawyers and the Birth of Constitutionalism*' (2018) *34*(3) *South African Journal on Human Rights* 517

Madlingozi T., 'On Settler Colonialism and Post-Conquest *Constitutionness*: The Decolonising Constitutional Vision of African Nationalists of Azania/South Africa' (2016) https://www.academia.edu/33747352/On_Settler_Colonialism_and_Post-Conquest_Constitutionness_The_Decolonising_Constitutional_Vision_of_African_Nationalists_of_Azania_South_Africa (last accessed 1 August 2021)

Magyar K.P. and Ranchod B., 'South Africa's New Constitution: The Indian Experience' (1985) *15*(1) *Africa Insight* 31

Maharaj M. and Jordan Z.P., *Breakthrough: The Struggles and Secret Talks That Brought Apartheid South Africa to the Negotiating Table* (Penguin Random House 2021)

Maree J., 'The Durban Moment: Turning Temporary Worker Action into a Permanent Democratic Trade Union Movement . . . and Then . . .?' Transformation: Critical (2019) *100*(1) *Perspectives on Southern Africa* 53

Meachham J., *Franklin and Winston: An Intimate Portrait of a Friendship* (Penguin Random House 2003)

Modiri J.M., 'Conquest and Constitutionalism: First Thoughts on an Alternative Jurisprudence' (2018) *34 South African Journal of Human Rights* 300

Moseneke D., *My Own Liberator* (Picador Africa 2016)

Neame S., *Drama of the Peace Process in South Africa: I Look Back 30 Years* (Best Red HSRC 2021)

Ngcukaitobi T., *The Land Is Ours: South Africa's First Black Lawyers and the Birth of Constitutionalism* (Penguin Random House 2018)

Ngcukaitobi T., *Land Matters: South Africa's Failed Land Reforms and the Road Ahead* (Penguin Random House 2021)

Philips I, 'The Political Role of the Freedom Charter' in Steytler N. (ed.), *The Freedom Charter and Beyond: Founding Principles for a Democratic South African Legal Order* (Wyvern 1991) 63

Polzin M., 'Constitutional Identity, Unconstitutional Amendments and the Idea of Constituent Power: The Development of the Doctrine of Constitutional Identity in German Constitutional Law' (2016) *14*(2) *International Journal of Constitutional Law* 411

Polzin M., 'Constitutional Identity as a Constructed Reality and a Restless Soul' (2017) *18*(7) *German Law Journal* 1599

Ramose M.B., 'Towards a Post-conquest South Africa: Beyond the Constitution of 1996' (2018) *34*(3) *South African Journal on Human Rights* 326

Rosenfeld M., 'Constitutional Identity' in Rosenfeld M. and Sajó A. (eds.), *The Oxford Handbook of Comparative Constitutional Law* (Oxford University Press 2012) 756

Roux T., 'The Global South and Liberal Constitutionalism: Incommensurable Opposites' IACL-IADC Blog (15 July 2021) https://blog-iacl-aidc.org/2021-posts/6-15-21the-global-south-and-liberal-constitutionalism-incommensurable-opposites (last accessed 15 August 2021)

Roux T.R., 'Constitutional Populism in South Africa' (2021) https://papers.ssrn.com/sol3/papers.cfm?abstract_id=3583270 18 (last accessed 6 July 2021)

SA History online, uMkhonto weSizwe (MK) (n.d.) https://www.sahistory.org.za/article/umkhonto-wesizwe-mk (last accessed 3 October 2022)

Seekings J., *The UDF: A History of the United Democratic Front in South Africa, 1983–1991* (New Africa Books 2000)

Simpson T., *History of South Africa: From 1902 to the Present* (Penguin Random House 2021)

Steytler I., '"Striking Back" and "Clamping Down" in South Africa: Responding to Adverse Judicial Decisions under Systems of Parliamentary Sovereignty and Constitutional Supremacy' (2020) *12 Hague Journal on the Rule of Law* 363

Steytler N., 'The Dynamic Relationship between Devolution and Constitutionalism in South Africa' in Fombad C. and Steytler N. (eds.), *Decentralisation and Constitutionalism in Africa* (Oxford University Press 2019) 151

Steytler N. and Mettler J., 'Federal Arrangements as a Peacemaking Device during South Africa's Transition to Democracy' (2001) *31*(4) *Publius: The Journal of Federalism* 93

Thompson L.M., *The Unification of South Africa: 1902–1910* (Clarendon Press 1960)

Thompson L.M., *A History of South Africa* (4th edn, Jonathan Ball 2014)

Truth and Reconciliation Commission, *Truth and Reconciliation Commission of South Africa Report* Vol 2 (Truth and Reconciliation Commission 1998)

Von Bogdandy A., Häußler S., Hanschmann F., and Utz R., 'State-Building, Nation-Building, and Constitutional Politics in Post-Conflict Situations: Conceptual Clarifications and an Appraisal of Different Approaches' (2005) *9*(1) *Max Planck Yearbook of United Nations Law* 579

Welsh D., 'Constitutional Changes in South Africa' *83* (1984) *African Affairs* 147

Welsh D., *The Rise and Fall of Apartheid* (Jonathan Ball 2009)

Wessels L., *Vereeniging: Die Onvoltooide Vrede* (Umuzi 2010)

7
Constitutional Identity and Disruption in Contemporary Ethiopia

Asnake Kefale

1. Introduction

Ethiopia has a long history of constitutions. Before the introduction of a modern constitution in 1931, religious texts served as a constitution; since then, however, Ethiopia has continued to suffer from constitutional disruptions. The 1931 Constitution was revised in 1955 but was suspended after the Marxist-Leninist military government of the Derg[1] assumed state power in a popular revolution in 1974. The 1987 Peoples' Democratic Republic of Ethiopia (PDRE) Constitution was then nullified by the Ethiopian Peoples' Revolutionary Democratic Front (EPRDF) when it assumed state power after its military victory over the Derg in May 1991. The EPRDF-led government introduced its own constitution, the Constitution of the Federal Democratic Republic of Ethiopia (FDRE), in 1995, but following the political changes that took place in Ethiopia in 2018, this current constitution, too, is under stress. In the context of these ongoing changes, there is heated debate about the future prospects of the 1995 Constitution. It is now difficult to tell whether the 1995 Constitution will be nullified like its predecessors, or if it will be reformed to meet the demands of the time.

This chapter argues that the key to understanding the problem of constitutional disruption, or discontinuity, in Ethiopia lies in examining the problematic identity of constitutions. Although 'constitutional identity' is a contested term,[2] it refers at bottom to an essential, constitutive part of the constitution which is 'permanent, stable, and relates to the essence of a particular political community'.[3] According to Jacobsohn, constitutional identity represents 'a mix of aspirations and commitments expressive of a nation's past'.[4] Since it is forged out of disharmonious elements, constitutional identity is not static; rather, it may be adjusted from time to time through 'interpretive activities occurring in courts, legislatures, and other public and private domains'.[5] However, such changes rarely culminate in the complete change of the constitution, as nations by and large remain faithful to the basic

[1] *Derg*, an Amharic-Geez word for 'committee', refers to the Provisional Military Administrative Council (PMAC) which ruled Ethiopia from 1974 to 1987.

[2] Michel Rosenfeld, 'Constitutional Identity' in Michel Rosenfeld and András Sajó (eds.), *The Oxford Handbook of Comparative Constitutional Law* (Oxford University Press 2012).

[3] Han Zhai, *The Constitutional Identity of Contemporary China: The Unitary System and Its Internal Logic* (Brill NV 2019) 15.

[4] Gary J. Jacobsohn, 'The Formation of Constitutional Identities' in Tom Ginsburg and Rosalind Dixon (eds.), *Comparative Constitutional Law* (Edward Elgar 2014) 129.

[5] Ibid.

Asnake Kefale, *Constitutional Identity and Disruption in Contemporary Ethiopia* In: *Constitutional Identity and Constitutionalism in Africa*. Edited by: Charles M. Fombad and Nico Steytler, Oxford University Press.
DOI: 10.1093/oso/9780198906308.003.0010

elements of their constitutional identity.[6] In other words, changing the core norms of the constitution changes the constitutional order.[7] It is because of this that there is emphasis on the protection and preservation of constitutional identity.[8]

In many cases, the core identities of constitutions are reflected in what Jacobsohn says are regime-defining characteristics expressly recognised in the text of the constitution. For instance, the American Constitution unambiguously guarantees a republican form of government throughout the federal system. Similarly, the French Constitution prohibits any change to the constitution that would alter the republican character of the government.[9]

Disharmony in the making of constitutions and their identities is expected, as the very processes through which constitutions are made and implemented involve competition between different political, ideological, and economic interests. The presence of disharmony, and attempts made by leaders to find solutions to harmonise interests, contributes to constitutional development. But, as Jacobsohn clearly points out, when there is a 'confrontational relationship between the constitution and the social order within which it operates',[10] it is inconceivable to expect the continuation of the constitutional order. Jacobsohn's understanding of matters speaks well to one of the key reasons for constitutional disruption in Ethiopia.

In this chapter, following Rosenfeld, I examine the three main aspects of constitutional identity: the text of the constitution; constitutional culture; and the interplay between the constitution and national identity.[11] I contend that the lack of an overarching constitutional identity in Ethiopia could be explained by limitations in the making of constitutions, an inability to reconcile foreign ideas with the country's socio-political identities, and disharmony between the constitutional principles and the reality on the ground.

Ethiopia has unique socio-political identities that have had a strong bearing on the history of constitution-making and -unmaking. The country has a long history of statehood, and it also survived European colonialism. As a result, constitution-making processes in Ethiopia were by and large driven by local actors. Moreover, the country is characterised by different kinds of diversity. In terms of ethnicity, it has more than eighty ethno-linguistic groups. Historically, ethnic relations in Ethiopia have been marked by inequality. Northern Ethiopia, which is predominantly inhabited by the Amhara-Tigrayan populations and from where the centre of Ethiopian statehood over several centuries came to the geographic south, played a dominant role in the politics of the country. Ethnic groups in the south, which were incorporated into the Ethiopian state at the end of the nineteenth century, were subjected to economic exploitation and political, linguistic, and cultural domination.[12] The two major policies of Ethiopian rulers since the middle of the nineteenth century were modernisation and centralisation of the Ethiopian empire state.[13] The other aspects of diversity that have significant impacts on the Ethiopian polity include religion and differences

[6] Yaniv Roznai, *Unconstitutional Constitutional Amendments: The Limits of Amendment Powers* (Oxford University Press 2019) 148.

[7] See Zhai (n. 3) 15.

[8] Ibid.

[9] Jacobsohn (n. 4) 129.

[10] Ibid. 130.

[11] Rosenfeld (n. 2) 756.

[12] Alem Habtu, 'Ethnic Pluralism as an Organising Principle of the Ethiopian Federation' (2004) *28*(2) *Dialectical Anthropology*.

[13] Christopher Clapham, *Haile Selassie's Government* (Praeger 1969).

between highland (peasant agriculture) and lowland (nomadic pastoralism) modes of livelihood.

Another element of Ethiopia's political identity that continues to have crucial ramifications for the making and unmaking of constitutions is the hierarchical nature of politics and the overwhelming influence of the state and its institutions on society.[14] Put differently, despite the introduction of constitutions and parliaments since 1931, as well as changes in regimes and ideologies since 1974, there is little institutional restraint on the powers of rulers. Owing to the dominance of the state and the limited appetite of Ethiopian regimes for dissent, political changes in the country generally come about through violent ruptures rather than peaceful reforms.

Ethiopia's socio-political identities have had a strong impact on the country's history of constitution-making and -unmaking. As discussed in the subsequent sections, the constitutions that were adopted before 1995 failed to recognise the country's ethno-linguistic diversity and sought to promote centralisation and modernisation; by contrast, the 1995 Constitution gave disproportionate attention to ethno-linguistic diversity, inadvertently promoting parochial ethnonationalism. Generally, the authoritarianism of Ethiopian politics has prevented the development of constitutionalism.

The next section of this chapter deals with the processes of making constitutions and their implications for the problematic identity of Ethiopian constitutions. One important thread that emerges in the history of Ethiopian constitution-making is limited public participation: protracted bargaining and compromise are alien to the history of Ethiopian constitution-making. The tradition that prevails is that a newly established regime invents its constitution without ensuring the participation of competing political actors; as a result, whenever there are changes in governments, constitutions are disrupted. The third section of the chapter examines how the adoption (or transplantation) of foreign constitutional principles undermined the development of a stable constitutional identity in Ethiopia. The four constitutions that were adopted in the country transplanted foreign constitutional ideas and gave limited attention to the need to harmonise foreign ideas with local histories and cultures. This contributed to the difficulty of developing strong identities that could ensure the continuity of the constitutions. The fourth section examines the disharmony between constitutions and society and how it contributes to the disruption of the former. Finally, the chapter makes concluding remarks.

2. Constitution-Making Processes

According to Lerner and Landau, constitution-making is 'the process of replacing the existing constitutional order completely'.[15] Replacing an existing constitutional order in its entirety with a new one happens by and large outside of the existing legal order, as few constitutions contain provisions that allow for their replacement.[16] In many cases, the moment of constitution-making comes after major political changes such as revolutions or decolonisation. Indeed, historically, revolutions and constitutions are intertwined. The great

[14] Yeshtila Wondemeneh Bekele, Darley Jose Kjosavik, and Nadarajah Shanmugaratnam, 'State-Society Relations in Ethiopia: A Political-Economy Perspective of the Post-1991 Order' (2016) 5 *Social Sciences* 2.

[15] Hanna Lerner and David Landau, 'Introduction to Comparative Constitution Making: The State of the Field' in David Landau and Hanna Lerner (eds.), *Comparative Constitution Making* (Edward Elgar Publishing 2019) 2.

[16] Ibid.

historic revolutions of England, the United States, and France led to the making of new (revolutionary) constitutions.[17] In the Ethiopian case, too, major political changes not only disrupted existing constitutions but also led to the making of new constitutions.

The making of a new constitution after regime change is unfettered by the existing constitutional order. In such cases, the makers of the constitution seek to legitimise the constitution-making process, and ultimately the end product as well, by claiming that the forces engaged in the making of the new constitution represent the aspirations and wishes of the people. In other words, the makers of the constitution invoke 'constituent power'.[18] Constitution-making processes may take several forms.[19] It is possible, however, to identify two major ways of making constitutions—imposed and negotiated. In the first case, constitutions are imposed by a range of actors, including colonial governments, revolutionary forces, military governments, and in some instances foreign occupation forces, after the ending of conflicts. In the second case, constitutions are the products of 'negotiation or consensus among a number of political forces'.[20]

How constitutions are made undoubtedly influences their identity and legitimacy. Where constitutions are imposed by political actors who control state power without the participation of others, this not only undermines the legitimacy of the constitution but also severely limits its ability to serve a succession of political regimes. As will be shown below, by and large the history of constitution-making in Ethiopia has been non-inclusive and more of an imposition than a result of protracted negotiation and compromise.

As is often said, the 1931 Constitution was not only Ethiopia's first written constitution but also 'given' by Emperor Haile Selassie upon his 'free will'.[21] The key role-player in its drafting was Tekle-Hawariat Tekle-Mariam, the then minister of finance who had been educated in pre-revolutionary Czarist Russia[22] and rose to prominence due to his education and service to the government. In his autobiography, Tekle-Hawariat said that, despite his opposition to the assignment, the emperor had instructed him to draft a constitution that would be useful to the country. He was given copies of the constitutions of Japan, Germany, and Italy, in addition to which British constitutional statutes.[23] Using these materials, Tekle-Hawariat wrote the first draft of the 1931 Constitution.

Subsequently, the emperor convened a meeting of the country's leading dignitaries, which included the hereditary nobility (*mesafinit*) and the appointed nobles (*mekwanint*).[24]

[17] Andrew Arato, 'Revolutions and Constitution Making' in David Landau and Hanna Lerner (eds.), *Comparative Constitution Making* (Edward Elgar Publishing 2019) 27.

[18] David Landau, 'Constituent Power and Constitution Making in Latin America', in David Landau and Hanna Lerner (eds.), *Comparative Constitution Making* (Edward Elgar Publishing 2019) 567.

[19] Rosenfeld (n. 2) .

[20] Ibid. 569.

[21] Before the introduction of the 1931 Constitution, three religious laws, namely the *fetha nagast* ('Law of the Kings'), the *kebra nagast* ('Glory of the Kings'), and the *serate mengist* ('Rules of Governance'), regulated religious life, state administration, and civil matters. See M. Torcini Corazza, 'State and Religion in the Constitution and Politics of Ethiopia' (2002) 9(1) *European Journal for Church and State Research—Revue Européenne des Relations Églises-État* 351.

[22] Tekelehariat Tekle Mariam, *My Autobiography of My Life* (Addis Ababa University Press 2006) Amharic title, yehiyiwetē tarīki otobayogirafi.

[23] Ibid. 401.

[24] In imperial Ethiopia, the nobility comprised two classes of officials. The first were the hereditary nobility, including descendants of the various royal families. In Amharic, they were called *mesafinit*. The second included those who came from ordinary (non-royal) families but rose to positions of prominence owing to their services. In Amharic, they were called *mekwanint*. Zewde Reta, *Haile Selassie I Government, Vol. 1, 1930–1955* (Shama Books 2005) Amharic title, *yek'edamawī ḫayilešilasē menigišit qutir 1 1930–1955*.

According to Zewde Reta's monumental history of Haile Selassie's government, there was stiff resistance on the part of the nobility to the emperor's plan of adopting a constitution by emulating the experiences of Europe.[25] Two of the major points raised by those who opposed the idea of introducing a constitution include, firstly, the fear that a European-style constitution would corrupt the thinking of the people of the country and lead astray of long-established traditions. Secondly, the nobility opposed the idea of establishing a representative institution (parliament), saying that, inasmuch as they themselves represented the people and knew what they wanted, it was pointless to establish such an institution.[26] Despite this opposition, some members of the nobility lent support to the emperor's idea of introducing a constitution.

In 1930, the emperor established an eleven-strong constitutional drafting committee composed of the *mesafinit* and *mekwanint*. He instructed it to prepare a constitution incorporating the following ideas. Firstly, it should ensure the succession of the crown to the dynasty of the emperor, Haile Selassie. Secondly, it should maintain the unity and the territorial integrity of the country. Thirdly, it should strengthen the power of the emperor. Fourthly, it should transform the imperial government from absolutist feudal rule to a government supported by a people's representative council. Fifthly, the constitution should establish a parliament advising the emperor on the enactment of laws.[27]

While the members of the committee agreed on most of the provisions of the draft constitution, sharp disagreements arose between the *mesafinit* and *mekwanint* on two of them. The first was the future status of the *mesafinit* and their successors in the administration of the provinces. Historically, the provinces were in the main ruled by hereditary rulers, and the *mesafinit* sought affirmation of this tradition in the constitution.[28] This was opposed by the *mekwanint*. Among the ranks of the hereditary nobility, the idea of affirming the status of the nobility was opposed only by Prince Ras[29] Imru Haile Selassie, who was known for his reformist attitudes.[30] Key members of the *mekwanint* opposed the position of the hereditary nobility, saying that limiting high offices to the *mesafinit* would mean denying Ethiopian citizens the right to serve their country in higher positions of authority.[31]

The second bone of contention was the role of the lower house of parliament (chamber of deputies). The *mekwanint* argued in favour of providing members of the lower house with a role in making laws. Accordingly, they proposed that its members could study problems encountered by the public at grassroots level and propose ideas for laws to the emperor. In contrast, the *mesafinit* held the view that, as ordinary men were to be appointed as members of the lower house, they would have neither knowledge nor experience of public administration; as such, giving them a role in law-making would not be prudent.[32] As the parties were unable to bridge their differences, the issues were brought to the attention of the emperor, who sided with the *mekwanint* on the issue of appointment. In his speech during the meeting called to discuss the controversial points, the emperor, as Reta recalled, said the

25 Ibid.
26 Ibid. 22.
27 Ibid. 24.
28 Imru Haile-Selassie, *From What I Saw and Remember* (Ababa University Press 2009) Amharic title, kayehutina kemasitawisew 184.
29 *Ras* is a royal title in the Amharic language.
30 Ibid.
31 See Reta (n. 24).
32 Ibid.

proposal of the *mesafinit* seeking to limit appointment to the hereditary nobility would be counterproductive, as it would perpetuate an archaic feudal system and thus be inimical to the aim of modernising the country.[33] He then ordered the inclusion of a provision that

> all Ethiopian subjects, provided that they comply with the conditions laid down by law and the decrees promulgated by the Emperor, may be appointed officers in the army or civil officials, or to any other posts or offices in the service of the State.[34]

The emperor also sided with the *mekwanint* regarding the limited role that was given to the chamber of deputies in the making of laws.

The 1931 Constitution was suspended during Italy's brief occupation of the country from 1935 to 1940, but after the restoration of the emperor in 1940, it came back into force, and in 1942, Parliament was reconvened. At the beginning of the 1950s, changing the 1931 Constitution, which had then been in force for more than twenty years, became an inevitability. Two factors made revision of the Constitution necessary. Firstly, it had become obsolete: in particular, the absence of universal suffrage was anachronistic in an era when African countries under colonial rule were heading towards independence. Secondly, the Ethiopia-Eritrea federation created by the United Nations (UN) in 1952 raised an urgent need for constitutional change. This was particularly so due to the constitutional asymmetry that emerged between Ethiopia and Eritrea: whereas the 1931 Ethiopian Constitution did not recognise basic rights and universal suffrage, the Eritrean Constitution recognised universal suffrage and freedom of association and speech.

Unlike the case with the 1931 Constitution, there was little documentation of the making of the revised Constitution of 1955, which was drafted over about six years. The task of preparing the draft was entrusted to a committee comprising five individuals, namely two Ethiopians and three American lawyers.[35] The research for and drafting of the constitution were carried out by expatriate members of the committee, with the initial draft having been written in English. The American lawyer and adviser to the emperor, John H. Spencer, played a prominent role in the drafting of the constitution. According to Bahru Zewde, 'the crown council closely supervised the drafting of the constitution'.[36] This body was composed of the key figures of the empire, which included members of the hereditary nobility representing the royal lines of Shoa, Tigray, and Gojam, as well as influential *mekwanint* and the patriarch of the Orthodox Church.[37] The council was known for its conservative views and ensured the protection of the prerogatives of the crown in the constitution. The revised Constitution was inaugurated in 1955 on the occasion of the silver jubilee of the coronation of the emperor.[38]

The revised 1955 Constitution remained in force for nineteen years until its suspension by the military regime in 1974. The Derg ruled the country without a formal constitution for about thirteen years. After consolidating its power, the military government engaged in the process of building the organs of a socialist state. In 1984, it established what it called the

[33] Bahru Zewde, *A History of Modern Ethiopia, 1855–1991* (2nd edn, James Currey 2002) 34.
[34] See article 21 of the Ethiopian Constitution of 1931.
[35] Zewde (n. 33) 206.
[36] Ibid.
[37] Ibid.
[38] Ibid.

vanguard Marxist-Leninist party, the Workers Party of Ethiopia (WPE), under the chairmanship of Colonel Mengistu Haile Mariam. The next task was the establishment of a socialist republic, for which a constitution was required. The drafting and adoption of the 1987 PDRE Constitution followed the model that was applied by countries of the former communist bloc. According to Negede Gobeze, the making of the 1987 PDRE and 1995 FDRE constitutions followed fairly standard practices of constitution making in the former Soviet Union and its east European satellites.[39]

In this tradition, according to Negede, the first step was the establishment of the constitutional commission tasked with the responsibility of drafting the constitution. Such commissions were formed by communist parties and made accountable to them. To create the pretence of broad public representation, the commissions were composed of people representing different sectors of society, among them workers, intellectuals, farmers, youth, and women. After completing the draft, the commissions would organise public discussion forums. These forums were, however, carefully stage-managed to confer legitimacy to the constitution-making process; comments gathered from public discussions did not lead to any substantial change to the draft constitution. After these symbolic public discussions, the draft constitution would be put to a referendum and approved by a large majority of voters.

To illustrate how the system worked, Negede offers the example of the drafting and adoption of the 1968 Constitution of the former German Democratic Republic (GDR). The constitutional commission held 750,000 public meetings, in which 11 million citizens participated and provided 12,354 comments. The commission, however, entertained only a few comments in modifying the draft, which was put to a referendum and approved by 94.9 per cent of voters.[40]

As will be shown below, what was said above about the former GDR resonates well with the processes of making the 1987 and 1995 Ethiopian constitutions. In both cases, the ruling parties—the WPE and EPRDF, respectively—tightly controlled the process. In the case of the 1987 Constitution, the Derg formally established the Constitutional Drafting Commission in 1986 through a proclamation. The Commission comprised 344 members and, to create the impression that it represented different sectors of society, its members were drawn from the peasantry, urban dwellers, youth, women, and professional associations. Moreover, it included academics and members of the WPE.[41] The Commission was housed at the former Institute for the Study of Ethiopian Nationalities (ISEN) and supported by the experts of this institution. Following the tradition of the former communist bloc, the Commission also organised public discussion forums that closely resembled those of the GDR.

In a bid to enhance popular participation, the draft constitution was translated into fifteen languages.[42] The Constitutional Commission held more than 25,000 public discussion forums and collected 500,000 submissions.[43] These massive numbers of submissions were, however, not seriously considered.[44] The Commission delivered the draft constitution to

[39] Negede Gobeze, *Constitution, Elections and Democracy in Ethiopia* (AESOP Publishers 2004), Amharic tile, *hige menigisit mirich'a ina dīmokirasī be'ītiyop'iya* 65.
[40] Ibid. 65.
[41] Geset Techane, *It Was Then, No 2* (Commercial Printing Press 2009) Amharic title, *neber qutir 2* 93.
[42] Ibid.
[43] Negede (n. 39) 98.
[44] Geset (n. 41) .

Colonel Mengistu Haile Mariam in September 1986,[45] and it was put to a referendum in November 1986. The latter saw a large turnout: of an estimated 14.5 million voters, 14 million were registered to vote, and of these, 96 per cent voted, with the constitution being accepted by 81 per cent of voters.[46]

The 1995 Constitution was developed through much the same process as the PDRE Constitution. On assuming power, the EPRDF in July 1991 convened the Peace and Democracy Conference, where a Transitional Charter was adopted that incorporated the United Nations Declaration on Human Rights (UDHR) and promised multi-party democracy and freedom of association and speech. The EPRDF's promises did not materialise, however.

For instance, the EPRDF prohibited the participation of the Ethiopian People's Revolutionary Party (EPRP) and the All Ethiopian Socialist Movement, better known by its Amharic acronym, MEISON, in the July 1991 conference on the grounds that they had allegedly failed to renounce violence. Even those ethnic organisations, such as the Oromo Liberation Front (OLF), which were allowed to participate in the conference and which became members of the Transitional Government of Ethiopia (TGE), claimed there was an absence of a level playing field for all political parties and left the transitional government. The withdrawal of the OLF and other parties from the transitional government followed the deeply flawed 1992 regional elections in which the EPRDF instituted itself and its allies as regional governing parties.[47]

The result was that the entire process of making the 1995 Constitution was under the tight control of the EPRDF.[48] The EPRDF dominated an interim unelected legislative organ, the Council of Representatives (CoR), and established the Constitutional Commission in 1992. The Commission was composed of twenty-nine members drawn from the CoR, political parties, and civic and professional associations.[49]

During the drafting process, the Constitutional Commission held various symposia to debate constitutional questions.[50] It also organised public discussions at grassroots level with two purposes—to provide civic education on constitutional issues and to gather the opinion of the people on key constitutional choices.[51] More than sixteen million citizens reportedly took part in these discussion forums. The Commission completed the preparation of the first draft of the constitution in 1994. Despite the presence of representatives of different political parties and civic associations in the commission, the EPRDF maintained the majority of the votes. As a result, during the drafting of the constitution, its wishes held sway in almost all decisions.[52]

After the constitution was drafted, it was submitted to the CoR, which discussed its every provision for about a month and approved the draft after making modifications.[53] This gave

45 Ibid.

46 Ibid.

47 National Democratic Institute for International Affairs (NDIIA), 'An Evaluation of the June 21, 1992 Elections in Ethiopia' (NDIIA 1992).

48 See Theodore M. Vestal, 'Analysis of the New Constitution of Ethiopia and the Process of Its Adoption' (1996) *3 Northeast African Studies,* New Series 21, 26

49 Tesgaye Regassa, 'The Making and Legitimacy of the Ethiopian Constitution: Towards Bridging the Gap between Constitutional Design and Constitutional Practice' (2010) *23 Africa Focus* 102.

50 Ibid. 93.

51 Lovise Aalen, *Ethnic Federalism in a Dominant Party State: The Ethiopian Experience 1991–2000* (Chr. Michelsen Institute 2002) 42.

52 Tesgaye (n. 49) 102.

53 Ibid.

the EPRDF an additional opportunity to pursue its political objectives in regard to the new constitution. Thereafter, the draft constitution was presented to the Constituent Assembly, the members of which had been elected in June 1994 from across the country. However, there had been little participation in the elections by opposition parties, which boycotted them, saying there was no ground for free and fair elections. In the end, the Constituent Assembly was dominated overwhelmingly by the EPRDF, which controlled 539 seats out of a total of 557.[54] The EPRDF's positions on key constitutional questions such as ethnicity, federalism, secession, and land ownership were thus included in the Constitution without bargaining and compromise.

The four constitutions under consideration in this chapter were written in differing historical and political contexts and also differed in their content and ideology; nevertheless, the processes by which they were made were profoundly similar to each other: by and large, they were not inclusive and did not involve bargaining and compromise. Constitution-making of this kind undermines the legitimacy of constitutions and limits their prospects for continuity. To put it another way, when there is political (regime) change, the new regime has no appetite for continuing with the existing constitution; similarly, the content and orientation of the existing constitution are found to be unsuitable to a changed political context.

3. The Transplantation of Foreign Ideas

The transplantation of constitutional ideas and principles is widespread across the world. As Tom Ginsburg and his colleagues note, constitution-making has been characterized by a 'long history of transnational flow of ideas about constitutions and how they should be made'.[55] It is, in other words, difficult to find any constitution that has not been influenced by foreign ideas.

In the Ethiopian case, its four constitutions were likewise influenced by foreign ideas. The very idea of establishing a constitution in Ethiopia could be seen as an aspect of the long-standing aspiration of Ethiopian rulers to modernise their systems of governance along European lines. In this respect, Emperor Tewodros (1855–68), who is credited with the birth of the modern Ethiopian state, had sought, for instance, to form a paid, standing army; make administrators and judges salaried officials; and regulate the power and land of the Ethiopian Orthodox Church.[56] Even before his rise to the throne, Tewodros had been interested not only in the formation of a standing army but also in adopting modern weaponry and Western-style military discipline.[57] However, opposition from the church and traditional nobility frustrated his plans for modernisation.

Emperor Menelik (1889–1913) was, in 1907, the first Ethiopian ruler to establish ministries, although this was more of a symbolic gesture than a case of instituting bureaucracies

[54] Sandara Fullerton Joireman, 'Opposition Politics and Ethnicity in Ethiopia: We Will All Go Down Together' (1997) 35 *Journal of Modern African Studies* 186.

[55] Tom Ginsburg, Terence C. Halliday, and Gregory C. Shaffer, 'Constitution-Making as Transnational Legal Ordering' in Gregory C. Shaffer, Tom Ginsburg, and Terence C. Halliday (eds.), *Constitution-Making and Transnational Legal Order* (Cambridge University Press 2019), 1.

[56] Margery Perham, *The Government of Ethiopia* (Faber & Faber 1970) 50.

[57] Bahru (n. 33).

along the lines of those in Europe. It was Emperor Haile Selassie, who ruled the country first as a regent for fourteen years (1916–30) and later as emperor for forty-four years (1930–74), who played a far more prominent role in modernising the country's governance. Unlike his predecessors, he had close contact with Europeans. His father, Ras Mekonnen, was not only Menelik's cousin but also a close confidante of the emperor, and served him as foreign minister; he had also twice led Menelik's diplomatic mission to Europe, in 1889 and 1902. Ras Mekonnen appeared to have been interested in adopting European ideas and practices. Indeed, he hired a French tutor for the future Haile Selassie during the latter's childhood. Haile Selassie, while a regent to Empress Zewditu (1916–30), undertook a visit to Europe in 1924 and visited five countries, including France, Britain, and Italy.[58] His belief was that the key to Ethiopia's development and independence was European-style modernisation and centralisation of power.[59]

The historian Bahru Zewde divides Haile Selassie's rule into two phases: a progressive phase, spanning from 1916 to 1955; and a reactionary one, extending from 1955 to the demise of his rule in 1974.[60] During the progressive phase, Haile Selassie undertook many measures intended to modernise the workings of the Ethiopian government. In his autobiography, the emperor listed some of the major changes he introduced. In 1921, under his direction, the government brought regulations from Europe and gave them to the ministries which were established under Menelik in 1907 but were functioning without (written) rules and regulations.[61] Secondly, he expanded modern, or European, education. Thirdly, in 1918, he removed the inherited nobility and appointed commoners to govern provinces, thereby paving the way for an end to feudalism.[62] In addition, Ethiopia's admission to the League of Nations in 1923 inspired the emperor to adopt the 1931 Constitution.

The adoption of the 1931 Constitution could be taken as a symbol of Haile Selassie's determination to modernise the empire's governance by transplanting ideas from foreign countries. Accordingly, as noted above, the committee tasked with the drafting of the 1931 Constitution considered the constitutions of Japan, Germany, and Italy, as well as constitutional documents from Britain. According to a memoir by one of the committee members, Prince Ras Imru Haile Selassie, remarkable differences between the British and Japanese constitutions, particularly regarding the role of the monarchy, left members of the commission puzzled as to which of the two would give better guidance to their work. The difficulty of choosing between them was compounded by the members' lack of knowledge about the emperor's preferences.[63] Later, the emperor appeared to suggest that what would be helpful to Ethiopia would be adopting elements from both of the constitutions.[64]

In due course, the drafters of the constitution drew heavily on the 1889 Meiji Constitution, which had become more appealing than the British constitution for two reasons. The first was the similarity between the Japanese and Ethiopian political systems—both were absolutist monarchies. Secondly, Ethiopian intellectuals, along with the emperor himself, were

[58] Haile Selassie I, King of Kings, *My Life and Ethiopia's Progress: Haile Selassie I, King of Kings. Volume 1* (Birehaena Selam Printing Press 1974) Amharic title, k'edamawī ḫayile šilasē niguše negešet, ḥiyiwet ēna ye'ītiyop'iya irimija k'ut'ir 1.

[59] Zewde (n. 24).

[60] Bahru Zewde, 'Hayla-Sellase: From Progressive to Reactionary' (1995) *2 Northeast African Studies* 99.

[61] Haile Selassie (n. 58) .

[62] Ibid. 49–54.

[63] Ibid. 186.

[64] Ibid.

attracted to Japan thanks to the economic and political progress it had made after the Meiji reforms. Japan's victory over Russia in 1905 was also a huge influence on Ethiopia.[65] The significant ideas that were adopted from the Meiji Constitution into the 1931 Constitution included the notion of consolidating the emperor's power by weakening the traditional nobility. In this respect, the 1931 Constitution provided that the emperor was 'sacred, his dignity is inviolable and his power indisputable'.[66] This article was borrowed directly from the Meiji Constitution, which provided that the 'emperor is sacred and inviolable'.[67]

Despite the similarities between the Meiji Constitution and the 1931 Ethiopian Constitution, there were differences too. A notable one was the Meiji Constitution's provision for the people of Japan to elect members of the Japanese Diet. In the Ethiopian case, according to article 32 of the 1931 Constitution, 'as a temporary measure, until the people are capable of electing them themselves, the members of the chamber of deputies shall be chosen by the dignitaries and the local chiefs'.[68]

In sum, the Meiji Constitution and the 1931 Ethiopian Constitution were both preoccupied with consolidating and centralising imperial power by introducing Western constitutional principles and institutions. Their main goal was to curb the power of provincial rulers and the traditional (hereditary) nobility.[69] In Japan, the Constitution contributed more effectively in this regard than in Ethiopia. For instance, the Meiji reforms led to the abolition of feudal ownership of land;[70] in contrast, the 1931 Ethiopian Constitution failed to bring changes to the country's highly inequitable land-tenure system.

While the 1931 Constitution was heavily influenced by the Meiji Constitution, the Revised 1955 Constitution was influenced by Western ideas. The participation of three American lawyers in the drafting of the constitution contributed to the adoption of American ideas and principles in the 1955 Revised Constitution. This influence was particularly significant in the framing of the division of power between the three branches of government as well as in the case of the provisions on human rights.[71]

Owing to the dominance of Marxist-Leninism among the forces that came to play a central role in Ethiopian politics after the 1974 revolution toppled Haile Selassie's government, the 1987 PDRE Constitution was profoundly influenced by the constitutional principles of the former Soviet Union and its satellites. Some of the major principles transplanted from the Soviet constitutional tradition include the following: Firstly, as in the Soviet Union and its East European satellites, the PDRE Constitution not only established a single-party system but, in article 6, also affirmed the vanguard role of the WPE.[72] Secondly, in articles 12 and 13, the Constitution provided for state ownership of the means of production and the establishment of a socialist economy.[73] Thirdly, the structure of government set out in the PDRE Constitution almost mirrored the Soviet Union's structure of government.

[65] Joseph Calvitt Clarke, *Alliance of the Colored Peoples: Ethiopia and Japan before World War II* (James Currey 2011) 7.

[66] Article 5 of the 1931 Ethiopian Constitution.

[67] Article 3 of the Constitution of the Empire of Japan, 1889.f

[68] 1931 Ethiopian Constitution.

[69] Stephen Vlastos, 'Opposition Movements in Early Meiji, 1868–1885' in Marius B. Jansen (ed.), *The Emergence of Meiji Japan* (Cambridge University Press 1997) 484.

[70] Ibid.

[71] See Edmond Keller, *Revolutionary Ethiopia: From Empire to People's Republic* (Indiana University Press 1988) 85.

[72] The 1987 PDRE Constitution.

[73] Ibid.

Accordingly, the legislature, which was named Shengo (an Amharic translation of the term 'assembly' or 'soviet'), was, in article 62, declared the highest organ of state power.[74] In the case of the Soviet Union, article 108 of its 1977 Constitution provided that the Supreme Soviet was the 'highest organ of State power'.[75] This organ was not, however, a full-time parliament. It only met once a year: when the Supreme Soviet was not in session, its powers were exercised by a smaller body called the Presidium[76] of the State Council.[77] The same was true in the Ethiopian case when the Shengo was not in session: its powers and prerogatives were exercised by the Council of State, a smaller body that brought together key figures of the government and WPE under the chairmanship of Colonel Mengistu Haile Mariam.

The 1995 Constitution adopted a range of ideas and principles from foreign countries. One can find in it not only European and American ideas but also provisions derived from international human rights conventions. As noted by constitutional law experts such as Ugo Mattie, the American influence in the Constitution is evident in the division of power between the three branches of government and in the federal system of government.[78]

Although the 1995 Constitution was adopted after the collapse of the Soviet Union and the communist bloc, the influence of the Soviet constitutional tradition is also apparent.[79] The ethno-federal structure established by the 1995 Constitution was strongly influenced by the Stalinist approach to the 'national question' and by the Soviet model of federalism. The EPRDF, which followed Stalin's theory of the nationalities even before it came to power, employed his understanding of the nation when it identified the key elements of the Ethiopian federation as 'nations, nationalities and peoples'.[80] Article 20(5) of the Constitution defines the latter as

> [a] group of people who have or share a large measure of common culture or similar customs, mutual intelligibility of language, belief in a common or related identity, a common psychological make-up, and who inhabit an identifiable, predominantly contiguous territory.[81]

Following the Soviet tradition, the 1995 Constitution recognised, too, the rights of nations, nationalities, and peoples to self-determination. Article 39 provides that '[e]very Nation, Nationality and People in Ethiopia has an unconditional right to self-determination, including the right to secession'.[82]

74 Ibid.

75 The 1977 Constitution of the USSR.

76 The presidium of the Soviet Union was elected by the Supreme Soviet. Among other things, it was responsible for legislation when the Supreme Soviet was not in secession and for constitutional interpretation. See István Kovács and J. Decsényi, *New Elements in the Evolution of Socialist Constitution* (Akadémiai Kiadó 1968); Herbert Hausmaninger, 'The Committee of Constitutional Supervision of the USSR' (1990) *23 Cornell International Law Journal 287*.

77 Negede (n. 39) 66.

78 Ugo Mattei, 'The New Ethiopian Constitution: First Thoughts on Ethnical Federalism and the Reception of Western Institutions' in Elisabetta Grande (ed.), *Transplants, Innovation, and Legal Tradition in the Horn of Africa* (L'Harmattan 1995) 111.

79 Negede (n. 39).

80 Stalin defined the nation as 'a historically constituted, stable community of people, formed on the basis of a common language, territory, economic life, and psychological make-up manifested in a common culture'. See J.V. Stalin, *Marxism and the National Question: Collected Works, Vol. 2* (Foreign Languages Publishing House 1954) 307.

81 The 1995 FDRE Constitution.

82 Ibid.

According to Negede Gobeze, the 1995 Constitution also borrowed the 'principle of unity of power' from the Soviet tradition.[83] Consequently, like the constitutions of the communist bloc, the FDRE Constitution, in article 50(3), provides that 'the House of People's Representatives is the highest authority of the Federal Government'.[84] This provision, Gobeze notes, reveals not only the influence of the Stalinist tradition but also the implicit desire of the EPRDF to consolidate its power by ensuring dominance in Parliament.[85] In Gobeze's view, the principle of unity of power is inimical to the separation of powers and multi-party democracy;[86] moreover, it does not allow for the creation of a boundary between the (vanguard) party and the state (or government). In this regard, even though it gives the impression that it institutionalised the independence of the judiciary, the 1995 Constitution contains no clear principles that serve to ensure judicial independence.[87]

Another dimension that the Constitution borrowed from the Soviet tradition is what is called 'programmatic positivism'.[88] According to this tradition, the constitution of a socialist state is an instrument which the communist party uses to advance its objectives; as a result, the vanguard party's key programmatic objectives are included in the constitution. In a liberal multi-party democracy, the constitution by and large leaves out programmatic policy choices, as it is political parties that win elections which come up with such choices. In the Ethiopian case, as succinctly pointed out by Gobeze, the 1995 Constitution contains the main political and economic programme objectives of the EPRDF. These include deeply controversial provisions on secession and state ownership of land. Both positions were pursued by the Tigray People's Liberation Front (TPLF), for long the dominant party in the EPRDF.

Interestingly, there is a similarity between the PDRE and FDRE constitutions on the question of land. Article 13(2) of the PDRE Constitution provided that 'natural resources, in particular land, minerals, water and forest, are state property'.[89] Likewise, article 40(3) of the FDRE Constitution provides that

> the right to ownership of rural and urban land, as well as of all-natural resources, is exclusively vested in the State and the peoples of Ethiopia. Land is a common property of the Nations, Nationalities and Peoples of Ethiopia and shall not be subject to sale or to other means of exchange.[90]

The inclusion of such a stringent provision on land in the FDRE Constitution in a country where more than 80 per cent of the population is engaged in agriculture does not allow political parties to develop alternative political and economic policies.[91] The programmatic nature of the FDRE Constitution becomes clear when one looks at the stringent

83 Negede (n. 39).
84 The 1995 FDRE Constitution.
85 Ibid.
86 Ibid.
87 Ibid.
88 Karl Loewenstein, 'Constitutions and Constitutional Law in the West and in the East' (1969) *30 The Indian Journal of Political Science* 234.
89 Ibid.
90 The 1995 FDRE Constitution.
91 Negede (n. 39).

protection given to the EPRDF's position on land and secession in the 1995 Constitution. It is almost impossible to amend the provisions on the two issues. Such an amendment requires not only two-thirds majorities in the two houses of parliament, but also support (a simple majority) in all of the regional councils. Gobeze concludes that it is easier for a member state of the federation to pursue secession than for land laws and policies to be reformed.[92]

Transplanting foreign ideas and principles remains an enduring feature of constitution-making in Ethiopia. While this is a phenomenon widespread across the world, the manner in which foreign ideas were incorporated in Ethiopia's two latest constitutions (i.e. those of 1987 and 1995) was counterproductive to constitutional development. In both cases, ideological or programmatic foreign ideas were incorporated in the constitutions, with little effort having been made to harmonise them with local cultures and traditions. While the 1987 Constitution appeared to be a political programme of the WPE, the 1995 Constitution adopted the principles of the Soviet constitutional tradition, doing so well after the collapse of the Soviet Union and other socialist federations. All these factors hindered the emergence of a stable constitutional identity that could ensure the succession of constitutions across changes of political regime.

4. Constitutional Disharmonies

According to Pratap B. Mehta, almost all constitutions face the problem of disharmony, which arises for two reasons—internal contradictions and divergences between the constitution and society.[93] The four Ethiopian constitutions under consideration in this chapter suffered both from contradictions and from divergences with the society they were meant to serve.

The 1931 Constitution was divided into seven chapters comprising fifty-five articles. It provided for the establishment of a bicameral parliament consisting of the Chamber of the Senate and the Chamber of Deputies. The members of the senate were appointed personally by the emperor from the nobility and local chiefs who served as military commanders, ministers, or judges. As provided in article 32 of the Constitution, the members of the Chamber of Deputies, 'temporarily, and until the people are in a position to elect them themselves, shall be chosen by the Nobility and the local Chiefs'.[94] Neither of the chambers of parliament had any legislative powers, but served instead as forums for discussing matters of interest to the emperor. In other words, Parliament was made to be advisory to the emperor and a channel of communication between him and his subjects.

The Constitution guaranteed several rights for Ethiopian subjects, such as the rights to movement, due process of law, property, and secrecy of correspondence. As mentioned, however, one of the objectives of the 1931 Constitution was to weaken the provincial nobility and consolidate the power of the emperor. Attainment of this objective was greatly accelerated at the end of the Italian occupation (1935–41). The first decree that Haile Selassie adopted immediately upon the restoration of the country's independence was

[92] Ibid.
[93] Pratap Bhanu Mehta, *The Oxford Handbook of the Indian Constitution* (Oxford University Press 2016).
[94] The 1931 Ethiopian Constitution.

Decree 1 of 1942, which brought about levels of centralisation unprecedented in Ethiopia's history.[95]

It is then possible to contend that the 1931 Constitution achieved its main objective—the consolidation of the power of the emperor. There were, nonetheless, disharmonies that were embedded in the Constitution. Firstly, the representativeness of the parliament established by the 1931 Constitution was limited. The members of the lower house, the Chamber of Deputies, were appointed by provincial and local officials rather than elected by the people. Even if the appointment of members of parliament was meant to be a temporary measure, this practice continued until 1955. Moreover, Parliament was not given a credible role in making laws.

Secondly, even though the 1931 Constitution was modelled on the 1889 Meiji Constitution, its impact on reducing the influence of the provincial nobility by reforming feudal ownership of land was non-existent in comparison to what Japan had experienced—there, the Meiji reforms led to the weakening of feudal ownership of land.[96]

Thirdly, the 1931 Constitution failed to recognise Ethiopia's diversity. As noted, the multi-ethnic empire, which was massively expanded by Emperor Menelik, was characterised by ethnic inequality.[97] The land-tenure system instituted in the newly conquered territories was exploitative and turned the majority of the peasants into tenants. The framers of the 1931 Constitution, in deciding to take Japan as their model, overlooked a fundamental difference between that country and Ethiopia: whereas Japan was ethnically and linguistically homogeneous, Ethiopia was characterised by ethno-linguistic and religious diversity. In other words, the goal of building a centralised state under Haile Selassie did not give recognition to the country's diversity. Not only was Amharic used as a medium of instruction in elementary schools—this in addition to serving its traditional function as the language of government—but the imperial government also prohibited publishing in other languages such as Affan Oromo and Tigrinya.[98]

Fourthly, another contradiction that accompanied the 1931 Constitution and its successors was the emergence of a hybrid government. As Mesfin Woldemariam noted, the Haile Selassie government was neither modern nor traditional but a mixture of traditional and modern norms and practices.[99] As a result, the system was imbued with many contradictions. On the one hand, the emperor stepped up the process of instituting a modern bureaucracy that mimicked Europe's; on the other hand, the educated elites who were put in charge of this bureaucracy and its ministries failed to carry out their functions as per the officially sanctioned rules and regulations of the government, thus engendering contradictions of various kinds.[100]

In comparison to the 1931 Constitution, the 1955 Constitution was more elaborate, containing 8 chapters and 131 articles. It introduced elections for the lower house of parliament and also recognised human rights. However, it suffered from several disharmonies. Some of the major contradictions include—firstly—the absence of formal restraints on the

[95] Imperial Ethiopian Government, Decree No. 1, Administrative Regulations, 1942.

[96] Vlastos (n. 68).

[97] Alem (n. 12) 100.

[98] See John Markakis, 'Ethnic Conflict in Pre-federal Ethiopia' in *Proceedings of the First National Conference on Federalism, Conflict and Peace Building* (Ministry of Federal Affairs and GTZ 2003).

[99] Mesfin W.M., *Mortar, Fear and Defeat* (Graphics Printers 2015) Amharic title, ādafinē, firihatina kishifet 90.

[100] Ibid.

emperor's powers. On the one hand, as per article 88, all laws passed by Parliament needed the assent of the emperor to come into force; on the other hand, the 'emperor could issue decrees and orders without consulting parliament'.[101]

Secondly, the exercise of the human and democratic rights that were included in the 1955 Constitution was subject to laws,[102] but the detailed laws that were meant to regulate the exercise of these rights were never introduced. Furthermore, despite the introduction of universal suffrage, the 1955 Constitution did not allow the formation of political parties.

Thirdly, the 1955 Revised Constitution failed to recognise the ethno-linguistic and religious diversity of the country and address ethnic inequality. The fundamental disharmony between the constitution and the identity of the country since the end of the 1960s was framed by the Ethiopian Student Movement (ESM) in terms of the 'nationalities question'.[103] The ESM, as the organised opposition of university students to imperial rule came to be known, passed through several stages before it reached a climax at the end of the 1960s.[104] At the initial stage of their activism, students were parochial in their concerns and focused on campus issues.[105] At the end of the 1960s, though, they came to challenge the politico-economic structure and ethnic inequality that prevailed in the country—and hence the 'national question' emerged as one of the central issues of Ethiopian politics.

The nationalities question had political and economic dimensions. In terms of politics, it highlighted the ethnic inequality that was embedded in the system and was critical in particular of the dominance of the Amhara political elite. In addition, students challenged the land-tenure system which in effect had turned the peasants of southern Ethiopia into tenants, and also inveighed against linguistic and cultural domination. As noted, the imperial government had prohibited publication in the Oromo and Tigrayan languages;[106] moreover, the Orthodox Church was declared a state religion, while Islam, which has a wide following in the country, was not officially recognised.[107]

The imperial government not only refrained from addressing these anomalies by reforming the 1955 Constitution, but also derailed benign efforts that certain provincial governors made in order to accommodate diversity. A case in point was the reformist Abebe Gebre, the first governor of the province of Bale, who ruled it from 1960 to 1963. His attempts to assign the local Oromo people to administrative positions and address the grievances of the people encountered stiff resistance from court officials, whose interest in the province was undermined by his reformist approach.[108] In the end, the failure of the imperial government to address these central questions—ethnic equality and the exploitative land-tenure system—contributed to its demise in 1974.

[101] Haile Kiros Asmerom, *Emergence, Expansion and Decline of Patrimonial Bureaucracy in Ethiopia, 1907–1974: An Attempt at Historical Interpretation* (PhD thesis, Vrije Universiteit Amsterdam 1978).

[102] For instance, article 41 of the Constitution provided that 'freedom of speech and the press is guaranteed throughout the Empire in accordance with the law'.

[103] Bahru (n. 33).

[104] Ibid.; Rani Ronning Balsvik, *Haile Selassie's Students: The Intellectual and Social Background to Revolution, 1952–1974* (Addis Ababa University 2005) 71.

[105] Kiflu Tadesse, *The Generation, the History of the Ethiopian People's Revolutionary Party: Part I, From the Early Beginnings to 1975* (Independent Publishers 1993) 35.

[106] Markakis (n. 97).

[107] See the Revised 1955 Constitution.

[108] Merid Abebe, *The Representative: Fitaurari Abebe Gebre's Biography* (Oscar Printers 2009) Amharic title, iniderasēwi yefītawirarī ābebe gebirē yeḥiyiwet tarīk 1 50.

The other major contradiction was the imperial regime's inability to respond to social, political, and economic change through reform of the political system. Instead of reforming an overly centralised system, the Haile Selassie government nullified the federal status of Eritrea in 1962.[109] This introduced another layer of contradiction. Ultimately, the failure of the government to address its structural weaknesses by effecting political and economic reform and limiting the power of the monarchy precipitated the 1974 revolution,[110] at which point the 1955 Constitution was suspended.

The Derg, which seized power in the revolution, led the country without a formal constitution for thirteen years and adopted the PDRE Constitution only in 1987—as noted, the latter was heavily influenced by the Soviet tradition. Divided into 4 parts and 17 chapters, it had 119 articles and, like the constitutions of other socialist countries of the time, contained provisions on political and economic systems, social and cultural policies, and freedoms, rights, and duties. The Constitution was, however, fraught with several contradictions.

The first and most pronounced disharmony was the imposition of a Marxist-Leninist ideology on a society that had a negligible working class and which was deeply religious. Secondly, even though the military government recognised the diversity of the country and declared the equality of the nationalities, it neither allowed the use of non-Amharic languages for administrative purposes nor tried seriously to address the demand for ethnic self-administration. Instead, it permitted only a form of asymmetrical regional autonomy in which some of the provinces affected by ethnic or regional insurgency were organised into five autonomous regions, namely Eritrea, Tigray, Dire Dawa, Ogaden, and Assab. The rest of the country was divided into twenty-five administrative zones.

The 1987 Constitution remained in force merely for five years, so it is difficult to discern its long-lasting impacts. As noted, when the EPRDF defeated the Derg and took control of state power in 1991, the PDRE Constitution was nullified and Ethiopia embarked on another round of constitution-making. The EPRDF promised radical change and a truly democratic system, but there are many contradictions, or disharmonies, between the theory and praxis of the 1995 Constitution.

To begin with the structure of the federal system, the 1995 Constitution has various federal and confederal characteristics. Unlike the majority of federations around the world, its second chamber does not provide the constituent units of the federation with a platform on which to participate in the making of federal laws: the power of making federal laws is accorded only to the lower house. This gives one the impression that the constitution-makers sought to establish a more centralised federal system. At the same time, though, this federal constitution has numerous confederal features. Firstly, article 8 provides that 'all sovereign power resides in the Nations, Nationalities and Peoples of Ethiopia'. Secondly, unlike the constitution of any other federation, the 1995 Constitution allows for unqualified internal secession, meaning that, in terms of article 47, a council of a particular ethnic group could demand, without any precondition, that a referendum be held in regard to establishing a new federating unit.[111] The Constitution, in articles 39(1) and 39(4), also allows ethnic communities to secede and establish independent states.[112]

[109] Tekeste Negash, *Eritrea and Ethiopia: The Federal Experience* (Nordiska Afrikainstitutet 1997).

[110] Christopher Clapham, *Transformation and Continuity in Revolutionary Ethiopia* (Cambridge University Press 1988) 32.

[111] The 1995 FDRE Constitution.

[112] Ibid.

The recognition of the right of secession makes Ethiopia unique in Africa. It has been regarded as an instrument to stabilise the country by preventing unwarranted centralisation, given that ethnic groups have an insurance policy enabling unconditional exit.[113] However, instead of cementing a federal union, a constitutional guarantee of secession could stimulate separatist nationalism.[114] Immediately after the introduction of the Constitution, Brietzke made the insightful point that recognition of the right of secession tends to prevent the development of the political art of compromise—an important ingredient in federal practice—and would thus encourage estranged political parties to pursue a separatist path instead of engaging peacefully within the system.[115] This observation well captures the separatist sentiment that parties of the Tigray region, including the TPLF, appear to have promoted, or tolerated, after political changes in 2018 removed the TPLF from the driver's seat of Ethiopian politics.

The other significant disharmony of the 1995 Constitution is the inoperability of the provision on ethnic self-determination and -administration for the majority of the country's ethnic groups. Although the Constitution grants all ethnic communities self-determination and -administration rights, what has happened on the ground is far from what is constitutionally guaranteed. Of an estimated eighty-five ethnic groups, only five (Tigray, Afar, Amhara, Oromo, and Somali) were allowed to have ethnic regions in which they are the majority. In contrast, several dozen smaller ethnic groups were either placed in multi-ethnic regions—such as the Southern Nations, Nationalities and Peoples Region (SNNPR) and Gambella and Benishangul-Gumuz regions—or incorporated as minority ethnic groups within regions dominated by other such groups.

Almost all of the multi-ethnic regions have experienced interethnic conflict around issues such as territory, representation, and the sharing of resources. In certain cases, some ethnic groups seek to separate themselves from the existing multi-ethnic regions and form their own region on the basis of the constitutional provision for internal secession contained in article 47.[116] By using this provision, the Sidaama ethnic group managed to separate itself from the SNNPR and establish a new region in 2020, a development that has placed the SNNPR under stress. In sum, the provision allowing ethnic communities to establish regions by separating themselves from existing regions contradicts the federal principle of maintaining the integrity of the members of a federation and has been a continuing source of instability.

Another crucial disharmony of the 1995 Constitution is its approach to constitutional interpretation and amendment. In the case of constitutional interpretation, this task was given to the upper house of parliament, the House of Federation (HoF), which it would be more appropriate to call a council of ethnic communities. In almost all other federations, constitutional interpretation rests with supreme or constitutional courts.[117] Because constitutional interpretation is an important element of the development of federations, it is

[113] GebreAb Barnabas, 'Ethnic and Religious Policies of the Federal Democratic Republic of Ethiopia' in *Proceedings of the First National Conference on Federalism, Conflict and Peace Building* (Ministry of Federal Affairs and GTZ 2003) 202.

[114] Paul H. Brietzke, 'Ethiopia's "Leap in the Dark": Federalism and Self-Determination in the New Constitution' (1995) *39 Journal of African Law* 32.

[115] Ibid.

[116] The 1995 FDRE Constitution.

[117] Michael Burgess, *Comparative Federalism: Theory and Practice* (Routledge 2006) 158; Ronald Watts, *Comparing Federal Systems* (McGill-Queen's University Press 1999) 100.

often assigned to an organ independent of the two orders of government and as impartial and politically non-partisan as possible, notwithstanding controversy about whether it is legitimate for the unelected judiciary to legislate in effect through constitutional interpretation.[118] In the Ethiopian case, the HoF is a partisan political organ with the power of constitutional interpretation.

Various explanations have been given as to why the framers of the constitution decided to give the HoF the power of constitutional interpretation. According to Assefa Fiseha, the decision arose from the consideration that, since the Constitution is a political covenant of nations, nationalities, and peoples, its interpretation should be left to its authors.[119] However, the reasons for this decision go further than such official justifications. Importantly, the EPRDF, which introduced federalism in a top-down manner with no constitutional bargaining, sought to control the institution that was put in charge of interpreting the Constitution. While the EPRDF was still internally united and in control of almost all government structures—namely, regional parliaments and both houses of the federal parliament—the HoF was not tasked with interpreting controversial constitutional questions. However, in the context of the political changes that have been under way since 2018—among them being division within the EPRDF and its transformation into the Prosperity Party in December 2019—there is now closer scrutiny of the HoF's role in interpreting the Constitution.

A case in point was the decision of the National Electoral Board of Ethiopia (NEBE) to postpone general elections in April 2020 due to the Covid-19 pandemic. The postponement was controversial, as the term of office of the sitting government was expected to end at the beginning of October that year. The federal government considered the implications of the postponement for the tenure of the government and came up with four options: constitutional interpretation by the HoF; amendment of the Constitution; declaration of a state of emergency; or dissolving Parliament and holding elections within six months thereafter. In contrast, opposition political parties proposed other options, such as the establishment of a transitional government or a caretaker government with limited powers.

Eventually, the House of Peoples' Representatives (HoPR), after deliberating on the four options, decided to ask that the Constitution be interpreted in view of its lack of clarity about the possibility of extending the term of a sitting government due to emergencies. The Council of Constitutional Interpretation (CCI), a body of mainly legal experts that advises the HoF on matters of constitutional interpretation, deliberated and recommended that elections be held six to nine months after the relevant authority (the Ministry of Health, the Ethiopian Public Health Institute, or the World Health Organization) indicated that COVID-19 was no longer a threat to public health. After endorsing the CCI's recommendations, the HoF ruled to extend the term of office of the federal parliament as well as executive and regional governments until the conduct of the next election. Some opposition parties, including the TPLF (as noted, a leading light in the former EPRDF), dismissed the HoF's constitutional interpretation and contended that the government of Prime Minister Abiy Ahmed would no longer be legitimate at the end of its five-year term in early October 2020.

[118] Watts (n. 117).

[119] Assefa Fiseha, *Federalism and the Accommodation of Diversity in Ethiopia: A Comparative Study* (rev. edn, Artistic Printing Enterprise 2007) 402–3.

Indeed, the TPLF-led Tigray region denounced the decision of the HoF to extend the terms of the federal and regional governments. In particular, it rejected the mandate of the federal government to postpone elections and went ahead with the establishment of its electoral commission in July 2020, after the NEBE had refused to manage planned regional elections, and held regional elections in September 2020.[120] This took place in spite of the fact that the federal constitution assigns electoral management to the NEBE[121] and that the HoF declared that such regional elections would be an affront to the Constitution.[122]

The TPLF won a landslide victory, taking control of more than 98 per cent of seats in the regional council and forming a new administration in October 2020.[123] The TPLF-led regional government then declared that, as the term of the federal government had been extended unlawfully, it would not recognise, and hence not work with, the federal government or its institutions.[124] The federal government, for its part, suspended relations with the Tigray regional council and executive.[125] As a result, financial transfers from the federal government to the region (in the form of federal subsidies) stood to be affected; as regards the provision of basic services in Tigray, the federal government said it would work with local *woreda* (district) and *kebele* (community) councils and administrations.[126] In turn, the TPLF said that any cessation of financial transfers was a declaration of war and that it would take serious action in response.[127] Tensions between the Tigray region and federal government escalated into armed conflict in November 2020, a conflict which continues at the time of writing.

The controversy about the postponement of elections—and thereafter the conflict between the Tigray region and federal government—emerged partly as a result of the 1995 Constitution's inability to institute an impartial platform for constitutional interpretation. Since the task of such interpretation is given to a political organ, the HoF, it is hard to conceive how its decisions on controversial political issues could enjoy wide acceptance. Constitutional interpretation is thus one of the key issues that need urgent attention and reform.

Another key disharmony embedded in the Constitution is its imperviousness to being changed through amendment. While stringent amendment procedures are common in many federations, including supermajority approval requirements, the approach of the 1995 Constitution is too inflexible. This potentially undermines opportunities for constitutional development through amendment. Notably, under article 105(10), the amendment

[120] Neamin Ashenafi, 'Tigray Establishes Regional Electoral Commission' *The Ethiopian Reporter* (18 July 2020) https://www.thereporterethiopia.com/article/tigray-establishes-regional-electoral-commission (last accessed 1 March 2022).

[121] See article 102 of the FDRE Constitution.

[122] Fana Broadcasting Corporate (FBC), 'Tigray's Planned Election Unconstitutional: House of Federation' (6 September 2020) https://www.fanabc.com/english/tigrays-planned-election-unconstitutional-house-of-federation (last accessed 1 March 2022).

[123] Neamin Ashenafi, 'Tigray Elections: Beyond the Polls' *The Ethiopian Reporter* (19 September 2020) https://www.thereporterethiopia.com/article/tigray-elections-beyond-polls (last accessed 1 March 2022).

[124] Borkena.com, 'TPLF Ordered Members of Parliament from the Region to Leave the House' *Borkena* (5 October 2020) https://borkena.com/2020/10/05/tplf-ordered-members-of-parliament-from-the-region-to-leave-the-house (last accessed 1 March 2022).

[125] Fana Broadcasting Corporate (FBC), 'Federal Government Severs Relationship with Tigray Regional State' (7 October 2020) https://www.fanabc.com/english/federal-govt-severs-relationship-with-tigray-regional-state (last accessed 1 March 2022).

[126] FBC (n. 120).

[127] Ezega News, 'Any Attempt to Stop Tigray Elections Tantamount to Declaration of War: TPLF' https://www.ezega.com/News/NewsDetails/8113/Any-Attempt-to-Stop-Tigray-Elections-Tantamount-to-Declaration-of-War-TPLF (last accessed 1 March 2022).

of some of the key, controversial provisions of the Constitution requires the unanimity of members of the federation.

All Ethiopian constitutions since 1931 have suffered from a gap between formal rules and practice. There is, to begin with, a poor tradition of constitutionalism. All the regimes discussed in this chapter not only exercised discretionary powers frequently but more often than not also acted with little legal restraint.[128] What Markakis said of the limited role of constitutions in Ethiopia during Haile Selassie's reign is just as pertinent to the current constitution:

> [T]he constitutional provisions amount to little more than a formal statement of the facts of political life in Ethiopia. Those provisions which run contrary to the basic political fact that is the unlimited power of an autocratic regime—are blithely ignored.[129]

A related problem that has undermined constitutionalism in Ethiopia is the heavy influence of ruling parties over state institutions, as was witnessed under both the Derg and EPRDF. As Tanchev Evgeni points out, a remarkable feature of Soviet constitutional history was 'the presence of unofficial, sometimes unpublished, party decisions that constituted more powerful rules than the legal and constitutional provisions'.[130] Similarly, under the Derg and EPRDF, the directives of these vanguard parties mattered far more than what the constitution and other laws said. Although the 1995 Constitution recognises political freedoms and human rights, their realisation was thwarted by the EPRDF's unwillingness to allow political pluralism. Put differently, the EPRDF's interests lay in maintaining a dominant-party system that left little room for opposition parties to participate in the political process. A good example of this outlook is found in a party publication dealing with preparation for the 2010 elections. Here, the EPRDF unashamedly declared that opposition forces in Ethiopia, irrespective of their differences, were rent-seekers that needed to be prevented from gaining ground.[131]

Furthermore, poor public awareness, as well as cynicism, has adverse implications for the implementation of constitutions. According to Haddis Alemayehu, the Ethiopian author and statesman, constitutions that proclaim popular sovereignty were introduced in Ethiopia as long ago as 1987, but people's views on political power have not changed significantly:

> The people of Ethiopia, the majority of whom are deeply religious . . ., believe that the source of power is God. When an evil person comes to power, the people allude that God allowed that to punish them for their misdeeds [*sic*]; likewise, when a kind person comes to power, they say that was because of God's will and happiness. As God must give power, the people firmly believe that they need to obey their rulers. There is no . . . doubt among the people that they could not do something about this.[132]

128 See Olimpiad Solomonovič Ioffe, *Soviet Law and Soviet Reality* (Martinus Nijhoff 1985) 1.

129 Markakis (n. 97) 277.

130 Tanchev Evgeni, 'Historical and Psychological Sources Shaping Constitutionalism and Constitutional Performance in the Post-Communist Societies: Reflections on Constitutionalism in Transition, or the Legacy of Transitory Constitutions' in Stanisław Frankowski and Paul B. Stephan III (eds.), *Legal Reform in Post-Communist Europe: The View from Within* (Martinus Nijhoff 1995) 154.

131 Addis Raey, '2010 Election Strategy' (2010) 3 *Addis Raey: Ideological Journal of the EPRDF* 14.

132 Haddis A., 'Ethiopianness in My View' in *Ethiopianess* (Ethiopianess Association 1993) Amharic title, 'ītiyop'iyawīnet be'inē āmelekaket' (ītiyop'iyawīneti mahiber) 18.

Similarly, John Markakis observes that 'few Ethiopians take their constitution seriously. Those who are aware of it regard it with profound cynicism, while the masses are unaware of its existence'.[133]

As discussed in this section, the four constitutions under consideration suffered from internal and external disharmonies. Internal disharmonies refer to inconsistencies within constitutions themselves, while external disharmonies refer to divergences between constitutions and the socio-political identities of the country. In sum, the 1931 and 1955 constitutions failed not only to recognise Ethiopia's religious and ethnic diversity but also to guarantee popular sovereignty. The 1987 Constitution did indeed recognise ethnic diversity, but neglected to respond to demands for autonomy, self-administration, and multiparty democracy; in addition, it imposed a Marxist-Leninist ideology on a deeply religious society. The 1995 Constitution, in many respects more advanced than the earlier constitutions, also has serious disharmonies. For instance, it gave more attention to diversity—that is, to ethnic rights—than to building a political structure that could strike a delicate balance between unity and diversity.

The strong wish of regimes to imprint their ideologies in the constitution (as witnessed with the 1987 and 1995 constitutions) also limits the possibility of using constitutions for the development of political identity. Moreover, the inability of leaders to address constitutional disharmonies through constitutional amendment and interpretation is another factor that leads to oft-repeated constitutional disruption.

5. Conclusion

This chapter argued that understanding the problematic identity of Ethiopian constitutions sheds important light on the constitutional disruptions the country has faced. While Ethiopia has had relatively long experience in making constitutions, no single constitution has been able to serve a regime other than the one that introduced it.

Problems of constitutional identity in Ethiopia were discussed by looking at three major issues. The first was constitution-making processes. Despite their differences, one major feature the four constitutions have in common is that there was limited political participation in the process of making them—in other words, there were few to no instances of bargaining and compromise. As a result, the constitutions were seen as instruments of the political regimes that invented them; consequently, whenever political change occurs, there is little appetite to allow for the continuation of the constitution.

Secondly, since the adoption of the 1931 Constitution, transplanting foreign ideas and principles has been common practice in the making of constitutions, becoming more profound and controversial in the case of those of 1987 and 1995. The 1987 PDRE Constitution, which by and large was copied from the former socialist countries, was alien to Ethiopia's culture and history; hence, when regime change occurred in 1991, there was little incentive to retain it. In turn, however, the 1995 FDRE Constitution transplanted Stalinist approaches to managing ethnic diversity, doing so well after the dissolution of the socialist federations that were created on the basis of Stalin's precepts. As discussed, inconsistencies

133 Markakis (n. 97) 277.

in the self-determination principles of the FDRE Constitution ultimately undermined the legitimacy of that constitution.

Thirdly, constitutions in Ethiopia have suffered from internal and external disharmonies. The 1931 Constitution had several internal inconsistencies. For instance, although it introduced a parliamentary institution, members of parliament were not elected and the parliament was not accorded a meaningful role in making laws. The chief external disharmony was the failure to appreciate the identity—that is, the ethnic diversity—of the country. The 1955 Revised Constitution also suffered from disharmonies. One of its internal inconsistencies was that it did not constrain the power of the emperor in spite of the adoption of universal suffrage and the election of members of the chamber of deputies. Moreover, the implementation of its human rights provisions was made contingent on other laws. The chief external disharmony was the divergence between the constitutional document and the composition of the society—in other words, the 1955 Revised Constitution failed to recognise the country's diversity. With the 1987 PDRE Constitution, a major internal disharmony was that it provided for political and economic rights, yet made their implementation contingent on other conditions. Its external inconsistencies were more profound: a Marxist-Leninist ideology was imposed on a society that was religious and followed a traditional way of life.

As for the 1995 Constitution, its internal consistencies include its hybrid mix of federal and confederal tendencies: on the one hand, it created a centralised federal system; on the other, it has confederal features, notably the secession provision and the requirement of unanimity among members of the federation in the event of amendment of its key provisions. In addition, this constitution leaves limited avenues open for constitutional development, given that it assigns its interpretation to a partisan political organ, the HoF, and imposes difficult conditions for constitutional reform through amendment. While the 1931 and the 1987 constitutions failed to recognise ethno-linguistic diversity, the 1995 Constitution not only elevated ethnicity as the country's key organising device but also recognised the unconditional rights of ethnic communities to create new regions within the existing federation or secede entirely and establish new states. This approach to self-determination undermines development of the political art of negotiation and compromise and tends towards destabilisation.

As noted, Ethiopia's pre-1995 constitutions were disrupted by political changes. Likewise, the 1995 FDRE Constitution is under stress thanks to political changes that have been under way since 2018. As the controversy about the postponement of the 2020 elections showed, the Constitution affords limited avenues for addressing disputes. Hence, it is important to consider constitutional reforms that would enable the Constitution to function in a multi-party context.

The creation of a more durable constitution in Ethiopia requires grand constitutional bargaining with a view either to reforming the existing constitution or to introducing a new one. Some of the key issues that need to be addressed in this exercise include challenges concerning shared and self-rule (unity and diversity), the introduction of systems that strengthen popular participation, and revisiting the system of constitutional interpretation.

As this chapter has underlined, however, one of the major trends in the making of constitutions in Ethiopia is the imposition of the ideas of those who succeed in gaining power. Unless this trend is reversed, it is difficult to imagine the invention of a more sustainable constitution. A durable constitution for Ethiopia would need to strike a balance between unity and diversity; crucially, it would need to limit the power of the executive through the introduction of the rule of law, the development of independent institutions such as the judiciary, and the creation of systems for safeguarding the human rights included in the Constitution and the international conventions which Ethiopia has ratified.

Bibliography*

Aalen L., *Ethnic Federalism in a Dominant Party State: The Ethiopian Experience 1991–2000* (Chr. Michelsen Institute 2002)

Addis R., '2010 Election Strategy' (2010) *3 Addis Raey: Ideological Journal of the EPRDF* 6, Amharic title, ye2002 *yemirich'a sitiratejīyachin*

Alem H., 'Ethnic Pluralism as an Organising Principle of the Ethiopian Federation' (2004) *28(2) Dialectical Anthropology* 91

Arato A., 'Revolutions and Constitution Making' in Landau D. and Lerner H. (eds.), *Comparative Constitution Making* (Edward Elgar Publishing 2019) 27

Assefa F., *Federalism and the Accommodation of Diversity in Ethiopia: A Comparative Study* (rev. edn, Artistic Printing Enterprise 2007)

Bahru Z., 'Hayla-Sellase: From Progressive to Reactionary' (1995) *2 Northeast African Studies* 99

Bahru Z., *A History of Modern Ethiopia, 1855–1991* (2nd edn, James Currey 2002)

Balsvik R.R., *Haile Selassie's Students: The Intellectual and Social Background to Revolution, 1952–1974* (Addis Ababa University 2005)

Bekele Y.W., Kjosavik D.J., and Shanmugaratnam N., 'State-Society Relations in Ethiopia: A Political-Economy Perspective of the Post-1991 Order' (2016) *5 Social Sciences* 1

Borkena.com (online news website), 'TPLF Ordered Members of Parliament from the Region to Leave the House' *Borkena* (5 October 2020) https://borkena.com/2020/10/05/tplf-ordered-members-of-parliament-from-the-region-to-leave-the-house (last accessed 1 March 2022)

Brietzke P.H., 'Ethiopia's "Leap in the Dark": Federalism and Self-Determination in the New Constitution' (1995) *39 Journal of African Law* 32

Burgess M., *Comparative Federalism: Theory and Practice* (Routledge 2006)

Clapham C., *Haile Selassie's Government* (Praeger 1969)

Clapham C., *Transformation and Continuity in Revolutionary Ethiopia* (Cambridge University Press 1988)

Clarke J.C., *Alliance of the Colored Peoples: Ethiopia and Japan before World War II* (James Currey 2011)

Corazza M.T., 'State and Religion in the Constitution and Politics of Ethiopia' (2002) *9*(1) *European Journal for Church and State Research—Revue Européenne des Relations Églises-État* 351

Evgeni T., 'Historical and Psychological Sources Shaping Constitutionalism and Constitutional Performance in the Post-Communist Societies: Reflections on Constitutionalism in Transition, or the Legacy of Transitory Constitutions' in Frankowski S. and Stephan P.B. (eds.), *Legal Reform in Post-Communist Europe: The View from Within* (Martinus Nijhoff 1995) 141

Ezega News (online news website), 'Any Attempt to Stop Tigray Elections Tantamount to Declaration of War: TPLF' (5 September 2020) https://www.ezega.com/News/NewsDetails/8113/Any-Attempt-to-Stop-Tigray-Elections-Tantamount-to-Declaration-of-War-TPLF (last accessed 1 March 2022)

Fana Broadcasting Corporate (FBC) (online news website), 'Tigray's Planned Election Unconstitutional: House of Federation' (6 September 2020) https://www.fanabc.com/english/tigrays-planned-election-unconstitutional-house-of-federation (last accessed 1 March 2022)

* Following the Ethiopian tradition, the first (given) names of Ethiopian authors are put in the list of bibliography, the names of their fathers are abbreviated like the other contributors. In addition, the transliteration of Amharic titles of works cited are given next to the English translation.

Fana Broadcasting Corporate (FBC) (online news website), 'Federal Government Severs Relationship with Tigray Regional State' (7 October 2020) https://www.fanabc.com/english/federal-govt-severs-relationship-with-tigray-regional-state (last accessed 1 March 2022)

Gebreab B., 'Ethnic and Religious Policies of the Federal Democratic Republic of Ethiopia' in *Proceedings of the First National Conference on Federalism, Conflict and Peace Building* (Ministry of Federal Affairs and GTZ 2003) 199

Geset T., *It Was Then, No 2* (Commercial Printing Press 2009) Amharic title, *neber qutir 2*

Ginsburg, T., Haillíday, T.C., Shaffer G.C., 'Constitution-Making as Transnational Legal Ordering' in Gregory C. Shaffer, Tom Ginsburg, and Terence C. Halliday (eds.), *Constitution-Making and Transnational Legal Order* (Cambridge University Press 2019) 1

Haddis A., 'Ethiopianness in My View' in *Ethiopianess* (Ethiopianess Association 1993) 17 Amharic title, *'ītiyop'iyawīnet be'inē āmelekaket'* (ītiyop'iyawīneti mahiber)

Haile Kiros A., *Emergence, Expansion and Decline of Patrimonial Bureaucracy in Ethiopia, 1907–1974: An Attempt at Historical Interpretation* (PhD thesis, Vrije Universiteit Amsterdam Thesis 1978)

Haile Selassie I, King of Kings, *My Life and Ethiopia's Progress: Haile Selassie I, King of Kings*. Volume 1 (Birhane and Selam Printing Press 1973) Amharic title, *k'edamawī ḫayile šilasē niguše negešet, ḥiyiwet ēna ye'ītiyop'iya irimija k'ut'ir 1*

Hausmaninger H., 'The Committee of Constitutional Supervision of the USSR' (1990) *23 Cornell International Law Journal* 287

Imru H.S., *From What I Saw and Remember* (Ababa University Press 2009) Amharic title, *kayehutina kemasitawisew*

István K. and Decsényi J., *New Elements in the Evolution of Socialist Constitution* (Akadémiai Kiadó 1968)

Jacobsohn G.J., 'The Formation of Constitutional Identities' in Ginsburg T. and Dixon R. (eds.), *Comparative Constitutional Law* (Edward Elgar Publishing 2014) 129

Joireman S.F., 'Opposition Politics and Ethnicity in Ethiopia: We Will All Go Down Together' (1997) *35 Journal of Modern African Studies* 186

Keller E., *Revolutionary Ethiopia: From Empire to People's Republic* (Indiana University Press 1988)

Kiflu T., *The Generation, The History of the Ethiopian People's Revolutionary Party: Part I, From the Early Beginnings to 1975* (Independent Publishers 1993)

Landau D., 'Constituent Power and Constitution Making in Latin America' in Landau D. and Lerner H., *Comparative Constitution Making* (Edward Elgar Publishing 2019) 567

Lerner H. and Landau D., 'Introduction to Comparative Constitution Making: The State of the Field' in Landau D. and Lerner H., *Comparative Constitution Making* (Edward Elgar Publishing 2019) 2

Loewenstein K., 'Constitutions and Constitutional Law in the West and in the East' (1969) *30 The Indian Journal of Political Science* 203

Markakis J., *Ethiopia: Anatomy of a Traditional Polity* (Oxford University Press 1974)

Markakis J., 'Ethnic Conflict in Pre-federal Ethiopia' in *Proceedings of the First National Conference on Federalism, Conflict and Peace Building* (Ministry of Federal Affairs and GTZ 2003) 11

Mattei U., 'The New Ethiopian Constitution: First Thoughts on Ethnical Federalism and the Reception of Western Institutions' in Grande E. (ed.), *Transplants, Innovation, and Legal Tradition in the Horn of Africa* (L'Harmattan 1995) 111

Mehta P.B., *The Oxford Handbook of the Indian Constitution* (Oxford University Press 2016)

Merid A., *The Representative: Fitaurari Abebe Gebre's Biography* (Oscar Printers 2009) Amharic title, *iniderasēwi yefītawirarī ābebe gebirē yeḥiyiwet tarīk*

Mesfin W.M., *Mortar, Fear and Defeat* (Graphics Printers 2015) Amharic title, *ādafinē, firihatina kishifet*

National Democratic Institute for International Affairs (NDIIA), 'An Evaluation of the June 21, 1992 Elections in Ethiopia' (NDIIA 1992)

Neamin A., 'Tigray Establishes Regional Electoral Commission' *The Ethiopian Reporter* (18 July 2020) https://www.thereporterethiopia.com/article/tigray-establishes-regional-electoral-commission - online version (last accessed 1 March 2022)

Neamin A., 'Tigray Elections: Beyond the Polls' *The Ethiopian Reporter* (19 September 2020) https://www.thereporterethiopia.com/article/tigray-elections-beyond-polls online version (last accessed 1 March 2022)

Negede G., *Constitution, Elections and Democracy in Ethiopia* (AESOP Publishers 2004) 65, Amharic tile, *hige menigisit mirich'a ina dīmokirasī be'ītiyop'iya*

Olimpiad S.I., *Soviet Law and Soviet Reality* (Martinus Nijhoff 1985)

Perham M., *The Government of Ethiopia* (Faber & Faber 1970)

Rosenfeld M., 'Constitutional Identity' in Rosenfeld M. and Sajó A. (eds.), *The Oxford Handbook of Comparative Constitutional Law* (Oxford University Press 2012) 756

Roznai Y., *Unconstitutional Constitutional Amendments: The Limits of Amendment Powers* (Oxford University Press 2019)

Stalin J.V., *Marxism and the National Question: Collected Works, Vol. 2* (Foreign Languages Publishing House 1954)

Tekelehariat T.M., *My Autobiography of My Life* (Addis Ababa University Press 2006) Amharic title, yehiyiwetē tarīki otobayogirafi

Tekeste N., *Eritrea and Ethiopia: The Federal Experience* (Nordiska Afrikainstitutet 1997)

Tesgaye R., 'The Making and Legitimacy of the Ethiopian Constitution: Towards Bridging the Gap between Constitutional Design and Constitutional Practice' (2010) *23 Africa Focus* 85

Vestal T.M., 'Analysis of the New Constitution of Ethiopia and the Process of its Adoption' (1996) *3 Northeast African Studies*, New Series 21, 26

Vlastos S., 'Opposition Movements in Early Meiji, 1868–1885' in Jansen M.B. (ed.), *The Emergence of Meiji Japan* (Cambridge University Press 1997) 367

Watts R., *Comparing Federal Systems* (McGill-Queen's University Press 1999)

Zewde R., *Haile Selassie I Government, Vol. 1, 1930–1955* (Shama Books 2005) Amharic title, *yek'edamawī ḫayilešilasē menigišit qutir 1 1930–1955*

Zhai H., *The Constitutional Identity of Contemporary China: The Unitary System and Its Internal Logic* (Brill NV 2019) 15

8

Rooting Constitutional Identity in African Countries without Pre-colonial Institutional Traditions but with National Values

The Cape Verdean Experience and the Role of the Constitutional Court

José Pina-Delgado

1. Introduction

Constitutional identity is an elusive and contested concept,[1] but, for practical purposes, it is reasonable to say that it is a broad, multilayered notion that encompasses the set of established constitutional principles, stable normative features, and institutional practices that characterise a certain constitutional order in regard to form of the state; its relations with individuals; the system and relationships between the political branches of government and with the courts; the territorial distribution of power; the protection and amendment of the constitution; and, in some cases, the incorporation of international law; national security; and the economic order.

The term does not equate to cultural identity, national identity, or identity of the people.[2] Nevertheless, it can reflect traces of all of these, as well as of universal values, foreign influences, and international legal developments. In this sense, a constitutional text or decision can be the source of a new constitutional identity if duly incorporated by the people as part of their own identity, independently of its national, foreign, or international origins. Thus, the dialectic between the identity of the people, national identity, cultural identity, other identities,[3] and the identity of the constitution is permanent, despite leading to different outcomes depending on the national or supranational context where it is applicable.

In an era marked by the globalisation of constitutional institutions,[4] an appeal to constitutional identity in its basic sense, that is, as a recognition of communitarian values, is sometimes viewed with distrust as a sign of breaking with universally established patterns

[1] See Gary Jacobson, 'Constitutional Identity' (2006) *68 Review of Politics* 361; Michel Rosenfeld, 'Constitutional Identity' in Michel Rosenfeld and András Sajó (eds.), *The Oxford Handbook of Comparative Constitutional Law* (Oxford University Press 2012) 756.

[2] See also José Luis Marti, 'Two Different Ideas of Constitutional Identity: Identity of the Constitution v. Identity of the People' in Alejandro Saiz Arnáiz and Carina Alcoberro (eds.), *National Constitutional Identity and European Integration* (Intersentia 2013) 17.

[3] See Michel Rosenfeld, 'The Identity of the Constitutional Subject' (1995) *16 Cardozo Law Review* 1049.

[4] See, for example, Bui Ngoc Son, 'Globalisation of Constitutional Identity' (2017) *26 Washington International Law Journal* 463.

José Pina-Delgado, *Rooting Constitutional Identity in African Countries without Pre-colonial Institutional Traditions but with National Values* In: *Constitutional Identity and Constitutionalism in Africa.* Edited by: Charles M. Fombad and Nico Steytler, Oxford University Press.
 DOI: 10.1093/oso/9780198906308.003.0011

of constitutional development, and, as such, as retrogression in the consolidation of a world of free, democratic, and stable countries and an enabler of more authoritarian forms of government instrumentally anchored in the past[5] or forged in ethnocultural understandings of constitutional identity.[6] Such a risk is indeed a reality, especially when the search for and imposition of those communitarian values result from artificial, selective, or static constructions of the shared ethos of an otherwise dynamic political community.

However, grounding the Constitution in a sense of shared basic values, regardless of its thickness or thinness, can be crucial if one intends to be represented by institutions that can be appropriated as 'ours', that appeal to one's collective evolution and reduce the distance between the formal constitution and the constitutional concrete order that marks the institutional experience in many parts of the world. A region such as Africa, which was subjected to colonialism, also inherited the legal institutions of foreign civilisations.[7] In such cases, one could stress that it is important for the constitutional experience to be effective—that is, to determine de facto collective life and individual behaviour in a community—and for constitutional identity to result not only from formulas absorbed from universal, regional, or external sources but also from the national identity as represented at a certain time, including from its traditional institutional values.

With this general context in mind, this chapter examines the experience of the Republic of Cape Verde's constitutional law in recognising communitarian values as part of its constitutional identity. Beginning with an account of the country's political and constitutional history before independence, the chapter analyses the context of approval and the main values of the fundamental laws that marked the former and current constitutional order so as to evaluate whether these reflect the cultural identity of the Cape Verdean people; the chapter also emphasises the efforts recently taken by the Constitutional Court of Cape Verde (CCCV) in strengthening that connection and rooting constitutional law in the local creole identity and in institutional traditions developed since colonial times. It ends with final remarks.

2. The Creation of a Creole Identity and Institutional Traditions before Independence

The development of what one can call an institutional identity was the result of a process spanning five centuries that led, on the one hand, to the creation of a creole cultural identity which is the foundation of the Cape Verdean nation, and, on the other, to the development of certain values concerning the legitimacy and exercise of power and individual rights, values which form the basis of shared communitarian institutional and legal preferences.

Since the colonial era, these processes moved at different speeds, albeit in an intermingled manner, given that the Cape Verde islands remained subject to Portuguese rule from the middle of the fifteenth century until independence in 1975.[8] With there being no

[5] See András Popp, 'Illiberalism as Constitutional Identity—the Case of Hungary' (2018) *59 Hungarian Journal of Legal Sciences* 378.

[6] Kriszta Kovács, 'The Rise of Ethnocultural Identity in the Jurisprudence of the East Central European Courts' (2017) *18 German Law Journal* 1703.

[7] For a discussion of this, see Chapter 1, 'Constitutional Identity and Constitutionalism in Africa: Concept and Key Issues', by Charles M. Fombad, in this volume.

[8] For a useful presentation, see Richard Lobban Jr., *Cape Verde: From Crioulo Colony to Independent Nation* (Westview Press 1995).

indigenous population, the first settlers from Europe to explore the main island of Santiago economically brought persons from the African mainland as slaves, initially to work on the land and subsequently to be traded to the Americas, as participation in the transatlantic traffic of people became the main economic activity of the archipelago.[9] Moreover, some followers of the Jewish faith, only formally converted to Christianity, reached the island seeking a space where they could more easily, albeit discreetly, observe the rituals of their real religious confession without being controlled, harassed, and punished by the state or by the Holy Office.[10]

For obvious reasons, neither African nor Jewish persons, despite their influence on the genetics of the people and on local cultural traditions, values, language, and culinary customs, were strong enough to determine the institutional design of a peripheral territory of a multi-continental empire.[11] These circumstances explain why there were no local or parallel legal traditions before the construction of the legal and administrative colonial apparatus. This was, as a matter of fact, the formal institutional ground zero, based on the traditional local governmental framework of the Lusitanian monarchy of the fifteenth, sixteenth, and seventeenth centuries, with its elected municipalities centred in a multifunctional collective organ that had executive, normative, and judicial powers, namely the City Council (*Câmara Municipal*), which shared local power in the colonies with the permanent representatives of the crown, the general-governor.[12] The scheme of colonial government—based on the free choice of rulers by residents in competitive elections and mainly on a power exercised by a collegial organ—proved to be essential to the development of a tradition of popular legitimation of power in the islands, as well as of dilution of public power by allocating it to different political organs, and of resistance to strong one-man rule.

Notwithstanding its colonial status, the fact was that, for diverse reasons, Cape Verdean society developed in a way that allowed its inhabitants to amalgamate European, African, and Jewish or at least Crypto-Jewish influences, thereby creating distinctive and hybrid cultural features[13] that led, very early on, to a sense of national identity. This perspective appears in the first work authored by a Cape Verdean, the Mestizo captain André Álvares d'Almada (1555–1650). Born in the islands and a product of local miscegenation, he was the grandson of an African slave[14] but still a member of the local ruling class—a 'man of governance', as it was put. His *Tratado Breve dos Rios da Guiné e de Cabo Verde*[15] is a 'historical, geographical, ethnographic, anthropological, botanic, economical and legal book crucial

[9] Toby Green, 'Building Slavery in the Atlantic World: Atlantic Connections and the Changing Institution of Slavery in Cabo Verde, Fifteenth–Sixteenth Centuries' (2011) *32 Slavery & Abolition* 227.

[10] Toby Green, *Masters of Difference: Creolisation and the Jewish Presence in Cabo Verde, 1497–1672* (PhD thesis, Centre of West African Studies, University of Birmingham 2006).

[11] A.J.R. Russel-Wood, *The Portuguese Empire, 1415–1808: A World on the Move* (John Hopkins University Press 1998).

[12] See Maria Teresa Avelino Pires, *O Município nas Ilhas de Cabo Verde—Séculos XIV a XVIII* (PhD thesis, UNL 2009); for the rules, see *Ordenações Manuelinas* (FCG 1985 [1512 or 1513?]), Book I, Tit. XLVI and f.; *Ordenações Filipinas* (FCG 1985 [1603]), Book I, Tit. LXV-LXVII, 133–53.

[13] Gabriel Fernandes, *Em Busca da Nação: Notas para a Reinterpretação do Cabo Verde Crioulo* (Editora UFSC/IBNL 2006).

[14] See 'Concessão do Hábito de Cristo a André Álvares de Almada [19 August 1598]' in *Monumenta Missionária Africana*, 2. Serie (Agência Geral do Ultramar 1963), v. III, 428–30.

[15] André Álvares d'Almada, *Tratado Breve dos Rios da Guiné e de Cabo Verde*, António Luís Ferronha (ed.) (Grupo de Trabalho do Ministério da Educação para as Comemorações dos Descobrimentos Portugueses, 1994 [1594]) (an English translation by P.E.H. Hair, with the title *Brief Treatise on the Rivers of Guinea* (Department of History—University of Liverpool 1984), can be found at https://search.library.wisc.edu/digital/AQ2XQZT2FQE3VB8C).

for the knowledge and understanding of West African peoples'.[16] From a political point of view, it is also a manifesto for defending Cape Verdean commercial interests in an area that locals considered their area of influence. In doing so, he appealed to a rationale that separated the interests of the Portuguese Crown from the collective aims of the Cape Verdean inhabitants.[17]

This amalgamation was the result of a process initiated in the middle of the sixteenth century that led local people (specifically free adult males with property), the *Filhos da Terra* ('sons of the land') or *Nobreza da Terra* ('land's nobility'), to gain, independently of their origin or race, access to local power,[18] replace the former ruling *Homens honrados brancos* ('honourable white men'),[19] and subsequently control municipalities, thereby enjoying political power in concurrence with the administrators appointed by the Portuguese Crown, especially in the periods in which they could fill power vacuums as acting governors.[20] In this manner, a modus vivendi was established and accepted, or at least tolerated, by the colonial power until the last quarter of the eighteenth century. It is true that impulses of centralisation in Europe—in an era of absolute power and excessive control of the municipalities by local elites—led the controversial First Minister of the Crown, the Marquis of Pombal,[21] to use criminal procedures in order to purge the non-compliant members of the island's ruling class or to gradually impoverish them by imposing chartered companies, namely the Grão-Pará and Maranhão Company, so as to control commerce in the islands.[22] Despite this collective setback, the municipal experience in colonial times ended up integrating the national institutional heritage[23] and had an indelible impact on the Cape Verdean way of conceiving political legitimacy and the exercise of power.

Additionally, the way that islanders saw the world was impacted on by their early experience of emigration to, and return migration from, liberal democratic America;[24] by the introduction of the press and printing facilities;[25] and by their enjoyment of some degree of personal liberty, or at least of pathways to individual freedom, through the frequent manumission of bondsmen and practice of religious tolerance, even in what was essentially a society driven by slavery.[26] At the same time, the relative absence of public authority on the islands, combined with natural resistance to the unjust laws of serfdom and the

[16] See José Pina-Delgado, 'A Primeira Obra Cabo-Verdiana. "Tratado Breve da Guiné do Cabo Verde" de André Álvares d'Almada' (2018) *1 Leitura. Revista da Livraria Pedro Cardoso* 33.

[17] José Pina-Delgado, 'Os escrúpulos de um Ilustre Santiaguense nos 'Tractos' da Guiné dos Séculos XVI–XVII: o Capitão André Álvares d'Almada e a Questão da Incerteza sobre a Presença dos Títulos Jurídicos da Escravatura' in Mário Silva, Leão de Pina, and Paulo Monteiro Júnior (eds.), *Estudos em Comemoração do Quinto Aniversário do ISCJS* (ISCJS 2012) 112–15.

[18] See 'Carta dos Moradores de Santiago a El-Rei [26 de Maio de 1546]' in *Monumenta Missionaria Africana*, 2. Serie (AGU 1963), v. II, 386–7.

[19] Iva Cabral, *A Primeira Elite Colonial Atlântica: Dos 'Homens Honrados Brancos' de Santiago à 'Nobreza da Terra' (Finais do séc. XV—Início do século XVII)* (Pedro Cardoso Livraria 2015).

[20] Maria Teresa Avelino Pires, *O Domínio do Poder e o Poder dos Homens: Os Governos Interinos Camarários das Ilhas de Cabo Verde—Séculos XVII e XVIII* (Chiado 2013).

[21] Kenneth Maxwell, *Pombal, Paradox of the Enlightenment* (Cambridge University Press 1995).

[22] See António Carreira, *As Companhias Pombalinas de Grão-Pará e Maranhão e Pernambuco e Paraíba* (2nd edn, Presença 1982 [1969]).

[23] See also Wladimir Brito, 'Cabo Verde: Institucionalização, organização e problemas do poder local' in José Melo Alexandrino (ed.), *Jornadas de Direito Comparado Lusófono* (AAFDL 2014) 73.

[24] Marilyn Halter, *Between Race and Ethnicity: Cape Verdean American Immigrants, 1860–1965* (UIP 1993).

[25] João Nobre Leite, *A Imprensa em Cabo Verde, 1820–1975* (FM 1998).

[26] António Carreira, *Cabo Verde: Formação e extinção de uma sociedade escravocrata (1460–1878)* (3rd edn, IPC 2000 [1972]).

discrimination experienced by African and Jewish persons, led to strong notions of personal liberty inflected with libertarian elements, especially so after the abolition of slavery in 1869.

This event finally resolved the existential paradox of the nation's construction, and created the conditions for the idea of a free mixed-race people having African and European blood with some grains of Semitic heritage; this solidified in the collective psyche. The fusion of blood and culture created a new people who, due to their origins, recognised persons independently of their features and station in life and saw them as integrated within a national community, precisely because the notion of the nation was marked not by racial homogeneity but by the continuous mutation of a hybrid culture that manages to reinvent itself with external contributions according to domestic certification criteria based on very thin values of freedom, tolerance, and equality. This development was perfectly captured by the famous abolitionist novel of 1856 written by José Evaristo d'Almeida (c. 1820–c. 1857) and entitled *The Slave.*[27] Besides attacking the practice of slavery, the book celebrates the local ethos by stressing its difference from Portuguese values and capacity to accommodate people irrespective of their physical characteristics and on the basis of their acceptance of values core to the hybrid culture developed by the islanders.

From then on, interpersonal interaction and the societal dynamics of the archipelago led to the gradual consolidation of the elements that represented the particularities of the Cape Verdean people and their special interests, all of which successive generations of intellectuals managed to promote or theorise.[28] Firstly, there were the politically and socially active 'nativists' of the late nineteenth century and of the early twentieth century, such as Luiz Loff de Vasconcellos (1861–1923), Eugénio de Paula Tavares (1867–1930), and Pedro Cardoso (1890–1942).[29] Subsequently, the second quarter of the century saw the so-called *Claridosos* ('The enlighteners')—formed by a group of essayists gathered around the journal *Claridade*[30]—seek to deepen understanding of Cape Verdean culture. In doing so, they contributed to the explanation of the 'creole adventure',[31] especially the process of creation of the national language.[32] It is true they were inclined to accommodate themselves to Portuguese official discourse by stressing the regional nature of Cape Verdean culture, but they were also vital for the promotion of intellectual and scientific studies on national identity.

Finally, younger intellectuals loosely linked with the chief promoters of that movement, including the judge and storyteller Gabriel Mariano (1928–2002)[33] and the physician and novelist Teixeira de Sousa (1919–2006), also played a decisive role.[34] They underlined the

[27] José Evaristo d'Almeida, *O Escravo* (2nd edn, ICL 1989 [1856]).

[28] See, for example, David Hopffer Almada, *Caboverdianidade & Tropicalismo* (Fundação Joaquim Nabuco & Editora Massangana 1992) 63–4.

[29] See Luiz Loff de Vasconcelos, *O Extermínio de Cabo Verde: Pavorosas Revelações* (Guimarães, Libânio & Co. 1905); Eugénio Tavares, *Eugénio Tavares pelos Jornais . . .*, Félix Monteiro (ed.) (ICLD 1997); Pedro Cardoso, *Textos Jornalísticos e Literários*, Manuel Brito-Semedo and Joaquim Morais (eds.) (IBNL 2008).

[30] See the published volumes in *Claridade: Revista de Arte e Letras* (2nd edn, Instituto Cabo-Verdiano do Livro e do Disco 1988).

[31] Manuel Ferreira, *A Aventura Crioula: ou Cabo Verde, uma Síntese Cultural e Étnica* (2nd edn, Plátano 1973).

[32] See the monumental Baltasar Lopes da Silva, *O Dialecto Crioulo de Cabo Verde* (IN—CM 1984 [1957]).

[33] Gabriel Mariano, 'Do Funco ao Sobrado ou o Mundo que o Mulato Criou' *Cultura Cabo-Verdiana: Ensaios* (Vega 1991 [1959]) 37.

[34] See Henrique Teixeira de Sousa, 'Sobrados, Lojas & Funcos: Contribuição para o Estudo da Evolução Social da Ilha do Fogo' (1958) (30) *Claridade: Revista de Arte e Letras* 2.

special nature of Cape Verdean identity, rejecting its characterisation either as a Portuguese regional identity or its pure African character[35] and emphasising its hybridity.

To this set of collective features one could add the qualities of what locals call *morabeza*—a mixture of affability and hospitality, tolerance and flexibility—along with an ardent desire for freedom, a wariness, even disdain, for authority, and a firm belief in the popular legitimation of public power.

3. Basic Laws Imported from Afro-Socialist Constitutionalism

The *Claridosos* were rejected by more engaged and activist intellectuals[36] as out of touch with social and political reality and for failing to achieve an autonomous status for Cape Verde akin to that of the Northern Atlantic islands of Azores and Madeira. Since the eighteenth century, the islands had experienced a crucial diminution of self-government in which municipalities were stripped of their political character and limited to purely administrative tasks in a system controlled by the governor and the non-elected administrators he appointed to manage the islands of the archipelago.[37] With the advent of the Portuguese Republic, Cape Verde's residents gained the opportunity of being elected to the parliament in Lisbon, but, despite the engaged role that many of the island's representatives played, their efficacy was highly limited.[38] The rise in Portugal of the fascist New State (*Estado Novo*) under Salazar led to the tightening of control of the colonies and the repression of all local demands. This in turn led, on the one hand, to the idea that for Cape Verdeans there was no advantage in integrating a decadent empire controlled by an 'underdeveloped' and poorly managed nation unable to guarantee the protection of the 'people of the islands' against cyclical famines and permanent food insecurity;[39] on the other hand, the international winds of full self-determination for colonial peoples saw the creation of independence movements, specifically the African Party for the Independence of Guinea and Cape Verde (Partido Africano para a Independência da Guiné e Cabo Verde; PAIGC).[40]

The main figure in the party was Amílcar Cabral (1924–1973), Cape Verdean by blood and Bissao-Guinean by birth. Although an accomplished intellectual, he was more interested in political action than in discussions about identity because he believed that thought and policies had to be rooted in the local reality and not in the purity of intellectual concepts. For Cabral, the need to develop an independent country free from external dependence made it necessary to ensure that the state was strong enough to be economically viable;

[35] See Gabriel Mariano, 'Negritude e Cabo-Verdianidade' (1958) *104 Boletim Cabo Verde* 7.

[36] Manuel Duarte, 'Caboverdianidade e Africanidade' [1951] in *Caboverdianidade, Africanidade e outros Textos* (Spleen 1999) 21; Amílcar Cabral, 'Apontamento sobre a Poesia Cabo-Verdiana' (1952) 28 *Boletim de Propaganda e Informação* 5, 7–8; Onésimo Silveira, *Consciencialização na Literatura Caboverdiana* (Edição CEI 1963).

[37] The incremental erosion of the island's autonomy is symbolised by the following acts: the *Carta Orgânica das Instituições Administrativas nas Províncias Ultramarinas* (1869); J.A. Ismael Gracias (commentary) (Imprensa Nacional, 1894); the Administrative Code for the Overseas Provinces of 1881; the Administrative Organisation of the Province of Cape Verde of 1892, the Organic Charter of the Colony of Cape Verde of 1926; the Portuguese Constitution of 1933 and the Colonial Act of 1933.

[38] See Eduardo Vera-Cruz Pinto, 'Para a História do Direito Político Cabo-Verdiano: O Contributo do Senador Vera Cruz' in Mário Silva, Leão de Pina, and Paulo Monteiro Júnior (eds.), *Estudos em Comemoração do Quinto Aniversário do ISCJS* (ISCJS 2012) 45–77, which discusses the role of one Cape Verdean politician.

[39] See the indictment by the Cape Verdean jurist, Duarte (n. 36) 33.

[40] See, for example, Amílcar Cabral, 'The Facts About Portugal's African Colonies' [1960] in Michael Wolfers (trans.), *Unity and Struggle: Speeches and Writings. Texts Selected by the PAIGC* (Monthly Review Press 1979) 17.

this led to a defence of the maintenance of the unity between Cape Verde and Guinea-Bissau, thus downgrading the importance of the cultural particularities of their respective peoples; it also resulted in an institutional design in which political power would be organised around a centralised state controlled by a vanguard party made up of the 'best sons and daughters of our land'.[41]

This model of organisation of the political community served as a loose blueprint for the two West African states.[42] This was so not only because of the Unity Project that was expected to create a Bissau-Guinean/Cape Verdean confederation of sorts, but also because, in regard to Cape Verde, the main categories of Cabral's political thinking and of its party ideology were duly inserted into the basic laws of the so-called First Republic as constitutional values. In 1975, at its first meeting, the Popular National Assembly announced the Proclamation of Independence and approved the first constitutional law of the country, namely the Law on the Political Organization of the State (*Lei de Organização Política do* Estado) (LOPE).[43]

The two instruments together formed the constitutional framework of Cape Verde from 1975 to 1980. The constitutional values were inserted in the former, and the basic principles and the architecture of the state in the latter. These values were the dignity of the people and their exclusive representation by the PAIGC, as reflected in article 1 of the LOPE, which sets out the principle that the PAIGC is the commanding political force of Cape Verdean society and that the people exercise sovereignty through the party, unity with Guinea-Bissau, anti-colonialism, anti-imperialism, and the country's African destiny.

The broad constitutional text that succeeded this in 1980[44] was drafted by Cape Verdean jurists, with minor contributions made by German Democratic Republic (GDR) public lawyers.[45] It retained the same values enshrined in the Proclamation of Independence, but, in its preamble, also recognised others, such as popular democracy, defence of the working classes, peace, progress, and the pursuit of happiness, justice, and fraternity. It was structured on the principles of revolutionary national democracy (article 3) and the supremacy of the party (article 4) within a centralised state that controlled society as well as the economy. This Basic Law, despite listing fundamental rights, made their applicability largely dependent on the enactment of statutes, thus in practice voiding them.[46] The law recognised a formal system of government in which power was exercised by the party through a non-permanent[47] and only formally powerful national assembly, as well as through the president of the Republic, a head of state whose main function was to represent the state, and through the government with its executive powers.[48]

[41] Ibid. 'Party Principles and Political Practice' [1969] in *Unity and Struggle: Speeches and Writings. Texts Selected by the PAIGC* 30.

[42] A useful presentation of Cape Verdean constitutional history from this moment on can be found in Mário Silva, *Contributo para a História Político-Constitucional de Cabo Verde, 1974–1992* (ISCJS/Almedina 2015).

[43] Ibid. 70–82.

[44] Constitution of Cape Verde of 1980 (original version); for further discussion, see Silva (n. 42) 116–48.

[45] See José Vicente Lopes, *Cabo Verde: Os Bastidores da Independência* (2nd edn, Spleen 2002 [1996]), quoting the testimony of one of the members of the draft committee that travelled to the GDR.

[46] For developments, see Mário Silva, *O Regime dos Direitos Sociais na Constituição Cabo-Verdiana de 1992* (Almedina 2004) 74–81.

[47] See, for example, Aristides R. Lima, *Reforma Política em Cabo Verde: Do paternalismo à modernização do Estado em Cabo Verde* (Grafedito 1992).

[48] See the analysis by Jorge Carlos Fonseca, 'O Sistema de Governo na Constituição Cabo-Verdiana' [1982] in Jorge Carlos Fonseca, *Cabo Verde: Constituição—Democracia—Cidadania* (Almedina 2011) 11–76.

With the advent of a postcolonial state, Cape Verdeans at last managed to enjoy stable self-determination, which raised the possibility of their living freely under a legitimate and participatory government. However, that potential was diminished significantly as national self-determination came at a price: the imposition of a political system dominated by a single party, one that had fought for the independence of Cape Verde and Guinea-Bissau and which functioned as a paternalistic entity with some social concerns.[49] The system showed some degree of solidarity, but lacked recognition of self-rule by the people, was devoid of meaningful freedom, and, despite its relative moderation—which some observers attributed to the need to adapt to Cape Verde's moderate mores[50]—instituted repressive policies when these were necessary for limiting political dissent.[51]

4. A Constitution Borrowed from a Former Colonial Power after a Democratic Transition

The political model adopted by post-independence rulers was later seen as incompatible with traditional Cape Verdean values.[52] It had been based on constitutional institutions with a Marxist-Leninist character and Afro-socialist-populist features, this due to the influence of other recently independent states in Africa as well as of Amílcar Cabral's political thought.[53] When the regime collapsed in the late 1980s and an amendment to the Constitution, reluctantly accepted by Cape Verdean rulers, introduced a multi-party system in 1990, the opposition—by appealing to long-repressed desires for freedom, political tolerance, and self-government by the people—managed to inflict a resounding defeat on the former one-party regime and win more than two-thirds of the seats in Parliament.

This allowed the new ruling party Movimento para a Democracia (Movement for Democracy), to stage a non-violent constitutional revolution in the country and use its power to approve a new Basic Law that rejected almost all of the constitutional values of the previous regime,[54] barring those of national independence and solidarity. This party embraced those values and constitutional solutions which it understood as reflecting the Cape Verdean ethos and its communitarian disposition—namely, human dignity, national independence, individual freedom, equality, popular sovereignty, solidarity, peace, and justice—and all other values were rejected, including the core constitutional principles of the *ancien régime*, namely national revolutionary democracy and the supremacy of the party and its leaders.

Before the adoption of the 1992 Constitution, proposals made by civil society organisations such as the Roman Catholic Church had appealed for other identity references, such as declaring God the 'supreme legislator';[55] other groupings advocated for a presidential regime and a quasi-federalist constitution[56] inspired by American constitutional institutions.

[49] See Lima (n. 47) 10.

[50] Onésimo Silveira, *A Democracia em Cabo Verde* (Colibri 2005) 12.

[51] Onésimo Silveira, *A Tortura em Nome do Partido Único: O PAICV e a sua Polícia Política (Depoimentos)* (Terra Nova & Ponto e Vírgula 1991); Humberto Cardoso, O partido Único em Cabo Verde. Um Assalto à Esperança (Imprensa Nacional de Cabo Verde1993) 63.

[52] Silveira (n. 50) 9–13.

[53] See Lima (n. 47) 9–10.

[54] See Carlos Veiga, 'Cabral e a Construção do Estado em Cabo Verde—Uma Apreciação Crítica' (2004) *19 Direito e Cidadania* 83–4.

[55] *Contribuição da Igreja Católica para a Elaboração da Nova Constituição: Critérios e Exigências para a Nova Ordem Constitucional* [September 1990], reproduced in *Vozdipovo* (11 September 1990) 3.

[56] *Proposta da UCID para a Constituição de 1992* (UCID 1992).

However, the new ruling party[57] and independent jurists[58] presented texts inspired by, if not identical to, the values and foundations of the 1976 Constitution of the Portuguese Republic.

The contrast between the old constitutional order and the newly emerging one was clearly evident in the constitutional debates[59] of 1992, where one of the framers said that 'during 1990, two completely different conceptions clashed in Cape Verde':

> On the one hand, [one sees] the continuity of the regime enshrined in the current constitution [of 1980] with its national-revolutionary democracy, with its mass organisations and deficits of protection of individual rights, freedoms, and safeguards, with its state-controlled economy, society and culture and reduced expression of the judiciary and local power.[60]

On the other hand, there was the project of change of the political regime, one advocating

> human rights, pluralism, right to difference and possibility of political transfer of power as fundamental principles of life in society, a subsidiary role and of development promotion for the State, the rise of an independent judicial system, of an autonomous local power, as well as the existence of real [individual] guarantees in the Constitution.[61]

The drafters of the Cape Verdean constitutional text chose to use a structure, form, and norms borrowed from the Portuguese Constitution after that country transitioned to democracy.[62] There were various reasons for this,[63] but the main one is that many of the framers were trained in Portugal,[64] in particular the Cape Verdean lawyers who led the party that controlled Parliament and formed the government, among them the first prime minister of the so-called Second Republic, Carlos Veiga, a prominent attorney,[65] and the minister of foreign affairs, Professor Jorge Carlos Fonseca,[66] who participated in discussions of the draft and represented the executive in the discussion of the constitutional bill.[67] In addition, the main drafter of the 1992 Constitutional bill, Professor Wladimir Brito, was a member of the faculty of the Minho Law School in Portugal.[68]

[57] *Uma Proposta de Constituição para Cabo Verde* (PAICV 1992).

[58] António Caldeira Marques, *Revisão da Constituição. Subsídios para o Debate*, reproduced in *Terra Nova* January–June 1990.

[59] See the constitutional debates on the *Actas das Sessões de Apresentação e Debate da Constituição da República [Parliamentary Records]*, 2nd Legislative Session, 4th Legislature (1992) (20 July 1992).

[60] Ibid. 46 (Member of Parliament Arnaldo Silva).

[61] Ibid. 46–7.

[62] For developments on this matter, see Jorge Carlos Fonseca, 'Do Regime de Partido Único à Democracia em Cabo Verde: As Sombras e a Presença da Constituição Portuguesa de 1976' (2006) *Special Edition Themis: Revista da Faculdade de Direito da UNL* 81.

[63] Ibid. 108–9.

[64] Ibid. 108.

[65] See Nuno Manalvo, *Carlos Veiga: biografia política. O rosto da mudança em Cabo Verde* (2nd edn, Aletheia 2009) 45–6.

[66] See 'Notas Bio-bibliográficas de Jorge Carlos Almeida Fonseca' in Lígia Dias Fonseca and Sofia Dupret Fonseca (eds.), *Liberdade Sempre! Homenagem a Jorge Carlos Almeida Fonseca por ocasião dos seus 70 anos* (Pedro Cardoso Livraria 2020) 9–27.

[67] *Actas das Sessões de Apresentação e Debate da Constituição da República* (n. 59).

[68] See 'Wladimir Brito' in José Vicente Lopes (Interviewer), *A Explicação do Mundo (Entrevistas)* (Spleen 2004) 144.

However, although the wording of the two constitutions provides some evidence in this regard, the conclusions that found a large one-directional influence[69] by the Portuguese Constitution on the Cape Verdean one and which held that the latter 'closely follows the Portuguese Constitution',[70] to the extent that the country has a largely plagiarised constitution,[71] have to be softened in certain respects, and for three reasons. First of all, it is not factually correct to say that the two constitutional structures and the wordings of their respective constitutional norms are the same.[72] The fact is that the drafters were able to insert constitutional sub-regimes not recognised by the Portuguese Constitution but modelled on other legal traditions—this had the effect of implementing meaningful changes in the island's Basic Law. This is the case in the *amparo* procedure (a constitutional complaint) and the writ of *habeas data*, inspired, respectively, by the Spanish Constitution of 1978 and Latin American sources,[73] as well as in the comprehensive conception of individual duties directly influenced by the African Charter on Human and Peoples' Rights.[74]

Secondly, certain structural options are rather distinct in degree, including the semi-presidential system of government, or the system of judicial review of legislation; some were simply worded differently due to internal concerns and challenges. Thirdly, and most importantly for the purposes of this chapter, if one looks beyond the text of the 'Large-C' Constitution and considers the political use of the Basic Law, the institutional practices, and the judicial decisions—that is, to use a symbolic expression, the 'small-c' constitution[75]—and, above all, if one considers the context of the adoption of the current Basic Law and all its amendments, the political and scholarly discussion, and the preparatory works, the probable conclusion would be different, or at least more nuanced. Both for pragmatic and substantive reasons of seeking inspiration in a functioning liberal democracy with which the country has historical ties and cultural affinities, the founding fathers used the Portuguese Constitution in order to adopt a constitutional skeleton, assimilate universal or foreign values on which to organise the Republic, and articulate traditional Cape Verdean values as well as communitarian aspirations.

As many authors from Cape Verde and elsewhere have noted, features of the Cape Verdean institutional and constitutional experience, whether considered generally[76] or in particular,[77] have arisen from deeply embedded cultural and national communitarian values. These include the notions that the people have the right to choose their leaders; that Cape Verdeans have the right to rule themselves; that the power of the state should be limited and not concentrated in one person; and that all individuals have worth. Conceptions like

[69] In general, see Jorge Bacelar Gouveia, 'Sistemas Constitucionais Africanos de Língua Portuguesa: a Caminho de um Paradigma' (2006) *Special Edition Themis: Revista de Direito da UNL* 119–41.

[70] See Jorge Miranda and E. Kafft Kosta, *As Constituições dos Estados de Língua Portuguesa: Uma Visão Comparativa* (Juruá 2013) 129.

[71] See Paulo Otero, *Direito Constitucional Português: Identidade Constitucional* (Almedina 2010) v. I 251.

[72] See also Fonseca (n. 62) 114–18.

[73] See José Pina-Delgado, 'Data Protection in the Internet: Cape Verde's National Report' in Dário Moura Vicente and Sofia de Vasconcelos Casimiro (eds.), *Data Protection in the Internet* (Springer 2019) 77.

[74] See José Pina-Delgado, 'As relações entre a Carta e a Constituição de Cabo Verde' in Paulo Pinto Albuquerque (ed.), *Comentário à Carta Africana dos Direitos Humanos e dos Povos* (Universidade Católica Editora 2020) 97.

[75] See Adam Shilton and Mila Versteeg, 'Small-c Constitutional Rights' (2022) *20*(1) *ICON* 141.

[76] In this sense, the notable essay authored by Silveira (n. 50) 17–69, and also Fafali Koudawo, *Cabo Verde e Guiné-Bissau: Da Democracia Revolucionária à Democracia Liberal* (INEP 2001) 162–4.

[77] Raul Araújo, *Os Sistemas de Governo de Transição Democrática nos P.A.L.O.P.* (Coimbra Editora 1997) 75; Leão de Pina, *Cultura Política, Valores Cívicos e Cidadania Democrática em Cabo Verde: Entre Adesão Formal e Embaraço Cultural* (ISCJS 2020).

these are so engrained in the Cape Verdean psyche that it was natural to reject one-party rule, the absence of self-determination, and a system in which the state was deemed superior to the persons whom it ruled. Consequently, the legal form of the community was modelled in such a manner that it managed to harmonise national independence, human rights, and the sovereignty of the people.

Although the people of Cape Verde have not lived independently for most of the country's five-century history, they have enjoyed some degree of autonomous rule for a considerable period. In other words, even though there has not been a system of full and universal freedom for all, part of the population has enjoyed some degree of freedom, to the limited extent possible in a slave and patriarchal society; prior to democratisation, people did not exercise sovereignty in the strict sense of the word, but at least experienced episodes of competitive elections in which they could choose local leaders.

As the CCCV stressed in a judgement dealing with the application of the democratic principle, despite the fact that 'a Cape Verdean national democracy was only possible after the foundation of the State of Cape Verde in 1975, [which] permitted [us to leave] our condition of colonial subjects and [enjoy the] democratization of 1990', one could not say 'there weren't periods in which part of the population was allowed to express their will about relevant matters of local governance'.[78]

5. Features of a Constitutional Tradition in the Making

5.1 The Structure and Substance of the Constitution

The ideas above serve to explain why liberal democracy found such fertile ground to thrive on in the archipelago[79] and why a political system inspired by its ideals has proven so stable for the past thirty years. The country has a moderate constitution reflecting elements of a liberal, democratic, republican, and social state.[80] The values recognised in the preamble and the first articles of the original version of the Basic Law include human dignity, freedom and individual autonomy, popular sovereignty, national independence, equality, solidarity, justice, and peace.

It is on these values that the constitutional edifice was erected, firstly, by translating them into constitutional principles and, secondly, by drafting all parts of the Constitution accordingly. The Constitution recognises a generous bill of rights, including civil and political rights, social rights, and rights of vulnerable persons; establishes a unitary state with local power attributed to elected municipal organs and a semi-presidential system of government; and envisages a market-oriented economic model based on the recognition of private property, free enterprise, and economic initiative balanced with the collective ends of social justice.

[78] Judgment No. 24/2016 of 20 October, *President of the Republic Request to Review the Constitutionality of a Norm of the Public Prosecutors Statute*, published by the Official Journal [*Boletim Oficial da República de Cabo Verde*, henceforth BOCV], I Serie, N. 61 (2 November 2016), 2033–54, 1.4.

[79] See Peter Meyns, 'Cape Verde: An African Exception' (2002) *13*(3) *Journal of Democracy* 153; Bruce Baker, 'Cape Verde: The Most Democratic Nation in Africa?' (2006) *44*(4) *Journal of Modern African Studies* 493.

[80] See José Pina-Delgado, 'Constituição de Cabo Verde de 1992—Fundação de uma República Liberal de Direito, Democrática e Social' in José Pina-Delgado and Mário Silva (eds.), *Estudos em Comemoração do XX Aniversário da Constituição da República de Cabo Verde* (ISCJS 2013) 113.

The Basic Law provides for an independent system of courts, including the CCCV, a Supreme Court of Justice (SCJ), and a Superior Court of Auditors. The system is characterised by robust mechanisms of judicial review, with tools in existence to control not only the acts or omissions of administrative organs but also legal norms (including acts of parliament, governmental or presidential decrees, regulations, international treaties, and international customary norms). The constitutional system recognises that the higher value of the Constitution places it above all other sources of the law, and adopts a friendly approach to international law, explicitly referring to customary international norms, treaty norms, and norms created by the organs of the international organisations of which Cape Verde is a member. The fundamental law is *lex suprema*, not *lex aeterna*, because, with some constraints linked to time, circumstances, or the domains covered by the eternity clause, it can be amended or have certain of its norms suspended in periods of declared constitutional necessity.

The fundamental traces of the identity of the Constitution emerge essentially, but not exclusively, from its values and principles as set out, for instance, in article 2, which reveals the content of the Cape Verdean *Rechtsstaat*, or in the eternity clause of article 290. These precepts recognise the pillars of popular sovereignty and human rights, and entail a liberal-democratic political community based on the conception of an independent nation with a unitary state that recognises local power; with a republican form of government anchored in competitive elections; with the dispersal of public power to different constitutional organs; with separation of the branches of the state, separation of state and church, and subordination of the military to civil authorities; with a strong system of independent courts and of judicial review of all public acts designed to protect rights; and with an open but regulated economy that shall produce not only wealth but also social justice.

5.2 National Values and Cape Verdean Constitutional Identity

Arguably, many of these features reflect political traditions and values that developed hand in hand with the formation of Cape Verde's creole identity. The framers of the Constitution, despite having borrowed extensively from the Portuguese Constitution of 1976, sought to adopt constitutional values that represented Cape Verdean cultural values by capturing aspects of the islanders' long-standing institutional and legal preferences. Thus, the Cape Verdean framers cloned a foreign body but added other parts and gave it its soul, thereby reflecting the logic of the construction of a political community that uses a Western structure to contain a mixed Euro-African mass of cultural inclinations and institutional attitudes.[81]

5.3 Neglect of the Constitution by Legislative and Judicial Powers

The problem is that the legal system does not exist solely in its constitutional dimension. Its values, principles, and rules must be developed to create regulatory regimes that cover

[81] See also Odair Varela, 'Cabo Verde: a Máquina Estatal da Modernidade (1614–1990)' in Cristina Montalvão Sarmento and Suzano Costa (eds.), *Entre África e Europa: Nação, Estado e Democracia em Cabo Verde* (Almedina 2013) 176.

all areas of social and individual existence. In a *Rechtsstaat*, and as such one ruled by law, this has to be achieved by means of acts and complementary regulations formulated by Parliament and other normative bodies and applied to concrete situations. The main issue in Cape Verde is that structural legislation was inherited from the colonial era and duly recognised by the former and current constitutional order insofar as it did not contradict the applicable constitutional values and principles of the day.[82] Most of this was repealed and replaced by legal codes approved after independence, as was the case with the Criminal Code, the Criminal Procedure Code, the Civil Procedure Code, and the Labour Code. The only main legislation that is in force since colonial times is the Portuguese Civil Code of 1966,[83] but the legal instruments enacted since independence still have strong Portuguese influences for the same reasons.[84] In general, they were drafted by scholars who studied or lectured in Portugal, or by Portuguese attorneys, and in most cases they evince a high degree of legislative borrowing; as a result, they fail to take into account almost any local particularity and often neglect cultural features proper to national traditions. It does not help that in Cape Verde bills are often approved without adequate time for maturation or discussion, which always facilitates uncritical legal transplants.

The legislator's lack of legal imagination and rationality is compounded by a certain incapacity, or at least a lack of confidence, among most judges to evaluate legislation independently so as to discover the meaning of norms. In a system strongly influenced by a 'scholar-made law' inherited from Portugal, judges do not feel comfortable attributing meaning to rules without help from textbooks or academic papers. Insofar as they have been trained professionally in the former colonial power,[85] they generally turn to Portuguese textbooks, scholarly papers, and case law to seek guidance on almost every single case,[86] even when the facts or normative wording are different. This sometimes leads to errors of law that have to be corrected by superior ordinary courts or the CCCV. The next section deals with the efforts of this judicial organ to anchor constitutional law, and by implication the legal system as a whole, in the national values recognised by the fundamental law.

6. The CCCV's Role in Preserving National Identity

The CCCV's competencies are stated by the Basic Law (in article 215(1)), the Constitutional Court Act, the Amparo and Habeas Data Act, and other legislation.[87] The competencies encompass powers to review legislation and decide constitutional complaints about violations of civil and political rights through the *amparo* procedure and of privacy-related rights

[82] See Law on the Political Organisation of the State of 1975, art. 22; Constitution of Cape Verde of 1980 (original version), art. 99; Constitution of Cape Verde of 1992, art. 293.

[83] See Dário Moura Vicente, 'O Código Civil na Lusofonia: Constantes e Variáveis' (2019) *4 Revista de Direito Civil* 59.

[84] See, for example, the conclusions of Michael Bogdan, 'The Law of the Republic of Cape Verde Twenty Five Years after Independence' (2000) *44*(1) *Journal of African Law* 86.

[85] See Fernando Loureiro Bastos, 'An Overview of Judicial and Executive Relations in Lusophone Africa' in Charles M. Fombad (ed.), *Separation of Powers in African Constitutionalism* (Oxford University Press 2018) 159, 162.

[86] Ibid. 162–3.

[87] For developments, see José Pina-Delgado, 'Constitutional Court of Cape Verde' in Rainer Grote, Frauke Lachenmann, and Rüdiger Wolfrum (eds.), *Max Planck Encyclopedia of Comparative Constitutional Law* (Oxford University Press 2022).

through *habeas data*. Notwithstanding the comprehensiveness of its material jurisdiction, this is a judicial organ with a minimum composition of three judges, who, in terms of article 215, paragraph 3, of the Constitutional Court Act, are elected by a two-thirds majority in Parliament for a non-renewable term of office of nine years.

Eligibility is relatively broad, with no special requirements of age or legal profession specified. According to the Constitution, one must only hold a law degree, be a Cape Verdean national of high standing and merit, capacity, and recognised morality, and not have been disqualified of one's civil and political rights (article 215(3)). The first composition of the Court deliberately did not include a single career judge, which angered this judicial sector.[88] Instead it comprised a former parliamentary chairperson and part-time lecturer of constitutional law; a scholar specialising in constitutional theory, basic rights, and international law; and a senior career prosecutor.[89]

The first justices shared another facet important for this essay. Unlike the case with other superior ordinary courts, they were not lawyers trained exclusively in Portugal but an interesting mix of open-minded holders of bachelor of law degrees—one of them in one of the main Portuguese law schools, the so-called *Clássica* at the University of Lisbon; another trained both in the former GDR (Leipzig) and in the Federal Republic of Germany after unification (Heidelberg); and the third with degrees from Brazil and a PhD from the Nova University of Lisbon Law School.[90]

These developments led the new court to (a) review the constitutional case law it inherited from the SCJ and impose on the ordinary courts a duty to apply any law in agreement with the Fundamental Law precepts; (b) cut dependence on foreign sources, namely scholar and jurisprudential; and, finally, (c) centre constitutional interpretation on domestic sources and, when justified, in national identity and values.

6.1 Reviewing Inherited Case Law and Enforcing the Duty to Apply Statutes in Consonance with the Constitution

The CCCV emerged only in 2015, despite its having been formally created by an amendment to the 1992 Basic Law approved by the Constitutional Act 01/1999 (article 130). During this period, the SCJ acted as a transitional surrogate duly mandated by the Basic Law, which led to the advancement of comprehensive case law in certain constitutional domains.[91] Thus, one of the first questions the autonomous constitutional court had to deal-with related to the use of SCJ-established jurisprudence. The CCCV, adopting a case-by-case analysis, quoted its predecessor's case law, variously to endorse it, develop it, or repeal it whenever it found it did not represent the best meanings of the Basic Law norms.[92] In this sense, it reviewed not only the content of specific constitutional norms[93] but also

[88] Simão Santos, *Sistema de Fiscalização da Constitucionalidade em Cabo Verde* (Almedina 2017) 304–5.

[89] See the profiles in CCCV, *Conheça o Tribunal Constitucional de Cabo Verde* (TC 2016) 8–9.

[90] Ibid. 8–9.

[91] The SCJ decisions as a constitutional jurisdiction are available in Portuguese at https://www.tribunalconstitucional.cv/index.php/acordaos-do-tc-1995-a-2015/ (last accessed 23 September 2022).

[92] All the decisions of the Constitutional Court of Cape Verde are available in Portuguese in https://www.tribunalconstitucional.cv/index.php/acordaos/ (last accessed 23 September 2022).

[93] Judgment No. 11/2017 of 22 June, *Maria de Lurdes v SCJ*, *BOCV*, I Serie, N. 42 (21 July 2017), 933–50, 2.1.6, putting aside the understanding of the SCJ concerning the possibility of using article 29(2) of the Universal Declaration on Human Rights to justify the limitation of a constitutional right.

the intensity of review and the tests it applies when establishing the meaning of the general values and principles[94] and even the approach used to analyse the admissibility of appeals in certain procedures.

This last question proved to be essential in the development of the CCCV's approach because it allowed the court to reinforce the constitutional complaints procedure, thus replacing the overly formalistic approach adopted by the SCJ with a more appeal-friendly one, advocated for by one of the justices in an individual opinion,[95] as well as to rationalise the purpose of the constitutional appeals procedures. In *Teixeira v SCJ*,[96] the CCCV stressed that the Basic Law has to illuminate the legal system in its entirety.[97] According to its reasoning, the 'principle of the subjection of all public entities' to the basic rights mentioned by article 18 imposes a duty to interpret any law of the republic in consonance with 'the Constitution and the Universal Declaration of Human Rights'.[98] Given that, by virtue of their training and personality, career judges may hinder the establishment of a new constitutional order by resisting its core values and principles and asserting those of the former system, the Court underscored that one of the justifications for inserting those procedures in the framework of a constitution of a new democracy was to avoid ordinary courts' consciously or unconsciously applying legislation without taking into account the Basic Law.[99] In this regard, it enforced that duty by directing the ordinary courts to act accordingly.

The relation of this development to the theme of this chapter is that the Court noticed that in many cases there was a subversion of the Constitution by interpretations made by ordinary courts; instead of taking into account the Constitution and even less so Cape Verdean institutional identity established content, ordinary courts often appealed to foreign—especially Portuguese—legal scholarships or case-law, with the argument that the constitutional and ordinary norms were identical, even in situations where they were not. This repeatedly lead to violations of rights by courts that have to be corrected by the CCCV, as was the case of the *Borges*[100] and of the *Hills*[101] decisions, as well as in a second *Teixeira* case.[102]

6.2 Reducing Interpretive Dependence on Foreign Sources

In the same vein, the CCCV, pursuing the aim of reducing dependence on foreign sources, had to highlight the obvious fact that as a court it is bound to follow Cape Verde's legislation as understood by the framers and the legislator and in keeping with international law received in the domestic legal system and also that decisions citing foreign legislation, scholarship, case law, and the like declare their limited relevance to determining the meaning of the Constitution and national legislative acts; and, finally, that the extensive use of foreign

[94] Judgment No. 07/2016 of 21 April, *BOCV*, I S., N. 35 (10 May 2016), 1225–51, 2.11–2.12, changing the levels of scrutiny aimed at evaluating violations of constitutional equality clauses.
[95] Dissenting Opinion, Constitutional Complaint 01/2016, *Emílio v SCJ*, *BOCV*, I S., N. 35 (10 May 2016), 1216–21.
[96] Judgment No. 08/2018, of 25 April, *BOCV*, I S., N. 25 (2 May 2018), 574–96.
[97] Ibid. 18.
[98] Ibid.
[99] Ibid.
[100] Judgment No. 24/2018 of 13 November, *BOCV*, I S., N. 88 (28 December 2018), 2132–53.
[101] Judgment No. 27/2018 of 20 December, *BOCV*, I S., N. 11 (31 January 2019), 146–78.
[102] Judgment No. 29/2019 of 30 July, *BOCV*, I S., N. 100 (24 September 2019), 1618–53.

sources to interpret the Constitution could even be argued to be a violation of the democratic principle, the principle of separation of powers, and the principle of the supremacy of the Constitution. In its decision in *PR Request to Review the Constitutionality of Certain Restrictive Norms of the Electoral Code*,[103] the CCCV stated that protecting freedoms depends largely on the legal traditions of a particular society, leading to a reasoning that despite acknowledging foreign developments related to the prohibition of releasing opinion polls in electoral periods, warned against the non-consideration of 'national variables' in constitutional adjudication. The CCCV, finally, stressed that it would deal with 'constitutional questions keeping in mind the particularities of our fundamental law and the differentiated social, identity related, political, cultural, historical, ethical and economic elements of our Political Community'.[104]
In two other cases dealing with electoral matters, the CCCV responded to an allegation made by a defendant to the effect that in Portugal and Brazil there was an understanding that blank votes should not be considered in the allocation of municipal council and municipal assembly seats, asserting that it (the Court) did not 'apply either Portuguese or Brazilian legislation'.[105] In *PAICV v National Electoral Commission (NEC)*, regarding the prohibition of donations of T-shirts with political messages, the plaintiff suggested that there was a universal, or at least, a shared, lusophone position on that matter—in response to which the Court reiterated that the 'definition of the electoral regime results from the will of the legislator';[106] hence, such legislation 'should be interpreted accordingly with predominantly local analytical elements, namely the normative construction adopted, the intentions of the legislator, the political context, that, for obvious reasons, are proper to each country'.[107] The Court then turned to the preparatory works of the Electoral Code and its case law to decide the appeal.

In another decision, on a *Request by the PR to Review the Constitutionality of the Enabling Act to Approve a New Regime on the Consumption and Smuggling of Drugs*, the CCCV stressed that the requirement of an enabling Act of Parliament to extensively display the content of the legislation to be approved by the Cabinet is determined by the will of the framers and not by an objective norm that, independently of recognition by the drafters, imposes itself upon the constitutional order.[108]

The Court has never espoused a xenophobic or parochial conception of constitutional adjudication. Besides adopting the doctrine that international law norms, as far as they bind the state, are sources of Cape Verdean law, and taking into consideration international rulings, particularly from African tribunals, it has maintained dialogue with foreign case law, legislation, and scholarship because it endorses the understanding that an open-minded creole nation marked by a cosmopolitan spirit is the soul of the country's constitutional identity. Thus, several important constitutional adjudication tests, ones designed to measure the proportionality of the limitation of rights, were drafted in the light of German jurisprudential and doctrinal developments.[109] Despite some level of originality, it took into

[103] Judgment No. 13/2016 of 7 June, *BOCV*, I S., N. 43 (24 July 2016), 1421–75.
[104] Ibid. 2.8.3.
[105] Judgment No. 22/2016 of 16 September, *BOCV*, I S., N. 59 (14 October 2016), 1994–2007.
[106] Judgment No. 30/2020 of 11 September, *BOCV*, I S., N. 139 (23 December 2020), 2182–98, 5.1.
[107] Ibid.
[108] Advice No. 02/2020 of 10 February, *BOCV*, I S., N. 25 (3 March 2020), 633–52, 639.
[109] Judgment No. 07/2016 of 21 April (n. 94) 4.3.2.

account developments of the same source to design a test to evaluate the violation of the principle of legitimate expectations.[110]

Notwithstanding its position, it developed another test, aimed at dealing with delays of criminal procedural decisions by ordinary courts, largely on the basis of the case law of the European Court of Human Rights, the African Court on Human and Peoples' Rights, the Supreme Court of the United States, and the Spanish Constitutional Court.[111] By the same token, despite leaning towards legal texts that directly discuss Cape Verdean law, it has cited scholarship from other countries, namely Portugal, Germany, and Brazil, especially concerning general legal theoretical issues.[112] Above all, the CCCV has sought to develop its constitutional jurisprudence by grounding its main positions in universal constitutional theory and the political philosophy of thinkers such as Locke, Rousseau, Rawls, and Habermas.[113]

The intensity of this dialogue has led to disputes between the justices. One of them rejected German-based arguments against the legitimacy of constitutional mutation[114] and for the understanding of human dignity as a constitutional value and a constitutional right,[115] because, according to him, they were rooted in that country's particular constitutional experience. Despite minor differences,[116] however, the Court has collectively underlined that foreign developments should not be treated as central to understanding the meaning of the Constitution. Instead, it began to look inwards. Firstly, it considered constitutional and public debates so as to understand the framers' motives in adopting the norms contained in the Constitution and the political context that led to its adoption; secondly, it has explicitly examined the cultural, political, institutional, and legal history of Cape Verde when interpreting constitutional matters, doing so in order to preserve the national dimension of constitutional identity.

6.3 Affirming National Values as Part of Constitutional Identity

The Court has proceeded on the premise that the 'State of Cape Verde is a new country with an ancestral nation, which developed a certain *ethos* that must be considered its collective heritage and [the basis for its] legal system, especially its values and principles'.[117] In doing so, it repeatedly emphasised the constitutional relevance of national culture.[118] The Court has thus endeavoured to root constitutional values in Cape Verdean history, reality, and national institutional values. Consequently, it has sought to find justifications for defining the scope of constitutional values according to local values and to look to national history to find anchorage for certain institutions that are considered part of Cape Verde's constitutional identity.

[110] Judgment No. 24/2016 of 20 October (n. 78) 5.3.1.
[111] Judgment No. 08/2018 of 25 April (n. 96) 5.3.3.
[112] For example, Judgment No. 27/2017 of 14 December and separate opinions, *BOCV*, I S., N. 82 (29 December 2017), 1784–819.
[113] For example, Judgment No. 13/2016 of 7 June (n. 103), quoting Milton, Locke, Spinoza, Pettit, Habermas, Arendt, Saint-Just, Beccaria, and Wittgenstein.
[114] Concurring Opinion to Judgment No. 27/2017 of 14 December (n. 112).
[115] Dissenting Opinion to Judgment No. 29/2017 of 5 December, *BOCV*, I S., N. 6 (1 February 2018), 85–93, I.
[116] Advice No. 01/2020 of 27 January, *BOCV*, I S., N. 14 (4 February 2020), 347–57, 8.3.
[117] Judgment No. 24/2016 of 20 October (n. 783) 5.5.3.
[118] Judgment No. 13/2016 of 7 June (n. 104) 2.7.3. and separate opinion.

6.3.1 National reasons for adopting and defining constitutional values

Since 2016, the Court, when dealing with general constitutional values, has attempted to anchor them in national culture and history. This was the case in regard to human dignity, which the Court—in the matter of *Request of the AG to Review the Constitutionality of a Norm of the Judicial Council's Act that Prohibits the Access to the Vice-Presidency of the Council to Career Judges Members*[119]—regarded simultaneously as a universal value and a Cape Verdean traditional value. To interpret the meaning of the concept of 'equal dignity' found in article 24 of the Constitution, it not only resorted to thinkers such as Cicero, Aquinas, and Kant but also invoked the thought of nineteenth-century and early twentieth-century national intellectuals such as J. Evaristo d'Almeida, Eugénio Tavares, and L. Loff de Vasconcelos, who had used the same concept to denounce slavery and racial discrimination and demand access to quality education and protection against hunger.

For this reason, the Court rejected the idea that in Cape Verde human dignity could be understood as imposing merely negative duties on the state, and stressed that it entailed a duty to protect individuals in situations of hardship and guarantee that they did not fall below standards of living considered undignified by the community. In a decision in 2019,[120] it adopted a test proposed in a dissenting opinion by an associate justice in a previous case that had appealed to the idea that the state violated the principle of justice when it acted on the basis of maxims of conduct incompatible with 'institutional public values adopted by the Cape Verdean Political Community'.[121]

Both cases dealt with the application of the constitutional principle of justice to fiscal relations between the public administration on the one hand and individuals and other private entities on the other. After acknowledging the difficulties of applying such a broad principle, the Court linked it to the constitutional pillars of human rights and democracy and the constitutional values of human dignity, freedom, solidarity, and the 'ethical traditions of the nation'.

6.3.2 National reasons for adopting constitutional regimes that represent Cape Verdean constitutional identity

In regard to the elements comprising Cape Verdean constitutional identity, the Court, probably due to its multilayered conception or for pragmatic purposes, has not always anchored these elements on national grounds, be they historical, cultural, political, or sociological. National independence was discussed in the decision on the matter *Request by MPs to Review the Constitutionality of the Status of Forces (SOFA) Agreement Concluded with the United States of America*. While acknowledging the existence of a principle of national independence linked to national sovereignty, the Court did not ground it in a specific historical or cultural basis, preferring to deal with questions through an approach based on abstract legal philosophy, constitutional theory, and international law.[122] The same occurred when, for different reasons, it had to deal with the principle of the separation of powers, linking it to the structure of a typical liberal-democratic constitution and appealing to Locke, Montesquieu, and *The Federalist Papers*.[123]

[119] Judgment No. 07/2016 of 21 April (n. 94) 2.3.

[120] Advice No. 01/2018 of 7 May, *BOCV*, I S., N. 28 (11 May 2018), 655–64, 18.1.4

[121] Dissenting opinion, Concrete Review of Constitutionality No. 9/2015, *Sal Hotéis v SCJ*, *BOCV*, I, N. 42 (21 July 2017), 911–25, 8.2.5.

[122] Judgment No. 10/2020 of 20 March, *BOCV*, I S., N. 86 (23 July 2020), 1731–53; 1753–82.

[123] Advice No. 02/2018 of 27 June, *BOCV*, I S., N. 44 (2 July 2018), 1141–56, 3.2.

Concerning other key structural features of the Cape Verdean Constitution, the Court has sought to establish a connection with local experience. In the matter of popular sovereignty and democracy, it stressed, in the framework of a decision on an electoral appeal, namely *Monteiro v NEC*, that these values find their remote roots in Cape Verde's history and in the islanders' *ethos*, inasmuch as the islanders developed a conviction that people should be consulted in regard to their choice of rulers through periodic, competitive, and free elections.[124]

The same is true of the Court's understanding of the constitutional centrality of local autonomy. In its decision *MPs Request to Review the Constitutionality of Article 13 of the Amendment Act to the Environment Tax Act*,[125] the Court considered that there was a constitutional guarantee of local autonomy that protected municipalities against acts liable to deprive them of a fair share of tax collected by the state, a guarantee based on the traditional historical role these entities played in the archipelago, enabling, even in colonial times, Cape Verdeans to enjoy some degree of popular rule.[126]

With regard to individual rights, it highlighted, in *PR Request to Control Certain Restrictive Norms of the Electoral Code*, the structural importance of freedom of the press and freedom of expression in the traditional openness of Cape Verdean society to criticisms articulated in public sphere.[127]

In *Maria de Lurdes v SCJ*, a constitutional complaint involving a discussion of the constitutional recognition of family outside marriage, the Court, citing historical evidence and a tradition of sexual tolerance, recalled that Cape Verdean society had always accepted different forms of family in the 'framework of the usual spirit of tolerance that, as a community, we constructed', and that it refused to limit the liberty to create a family to the liberty to contract marriage. The Court concluded that the Constitution should thus be interpreted in a plural sense when it came to interpreting the scope of the liberty to create a family.[128]

7. Conclusion

The process of constructing Cape Verdean national identity was the result of a creolisation that, paradoxically, went hand in hand with cosmopolisation. In this same sense, the country's constitutional identity is the result of a patchwork of norms that represent (a) universal values; (b) regional values, both European and African; and (c) values created by the national experience of hybridisation. There is nothing wrong with that, so long as the textual forms representing universal or Western constitutional values—which, alongside African values, are also Cape Verdean values—do not lead to an artificial understanding of the archipelago's constitutional identity that disregards the national dimension (which unfortunately is often the case).

If one adopts a multilayered conception of a constitutional identity that couples universal, regional, foreign, and national elements with such a context, the main issue in Cape Verde is how to preserve the 'national' aspect of constitutional identity. This is the task that the

[124] Judgement No. 07/2018 of 29 March, *BOCV*, I S., N. 21 (11 April 2018), 505–28, 9.
[125] Judgement No. 01/2017 of 12 January, *BOCV*, I S., N. 10 (27 February 2017), 218–60.
[126] Ibid. 1.1.6.
[127] Judgment No. 13/2016 of 7 June (n. 103).
[128] Judgment No. 11/2017 of 22 June (n. 93) 2.1.10.

CCCV took upon itself in cases in which it had to deal with constitutional values by trying to base them on Cape Verdean cultural and institutional traditions—traditions which are the result not of the recovery of pre-colonial models but rather of the nationalisation of colonial institutions and legal preferences adopted by an Afro-European-Jewish creole nation that created a particular culture and developed certain values.

Bibliography

Almada D.H., *Caboverdianidade & Tropicalismo* (Fundação Joaquim Nabuco & Editora Massangana 1992) 63

Araújo R., *Os Sistemas de Governo de Transição Democrática nos P.A.L.O.P.* (Coimbra Editora 1997) 75

Baker B., 'Cape Verde: The Most Democratic Nation in Africa?' (2006) *44*(4) *Journal of Modern African Studies* 493

Bastos F.L., 'An Overview of Judicial and Executive Relations in Lusophone Africa' in Fombad C.M. (ed.), *Separation of Powers in African Constitutionalism* (Oxford University Press 2018) 159

Bogdan M., 'The Law of the Republic of Cape Verde Twenty Five Years after Independence' (2000) *44*(1) *Journal of African Law* 86

Brito W., 'Cabo Verde: Institucionalização, organização e problemas do poder local' in José Melo Alexandrino (ed.), *Jornadas de Direito Comparado Lusófono* (Associação Académica da Faculdade de Direito de Lisboa 2014) 73

Cabral A., 'Apontamento sobre a Poesia Cabo-Verdiana' (1952) *28 Boletim de Propaganda e Informação* 5

Cabral A., 'Party Principles and Political Practice' in *Unity and Struggle: Speeches and Writings. Texts Selected by the PAIGC* (trans. Michael Wolfers, Monthly Review Press 1979 [1969]) 30

Cabral A., 'The Facts about Portugal's African Colonies' in *Unity and Struggle: Speeches and Writings. Texts Selected by the PAIGC* (trans. Michael Wolfers, Monthly Review Press 1979 [1960]) 17

Cabral I., *A Primeira Elite Colonial Atlântica: Dos 'Homens Honrados Brancos' de Santiago à 'Nobreza da Terra' (Finais do séc. XV—Início do século XVII)* (Pedro Cardoso Livraria 2015)

Cardoso H., *O partido Único em Cabo Verde. Um Assalto à Esperança* (Imprensa Nacional de Cabo Verde1993)

Cardoso P., *Textos Jornalísticos e Literários*, Manuel Brito-Semedo and Joaquim Morais (eds.) (Instituto da Biblioteca Nacional e do Livro 2008)

Carreira A., *As Companhias Pombalinas de Grão-Pará e Maranhão e Pernambuco e Paraíba* (2nd edn, Presença 1982 [1969])

Carreira A., *Cabo Verde: Formação e extinção de uma sociedade escravocrata (1460–1878)* (3rd edn, Instituto da Promoção Cultural 2000 [1972])

'Carta dos Moradores de Santiago a El-Rei [26 de Maio de 1546]' in *Monumenta Missionaria Africana*, 2. Serie (Agência Geral das Colónias 1963), v. II, 386

Claridade: Revista de Arte e Letras (2nd edn, Instituto Cabo-Verdiano do Livro e do Disco 1988)

'Concessão do Hábito de Cristo a André Álvares de Almada [19 de Agosto de 1598]' in *Monumenta Missionária Africana*, 2. Serie (Agência Geral do Ultramar 1963), v. III, 428

Contribuição da Igreja Católica para a Elaboração da Nova Constituição: Critérios e Exigências para a Nova Ordem Constitucional [September 1990], reproduced in *Vozdipovo* (11 September 1990)

da Silva B.L., *O Dialecto Crioulo de Cabo Verde* (Imprensa Nacional - Casa da Moeda 1984)

d'Almada A.A., *Brief Treatise on the Rivers of Guinea*, P.E.H. Hair (trans.) (Department of History—University of Liverpool 1984)

d'Almada A.A., *Tratado Breve dos Rios da Guiné e de Cabo Verde*, António Luís Ferronha (ed.) (Grupo de Trabalho do Ministério da Educação para as Comemorações dos Descobrimentos Portugueses 1994 [1594])

d'Almeida J.E., *O Escravo* (2nd edn, Instituto Cabo-Verdiano do Livro 1989 [1856])

de Pina L., *Cultura Política, Valores Cívicos e Cidadania Democrática em Cabo Verde: Entre Adesão Formal e Embaraço Cultural* (Instituto Superior de Ciências Jurídicas e Sociais 2020)

de Sousa H.T., 'Sobrados, Lojas & Funcos: Contribuição para o Estudo da Evolução Social da Ilha do Fogo' (1958) *1 Claridade: Revista de Arte e Letras* 2

de Vasconcelos L.L., *O Extermínio de Cabo Verde: Pavorosas Revelações* (Libânio & Co. 1905)

Duarte M., 'Caboverdianidade e Africanidade' in *Caboverdianidade, Africanidade e outros Textos* (Spleen 1999 [1951]) 21

Fernandes G., *Em Busca da Nação: Notas para a Reinterpretação do Cabo Verde Crioulo* (Editora UFSC/IBNL 2006)

Ferreira M., *A Aventura Crioula: ou Cabo Verde, uma Síntese Cultural e Étnica* (2nd edn, Plátano 1973)

Fonseca J.C., 'Do Regime de Partido Único à Democracia em Cabo Verde: As Sombras e a Presença da Constituição Portuguesa de 1976' (2006) *Special Edition Themis: Revista da Faculdade de Direito da UNL* 81

Fonseca J.C., 'O Sistema de Governo na Constituição Cabo-Verdiana' in Fonseca, J.C, *Cabo Verde: Constituição—Democracia—Cidadania* (Almedina 2011 [1982]) 11

Gouveia J.B., 'Sistemas Constitucionais Africanos de Língua Portuguesa: a Caminho de um Paradigma' (2006) *Special Edition Themis: Revista da Faculdade de Direito da UNL* 119

Gracias, J.A.I., *Carta Orgânica das Instituições Administrativas nas Províncias Ultramarinas* (Imprensa Nacional, 1894 [1869])

Green T., *Masters of Difference: Creolization and the Jewish Presence in Cabo Verde, 1497- 1672* (PhD thesis, Centre of West African Studies, University of Birmingham 2006)

Green T., 'Building Slavery in the Atlantic World: Atlantic Connections and the Changing Institution of Slavery in Cabo Verde, Fifteenth–Sixteenth Centuries' (2011) *32 Slavery & Abolition* 227

Halter M., *Between Race and Ethnicity: Cape Verdean American Immigrants, 1860–1965* (University of Illinois Press 1993)

Jacobson G., 'Constitutional Identity' (2006) *68 Review of Politics* 361

Koudawo F., *Cabo Verde e Guiné-Bissau: Da Democracia Revolucionária à Democracia Liberal* (Instituto Nacional de Estudos e Pesquisas 2001) 162

Kovács K., 'The Rise of Ethnocultural Identity in the Jurisprudence of the East Central European Courts' (2017) *18 German Law Journal* 1703

Leite J.N., *A Imprensa em Cabo Verde, 1820–1975* (Fundação Macau 1998)

Lima A.R., *Reforma Política em Cabo Verde: Do paternalismo à modernização do Estado em Cabo Verde* (Grafedito 1992)

Lobban R. Jr., *Cape Verde: From Crioulo Colony to Independent Nation* (Westview Press 1995)

Lopes J.V., *Cabo Verde: Os Bastidores da Independência* (2nd edn, Spleen 2002 [1996])

Manalvo N., *Carlos Veiga: biografia política. O rosto da mudança em Cabo Verde* (2nd edn, Aletheia 2009)

Mariano G., 'Negritude e Cabo-Verdianidade' (1958) *104 Boletim Cabo Verde* 7

Mariano G., 'Do Funco ao Sobrado ou o Mundo que o Mulato Criou', *Cultura Cabo-Verdiana: Ensaios* (Vega 1991 [1959]) 37

Marques A.C., *Revisão da Constituição: Subsídios para o Debate,* reproduced in *Terra Nova* Mindelo N. 166–171, January–June 1990

Marti J.L, 'Two Different Ideas of Constitutional Identity: Identity of the Constitution v. Identity of the People' in Arnáiz A.S. and Alcoberro C. (eds.), *National Constitutional Identity and European Integration* (Intersentia 2013) 17

Maxwell K., *Pombal, Paradox of the Enlightenment* (Cambridge University Press 1995)

Meyns P., 'Cape Verde: An African Exception' (2002) *13(3) Journal of Democracy* 153

Miranda J. and Kafft Kosta E., *As Constituições dos Estados de Língua Portuguesa: Uma Visão Comparativa* (Juruá 2013)

'Notas Bio-bibliográficas de Jorge Carlos Almeida Fonseca' in Fonseca L.D. and Fonseca S.D. (eds.), *Liberdade Sempre! Homenagem a Jorge Carlos Almeida Fonseca por ocasião dos seus 70 anos* (Pedro Cardoso Livraria 2020) 9

Otero P., *Direito Constitucional Português: Identidade Constitucional* (Almedina 2010) v. I

Pina-Delgado J., 'Os escrúpulos de um Ilustre Santiaguense nos "Tractos" da Guiné dos Séculos XVI–XVII: o Capitão André Álvares d'Almada e a Questão da Incerteza sobre a Presença dos Títulos Jurídicos da Escravatura' in Silva M., de Pina L., and Júnior P.M. (eds.), *Estudos em Comemoração do Quinto Aniversário do ISCJS* (Instituto Superior de Ciências Jurídicas e Sociais 2012) 112

Pina-Delgado J., 'Constituição de Cabo Verde de 1992—Fundação de uma República Liberal de Direito, Democrática e Social' in Pina-Delgado J. and Silva M. (eds.), *Estudos em Comemoração do XX Aniversário da Constituição da República de Cabo Verde* (Instituto Superior de Ciências Jurídicas e Sociais 2013) 113

Pina-Delgado J., 'A Primeira Obra Cabo-Verdiana. 'Tratado Breve da Guiné do Cabo Verde' de André Álvares d'Almada' (2018) *1 Leitura. Revista da Livraria Pedro Cardoso* 33

Pina-Delgado J., 'Data Protection in the Internet: Cape Verde's National Report' in Vicente D.M. and de Vasconcelos Casimiro S. (eds.), *Data Protection in the Internet* (Springer 2019) 77

Pina-Delgado J., 'As relações entre a Carta e a Constituição de Cabo Verde' in Paulo Pinto Albuquerque (ed.), *Comentário à Carta Africana dos Direitos Humanos e dos Povos* (Universidade Católica Editora 2020) 97

Pina-Delgado, J., 'Constitutional Court of Cape Verde' in Grote R., Lachenmann F., and Wolfrum R. (eds), *Max Planck Encyclopedia of Comparative Constitutional Law* (Oxford University Press 2022).

Pinto E.V., 'Para a História do Direito Político Cabo-Verdiano: O Contributo do Senador Vera Cruz' in Silva M., de Pina L., and Júnior P.M. (eds.), *Estudos em Comemoração do Quinto Aniversário do ISCJS* (Instituto Superior de Ciências Jurídicas e Sociais 2012) 45

Pires M.T.A., *O Município nas Ilhas de Cabo Verde—Séculos XIV a XVIII* (PhD thesis, Universidade Nova de Lisboa 2009)

Pires M.T.A, *O Domínio do Poder e o Poder dos Homens: Os Governos Interinos Camarários das Ilhas de Cabo Verde—Séculos XVII e XVIII* (Chiado 2013).

Popp A., 'Illiberalism as Constitutional Identity—the Case of Hungary' (2018) *59 Hungarian Journal of Legal Sciences* 378

Rosenfeld M., 'The Identity of the Constitutional Subject' (1995) *16 Cardozo Law Review* 1049

Rosenfeld M., 'Constitutional Identity' in Rosenfeld M. and Sajó A. (eds.), *The Oxford Handbook of Comparative Constitutional Law* (Oxford University Press 2012) 756

Russel-Wood A.J.R., *The Portuguese Empire, 1415–1808: A World on the Move* (John Hopkins University Press 1998)

Santos S., *Sistema de Fiscalização da Constitucionalidade em Cabo Verde* (Almedina 2017)

Shilton A. and Versteeg M., 'Small-c Constitutional Rights' (2022) *20*(1) *International Journal of Constitutional Law* 141

Silva M., *O Regime dos Direitos Sociais na Constituição Cabo-Verdiana de 1992* (Almedina 2004)

Silva M., *Contributo para a História Político-Constitucional de Cabo Verde, 1974–1992* (ISCJS/ Almedina 2015)

Silveira O., *Consciencialização na Literatura Caboverdiana* (Edição Casa dos Estudantes do Império 1963)

Silveira O., *A Tortura em Nome do Partido Único: O PAICV e a sua Polícia Política (Depoimentos)* (Terra Nova & Ponto e Vírgula 1991)

Silveira O., *A Democracia em Cabo Verde* (Colibri 2005)

Son B.N., 'Globalisation of Constitutional Identity' (2017) *26 Washington International Law Journal* 463

Tavares E., *Eugénio Tavares pelos Jornais . . .*, Félix Monteiro (ed.) (Instituto Cabo-Verdiano do Livro e do Disco 1997)

Varela O., 'Cabo Verde: a Máquina Estatal da Modernidade (1614–1990)' in Sarmento C.M. and Costa S. (eds.), *Entre África e Europa: Nação, Estado e Democracia em Cabo Verde* (Almedina 2013) 176

Veiga C., 'Cabral e a Construção do Estado em Cabo Verde—Uma Apreciação Crítica' (2004) *19 Direito e Cidadania* 83

Vicente D.M., 'O Código Civil na Lusofonia: Constantes e Variáveis' (2019) *4 Revista de Direito Civil* 59

'Wladimir Brito' in José Vicente Lopes (Interviewer), *A Explicação do Mundo (Entrevistas)* (Spleen 2004) 144

9

Cameroon and the Crisis of Constitutional Identity

Is Anglophone Identity Compatible with a Cameroonian Constitutional Identity?

Carlson Anyangwe and Charles M. Fombad

1. Introduction

Since 2016, Cameroon has been in the grip of a profound crisis that has led to military occupation of its anglophone regions in operations against groups calling for a separate state called Ambazonia. As far as the francophone-dominated government is concerned, these operations, which have resulted in the death of thousands of people, including civilians, as well as the burning of villages and looting of property, are aimed at eliminating what it refers to as a handful of 'terrorists' threatening the unity of the country. In spite of half-hearted pressure from the international community, the government has relentlessly—yet unsuccessfully—pursued what is turning out to be a scorched-earth policy, using sophisticated weapons and disproportionate force against young men armed mostly with traditional hunting guns.

Cameroon's apparent political stability until 2016 should impress even the most casual observer as singular and extraordinary. In many respects, the union in 1961 of English-speaking Cameroon (the former British Southern Cameroons) and French-speaking Cameroon (the former Republic of Cameroon) was, unlike many such unions elsewhere in the world, doomed from the start, as it brought together communities with strong and distinct colonial heritages, identities, and loyalties.

When the two communities came together under a federal arrangement, the country's first leader, President Ahmadou Ahidjo, in expressing the optimism of the era, declared that 'the Federal Republic of Cameroon should serve as a bridge between French-speaking Africa and English-speaking Africa, in the exact measure in which reunification has demonstrated the possibility of a fruitful cohabitation between them'.[1] However, confronted with two states with divergent and potentially antagonistic inherited colonial constitutional cultures, languages, and attitudes, as well as populations with differing interests and conflicting demands, the Cameroonian leadership has had a hard time finding a satisfactory constitutional and institutional framework for creating a sense of common citizenship and common destiny.

[1] Cited in Victor J. Ngoh, 'Dismantling the Federal System' in Victor J. Ngoh (ed.), *Cameroon: From Federal to Unitary State 1961–1972* (Design House 2004) 143.

Carlson Anyangwe and Charles M. Fombad, *Cameroon and the Crisis of Constitutional Identity* In: *Constitutional Identity and Constitutionalism in Africa*. Edited by: Charles M. Fombad and Nico Steytler, Oxford University Press.
 DOI: 10.1093/oso/9780198906308.003.0012

Unsurprisingly, English speakers have not only had a hard time for being anglophone and Cameroonian, but also, and perhaps most importantly, have hardly ever felt part of the French-speaking community's attempts to develop a Cameroonian constitutional identity. This raises a fundamental question, namely whether an anglophone identity is compatible with a Cameroonian constitutional identity. At the heart of the crisis of constitutional identity in Cameroon is the challenge of reconciling a French-based constitutional culture—centred around a philosophy of a highly centralised governance system, weak respect for the rule of law, and intolerance of opposing views—with an English constitutional culture which is its very antithesis.

As Gary Jacobsohn has opined, the substance of a country's constitutional identity depends to a large extent on how the constitution reflects the essentials of constitutionalism as well as the country's unique history and circumstances.[2] The union between two communities ordinarily would have provided constitutional drafters with an opportunity for innovation and creativity. This is particularly important in an era when African countries are increasingly attempting to construct constitutional identities that reflect the history, culture, fears, desires, and aspirations of all the citizens in the body politic. This did not happen in Cameroon in 1961, and the prospects of its ever coming to pass in the future have grown evermore distant. It is again Jacobsohn who warned that constitutional identity, as in the case under study, present-day Cameroon, is 'dangerous . . . when it is inspired by a felt need to eliminate contradiction or incongruity', whether such 'contradiction or incongruity' be real or perceived.[3]

Section 2 of this chapter proceeds to provide brief historical context to the discussion. Section 3 examines the federal framework that formed the basis for the union between the British Southern Cameroons and the Republic of Cameroon. It underlines that the union was not only flawed but that, almost immediately after the formation of the federation, the francophone-dominated government began to dismantle it. Section 4 shows that, in 1972, there was in effect a 'divorce', one that led to the forced 'cohabitation' of the two communities as the process of anglophone de-identification gathered speed. Section 5 examines the crisis of 2016 to which this inevitably led. It is against this background that section 6 examines the key issue of whether an anglophone identity is compatible with a Cameroonian constitutional identity. The various options are briefly examined, after which the discussion ends in section 7 with several concluding remarks. As long as the anglophone minority is not allowed to retain its distinctive identity and no attempt is made to reflect this in the constitution, the divorce *nisi* of 1972 is very likely to end with a final separation of the two communities.

2. Historical Background

Much has been written on Cameroon's post-independence history, the reunification of the two former trust territories, and the painful first two decades of independence.[4] It is

[2] Gary J. Jacobsohn, 'Constitutional Identity' in Sujit Choudhry, Madhav Khosla, and Pratap B. Mehta (eds), *The Oxford Handbook of the Indian Constitution* (Oxford University Press 2016) 110–26.

[3] Gary J. Jacobsohn, *Constitutional Identity* (Harvard University Press 2010) 11.

[4] Edwin Ardener, 'The Nature of the Reunification of Cameroon' in Arthur Hazlewood (ed.), *African Integration and Disintegration: Case Studies in Economic and Political Union* (Oxford University Press 1967) 293; Edwin Ardener, *Eyewitness to the Annexation of Cameroon 1883–1887* (Government Press 1968); Jean F. Bayart, 'The

unnecessary to go into these details here. However, for an understanding of the quandary in which the country finds itself today, it is important to highlight certain pertinent aspects of this history.

In the 1500s, the Portuguese were reputedly the first Europeans to arrive on Cameroon's coast, but malaria prevented settlement and conquest of the interior until the late 1870s. The name of the country is derived from *Camarões*, meaning 'shrimps', because the Portuguese explorer Fernando Po named the River Wouri *Rio dos Camerões* ('Shrimp River') for its many shrimps. After the Berlin Conference of 1884, all of present-day Cameroon and parts of several of its neighbours became the German colony of *Kamerun*, with a capital first at Buea and later Yaoundé. This lasted for thirty-two years until 1916, when a British and French expeditionary force defeated the Germans in Cameroon and partitioned the territory in two. The British took two small, disconnected portions, which they called Northern and Southern Cameroon, whilst the French took the larger portion, comprising about four-fifths of the territory.

This rather arbitrary division was later recognised by the League of Nations when, on 28 June 1919, it conferred mandates on these two countries to administer the territories. The mandates were superseded by trusteeship agreements on the creation of the United Nations (UN) in 1945. Britain in effect administered its two disconnected portions as appendages of its neighbouring colony of Nigeria: the Southern Cameroons was administered as part of Eastern Nigeria and the Northern Cameroons as part of the Sarduana Province of Nigeria. After the UN-sponsored plebiscite of 11 February 1961, the Southern Cameroons voted in favour of reuniting with the former French Trust territory of Cameroon, which had become independent as the Republic of Cameroon on 1 October 1960, while the Northern Cameroons opted to remain in the Federation of Nigeria, which is still the case today. On 1 September 1961, the Southern Cameroons and Republic of Cameroon were formally joined in a union and adopted the name 'Federal Republic of Cameroon'.

The British and French portions of the former German Kamerun had existed separately from 1916 to 1961, that is, a period of forty-five years.[5] So, in practical terms, prior to reunification in 1961, the two Cameroonian communities had not only undergone

Political System' in Richard Joseph (ed.), *Gaullist Africa: Cameroon under Ahmadou Ahidjo* (Fourth Dimension Publishing 1968) 45–69; Jean F. Bayart, 'L'Etat au Cameroun' (1979) *Outre-Mers Revue d'Histoire* 484; Jacques Benjamin, 'Dix Ans de Fédéralisme Camerounais 1961–1970' in Roman Serbyn (ed.), *Fédéralisme et Nations* (Les Presses de L'Université du Québec 1971) 279; Jacques Benjamin, *Les Camerounais Occidentaux: La Minorité dans un état Bicommunautaire* (Les Presses de L'Université Montréal 1972); Mark de Lancey, *Cameroon Dependence and Independence* (1st edn, Westview Press 1989); David E. Gardiner, *Cameroon: United Nations Challenge to French Policy* (Oxford University Press 1963); Willard R. Johnson, 'The Cameroon Federation: Political Union between English and French Speaking Africa' in William Lewis (ed.), *French-Speaking Africa* (Walker 1965) 206–11; Willard R. Johnson, *The Cameroon Federation: Political Integration in a Fragmentary Society* (Princeton University Press 1970); Richard A. Joseph, *Radical Nationalism in Cameroon: Social Origins of the U.P.C. Rebellion* (Clarendon Press 1977); Richard A. Joseph (ed.), *Gaullist Africa: Cameroon under Ahmadou Ahidjo* (Fourth Dimension 1978); Victor T. Le Vine, *The Cameroons from Mandate to Independence* (University of California Press and Cambridge University Press 1964); Victor T. Le Vine, *The Cameroon Federal Republic* (Cornell University Press 1971); Victor T. Le Vine, 'Political Integration, and the United Republic of Cameroon' in David Smock and Kwamena Bentsi-Enchill (eds.), *The Search for National Integration in Africa* (Free Press 1976) 61–75; Joseph Takougang and Milton Krieger, *African State and Society in the 1990s* (Westview Press 1998).

[5] Before Germany formally colonised Cameroon in 1884, there had been a British imperium over the territory from 1846. Hence, in a sense, there was a British influence in English-speaking Cameroon that, but for the thirty-two years of German rule, lasted for eighty-three years (i.e. 1846–84 and 1916–61).

two entirely different colonial experiences but had lived longer apart than together as a body politic. There appears to have been no compelling historical, geographical, or other reasons for the reunion other than the convenience of the UN and the British, along with, perhaps, nostalgia on the part of some Cameroonian politicians on either side of the 1916 divide. In fact, it has been shown that there were no great numbers of partitioned peoples on the intra-Cameroon boundary of 1916 to lend any weight to the idea of a union based on ethnicity.[6]

The reunification brought together not only two historically contrasting cultural experiences, one English and the other French, but also a wondrous mosaic of tribes, estimated at about 250, that speak about 280 different languages; anglophones make up about 20 per cent of the current population, estimated at 26,392,497 as at 11 April 2020.[7] Colonialism was the only glue that held these human units together in any shape recognisable in an atlas. Cameroon, with perhaps the exception of Somalia, is thus unique in Africa in having within its borders two territories that had undergone distinctly different colonial experiences. It is, however, different from Somalia in that the union in July 1960 between the former British Somaliland and Italian Somaliland brought together a people with a strong linguistic, cultural, religious, and ethnic bond, elements entirely missing in Cameroon's case.[8] Confronted with the heterogeneity of the country's population and its varied interests and conflicting demands, Cameroon's leadership at independence and reunification faced the major challenge of having to find a satisfactory constitutional framework for creating a sense of common citizenship and destiny.

3. Reunification of the British Southern Cameroons and Republic of Cameroon

As noted earlier, so much has been written about the intrigues of the reunification process that it is unnecessary here to delve into them any further. However, understanding the psychology of those who are supposed to have voted in favour of reunion with the Republic of Cameroon is important in gaining a full appreciation of some of the reasons for the current rumblings of discontent with the status quo.[9] Two points are worth noting. Firstly, the 1961 federal constitution that served as the basis for the union between the former British Southern Cameroons and the Republic of Cameroon turned out to be a sham; and secondly, the process of dismantling the union began almost immediately after the union was formed.

[6] See Ardener 1967 and 1968 (n. 4); Ndiva Kofele-Kale (ed.), *An Experiment in Nation Building: The Bilingual Cameroon Republic since Reunification* (Westview Press 1980); Ian Brownlie, *African Boundaries: A Legal and Diplomatic Encyclopaedia* (Hurst & Co 1919).

[7] See Worldometer, 'Cameroon Population' https://www.worldometers.info/world-population/cameroon-population/ (last accessed 20 November 2022).

[8] As the rest of the discussion will show, it is not insignificant that, since May 1991, the former British Somaliland and Italian Somalia have reverted to their former status as separate countries.

[9] Richard Björnson, *The African Quest for Freedom and Identity: Cameroon Writing and the National Experience* (1st edn, Indiana University Press 1991); De Lancey (n. 4); Gardiner (n. 4); Johnson 1965 (n. 4); Joseph 1978 (n. 4); Kofele-Kale (n. 6); Le Vine 1964 and 1971 (n. 4); and Nfor N. Susungi, *The Crisis of Unity and Democracy in Cameroon* (Nfor N. Susungi 1991).

3.1 The 1961 Federal Constitution: A Sham Federation Ab Initio

Before the reunification of the two territories, the French Cameroons, under the leadership of Ahmadou Ahidjo, had been granted independence already on 1 October 1960. Its constitution was based on a document produced by a constitutional consultative committee, created in 1959, composed mainly of foreign experts. Significantly, it excluded the banned Union des Populations du Cameroun (UPC), the country's most popular indigenous party, which represented a substantial part of national political opinion. The draft constitution that emerged was essentially a replica of the Constitution of France's Fifth Republic, with a strong executive and a highly centralised system of government. Although a narrow majority in a referendum later approved it, this constitution, which has formed the basis of virtually all subsequent constitutions of the unified Cameroon, could hardly be described as a document grounded in public participation.[10] Thus, by the time of reunification, the francophone part of the country was not only independent but had a fully functioning constitution in place.

As regards the anglophones of the former Southern Cameroons, there is now sufficient evidence to show that they were placed on the horns of a dilemma and given what amounted to a Hobson's choice. The period of British administration as part of Nigeria was an unhappy experience for the Southern Cameroonians. It was marked by general neglect by the British, and domineering, often humiliating treatment by Nigerians, especially the Igbos. Contrary to the expressed wishes of the dominant political forces in the Southern Cameroons at the time, the UN, with the complicity of the British, refused to put the issue of the desire for the separate existence of the Southern Cameroonians to voters in the 1961 plebiscite. Although the voters in the Southern Cameroons, unlike those in the Northern Cameroons, voted by a seven to three majority in favour of union with the former French Cameroons, there is overwhelming evidence to suggest that the third alternative of either independence or continued trusteeship would have carried the day had it been provided.[11] In fact, the vote in favour of reunification was more of a rejection of continued ties with Nigeria than a vote for the union with the French Cameroons.[12] France's tactics in brutally suppressing the UPC rebellion in its part of the territory, and French policies in general, had created deep suspicion and dislike among anglophones for the 'French way'.[13]

With the intense prodding of the British (based on the self-serving Sydney Phillipson Report of 1958 which concluded that the Southern Cameroons was not economically viable as an autonomous entity) and the connivance of the UN, the anglophones were forced to choose the lesser of the two evils. As N.N. Susungi aptly puts it, the reunification was far from the reunion of two prodigal sons unjustly separated at birth and much like a loveless arranged marriage, courtesy of the UN, between two people who hardly knew each other.[14]

In joining the former French Cameroons, the anglophones hoped to enter into a loose voluntary association in which they would retain a significant level of political and economic

[10] See Le Vine 1964 (n. 4) and John M. Mbaku, 'Constitutional Federalism and Policy Reform in Cameroon: Lessons for Africa' (1997) *2*(1) *Makerere Political Science Review* 20.

[11] See De Lancey (n. 4) and Gardiner (n. 4).

[12] Alain D. Olinga, 'La Question Anglophone dans le Cameroun d'Aujourd'hui' (1994) *48*(3) *Révue Juridique et Politique* 292.

[13] De Lancey (n. 4).

[14] Ibid.

autonomy. In fact, the anglophone leader at the time, John Ngu Foncha, had insisted on a confederation and finally settled on a loose federation, which he felt was the only way of guaranteeing a large degree of autonomy as well as equality of partnership and preservation of the anglophones' cultural heritage. However, owing to the latter's weak negotiating position, the limited concessions Ahidjo was prepared to make were contained in a document called the 'transitional and special dispositions', annexed to the 1960 Constitution of the then independent former French Cameroons.

The union gave birth to the Federal Republic of Cameroon, a two-state federation consisting of West Cameroon, made up of the former British Southern Cameroons, and East Cameroon, covering the former Republic of Cameroon. Article 1 of the Constitution made it clear that 'the Federal Republic of Cameroon' was formed from the 'territory of the Republic of Cameroon' and the 'territory of the Southern Cameroons'. However, as Ardener points out, the francophone sector made few, if any institutional adjustments, with the result that the federal and East Cameroon state institutions were basically the same in 'origin as well as in function'.[15] Pierre Messmer, one of the last French high commissioners and a close adviser to Ahidjo, notes in a book published recently that they knew at the time that the so-called federal constitution was '*une constitution faussement fédérale*' ('constitution containing a sham federation'), one that was '*sauf en apparence, une annexion*' ('save for appearances, an annexation') of West Cameroon, such that '*Le Cameroun réunifié est un pays bilingue francophone*' ('the unified Cameroon is a bilingual francophone country').[16] The federation, in short, was a sham ab initio.

In regard to such sham constitutions, Walter Murphy observes that their principal function is to deceive.[17] Under this 'new' constitution, West Cameroon lost most of the limited autonomy it had enjoyed as part of the Nigerian federation. Articles 5 and 6 of the Constitution stated the responsibilities of the federal government in such vague and broad terms as to include any powers that it might wish to assume. The federated states had almost no powers. They were, however, allowed to retain separate constitutions which, although parliamentary in nature, reflected the British and French constitutional traditions in the two different federated states.[18] Article 59 stated that the Constitution 'shall be published in French and English, the French text being authentic'. Therefore, from the very beginning of the union, the English language was officially given second-class status. This inferior status of the English language in the federation has remained a reality, as is shown below, notwithstanding that the Constitution was subsequently amended to grant equal status to English and French.

The Southern Cameroons delegation at the negotiations leading to the so-called federal constitution had argued for the inclusion of a proviso sanctioning peaceful withdrawal from the federation should this become necessary, but this was never included. In fact, in spite of the Southern Cameroons delegation's presence, the constitution was drafted almost entirely

[15] Ibid.

[16] Pierre Messmer, *Les Blancs, S'en Vont: Récits de Décolonisation* (Albin Michel 1998).

[17] Walter Murphy, 'Constitutions, Constitutionalism, and Democracy' in Douglas Greenberg , Stanley Katz, Melanie Oliviero, and Steven Wheatley (eds), *Constitutionalism and Democracy: Transitions in the Contemporary World* (1st edn, Oxford University Press 1993) 3–13.

[18] For the Constitution of the State of West Cameroon, see Henry N.A. Enonchong, *Cameroon Constitutional Law: Federalism in a Mixed Common Law and Civil Law System* (Centre d'Edition et de Production de Manuels et Auxiliaires de L'enseignement 1967) 267–91.

by Ahidjo with the help of his French advisers, after which he promulgated it into law. The Southern Cameroons' parliament was never given an opportunity to debate and approve it.

Nevertheless, the Constitution contained a few safeguards. Article 9 provided that the 'President of the Federal Republic and Vice President . . . must not be natives of the same Federated State', and article 46 allowed for the continuous application of the previous legislation of the federated states provided it were not in conflict with the provisions of the Constitution. Perhaps the most significant provisions were articles 18 and 47. Article 18 provided that before a federal bill is promulgated into law by the president, he may request a second reading at the request of either of the prime ministers of the federated states. On such a second reading, the law could be considered as adopted only if the simple majority of deputies required to approve it included the votes of a majority of the deputies of each of the federated states. The truly critical provision was article 47, which stated, inter alia, that 'any proposal for the revision of the present Constitution which impairs the unity and integrity of the Federation shall be inadmissible'. Although it turned out to be a heavily centralised federation that left almost all powers in the hands of the president, there was at least article 47 to ensure that the federal character of the country would never be changed. Nonetheless, the dismantling of the weak federation began almost immediately after the union came into existence.

3.2 The Incremental Dismantling of the Federation

The people of the former British Southern Cameroons had wanted, at best, a confederation or, at worst, a loose federation. Hence, the 1961 Constitution was for them a very unsatisfactory compromise. Their only consolation was that they had a separate state with their own prime minister and government. Had this unsatisfactory 'bargain' been implemented in good faith, it may have given them some consolation. However, this did not come to pass, and it was not long before President Ahidjo began the process of dismantling it.

Soon after the inception of the federation in October 1961, Ahidjo, by Decree No. 61-DF of 15 December 1961, created a system of regional administration in which West Cameroon was designated as one of six regions. This basically ignored the 'federal' character of the country. Powerful federal inspectors, who, in the case of West Cameroon, virtually overshadowed the prime minister with whom there were frequent conflicts of jurisdiction, headed these regions. The federal inspector was authorised to use the armed forces, gendarmes, and police to reinforce his authority. The gendarmes in turn were generally so eager to demonstrate their powers that they regularly and arbitrarily stopped and searched the vehicles of senior West Cameroon government officials, among them ministers and members of parliament.

This provoked John Ngu Foncha, the prime minister of West Cameroon, to write one of the many confidential letters he sent to President Ahidjo in protest at this administrative system:

> By this administrative division, West Cameroon has the same status as any of the five administrative regions in which East Cameroon is divided. We regret that this is inconsistent with the status of West Cameroon as a state in our federation of two states. Furthermore, we cannot at the same time regard West Cameroon as a state in the federation and as a

> province in the same federation. The powers given to the Inspector of Administration are far more extensive than those of either the Prime Minister of West Cameroon or the House of Assembly and Government [of West Cameroon]. This system is anachronistic and in fact *a resuscitation of what existed in the early colonial system.* It is also derogatory to the authority and dignity of our Prime Minister and our government. It is tending to change the system of administration in this state and is causing a great deal of frustration and disappointment among citizens of West Cameroon. It is adversely affecting the operation not only of the state government but also of the federal machinery.[19]

Ahidjo ignored this and other letters, and proceeded with his policy of eradicating aspects of anglophone economic and cultural heritage and integrating the anglophone community into the francophone-dominated federal state.[20] In 1962, without Ahidjo's bothering to consult the West Cameroon government, the Nigerian pound in West Cameroon was replaced with Communauté Française d'Afrique (CFA) francs. The imperial system of weights and measures was changed to the metric system in operation in East Cameroon; the system of right-hand driving in East Cameroon was extended to West Cameroon; and the pass system (*laissez-passer*) in force in East Cameroon was likewise applied in West Cameroon.

Similarly, the movement of imported and exported goods through the West Cameroon ports of Limbe and Tiko was diverted to Douala owing to economic policies that promoted imports from East Cameroon and France instead of Nigeria and Britain. As a result of this and general neglect, these two once-bustling places were reduced to ghost towns within a few years after reunification. The West Cameroon Electricity Corporation (PowerCam), which produced relatively cheap electricity, was closed down in favour of more expensive electricity produced in East Cameroon by a French company. Foncha was able to stop attempts by Ahidjo to harmonise the educational and legal systems in favour of what was obtaining in East Cameroon. Although the Constitution provided for a bilingual system, the reality of 'bilingualism in French' had begun to show itself, as French became the official language of administration as well as the police, army, and university.[21]

Much of the literature on this period highlights not only the frequent protests by West Cameroonian leaders at anglophones' steady loss of autonomy and identity but also these leaders' blatant lack of involvement in the decision-making process. The increasingly autocratic Ahidjo was able to exploit differences among political elites in a West Cameroon, where a vibrant multi-party system held sway. Having used a mixture of intimidation, co-option, and patronage to induce the different political parties in East Cameroon to join his party, Ahidjo did the same in West Cameroon, and by 1966 all the political parties had joined his party to create the Cameroon National Union (CNU).

Because the Constitution did not provide an autonomous source of finance, the West Cameroon government could not function properly, seeing as it depended entirely on erratically provided subventions from the federal government, which controlled major sources of revenue. By 1965, relying on articles 5 and 6 of the Constitution, Ahidjo had effectively

[19] This is cited in Piet Konings and Francis B. Nyamnjoh, *Negotiating an Anglophone Identity: A Study of the Politics of Recognition and Representation in Cameroon* (Brill 2003), 53. Emphasis added.

[20] For a detailed discussion of anglophone de-identification, see ibid.

[21] For example, an anglophone lecturer was dismissed from the Faculty of Law and Economics at the supposedly bilingual University of Yaoundé in the 1980s for 'inefficient delivery of his lessons' merely because he had dared to teach a course in English. See ibid. 70–1.

assumed most of the powers previously exercised by the governments of the two states. Hence, after having united the country's parties within the CNU, he felt sufficiently confident to let rumours circulate about his plans to reconfigure the federation in such a manner that parts of it would be merged with administrative divisions in East Cameroon. The prime minister of West Cameroon, Augustine Jua, reacted strongly:

> It must be emphasised that the Federal Republic of Cameroon is a federation of two states with different backgrounds, cultures and traditions; the present arrangement was in fact envisaged as the most ideal solution to reunification . . . Any exercise, therefore, that is designed to alter this arrangement . . . will clearly alter the basis on which the entire Federation rests and will throw our present system of government into complete disarray . . . It is equally clear that since ours is a democratic republic, a matter of far-reaching significance and consequences cannot be conceived and executed in secret without the full knowledge and concurrence of the people of West Cameroon through their accredited representatives, to wit, the West Cameroon Government.[22]

With the establishment of the one-party state in 1966, it was easy for Ahidjo to consolidate his centralisation agenda by appointing to positions of power only those West Cameroonian politicians who would not challenge his policies of ending the federation. Hence, when on 6 May 1972 he announced in the National Assembly that he had decided to transform the federation into a unitary state and schedule a referendum for 20 May 1972, there was, other than in name, no meaningful federation left to replace. Outspoken West Cameroonian politicians such as Augustine Jua and John Foncha had been systematically sidelined.

4. The 1972 'Divorce', Forced 'Cohabitation', and Intensive De-identification

The imposition of homogeneity and de-identification of anglophones were vigorously pursued by illegal as well as legal means. For example, Decree No. DF 72-270, through which Ahidjo abrogated the federal façade and created the unitary state, disregarded article 47(1) of the federal constitution, which had laid down a special procedure for amendment and expressly prohibited any revisions that impaired the 'unity and integrity of the federation'. This was in many ways the last nail in the coffin of the sham federal union, and it brought about the divorce of the former West Cameroon and former East Cameroon. It established a forced cohabitation between the two entities at the behest and under the control of the dominant francophone majority. There can be no surprise at what happened, for, as Linz and Stephen point out, it is meaningless to speak of federalism under authoritarian or other dictatorial systems.[23] In the aftermath of this divorce, policies of 'divide and rule', systematic francophonisation, and discrimination against and marginalisation of anglophones became the modus operandi of Ahidjo and his successor, Paul Biya. Certain aspects of this are briefly examined below.

[22] Cited in ibid. 62–3.

[23] Cited in Michael C. Davis, 'The Case for Chinese Federalism' (1999) *10*(2) *Journal of Democracy* 124, 130.

4.1 The 1972 'Divorce'

Even if it did not declare this in as many words, it was understood and accepted by all that the 1961 Constitution brought together two distinct, separate communities, the cultural, linguistic, and other bases of whose identity needed to be protected. The eternity clause in article 47 may have been simply one of the numerous provisions copied unthinkingly from the French 1958 Constitution, but it became particularly significant in Cameroon view of the need to protect the demographically and geographically smaller anglophone minority in the federation.

The so-called referendum in 1972 that ushered in the unitary state was illegal for at least three reasons. Firstly, article 47 prohibited any change to the federal character of the country. This character was at the core of the reunification of the two territories, and changing it amounted to the total destruction of the basis on which the two communities came together. As the Indian Supreme Court said in *Kesavananda Bharati v State of Kerala*, 'one cannot legally use the constitution to destroy itself'.[24] The change substantially transformed, indeed negated, the defining political commitment of the constitutional order, one which had been central to the country's self-understanding and its emerging constitutional identity—what could be seen, in the words of Ran Hirschl, as a 'foundational collective identity'.[25] Walter Murphy rightly points out that to amend a constitution does not mean 'to deconstitute and reconstitute' it, to replace one system with another, or to abandon its primary principles.[26] What happened was nothing short of what Gary Jacobsohn has described as constitutional identity theft.[27]

Secondly, given that the unitary state and centralisation are at the heart of the Gallic constitutional tradition on which the constitutional system of East Cameroon is built, the results of the referendum were a foregone conclusion owing to the overwhelming francophone majority in the federation. Francophone political actors simply used this majority to enforce a system of governance which they knew the anglophones did not like and had wanted to avoid since the inception of the union.

Finally, given that by 1972 most West Cameroonians were already disillusioned with the union, most of them voted more out of fear than anything else. As Konings and Nyamnjoh point out,

> [The] ballot was far from secret, election results were arranged beforehand, and it was neither politically wise nor politically safe to hold and express views different from the President's, let alone oppose in words or deeds any of his plans or actions.[28]

Although each voter was supposed to be given a 'yes' and 'no' ballot, as was common in elections before 1990, most polling stations had only the 'yes' ballots, leaving voters with the

[24] 1973 SC1461 (1973) 1624.

[25] Ran Hirschl, *Towards Juristocracy: The Origins and Consequences of the New Constitutionalism* (Harvard University Press 2004).

[26] Walter F. Murphy, 'Merlin's Memory: The Past and Future Imperfect of the Once and Future Polity' in Sanford Levinson (ed.), *Responding to Imperfection: The Theory and Practice of Constitutional Amendment* (Princeton University Press 1995) 177.

[27] Jacobsohn (n. 3).

[28] Konings and Nyamnjoh (n. 19) 65.

choice between 'yes' and 'yes' ballots! Hence, the referendum was as bogus as the constitution it was designed to replace.[29]

This has to be seen in the context of Ahidjo's plans. From the outset of his political career, he regarded national unity as a prerequisite for maintaining peace and promoting national development.[30] The main argument made for dismantling the federal system was that it not only encouraged division and regionalism but was costly to maintain, depleting scarce resources that could have been used to speed up economic development. However, there was also some suspicion that Ahidjo was worried that disgruntled anglophones might be tempted to try to secede from the federation, emboldened as they were by the discovery of oil in West Cameroon in 1967. His concerns must have been reinforced by the civil war that broke out in Nigeria when in 1967 the Igbos wished to secede and create a Biafran state.[31]

Be that as it may, Ahidjo used the slogan of national unity as the ideological justification for the progressive elimination of anglophone particularities after 1972. His successor, Paul Biya, came to power in 1982 on a wave of popular support and did not disappoint with his initial promises of greater democracy as well as 'rigour and moralisation'. He affirmed his commitment to political stability and national unity, which he described as 'the cardinal historic task of highest priority'.[32] Declaring the 'consolidation of national unity to be the indispensable foundation' of nation-building, he rejected the 'collection and juxtaposition of our diversities' and pronounced himself 'firmly convinced that we should move on a higher level of unification, which is that of national integration'.[33]

After a false dawn of promised relaxation of some of the restrictions put in place by the previous regime, an attempted coup d' état in 1984 was brutally suppressed. This gave Biya the pretext to reimpose the full repressive machinery which he had inherited. This included transforming the already highly centralised state machinery into one of the most bureaucratic, but inefficient, lethargic, and corrupt, administrations in Africa.[34] What many considered as one of the last visible and nominally significant symbols of the 1961 union was removed when Law No. 84/001 of 1984 abolished the appellation 'United Republic of Cameroon' (adopted in 1972 after the referendum) and replaced it with 'Republic of Cameroon'—significantly, the name the French-administered portion of the country adopted when it became independent in 1960. No convincing reasons were given for the change, but it left restive anglophones jittery. Since then, the process of eliminating any anglophone sense of belonging in, and self-identification with, Cameroonian society has gathered momentum thanks to a policy of 'divide and rule'.[35]

[29] For arguments maintaining that the 1972 referendum was illegal, see Carlson Anyangwe, *Betrayal of Too Trusting a People: The UN, the UK and the Trust Territory of the Southern Cameroons* (Langaa Research and Publishing Common Initiative Group (RPCIG) 2009) 103.

[30] Ahmadou Ahidjo, *Contribution to National Construction* (Présence Africaine 1964).

[31] Konings and Nyamnjoh (n. 19) 64.

[32] Paul Biya, *Communal Liberalism* (Macmillan 1987), 26–30.

[33] Mario J. Azevedo (ed.), *Cameroon and Chad in Historical Contemporary Perspectives* (E Mellen Press 1988).

[34] See Charles M. Fombad, 'Endemic Corruption in Cameroon: Insights on Consequences and Control' in R. Hope and Bornwell Chikulo (eds.), *Corruption and Development in Africa: Lessons from Country Case Studies* (Palgrave Macmillan 2000) 234; Charles M. Fombad, 'The Dynamics of Record-Breaking Corruption and Political Opportunism in Cameroon' in John M. Mbaku and Joseph Takougang (eds.), *The Leadership Challenge in Africa: Cameroon under Paul Biya* (Africa World Press 2003) 357.

[35] Some of these issues are discussed in Carlson Anyangwe, *Imperialistic Politics in Cameroun: Resistance and the Inception of the Restoration of the Statehood of Southern Cameroons* (Langaa RPCIG 2008), 82–111.

4.2 The Politics of 'Divide and Rule'

It is useful to preface discussion of the policy of 'divide and rule' with an explanation of who, in the Cameroonian context, an 'anglophone' is. Although scholars are not fully agreed on the definition,[36] it is clear that this categorisation is not based simply on the ability to speak English or a dialect of it, or on having been born in the North West or South West regions of Cameroon. The term refers instead to those people whose ancestry can be traced to the two anglophone regions and who were brought up in a milieu where they acquired an anglophone education and culture. In other words, it applies to people who identify themselves through upbringing, culture, history, and ethnic roots with these two regions. In spite of intermarriage between many anglophones and francophones, political elites since independence have perpetuated the colonial policy of creating and exploiting rivalries between ethnic communities—here, meaning between anglophones and francophones, as well as, more importantly, between ethnic groups within the two anglophone regions.

Much of the literature on anglophones highlights the extraordinary lengths to which various francophone-dominated governments have gone to sow division and create intra-anglophone conflict.[37] This started as early as December 1961, when Ahidjo divided the former West Cameroon federated state into the two separate regions we have today. Thereafter, he began co-opting elites from each of these regions, particularly those whom he considered a threat to his goal of assimilating the anglophone community. Indeed, Ahidjo and his successor, Biya, created a scenario in which anglophones from the two regions were made to compete against each other for the few positions that were reserved for them. Often an appointment of an anglophone from one region was made to look like a loss to anglophones in the other region. The anglophones appointed as government ministers used their cabinet positions not only to defend the system but also to promote division among anglophones from their two regions, thereby seeking to prevent them from forming a united front in the face of a regime determined to sideline and silence them. In general, ruling-party supporters and other elites from the two anglophone regions, as well as prominent traditional leaders, were regularly given space on government-owned and -controlled media in order to discredit any critics of the government's policies of discrimination and marginalisation of the two anglophone regions.

4.3 Discrimination and Marginalisation of Anglophones

In many respects, the union of the former British Southern Cameroons and the Republic of Cameroon appears to have resulted in the replacement of one form of colonial rule with

[36] For discussion of this, see Joseph L. Nfi, 'The Anglophone Identity in Cameroon 50 Years after Reunification' (2014) *2*(2) *International Journal of Advanced Research* 121; Micheal Ndobegang, 'The Anglophone Francophone Divide in Cameroon: Diagnosis of a National Disconnection' (2014) *2*(2) *International Journal of Advanced Research* 121, cited in Government of the United Kingdom, 'Home Office, Country Policy and Information Note "Cameroon: Anglophones" (29 December 2020) 11 https://www.gov.uk/government/publications/cameroon-country-policy-and-information-notes (last accessed 20 November 2022); Victor J. Ngoh, *History of Cameroon since 1800* (Presprint 1996).

[37] See, for example, Ngoh (n. 1); George Ngwane, *The Anglophone File* (Presbook 1994); Micheal Rowlands, 'Accumulation and the Cultural Politics of Identity in the Grassfields' in Peter Geschiere and Piet Konings (eds.), *Itinéraires d'Accumulation au Cameroun* (Karthala 1993) 91.

another. Since 1961, as analysis of the fate of anglophone Cameroon shows, the policies of the francophone-dominated government have been as repressive, coercive, and extractive as those of the colonial government. It is not difficult to see why anglophones feel so little sense of any attachment to the government, given that it has alienated itself from them and shown negligible interest in their well-being beyond exploiting the two regions for all it can extract. At the heart of what is usually called the 'anglophone problem'[38] is a profound sense of discrimination, marginalisation, and exclusion from the social, political, and economic life of the country.

For a start, Cameroon's bilingual and bi-cultural nature, one of its greatest sources of pride, has turned out to be its most enduring contradiction. The anglophones, who make up about 20 per cent of the total population and occupy about 9 per cent of the total land surface, have since reunification in 1961, never been made to feel a sense of belonging in the country. A perception of marginalisation in the face of a government policy of assimilation that entails elimination of anglophone particularities looms large and runs deep. For many anglophones, the straw that broke the camel's back came in 1992, when the Supreme Court, whilst acknowledging gross irregularities in the presidential elections, proceeded to declare Biya the winner in a contest that many, including international observers, believed Ni Fru Ndi—an anglophone—had won. This, more than anything else, reinforced the long-standing anglophone feelings that, no matter their merits, they are destined to play second fiddle to francophones. Many analysts agree that anglophones have had a hard time being both anglophone and Cameroonian.[39]

With the possible exception of the three regions of the Centre, South, and East—Biya's support base—the entire country has suffered during the four decades of his misrule, marked as it has been by gross mismanagement, incompetence, corruption, cronyism, and poor economic performance; however, the anglophone regions have been the worst affected. The case is especially painful for the South West region, which is not only the country's breadbasket in terms of agricultural produce but its main source of oil wealth. This has led to a feeling that the two regions are a mere appendage—useful for their resources but not for their people.[40]

In fact, while it has been suggested that the two anglophone regions account for about 60 per cent of Cameroon's gross domestic product (GDP), there is little infrastructural development in the regions to show for this.[41] Oil output and oil revenue have remained a state secret. All the general managers and most of the senior staff of the parastatal that manages the oil in Limbe, the Societé Nationale de Raffinage (SONARA), have been francophones; the company pays its taxes not to the Limbe Council in the anglophone region where the oil

[38] Besides some of the other works already referred to, see Jean F. Bayart, 'The Neutralisation of Anglophone Cameroon' in Joseph (n. 4); Piet Konings, 'Le Problème Anglophone au Cameroun dans les Années 1990' (1986) *62 Politiques Africaine* 25; Piet Konings and Francis B. Nyamnjoh, 'The Anglophone Problem in Cameroon' (1997) *35*(2) *Journal of Modern African Studies* 207; Eko Lyombe, 'The English-Language Press and the "Anglophone Problem" in Cameroon: Group Identity, Culture and the Politics of Nostalgia' (2003) *20*(1) *Journal of Third World Studies* 79–102; Victor Ngoh, 'The Origin of the Marginalisation of Former Southern Cameroonians (Anglophones), 1961–1966: An Historical Analysis' (1999) *16*(1) *Journal of Third World Studies* 165; Francis B. Nyamnjoh, 'Cameroon: A Country United by Ethnic Ambition and Difference' (1999) *98*(380) *African Affairs* 101.

[39] Bayart (n. 38); Benjamin, 1972 (n. 4); Konings 1986 (n. 38); Albert Mukong (ed.), *The Case for Southern Cameroons* (CAMFECO 1990); Frank Stark, 'Federalism' in Kofele-Kale (n. 6).

[40] Jonathan Derrick, 'Cameroon: One Party, Many Parties and the State' (1992) *22*(3) *African Insight* 165.

[41] See Yoletta Nyange, 'State of Confusion' *The Tortoise Quarterly* (9 April 2020) https://bit.ly/3U0mZLc (last accessed 20 November 2022).

is located, but to the Douala council in the francophone littoral region where the oil is taken via huge pipelines for export. The natural deep-sea port in Limbe was long ago abandoned in favour of the Douala port, which has to be dredged regularly at enormous cost.

Whilst there has been little serious investment of any sort in any of the two anglophone regions since their reunification with the then Republic of Cameroon in 1961,[42] francophones were soon appointed to head most of the successful enterprises, such as banks and marketing boards, that were doing well in the days of West Cameroon. It did not take long for them to be declared bankrupt.[43] There was one exception: the Cameroon Development Corporation (CDC). This is the largest agro-industrial enterprise in Cameroon and the second-largest employer of labour after the government. Its contribution to the social and economic life of the anglophone regions has been enormous, and its origins go back to the German colonial period. For the past four decades, the francophone-dominated government has struggled against persistent opposition by the anglophone community to sell this corporation, which remains one of the few symbols of anglophone pride and a critical economic lifeline to the people.[44] In spite of resistance, the government went ahead and sold some parts of the CDC.

It is no surprise that the economy of the two anglophone regions, which was already in dire straits before the 2016 crisis, virtually collapsed. The government's level of investment in these regions is consistently amongst the lowest across the country. For example, in Cameroon's public investment budget for 2017, they were allocated a combined USD 153 million; by contrast, the South Region, from which Biya originates, was allocated USD 225 million. To underscore the disparities, the following facts bear repeating: while the two anglophone regions make up only 20 per cent of the population but contribute almost 60 per cent of GDP, the South Region makes up only about 3 per cent of the population.[45]

Since the end of the sham federation, there has been an intensification of the policy of 'de-identification' of anglophones from their distinct heritage and 'persona' through a careful process of 'Gallicising' most aspects of social, economic, and educational life to conform to French models. This process of 'de-anglophonisation' and 'francophonisation' that started under Ahidjo has continued with even more vigour under Biya. In pursuing their policies of 'national unity and integration', the two leaders regarded the persistence of anglophone 'idiosyncrasies' as an obstacle. As noted earlier, Biya has rejected what he terms the 'collection and juxtaposition of our diversities'.[46] It came as a shock to anglophones to realise that, upon having agreed to join a bilingual union in which inherited colonial differences in language and institutions were to be respected and integrated into a new collective national

[42] Most schools and hospitals in the two regions were built by missionary bodies before 1972. Many of the schools built after 1972 were not completed because the money allocated for them was embezzled with the complicity of the supervising authorities before they could be completed.

[43] Such was the case with the highly successful West Cameroon bank, Cameroon Bank. The West Cameroon Marketing Board, which was established to protect farmers against fluctuations in the price of important export commodities such as coffee, cocoa, and tea, accumulated enormous reserves for this purpose. After the 1972 referendum, its headquarters, as well as these reserves, were transferred from Limbe to Douala in the francophone part of the country.

[44] The struggle for the preservation of this anglophone economic legacy is discussed in Konings and Nyamnjoh (n. 38).

[45] This and many similar anomalies are revealed in the appropriately entitled study by Roxana Willis , James Angove, Caroline Mbinkar, and Joseph McAuley, 'We Remain Their Slaves: Voices from the Cameroon Conflict: A Working Paper' (Oxford University Press 2020) 17.

[46] Biya 1987 (n. 32).

experience, they were being buried under the weight of the dominant francophone way of life.[47] For example, until fairly recently, anglophone certificates and diplomas were regarded as inferior to their French equivalents. This was in fact the cause of the early obsession with the harmonisation of educational systems, and served as a pretext for seeking to replace the anglophones' educational system with that of the francophones. It is this relentless, insensitive pursuit of the policy of harmonisation—not only in education but also in the legal system—that has led to the upheavals that threaten to be the final nail on the coffin of the moribund marriage between the anglophones and francophones in Cameroon.

Firstly, consider the legal system.[48] The legal premise for the continuous coexistence of the two distinct legal systems and the two legal districts can only be inferred from certain vague provisions in the different constitutions. In the case of the 1996 Constitution, article 68 allows for the continuous use of 'legislation applicable in the federal state of Cameroon and in the federated states . . . as long as it is not amended by subsequent laws and regulations'. Ahidjo often cited the coexistence of the common law system in the anglophone regions and the civil law system in the francophone regions as an example of his policy of 'unity in diversity'. The reality, however, is that the common law system in the anglophone regions has barely survived, having been attenuated by a policy that has seen substantial parts of it replaced with French civil law under the pretext of the harmonisation of laws.

This one-sided invasion of civil law principles started with so-called uniform laws, such as the Labour Code and the Penal Code, but in almost all cases these 'harmonised' laws were based entirely on civil law principles that are often at odds with the common law substratum of the legal system in the anglophone regions. This has led to confusion and uncertainty about the interpretation of these laws in the anglophone regions.[49] Furthermore, successive ministers of justice have treated the anglophone legal system with contempt. Although one of them was fired in 1985 for unleashing a torrent of verbal attacks on the system, this did not disguise the growing impatience at the highest government level with its continued existence.

When, in December 1996, Cameroon became a party to the treaty setting up the Organisation for the Harmonisation of Business Laws in Africa, the effect of which was to replace all the business laws in member states with uniform laws based on the French civil law, it nearly sounded the dead knell for the common law system in the anglophone provinces. Ironically, some analysts have cited Cameroon as an example of how Organisation for the Harmonization of Business Law in Africa (in French: 'Organisation pour l'Harmonisation en Afrique du Droit des Affaires' or OHADA) could work in anglophone Africa, but they ignore, or gloss over, the many anomalies it has created.[50] Three problems should be noted in particular. Firstly, the OHADA regime was imposed on anglophone Cameroonians without

[47] Ndiva Kofele-Kale, 'Ethnicity, Regionalism, and Political Power: A Post-Mortem of Ahidjo's Cameroon' in Michael Shatzberg and Ira W. Zartman (eds.), *The Political Economy of Cameroon* (Praeger 1986) 53–82.

[48] Aspects of this are discussed in Charles M. Fombad, 'An Experiment in Legal Pluralism: The Cameroonian Bi-Jural/Uni-Jural Imbroglio' (1997) *16 University of Tasmania Law Review* 209; Charles M. Fombad, 'Cameroonian Bi-Juralism: Current Challenges and Future Prospects' (1991) *5 Fundamina Journal of Legal History* 22.

[49] For discussion of this, see Charles M. Fombad, 'The Scope for Uniform National Laws in Cameroon' (1991) 29(3) *Journal of Modern African Studies* 443.

[50] See, for example, the otherwise excellent paper by Gustav Kalm, 'Building Legal Certainty through International Law: OHADA Law in Cameroon' (2011) https://www.academia.edu/38335634/Building_Legal_Certainty_Through_International_Law_OHADA_Law_in_Cameroon (last accessed 20 November 2022), who fails to say anything about whether or not OHADA has brought legal certainty in the anglophone regions of Cameroon.

warning, consultation or discussion. English common-law principles of business law were swept aside overnight and replaced with OHADA's. Hardly any anglophone scholars, lawyers, or judges were prepared for the dramatic change. As a result, some anglophone judges initially refused to apply the OHADA acts,[51] and gave in only under pressure from the minister of justice. A senior anglophone judge indicated that 'many sitting judges did not know about OHADA until after the first OHADA laws were already in effect', and were 'furious and embarrassed to have learned about OHADA for the first time not from the government or from OHADA, but rather from counsel pleading a case'.[52] OHADA therefore applies in anglophone Cameroon today not because the people directly or indirectly wanted it, but because the government imposed it. So far, there is nothing to suggest that if the people of this region had a choice, they would opt for OHADA.

Secondly, the constitutionality of the OHADA regime in Cameroon is questionable. One of the main reasons for this is that the imposition of the French language and French texts in a country where the Constitution expressly sanctions bilingualism might have been removed with the amendment of article 42 of the treaty to make English a working language, but there remain many nagging questions. Unfortunately, because individual citizens have no standing to challenge violations of the Constitution before the courts, the OHADA constitutional questions will never be tested in court.[53] Thirdly, anglophone judges have had great difficulty in interpreting Cameroonian harmonised laws, drawn largely from French laws, in a manner which is consistent with francophone judges, mainly because of the differences in rules of interpretation and procedure in English law.[54] It will thus be even harder for them to interpret and apply OHADA texts, which make little pretence at incorporating common law principles, in a manner consistent with interpretations by francophone judges, especially those at the Common Court of Justice and Arbitration (CCJA), the supranational court based in Dakar which has the final say in the interpretation of OHADA uniform laws.

As if the imposition of a civil law-based commercial law regime in the anglophone regions were not enough, by 2016—one of the last straws that led to the crisis—the common law system in the two anglophone regions was almost completely run by francophone Cameroonians who had little knowledge of English and less of the English law on which the system is based.[55]

A third and equally troubling aspect of the 'de-identification' process has been the attempt to impose the francophone system of education on anglophones. In addition to looking down on Anglo-Saxon education, the Biya regime, after making numerous subtle but significant changes to the education system and the calendar in conformity with the

[51] See Justice Paul Ayah in *Akiangan Fombin Sebastian v Foto Joseph & Others*, suit no. HCK/3/96 of 6 January 2000.

[52] Claire M. Dickerson (ed.), *Unified Business Laws for Africa: Common-Law Perspectives on OHADA* (GMB 2009) 45.

[53] For discussion of the absence of an effective mechanism for constitutional review in Cameroon, see Fombad 2003 (n. 34).

[54] Fombad 1991 (n. 49).

[55] A 'Position statement of the SDF members of the National Assembly of Anglophone extraction', signed by fifteen members of the SDF in Yaoundé on 16 November 2016, provided the following evidence of what it referred to as the flooding of the common law system by magistrates trained in the civil law system: (i) 58 of the 148 magistrates (39.2 per cent) were francophones trained in the civil law; (ii) 54 of the 89 lawyers (60.7 per cent) in the legal department in the South West Region were francophone; (iii) 20 of the 50 magistrates (40 per cent) in the Buea bench and legal department were francophone; (iv) 28 of the 30 bailiffs (93.2 per cent) appointed to the two regions were francophone; 67 of the 128 magistrates (52.3 per cent) in the North West Region were francophone; and 64 of the 97 (65.9 per cent) magistrates in the legal department of the North West Region were francophone.

francophone system, tried in 1983 to replace the anglophone General Certificate of Education (GCE) Ordinary and Advanced level with its francophone equivalent, the *Baccalauréat* (BAC). Faced with this unwarranted assault on one of the pillars of its education system, the anglophone community took to the streets daily for more than a week, in spite of the armed troops that were sent to disperse them, until the government was forced to shelve its plans. Nevertheless, the protesters were labelled by the government-controlled media as enemies of national integration.[56] Another minister of national education tried in 1989 to revive the harmonisation plans, but once again, after fierce opposition and widespread demonstrations, the minister was sacked and the implementation of the scheme halted.

From 1992, concerns about the falling standards of the GCE led a number of teachers' unions, students, church associations, and parents to agitate for the creation of an autonomous GCE board to take over the management of the examinations from the ministry of national education. It was again only after numerous demonstrations which the government unsuccessfully tried to break up that a reasonably autonomous GCE board was approved. The government grudgingly provided it with financial support of CFA 166 million for its first year and CFA 44 million for its second—but in its third year nothing was provided, and the Board had to depend on the benevolence of teachers and parents. However, by 1995, the government had undermined the efforts by the anglophone community to preserve its education system by making strategic appointments to the GCE board in a manner that restricted its independence. This in effect left the Board and education system in the anglophone regions under the direct control of the francophone minister of national education.

By 2016, the inherited Anglo-Saxon educational system had been so undermined by the extensive appointment of francophone teachers with little understanding of English as teachers in primary and secondary schools in the anglophone regions that parents and teachers had no alternative but to act. Apart from this, the policy of anglophone 'deculturalisation' and marginalisation was reinforced by derogatory references to English speakers as '*les Biafrais*' (i.e. Biafrans, evoking memories of the Nigerian civil war) and '*les ennémis dans la maison*' ('the enemies within the house').[57] Repeated anglophone demands for a return to federalism were dismissed as evidence of lack of patriotism and a smokescreen for secessionism.

Frustrated by the regime's intransigence, and galvanised by general hardship in which, as most analysts agree, anglophones have suffered more than any other group, an alarming number of pressure groups sprouted, starting with the first All Anglophone Conference (AAC 1) held in Buea in 1993. Moderate demands for a return to the federation—made, for example, by the Cameroon Anglophone Movement (CAM), now the Southern Cameroons Restoration Movement (SCARM), and the Southern Cameroons National Council (SCNC)—were brushed aside. What slowly emerged thereafter were radical factions, such as the Ambazonia, the Southern Cameroons Liberation Front, and the Free West Cameroon Movement, which advocate outright secession, by force of arms if necessary.

56 See *The Messenger* (25 November 1993) 11.

57 Dickson Eyoh, 'Conflicting Narratives of Anglophone Protest and the Politics of Identity in Cameroon' (1998) *16 Journal of Contemporary African Studies* 249; Derrick (n. 40); Takougang and Krieger (n. 4); Achille Mbembe, 'Epilogue. Crise de Légitimité, Restoration Autoritaire et Déliquescence de L'État' in Peter Geschière and Piet Konings (eds.), *Pathways to Accumulation in Cameroon* (Karthala 1993) 345–74.

5. The 2016 Crisis and Its Aftermath

After years of unrelenting assault on all aspects of their social, political, educational, cultural, and economic identity, it was becoming clear to anglophones that unless action were taken, the anglophone identity in Cameroon would be eradicated. This was fuelled by a feeling that the process of 'francophonisation' and assimilation of anglophones had reached a turning point.[58] It was out of this fear that in mid-October 2016, lawyers in the two anglophone regions started a protest action against the domination of the judiciary by francophones who have little or no knowledge or training in common law. This was followed a few weeks later by a strike by teachers, leading to the closure of schools. The teachers complained that French-speaking and -trained teachers had been deployed to the two anglophone regions to teach subjects in French to children who do not understand this language. They also complained that competitive public examinations to gain admission into professional schools in the country are poorly translated from French to English, making it difficult for anglophones to gain admission to these schools.

An anglophone newspaper, the *Guardian Post Daily*, in a report headlined 'Anglophone marginalisation: Facts and figures speak!', painted the following bleak picture of the low level of anglophone representation in the top echelon of the Cameroonian public service in 2016:

- only 76 anglophones appointed amongst Biya's 700 ministers in 34 years;
- only 6 anglophones present in the 63-member government;
- only 1 anglophone minister with a portfolio out of 38 (the rest being deputy ministers);
- less than 15 anglophones out of more than 130 general managers of state corporations;
- only 10 anglophones out of more than 130 board chairmen of state corporations;
- only 3 anglophone directors of general administration out of 38 directors-general of government ministries in the country;
- no anglophone secretary general at the presidency and ministries of finance, territorial administration, and defence, or as general manager of SONARA since independence;
- no operational airport or seaport in anglophone Cameroon;
- no anglophone on the Douala Stock Exchange Board;
- only 4 anglophone secretary generals out of 38 secretary generals in government ministries;
- no referral hospital in anglophone Cameroon;
- only 6 anglophones out of more than 36 ambassadors;
- only 6 anglophones out of 58 senior divisional officers; and
- only 3 anglophone army generals out of 33 such generals in the country.

Moreover, at a time when many anglophones, including those with degrees, were unemployed, most senior administrative positions at the regional, divisional, and

[58] In a panel discussion on 12 November 2019 at the Second Paris Peace Summit in France, Paul Biya, in response to a question by Mohammed Ibrahim, a Sudanese-British billionaire who was moderating the panel, said: 'We tried assimilating their system into the majority francophone system but because of identity differences, it failed.' This was the first time he had admitted to pursuing a policy of assimilation of anglophones and acknowledged that there were indeed 'identity' problems. See Amos Fofung, 'Cameroon: From Biya, a Mea Culpa on the Anglophone Crisis in Paris' (12 November 2019) https://panafricanvisions.com/2019/11/cameroon-from-biya-a-mea-culpa-on-the-anglophone-crisis-in-paris/ (last accessed 20 November 2022).

subdivisional levels in the anglophone regions were held by francophones. Almost all the senior security officials in the two regions were also francophones. It was thus difficult to resist the feeling that a francophone colonisation was under way. Most of these francophone officials are arrogant and speak to the people mainly in French, and since they owe their positions and hence loyalty to those who appointed them in Yaoundé, spend their time enriching themselves from budgets meant for local development. In other words, the patronage system and its accompanying looting of budgets for personal benefit were especially prevalent in the anglophone regions, which were subject to few checks from the central government.

The level of frustration among anglophones was such that, by December 2016, daily life in the two regions had ground to a halt due to a general strike and demonstrations calling for a return to the federal system. The government's response was swift: armed troops were dispatched throughout the regions, and in many places street demonstrations were violently suppressed, resulting in the deaths of numerous demonstrators and the detention of many more. In his traditional 31 December New Year speech, President Biya, as in the past, pretended there was no 'anglophone problem' and reiterated his view that the strikes and demonstrations were the 'acts of a group of manipulated and exploited extremist rioters'.[59] He reaffirmed his determination to defend the unity of the country.

As at the time of writing,[60] the situation in Cameroon had degenerated into a civil war. At the start of the crisis, the government must have assumed that its violent response would break the strikes and demonstrations and, as in the past, reduce the anglophones to silence and submission. The international situation favoured such an outcome. Europe was too preoccupied with the uncertainties caused by Brexit and the rise of right-wing populist governments in countries such as Italy, Poland, and Hungary to bother about what was happening in Cameroon. Similarly, with Donald Trump, a populist, in the White House and preoccupied with his rhetoric of 'America first', there was not likely to be much interest in what to the international community looked like a small conflict. A greater distraction for the international community was the Covid-19 pandemic.

With the French firmly on his side, and using arms previously supplied by them as well as the United States (US), the United Kingdom (UK), Germany, and Russia to fight the insurgency brought about by attempts by Boko Haram to create an Islamic state that would include parts of Cameroon, Chad, Nigeria, and Niger,[61] Biya resolutely went for what he assumed was going to be a quick military victory. Although the US, the UK, and Germany were later to prohibit any use of the weapons they supplied in the anglophone region, Biya has been able to obtain a steady supply of sophisticated arms from other countries, mainly China, Israel, the United Arab Emirates, and Ukraine. The distraction caused by Covid-19

[59] The continuous refusal, against all logic, to recognise the so-called anglophone problem, and the firm belief by the ruling clique that it should use force to suppress the demonstrations, is driving many moderate anglophones into the extremist camp of those who believe the only solution is secession. Some of these pro-secessionist groups, such as the Southern Cameroons Youth League, the Southern Cameroons National Council, and the Ambazonia Movement, are gaining supporters and becoming increasingly militant.

[60] June 2020.

[61] The Boko Haram insurgency, which began in the northern part of Nigeria, was able to spread easily into the northern part of Cameroon because, much like the two anglophone regions, it has been neglected by successive governments, particularly so by the Biya administration. See further Edward B. Rackley, 'Cameroon's Far North: Responding to Boko Haram' https://reliefweb.int/sites/reliefweb.int/files/resources/Cameroons%20Far%20North%20-%20Responding%20to%20Boko%20Haram.pdf (last accessed 20 November 2022); Jean C.G. Kouma, 'Cameroon Fighting Boko Haram' (2017) *17*(4) *RUDN International Relations* 727.

was a perfect gift for Biya, enabling him to continue his scorched-earth military operations in the two anglophone regions while the attention of the international community was focused on the virus.

In the early stages, the conflict took a decisive turn when, on 1 October 2017, shocked by the extent of military operations against unarmed peaceful demonstrators, numerous local groups that had taken up arms to defend themselves declared an independent state called the Republic of Ambazonia. Since then, there has been continuous fighting between the Cameroonian army and various groups of poorly armed separatists.

What is likely to leave a lasting impression and hamper the search for a durable solution to keep the country unified is the nature of the military operation in the anglophone regions. Reports by human rights organisations indicate that security forces have been responsible for the destruction of homes and other property; for example, some estimate that more than three hundred villages were burnt to punish local populations perceived as supporting the separatists.[62] Security forces have also been accused by rights groups of indiscriminate arrests, torture, extrajudicial killings, forced disappearances, and inhumane treatment of detainees, including rape, sexual assault, and sexual exploitation. Armed separatist groups which have tried to enforce a school boycott since 2016 as well as numerous lockdowns have been accused of the assassination of government officials, kidnappings, and attacks on schools and teachers. Nevertheless, there is no moral equivalence between their actions and those of the government forces. The military operations by the government and the crimes committed in the process are disproportionate in force, duration, effect, and reach. They have led to a humanitarian crisis in which more than 20,000 anglophones, including children, the elderly, and persons with disabilities, are believed to have been killed, with many burnt to death in their homes as part of the army's scorched-earth policy. It was also estimated that more than 40,000 anglophones had fled to Nigeria and that there were over 650,000 internally displaced anglophones.

Several observations need to be made about the government's handling of this crisis. Firstly, the number of atrocities the army has committed lends credence to the suggestion that its actions qualify as genocide or crimes against humanity.[63] In one atrocity that attracted international condemnation, Human Rights Watch reported that government forces and an armed local group supported by them killed at least twenty-one civilians, including thirteen children and a pregnant woman, in Ngarbuh village in the North West Region.[64] They also burned five homes, pillaged scores of other properties, and beat residents. Some of the bodies of the victims were found burnt inside their homes. As usual, the

[62] See, for example, 'English-Speaking Villages Are Burning in Cameroon' *The Economist* (Buea, 7 November 2019) https://www.economist.com/middle-east-and-africa/2019/11/07/english-speaking-villages-are-burning-in-cameroon (last accessed 20 November 2022); Atia Azohnwi, 'Cameroon—Anglophone Crisis: 206 Villages Burnt in North West, South West Regions since 2017' (24 May 2019) http://www.cameroon-info.net/article/cameroon-anglophone-crisis-206-villages-burnt-in-north-west-south-west-regions-since-2017-343365.html (last accessed 20 November 2022); Nyange (n. 41).

[63] See 'This Is a Genocide: Villages Burn as War Rages in Blood-Soaked Cameroon' *The Guardian* (30 May 2018) https://www.theguardian.com/global-development/2018/may/30/cameroon-killings-escalate-anglophone-crisis (last accessed 20 November 2022); 'Horrific Violence Escalates Further in Anglophone Regions' *Genocide Watch* (18 September 2018) https://www.genocidewatch.com/single-post/2018/09/28/Cameroon-Horrific-violence-escalates-further-in-Anglophone-regions (last accessed 20 November 2022); Azeem Ibrahim, 'Should We Worry about Genocide in Cameroon?' *AL Arabiya* (20 May 2020) https://english.alarabiya.net/en/views/news/middle-east/2019/03/18/Should-we-worry-about-genocide-in-Cameroon- (last accessed 20 November 2022).

[64] 'Cameroon: Civilians Massacred in Separatist Area' *Human Rights Watch* (25 February 2020) https://www.hrw.org/news/2020/02/25/cameroon-civilians-massacred-separatist-area (last accessed 20 November 2022).

government denied any involvement and promised to investigate the incident, but a few days later, Mallam Danjuma, the young man who informed the world about the atrocities, was picked up by the army and tortured to death.[65]

What more evidence is needed to confirm the views of many anglophones that there is a deliberate government policy to displace anglophones from their homeland as part of the grand project of total assimilation? In spite of the international condemnation that followed the atrocities in Ngarbuh, there have been many other such incidents, with the government simply intensifying its military operations in the two regions.[66] It is not surprising that General René Claude Meka, the commander of the Joint Chiefs of Staff, declared that 'all the Ambazonia gangsters will be exterminated. Everything's in place to eradicate the roaches'.[67]

Military operations against anglophones have extended beyond the territory of the two regions. There have been reports that security forces conduct regular checks in those neighbourhoods in the francophone major cities, such as Douala and Yaoundé, where anglophones are found in large numbers and where those internally displaced by the war have taken refuge. Their documents are often checked, and many of them are regularly arrested, detained, and released with no reasons being given.

Secondly, nothing signals the extremes to which the regime is prepared to go in order to silence anglophones more than the abduction, with the complicity of Nigeria, of 47 Cameroonian activists residing in Nigeria in January 2018, including the 'interim president' of the 'Republic of Ambazonia' and members of his cabinet. This group was illegally arrested in Nigeria, in violation of international laws regarding the treatment of aliens and refugees, and extradited to Cameroon. After being held incommunicado for several months, they were eventually allowed to meet lawyers after pressure from the International Committee of the Red Cross. The detention of this group and thousands of other anglophone activists caused many anglophones, especially those in the diaspora in countries such as the UK, the US, Germany, and South Africa, to mobilise resources to support the armed groups that had begun to attack the security forces. It was only in August 2019 that the 'interim president' of Ambazonia, Dr Julius Ayuk Tabe (Sisiku), and nine others were tried in what many regard as a sham trial before a military tribunal, convicted of secession, terrorism, and hostility towards the state, and sentenced to life imprisonment.[68] To complete what was at best a farcical trial, the court fined the ten the absurd sum of CFA 250 billion francs (about USD 350 million or GBP 286 million). To maintain the climate of fear, intimidation, and oppression against the anglophones, many other activists have been sentenced by the military court to long terms of imprisonment, though nobody knows exactly how many more activists are in detention, where they are being detained, and how many of them have died in

[65] See 'Cameroon: Alleged Eye Witness of the Ngarbuh Killings Murdered in Bui' *Journal du Cameroun.com* (2 March 2020) https://www.journalducameroun.com/en/cameroon-alleged-eye-witness-of-ngarbuh-killings-murdered-in-bui/ (last accessed 20 November 2022).

[66] At the time of the Ngarbuh massacres, about 481 similar incidents had been reported.

[67] See Linda Akwangse, 'All Amba Gangsters Will Be Wiped Out! Says Army General Rene Claude Meka' (29 July 2020) http://www.cameroon-info.net/article/cameroon-anglophone-crisis-all-amba-gangsters-terrorists-will-be-wiped-out-general-rene-348861.html (last accessed 20 November 2022).

[68] See Ruth McClean and Brenda Kiven, 'Cameroon Anglophone Separatist Leader Handed Life Sentence' *The Guardian* (Douala, 20 August 2019)
https://www.theguardian.com/world/2019/aug/20/cameroon-anglophone-separatist-leader-ayuk-tabe-handed-life-sentence (last accessed 20 November 2022).

detention.[69] To underline the desperation of the government, despite its success in Nigeria, it has failed in its numerous attempts to exert bilateral pressure on several countries to take legal action against Cameroonian anglophones living in their territories who support opposition groups in the anglophone regions.[70]

Thirdly, in September 2019, the government finally gave in to relentless international pressure to negotiate with the anglophone leaders. The agenda for the dialogue was predetermined by the government and, when the meeting took place, the government did not involve any of the separatist leaders, many of whom were in prison or in the diaspora, nor did it invite the moderate anglophones who support federalism. Only those anglophones who support the unitarist state agenda were involved. At the end of the dialogue on 5 October 2019, the main proposals included the

- adoption of a special status for the two anglophone regions;
- restoration of the House of Traditional Chiefs;
- election of local governors;
- immediate relaunch of certain airport and seaport projects in the two regions;
- rapid integration of ex-combatants into society;
- restoration of the country's former name, the United Republic of Cameroon; and
- implementation of the law that government officials declare their assets, in order to tackle corruption.

Although a special session of Parliament in 2019 passed a bill granting the two anglophone regions a special status, this has had no impact on the francophone-anglophone conflict. Most anglophones regarded the dialogue as a 'non-event', and even most international observers agree that the government has done little to nothing to deal with the core grievances of the anglophones.[71] In the full glare of the international community, the Biya government displayed its unwillingness to see the anglophone problem for what it is. There has therefore been no serious or genuine attempt by the government to engage key anglophone leaders in resolving this conflict due to its blind and misguided belief in military victory. This was not the first time Biya had an opportunity to resolve this long-festering problem but missed it. The other occasion was when, again under national and international pressure, he decided to set up a committee to revise the 1972 Constitution. It is an issue which is discussed below.

A final point to be noted has to do with the character of the two leaders who led Cameroon into the quagmire in which it finds itself today. Ahidjo, through the creation of a highly effective and much-feared repressive machinery, ensured that threats to his authority were

[69] For an indication of the numerous separatist and militia groups fighting government forces in the North West and South West regions, see UK Home Office (n. 36) 56.

[70] See United States Department of State, '2019 Country Reports on Human Rights Practices: Cameroon' https://www.state.gov/reports/2019-country-reports-on-human-rights-practices/cameroon/ (last accessed 20 November 2022).

[71] See, for example, International Crisis Group, 'Cameroon's Anglophone Dialogue: A Work in Progress' *International Crisis Group* (26 September 2019) https://www.crisisgroup.org/africa/central-africa/cameroon/cameroons-anglophone-dialogue-work-progress (last accessed 20 November 2022); Josiane Kouagheu, 'Cameroon Peace Talks Falter as Separatists, Politicians Boycott' *Reuters* (Yaounde, 30 September 2019) https://www.reuters.com/article/us-cameroon-separatists-dialogue/cameroon-peace-talks-falter-as-separatists-politicians-boycott-idUSKBN1WF1NZ (last accessed 20 November 2022).

all but eliminated during a reign that lasted until he resigned voluntarily in 1982. He often declared that he stood between Cameroon and bloody civil war—a common argument also made by his contemporaries, to the effect that Africans had to choose between authoritarian government and anarchy.[72] But for all his authoritarianism, Ahidjo is considered by many analysts to have been a shrewd pragmatist who managed not only to maintain peace but ensure a measure of social and economic prosperity that made Cameroon the envy of its neighbours. In this vein, Williard Johnson, quite prematurely and without cogent evidence, was able to suggest in 1980 that Cameroon had 'made great strides in achieving a sense of common Cameroonian nationality among its diverse peoples'.[73] The views of another eminent scholar on Cameroon, Le Vine, are also worth noting:

> [I]t was Ahidjo's tactics that made the difference in the final analysis. He treated his opponents firmly, sometimes harshly, but made sure that even his bitterest enemies had both the chance of joining his side and actively sharing in the perquisites of power. That he was never vindictive is to his credit. The style of the regime appears to have been actively reconciliationist, pragmatic and tactically consistent.[74]

Ahidjo, never wanting to be overshadowed, carefully selected his successor. Unlike Ahidjo, Biya adopted a management style that allowed little participation in the spoils system outside his own Beti ethnic group and its close affiliates in, from, and around the Centre, South, and East provinces who, although constituting less than 25 per cent of the population, occupy most of the senior positions in the administration, the military, and parastatals. To a large extent, he pursued the same methods and policies as his predecessor, that is, centralisation, co-option, coalition-building, and repression.

However, he has lacked the political acumen of Ahidjo. Biya's longevity in power has astonished his early critics, given that what has been confirmed throughout his four decades in office is his reputation as a weak, indecisive leader, something which Ahidjo himself admitted to knowing in the many interviews he gave after leaving power, especially after the failed 1984 coup.[75] Evidence of this appeared in early diplomatic intelligence reports assessing Biya's ability.[76] This explains why Biya is perceived as a hostage to a hard-line ethnic clique determined to hold on to power at all costs. It is thus no surprise that this lacklustre leader has been described as an 'absentee president', one leaving most of the self-serving extremists who surround him to run the country.[77] To this clique, and the francophone elites

[72] Derrick (n. 40) 165.

[73] See his chapter in Kofele-Kale (n. 5).

[74] Le Vine 1971 (n. 4). In fact, Milton Krieger, 'Cameroon's Democratic Crossroads, 1990–94' (1994) 32(4) *Journal of Modern African Studies* 605, 606 points out that, for all his authoritarianism and 'selective' repression, President Ahidjo demonstrated good negotiating skills with local elites and good marketing skills abroad.

[75] Like most people with such a temperament, Biya has never hesitated to resort to military force, even in situations where a little bit of negotiation could have solved the problem. This often has led him to overreact to even the least threat to his authority.

[76] See, for example, the redacted Central Intelligence Agency (CIA) report, 'Cameroon: Challenges to Biya's Leadership. An Intelligence Report' (December 1984) https://www.cia.gov/library/readingroom/docs/CIA-RDP85S00317R000300120003-2.pdf (last accessed 20 November 2022) which, as early as 1984, pointed out that Biya's 'instincts and talents . . . for firm leadership remain in doubt'. It adds that there were doubts about 'Biya's ability to establish his credibility as a leader and reshape the country's political institutions'.

[77] 'Paul Biya: Cameroon's Absentee President' *BBC News* (5 October 2018) https://www.bbc.com/news/world-africa-43469758 (last accessed 20 November 2022).

from other regions who have been co-opted to share in the spoils of a profoundly corrupt system, the anglophone issue is a nuisance that must be suppressed at all costs. This leaves us with one major question, to which we now turn.

6. Is Anglophone Identity Compatible with a Cameroonian Constitutional Identity?

The unilateral abrogation of the federal constitution in 1972 destroyed not only the basis on which the British Southern Cameroons and then Republic of Cameroon united, but also any sense of identification by the former with what emerged from the ashes of that union. This is in line with the principle that you cannot destroy what you purport to amend or modify and still call the process one of amending or modifying a constitution. Constitutions are living things that must necessarily evolve with time and change in circumstance.[78] In the process, they must retain their identity. For constitutional change to retain the constitution's identity, such changes must reflect societal consensus on, and strive to establish, the principles, rules, structures, and institutions that best reflect the aspirations, desires, hopes as well as the fears and needs of the people. This did not happen with the fundamental constitutional change of 1972.

An opportunity came in the mid-1990s to correct this. After the protests and demonstrations of the early 1990s and calls for a revision of the 1972 Constitution, particularly by the anglophone community, a new constitution was adopted—or, more accurately, imposed—by the Biya regime. The process of making this constitution gave Biya another golden opportunity to incorporate the best aspects of the common law and civil law constitutional traditions in a new constitutional dispensation that would move the country away from an authoritarian system that had become all the more repressive as he entrenched himself in power. Since an authoritarian regime is by definition inadequately restrained by a constitution having the force of a supreme and overriding law, a genuine transition from authoritarianism to constitutional democracy would perforce require a fundamental constitutional change.[79] Unfortunately, the opportunity for this was squandered, providing fertile ground for the conflict that has engulfed the nation. The crisis of constitutional identity in Cameroon results not just from a flawed framework that negates the essentials of constitutionalism, but from its failure to reflect the unique histories and circumstances of the two countries that unified with each other.

Firstly, going against the grain of post-1990 constitutional developments on the continent, Biya imposed, and Cameroonians adopted, a constitution which is the very negation of constitutionalism. From a comparative African constitutional law perspective, only the Eritrean 1992 Constitution is more retrogressive. Secondly, as a result of this constitution, legal avenues for anglophones to find their lost sense of constitutional self-identification as anglophones and Cameroonians were blocked.

[78] See Charles A. Beard, 'The Living Constitution' (1936) *185*(1) *Annals of the American Academy of Political and Social Science* 29; Scott Dobson, 'A Darwinist View of the Living Constitution' (2008) *61*(5) *Vanderbilt Law Review* 1319.

[79] Ben Nwabueze, *Democratisation* (Spectrum Law Publishing 1993) 80.

6.1 A Constitutional System Negating the Fundamentals of Constitutionalism

A constitution that does not entrench the fundamental principles of modern constitutionalism is as good as no constitution at all. In this regard, modern constitutionalism dictates that a constitution should establish a system of governance in which the government is not only limited in a way that protects its citizens from arbitrary rule, but also that such a government is able to operate efficiently and in such a manner that it can be effectively compelled to operate within its constitutional limitations. In other words, constitutionalism combines the idea of a government limited in its action and accountable to its citizens for its actions. It encompasses two critical dimensions: firstly, the existence of certain limitations imposed on the state, particularly in its relations with citizens, based on a clearly defined set of values; and, secondly, the existence of a clearly defined mechanism for ensuring that limitations on the government are legally enforceable. At least six core elements are critical for enhancing the prospects of constitutionalism in any constitution. These are provisions that recognise, entrench, and protect fundamental human rights; the separation of powers; judicial independence; checks against arbitrary amendment of the constitution; judicial review; and institutions to support and sustain democracy. What matters is the implementation of these core elements in a way that promotes not just constitutionalism but respect for the rule of law and good governance.

Judged by these core minimum requirements for promoting constitutionalism, the 1996 Constitution did no more than obfuscate, consolidate, and reinforce the pre-existing authoritarian system provided for under the 1972 Constitution. Although it made provision, for the first time since 1966, for multi-party elections, it has merely allowed opposition parties to participate in elections they have no chance of ever winning. This explains why, although an anglophone, the founding leader of the main opposition Social Democratic Front (SDF) was widely considered to have won the 1992 presidential elections. Paul Biya, with French support, was able to declare himself the winner.[80] In fact, the prospects for constitutionalism, good governance, accountability, and democracy have been substantially compromised by this constitution in several ways.

Firstly, the few references to human rights appear only in the preamble to the Constitution. Although article 65 states that the preamble is 'part and parcel' of the Constitution, the vague and hortatory language in which these few rights are formulated do not make them justiciable. Secondly, the separation of powers and judicial independence are substantially compromised by several provisions that render these two important branches subservient to the president. For example, although the High Council of Magistracy makes decisions on judicial appointments, promotions, and transfers, this is an illusion because it is the president himself who convenes and presides over this body. As if this were not enough, the body only has powers, according to article 37(3) of the Constitution, to 'give its opinion', to the president! The absence of an effective system of judicial review as well as institutions that can hold the president accountable effectively places him above, rather than as subject to the Constitution.

[80] This is discussed in Charles M. Fombad and Jonie Fonyam, 'The Social Democratic Front: The Opposition and the Transition' in John M. Mbaku and Joseph Takougang (eds.), *The Leadership Challenge in Africa: Cameroon under Paul Biya* (Africa World Press 2004) 453.

Thirdly, besides the judiciary, most key institutions, such as the public services, security forces, and regional and divisional administration, are under the control of the president. He can rule by decree and violate the Constitution with impunity since there is no credible mechanism in place to hold him in check. For example, because some of the 'new' institutions that were introduced in the 1996 Constitution were established only more than a decade or two later, it was unclear whether Cameroon was being governed under the 1972 or 1996 constitution. An example is the Constitutional Council provided for in this new constitution—it was established only twenty-two years later in 2018.

Finally, Cameroon is by all standards one of the most centralised and dysfunctional systems in the world. Almost everything is run from the presidency. During the stage-managed discussions that led to this constitution, the anglophones submitted elaborate proposals for a federal constitution, but these were rejected out of hand. As a result, the delegation walked out of the proceedings. The response to persistent anglophone demands for a return to the federal system was the introduction of elaborate but vaguely worded provisions on an obscure system of decentralisation. On close analysis, these provisions basically do no more than decentralise an authoritarian, corrupt, and repressive system or, put simply, decentralise despotism.[81]

6.2 The Compatibility of Anglophone Identity with Cameroonian Constitutional Identity

At the heart of the Cameroonian political crisis is the inability of the ruling elites to create an inclusive Cameroonian national identity that integrates, amongst other things, the two dominant but distinct anglophone and francophone identities in a manner paving the way for a common Cameroonian constitutional identity to emerge. Most of the literature on constitutional identity affirms the fundamental principle that constitutional identity arises from a process characterised by the reconciliation and preservation of the different identities, conflicts, and tensions within the country. As Michel Rosenfeld puts it, '[C]onstitutional identity is determined by the need for dialectical mediation of existing, evolving, and projected conflicts and tensions between identity and difference.'[82] A constitutional identity which is perceived as contrived and imposed and that makes no effort at building a collective sense of self-identity from common and divergent identities, especially in a complex society like Cameroon, is unlikely to secure general acceptance and legitimacy.

As noted, the era of German colonial rule that brought different ethnic groups into one country lasted for only thirty-two years and hardly created any sense of a common Cameroonian identity among these groups. A greater sense of self-identification emerged during separate British and French colonial rule, which lasted for forty-six years.[83] At the time of reunification in 1961, it was clear that in spite of the numerous ethnic groups, two distinct communities, each with heavy colonial baggage, were coming together. After

[81] See Charles M. Fombad, 'Cameroon and the Anomalies of Decentralisation with a Centralist Mindset' in Charles M. Fombad and Nico Steytler (eds.), *Decentralisation and Constitutionalism in Africa* (Oxford University Press 2019) 326–64.

[82] Michel Rosenfeld, 'Constitutional Identity' in Michel Rosenfeld and András Sajó (eds.), *The Oxford Handbook of Comparative Constitutional Law* (Oxford University Press 2012) 761.

[83] Or even longer in the case of the anglophone association with the British (see n. 5).

almost sixty years of the union, there are serious questions as to whether one can detect any sense of a common destiny or identity between the two communities, or more precisely, between the anglophone and francophone ways of living.

All the evidence points to a forced union in which the dominant francophone majority from the very start in 1961 worked on the patently false premise that all that had happened was that part of their territory was being returned to them and not that two separate communities had entered into a voluntary federal union. This explains why, within a few months of what was assumed to be a union amongst equals, the dominant francophone elites embarked on a process of deconstructing the anglophone identity and replacing it with a francophone, let alone a Cameroonian, identity. Using slogans such as 'national integration', 'national unity', and 'harmonisation' as ideological justification, they have tried to 'francophonise' the anglophones and eliminate all traces of their British inheritance. The past sixty years can therefore be described as a period of the anglophones' struggle, firstly, to retain their distinct identity; secondly, to prevent its destruction; thirdly, to resist the imposition on them of an alien identity; and finally, to gain acceptance as anglophones and Cameroonians.

The struggle for the preservation of anglophone identity has been resisted by the dominant francophone elites not only by legal and illegal means, but more recently through the full, coercive, and violent force of the army that has been unleashed on a largely defenceless population in the North West and South West regions. There is no doubt that the imposition of a unitary state from 1972 was a flagrant violation of the 1961 Constitution that destroyed the basis on which the two distinct communities had come together. These are profound changes that the anglophones repeatedly and consistently petitioned against, only to have been ignored by Ahidjo and Biya's governments.

The plight of anglophones is worsened by the fact that what has been imposed on them and the rest of the ordinary citizens is a harsh, repressive, and autocratic system that is the very negation of the fundamental tenets of constitutionalism. In fact, the only other countries in Africa where authoritarianism has been constitutionally legitimised on this scale are Eritrea and Eswatini. In describing the anomalous situation in which anglophones find themselves in Cameroon, one prominent anglophone journalist, Victor Epie Ngome, famously described it thus: 'they [i.e. the ruling Francophone elites] keep you forcibly in the nation but kill the nation in you'.[84]

The two communities differ fundamentally in many respects—in colonial history and cultural baggage in regard to matters such as legal and education system, world view, and, perhaps most importantly, constitutional tradition and system of governance. Most historical accounts of the union of the two Cameroons show that the danger signs were as clearly visible at the outset as they are today. For example, Lord Thompson, a British member of parliament, expressed his concerns in August 1961 thus:

> There can be no doubt that given the difficulties facing the two countries, with different systems of administration and different languages, federation is the only practical system, certainly in the interests of Southern Cameroonians. But there is no clarity as to how far this is a definite commitment from the Republic of Cameroon.[85]

[84] Cited in Konings and Nyamnjoh (n. 19) 127.
[85] Ibid. 41.

The international community, and particularly the British, did little to protect the anglophones, given that it was a trust territory administered under the auspices of the UN, when compared to the francophones who were advised by French experts throughout the negotiations leading to the unification. In spite of the awareness that a federal arrangement was the best way to keep the two communities together, the international community has watched with indifference at the effective recolonisation of the anglophone regions by the dominant francophone regime. This is exemplified by the muted international reaction to atrocities committed in anglophone regions by the ill-disciplined Cameroonian army.[86]

It therefore seems that the Cameroonian government has affirmed through its declarations and actions that an anglophone identity is incompatible with a Cameroonian constitutional identity. A change in the status quo is imperative; the manner and direction of the change will determine the future of the country. The enduring wisdom found in the words of two great American presidents is of some relevance. The first is Abraham Lincoln:

> This country . . . belongs to the people who inhabit it [and one could add, 'and not its rulers and elites']. Whenever they should grow weary of the existing government, they can exercise their constitutional right of amending it, or their revolutionary right to dismember or overthrow it.[87]

The other immortal words are those of John F. Kennedy: 'Those who make peaceful revolution impossible will make violent revolution inevitable.'[88]

Three options are possible in dealing with Cameroon's political crisis. Firstly, if the government persists in its current hard-line militarist policy, the militant groups fighting for secession will continue to win support. The case for separation of the two communities is strong. Azevedo's assertion in 1984 that Cameroon is 'two different countries in one' is as true today, if not more so, as it was four decades ago.[89] Neither the Ahidjo nor Biya government have done anything to prove to the anglophones that there are benefits to continued association with the francophones. The unreasonable refusal for the past sixty years to acknowledge anglophone grievances has emboldened desperate young people who experience nothing but exclusion to risk their lives and take up traditional hunting rifles to fight an army equipped with modern weapons and strike back at a government they see as alien to them.

A second option is the return to the two-state federation. This is nothing short of a return to legality and, in a sense, a return to the road along which a Cameroonian constitutional identity can evolve with time. Well thought-out and reasonable proposals as to what a new federal framework could look like were submitted to the government before it imposed the

86 The international community's indifference to what is unfolding in Cameroon is, in the aftermath of the Rwanda genocide, shocking. While the AU's approach has been 'see no evil, hear no evil', the silence of the rest of the international community, especially the British, French, and Chinese, is motivated by a desire to exploit the country's natural and mineral resources by taking advantage of a weak, incompetent, and absentee dictator whose only interest is in holding on to power. See Willis et al. (n. 45).

87 Abraham Lincoln, 'Inaugural Address' in Donald P. Kommers, John E. Finn. and Gary J. Jacobsohn, *American Constitutional Law: Cases and Comparative Notes* (Rowman & Littlefield 2004), 1050.

88 See John F. Kennedy, 'Berkley Poster Collection' (University of British Columbia Library 1973) https://open.library.ubc.ca/collections/berkpost/items/1.0001355 (last accessed 20 November 2022).

89 Mario J. Azevedo (ed.), *Cameroon and Its National Character* (EUGA 1984), 5.

1996 Constitution. The government has consistently equated federalism with secession, but it is the only means by which the union can be saved.

The third option is to perpetuate the current decentralised framework, which has been embellished with Law 2019/024 to Institute the General Code of Regional and Local Authorities—this law supposedly grants the North West and South West regions a special autonomous status. As noted before, the 1996 Constitution does nothing other than reinforce the existing authoritarian and repressive system. Any process of decentralisation under its weak framework serves only to decentralise a totalitarian system of governance, with there being scant prospect that any of the core elements of constitutionalism will be respected. The present centralised and dysfunctional unitary system is the least desirable of the three options, yet it is the one the government is stubbornly holding on to. It is difficult to see how a system whose philosophy is to persecute any anglophone who disagrees with its policies and label him or her a 'terrorist' could ever earn the trust of the people it is meant to serve. How could anglophones, who, as mentioned, are referred to with contempt as 'slaves', 'cockroaches', 'rats', and 'dogs', be expected to consent to live under a system that dehumanises them?[90]

The misguided attempts by a government that operates without regard for the rule of law or principles of constitutionalism to impose homogeneity by brute force poses an existential threat to the country. Cameroon stands prominent among those African countries which have refused to look beyond their inherited Gaullist centralism and adapt a constitutional framework reflective of their diverse heritage. It has, in short, refused to wean itself from the autocratic tradition of the French Fifth Republic and carve out its own constitutional identity.

7. Conclusion

The repressive unitary system in Cameroon today negates the defining political commitment of the 1961 constitutional order that brought anglophones into a union with francophones. The crisis in the country raises serious questions about the ability of Africans in the twenty-first century to rise above their colonised mindsets and design institutions that are effective in addressing their most pressing, recurrent governance challenges and other impediments to progress. Cameroon is the perfect laboratory where such a development could have taken place—one extracting the best of the British common law and French civil law traditions and combining them with elements of traditional culture to form a system uniquely suited to the country's circumstances. Unlike most African states, Cameroon has had to grapple not only with ethnic, religious, cultural, and linguistic diversity but also with the more serious problem of having, within the same state, two distinct communities with contrasting legacies and worldviews. The 1961 federal Constitution, in spite of its flaws, at least allowed these two communities to retain their distinctive identities within a union that held out the prospect of evolution towards a common Cameroonian constitutional identity.

As pre-commitment devices, constitutions should stand like mirrors reflecting their societies in all their complexity. From this perspective, the federal constitution was a reflection of two communities and should have provided a solid foundation for unity in diversity.

[90] See Willis et al. (n. 45) 22–3.

However, it was dismantled illegally and a unitary system of governance was imposed in its place. In other words, rather than seizing the opportunity to devise a creative solution for fashioning the two traditions into a unique system, the dominant francophone majority opted for the much cruder route of simply imposing a unitary system on the anglophone minority.

As we have seen, the sixty years during which Cameroon has been 'reunified' have been marked by systematic efforts to de-identify anglophones through marginalisation, discrimination, and economic disenfranchisement. Throughout this period, anglophones have resisted attempts, some subtle and others involving force and intimidation, to 'francophonise' them and eliminate those aspects of their history and culture that they treasure. The last straw was the attempt to impose francophone teachers on anglophone children in English primary and secondary schools, and the appointment to the two regions of numerous francophone judges and state prosecutors who had no knowledge of the common law system. All this occurred at a time of unemployment among anglophone youths, many of whom had university educations but little prospect of employment even in their own part of the country. Faced with a state and government that was hardly representative of them, was repressive, sought to impose an alien culture on them, and appointed disdainful francophones to run most affairs in the North West and South West regions, it was inevitable that the people would react as they finally did.

Since the demise of the federation in 1972, anglophones have clamoured for its return. In a recent interview, Cardinal Christian Tumi opined that 'many think if we had remained faithful to the Federal Republic of Cameroon, we would not have had the problems we have now'.[91] There is no doubt that only a federal constitution can provide the foundation for a common constitutional identity that incorporates elements of what the two communities hold dear, cherish, and wish to retain. It is also only such a federal framework that will provide space for the creative thinking that is needed to adopt a long-lasting solution to political problems that have been festering for so long. Constitutional identity cannot be imposed, particularly in a complex society like Cameroon where competing identities are at stake. It must be developed by a societal consensus that reconciles the past with the present, and fully takes account of, and reconciles, the diverse interests, aspirations, fears, and concerns of all the different sectors of the community. Most anglophones believe that only a return to a federal system would enable them to retain their identity, regain their self-confidence, and start the process of developing their community. The alternative is either secession or continued association with a stifling unitary system that lacks any of the minimum protection provided in a governance system based on the principles of constitutionalism, the rule of law, and democracy.

Cameroon's constitutional identity crisis cannot be wished away, nor will it be solved by the government's pretending that it does not exist and trying to mis-frame it to suit its own agenda. As Jacobsohn has observed, 'the future of constitutional identity is inscribed in its past'.[92] A constitution is a precious artefact that should not be destroyed at the whim of opportunistic politicians who put their interests above those of the country, as has been the case in Cameroon. Given that the 1996 Constitution fails to incorporate the core elements of modern constitutionalism, it is difficult to see the basis for any meaningful interaction

[91] Cited in UK Home Office (n. 36) 15.
[92] Jacobsohn (n. 3) 396.

that would resolve the country's problems. Neither anglophones nor any other group should have to sacrifice their distinct identity and culture in order to enable the government to impose what it considers as the country's constitutional identity. Governments must manage identity issues, especially those concerning the constitution, in a manner that addresses the legitimate needs and aspirations of all groups within the country. It is such group identity that lays the foundation for the emergence, growth, and consolidation of a constitutional identity over time.

At the end of the day, the political stability needed to promote peace, security, and development in Cameroon can take root only within the framework of a constitution that promotes the fundamental principles of constitutionalism while taking full account of the country's past history and the need to allow the anglophone community to express their group identity within the national collective identity.

Bibliography

Ahidjo A., *Contribution to National Construction* (Présence Africaine 1964)

Akwangse L., 'All Amba Gangsters Will Be Wiped Out!' Says Army General Rene Claude Meka' (29 July 2020) http://www.cameroon-info.net/article/cameroon-anglophone-crisis-all-amba-gangsters-terrorists-will-be-wiped-out-general-rene-348861.html (last accessed 20 November 2022)

Anyangwe C., *Imperialistic Politics in Cameroon: Resistance and the Inception of the Restoration of the Statehood of Southern Cameroons* (Langaa Research and Publishing Common Initiative Group (RPCIG) 2008)

Anyangwe C., *Betrayal of Too Trusting a People: The UN, the UK and the Trust Territory of the Southern Cameroons* (Langaa RPCIG 2009)

Ardener E., 'The Nature of the Reunification of Cameroon' in Hazelwood A. (ed.), *African Integration and Disintegration: Case Studies in Economic and Political Union* (Oxford University Press 1967) 293

Ardener E., *Eyewitness to the Annexation of Cameroon* (Government Printer 1968)

Azevedo M.J. (ed.), *Cameroon and Its National Character* (EUGA 1984)

Azevedo M.J. *Cameroon and Chad in Historical Contemporary Perspectives* (E Mellen Press 1988)

Azohnwi A., 'Cameroon—Anglophone Crisis: 206 Villages Burnt in North West, South West Regions since 2017' (24 May 2019) http://www.cameroon-info.net/article/cameroon-anglophone-crisis-206-villages-burnt-in-north-west-south-west-regions-since-2017-343365.html (last accessed 20 November 2022)

Bayart J.F., 'The Political System' in Joseph R. (ed.), *Gaullist Africa: Cameroon under Ahmadou Ahidjo* (Fourth Dimension Publishing 1968) 45

Bayart J.F., 'The Neutralisation of Anglophone Cameroon' in Joseph R. (ed.), *Gaullist Africa: Cameroon under Ahmadou Ahidjo* (Fourth Dimension 1978) 82

Bayart J.F., 'L'Etat au Cameroun' (1979) *Outre-Mers Revue d'Histoire* 484

Beard C.A., 'The Living Constitution' (1936) *185*(1) *Annals of the American Academy of Political and Social Science* 29

Benjamin J., 'Dix Ans de Fédéralisme Camerounais 1961–1970' in Serbyn R. (ed.), *Fédéralisme et Nations* (Les Presses de L'Université du Québec 1971) 279

Benjamin J., *Les Camerounais Occidentaux: La Minorité dans un état Bicommunautaire* (Les Presses de L'Université Montréal 1972)

Biya P., *Communal Liberalism* (Macmillan 1987)

Björnson R., *The African Quest for Freedom and Identity: Cameroon Writing and the National Experience* (1st edn, Indiana University Press 1991)

Brownlie I., *African Boundaries: A Legal and Diplomatic Encyclopaedia* (Hurst & Co 1919)

'Cameroon: Civilians Massacred in Separatist Area' *Human Rights Watch* (25 February 2020) https://www.hrw.org/news/2020/02/25/cameroon-civilians-massacred-separatist-area (last accessed 20 November 2022)

'Cameroon: Alleged Eye Witness of the Ngarbuh Killings Murdered in Bui' Journal du Cameroun.com (2 March 2020) https://www.journalducameroun.com/en/cameroon-alleged-eye-witness-of-ngarbuh-killings-murdered-in-bui/ (last accessed 20 November 2022)

Central Intelligence Agency, 'Cameroon: Challenges to Biya's Leadership: An Intelligence Report' (December 1984) https://www.cia.gov/library/readingroom/docs/CIA-RDP85S00317R000300120003-2.pdf (last accessed 20 November 2022)

Choudhry S., Khosla M., and Mehta P.B., *The Oxford Handbook of the Indian Constitution* (Oxford University Press 2016)

Davis M.C., 'The Case for Chinese Federalism' (1999) *10*(2) *Journal of Democracy* 124

De Lancey M., *Cameroon Dependence and Independence* (1st edn, Westview Press 1989)

Derrick J., 'Cameroon: One Party, Many Parties and the State' (1992) *22*(3) *African Insight* 165

Dickerson C.M. (ed.), *Unified Business Laws for Africa: Common-Law Perspectives on OHADA* (GMB 2009).

Dobson S., 'A Darwinist View of the Living Constitution' (2008) *61*(5) *Vanderbilt Law Review* 1319

'English-Speaking Villages are Burning in Cameroon' *The Economist* (Buea, 7 November 2019) https://www.economist.com/middle-east-and-africa/2019/11/07/english-speaking-villages-are-burning-in-cameroon (last accessed 20 November 2022)

Enonchong H.N.A., *Cameroon Constitutional Law: Federalism in a Mixed Common Law and Civil Law System* (Centre d'Edition et de Production de Manuels et Auxiliaires de L'enseignement 1967)

Eyoh D., 'Conflicting Narratives of Anglophone Protest and the Politics of Identity in Cameroon' (1998) *16 Journal of Contemporary African Studies* 249

Fofung A., 'Cameroon: From Biya, a Mea Culpa on the Anglophone Crisis in Paris' (12 November 2019) https://panafricanvisions.com/2019/11/cameroon-from-biya-a-mea-culpa-on-the-anglophone-crisis-in-paris/ (last accessed 20 November 2022)

Fombad C.M., 'The Scope for Uniform National Laws in Cameroon' (1991) *29*(3) *Journal of Modern African Studies* 443

Fombad C.M., 'An Experiment in Legal Pluralism: The Cameroonian Bi-Jural/Uni-Jural Imbroglio' (1997) *16 University of Tasmania Law Review* 209

Fombad C.M., 'Cameroonian Bi-Juralism: Current Challenges and Future Prospects' (1999) 5 Fundamina Journal of Legal History 22

Fombad C.M., 'Endemic Corruption in Cameroon: Insights on Consequences and Control' in Hope R. and Chikulo B. (eds.), *Corruption and Development in Africa: Lessons from Country Case Studies* (Palgrave Macmillan 2000) 234

Fombad C.M., 'The Dynamics of Record-Breaking Corruption and Political Opportunism in Cameroon' in Mbaku J.M. and Takougang J. (eds.), *The Leadership Challenge in Africa: Cameroon under Paul Biya* (Africa World Press 2003) 357

Fombad C.M., 'Cameroon and the Anomalies of Decentralisation with a Centralist Mindset' in Fombad C.M. and Steytler N. (eds.), *Decentralisation and Constitutionalism in Africa* (Oxford University Press 2019) 326

Fombad C.M. and Fonyam J., 'The Social Democratic Front: The Opposition and the Transition' in Mbaku J.M. and Takougang J. (eds.), *The Leadership Challenge in Africa: Cameroon under Paul Biya* (Africa World Press 2004) 453

Gardiner D.E., *Cameroon: United Nations Challenge to French Policy* (Oxford University Press 1963)

Government of the United Kingdom, 'Home Office, Country Policy and Information Note "Cameroon: Anglophones"' (29 December 2020) https://www.gov.uk/government/publications/cameroon-country-policy-and-information-notes (last accessed 20 November 2022)

Hirschl R., *Towards Juristocracy: The Origins and Consequences of the New Constitutionalism* (Harvard University Press 2004)

'Horrific Violence Escalates Further in Anglophone Regions' *Genocide Watch* (18 September 2018) https://www.genocidewatch.com/single-post/2018/09/28/Cameroon-Horrific-violence-escalates-further-in-Anglophone-regions (last accessed 20 November 2022)

Ibrahim A., 'Should We Worry about Genocide in Cameroon?' *AL Arabiya* (20 May 2020) https://english.alarabiya.net/en/views/news/middle-east/2019/03/18/Should-we-worry-about-genocide-in-Cameroon- (last accessed 20 November 2022)

International Crisis Group, 'Cameroon's Anglophone Dialogue: A Work in Progress' (26 September 2019) https://www.crisisgroup.org/africa/central-africa/cameroon/cameroons-anglophone-dialogue-work-progress (last accessed 20 November 2022)

Jacobsohn G.J., 'Constitutional Identity' (2006) *68*(3) *The Review of Politics* 361

Jacobsohn G.J., *Constitutional Identity* (Harvard University Press 2010)

Jacobsohn G.J., 'Constitutional Identity' in Choudhry S., Khosla M., and Mehta P.B. (eds), *The Oxford Handbook of the Indian Constitution* (Oxford University Press 2016) 110

Johnson W.R., 'The Cameroon Federation: Political Union between English and French Speaking Africa' in Lewis W.H. (ed.), *French-Speaking Africa* (Walker 1965) 206

Johnson W.R., *The Cameroon Federation: Political Integration in a Fragmentary Society* (Princeton University Press 1970)

Joseph R.A., *Radical Nationalism in Cameroon: Social Origins of the U.P.C. Rebellion* (Clarendon Press 1977)

Joseph R.A. (ed.), *Gaullist Africa. Cameroon under Ahmadou Ahidjo* (Fourth Dimension 1978)

Kalm G., 'Building Legal Certainty through International Law: OHADA Law in Cameroon' (2011) https://www.academia.edu/38335634/Building_Legal_Certainty_Through_International_Law_OHADA_Law_in_Cameroon (last accessed 20 November 2022)

Kennedy J.F., 'Berkley Poster Collection' (University of British Columbia Library 1973) https://open.library.ubc.ca/collections/berkpost/items/1.0001355 (last accessed 20 November 2022)

Kofele-Kale N. (ed.), *An Experiment in Nation Building: The Bilingual Cameroon Republic Since Reunification* (Westview Press 1980)

Kofele-Kale N., 'Ethnicity, Regionalism, and Political Power: A Post-Mortem of Ahidjo's Cameroon' in Shatzberg M. and Zartman I.W. (eds.), *The Political Economy of Cameroon* (Praeger 1986) 53

Konings P, 'Le Problème Anglophone au Cameroun dans les Années 1990' (1986) *62 Politiques Africaine* 25

Konings P. and Nyamnjoh B., 'The Anglophone Problem in Cameroon' (1997) *35*(2) *Journal of Modern African Studies* 207

Konings P. and Nyamnjoh F., *Negotiating an Anglophone Identity: A Study of the Politics of Recognition and Representation in Cameroon* (Brill 2003)

Kouagheu J., 'Cameroon Peace Talks Falter as Separatists, Politicians Boycott' *Reuters* (Yaounde, 30 September 2019) https://www.reuters.com/article/us-cameroon-separatists-dialogue/cameroon-peace-talks-falter-as-separatists-politicians-boycott-idUSKBN1WF1NZ (last accessed 20 November 2022)

Kouma J.C.G., 'Cameroon Fighting Boko Haram' (2017) *17*(4) *RUDN International Relations* 727

Krieger M., 'Cameroon's Democratic Crossroads, 1990–94' (1994) *32*(4) *Journal of Modern African Studies* 6005

Le Vine V.T., *The Cameroons from Mandate to Independence* (University of California Press and Cambridge University Press 1964)

Le Vine V.T., *The Cameroon Federal Republic* (Cornell University Press 1971)

Le Vine V.T., 'Political Integration, and the United Republic of Cameroon' in Smock D. and Bentsi-Enchill K. (eds.), *The Search for National Integration in Africa* (Free Press 1976) 61

Levinson S. (ed.), *Responding to Imperfection: The Theory and Practice of Constitutional Amendment* (Princeton University Press 1995)

Lincoln A., 'Inaugural Address' in Kommers D.P., Finn J.E., and Jacobsohn G.J., *American Constitutional Law: Cases and Comparative Notes* (Rowman & Littlefield 2004) 1050

Lyombe E., 'The English-Language Press and the "Anglophone Problem" in Cameroon: Group Identity, Culture and the Politics of Nostalgia' (2003) *20*(1) *Journal of Third World Studies* 79

Mbaku J.M., 'Constitutional Federalism and Policy Reform in Cameroon: Lessons for Africa' (1997) *2*(1) *Makerere Political Science Review* 20

Mbembe A., 'Epilogue: Crise de Légitimité, Restoration Autoritaire et Déliquescence de L'Etat' in Geschiere P. and Konings P. (eds.), *Pathways to Accumulation in Cameroon* (Karthala 1993) 345

McClean R. and Kiven B., 'Cameroon Anglophone Separatist Leader Handed Life Sentence' *The Guardian* (Douala, 20 August 2019) https://www.theguardian.com/world/2019/aug/20/cameroon-anglophone-separatist-leader-ayuk-tabe-handed-life-sentence (last accessed 20 November 2022)

Messmer P., *Les Blancs, s'en vont: Récits de Décolonisation* (Albin Michel 1998)

The Messenger (25 November 1993) 11

Mukong A. (ed.), *The Case for Southern Cameroons* (CAMFECO 1990)

Murphy W., 'Constitutions, Constitutionalism, and Democracy' in Greenberg D., Katz S, Oliviero M., and Wheatley S. (eds.), *Constitutionalism and Democracy: Transitions in the Contemporary World* (1st edn, Oxford University Press 1993) 3

Murphy W.F., 'Merlin's Memory: The Past and Future Imperfect of the Once and Future Polity' in Levinson S. (ed.), *Responding to Imperfection: The Theory and Practice of Constitutional Amendment* (Princeton University Press 1995) 177

Ndobegang M., 'The Anglophone Francophone Divide in Cameroon: Diagnosis of a National Disconnection' (2014) *2*(2) *International Journal of Advanced Research* 121

Nfi J.L., 'The Anglophone Identity in Cameroon 50 Years after Reunification' (2014) *2*(2) *International Journal of Advanced Research* 121

Ngoh V.J., *History of Cameroon since 1800* (Presprint 1996)

Ngoh V.J., 'The Origin of the Marginalisation of Former Southern Cameroonians (Anglophones), 1961–1966: An Historical Analysis' (1999) *16*(1) *Journal of Third World Studies* 165

Ngoh V.J., 'Dismantling the Federal System' in Ngoh V.J. (ed.), *Cameroon: From Federal to Unitary State 1961–1972* (Design House 2004) 143

Ngwane G., *The Anglophone File* (Presbook 1994)

Nwabueze B., *Democratisation* (Spectrum Law Publishing 1993)

Nyamnjoh F.B., 'Cameroon: A Country United by Ethnic Ambition and Difference' (1999) *98*(380) *African Affairs* 101

Nyange Y., 'State of Confusion' *The Tortoise Quarterly* (9 April 2020) https://bit.ly/3Uqkdid (last accessed 20 November 2022)

Olinga A.D., 'La Question Anglophone dans le Cameroun d'aujourd'hui' (1994) *48*(3) *Révue Juridique et Politique* 292

'Paul Biya: Cameroon's Absentee President' *BBC News* (London, 5 October 2018) https://www.bbc.com/news/world-africa-43469758 (last accessed 20 November 2022)

Rackley E.B., 'Cameroon's Far North: Responding to Boko Haram' (31 March 2017) https://reliefweb.int/sites/reliefweb.int/files/resources/Cameroons%20Far%20North%20-%20Responding%20to%20Boko%20Haram.pdf (last accessed 20 November 2022)

Rosenfeld M., 'Constitutional Identity' in Rosenfeld M. and Sajó A. (eds.), *The Oxford Handbook of Comparative Constitutional Law* (Oxford University Press 2012) 756

Rowlands M., 'Accumulation and the Cultural Politics of Identity in the Grassfields' in Geschiere P. and Konings P. (eds.), *Itinéraires d'Accumulation au Cameroun* (Karthala 1993) 91

Stark F., 'Federalism' in Ndiva Kofele-Kale (ed.), *An Experiment in Nation Building: The Bilingual Cameroon Republic since Reunification* (Westview Press 1980) 101

Susungi N.N., *The Crisis of Unity and Democracy in Cameroon* (N.N. Susungi 1991)

Takougang J. and Krieger M., *African State and Society in the 1990s* (Westview Press 1998)

'This Is a Genocide: Villages Burn as War Rages in Blood-Soaked Cameroon' *The Guardian* (30 May 2018) https://www.theguardian.com/global-development/2018/may/30/cameroon-killings-escalate-anglophone-crisis (last accessed 20 November 2022)

United States Department of State, '2019 Country Reports on Human Rights Practices: Cameroon' https://www.state.gov/reports/2019-country-reports-on-human-rights-practices/cameroon/ (last accessed 20 November 2022)

Willis R., Angove J., Mbinkar C., and McAuley J., 'We Remain Their Slaves: Voices from the Cameroon Conflict: A Working Paper' (Oxford University Press 2020)

Worldometer, 'Cameroon Population' (2022) https://www.worldometers.info/world-population/cameroon-population/ (last accessed 20 November 2022)

10

Taking Power from the People

Shifting Constitutional Identity in Egypt

Sherif A. Elgebeily

1. Introduction

The notion of constitutional identity is contested, with little consensus as to how it may be defined.[1] While some define constitutional identity as 'the identity of the constitution',[2] I prefer the view that a constitution's identity is a weathervane for its people, and that at least part of the struggle in defining the term 'constitutional identity' stems from the widely differing views and experiences of the people themselves. How can one realistically argue that the Constitution of the United States (US)—which was drafted more than two hundred years ago for a nation originally formed of thirteen disparate states—is analogous in its identity to that of Britain, the nation from which the US liberated itself and which has no written constitution at all? Indeed, part of the identity of the US Constitution derives from the quasi-deification of its founding fathers, the fact that it was written down, and the struggle for independence from the British. The identity of a constitution is inextricably linked in many ways to the identity of the people themselves: for each people, a constitution.

This is not to say, however, that among constitutions in general there are not commonalities, whether borrowed or shared. There are constitutional models—the German, French, British, American, Spanish, and postcolonial, to name but a few—each of which has offered different elements to countries seeking to draw on them for inspiration. David Law has distinguished at least three different 'styles' of preamble, depending on political leanings,[3] and it is not uncommon for states to borrow articles or concepts when drafting their own. South Africa, for example, drew significantly from the constitutions of other states. The section incorporating the Bill of Rights, headed by a human-dignity provision, is similar in nature to the German Constitution. Its progressive nature also owes much to the Basic Law of Germany, and its diversity of official and recognised languages is a nod to the Canadian Constitution. Yet even the choice of what to borrow (or, indeed, omit) speaks volumes about the relative weight that a nation attributes to civil and political rights, or economic, social, and cultural rights.

[1] See, for example, Monica Claes and Jan-Herman Reestman, 'The Protection of National Constitutional Identity and the Limits of European Integration at the Occasion of the Gauweiler Case' (2015) *16 German Law Journal* 917, 937; Gerhard van der Schyff, 'EU Member State Constitutional Identity: A Comparison of Germany and the Netherlands as Polar Opposites' (2016) *76 Zeitschrift Für Ausländisches Öffentliches Recht und Völkerrecht* 167.

[2] Tímea Drinóczi, 'Constitutional Identity in Europe: The Identity of the Constitution—a Regional Approach' (2020) *21 German Law Journal* 105.

[3] David Law, 'Constitutional Archetypes' (2016) *95 Texas Law Review* 153.

Sherif A. Elgebeily, *Taking Power from the People* In: *Constitutional Identity and Constitutionalism in Africa.* Edited by: Charles M. Fombad and Nico Steytler, Oxford University Press. © Sherif A. Elgebeily 2024. DOI: 10.1093/oso/9780198906308.003.0013

This chapter deals with Egypt, where identities are multiple and have been subject to both external and internal influences, and asks: What is the indigenous constitutional identity of Egypt? In its earliest constitutions, Egypt was influenced by Islamic, Ottoman, and British occupations and, as a result, their laws and codes. Cultural and societal influences can be seen not only in statues and street names but also in clauses of the first constitution that persist all the way through to the current Constitution of 2014, last amended in 2019 and one in which Islam is a state religion, Arabic is the state language, and provision is made for a bicameral legislature. Egypt has not always been a republic and underwent a rapid, deep, and permanent change in identity from a British-influenced monarchy under King Farouk to a state with a socialist Arab-nationalist ideology under Gamal Abdel Nasser in 1952. Though formally non-aligned, Egypt was influenced by the leftist political ideology of the Union of Soviet Socialist Republics (USSR) and, under a newly established pan-Arab movement, its constitution shifted to one focused on economic, social, and cultural rights.

Though many documents have been called constitutions in Egypt's history, only four have been classified as official—those of 1923, 1956, 1971, and 2014. There certainly have been attempts to introduce new constitutions in interim periods, however. In 1930, a brief attempt to introduce, among other contentious clauses, the right to vote only for those with a certain level of wealth led to a return to the 1923 Constitution. There was a revolutionary, provisional constitution in 2011 following the deposal of Mubarak, and a short-lived pro-Islamist constitution in 2012 adopted by the Muslim Brotherhood after Mohammed Morsi's election.

In 1958, following the creation of the United Arab Republic (UAR) consisting of Egypt and Syria, a new seventy-three-clause constitution was drafted principally to merge the legislatures, executives, and judiciaries of two previously independent nations. In terms of identity, however, the text confers nationality of the UAR to Egyptians and Syrians[4] and positions the UAR's people as 'part of the Arab Nation'.[5] This positioning is indicative of the wider political context—Nasserism—that saw Arab nationalism rise, build a base in the Middle East, and lead to the unification of Syria and Egypt. It is noteworthy that, under the 1958 Constitution, multiple identities could coexist simultaneously: Egyptians and Syrians could at once be part of both the UAR and the Arab Nation.

As a geopolitically important bridge between Africa and the Middle East, and as one of only two Arab countries to have normalised relations with Israel, Egypt is a lynchpin of the region. Its prized status has meant that it has had little difficulty in forming international partnerships, first under the socialist banner of Arab nationalism, then, during the Sadat and Mubarak eras, with the US, and more recently with Africa and the European Union. What implications has this foreign-policy shift over the years had on the Egyptian constitution, which has transitioned from socialist ideals under Nasser to militaristic capitalism under Sisi? It seems clear that the constitution has evolved to reflect different priorities and stances, but can this identity be mapped onto the evolution of Egypt's own identity?

Internally as well, developments meant that, in order to remain relevant, the constitution had to change to accommodate new realities. As the population rapidly grew, Egypt's

[4] Provisional Constitution of the United Arab Republic, 1958, art. 2.
[5] Ibid art. 1.

demographics changed, calls increased for a more transparent, representative government, and in turn the constitution followed. Women, youth, and agricultural workers were guaranteed more seats in the legislature; greater powers were delegated to local government; and independent bodies were established to oversee the executive. Following the 2011 revolution, the constitution changed to reflect a newly envisioned future where human rights were protected. Egypt is religiously and ethnically diverse, with a 10 per cent Coptic Christian and 90 per cent Sunni Muslim population, and at times this has been a fraught relationship; yet the non-applicability of Islamic law to Copts was recognised only recently, in the 2014 Constitution. Could religious pluralism be said to form part of Egypt's constitutional identity?

In recent years, amendments in 2016 and 2019 drastically shifted the meaning and content of the Egyptian constitution, arguably away from the notion of giving representation to the people and in a more autocratic direction reminiscent of the 1923 Constitution and its enshrinement of hereditary monarchy. Increased personal powers for the president, a weakening of the separation of powers, retraction of oversight of the military, and other worrying trends have crept into newer incarnations of the constitution. More control granted to the military has meant new clauses and insertions; a desire for less competition from rivals to the president has meant the addition of language that in effect would bar competitors from contesting power. Rather than their being amendments that reflect developments in the population, the 2014 amendments maintain key elements of Egypt's constitutional identity while stifling dissent and diversity of thought. Has this become the new norm for Egypt?

In the course of all these changes, and in response to influences varying in size and importance, the Egyptian constitution has altered dramatically, first from the constitution of a hereditary monarchy to a revolutionary constitution, next to a unificatory constitution with Syria, then to an open-market constitution, then a constitution based on Islamic law, and, latterly, to a centralist constitution edifying a 'strongman leader'.

Some elements, however, have remained consistent, and this chapter will look at the evolution of the Egyptian constitution by focusing on three defining features: firstly, the increased role of the military in and over the constitution, including the military's protection from being bound by its articles; secondly, de facto centralised government control; and thirdly, the role of religion. This chapter will examine what fundamental elements of the constitution have been shared throughout Egypt's history and how the Egyptian constitution—like a chameleon—has changed to match the environment in which it exists. It will explore the concept of constitutional identity by examining the constitutions of the twentieth and twenty-first centuries and reflecting on the reasons for their evolution. It will show that the Egyptian state has contained constitutional articles tailored to the country's own history and social characteristics.

The chapter looks at the evolving constitutions of Egypt through several lenses. Section 2 considers the political shift in the country and examines how the constitution has either led or reflected developments at grassroots level. Thereafter, section 3 reflects on the role of religion, finding that the country has evolved—societally and constitutionally—from one with a relatively secular and religiously lax initial constitution to a country where religion plays a far more significant role. Section 4 engages with the role of the military, which for assorted reasons has been a part of Egypt's identity since the 1952 revolution, a point at which Gamal Abdel Nasser and his Free Officer colleagues staged a military coup to seize control of the country.

2. The Political Shift in Egypt

At its most fundamental level, 'constitutional identity' refers to the notion that a constitutional text is shaped by the idiosyncrasies of a nation, that it is impacted on by desires and necessities to address issues specific to that nation, and that it reflects the nation's history, current status, and desired future progression. The Egyptian constitution in its various iterations exemplifies this. Each new constitution has looked at where the country has been, taken stock, and set out on a path either redesigning itself entirely qua constitution or continuing on an existing path with minor modifications. In fact, as one commentator points out,

> since the beginning of Nasser's rule, the Egyptian state has undergone, not two, but three crucial transitions: a transition from populist authoritarianism under Nasser to post-populist or hybrid authoritarianism under Anwar Sadat and Hosni Mubarak, and a subsequent transition to bureaucratic authoritarianism under El-Sisi. Each of these transitions has led to the creation of a new type of regime based on a distinct set of interests, social and economic policies, and political institutions and instruments.[6]

Since its independence in 1923, Egypt has been through a range of identities, but some elements have been present throughout. One of the oldest forms of Egypt's constitutional identity is visible in its oldest tenets, namely that Islam is the state religion and Arabic is the national language. As this suggests, a society shapes its constitution, moulding it to fit itself; however, as this chapter shows, a constitution may also elicit change in a society and shape a national identity.

2.1 From Colony to Monarchy

Egypt's first constitution in 1923 was published as a royal decree marking the country's emergence as an independent nation.[7] To understand the identity of the 1923 Constitution, it is necessary to consider its content against the backdrop of political developments at the time. In 1882, Egypt was occupied by Britain in the Anglo-Egyptian War and, though it remained formally outside the British Empire, it was a de facto British protectorate. In 1914, at the outset of the First World War, Ottoman ties to the country were cut and the 1919 Egyptian Revolution became a turning point in law, if not in practice, for liberty, independence, and democracy. While Britain continued to dominate Egypt's politics and economy through its control of the Suez Canal and military presence in Egyptian cities for another thirty years, on 22 February 1922 the Unilateral Declaration of Egyptian Independence brought an end to Britain's control over Egypt.[8]

[6] Diana Shehata, 'Sixty Years of Egyptian Politics: What Has Changed?' *The Cairo Review of Global Affairs* (2018) https://thecairoreview.com/essays/sixty-years-of-egyptian-politics-what-has-changed/ (last accessed 27 September 2022).

[7] Royal Decree No. 42 of 1923 (1923 Constitution).

[8] 'Statement on Egypt, February 1922' *Hansard 1803–2005* https://api.parliament.uk/historic-hansard/lords/1922/feb/28/statement-on-egypt (last accessed 27 September 2022); 'The Anglo-Egyptian Treaty Negotiations' *Bulletin of International News* (1928) 4(19) New Series 3–11.

It is not surprising, therefore, that the preamble of the 1923 Constitution outlines what appeared to be important rights for any free nation—greater equality among citizens and a more just country. The preamble was used as a means to introduce Egypt on the world stage as a newly independent state with democratic goals and the capacity for self-rule. The 1923 Constitution aimed to establish

> a constitutional system similar to the most advanced constitutional systems in the world, under which our nation can happily and satisfactorily live and pursue the path of an absolutely free life, and which ensures active participation in running state affairs and overseeing the drafting and enforcement of laws, and brings a sense of comfort and assurance about our nation's present and future, while maintaining the national qualities and distinctions which constitute the great historical heritage thereof.[9]

Britain had deemed Egypt incapable of governing itself[10] and the 1923 Constitution explicitly rebuts this belief, stating that the 'People of Egypt . . . assume control ourselves and take the command of [our] affairs from now on'.[11] Throughout Egypt's time as a formal protectorate, its citizens were denied access to their own political systems. The Constitution aimed to redress this too: Egyptians alone were permitted to hold public, civil, or military positions,[12] and only Egyptians were permitted to assume the role of ministers.[13] Under the 1923 Constitution, Egyptians were equal under the law[14] and had equal civil and political rights irrespective of 'origin, language, or religion'.[15] The Constitution contained many nascent human rights and rule-of-law clauses, including freedom from arbitrary imprisonment,[16] the right to privacy,[17] prohibition of ex post facto law,[18] a free press,[19] freedom of belief[20] and opinion,[21] and freedom of assembly.[22]

2.2 From Monarchy to Socialist Democracy

Though Egypt was independent in name following the 1923 Constitution, the British continued to exercise power within its borders, notably over its natural resources and the Suez Canal.[23] In the two decades following the introduction of the 1923 Constitution, political groups from left and right alike gathered momentum in pushing for an end to monarchy in Egypt. In a bloodless coup on 23 July 1952, the Free Officers, a group of young military

[9] Egyptian Constitution of 1923, preamble.
[10] Lisa Pollard, *Nurturing the Nation: The Family Politics of Modernizing, Colonizing and Liberating Egypt, 1805–1923* (University of California Press 2005) 2.
[11] Egyptian Constitution of 1956, preamble.
[12] Egyptian Constitution of 1923, art. 3.
[13] Ibid. art. 58.
[14] Ibid. art. 3.
[15] Ibid. art. 3.
[16] Ibid. art. 5.
[17] Ibid. art. 4.
[18] Ibid. arts 6, 27.
[19] Ibid. art. 15.
[20] Ibid. art. 12.
[21] Ibid. art. 14.
[22] Ibid. art. 20.
[23] Laila Morsy, 'Farouk in British Policy' (1984) *20*(4) *Middle Eastern Studies* 193, 203.

officers led by Colonel Gamal Abdel Nasser, ousted King Farouk and drove him into exile.[24] Nasser's was the first military coup to take place in the Middle East and set the tone for others, including in neighbouring Libya.[25] So impactful was this revolution and the role of the military that from this day, with the exception of the Morsi administration of 2012–13 which itself was ended by a military coup, Egypt's head of state has been a member of the armed forces.

The 1952 revolution was built upon six principles: the abolition of imperialism; eliminating feudalism; ending monopoly and the domination of capital over the government; establishing social justice; building a strong national army; and developing a sound democratic system. Anwar Sadat, the Free Officer revolutionary colleague of Nasser and future president of Egypt, summarised matters as follows:

> The problem was to get Egypt out of the Middle Ages, to turn it from a semi-feudal country into a modern, ordered, viable State, while at the same time respecting the customs of the people. On this last point, respecting the customs of the people does not mean chaining them down to a dead past, it means respecting the essential and invisible continuities in a nation's life. We would conserve everything that did not impede the real progress of the community.[26]

Though it would be another four years until the 1956 Constitution was drafted and approved, it served as a written manifesto of these efforts. As an iteration of Egypt's constitutional identity, the 1956 Constitution is arguably the most important of them all. It both marks a seismic shift in the country's political development and lays the foundation upon which later constitutions would be built. Indeed, it served as the basis for the 1971 Constitution and heralded the beginning of Egypt's new identity as a democratic republic, in the process establishing principles that would remain in effect for decades thereafter.

Underpinning the 1952 revolution was a sense of Egyptian nationalism, and the 1956 Constitution accordingly marked a fundamental change for both the political status of Egypt and its constitution. The revolution of 1952 replaced the monarchy with a socialist democratic republic,[27] as a result of which the benefits afforded to the monarchy in the 1923 Constitution were incompatible with the new republic, founded on socialist values, which its new president, Gamal Abdel Nasser, had created. The 1923 Constitution stipulated that the throne of the Egyptian Kingdom was hereditary[28] and that the king as head of state was inviolable[29] and accorded with a wide range of summary powers—all of which a people's republic could not countenance. Nasser had risen to power with pledges of progressive socialism. Reflecting Egypt's identity as a republic, one severing all links with its previous identity as a monarchy, the 1956 Constitution thus prohibits the president from being related to the Egyptian royal family.[30]

[24] Pierre Crabites, 'Britain's Debt to King Farouk' (1941) *19 Foreign Affairs* 852.

[25] Stephen Blackwell, 'Saving the King: Anglo-American Strategy and British Counter-Subversion Operations in Libya, 1953–59' (2003) *39*(1) *Middle Eastern Studies* 1, 9.

[26] Anwar El Sadat, *Revolt on the Nile* (Allan Wingate 1957) 53.

[27] Derek Hopwood, *Egypt: Politics and Society 1945–1981* (George Allen & Unwin 1982) 37.

[28] Egyptian Constitution of 1923, art. 32.

[29] Ibid. art. 33.

[30] Ibid art. 120.

As a result of the Nasser administration's efforts to reduce British control of Egyptian politics, economics, and assets, numerous clauses of the 1956 Constitution are dedicated to development and the state's reclamation of natural resources.[31] The preamble makes reference to both 'aggressive external monarchy and manipulative internal monarchy', which is almost certainly an allusion to the British and Egyptian monarchies. Nasser himself, in a 1955 *Foreign Affairs* article, described the revolution as 'an effort to free the country from a foreign yoke'[32]:

> From the outset, the British sapped the strength and the moral energies of Egypt . . . British advisers were installed in every department of government and vested with power to exercise full control. The Egyptians had to pay the cost of occupation and open the country to British companies and foreign agencies. Chartered monopolies dominated the Egyptian market.[33]

The 1956 Constitution imbued the Egyptian people with the idea that the country belonged to them communally rather than to the monarch, as had been the case previously. Patriotism among Egyptians rose,[34] and a new socialist youth generation was created through the formation of the Socialist Youth Organization (SYO).[35] The SYO set up summer youth camps that included lectures, study, exercise, and religious studies.[36] Initiatives were adopted to enable citizens to benefit from their homeland, the aims being to secure, inter alia, an end to feudalism,[37] the protection of small agricultural lands,[38] social insurance,[39] universal health care,[40] and shared natural wealth.[41] At the same time, additional national duties were included, such as conscription,[42] a prohibition on renouncing nationality,[43] maintenance of public order and societal morals,[44] and contribution to public life, including voting.[45]

The 1956 Constitution was adopted in June 1956 by means of a national referendum. Egyptian citizens' engagement in the political future of the country was illustrated by the 96.5 per cent voter turnout, with the Constitution being overwhelmingly approved by 98 per cent of those voting.[46] The 1956 Constitution instilled a sense of ownership and national identity in Egyptians that Nasser leveraged a month later to rally support for the nationalisation of the Suez Canal,[47] to this day a major source of revenue for the country.[48] He

[31] Ibid. art. 26

[32] Gamal Abdel Nasser, 'The Egyptian Revolution' (1955) 33(2) *Foreign Affairs* 199.

[33] Ibid. 200.

[34] Saleh Omar, 'Arab Nationalism: A Retrospective Evaluation' (1992) *14*(4) *Arab Studies Quarterly* 23.

[35] ASU Programme for Youth, 'Pioneers of the Future' *Arab Observer* (14 February 1966) 8

[36] James B. Mayfield, *Rural Politics in Nasser's Egypt: A Quest for Legitimacy* (University of Texas Press 1971) 157.

[37] Egyptian Constitution of 1956, art. 12.

[38] Ibid. art. 13.

[39] Ibid. art. 21.

[40] Ibid. art. 56.

[41] Ibid. art. 26.

[42] Jack Crabbs, 'Politics, History, and Culture in Nasser's Egypt' (1975) 6(4) *International Journal of Middle East Studies* 386.

[43] Egyptian Constitution of 1956, art. 30.

[44] Ibid. art. 60.

[45] Ibid. art. 61.

[46] 'Egypt's Referendums Poll Results 1956–2012' *Ahramonline* (2014) http://english.ahram.org.eg/NewsAFCON/2019/91674.aspx (last accessed 27 September 2022).

[47] Crabbs (n. 42) 414.

[48] https://www.reuters.com/article/egypt-suezcanal-idUSL8N2AU0H7 (last accessed 18 November 2022); https://www.reuters.com/article/egypt-canal-minister/egypt-sees-suez-canal-zone-making-up-30-35-pct-of-economy-minister-idUSL5N0W74WT20150305 (last accessed 27 September 2022).

aimed to launch major development projects in Egypt, including the reclamation of desert land,[49] but by far the largest and most prestigious project was the Aswan Dam, which Nasser claimed would 'increase agricultural output by almost 50 percent'.[50]

The construction of such a large project, particularly in the absence of Western financial support,[51] remains a major source of pride for Egyptians. Patriotic songs by famous singers such as Abdel Halim Hafez[52] evoked 'a mythical narrative that intertwine[d] the "story of a people" and the story of its army with the late president Gamal Abdel Nasser as the ultimate bearer of victory and liberation'.[53] This populist image, along with its leaning towards the armed forces, resonated with the people, and is discussed in the next section.

2.3 Sequential Shifts in Values

The core values of Egyptian society also shifted following the deposition of King Farouk. As Nasser ushered in an era of socialism typified by the nationalisation of public resources[54] and a shift towards industrialisation, the population began to acclimatise to a more cohesive, communal way of life. In stark contrast to King Farouk, who was descended from several generations of royalty, Nasser himself came from a humble background in Alexandria and saw that his allegiance was to the people, who revered him in turn.[55] He aimed to improve the standard of living of Egyptians and to end what he saw as their exploitation. By contrast, under King Farouk, large swathes of land had been owned by elites, and the existence of feudal class meant that many ordinary citizens lived in poverty.

The new constitution introduced the mantra that 'social solidarity is fundamental to Egyptian society'.[56] The articles of the 1956 Constitution provided foundations for a planned economy,[57] the prohibition of aristocracy,[58] the limiting of agricultural holdings,[59] and the development of cooperatives[60] and a social security programme.[61] As a counterbalance to these unequivocally socialist objectives, private economic activity remained permitted, provided that it did not adversely affect the public interest.[62]

49 Nasser (n. 32) 204.
50 Ibid.
51 Ragaei El Mallakh, 'Some Economic Aspects of the Aswan High Dam Project in Egypt' (1959) *35*(1) *Land Economics* 15, 15; Joachim Joesten, 'Nasser's Daring Dream: The Aswan High Dam' (1960) *16*(2) *The World Today* 55.
52 عبد الحليم حافظ حكاية شعب * عيد النصر ٢٣ ديسمبر ١٩٦١ حفل بورسعيد, https:// www.yout ube.com/ watch?v= Z2xCH-Zpzag (last accessed 27 September 2022).
53 Menna Khalil, 'The People and the Army Are One Hand: Myths and Their Translations' in Samia Mehrez (ed.), *Translating Egypt's Revolution: The Language of Tahrir* (The American University in Cairo Press 2012) 256.
54 Peter Mansfield, 'Nasser and Nasserism' (1973) *28*(4) *International Journal* 670, 677.
55 'For 18 Years Nasser Had Almost Hypnotic Power in His Leadership of Egyptians' *New York Times* (29 September 1970) https://www.nytimes.com/1970/09/29/archives/for-18-years-nasser-had-almost-hypnotic-power-in-his-leadership-of.html (last accessed 27 September 2022); Amira Nowaira, 'Egypt 1967—a Very Personal Defeat' *The Guardian* (Egypt, 27 May 2010) https://www.theguardian.com/commentisfree/2010/may/27/egypt-1967-very-personal-defeat (last accessed 27 September 2022).
56 Egyptian Constitution of 1956, art. 4.
57 Ibid. art. 9.
58 Ibid. art. 29.
59 Ibid. art. 12.
60 Ibid. art. 16.
61 Ibid. art. 28.
62 Ibid. art. 8.

Alongside nationalisation and other socialist initiatives, however, there was an almost inevitable enlargement and bureaucratisation of the state apparatus—a phenomenon still visible today in Egypt.[63] The nationalisation of the Suez Canal led to an exodus of foreign expertise, which Nasser aimed to replace with home-grown talent. To this end, he guaranteed employment for all university graduates,[64] later extending this to vocational secondary schools and technical institutes.[65] These guarantees created a pipeline whereby the guarantee of employment led to a greater number of university graduates who, in turn, needed jobs once emerging from university. Although the transition from Nasser to Sadat led to the replacement of social development in 1973,[66] Sadat, rather than pivoting away from the 1970s path of guaranteed public sector employment, expanded it until 1976 to include demobilised military conscripts.[67] Today, 17.5 per cent of Egypt's 32-million-strong labour force,[68] amounting to 5.6 million people, is employed by the government.[69] This stems from the 1956 Constitution, which guarantees that 'Egyptians have a right to work, and the state shall ensure this'.[70]

2.4 Egypt as an Arab Nation

Nasser forged solidarity not only among Egyptians but also among Arab states.[71] Between 1952 and 1970, the year that he died, Arab unity was at its strongest,[72] and the wars against Israel in 1956 and 1967 highlighted the importance of the Palestinian issue in his foreign-policy agenda.[73] At the time of the revolution in 1952, Egypt was still reeling from its 1948 defeat in Palestine—a war Nasser believed he could have won had it not been for the '[m]ismanagement and corruption by [King Farouk's] clique, which included trading in defective arms'.[74] His initial plan was to reclaim fifty thousand acres of the Sinai Peninsula for the benefit of Palestinian refugees.[75]

Every constitution since 1956 has reaffirmed Egypt's identity as an 'Arab' nation. The failed endeavour in 1958 to create a Syrian-Egyptian constitution saw the merged states renamed as the United Arab Republic,[76] a title Egypt retained for ten years even after Syria's withdrawal in 1961. Despite three constitutional amendments under Sadat and Mubarak

63 Ragui Assaad, 'The Effects of Public Sector Hiring and Compensation Policies on the Egyptian Labor Market' (1997) *11*(1) *The World Bank Economic Review* 85–118.

64 Ibid.

65 Law 14 of 1964.

66 Ibrahim El-Issawy, *Labour Force, Employment, and Unemployment* (International Labour Office 1983).

67 Bent Hansen and Samir Radwan, *Employment Opportunities and Equity in a Changing Economy: Egypt in the 1980s* (International Labour Office 1982).

68 World Bank, 'Labor Force, Total—Egypt' https://data.worldbank.org/indicator/SL.TLF.TOTL.IN?locations=EG (last accessed 27 September 2022).

69 Amr Emam, 'Egypt Struggles with Bloated Public Sector' *The Arab Weekly* (18 November 2018) https://thearabweekly.com/egypt-struggles-bloated-public-sector (last accessed 27 September 2022).

70 Egyptian Constitution of 1956, art. 52.

71 'Arab Unity: Nasser's Revolution' *Al Jazeera* (20 June 2008) https://www.aljazeera.com/focus/arabunity/2008/02/200852517252821627.html (last accessed 27 September 2022).

72 *New York Times* (n. 55).

73 Nabil Fahmy, 'Palestine, an Arab Issue' *The Cairo Global Affairs Review* (2017) https://www.thecairoreview.com/essays/palestine-an-arab-issue/ (last accessed 27 September 2022); Mansfield (n. 54) 676.

74 Nasser (n. 32) 199–211, 202.

75 Ibid. 205.

76 Egyptian Constitution of 1958, art. 2.

in 1980, 2005, and 2007, the 1971 Constitution described Egypt as an 'Arab Nation . . . convinced that Arab Unity is a call of history and of the future'.[77] The 2012 Constitution, drafted under a Muslim Brotherhood presidency, expanded Egypt's identity and envisaged the Egyptian people as forming 'part of the Arab and Islamic nations . . . [and being] proud of belonging to the Nile Valley, to the African continent and to Asia'.[78] Most recently, the 2014 Constitution reaffirmed this, stating that 'Egypt is part of the Arab nation . . . [p]art of the Muslim world, belongs to the African continent, [and] is proud of its Asian dimension'.[79]

However, this 'Arab identity' has all but disappeared today among many Egyptians.[80] 'Arab' has become a well-nigh pejorative term in Egypt, and is used to refer to wealthy visitors from the Gulf who exploit Egypt in a variety of ways.[81] Many Egyptians see themselves as different from Arabs, with Egyptian culture, history, mannerisms, characteristics, music, food, and even appearance viewed as more refined, mature, and sophisticated than the ways of the nouveau riche across the Red Sea.[82]

2.5 Relative Stability under the 'Permanent Constitution' of 1971

The constitutions of 1923 and 1956 were landmarks in the country's political development, and represented a sovereign monarchy and a republic, respectively. Sadat's assumption of power in Egypt following Nasser's death from heart attack in 1970 marked the first time in Egypt's history that a transition between presidents was legal rather than the result of a coup d'état. Sadat's presidency was seen as a continuation of Nasser's regime, and his tenure was seen by many—initially at least—as destined to be short.[83] There was no need, therefore, for a lengthy scene-setting preamble as in 1923 and 1956, and the 1971 Constitution maintained the country's political and economic leaning towards socialism.

The 1971 Constitution marked Egypt's first non-revolutionary transition of power in modern history and remained valid for more than forty years after its enactment under President Sadat. Despite being referred to as 'The Permanent Constitution of Egypt', it was amended multiple times by both Sadat and his successor, Hosni Mubarak, underscoring the balance required between the foundational constitutional elements it contained and the need for flexibility to accommodate Egypt's changing society. When Mubarak came to power in 1981, he opted to amend the existing 1971 Constitution rather than replace it.

Unlike Nasser, Sadat did not shift Egypt immediately to another trajectory in terms of its political and economic system. In many ways, the 1971 Constitution was initially a continuation of Nasser's socialist course. Nationalisation may have been restricted to public

[77] Egyptian Constitution of 1971, preamble.

[78] Egyptian Constitution of 2012, art. 1.

[79] Egyptian Constitution of 2014, art. 1.

[80] For a discussion of Arab identity more widely, see Martin Kramer, 'Arab Nationalism: Mistaken Identity' (1993) *122*(3) *Daedalus* 171; Baher Ibrahim, 'An Egyptian, and an Arab' *The Guardian* (8 July 2010) https://www.theguardian.com/commentisfree/2010/jul/08/egyptian-arab-cultural-identity (last accessed 27 September 2022); Mohammed Nossier, 'Will Arabizing Education Strengthen Egyptian Identity?' *Arab News* (8 June 2018) https://www.arabnews.com/node/1318291 (last accessed 27 September 2022).

[81] Massoud Hayoun, 'The Coming Arab Identity Crisis' *The Atlantic* (8 March 2012) https://www.theatlantic.com/international/archive/2012/03/the-coming-arab-identity-crisis/254144/ (last accessed 27 September 2022).

[82] 'The Rise and Fall of Egyptian Arabic' *The Economist* (8 March 2022) https://www.economist.com/prospero/2018/01/31/the-rise-and-fall-of-egyptian-arabic (last accessed 27 September 2022).

[83] 'Anwar el-Sadat: The Daring Arab Pioneer of Peace with Israel' *The New York Times* (7 October 1981).

services with compensation guaranteed,[84] but Sadat's capitalist development plan was published only after the 1971 Constitution,[85] so the constitutional references to a development plan[86] were not to mark a new change in tack. Moreover, the 1971 Constitution included several socialist elements that built on the 1956 Constitution, including what to do with surplus of productivity to the state development plan,[87] citizens sharing in national revenue,[88] and workers sharing in the management and profits of projects.[89]

Nevertheless, when Sadat assumed power the economy was in distress. 'The economic legacy Nasser left me was in even poorer shape than the political', he wrote in his autobiography.[90] Nationalisation and industrialisation, along with two wars against Israel in 1956 and 1967, had severely affected the economy.[91] Sadat aimed at boosting Egypt's economy by relinquishing state control of the economy in favour of greater private sector involvement and foreign investment. *Al-infitah al-iktisadi*, or 'the economic opening', was the keystone of his October Paper, published in 1974 and taking its name from the 6 October War with Israel in 1973:

> We have the three national economy sectors, the public sector, the private sector and the co-operative sector. With the outward-looking economic policy there would be wider vistas for Arab and foreign investments. All these activities should fall within the framework of the plan that draws up the strategic targets to bring about a radical change in the country's image and lays down the detailed plans to ensure the realisation of these targets.[92]

The 'economic opening' involved overlooking political and ideological differences between nations in favour of establishing cooperative ties, the premise thereof being that 'versatile and varied international economic relations constitute the material basis for the freedom of [Egypt's] political movement'.[93] This economic shift did not require a change in the constitution, which remained unaltered until 1980, and saw an influx of foreign investment, with Egyptians looking to newly oil-rich Gulf states for employment. Remittances soared,[94] tourism grew,[95] and foreign assistance for Egypt's economic development increased.[96]

It was only under Mubarak in 2007 that the constitution was amended to embed a further shift towards capitalism and the intervention of the state: national production was placed under the sponsorship of the state in place of the means of production being controlled by the people;[97] public ownership was now represented in the ownership of the

[84] Egyptian Constitution of 1971, art. 5.
[85] Mohamed Anwar El Sadat, 'Tasks of the Stage; or a Comprehensive Civilisation Strategy' (1974) The October Working Paper https://sadat.umd.edu/resources/written-works (last accessed 27 September 2022).
[86] Egyptian Constitution of 197, arts 24, 32.
[87] Egyptian Constitution of 1971, art. 24.
[88] Egyptian Constitution of 1971, art. 25.
[89] Egyptian Constitution of 1971, art. 26.
[90] Anwar El Sadat, *In Search of Identity: An Autobiography* [Arabic] (HarperCollins 1978).
[91] Marvin G. Weinbaum, 'Egypt's "Infitah" and the Politics of US Economic Assistance' (1985) *21*(2) *Middle Eastern Studies* 206.
[92] Anwar Sadat (n. 85) 56.
[93] Ibid. 64.
[94] Saad Edin Ibrahim, 'Governance and Structural Adjustment: The Egyptian Case' in Saad Eddin Ibrahim (ed.), *Egypt, Islam and Democracy: Critical Essays* (The American University in Cairo Press Cairo 1996) 141.
[95] Matthew Gray, 'Economic Reform, Privatization and Tourism in Egypt' (1998) *34*(2) *Middle Eastern Studies* 91, 94.
[96] Saad Eddin Ibrahim, 'An Islamic Alternative in Egypt: The Muslim Brotherhood and Sadat' (1982) *4*(1/2) *Arab Studies Quarterly* 75, 78.
[97] Egyptian Constitution of 1971, art. 24.

state;[98] public ownership was no longer inviolable but rather had sanctity;[99] safeguarding Egypt's socialist achievements was no longer a national duty;[100] and references to socialist elements were removed.[101] The upper house of the legislature no longer worked towards preservation of the principles of the 23 July 1952 Revolution and the 15 May Revolution of 1971,[102] reflecting the 'crony capitalist'[103] trajectory the state had been following in practice even before the constitutional amendments.

2.6 The Arab Spring

Much has been written about the causes of the revolution in 2011 that deposed Mubarak.[104] In many ways, the 2014 Constitution is a reflection of them. In the Constitution's poetic preamble, the 2011 revolution is seen as a continuation of the Egyptian aspiration to achieve the goals of freedom and social justice that motivated the 1919 and 1952 revolutions.[105] The famous slogan chanted on the streets, 'Bread, Freedom, and Social Justice',[106] is noted in the constitution as underpinning 'the homeland's free will'.[107]

A new constitution was required to address modern Egypt; one befitting of a fairer society far removed from the crony police state into which Mubarak's Egypt had developed and the Islamist state that Morsi was leading it towards. The frustrations of the middle classes and the youth—unemployed and underrepresented—seem to be at the heart of the 2014 Constitution. Favouritism, or 'wasta',[108] is prohibited in appointments to public posts.[109] Furthermore, the Constitution refers explicitly to gender equality 'in all civil, political, economic, social, and cultural rights in accordance with the provisions of the Constitution'.[110] This includes 'appropriate representation of women in the houses of parliament'[111] and in at least one-quarter of all seats in local councils.[112] In a reference to domestic violence,[113]

[98] Ibid. art. 30.
[99] Ibid. art. 33.
[100] Ibid. art. 59.
[101] Ibid. arts 73, 179, 180.
[102] Ibid. art. 194.
[103] Clement M. Henry and Robert Springborg, *Globalisation and the Politics of Development in the Middle East* (Cambridge University Press 2010) 154; 'Friends in High Places' *The Economist* (9 October 2014) https://www.economist.com/business/2014/10/09/friends-in-high-places (last accessed 27 September 2022); Philip Marfleet, 'Mubarak's Egypt: Nexus of Criminality' (2013) *2*(2) *State Crime Journal* 112; Ibrahim G. Aoudé, 'Egypt: Revolutionary Process and Global Capitalist Crisis' (2013) *35*(3) *Arab Studies Quarterly* 241.
[104] Wael Ghonim, *Revolution 2.0: The Power of the People Is Greater Than the People in Power* (Houghton Mifflin Harcourt 2012); Alaa Al Aswany, *On the State of Egypt: What Caused the Revolution* (Penguin Random House 2011); Sherif Khalifa, *Egypt's Lost Spring: Causes and Consequences* (ABC-CLIO 2015); Bahgat Korany and Rabab El-Mahdi, *Arab Spring in Egypt: Revolution and Beyond* (The American University in Cairo Press 2012); Kamal Eldin Osman Salih, 'The Roots and Causes of the 2011 Arab Spring' (2013) *35*(2) *Arab Studies Quarterly* 184; Ann M. Lesch, 'Egypt's Spring: Causes of the Revolution' (2011) *18*(3) *Middle East Policy Washington* 35; Hazem Fahmy, 'An Initial Perspective on "The Winter of Discontent": The Root Causes of the Egyptian Revolution' (2012) *79*(2) *Social Research: An International Quarterly* 349.
[105] Egyptian Constitution of 2014, preamble.
[106] 'عيش حرية عدالة اجتماعية'
[107] Egyptian Constitution of 2014, preamble.
[108] Robert B. Cunningham, Yasin K. Sarayrah, and Yasin E. Sarayrah, 'Taming "Wasta" to Achieve Development' (1994) *16*(3) *Arab Studies Quarterly* 29.
[109] Egyptian Constitution of 2014, art. 14.
[110] Ibid. art. 11.
[111] Ibid.
[112] Ibid art. 180.
[113] https://www.amnestyusa.org/files/mde_120042015.pdf

the Constitution also commits the state to 'the protection of women against all forms of violence'.[114] Similarly, in a country where more 60 per cent of the population is under thirty years of age,[115] the Constitution takes note of the burgeoning youth population, stipulating that at least one-quarter of all local council seats are guaranteed for youths under thirty-five;[116] youth representation in Parliament is also guaranteed, although the specific number is subject to national law.[117] Yet in reality, as the next section shows, Egypt rapidly developed into a military-controlled state with fewer freedoms than it had under Mubarak.

3. The Role of the Military in Egypt

In the 1923 Constitution, there were a mere three articles on the armed and police forces, with these stating that domestic law shall regulate the military,[118] conscription,[119] and the police authorities.[120] By contrast, the 2014 Constitution enshrined the constitutional right of the military to select the minister of defence,[121] removed financial scrutiny by permitting the armed forces' budget to be incorporated as a single figure in the state budget,[122] expanded the jurisdiction of military tribunals by allowing domestic laws to classify typically civilian public property as military,[123] and cemented the role of the National Defence Council as a gatekeeper for any laws related to the armed forces.[124] These changes were in keeping with a shift that took place gradually due to the military's increasing influence on political leadership since the 1952 revolution.

The 1956 Constitution established the defence of the country as a sacred duty[125] and introduced mandatory military service. This was said to have instilled 'a new philosophy of patriotism, in which there will be no room for the traditional practice of permitting potential conscripts to buy their release'.[126] Paramilitary units were also prohibited, thus centralising military forces under the control of the state.[127] The bolstering of support for the military under the 1956 Constitution is most likely attributable to Nasser himself as well as to the revolution's military origins, but under Nasser's commander in chief of the armed forces, Abdel Hakim Amer,

> the military essentially operated as a political power center independent of the state ... [and] little or no attempt was made to control them by means of security surveillance, the vetting of officers, or ideological indoctrination in the principles of pan-Arabism and socialism.[128]

[114] Ibid.
[115] Population Council, 'Survey of Young People in Egypt' https://www.popcouncil.org/research/survey-of-young-people-in-egypt (last accessed 30 September 2022)
[116] Egyptian Constitution of 2014, art. 180.
[117] Ibid. art. 244.
[118] Egyptian Constitution of 1923, art. 146.
[119] Ibid. art. 147.
[120] Ibid. art. 148.
[121] Egyptian Constitution of 2014, art. 234.
[122] Ibid. art. 203.
[123] Ibid. art. 204.
[124] Ibid. art. 203.
[125] Egyptian Constitution of 1956, art. 58.
[126] Curtis F. Jones, 'The New Egyptian Constitution' (1956) *10*(3) *Middle East Journal* 300, 305.
[127] Egyptian Constitution of 1956, art. 170.
[128] Ahmed S. Hashim, 'The Egyptian Military Part One: From the Ottomans through Sadat' (2011) *18*(3) *Middle East Policy* 69.

Nasser's doctrine that '[t]he army is a basic factor in Egyptian life'[129] continued to hold sway during the era of Sadat and Mubarak under the 1971 Constitution, survived the 2011 revolution, and remains in effect under the modern-day Sisi administration.

3.1 The Military as Saviour

Nasser recognised that one of the most characteristic traits of modern Egypt is the inextricability of its cultural identity from its military and experience of warfare. Populist sentiment has been at the heart of the military's power since the 1952 revolution, when the armed forces came to be revered as the saviours and guardians of the Egyptian people.[130] Similarly, in the wars of 1956, 1967, and 1973, the military was seen as the protector of the nation against the foreign aggressors of Britain, France, and Israel. Jingoism has long been a major element of Egyptian culture, with military parades, reverence to fallen military heroes, and monuments, landmarks, cities, and streets named in commemoration of famous victories adding to the persistent rumble of the armed forces in the background of Egyptian society.[131] Mostafa highlights the pervasive nature of the military in all aspects of life:

> This solid belief [in the centrality the military] was not only formed through studying history books at school or listening to endless debates and discussions within family circles about the heroism and patriotism of the Egyptian army, or by watching countless political speeches which hail the army and its achievements and victories, but more importantly through many films we have watched, songs we have fondly memorised, radio programmes and TV drama series we have listened to and seen over and over again while growing up, and countless images on TV, in documentaries, and in cinema, which reflect the courage and discipline of our national army. Until this day, if you ask young boys in Egypt what they would like to become when they grow up, most of them are likely to give you one of two answers: an army officer or a police officer.[132]

Who, then, would not aspire to join the armed forces? Apart from the honour of belonging to a prestigious sector of society, benefits afforded to members of the armed forces under Mubarak[133] included private hospitals, discounted holidays at Egypt's beauty spots, discounted housing in specialised compounds, and, at higher levels, well-paid, prestigious jobs in the public sector.[134]

[129] *The New York Times* (22 October 1955).

[130] Dalia Said Mostafa, *The Egyptian Military in Popular Culture: Context and Critique* (Palgrave Macmillan 2016) 8.

[131] Magdi Abdelhadi, 'Egyptians Look to Military "Saviour"' *BBC* (23 June 2009) http://news.bbc.co.uk/1/hi/world/middle_east/8113349.stm (last accessed 27 September 2022).

[132] Mostafa (n. 130) 8.

[133] Hicham Bou Nassif, 'Wedded to Mubarak: The Second Careers and Financial Rewards of Egypt's Military Elite, 1981–2011' (2013) *67*(4) *Middle East Journal 509*; Yezid Sayigh, 'Above the State: The Officers' Republic in Egypt' (2012) *The Carnegie Papers* https:///www.files.ethz.ch/isn/157113/CMEC_33_officers_republic1.pdf (last accessed 27 September 2022); Zeinab Abul-Magd, 'The Egyptian Republic of Retired Generals' *The Middle East Channel* (Limassol, 8 May 2012); Shana Marshall, 'Egypt's Other Revolution' *Jadaliyya*.

[134] Yezid Sayigh, 'Owners of the Republic: An Anatomy of Egypt's Military Economy' *Carnegie Middle East Centre* (18 November 2019) https://carnegie-mec.org/2019/11/18/mapping-informal-military-economy-officers-republic-pub-80337 (last accessed 27 September 2022).

However, when it became clear that Mubarak's '*Gamalakeeya*'[135] meant that he intended to pass power down to his son, Gamal, despite Egypt being a republic rather than a monarchy, branches of the military began turning against Mubarak. Eventually, this turned into outright opposition to the regime, and—in contrast to the police who attacked protestors in the 25 January uprisings—the army was welcomed on the streets for its protection of the people.[136] The military, then, was a literal saviour of the people from the state itself, establishing a tripartite relationship: the people, the state, and the armed forces. Whereas previously the armed forces had been synonymous with the state, their allegiance was now up for debate and their decision to side with the protestors, particularly against the backdrop of conscription in Egypt, established their dual function as both representatives and protectors of the people.

This is evident in the 2014 Constitution. One of the most famous slogans of the revolution, 'The people and the army are one hand',[137] is alluded to in its preamble, which credits the army with delivering 'victory to the sweeping popular will'.[138] The 2011 revolution was 'but an extension to a process of national struggle . . . [and] the capstone of two great revolutions in [Egypt's] modern history'.[139] The martyrs and the wounded of the 2011 revolution are also explicitly referred to in a commitment by the state to honour

> the martyrs of the nation, caring for the wounded of the revolution, elderly war veterans, the wounded, and families of those missing in war, as well as their equals, and the wounded in security operations, their wives, children and parents.[140]

In this way, the armed forces were able to weld themselves constitutionally to the aims of the 2011 revolution, thereby adding a veneer of legitimacy to their continued control of the political arena—control which was portrayed as in alignment with the 2011 protestors' demands.

3.2 The Expansion of the Armed Forces under Sisi

A split rapidly emerged between the armed forces and the 2011 protestors, however, and the Supreme Council for the Armed Forces (SCAF) replaced Mubarak as the immediate target of protest vitriol. The military police, which had taken to the streets after the national police vanished for fear of reprisals,[141] 'began killing protesters at demonstrations, and arresting, torturing and imprisoning many of them in military prisons';[142] anti-Mubarak chants gave way to ones calling for the downfall of military rule and death penalty for the

[135] 'جملكية' This is an amalgam of the two Egyptian words, *gomhoreeya* ('republic') and *malakeeya* ('monarchy'), that signified Mubarak's rule of Egypt.

[136] Khalil (n. 53) 250.

[137] الجيش والشعب إيد واحدة

[138] Egyptian Constitution of 2014, preamble.

[139] Ibid.

[140] Ibid. art. 16.

[141] Dina Zayed and Sherine El Madany, 'Egypt Vigilantes Defend Homes as Police Disappear' *Reuters* (London, 29 January 2011).

[142] Dalia Said Mostafa, *Transformation of the Popular War Hero's Image under Mubarak in the Egyptian Military in Popular Culture: Context and Critique* (Palgrave Macmillan 2017) 122.

SCAF commander, Field Admiral Tantawi.[143] Following the 2013 military coup that overthrew the Morsi regime, the armed forces once again found themselves in favour, this time for having rescued the country from a potential Islamist future.[144]

In contrast to the 'permanent' Constitution of 1971, the 2014 Constitution was 'born to be amended, as some of its architects made clear when they wrote it'.[145] As military control under Sisi grew stronger despite his nominal transition into a civilian, so the constitution reflected profound changes in Egyptians' way of life. The 2019 constitutional amendments expanded the role of the armed forces to include 'safeguarding the constitution and democracy, maintaining the foundations of the state and its civilian nature, the gains of the people, and the rights and freedoms of the individual'.[146] It is not clear how this intersects with the roles of the legislature, judiciary, or indeed the Supreme Constitutional Court. The jurisdiction of military courts was also extended to include all attacks against the military and its installations, as opposed to direct attacks, as was the case prior to the amendment.[147] With the expansion of the armed forces into traditionally civilian industries, 'military installations' include factories, roads, and other property owned by the military. Most recently, in response to the Covid-19 pandemic, Sisi ratified constitutional amendments that grant security agencies power to detain suspects and seize property without judicial review.[148] Sisi is now 'authorised to order the military prosecution to conduct preliminary investigations into offences deemed a violation of the emergency law'.[149]

4. Religion in Egypt

Prior to 1980, Egyptian constitutions had been largely secular in nature. Although the 1923 Constitution stated that 'Islam is the national religion', this was the first time that Islamic law, or Sharia, was included in the constitution as '*a* principal source of legislative rules' (emphasis added).[150] This article was amended in 1980 to state that Sharia was '*the* principal source of legislation' (emphasis added).[151] Nonetheless, Islam has been an unwavering part of Egyptian identity and culture since even before the 1923 Constitution. Friday prayers are perhaps the most overt example of this, with shops and businesses closing and the vast majority of the population filing into local mosques for a congregational prayer before, in most cases, resuming their weekend rest.

Aspects of religion have been integrated into daily speech. Inshallah, literally meaning 'God willing', is a nebulous term that can mean anything from an expression of good

143 Ibid.

144 https://www.economist.com/briefing/2013/07/06/the-second-time-around (last accessed 27 September 2022).

145 Nathan J. Brown, 'Correcting the "Corrective Revolution"' *Diwan* (27 February 2019) https://carnegie-mec.org/diwan/78461 (last accessed 27 September 2022).

146 Egyptian Constitution of 2014, art. 200.

147 Ibid. 204.

148 Law 22 of 2022.

149 'Coronavirus in Egypt: Sisi Signs Off New Emergency Powers for Security Forces' *Middle East Eye* (8 May 2020) https://www.middleeasteye.net/news/coronavirus-egypt-emergency-law-sisi-army-new-powers (last accessed 27 September 2022).

150 Egyptian Constitution of 1971, art. 2.

151 Ibid.

intentions to an empty promise.[152] Despite the popular support for a military coup or a Muslim Brotherhood presidency, Islam remains a deeply rooted part of Egyptian culture. However, a centrist approach resonates more with the people than the stricter Shariah-imposing regimes.[153] Religion, therefore, is not simply about the power given to a religious institution like Al-Azhar to regulate daily life, but also concerns the extent to which a population feels that religion is part of its identity. This could be an internal identity, such as the extent to which one follows the tenets of Islam, or an external identity that emerges only when juxtaposed with 'an other', such as a foreigner or the adherent of another religion (or none).

4.1 Religious Diversity

In principle, the 1956 Constitution, like the 1923 Constitution before it,[154] guaranteed Egyptians equality and freedom from discrimination on grounds of religion.[155] Egyptian identity was contingent upon wider factors than adherence to a certain faith, such as service to country or a shared language. One of the most notable inclusions in the 2014 Constitution is the explicit mention, for the first time, of the diversity of religion in Egypt. While Sharia remains the principal source of legislation,[156] 'the principles of the laws of Egyptian Christians and Jews are the main source of laws regulating their personal status, religious affairs, and selection of spiritual leaders'.[157] In actuality, though, religious freedoms have been stifled in numerous ways for decades. Not least of all is the fact that in Egypt there is no recognition of religions other than Islam, Christianity, and Judaism, as reflected in the somewhat paradoxical 'absolute' freedom of belief for 'followers of revealed religions'[158] in the 2014 Constitution.

4.1.1 Judaism in Egypt

Particularly so after the 1948 war, Zionism and Judaism were, in many circles, increasingly conflated. A series of reprisals against Egyptian Jews and the proximity of a new, welcoming homeland on Egypt's border triggered an exodus of thousands of Egyptian Jews in the early 1950s.[159] Under Nasser, Arab nationalism was strongly linked to an anti-Zionist, Palestinian cause and, due to the lack of distinction between Israel the state and Jews the people, violence against Jewish Egyptians following the 1956 and 1967 wars led to further emigration.[160] This continued even after Egypt and Israel signed a peace treaty in 1979, so

[152] For a discussion of this nebulous term, see Rebecca Clift and Fadi Helani, 'Inshallah: Religious Invocations in Arabic Topic Transition' (2010) *39*(03) *Language in Society* 357.

[153] Pakinam El Sharkawy, 'Islamic-Secular Hybrid and the Egyptian State' (2013) *7*(1) *Journal of Middle Eastern and Islamic Studies (in Asia)* 17; Fauzi M. Najjar, 'The Debate on Islam and Secularism in Egypt' (1996) *18*(2) *Arab Studies Quarterly* 1.

[154] Egyptian Constitution of 1923, art. 3.

[155] Egyptian Constitution of 1956, art. 31.

[156] Egyptian Constitution of 2014, art. 2.

[157] Ibid. art. 3.

[158] Ibid. art. 64.

[159] David Kenner, 'What Happened to the Jews of Egypt?' *Foreign Policy* (Washington, 27 March 2013).

[160] Michael M. Laskier, 'Egyptian Jewry under the Nasser Regime, 1956–70' (1995) *31*(3) *Middle Eastern Studies* 573, 581.

much so that it is estimated that only thirty members of the Egyptian Jewish community remain in Egypt.

4.1.2 Christianity in Egypt

Christians have lived alongside Muslims in Egypt for centuries without descending into sectarian conflict. Yet there is a difference between the legal toleration of Christians, as can be found in the constitution, and their social toleration by a majority Muslim nation with Islam as the state religion and Islamic law as *the* principle source of legislation.[161] Estimates of Egypt's Coptic Christian population are disputed at between 8 and 15 per cent, but the 2014 Constitution was the first effort to reflect its existence explicitly in a constitutional document. This is not to say that Christians are granted full rights in modern Egypt. Discrimination comes in the form of being overlooked for jobs, promotion, and better university grades; it comes, too, in such forms as boycotts of shops, or getting poorer hospital treatment.[162] Far more overtly, violence against Christians has led to church closures,[163] terrorist attacks,[164] and multiple deaths.[165]

Coptic Christians in particular see themselves, even if misguidedly, as the direct descendants of the Ancient Egyptians[166] and have a deeply embedded sense of identity as Egyptian.[167] A by-product of Nasser's Arab nationalism was the erasure of this pre-Arab identity, as he sought to weave a new narrative in which Egypt was an integral part of a pan-Arab State future. Under Sadat, Coptic Christians faced further crackdowns when the relationship between him and the Coptic patriarch, Pope Shenouda, soured following demands to increase the representation of Copts in civil service positions and an open contestation of the population census;[168] in 1981, Sadat banished Shenouda to a monastery,[169] where he would remain until 1985, four years after Mubarak assumed power. Sectarian tensions were rising as Sadat sought to replace Nasserists with Islamist groups to bolster his position as president.[170] In addition, until 1998, Christians were required to obtain presidential approval for repairs to churches.[171]

[161] David Zeidan, 'The Copts: Equal, Protected or Persecuted? The Impact of Islamisation on Muslim-Christian Relations in Modern Egypt' (1999) *10*(1) *Islam and Christian-Muslim Relations* 53, 60.

[162] Harriet Sherwood, 'Christians in Egypt Face Unprecedented Persecution, Report Says' *The Guardian* (10 January 2018).

[163] Amira El-Fekki and Jared Malsin, 'Anti-Christian Violence Surges in Egypt, Prompting an Exodus' *The Wall Street Journal* (29 August 2019).

[164] Agence France-Presse, 'Seven Coptic Christians Killed by Isil in Egypt Bus Attack' *The Telegraph* (London, 2 November 2018).

[165] Minorities at Risk Project, 'Chronology for Copts in Egypt' (2004) https://www.refworld.org/docid/469f38841c.html (last accessed 30 September 2022).

[166] Jacques van der Vliet, 'The Copts: "Modern Sons of the Pharaohs"?' (2009) *89*(1) *Church History and Religious Culture* 279.

[167] Elizabeth Iskander, 'The "Mediation" of Muslim-Christian Relations in Egypt: The Strategies and Discourses of the Official Egyptian Press during Mubarak's Presidency' (2012) *23*(1) *Islam and Christian-Muslim Relations* 31, 34.

[168] Olfat M. El Tohamy, 'Why Sadat Cracked Down on Copts' *The Christian Science Monitor* (Cairo, 22 September 1981).

[169] 'Egypt Ends Banishment of Coptic Pope' *Associated Press* (1 January 1985).

[170] Vivian Ibrahim, 'Tracing the Coptic Question in Contemporary Egypt' in Paul S. Rowe (ed.), *Routledge Handbook of Minorities in the Middle East* (Routledge 2018) 82.

[171] Naiem Girgis, *Egypt's Identities in Conflict: The Political and Religious Landscape of Copts and Muslims* (McFarland 2018).

4.1.3 Islam in Egypt

Although Nasser was a secularist, he faced a conundrum on the topic of religion. On the one hand, he recognised the central role of Islam in Egyptian society. Religion is deeply rooted in many facets of daily life for Egyptians—in morality, prayer five times a day, charity-giving, family life, and even one's duty to one's country. On the other hand, Nasser was deeply sceptical of political Islam and perceived it as a threat—both personally and politically—early on in his tenure as president, writing that

> [r]eactionary religious groups such as the Moslem Brotherhood are neither genuinely political nor genuinely religious. Their ultimate aim is power and to realize it they adopt methods contrary to the spirit of Islam and the spirit of the age. Islam derives from a comprehensive philosophy which never fails to accommodate various human feelings and aspirations. In this sense it is not only humanitarian but elastic and tolerant. It has its ubiquitous principles applicable to time and place and mindful of the rights of man. It condemns intolerance, terrorism, prejudice and organized hatred. Its teachings form the core of true democracy.[172]

Nasser aimed to eliminate political Islam by quashing its major outlets. Following an assassination attempt on him by a member of the Muslim Brotherhood in 1954, a brutal crackdown on the organisation ensued,[173] one that lasted until Sadat took office and which was resumed under Mubarak.

Nasser also sought to control religion, bringing Al-Azhar University, one of the Muslim world's oldest, most revered universities and a leading institution for Islamic jurisprudence,[174] under the control of the state. Al-Azhar became a state institution, and its leading scholars would thereafter be selected by the government.[175] Despite a tense relationship between Al-Azhar and President Morsi, the 2012 Constitution gave Al-Azhar a number of new powers[176] and further structural autonomy.[177] Al-Azhar has preferred to exist within a more secular regime than that of the Muslim Brotherhood, which positioned itself as closer to the truth of religion.[178] This explains the ease with which the university transitioned to a Sisi administration following the 2013 military coup.[179] Under Sisi, Al-Azhar has remained a beneficial means of legitimising state actions and has been used to sign off on controversial state policies.[180]

[172] Nasser (n. 32) 209.

[173] Khalil al-Anani, *Inside the Muslim Brotherhood: Religion, Identity, and Politics* (Oxford University Press 2018) 6.

[174] Masooda Bano and Keiko Sakurai (eds.), *Shaping Global Islamic Discourses: The Role of al-Azhar, al-Medina and al-Mustafa* (Edinburgh University Press 2015).

[175] Ahmed Morsy, 'An Independent Voice for Egypt's al-Azhar?' *Sada* (13 July 2011) https://carnegieendowment.org/sada/45052 (last accessed 30 September 2022).

[176] Rachel M. Scott, 'What Might the Muslim Brotherhood Do with Al-Azhar? Religious Authority in Egypt' (2012) *52*(2) *Die Welt Des Islams* 131.

[177] Masooda Bano, 'Al-Azhar University: A Crisis of Authority' in Masooda Bano (ed.), *Modern Islamic Authority and Social Change: Evolving Debates in Muslim Majority Countries* (Edinburgh University Press 2018) 53–78.

[178] Sonia Alianak, *Middle Eastern Leaders and Islam: A Precarious Equilibrium* (Peter Lang 2007) 197.

[179] Masooda Bano and Hanane Benadi, 'Regulating Religious Authority for Political Gains: Al-Sisi's Manipulation of Al-Azhar in Egypt' (2018) *39*(8) *Third World Quarterly* 1, 2.

[180] Malika Zeghal, 'The Recentering of Religious Knowledge and Discourse: The Case of Al-Azhar in Twentieth Century Egypt' in Robert Hefner and Muhammad Qasim (eds.), *Schooling Islam: The Culture and Politics of Modern Muslim Education* (Princeton University Press 2007) 105.

It was under Sadat that Islamic law became more constitutionally enshrined and the ban on the Muslim Brotherhood was relaxed.[181] The 1980 amendment to article 2 of the 1971 Constitution placed Islamic law at the pinnacle of law-making, prohibiting any domestic law from contravening the prevailing principles of Islamic law. Gender equality in the 'fields of political, social, cultural and economic life [must be] without violation of the rules of Islamic jurisprudence'.[182] Societal changes began to be noticed, including an uptick in the number of women wearing headscarves,[183] which would have been a rarity in the 1950s and 1960s. Indeed, the idea of all women wearing headscarves in Egypt was laughable to Nasser,[184] and Egyptian women's fashion looked to the West for inspiration (including bikinis and short skirts).[185]

Nevertheless, the interpretation of the constitutionality of national laws against the threshold of article 2 is not clear-cut. The sole institution with jurisdiction to exercise judicial review of constitutional matters is the Supreme Constitutional Court;[186] the incompatibility of domestic laws with Sharia, and by implication the constitution, has been challenged in this forum on countless occasions by members of the Islamic community. This suggests that understandings of the purpose and meaning of article 2, and of how Sharia should be interpreted, differ between groups.

The marriage of convenience between Sadat and the Muslim Brotherhood was relatively short-lived. After Sadat's assassination in 1981 by members of its splinter group al-Jihad,[187] the Muslim Brotherhood was once again driven underground by Mubarak, who, like Nasser, saw it as a threat to his political power.[188] Yet they still coexisted in silence: 'The government turned a blind eye to Islamist grassroots power. In return, the Islamists did not confront state corruption and inefficiency.'[189] From a constitutional standpoint, though, references to Islam were not removed; rather, to counter the power of the Muslim Brotherhood, Mubarak expanded the powers of the military. The Muslim Brotherhood—which during the Mubarak era increasingly provided a safety-net of social welfare for poorer Egyptians—was highly popular among the lower-middle class, which has seen particularly rapid growth.[190]

This policy of non-confrontation led, however, to the Muslim Brotherhood's successful participation in parliamentary elections since as early as 1984.[191] In the 2005 parliamentary elections, Muslim Brotherhood candidates, standing as independents under the banner 'Islam is the solution',[192] won 88 of the 454 seats in the chamber, quintupling their

[181] Ibrahim (n. 96).

[182] Egyptian Constitution of 1971, art. 11.

[183] Toqa Ezzidin, 'Depiction of Hijab in Egyptian Media: Why Does It Often Backfire?' *Egyptian Streets* (Cairo, 1 November 2017).

[184] https://www.youtube.com/watch?v=_ZIqdrFeFBk (last accessed 27 September 2022).

[185] 'Difference between Egyptian Fashion in 1950s vs. Now' *Egypt Today* (Cairo, 24 July 2017).

[186] Egyptian Constitution of 1971, art. 175.

[187] Ephraim Kahana and Sagit Stivi-Kerbis, 'The Assassination of Anwar al-Sadat: An Intelligence Failure' (2013) *27 International Journal of Intelligence and Counterintelligence* 178.

[188] Joel Campagna, 'From Accommodation to Confrontation: The Muslim Brotherhood in the Mubarak Years' (1996) *50*(1) *Journal of International Affairs* 278, 280.

[189] Ahmed Abdalla, 'Egypt's Islamists and the State: From Complicity to Confrontation' *Middle East Report* (July–August 1993) 29.

[190] Ibrahim (n. 96) 76.

[191] Carrie Rosefsky Wickham, 'The Muslim Brotherhood after Mubarak' *Foreign Affairs* (3 February 2011) https://www.foreignaffairs.com/articles/egypt/2011-02-03/muslim-brotherhood-after-mubarak (last accessed 30 September 2022).

[192] 'الإسلام الحل'

previous seats and catapulting them to the forefront as the largest opposition bloc. The Muslim Brotherhood, then, was simultaneously tolerated and vilified under Mubarak, who evidently understood the need to appease the public by allowing the movement space in which to operate politically in small groups as long as it did not disturb the broader status quo.[193]

Prior to the introduction of the most recent constitution in 2014, political Islam gained even further traction during mass protests in February 2011. After constitutional amendments received unexpected and overwhelming approval in the 2011 referendum, the theory arose that the Muslim Brotherhood had leveraged its network to convince illiterate members of the population in rural areas to vote yes.[194] Whether this is true or not, the credence given to the theory highlights the grassroots power that the Muslim Brotherhood was believed to have had in 2011. Indeed, in 2012, following the removal of Mubarak, two Islamist parties, the Muslim Brotherhood's Freedom and Justice Party and the Salafi Nour Party, won a combined 71 per cent of seats in the parliament's lower house and almost 90 per cent in the upper house.[195]

The Muslim Brotherhood is currently once again reviled by the leadership. Sisi has taken two main approaches to its suppression,[196] on the one hand jailing its leadership,[197] including former president Mohammed Morsi, who later died in prison,[198] and, on the other, isolating it by linking it to violent Islam.[199] However, the Muslim Brotherhood has been in this position before: 'Each time its organization was decimated, and observers wrote its obituary. But it has always reemerged.'[200] There have been numerous explanations as to how it has been capable of surviving repeated crackdowns,[201] but perhaps the most salient is that it remains popular with its core base. A 2018 poll revealed that 33 per cent of Egyptian Muslims held a positive view of the Muslim Brotherhood and 6 per cent, a 'very positive view'.[202]

[193] 'Many Egyptians Miss Their Deposed President, Hosni Mubarak' *The Economist* (19 August 2019) https://www.economist.com/middle-east-and-africa/2019/08/22/many-egyptians-miss-their-deposed-president-hosni-mubarak (last accessed 27 September 2022).

[194] Said Shehata, 'Islamism in Egypt: Legitimate Concerns?' *Ahramonline* (20 April 2011) http://english.ahram.org.eg/NewsContent/4/0/10405/Opinion/Islamism-in-Egyptlegitimate-concerns.aspx (last accessed 20 April 2011).

[195] '2012 Egyptian Parliamentary Elections' *Carnegie Endowment for International Peace* (22 January 2015) https://carnegieendowment.org/2015/01/22/2012-egyptian-parliamentary-elections-pub-58800 (last accessed 30 September 2022).

[196] Barbara Zollner, 'Surviving Repression: How Egypt's Muslim Brotherhood Has Carried on' *Diwan* (11 March 2019) https://carnegie-mec.org/2019/03/11/surviving-repression-how-egypt-s-muslim-brotherhood-has-carried-on-pub-78552 (last accessed 30 September 2022).

[197] 'Court Jails Egyptian Muslim Brotherhood Leader for Life: Sources' *Reuters* (London, 12 August 2018) https://www.reuters.com/article/us-egypt-court/court-jails-egyptian-muslim-brotherhood-leader-for-life-sources-idUSKBN1KX0I0 (last accessed 30 September 2022).

[198] Mona Eltahawy, 'Mohamed Morsi Died in a Soundproof Cage' *New York Times* (18 June 2019) https://www.nytimes.com/2019/06/18/opinion/morsi-death-egypt.html (last accessed 30 September 2022).

[199] Statement by H.E. president of the Arab Republic of Egypt Abdel Fattah El Sisi at the 71st Session of the United Nations General Assembly (20 September 2016) https://www.sis.gov.eg/Story/106007/Statement-by-H.E.-President-of-the-Arab-Republic-of-Egypt-Abdel-Fattah-El-Sisi-at-the-71st-session?lang=en-us&lang=en-us (last accessed 30 September 2022).

[200] Ibrahim (n. 96) 76.

[201] Zollner (n. 196).

[202] David Pollock, 'In Egypt, One-Third Still Like the Muslim Brotherhood; Half Call U.S. Ties "Important"' *Fikra Forum* (10 December 2018) https://www.washingtoninstitute.org/fikraforum/view/in-egypt-one-third-still-like-the-muslim-brotherhood-half-call-u.s.-ties-im (last accessed 30 September 2022).

5. Lack of Political Freedoms

Despite peaceful transitions of power between Nasser, Sadat, and Mubarak, every change in leadership has come with severe crackdowns on the political freedoms of those most closely affiliated with the former incumbent. This, in reality, has translated to a lack of political freedoms for the Egyptian people. A hallmark of Egypt's identity since the 1952 revolution sought to establish Egypt as an independent, democratic state is precisely the absence of such freedoms. The text of the constitutions, however, has not reflected this reality. In spite of its overt inclusion of progressive language on freedom of political belief, the relevant provisions are often subject to the whims of those in power thanks to their control of the executive and its de jure or de facto control in turn of levers of power such as the legislature or judiciary.

5.1 One-Party Politics under Nasser

After the deposal of King Farouk, Egypt rapidly evolved into a one-party state under Nasser as freedoms began to be stifled.[203] In January 1953, the Revolutionary Command Council dissolved all political parties and confiscated their funds; shortly thereafter, Egypt's new single political organisation, the National Liberation Rally, was established. The justification for this seems to have been that 'the task of national consolidation which the "revolution" had set for itself demanded the unity of the Egyptian people, and a mass of conflicting political forces could only divert the people from rallying around the "revolutionary vanguard"'.[204]

The 1956 Constitution creates a superficial illusion of political freedom. Articles on national governance exist, but are moderated by the state. The rights to assembly,[205] freedom of opinion,[206] the free press,[207] freedom of correspondence,[208] and the right to privacy at home[209] are all made subject to domestic law. The president is elected by means of a general referendum on the candidate chosen by the House of Representatives;[210] members of this House are themselves selected 'by means of a secret national ballot';[211] the president chooses his successor; and, at any event, he has the power to dissolve the House of Representatives.[212]

5.2 The 1971 Constitution under Sadat and Mubarak

The two transitions of power following Nasser's death were peaceful, at least in the sense that they did not stem from popular revolution. Nonetheless, shortly after assuming power,

[203] Mansfield (n. 54) 670, 673.
[204] Peter Johnson, 'Egypt under Nasser' (1972) *10 MERIP Reports* 3, 4.
[205] Egyptian Constitution of 1956, art. 47.
[206] Ibid. art. 44.
[207] Ibid. art. 45.
[208] Ibid. art. 42.
[209] Ibid. art. 41.
[210] Egyptian Constitution of 1958, art. 121.
[211] Ibid. art. 67.
[212] Ibid. art. 111.

Sadat began a purge of Nasserists in government[213] under the guise of a programme of major national reform. In the so-called Rectification Movement, he set about moving Egypt away from the pro-Soviet, left-wing nation of Nasser by expelling many of the remaining Nasser loyalists from government.[214] The date of the Movement's launch, 15 May 1971, became a public holiday to mark the event, and it is also commemorated in the name of a city, 15th of May City. By 1978, Nasser's Arab Socialist Union had been dismantled, and Sadat's National Democratic Party (NDP) would remain in power for more than forty years during Sadat and Mubarak's presidencies before being toppled in the Arab Spring. The Rectification Movement also became a turning-point in political opposition to Sadat. In July 1975, Sadat granted amnesty to all political prisoners jailed prior to the Rectification Movement, and in the following year restored voting rights to more than five thousand citizens who had been 'politically isolated'.[215]

5.3 The State of Emergency in Egypt

States of emergency have long been a part of the daily life and even identity of many an Egyptian. Until the 2011 revolution, few had known a life outside of emergency laws. Egypt spent all but seventeen months of Sadat's eleven-year tenure under a state of emergency; then, after Sadat's assassination in 1981, Mubarak imposed a continuous emergency law on Egypt for more than three decades until the protests of 2011 forced him to lift it. Previous presidents had also demonstrated good form in utilising this tactic:

> In 1954, Nasser cited the need 'to secure the Revolution first' to justify the exceptional People's Courts. More recently, Mubarak explained in 1998 that renewing the emergency law was necessary 'in order to confront terrorism [and] protect democracy and stability'. In 2000, arguing for the three-year extension of the law that passed that year, the minister of the interior insisted emergency rule was 'an indispensable deterrent . . . [to] guard . . . against the criminal forces who are still intent on seizing all possible opportunities to incite unrest and hit national interests'. Three years later, Egypt's prime minister assured the parliament that another extension was needed. . . . In other words, not surprisingly, the past half century of nearly continuous emergency rule in Egypt has been essential to the very existence of the state.[216]

Although Sadat restored opposition and social movement, guaranteeing the 'freedom of press, printing, publication, and mass media',[217] he limited these through constitutional powers of 'censorship of newspapers, publication, and mass media in a state of emergency'.[218] The 1971 Constitution permitted the president to unilaterally declare a state of

[213] Raymond A. Hinnebusch, 'Egypt under Sadat: Elites, Power Structure, and Political Change in a Post-Populist State' (1981) *28*(4) *Social Problems* 442.

[214] 'ثورة التصحيح'

[215] John Waterbury, *The Egypt of Nasser and Sadat: The Political Economy of Two Regimes* (Princeton University Press 1983) 373.

[216] Sadiq Reza, 'Endless Emergency: The Case of Egypt' (2007) *10*(4) *New Criminal Law Review* 544.

[217] Egyptian Constitution of 1971, art. 48.

[218] Ibid.

emergency,[219] which also enabled him to issue decrees with the force of law.[220] Despite the reopening of some political freedom under Sadat for groups such as the New Wafd Party,[221] 'Egyptians in the seventies did not yet enjoy the full freedoms that were their legitimate rights, although the relaxations of control "[did] allow [Egyptians] to meet, speak, discuss, and criticise" '.[222]

Political freedoms continued to be restricted under the Mubarak presidency. The NDP maintained its control over Parliament, with constitutional amendments in March 2007 strengthening the emergency powers bestowed upon the president. In total, thirty-four articles of the 1971 Constitution were amended,[223] as a result of which protections against warrantless arrests, detention, home entry, and surveillance or seizure of correspondence were suspended.[224] The amendment of article 179 also constitutionalised Mubarak's prerogative to refer terrorism offences to emergency or military courts. Prior to 2007, this power had been statutory under the Emergency Law and the Code of Military Justice, but had been challenged in court,[225] which perhaps explains the rationale for enshrining it in the constitution and removing it from the jurisdiction of constitutional courts.

5.4 Contemporary Egypt under Sisi

After brief respites between 2012 and 2017, a more permanent emergency law has resurfaced under Sisi. This is despite the existence of constitutional protections to avoid its misuse, protections that include the restriction of a state of emergency to three months, after which an extension of a further three months must be sought from Parliament.[226] These measures have brought Egypt back to pre-2011 levels of exigent state power to curtail freedoms and political freedoms.[227] Originally created by Nasser, the Emergency Law[228] permits mass surveillance and allows security forces to detain and interrogate suspects indefinitely. One may draw several similarities between Sisi and Nasser:

> [B]oth leaders led military movements, which were described as popular revolutions. Both entered an extended confrontation with the Muslim Brotherhood. Both of their states repressed all opposition and sought to curb the independence of the media and of civil society organizations, and both relied on their personal charisma to build legitimacy.[229]

219 Ibid. art. 148.
220 Ibid. art. 108.
221 Raymond A. Hinnebusch, 'The Reemergence of the Wafd Party: Glimpses of the Liberal Opposition in Egypt' (1984) *16*(1) *International Journal of Middle East Studies* 99.
222 Raymond William Baker, 'Fighting for Freedom and the Rule of Law' in Raymond William Baker (ed.), *Sadat and After: Struggles for Egypt's Political Soul* (Harvard University Press 1990) 66–7.
223 Michael Slackman, 'As Egypt Votes on Laws, Cynicism Rules the Street' *New York Times* (26 March 2007).
224 Egyptian Constitution of 1971, art. 179. For a discussion, see Reza (n. 216) 541.
225 Nathan J. Brown, *The Rule of Law in the Arab World: Courts in Egypt and the Gulf* (Cambridge University Press 1997) 98; Maye Kassem, *Egyptian Politics: The Dynamics of Authoritarian Rule* (Lynne Rienner Publishers 2004) 36.
226 Egyptian Constitution of 2014, art. 154.
227 Mohamed Abdellah and Mahmoud Mourad, 'Eight Years after Uprising, Egyptians Say Freedoms Have Eroded' *Reuters* (London, 24 January 2019).
228 Law 162 of 1958.
229 Shehata (n. 6).

Egypt has been under a perpetual state of emergency again since April 2017, at which time an estimated sixty thousand political prisoners had been incarcerated.[230] Forcible disappearances[231] have increased, and since 2011 at least nineteen new prisons have been built to house new detainees in Egypt's penal system.[232]

The amendments to the 2014 Constitution that expanded Sisi and the armed forces' powers were themselves the reason for a major crackdown on information in the run up to elections in 2019. Independent websites campaigning against the amendments were shut down,[233] as were websites calling for citizens to vote against them.[234] Mainstream media were instructed not to report on the amendments,[235] and opposition figures were arrested on charges of 'publishing false news'.[236] In May 2020, Sisi signed into law new amendments to the emergency law[237] in response to the global Covid-19 pandemic. As Human Rights Watch notes,[238] only five of the eighteen amendments are linked to public health; by annexing them to the existing emergency law, the resulting powers can be exercised whenever future states of emergency are declared, irrespective of whether a health crisis exists or not.

6. Conclusion

This chapter has discussed pertinent elements of the constitutions which Egypt has had since its rebirth as an independent nation in 1923 and as a republic in 1952. Outwardly, certain aspects of constitutional identity have not changed—the centrality of the armed forces, Islam's position as the state religion, and the lack of full political freedom for citizens—but in their substance they have indeed changed drastically.

Religion has been the foundational pillar of Egyptian society. Friday is customarily a national day of prayer, and given that Egypt is a majority Muslim nation, elements of Islamic morality underpin its codes of honour, respect, and social acceptability. This has grown in recent decades, and Egypt has shifted from a more secular nation under Nasser to a country that, in the first free elections of its entire history, voted to elect the Islamist Muslim Brotherhood candidate Mohammed Morsi as president in 2012. However, while this strand of Islamist support remains in force in Egypt, it is not endorsed by the majority. The failure of the Muslim Brotherhood in Egypt suggests at least three things.

Firstly, the election of the Muslim Brotherhood to power was due at least in some small part to the rejection of the 'other candidate', Ahmed Shafik, a remnant of the Mubarak

230 Human Rights Watch, '"We Are in Tombs": Abuses in Egypt's Scorpion Prison' (8 September 2016) https://www.hrw.org/report/2016/09/28/we-are-tombs/abuses-egypts-scorpion-prison (last accessed 30 September 2022).

231 Amnesty International, 'Egypt: Hundreds Disappeared and Tortured Amid Wave of Brutal Repression' (23 July 2016) https://www.amnesty.org/en/latest/news/2016/07/egypt-hundreds-disappeared-and-tortured-amid-wave-of-brutal-repression/ (last accessed 30 September 2022).

232 Al-Masry Al-Youm, 'Nineteen New Prisons Built in Egypt since 2011: Rights Group' *Egypt Independent* (9 September 2016) https://egyptindependent.com/nineteen-new-prisons-built-egypt-2011-rights-group/ (last accessed 30 September 2022).

233 https://bit.ly/2X8ugMH (last accessed 30 September 2022).

234 https://bit.ly/2X5ccmN (last accessed 30 September 2022).

235 https://bit.ly/2WESZcC (last accessed 30 September 2022).

236 https://bit.ly/2X217CU (last accessed 30 September 2022).

237 https://bit.ly/3gaj5Mm (last accessed 30 September 2022).

238 Human Rights Watch, 'Egypt: Covid-19 Cover for New Repressive Powers' (7 May 2022) https://www.hrw.org/news/2020/05/07/egypt-covid-19-cover-new-repressive-powers (last accessed 30 September 2022).

administration, owing to the desire for a total break with this administration's recent history. Secondly, religion in Egyptian identity is more secular in nature than the ideologies of the Muslim Brotherhood. The reality of this may even reflect the constitutional protections afforded to other 'revealed' (Abrahamic religions in Egypt, although the country still has far to go, both ideologically and constitutionally, to reach full religious pluralism. Finally, the rapid downfall of Morsi and the Muslim Brotherhood after attempts to change the constitution in 2012 highlight that, in Egypt, the armed forces are always waiting in the wings.

The armed forces now occupy a confusing space, one where they are at the same time saviours and oppressors, where patriotism and nostalgia about bygone wars collide with the military's ongoing encroachment into the political sphere, and where there are notable crackdowns against dissidents and opposition. Since the Egyptian peace treaty with Israel in 1979, a good deal of the raison d'être of the armed forces has evaporated. A new enemy, going under the umbrella term of terrorism, makes the military look inward to its own citizens rather than to an external invader, as in previous wars. Under this guise of affording protection against terrorism, the armed forces have steadily engulfed private businesses and lives, as well as eliminating checks on their powers through constitutional amendments that subordinated the judiciary and legislature to the executive branch, itself but a civilian facade for military rule. Since 1952, reverence for the military has been part of Egyptian identity, and never has the population loathed it in the way that many do now.

Since its first constitution in 1923, Egypt has seen ebbs and flows of political suppression by its leadership, despite the constitution's shifting only slightly in the protections granted. One element that has remained fairly constant is the loophole granted in the constitution for protections to be curtailed subject to domestic law. Coupled with an expansion of the powers of the executive, this has resulted in domination by political parties under Nasser, Sadat, and Mubarak, as well as, in recent years, a rubber-stamp judiciary in which the majority of its members are pro-Sisi.

The constitution seems, on the face of it, to offer guarantees of multi-party representation, along with an array of rights to freedom of political participation, dissent, and expression, as well as to freedom from arbitrary arrest and detention. However, the constitutionally permitted suspension of these freedoms under a state of emergency which has been almost ever-present since the 1952 military coup has meant that many of these rights are mere lip service to notions of what a democratic nation should look like, without there being interest in supporting the facade with substantive content that would give them meaning. In this way, Egypt has made a full circle back to the Constitution of 1923, which, in its preamble, concerned itself with referring to the perceived attributes of a free state, with little thought of how these might conflict with a monarchy.

There is talk of a new constitution on the horizon for Egypt, one that critics expect to take shape towards the end of Sisi's third term in 2030.[239] Justifications for amendment and replacement of Egypt's constitution have come from unlikely sources, including the head of the National Elections Authority, who, tasked with managing Egypt's elections and referenda,[240] has concluded that a constitution should 'fit the situation of its society'.[241] It is likely,

[239] https://www.almanassa.net/ar/story/12141 (last accessed 30 September 2022).
[240] Egyptian Constitution of 2014, art. 208.
[241] http://gate.ahram.org.eg/News/2144732.aspx (accessed 30 September 2022).

though, that were another constitution to be drafted, it would significantly expand the existing powers of the president and military.

Bibliography

'2012 Egyptian Parliamentary Elections' *Carnegie Endowment for International Peace* (22 January 2015) https://carnegieendowment.org/2015/01/22/2012-egyptian-parliamentary-elections-pub-58800 (last accessed 30 September 2022)

Abdalla A., 'Egypt's Islamists and the State: From Complicity to Confrontation', *Middle East Report* (July–August 1993) 29

Abdelhadi M., 'Egyptians Look to Military "Saviour"' *BBC* (Cairo, 23 June 2009) http://news.bbc.co.uk/1/hi/world/middle_east/8113349.stm (last accessed 27 September 2022)

Abdellah M. and Mourad M., 'Eight Years after Uprising, Egyptians Say Freedoms Have Eroded' *Reuters* (London, 24 January 2019)

Abdel-Nasser G.A., 'The Egyptian Revolution' (1955) *33*(2) *Foreign Affairs* 199

Abul-Magd Z., 'The Egyptian Republic of Retired Generals' *The Middle East Channel* (Limassol, 8 May 2012)

Agence France-Presse, 'Seven Coptic Christians Killed by Isil in Egypt Bus Attack' *The Telegraph* (London, 2 November 2018)

Al-Anani K., *Inside the Muslim Brotherhood: Religion, Identity, and Politics* (Oxford University Press 2018)

Al-Aswany A., *On the State of Egypt: What Caused the Revolution* (Penguin Random House, 2011)

Alianak S., *Middle Eastern Leaders and Islam: A Precarious Equilibrium* (Peter Lang 2007)

Al-Youm A., 'Nineteen New Prisons Built in Egypt since 2011: Rights Group' (9 September 2016) https://egyptindependent.com/nineteen-new-prisons-built-egypt-2011-rights-group/ (last accessed 30 September 2022)

Amnesty International, 'Egypt: Hundreds Disappeared and Tortured Amid Wave of Brutal Repression' (23 July 2016) https://www.amnesty.org/en/latest/news/2016/07/egypt-hundreds-disappeared-and-tortured-amid-wave-of-brutal-repression/ (last accessed 30 September 2022)

Amr Emam A., 'Egypt Struggles with Bloated Public Sector' *The Arab Weekly* (18 November 2018) https://thearabweekly.com/egypt-struggles-bloated-public-sector (last accessed 27 September 2022)

'The Anglo-Egyptian Treaty Negotiations' *Bulletin of International News* (1928) *4*(19) *New Series* 3–11

'Anwar El-Sadat: The Daring Arab Pioneer of Peace with Israel' *The New York Times* (7 October 1981) https://www.nytimes.com/1981/10/07/obituaries/anwar-el-sadat-daring-arab-pioneer-peace-with-israel-sadat-s-innovations-sprang.html (accessed 16 October 2023)

Aoudé I.G., 'Egypt: Revolutionary Process and Global Capitalist Crisis' (2013) *35*(3) *Arab Studies Quarterly* 241

'Arab Unity: Nasser's Revolution' *Al Jazeera* (20 June 2008) https://www.aljazeera.com/focus/arabunity/2008/02/200852517252821627.html (last accessed 27 September 2022)

Assaad R., 'The Effects of Public Sector Hiring and Compensation Policies on the Egyptian Labor Market' (1997) *11*(1) *The World Bank Economic Review* 85

ASU Programme for Youth, 'Pioneers of the Future' *Arab Observer* (14 February 1966)

Baker W., 'Fighting for Freedom and the Rule of Law' in Baker W. (ed.), *Sadat and After: Struggles for Egypt's Political Soul* (Harvard University Press 1990) 66

Bano M., 'al-Azhar University: A Crisis of Authority' in Bano M. (ed.), *Modern Islamic Authority and Social Change: Evolving Debates in Muslim Majority Countries* (vol. 1, Edinburgh University Press 2018) 53

Bano M. and Benadi H., 'Regulating Religious Authority for Political Gains: Al-Sisi's Manipulation of Al-Azhar in Egypt' (2018) *39*(8) *Third World Quarterly* 1

Bano M. and Sakurai K. (eds.), *Shaping Global Islamic Discourses: The Role of al-Azhar, al-Medina and al-Mustafa* (Edinburgh University Press 2015)

Blackwell S., 'Saving the King: Anglo-American Strategy and British Counter-Subversion Operations in Libya, 1953–59' (2003) *39*(1) *Middle Eastern Studies* 1

Brown N.J., *The Rule of Law in the Arab World: Courts in Egypt and the Gulf* (Cambridge University Press 1997)

Brown N.J., 'Correcting the "Corrective Revolution"' *Diwan* (27 February 2019) https://carnegie-mec.org/diwan/78461 (last accessed 27 September 2022)

Campagna J., 'From Accommodation to Confrontation: The Muslim Brotherhood in the Mubarak Years' (1996) *50*(1) *Journal of International Affairs* 278

Claes M. and Reestman J.H., 'The Protection of National Constitutional Identity and the Limits of European Integration at the Occasion of the Gauweiler Case' (2015) *16 German Law Journal* 917

Clift R. and Helani F., 'Inshallah: Religious Invocations in Arabic Topic Transition' (2010) *39*(03) *Language in Society* 357

'Coronavirus in Egypt: Sisi Signs Off New Emergency Powers for Security Forces' *Middle East Eye* (8 May 2020) https://www.middleeasteye.net/news/coronavirus-egypt-emergency-law-sisi-army-new-powers (last accessed 27 September 2022)

'Court Jails Egyptian Muslim Brotherhood Leader for Life: Sources' *Reuters* (London, 12 August 2018) https://www.reuters.com/article/us-egypt-court/court-jails-egyptian-muslim-brotherhood-leader-for-life-sources-idUSKBN1KX0I0 (last accessed 30 September 2022)

Crabbs J., 'Politics, History, and Culture in Nasser's Egypt' (1975) *6*(04) *International Journal of Middle East Studies* 386

Crabites P., 'Britain's Debt to King Farouk' (1941) *19 Foreign Affairs* 852

Cunningham R.B., Sarayrah Y.K., and Sarayrah Y.E., 'Taming "Wasta" to Achieve Development' (1994) *16*(3) *Arab Studies Quarterly* 29

'Difference between Egyptian Fashion in 1950s vs. Now' *Egypt Today* (Cairo, 24 July 2017)

Drinóczi T., 'Constitutional Identity in Europe: The Identity of the Constitution—a Regional Approach' (2020) *21 German Law Journal* 105

'Egypt Ends Banishment of Coptic Pope' *Associated Press* (1 January 1985)

'Egypt's Referendums Poll Results 1956–2012' *Ahramonline* (2014) http://english.ahram.org.eg/NewsAFCON/2019/91674.aspx (last accessed 27 September 2022)

El Mallakh R., 'Some Economic Aspects of the Aswan High Dam Project in Egypt' (1959) *35*(1) *Land Economics* 15

El Sadat A., *Revolt on the Nile* (Allan Wingate 1957)

El Sadat A., 'Tasks of the Stage; or a Comprehensive Civilisation Strategy' (1974) *The October Working Paper* https://sadat.umd.edu/resources/written-works (last accessed 27 September 2022)

El Sadat A., *In Search of Identity: An Autobiography* [Arabic] (HarperCollins 1978)

El Sharkawy P.E., 'Islamic-Secular Hybrid and the Egyptian State' (2013) *7*(1) *Journal of Middle Eastern and Islamic Studies (in Asia)* 17

El Tohamy O.M., 'Why Sadat Cracked Down on Copts' *The Christian Science Monitor* (Cairo, 22 September 1981)

El-Fekki A. and Malsin J., 'Anti-Christian Violence Surges in Egypt, Prompting an Exodus' *The Wall Street Journal* (29 August 2019)

Ezzidin T., 'Depiction of Hijab in Egyptian Media: Why Does It Often Backfire?' *Egyptian Streets* (Cairo, 1 November 2017)

Fahm N., 'Palestine, an Arab Issue' *The Cairo Global Affairs Review* (2017) https://www.thecairoreview.com/essays/palestine-an-arab-issue/ (last accessed 27 September 2022)

Fahmy H., 'An Initial Perspective on "The Winter of Discontent": The Root Causes of the Egyptian Revolution' (2012) *79*(2) *Social Research: An International Quarterly* 349

'For 18 Years Nasser Had Almost Hypnotic Power in His Leadership of Egyptians' *New York Times* (29 September 1970) https://www.nytimes.com/1970/09/29/archives/for-18-years-nasser-had-almost-hypnotic-power-in-his-leadership-of.html (accessed 27 September 2022)

'Friends in High Places' *The Economist* (9 October 2014) https://www.economist.com/business/2014/10/09/friends-in-high-places (last accessed 27 September 2022)

Ghonim W., *Revolution 2.0: The Power of the People Is Greater Than the People in Power* (Houghton Mifflin Harcourt 2012)

Girgis N., *Egypt's Identities in Conflict: The Political and Religious Landscape of Copts and Muslims* (McFarland 2018)

Gray M., 'Economic Reform, Privatization and Tourism in Egypt' (1998) *34*(2) *Middle Eastern Studies* 91

Hansen B. and Radwan S., *Employment Opportunities and Equity in a Changing Economy: Egypt in the 1980s* (International Labour Office 1982)

Hashim A.S., 'The Egyptian Military Part One: From the Ottomans through Sadat' (2011) *18*(3) *Middle East Policy* 69

Hayoun M., 'The Coming Arab Identity Crisis' *The Atlantic* (8 March 2012) https://www.theatlantic.com/international/archive/2012/03/the-coming-arab-identity-crisis/254144/ (last accessed 27 September 2022)

Henry C.M. and Springborg R., *Globalisation and the Politics of Development in the Middle East* (Cambridge University Press 2010)

Hinnebusch R.A., 'Egypt under Sadat: Elites, Power Structure, and Political Change in a Post-Populist State' (1981) *28*(4) *Social Problems* 442

Hinnebusch R.A., 'The Reemergence of the Wafd Party: Glimpses of the Liberal Opposition in Egypt' (1984) *16*(1) *International Journal of Middle East Studies* 99

Hopwood D., *Egypt: Politics and Society 1945–1981* (George Allen & Unwin 1982) 37

Human Rights Watch, '"We Are in Tombs": Abuses in Egypt's Scorpion Prison' (8 September 2016) https://www.hrw.org/report/2016/09/28/we-are-tombs/abuses-egypts-scorpion-prison (last accessed 30 September 2022)

Human Rights Watch, 'Egypt: Covid-19 Cover for New Repressive Powers' (7 May 2022) https://www.hrw.org/news/2020/05/07/egypt-covid-19-cover-new-repressive-powers (last accessed 30 September 2022)

Ibrahim B., 'An Egyptian, and an Arab' *The Guardian* (8 July 2010) https://www.theguardian.com/commentisfree/2010/jul/08/egyptian-arab-cultural-identity (last accessed 27 September 2022)

Ibrahim El-Issawy I., *Labour Force, Employment, and Unemployment* (International Labour Office 1983)

Ibrahim S.E., 'An Islamic Alternative in Egypt: The Muslim Brotherhood and Sadat' (1982) *4*(1/2) *Arab Studies Quarterly* 75

Ibrahim S.E., 'Governance and Structural Adjustment: The Egyptian Case' in Ibrahim S.E. (ed.), *Egypt Islam and Democracy: Critical Essays* (The American University in Cairo Press Cairo 1996) 141

Ibrahim V., 'Tracing the Coptic Question in Contemporary Egypt' in Rowe P.S. (ed.), *Routledge Handbook of Minorities in the Middle East* (Routledge 2018) 82

Iskander E., 'The "Mediation" of Muslim-Christian Relations in Egypt: The Strategies and Discourses of the Official Egyptian Press during Mubarak's Presidency' (2012) *23*(1) *Islam and Christian-Muslim Relations* 31

Joesten J., 'Nasser's Daring Dream: The Aswan High Dam' (1960) *16*(2) *The World Today* 55

Johnson P, 'Egypt under Nasser' (1972) *10 MERIP Reports* 3

Jones C.F., 'The New Egyptian Constitution' (1956) *10*(3) *Middle East Journal* 300

Kahana E. and Stivi-Kerbis S., 'The Assassination of Anwar al-Sadat: An Intelligence Failure' (2013) *27 International Journal of Intelligence and Counterintelligence* 178

Kassem M., *Egyptian Politics: The Dynamics of Authoritarian Rule* (Lynne Rienner Publishers 2004)

Kenner D., 'What Happened to the Jews of Egypt?' *Foreign Policy* (Washington, 27 March 2013)

Khalifa S., *Egypt's Lost Spring: Causes and Consequences* (ABC-CLIO 2015)

Khalil M., 'The People and the Army Are One Hand: Myths and Their Translations' in Mehrez S. (ed.), *Translating Egypt's Revolution: The Language of Tahrir* (The American University in Cairo Press 2012) 256

Korany B. and El-Mahdi R., *Arab Spring in Egypt: Revolution and Beyond* (The American University in Cairo Press 2012)

Kramer M, 'Arab Nationalism: Mistaken Identity' (1993) *122*(3) *Daedalus* 171

Laskier M.M., 'Egyptian Jewry under the Nasser Regime, 1956–70' (1995) *31*(3) *Middle Eastern Studies* 573

Law D., 'Constitutional Archetypes' (2016) *95 Texas Law Review* 153
Lesch A.M., 'Egypt's Spring: Causes of the Revolution' (2011) *18*(3) *Middle East Policy Washington* 35
Mansfield P., 'Nasser and Nasserism' (1973) *28*(4) *International Journal* 670
'Many Egyptians Miss Their Deposed President, Hosni Mubarak' *The Economist* (19 August 2019) https://www.economist.com/middle-east-and-africa/2019/08/22/many-egyptians-miss-their-deposed-president-hosni-mubarak (last accessed 30 September 2022)
Marfleet P., 'Mubarak's Egypt: Nexus of Criminality' (2013) *2*(2) *State Crime Journal* 112
Mayfield J.B., *Rural Politics in Nasser's Egypt: A Quest for Legitimacy* (University of Texas Press 1971)
Millet, F., 'L'Union Europèenne Et L'Identité Constitutionelle Des États Members' (2013)
Minorities at Risk Project, 'Chronology for Copts in Egypt' (2004) https://www.refworld.org/docid/469f38841c.html (last accessed 30 September 2022)
'Mohamed Morsi Died in a Soundproof Cage' *New York Times* (18 June 2019) https://www.nytimes.com/2019/06/18/opinion/morsi-death-egypt.html (last accessed 30 September 2022)
Morsy A., 'An Independent Voice for Egypt's Al-Azhar?' *Sada* (13 July 2011) https://carnegieendowment.org/sada/45052 (last accessed 30 September 2022)
Morsy L., 'Farouk in British Policy' (1984) *20*(4) *Middle Eastern Studies* 193
Mostafa D.S., *The Egyptian Military in Popular Culture: Context and Critique* (Palgrave Macmillan 2016)
Mostafa D.S., *Transformation of the Popular War Hero's Image under Mubarak in the Egyptian Military in Popular Culture: Context and Critique* (Palgrave Macmillan 2017)
Najjar F.M., 'The Debate on Islam and Secularism in Egypt' (1996) *18*(2) *Arab Studies Quarterly* 1
Nassif H.B., 'Wedded to Mubarak: The Second Careers and Financial Rewards of Egypt's Military Elite, 1981–2011' (2013) *67*(4) *Middle East Journal* 509
Nossier M., 'Will Arabizing Education Strengthen Egyptian Identity?' *Arab News* (8 June 2018) https://www.arabnews.com/node/1318291 (last accessed 27 September 2022)
Nowaira A., 'Egypt 1967—a Very Personal Defeat' *The Guardian* (27 May 2010) https://www.theguardian.com/commentisfree/2010/may/27/egypt-1967-very-personal-defeat (last accessed 27 September 2022)
Omar S., 'Arab Nationalism: A Retrospective Evaluation' (1992) *14*(4) *Arab Studies Quarterly* 23
Pollard L., *Nurturing the Nation: The Family Politics of Modernizing, Colonizing and Liberating Egypt, 1805–1923* (University of California Press 2005)
Pollock D., 'In Egypt, One-Third Still Like the Muslim Brotherhood; Half Call U.S. Ties "Important"' *Fikra Forum* (10 December, 2018) https://www.washingtoninstitute.org/fikraforum/view/in-egypt-one-third-still-like-the-muslim-brotherhood-half-call-u.s.-ties-im (last accessed 30 September 2022)
Population Council, 'Survey of Young People in Egypt' https://www.popcouncil.org/research/survey-of-young-people-in-egypt (last accessed 30 September 2022)
Reza R., 'Endless Emergency: The Case of Egypt' (2007) *10*(4) *New Criminal Law Review* 544
'The Rise and Fall of Egyptian Arabic' *The Economist* (8 March, 2022) https://www.economist.com/prospero/2018/01/31/the-rise-and-fall-of-egyptian-arabic (last accessed 27 September 2022)Salih K.E.O., 'The Roots and Causes of the 2011 Arab Spring' (2013) *35*(2) *Arab Studies Quarterly* 184
Sayigh Y., 'Above the State: The Officers' Republic in Egypt' (2012) *The Carnegie Papers* https://www.files.ethz.ch/isn/157113/CMEC_33_officers_republic1.pdf (last accessed 27 September 2022)
Sayigh Y., 'Owners of the Republic: An Anatomy of Egypt's Military Economy' (2019) https://carnegie-mec.org/2019/11/18/mapping-informal-military-economy-officers-republic-pub-80337 (last accessed 27 September 2022)
Scott R.M., 'What Might the Muslim Brotherhood Do with Al-Azhar? Religious Authority in Egypt' (2012) *52*(2) *Die Welt Des Islams* 131
'The Second Time around' *The Economist* https://www.economist.com/briefing/2013/07/06/the-second-time-around (last accessed 27 September 2022)
Shehata D., 'Sixty Years of Egyptian Politics: What Has Changed?' *The Cairo Review of Global Affairs* (2018) https://www.thecairoreview.com/essays/sixty-years-of-egyptian-politics-what-has-changed/ (last accessed 27 September 2022)

Shehata S., 'Islamism in Egypt: Legitimate Concerns?' *Ahramonline* (20 April 2011) http://english.ahram.org.eg/NewsContent/4/0/10405/Opinion/Islamism-in-Egyptlegitimate-concerns.aspx (last accessed 20 April 2011)

Sherwood H., 'Christians in Egypt Face Unprecedented Persecution, Report Says' *The Guardian* (10 January 2018)

Slackman M., 'As Egypt Votes on Laws, Cynicism Rules the Street' *New York Times* (26 March 2007)

'Statement by H.E. President of the Arab Republic of Egypt Abdel Fattah El Sisi at the 71st session of the United Nations General Assembly' (20 September 2016)

'Statement on Egypt, February 1922' *Hansard 1803–2005* https://api.parliament.uk/historic-hansard/lords/1922/feb/28/statement-on-egypt (last accessed 27 September 2022)

Van der Schyff G., 'EU Member State Constitutional Identity: A Comparison of Germany and the Netherlands as Polar Opposites' (2016) *76 Zeitschrift Für Ausländisches Öffentliches Recht Und Völkerrecht* 167

Van der Vliet J., 'The Copts: "Modern Sons of the Pharaohs"?' (2009) *89*(1) *Church History and Religious Culture* 279

Waterbury J., *The Egypt of Nasser and Sadat: The Political Economy of Two Regimes* (Princeton University Press 1983)

Weinbaum M.G., 'Egypt's "Infitah" and the Politics of US Economic Assistance' (1985) *21*(2) *Middle Eastern Studies* 206

Wickham C.R., 'The Muslim Brotherhood after Mubarak' *Foreign Affairs* (3 February 2011) https://www.foreignaffairs.com/articles/egypt/2011-02-03/muslim-brotherhood-after-mubarak (last accessed 30 September 2022)

World Bank, 'Labor Force, Total—Egypt' https://data.worldbank.org/indicator/SL.TLF.TOTL.IN?locations=EG (last accessed 27 September 2022)

Zayed D. and El Madany S., 'Egypt Vigilantes Defend Homes as Police Disappear' *Reuters* (London, 29 January 2011)

Zeghal M., 'The Recentering of Religious Knowledge and Discourse: The Case of Al-Azhar in Twentieth Century Egypt' in Hefner R. and Qasim M. (eds.), *Schooling Islam: The Culture and Politics of Modern Muslim Education* (Princeton University Press 2007) 105

Zeidan D., 'The Copts: Equal, Protected or Persecuted? The Impact of Islamization on Muslim-Christian Relations in Modern Egypt' (1999) *10*(1) *Islam and Christian-Muslim Relations* 53

Zollner B., 'Surviving Repression: How Egypt's Muslim Brotherhood Has Carried on' *Diwan* (11 March, 2019) https://carnegie-mec.org/2019/03/11/surviving-repression-how-egypt-s-muslim-brotherhood-has-carried-on-pub-78552 (last accessed 30 September 2022)

PART 3
CONCLUSION

11

Fostering a Sense of Constitutional Identity amid the Travails of African Constitutionalism

Charles M. Fombad

1. Introduction

Most contemporary studies on constitutional identity focus on countries in the Global North. These studies show that there is no general agreement on the definition of the concept or even its nature and scope. Nevertheless, most scholars agree that constitutional identity reveals tensions and disharmonies that are internal and external to a constitutional order. Since independence, and particularly after the wave of constitutional reform that began in the 1990s, African countries have grappled, in both design and practice, with the numerous disharmonies. The chapters in this volume take us on a journey through the challenges these countries have encountered in their efforts to design constitutions that strive not only to promote constitutionalism but also to do so in a manner that reflects the constitutional identity of the country. It is a broad overview that covers countries whose constitutional systems are rooted in one or other of the continent's two dominant constitutional traditions—the common law and civil law—and which also considers the possible impact of indigenous legal systems and institutions on constitutional identity. The chapters prompt a series of questions. These revolve around the relevance of constitutional identity to the fostering of constitutionalism and good governance. Is the former an end in itself or a means to the latter? What lessons could we draw from the studies?

In attempting to respond to these questions, the chapter proceeds as follows. Section 2 offers some thoughts on constitutional identity in the African context. Section 3 examines certain of the factors that appear to impede the fostering of a sense of constitutional identity. This provides the background against which section 4 considers ways of promoting constitutional identity in a manner that enhances, rather than undermines, efforts to entrench a culture of constitutionalism and good governance. The chapter ends with some concluding remarks.

2. Constitutional Identity and the African Context

It is mainly in the past three decades that the issue of constitutional identity has attracted the attention of Western scholars, with the seminal works being those by Gary Jacobsohn and Michel Rosenfeld. Given that there has been little research on this from an African perspective, Charles Fombad's introductory chapter to this volume poses the question of whether the notion of constitutional identity is of any relevance to Africa's present constitutional

Charles M. Fombad, *Fostering a Sense of Constitutional Identity amid the Travails of African Constitutionalism* In: *Constitutional Identity and Constitutionalism in Africa.* Edited by: Charles M. Fombad and Nico Steytler, Oxford University Press.
DOI: 10.1093/oso/9780198906308.003.0014

predicaments. Is it an illusion and distraction, or does it raise important issues of constitutional governance that need to be addressed? The answers depend in part on what is understood by this concept.

There are probably as many definitions of 'constitutional identity', and explanations of its nature, scope, and manifestations, as there are writers on the topic. However, as Fombad points out, it is possible to move away from the often restrictive Americo-Eurocentric perspective of the existing definitions, which do not reflect the historical, socio-economic, and other factors that influence the evolution of African constitutions and the challenges associated with them. In a general sense, constitutional identity develops from the political aspirations expressed in the constitution as interpreted and applied by the executive, judiciary, and legislature as well as the surrounding culture. It is a dynamic phenomenon influenced by several elements, some more dominant than others, which vary not only from country to country but also over time.

A good example of the fluctuating nature of the elements that combine to define a country's constitutional identity is found in Sherif Elgebeily's aptly entitled chapter, 'Taking Power from the People: Shifting Constitutional Identity in Egypt'.[1] He shows how the constitutional identity of the Egyptian Constitution has been marked by the centrality of the armed forces—the constitutional status of which has increased over the years in the different constitutions the country has adopted—by the role of Islam as a state religion, and by the distinct lack of full political freedoms for citizens. Egypt's constitutional identity is therefore inextricably linked with the military presence, *de lege* in the constitution and/or de facto in political life. Similarly, in 'A Century of South African Constitutional Identities', Nico Steytler, in examining South Africa's search for a constitutional identity, describes how the country evolved from racially exclusive apartheid constitutionalism (evident in the 1909, 1961, and 1983 constitutions) to a more inclusive democratic constitutionalism (starting with the 1993 Interim Constitution and culminating in the present 1996 Constitution).[2]

A number of key elements may combine to give African constitutions a sense of constitutional identity. Firstly, the coexistence and evolution of various identities at both the national (from local to regional) and international (from sub-regional, regional, to global) levels may combine and contribute to the establishment of the constitutional identity of a particular polity. The close interaction of these identities over time may result in a dominant identity emerging in the constitution as a whole, or some aspects of it, such as values, principles, or institutions, acquiring a distinctive characteristic associated with the country. Examples are the eternity clauses which some authors suggest have become a distinctive feature of the French, German, and Italian constitutions.[3] Based on this, one can argue that the peculiar 'state institutions supporting constitutional democracy' developed in the 1996 South African Constitution and replicated in the 2010 Kenyan and 2013 Zimbabwean constitutions have given these constitutions a distinct constitutional identity, or alternatively, made these institutions a peculiar feature of the constitutional identity of these constitutions.[4]

[1] See Chapter 10 of this volume.
[2] See Chapter 6 of this volume.
[3] See Chapter 1 of this volume.
[4] For a detailed discussion of these institutions, see Charles M. Fombad, 'The Role of Emerging Hybrid Institutions of Accountability in the Separation of Powers Scheme in Africa' in Charles M. Fombad (ed.), *Separation of Powers in African Constitutionalism* (Oxford University Press 2016) 325–44.

Secondly, whilst the constitutional text is indicative of the nature of the constitutional order, it is long and consistent experience which shows that the document and its principles resonate with the praxis of the body politic. Thirdly, constitutional identity relates to something of such constitutive essence at the heart of the constitution that it may be regarded as stable and deserving of preservation and special protection from arbitrary and casual change. This usually involves core aspects of the constitution whose continuity is identified with the continuity of the polity as a whole. For example, as Carlson Anyangwe and Fombad argue in 'Cameroon and the Crisis of Constitutional Identity: Is Anglophone Identity Incompatible with a Cameroonian Constitutional Identity?', the federal arrangement was at the heart of the reunification of the former British Cameroons and French Cameroon. By dismantling this and imposing a unitary system, a critical aspect of the country's mutually agreed constitutional identity was displaced in favour of an imposed one.[5] There is no doubt that constitutional identity is not static but rather a dynamic concept that develops through a process of negotiating the values and principles that should serve as elements of the self-identification of the community. However, any modifications to a constitution necessitated by changing circumstances must be effected within the institutional framework laid down in the constitution and be consistent with the consensus of the social and political community as a whole. This lack of social and political consensus, according to Anyangwe and Fombad, has rendered the incompatibility of anglophone identity with that of the broader imposed Cameroonian constitutional identity.

Fourthly, constitutional identity serves a legitimating and safeguarding function that helps to identify, preserve, and protect national identity from the unavoidable competition brought about through the encroaching forces of supranational, regional, and global constitutionalism. Whilst the forces of the latter are inevitable in the modern world, they should never be allowed to overwhelm and denude national constitutional identity of its relevance and essence.

Finally, and perhaps most importantly for Africa, constitutional identity provides the stimulus for debate aimed at developing constitutional principles, values, and institutions adapted to addressing the continent's peculiar governance challenges. The chapters in this volume underscore the numerous challenges that most African countries face.

3. Forging Constitutional Identity in Challenging Circumstances

Inherent in the process of developing a sense of constitutional identity is the need for every society to confront the actual and potential economic, social, cultural, political, and other dynamic forces within the polity as it develops. This has been particularly difficult in Africa owing to its short history of constitutional governance, which dates only to the independence constitutions. Diverse elements potentially constitutive of the constitutional identity of most African countries are competing for influence and dominance, and give rise to disharmonies that need to be reconciled and harmonised. The main disharmonic factors that have remained formidable challenges include the undermining of constitutionalism through autocratic constitutionalism; the problem of promoting unity in diversity;

[5] See Chapter 9 of this volume.

the continually debilitating effects of the colonial and apartheid legacies; the challenge of reconciling national factors with competing international and universal ones; and the elusive search for an authentic African constitutional identity which incorporates and reflects diverse indigenous cultures, laws, principles, values, doctrines, and institutions.

3.1 The Emergence of Autocratic Constitutionalism: The Civilian-Military Autocracies

While there is no doubt that—with the exception of a few countries such as Libya and Somalia, both ravaged by civil conflict, and Eritrea and Eswatini, the two exceptional constitutional aberrations—considerable strides have been made in African countries, at least in principle, to embed a culture of constitutionalism, good governance, and respect for the rule of law, the trajectory of constitutional development in the different countries, as the case studies show, is particularly revealing of the travails of constitutionalism on the continent.[6]

What Elgebeily's chapter on Egypt's 'chameleon' constitution well illustrates is the growing phenomenon of civilian-military autocracies that employ the symbolism and trappings of constitutionalism and democracy as a façade to mask their despotic systems. He points out that, particularly since the 1950s, Egypt has degenerated incrementally into a military-controlled state. This state's pronounced militaristic identity has been reinforced by the present leader, Sisi, with the military enjoying a strong presence in almost all aspects of social, political, and economic life. What can no longer be ignored is the military's direct or indirect influence on African constitutionalism more widely, whether prior to the 1990s, in countries such as Burundi, the Democratic Republic of the Congo (DRC), Rwanda, Togo, and Uganda, or recently, in the likes of Burkina Faso, Guinea, Central African Republic, Mali, Sudan, and Zimbabwe. This is especially so given the subtle, 'soft' form this influence takes in comparison to the 'hard', violent coup d'états of the past. It is the increasing use of autocratic legalism in these soft and not-so-soft coups in the past few years[7] that has led Gary Jacobsohn to raise the issue of whether 'the concept of constitutional identity should be applied sparingly, and only in instances where the norms of constitutionalism can plausibly be said to have been met'.[8]

Another defining feature of Africa's constitutional autocracies is the number of dynasties that are emerging, particularly in francophone Africa. Elgebeily suggests that former president Mubarak ran out of favour with the military establishment that supported his long reign when it became clear that he wanted to pass power down to his son, Gamal. There were also rumours that one of the factors that precipitated the coup in Conakry in 2021 was what were seen as plans by the disgraced former president, Alpha Condé, to have his only son and presidential adviser, Alpha Mohamed Condé, replace him when he died or became

[6] In Charles M. Fombad and Nico Steytler (eds.), *Democracy, Elections, and Constitutionalism in Africa* (Oxford University Press 2021), we drew attention to the global democratic recession, which is particularly serious in Africa, and the impact it is having on constitutionalism on the continent.

[7] See further Charles M. Fombad, 'Reversing the Surging Tide towards Authoritarian Democracy in Africa' in Charles M. Fombad and Nico Steytler (eds.), *Democracy, Elections, and Constitutionalism in Africa* (Oxford University Press 2021) 463.

[8] Gary Jacobsohn, 'How to Think about the Reach of Constitutional Identity' (2023) *1*(1) *Comparative Constitutional Studies* 1.

too ill to hold on to power. Although there were several father-to-son successions in the past,[9] they are emerging in post-1990 Africa as a new method of perpetuating dictatorship.

This re-emergent culture of father-to-son succession began surfacing in 2001 when, with the help of the military, former president Joseph Kabila replaced his assassinated father, Laurent Kabila, in the DRC.[10] In Togo, the army was also instrumental in Faure Gnassingbe's replacing his deceased father, Gnassingbe Eyadema, in 2005. Gabon's Ali Bongo took over in 2009 from his father, Omar Bongo, who had been in power for forty-two years; Bongo is now seriously handicapped after a stroke and barely able to walk, and is himself making preparations for his own son, Noureddin Bongo Valentin, to take over. In 2021, the army was instrumental in the replacement of the late Chadian president, Idriss Déby (who had been in power for thirty-one years) by his son, General Mahamat Déby. Equatorial Guinea's President Teodoro Obiang Nguema Mbasogo, in power for the past forty-three years, appointed his son, Teodoro Nguema Obiang Mangue, whom he has been grooming as successor, as vice president in 2016. Similar dynastic successions are in the making in other countries. For example, Paul Biya, in power in Cameroon for forty years, is openly planning to hand over to his son, Franck Biya. In Congo-Brazzaville, Denis Christel Sassou Nguesso, son of President Denis Sassou Nguesso, who has been in power for thirty-seven years, is being prepared for succession. In Uganda, General Muhoozi Kainerugaba is being prepared to replace his father, Yoweri Museveni, who has been president for the past thirty-six years. This trend suggests that constitutionalism on the continent is acquiring dynastic features.

3.2 Grappling with Diversity

A strong sense of nationhood built around factors such as a common culture, common language, common history, and common ethnicity usually provides the foundation not only for national identity but also for constitutional identity. Constructing constitutional identities in Africa, the most ethnically heterogeneous continent in the world and one fragmented by, inter alia, ethnic, racial, cultural, linguistic, and cultural divisions, has not been easy. Efforts, especially in the immediate post-independence period, to eradicate ethnicity with a view to promoting national unity, development, and nationhood not only failed to achieve their intended purposes but also remain a major challenge. This is because most African countries have failed to give diversity constitutional recognition and protection and use it to foster constitutionalism, democracy, and good governance. Reconciling the multiplicity of identities in Africa and giving every citizen a sense of belonging to the nation remains as critical today, if not more so, than it was at independence after the colonial powers formally departed. As Francis Deng notes, virtually every African conflict has some ethnoregional dimension to it.[11]

[9] Three cases of the sons of a founding father (the first president or prime minister after independence) coming to power can be identified because these came decades later: former president Ian Khama of Botswana, who came to power twenty-seven years after his father left office; former president Uhuru Kenyatta, who became president thirty-four years after his father; and Prime Minister Navin Ramgoolam, who was elected thirteen years after his father left power.

[10] See Issa Sikiti da Silva, 'The Rise of Africa's Political Dynasties' (5 April 2022) https://www.newsafrica.net/article/the-rise-of-africa-s-political-dynasties (accessed 10 October 2023).

[11] Francis M. Deng, 'Ethnicity: An African Predicament' (1 June 1997) https://www.brookings.edu/articles/ethnicity-an-african-predicament/

A strong illustration of the challenges of accommodating diversity in modern African constitutionalism is provided by Anyangwe and Fombad in their discussion of the ongoing crisis in Cameroon.[12] James Tully, in his critique of modern constitutionalism, which he labels the 'empire of uniformity', argues for a constitutionalism 'informed by the spirit of mutual recognition and accommodation of cultural diversity'.[13] Cameroon is one of the extreme cases in Africa of the situation where two inherited, and potentially conflicting, colonial cultures that are expressed in language, history, legal tradition, and style of governance (externally divisive elements) are proving difficult to reconcile with other factors (internally unifying ones) such as geography, indigenous culture, colonial experience, and tribal affinities. As Anyangwe and Fombad observe, a constitutional identity which is perceived to be contrived and imposed by a dominant community that makes little effort to build a sense of collective self-identity from common and divergent identities is bound to fail in securing general acceptance and legitimacy.

In sharp contrast to the Cameroonian situation, case studies by Karl Kössler of two African countries (Ethiopia and South Africa) and two European ones (Bosnia and Herzegovina, and Spain) demonstrate how the constitution is being used to develop a pluralist constitutional identity in these ethnically diverse countries. Kössler rightly points out that the lessons to be drawn from these studies is that lack of pluralism in the framing of the image of the people both reflects and fuels intergroup tensions, as it may either undergird tendencies towards disintegration or hinder integration in the first place. Nico Steytler's analysis of the struggle to reimagine South Africa's constitutional identity shows how, in spite of a widely acclaimed 'Rolls-Royce' constitution, the deeply rooted disharmonies sown by apartheid created strong fault lines that leave the majority of the population in abject poverty and with limited access to land. This has led some decolonialist scholars to question whether a constitution that fails to right the historical injustices of land seizures, marginalisation, and economic exclusion of the majority could ever create a sense of belonging and national constitutional identity.[14]

In Africa's complex multi-ethnic communities, it must be recognised that homogenisation is not synonymous with unity or even constitutional identity. Given the dynamic nature of constitutional identity, the acceptance of diversity as a feature of African society means there must be continuous dialogue and engaged activism at all levels and at all times to develop mirror images of the constitution and the country in which every citizen can see him- or herself reflected. This must be premised on an acceptance of the inevitability of diversity and recognition of the fact that it should not necessarily fuel conflict. For now, in a number of African states, such as Cameroon, Mali, Senegal, and the DRC, there is a perception amongst certain minorities that the country is held together by repression and authoritarian leadership with no regard to the will and desire of the people. One lesson Africa can learn from Europe, where societies have become more and more heterogeneous since the 1950s, is that ethnicity is a reality of the modern state. It can no longer be wished away: homogenisation is a myth. As the European Union (EU) has shown, a pragmatic approach to constitutional identity—one that involves recognising a place for national constitutional identity and a place for EU constitutional identity—is the way to go. Constitutionalism

[12] See Chapter 9 of this volume.
[13] Quoted by Heinz Klug in Chapter 3 of this volume.
[14] See Chapter 6 of this volume.

cannot be sustained in a country held together by repression and coercion rather than a consensual constitutional bond.

3.3 Living with the Legacy of Apartheid and Colonialism

Like Africa's rich ethnic diversity, the legacy of apartheid and colonialism will remain a permanent birthmark. In principle, in African countries that inherited one or the other of the two dominant constitutional cultures—the common law and civil law constitutional cultures—it should be no obstacle to developing constitutions with distinct identities. Nevertheless, it is important to note that the struggle to reconcile foreign ideas with a country's socio-political realities is true not only of African countries that underwent the painful experience of colonialism but—as Asnake Kefale shows in his chapter, 'Constitutional Identity and Disruption in Contemporary Ethiopia'—also of a country like Ethiopia, which narrowly escaped the disruptive effects of colonialism.[15] The enduring impact of the colonial legacy on the dynamics of constitutional identity development in Africa could be viewed from at least three perspectives.

The first is to see what positives could be drawn from this legacy. It may be argued that the contemporary preoccupation with decolonisation and Africanisation of laws and legal systems does not necessarily entail that the colonial legal edifice must be dismantled and abandoned. Instead, the decolonisation and Africanisation process can be seen as providing an opportunity for African legal experts from the continent's different legal traditions to seek to understand each other, engage in a constructive trans-systemic dialogue, and explore how common solutions could be crafted for the common problems afflicting the continent. This entails creative thinking in the process of adapting and adjusting legal systems in a manner that takes into account the social, economic, and political realities of the continent. Some of the chapters in this volume highlight examples of ways in which this should be done—and ways in which it should not. The latter, as we will see, relate to situations where colonial legal systems are allowed to be an albatross around the neck of African legislators; as regards the former, the best examples, alluded to earlier, are the peculiar state institutions supporting constitutional democracy, as developed under the Kenyan, South African, and Zimbabwean constitutions. They have enormous potential to safeguard constitutionalism and democracy, provided they are not captured and rendered impotent by overbearing executives.[16] Whilst it is now clear that more needs to be done to enable such institutions to be truly efficient and effective, they mark an important contribution to global constitutionalism.[17]

The second perspective considers the negative impact of the colonial heritage. The latter's potentially enduring impediment to legal development is highlighted in the chapter by Charles Fombad and Trésor Makunya, 'The Struggle for Constitutional Identity in

[15] The other country which was not formally colonised is Liberia.

[16] The risk of their being captured and neutralised is very high, as can be seen from a comparison of the record of South Africa's former public protector, Advocate Tuli Madonsela, and that of her successor, Advocate Busisiwe Mkhwebane. See, for example, Sarah Evans and Kyle Cowan, 'Insurgent or Independent: The Many Lives of Busisiwe Mkhwebane' (13 March 2020) https://www.news24.com/news24/opinions/analysis/analysis-insurgent-or-independent-the-many-lives-of-busisiwe-mkhwebane-20200312 (accessed September 2022).

[17] For some suggestions as to how their effectiveness could be enhanced, see Fombad (n. 4).

Francophone Africa', which looks at the situation in francophone Africa.[18] It is undeniable that inherited colonial systems are one of the competing elements that needs to be reconciled and harmonised in order to develop African constitutional identities. As the authors argue, the French legal system's continued predominance since independence and the French government's exploitation of its colonial links to perpetuate this legal system in its former colonies in Africa has made illusory any prospect of a distinct legal or constitutional identity emerging within them. In spite of the heightened desire for change on the continent and the realisation that sustaining constitutionalism and democracy requires measures designed to address the characteristic challenges of each country, obdurate reliance on the Gaullist constitutional model in francophone Africa persists mainly because it suits the temperament and strategic interests of francophone African leaders, the ruling elites, and the French. It is clear that this has been due largely to the slow pace of legal modernisation on the continent. This is what led to the advent of the Organisation for the Harmonisation of Business Law in Africa (OHADA), which provides a much-needed framework for promoting and facilitating intra-African trade. However, although it is African in name, it has a French identity.

A third perspective draws on the positives of the colonial legacy (as providing a framework for cross-systemic borrowing) as well as the negatives (as giving room for obsessive attachment to the Gaullist model as disguised in OHADA). The contention here is that this provides an opportunity for the African Union (AU) and Regional Economic Communities (RECs) to initiate, in a more decisive and proactive manner, measures to facilitate mobility between, and compatibility among, the continent's diverse legal systems.[19] This would not only enhance unity and understanding between countries belonging to the two dominant legal traditions, but also facilitate the process of negotiating and adopting AU legal instruments, such as declarations, treaties, and conventions, given that it is in this process that the conflicting approaches of the two legal traditions usually come to the fore.[20] In fact, article 44(2)(A)(b) of the African Union's Charter on Democracy, Elections and Governance (ACDEG) specifically mandates the AU Commission to 'promote the creation of favourable conditions for democratic governance in the African continent, in particular by facilitating the harmonisation of policies and laws of state parties'. In this regard, the AU could learn from the strides made by the EU in developing a legal lingua franca in Europe, even if this is due mainly to its more advanced supranational framework. From this perspective, the EU is an exemplar of what is happening in other regions of the world.[21] An African legal system could emerge eventually from the present interaction between the diverse legal systems. This has happened already with the imposed languages: the emergence of the Afrikaans language in South Africa distinct from European languages represents one of the most successful decolonising initiatives on the continent.[22] The same can be said of Swahili spoken

[18] See Chapter 4 of this volume.

[19] See Charles M. Fombad, 'Fostering a Constructive Intra-African Legal Dialogue in Post-Colonial Africa' (2022) *66*(1) Journal of African Law 1–22.

[20] See 'Its Shakespeare vs Molière in the African Union' (ISS/PSC Report, 27 November 2015) https://issafrica.org/pscreport/psc-insights/its-shakespeare-vs-moliere-in-the-african-union (last accessed 13 January 2022).

[21] See H. Dedek and A. Mestral, 'Born to be Wild: The "Trans-systemic" Programme at McGill and the Denationalization of Legal Education' (2009) *10*(6–7) *German Law Journal* 889.

[22] See P. Mbude, 'Decolonising Education: Lessons from the Afrikaans Language' (17 May 2018) https://www.news24.com/citypress/news/decolonising-education-lessons-from-the-afrikaans-language-20180517 (last accessed 13 January 2023).

in East Africa and, to a lesser extent, pidgin English spoken in West Africa. In this way, better use can be made of the disharmonic elements of the colonial heritage and its enduring potential, in certain jurisdictions, to remain a source of neocolonial capture, regardless of the elements' suitability, relevance, and context.

3.4 Reconciling National Identity with the Imperatives of Global Constitutionalism

Going beyond the difficulties of reconciling the past social and constitutional legal order with the present are the even more challenging imperatives of developing constitutional identities that reflect the changing pluri-legal culture emerging as a result of globalisation, internationalisation, and regional integration. As Roscoe Pound once put it, 'History of a system of law is largely a history of borrowings of legal materials from other legal systems and of assimilation of materials from outside of the law.'[23]

The reality is that the contemporary framework within which modern law is developing has ceased to be a single jurisdiction and the sources of legal rules are increasingly international and trans-systemic in nature. Future progressive constitutional developments in Africa depend on how efforts to get the best out of its diverse inherited legal traditions can be combined with contemporary international standards of constitutionalism and governance and still be able to deal with local problems. The 'internationalised' elements of global constitutional identity, which deal with issues such as human rights protection, judicial independence, the role of the legislature, accountability institutions, are sometimes in competition with local standards, which are often influenced by the inherited legal system. Although countries have the sovereign right to determine the content of their constitutions, the 'internationalised' elements of global constitutionalism reflected in global and AU treaties, conventions, and instruments for promoting constitutionalism, respect for the rule of law, and good governance set a minimum standard with which all civilised countries must comply. Non-conformity with most of the basic elements of constitutionalism has made it difficult for some of the countries discussed in this volume—Cameroon being a typical example—to develop a sense of constitutional identity. Transcending the internationalised identity is the equally difficult problem of African constitutional designers using Africa's unique indigenous institutions, values, and principles to develop a distinct constitutional identity.

3.5 Reflecting Indigenous Institutions and Values in African Constitutional Identities

Whilst the real or apparent dissonances between national aspirations and the 'universalist' components of constitutional identity are fairly familiar, what is less so, particularly from the perspective of constitutional identity, is the role and place of traditional rulers, institutions, and law in regard to constitutional identity. The wave of democratisation and constitutional

[23] In R. Pound, *The Formative Era of American Law* (Brown & Co. 1938) 94.

reforms in the 1990s that saw the replacement of autocratic rulers with democratically elected rulers and modern institutions of governance may have signalled the end of these unelected, mainly male, traditional leaders and the institutions associated with traditional governance. However, in the more than three decades since these developments, such institutions have not withered away, as was assumed by many modernists who considered them archaic.

A number of chapters in this volume touch on the African indigenous regime in general. They raise critical issues concerning how some understudied and controversial aspects of this regime have been incorporated in present-day African legal systems, especially the post-1990 constitutions. This is particularly important given that an Afrobarometer survey of twenty-two countries between late 2019 and early 2021 shows that Africans consistently express greater trust in traditional chiefs than elected leaders. In fact, nearly two-thirds (64 per cent) trust traditional leaders 'somewhat' or 'a lot', compared to 49 per cent for presidents, 43 per cent for local councillors, and just 39 per cent for members of parliament.[24]

Unsurprisingly, the highest levels of trust are among the elderly and uneducated, who live mainly in rural areas where the influence of traditional authority is felt the most and where there is usually limited governmental authority and presence, especially in the delivery of basic services. Whilst nearly half (49 per cent) of those surveyed think that chiefs strengthen democracy, Africans who strongly favour democracy as their preferred system of government appear to be entirely comfortable with the coexistence of traditional or unelected institutions and democratic or electoral ones. It is not clear whether these sentiments are based on a genuine reflection of what these traditional authorities can do or are actually doing. A contributory factor to the resurgence of interest in traditional authorities and traditional values and principles goes beyond the recent fascination with decolonisation and Africanisation. The fact is that the euphoria that came with the replacement of autocratic rulers in the 1990s has waned seeing as the new generation of leaders have failed to deliver the development, accountability, and inclusive governance that the new era of democracy and constitutionalism promised.

The evidence, therefore, is that the role and impact of traditional leaders and institutions in Africa's stride towards democratic and accountable governance is not going to disappear overnight. The challenge going forward is how to negotiate and reconcile traditionalism with modernism and ensure that traditional systems of governance can be integrated in a constructive manner to complement and strengthen modern democratic governance and constitutionalism. This calls for a careful assessment of what aspects of it need to be integrated, what contribution to democracy, constitutionalism, and good governance they can make, and how best this could be achieved. However, in spite of the overall resilience of African traditional regimes, their future is uncertain.

As Heinz Klug points out, the constitutional provisions in African constitutions recognising traditional authorities vary considerably in both the form of the recognition and the roles assigned to the authorities. In most instances, the provisions are more symbolic than substantive in nature and scope.[25] The same is true of the limited attempts to recognise and

[24] See Carolyn Logan and Luyando Mutale Katenda, 'Africans Have a Strong Message for Their Traditional Chiefs: Don't Tell Us How to Vote' (23 April 2021) https://www.washingtonpost.com/politics/2021/04/23/africans-have-strong-message-their-traditional-chiefs-dont-tell-us-how-vote/ (accessed in January 2023); and 'Relevance of African Traditional Institutions of Governance' (2007) https://repository.uneca.org/bitstream/handle/10855/3086/bib.%2025702_I.pdf?sequence=1 (accessed January 2023).

[25] See Chapter 3 of this volume.

integrate African traditional values, principles, and doctrines, the meagreness of which is evident in the coincidental manner in which traditional courts of justice feature in most constitutions. By contrast, George Ayittey's chapter dispels the widespread fallacy that pre-colonial Africans had neither history nor viable institutions and laboured under tyrannical rulers.[26] In pre-colonial Africa, there were traditional principles of checks and balances that in many respects operated more or less like modern principles of checks and balances. Like their Western equivalents, these traditional systems of checks and balances—which provided diverse ways of dispersing powers at different levels of the community and creating different centres of power to check each other—could be adjusted and adapted to address the changing governance demands and needs of contemporary societies.[27] Given the high level of accountability in traditional African societies, it is unlikely that pre-colonial traditional African rulers would have gotten away with the egregious crimes modern leaders commit against their people by, for example, killing opponents, locking them in prison, and plundering national treasuries and hiding the loot in banks overseas whilst their people live in misery.

Cape Verde provides us with a unique experience.[28] This is one of the few African countries which had no pre-colonial traditional culture or institutions and instead developed a self-created hybrid national cultural identity based on free intermarriage of the cultures of its European and African settlers. Despite the Cape Verdean Constitution's extensive borrowings from the Portuguese Constitution of 1976, its framers factored in many aspects of the country's history and hybrid culture, which is true as well of the way in which it has been interpreted by the Constitutional Court. This might not be patently obvious, but at least the Constitutional Court has underscored the importance of what is Cape Verdean in the legal system. The Court has also limited the use of foreign jurisprudence, especially what it refers to as so-called Lusophone approaches to the interpretation of the Constitution. This is in sharp contrast to what obtains in most other countries on the continent, particularly those in francophone Africa,[29] and raises some puzzling questions for the future.

4. Reconciling the Search for a Constitutional Identity with the Promotion of Constitutionalism

Besides the EU, Africa—more specifically, the AU, with its RECs—has developed a highly sophisticated framework for promoting constitutionalism, good governance, and respect for the rule of law. These provide building blocks for promoting the unity, peace, and political stability needed for economic progress and development. There are, however, many lessons that Africa could learn from the measures adopted by the EU to use national constitutional identity as a means to establish a broad EU constitutional identity. At present, the AU and its RECs are caught between, on the one hand, laudable ideas and ideals that lay the foundation for achieving similar goals and, on the other, vacuous political rhetoric and realism. Put differently, these organisations are caught between the quagmire of promoting

[26] See Chapter 2 of this volume.
[27] See Chapter 2 of this volume.
[28] See Chapter 8 of this volume.
[29] This is pointedly raised in Chapters 4 and 9 of this volume.

a sense of constitutional identity which is based on the fundamentals of constitutionalism and respect for the rule of law at the national level and keeping alive the fading hopes of a pan-Africanism at the continental level. These are not mutually exclusive and indeed can be pursued concurrently. However, the lack of political will and visionary leadership at the level of the AU remains an impediment. In spite of Africa's heterogenous nature in terms of ethnicity, religion, legal, and colonial heritage, as well differences in levels of economic development, more decisive continental leadership could exploit the continent's common past and common destiny to construct a mutually complementary cosmopolitan continental and national identity. Nevertheless, the foundation for a strong cosmopolitan continental identity that could feed and enhance national constitutional identity is there. The values and principles contained in articles 3 and 4 of the 2000 AU Constitutive Act and articles 2 and 3 of the 2007 ACDEG reflect the shared constitutional identity of AU member states. The underlying philosophy of these two key instruments of the AU agenda on constitutionalism strive to ensure that member states' constitutional identity may not be manipulated in such a way as to violate and undermine the AU's shared values. The ACDEG gives AU, particularly the Commission, extensive powers to develop benchmarks and guidelines to facilitate the implementation of the AU's shared values and principles as well as take the lead in facilitating 'appropriate ways and means to increase' the integration and effectiveness of traditional authorities and systems within the larger democratic system.[30] This needs to be urgently done.

At the national level, African courts, particularly constitutional courts, have an important role to play in shaping the interpretation and application of the post-1990 constitutions in a manner which reflects the attempts by the drafters to address the peculiar challenges of each country and ensure that the fundamentals of modern constitutionalism are safeguarded. This calls for a principled and rights-sensitive approach to constitutional interpretation that takes account of the radical political, economic, and social changes of our times and the revulsion against dictatorship. This means judges should go beyond their traditional role as interpreters of the constitution and strive to do justice by giving effect to contemporary social conditions and values. The notion of progressive or transformative judicialism—or what has been referred to as judicial activism—has been quite successful in promoting and sustaining constitutionalism in South Africa against numerous challenges.[31] What such activism requires is a conscious effort to abandon the conservative, inward-looking culture that was characteristic of the old pre-1990 African judiciaries.

The similarity of the experiences African countries have had under colonialism and its aftermath and in dealing with ethnic, cultural, and religious diversity means that they can learn from each other. This is not to blindly copy what obtains in other jurisdictions but to attempt to draw inspiration from their rich and dynamic jurisprudence. The benefits of this will be completely lost if national legal experts and judges are too unbending and stuck in the past to see the benefits of learning from what is happening elsewhere on the continent and using this to develop legal principles adapted to dealing with our peculiar problems. So far, there have been no significant efforts to cultivate intra-African judicial dialogue either

[30] See articles 27(9), 35, and 44 (2)(A)(a) of the ACDEG.

[31] See generally Theunis Roux, 'Judicial Activism' in *Elgar Encyclopedia on Comparative Law* (16 September 2021) https://papers.ssrn.com/sol3/papers.cfm?abstract_id=3923921 (last accessed January 2023); Hugh Corder, 'Judicial Activism of a Special Type: South Africa's Top Courts since 1994' in Brice Dickson (ed.), *Judicial Activism in Common Law Supreme Courts* (Oxford University Press, 2007) 323–62.

in terms of cross-fertilisation, borrowing, or migration of constitutional ideas from one African constitution to another, or through the use by judges of jurisprudence from other African jurisdictions. The progressive nature of South Africa's 1996 Constitution and high quality of the judgements delivered by the country's Constitutional Court, which in certain areas of the law such as socio-economic rights has laid down principles that are adopted the world over, suggests that we do not need to continue to look beyond the continent and copy Western constitutional models. Some of these innovative judgements could contribute to the emergence of a national constitutional identity that reflects African realities.

5. Conclusion

The concept of constitutional identity provides opportunities for understanding and appreciating the nature, scope, and content of constitutions as well as the challenges that may expose their limitations. It is of such critical importance today that constitutional designers must take account of it not only during the design of the constitution but also during its revision. If for any reason citizens do not self-identify with the constitution and feel that it does not reflect their aspirations or address their most pressing problems, they are unlikely to respect it.

From the perspective of the emerging theories of constitutional identity examined in this volume, particularly those advanced by Gary Jacobsohn and Michel Rosenfeld, it must be assumed that the post-1990 new or substantially revised constitutions signalled a fundamental departure from the colonial and postcolonial as well as post-apartheid constitutional architecture. It is now clear, however, that these constitutions have not entirely succeeded in reconciling and harmonising the diverse conflicting elements, such as the social, economic, legal, and political differences that were crucial to adopting constitutions that give all citizens a sense of common identity and destiny. Unsurprisingly, three decades after these fundamental constitutional revisions, the erosion of some of the progressive and transformative ideas they contain has resulted in a slow but steady revival of competitive authoritarianism.

Whilst it is inevitable that, as societies evolve, the diverse elements of constitutional identity will compete for dominance and give rise to disharmonies, a foundation for constitutionalism is needed to manage the changes and challenges that may arise therefrom. It is from this perspective that one can explain the relative success of South Africa and the dismal failure of Cameroon in managing the crisis of constitutional identity playing out in both countries. Both cases starkly reflect the paradox and dialectic created by the legacy of colonialism, reinforced in the latter by apartheid. Nevertheless, the absence of a basic framework for constitutionalism in Cameroon has led to a political crisis, whereas in South Africa, in spite of the enormity of the contradictions dividing the society, the solid constitutional framework has provided avenues for continuous engagement in the search for a compromise.[32]

Nevertheless, the quest for fostering a sense of constitutional identity in modern African constitutions goes beyond the legacy of colonialism, however profound the situation may

[32] Cee Chapter 6 for South Africa and Chapter 9 for Cameroon, both in this volume.

be, especially in the South African context, still reeling from the ravages of decades of black-majority exclusion, especially with respect to the land question and the economy. Scholars who have advocated for the decolonisation and Africanisation of these constitutions have so far not come up with any concrete and innovative constitutional principles, doctrines, or institutions to address this. Whilst incorporating traditional institutions, principles, and values in these constitutions remains a possibility, there also remains a major challenge in reconciling these with many fundamental human rights principles and basic principles of constitutionalism in general. As we have seen, there has been more success in incorporating most of the basic principles of global constitutionalism in African constitutions. However, in most of these constitutions, this has either been done in a symbolic manner or there has been a lack of effective implementation. This breeds insecurity. People would not normally reflect or even seek to assert their identity or distinctiveness from others unless they feel threatened and insecure.

The aspiration to decolonise and Africanise African constitutions and incorporate some traditional institutions, values, and principles on their own may only provide African constitutions with a false sense of constitutional identity. These will be meaningful only if they are able to address our present predicaments—unemployment, poverty, inequality, repressive and dictatorial rule, and other challenges that impede the continent's development. In the final analysis, the future will depend on how African constitutional designers incorporate in constitutions those distinct features that deal with our peculiar challenges; above all, it will depend on ensuring that these constitutions entrench the fundamental elements of modern constitutionalism—democracy and respect for the rule of law—not only as part of the constitutional identity but also as an integral part of the DNA of the constitutional system.

Bibliography

Corder H., 'Judicial Activism of a Special Type: South Africa's Top Courts Since 1994' in Dickson, B. (ed.), *Judicial Activism in Common Law Supreme Courts* (Oxford University Press 2007) 323

da Silva I.S., 'The Rise of Africa's Political Dynasties' (5 April 2022) https://www.newsafrica.net/article/the-rise-of-africa-s-political-dynasties (accessed 10 October 2023)

Dedek H. and Mestral A, 'Born to Be Wild: The "Trans-systemic" Programme at McGill and the De-nationalization of Legal Education' (2009) *10*(6–7) *German Law Journal* 889

Deng F.M., 'Ethnicity: An African Predicament' (1 June 1997) https://www.brookings.edu/articles/ethnicity-an-african-predicament/

Evans S. and Cowan K., 'Insurgent or Independent: The Many Lives of Busisiwe Mkhwebane' (13 March 2020) https://www.news24.com/news24/opinions/analysis/analysis-insurgent-or-independent-the-many-lives-of-busisiwe-mkhwebane-20200312 (last accessed September 2022)

Fombad C.M., 'The Role of Emerging Hybrid Institutions of Accountability in the Separation of Powers Scheme in Africa' in Fombad C.M. (ed.), *Separation of Powers in African Constitutionalism* (Oxford University Press 2016) 325

Fombad C.M. (ed.), *Separation of Powers in African Constitutionalism* (Oxford University Press 2016)

Fombad C.M., 'Reversing the Surging Tide towards Authoritarian Democracy in Africa' in Fombad C.M. and Steytler N. (eds.), *Democracy, Elections, and Constitutionalism in Africa* (Oxford University Press 2021) 463

Fombad C.M., 'Fostering a Constructive Intra-African Legal Dialogue in Post-Colonial Africa' (2022) *66*(1) *Journal of African Law* 1

Fombad C.M. and Steytler N. (eds.), *Democracy, Elections, and Constitutionalism in Africa* (Oxford University Press 2021)

'It's Shakespeare vs Molière in the African Union' (ISS/PSC Report, 27 November 2015) https://issafrica.org/pscreport/psc-insights/its-shakespeare-vs-moliere-in-the-african-union (last accessed 13 January 2022)

Jacobsohn, G., 'How to Think about the Reach of Constitutional Identity' (2023) *1*(1) *Comparative Constitutional Studies* 1

Logan C. and Katenda L.M., 'Africans Have a Strong Message for Their Traditional Chiefs: Don't Tell Us How to Vote' (23 April 2021) https://www.washingtonpost.com/politics/2021/04/23/africans-have-strong-message-their-traditional-chiefs-dont-tell-us-how-vote/ (last accessed January 2023)

Mbude P., 'Decolonising Education: Lessons from the Afrikaans Language' (17 May 2018) https://www.news24.com/citypress/news/decolonising-education-lessons-from-the-afrikaans-language-20180517 (last accessed 13 January 2023)

Pound R., *The Formative Era of American Law* (Brown & Co. 1938) 94

'Relevance of African Traditional Institutions of Governance' (2007) https://repository.uneca.org/bitstream/handle/10855/3086/bib.%2025702_I.pdf?sequence=1 accessed January 2023

Roux T., 'Judicial Activism', in *Elgar Encyclopedia on Comparative Law* (16 September 2021) https://papers.ssrn.com/sol3/papers.cfm?abstract_id=3923921 (last accessed January 2023)

Index

For the benefit of digital users, indexed terms that span two pages (e.g., 52–53) may, on occasion, appear on only one of those pages.

Please see individual countries for entries relating to that country